TEACHING
THE LANGUAGE ARTS
IN THE ELEMENTARY
SCHOOL

Third Edition

TEACHING THE LANGUAGE ARTS IN THE ELEMENTARY SCHOOL

Martha Dallmann

Professor Emeritus of Education
Ohio Wesleyan University
Professor Emeritus of Elementary Education
St. Cloud State University

wcb

WM. C. BROWN COMPANY PUBLISHERS
Dubuque, Iowa

To
My Mother Christine Bizer Dallmann
And
My Sister Marie Dallmann

Contents

Preface

During the time that has elapsed since the second edition of *Teaching the Language Arts in the Elementary School* was published—in 1971—changes in the language arts program that had previously come to the forefront of educational thinking have continued to receive serious consideration. Notable among these are: the recognition of the desirability of the use of methods of inquiry and self-discovery in acquiring many learnings; the realization of the importance to teaching of the existing interrelationships between the various facets of the language arts; the perception of the dire needs of the economically and/or culturally disadvantaged child; and the problems initially encountered, upon entrance to school, by the child from a non-English-speaking home.

The purpose of the book continues to be to present a workable relationship between theory and practice. While a considerable part of the book offers practical suggestions for teaching various phases of the language arts, these are not considered as isolated devices or procedures. Rather they are shown as they fit in with the guiding principles and other theoretical considerations that are presented in a clear-cut manner in connection with each facet of the language arts. Although the interrelationship between theory and practice is stressed, the placement in the book of the theoretical and the practical is such that the reader should have no problem in locating either. Typically when a topic is presented, guidelines for teaching it are first given and other matters of general importance are discussed. Thereupon suggestions are presented as to how the theory can be implemented. The ease with which the reader can find suggestions on theory when theory is wanted and on practical application when that is desired adds to the value of the book.

As in earlier editions, a variety of types of specific methods and procedures is recommended. Some are given in terms of possible practice exercises, some in the form of teaching plans or other descriptions of illustrative classroom situations, and still others as purposeful procedures that can be incorporated as part of the ongoing classroom activities. They are made more meaningful through a large number of pictorial illustrations that are scattered throughout much of the book. It is recommended that at all times only those procedures that seem best to fit the needs of the pupils should be selected by a teacher. It is hoped that the ideas that are presented will suggest to the teacher many that are especially well adapted to the various individuals in his or her charge.

Teaching the Language Arts in the Elementary School is divided into three parts. Part One, "Basic Considerations," simply and directly sets forth principles of child growth and development. It is these principles that should serve as part of the foundation for teaching the language arts. Part Two, "Developmental Procedures in Guiding Growth in Communication Skills," emphasizes, with attention to both theory and practice, means by which the teacher can guide the child in both oral and written communication. It is by far the longest part of the book. Part Three, "Specialized Procedures and Resources," begins with a chapter on "Creativity Through Dramatic Expression and Choral Speaking." Succeeding it is a chapter on "Adapting Instruction to Individual Differences." The final chapter gives a somewhat detailed index of many of the resources in the area of the language arts that may prove helpful to the classroom teacher.

While the basic organizational pattern of this third edition continues to be the same as in previous editions, there are some changes in it. The chapter on "Adapting Instruction to Individual Differences" is new, as a separate chapter, to this edition. Another change in the organization is that two chapters that were included in earlier editions no longer appear as chapters in this third edition. They are the chapters on evaluation and on il-

lustrative teaching situations. For the sake of greater continuity in the presentaton of the subjects dealt with in this book, types of materials that formerly were included in these two chapters are now incorporated in the various chapters of the book that deal with those phases of teaching. For example, evaluation of handwriting is taken up in the chapter on handwriting; illustrative teaching situations dealing with written communication are now included in the chapter on that topic. A change has also been made in the placement of material on creative writting. While in the second edition it was presented in a chapter on "Guiding Growth Through Creative Expression," in this third edition it appears as part of the chapter "Guiding Growth in Written Communication.' The change had been suggested so that students reading the book would, it is hoped, not be tempted to think of creative writing as merely an adjunct to practical writing, but would recognize the prominent and integrated role that it should play in a program of written expression.

Within the chapters of the book that have been retained changes have also been made. Bibliographies have been updated, lists of instructional materials have been revised, and photographs and other illustrations have been replaced where such substitution has been deemed advisable.

It is hoped that the changes made in this edition will add to the usefulness of the book to teachers and to prospective teachers.

Martha Dallmann
St. Cloud, Minnesota

Acknowledgments

It is impossible to write a book on teaching the language arts in the elementary school without accumulating a great indebtedness. In a sense a book in this area is the result of the combined efforts of many persons, known and unknown to an author. Publishers of materials in the language arts, teachers in the public schools and in the colleges in which the writer of this book has worked in some capacity, student teachers she has supervised, students in her classes through the years, and boys and girls in the elementary schools have helped the author gain the insight into the problems of teaching the language arts that is reflected, it is hoped, in this book. To all these she is grateful.

The author wishes to acknowledge her gratitude to the school administrators who provided photographs that make clearer the verbal content of the book. She is grateful to the publishing companies who gave permission to reproduce copyrighted material. She also acknowledges the fact that some of the photographs of illustrative materials and parts of the text appeared in articles she wrote for the magazine *Grade Teacher* (now titled *Teacher*).

The writer is indebted to many former students for the photographs of projects they had done in connection with work in the author's classes as well as the parts of the wording of some of the descriptions that are included. It is with regret that credit cannot be given in the case of some where records do not indicate who made the illustrative material. The writer is greatly indebted to Dr. Lowry Harding, editor when the manuscript for the first edition was being written, for his interest in the project and for the helpful suggestions he gave in the course of the preparation of that manuscript. Acknowledgment is also made of the debt to the late Dr. John DeBoer, senior author of the first three editions of *The Teaching of Reading*. published by Holt, Rinehart and Winston, Inc., which he wrote with the author of this book. The writing of *The Teaching of Reading*, including the fourth edition in which Dr. Roger Rouch and Dr. Lynette Chang served as co-authors, has had a marked influence on the content of the parts on reading in this book. Gratitude is also due all persons named in the acknowledgments of earlier editions whose names are not given here.

A list of persons named in these acknowledgments would be incomplete without mention of two individuals, Maria Dallmann, sister of the author, for her painstaking reading of the first edition, and Mrs. Christine Bizer Dallmann, the writer's mother, for her inspiration and for her interest in the writing activities of the author.

Martha Dallmann
St. Cloud, Minnesota

1

BASIC CONSIDERATIONS

1

Child Development and the Language Arts

The language arts program in the modern elementary school, like that of some of the other areas of the school curriculum, has been undergoing many changes during recent years. While in some respects these changes in the approach to development in the skills of communication have been less spectacular than those, for example, in mathematics, they nevertheless have been highly significant and, in many schools, far-reaching.

Many of the encouraging trends affecting the teaching of the language arts during the 1960s are continuing to be felt during the current decade. Among these are the following:

1. Increased attention is being given to the preschool child through programs such as Operation Head Start. In these programs considerable emphasis is being placed upon the development of skill in communication.

2. The urgent problems of the inner-city child and of other culturally or economically disadvantaged elementary school children and preschool children are being taken seriously and bold attempts are being made to eradicate some of the deplorable conditions created by poverty and lack of educational opportunities. The language handicaps of these boys and girls are being recognized and serious attempts are being made to adjust the educational program to their needs.

3. Solutions to problems of the child to whom English is a second language—not the one spoken at home—are increasingly becoming matters of grave concern.

4. The greater emphasis in teacher-education programs on the study of language is resulting in elementary school language arts programs in which boys and girls learn more about the characteristics of their own language. Thus knowledge acquired by studies of linguists is being utilized in many language arts programs.

5. Extensive and comprehensive studies for the improvement of teaching procedures, under the direction of well-qualified staff, are being funded by the government and private agencies. Some of these programs deal specifically with the language arts.

In addition to the continuation of the emphases just listed, the following are characteristic of many language arts programs during the early years of the 1970s.

1. The language arts programs are less subject-centered than were those in a large number of schools in the late fifties and the early sixties. During that period, immediately following 1957, undue stress was placed by numerous writers of educational materials and by other educators on a subject-centered curriculum. However, this overemphasis on an intellectualized curriculum was opposed by those, in and outside of schools, who felt that such an approach placed the proficiency of the child in various skills above the well-being of the child as a whole. The opposition staunchly maintained that the chief concern of the school should not be what Ivan can do that Johnny can't; that the child should not be made the focus of international rivalry nor political strategy; that more important than excellence in the performance of skills is the welfare of the child as he grows up in a social order that has pride in how much the individual counts. Fortunately, many educators now recognize that wise concentration on the best interests of the child will also aid him in achieving according to the level of his ability in all areas of the curriculum, including the language arts.

2. Of late more emphasis is being placed on the inductive rather than only the deductive method in teaching various phases of the language arts. In other words, the child is being provided with greater opportunity to use what has been termed the "self-discovery method," under the guidance of the teacher. Further discussion as well as examples of this method are given in chapter 3 as well as in connection with various other chapters of Part Two of this book.

Teachers of the language arts who have as their all-encompassing objective the welfare of the child, recognize that to accomplish effectively the aims of a desirable program in the language arts the techniques and procedures should be in harmony with what is known in the field of child growth and development. They realize that without knowledge of the tenets emphasized by specialists in that field, teachers may have goals in mind that are too limited. They know that without such guidance teachers may be content to settle for aims that deal only or primarily with skills, ignoring the contribution that the language arts can make to the personality of the growing individual. Because the author concurs with educators with such beliefs, throughout this book the relationship that should exist between the two areas is recognized.

Since incidental references to the contributions of the field of child development that are made in subsequent chapters are not sufficient to emphasize and demonstrate the known points, this first chapter is devoted exclusively to pointing out the relationship between child development and the language arts and the impact that knowledge of the former should have on teaching the latter. For the same reason the second chapter deals with a consideration of the developmental patterns of growth as they affect the program of the language arts.

The relationship between child development and the language arts is not one-way. It is reciprocal. An application of knowledge from the field of child growth and development affects the pupil's learning in major aspects of the language arts favorably—in listening, speaking, reading, and writing. At the same time, acquisition of abilities and skills in the language arts can—indeed, should—have a beneficial influence on the growth and development of the child. Let us now turn our attention to the first of these two points.

BEARING OF KNOWLEDGE OF CHILD DEVELOPMENT ON TEACHING THE LANGUAGE ARTS

What then are the "big ideas" from the field of child growth and development that the teacher should keep in mind in relation to teaching the language arts?

Behavior Is Caused

One of the most important emphases of students of child growth and development is embodied in the statement that has become almost the motto of that branch of study, namely "Behavior is caused." Manifold application can be made of this principle to the teaching of the language arts. It is pertinent to all phases of diagnosis and evaluation, ranging from the most casual to the specially planned highly technical. It is significant whether the appraisal deals with data like the child's ability to use *there* and *there* correctly or whether it is concerned with more intangible and more complex factors such as the attitude of the learner toward achieving excellence in speaking or the degree of assurance and poise with which he gives a report or tells a story to his classmates.

The teacher of the language arts who shapes his instructional program in harmony with the principle that all behavior is caused will not, for example, be satisfied with noting errors made in written or oral communication of an informal type nor will he stop short of careful analysis of results when a standardized test has been administered in any aspect of the language arts. He will try to determine what caused the child to perform as he did. He will endeavor to be understanding when dealing with persons, including those with very serious shortcomings, as he realizes that somehow, somewhere the reactions have been brought about by factors for which, in many instances, the individual may not be responsible, at least not at the time. Praise will then not be reserved for the child who habitually has a high rating but will be given primarily to the person who has overcome deficiencies, especially if he has done so against heavy odds. Blame will all but disappear as far as the teacher's attitude toward the learner is concerned. This statement, however, is not to be interpreted to mean that the teacher will not point out to the child his shortcomings; nor does it mean that he may not reprove the pupil for some of his actions. Rather, it means that his attitude toward the learner will be one of sympathy as he attempts to assist him in overcoming difficulties and tries to help him attain ever higher goals.

Multiple Causes of Behavior

The tenet that the causes of behavior are multiple is parallel in significance to the generalization that behavior is caused. Even so-called simple reactions are the result of many factors. As the teacher tries to ascertain what brought about obtained results, he should not be satisfied when one cause has been found, even though some of the influencing factors may be so hidden that at first glance they seemingly defy discovery.

One warning should be given here. Important though it is that the teacher, as well as, in many cases, the learner himself, be conscious of the fact that shortcomings shown through evaluative procedures are the result of many factors, an almost endless search for them should not be carried on. There are teachers, though relatively few, who strive so hard to make thorough analyses that time that they should devote to teaching is used for evaluation. After a few factors likely to be significant in bringing about a problem have been determined, the teacher should usually begin to plan corrective measures with these in mind while at the same time he remains alert to other factors that he may in the course of time suspect of being contributive.

The Concept of "the Whole Child"

Unfortunately the expression 'the whole child" has become almost a cliche. Statements made concerning "the whole child" are at times so vague that they may obscure rather than clarify known facts about learning.

Let us not, however, ignore the importance of the concept of "the whole child" because the term is at times used in a setting in which little help is given toward understanding the child's potentialities and shortcomings. It is far too significant a concept to be slighted because of misuse.

Studies of child growth and development demonstrate the fact that the living organism has a unity, a wholeness, that constitutes its pattern of development. Each human being has a basic pattern according to which he grows, a pattern in many respects similar to those of other human beings, but nevertheless one singularly unique to him alone. In accordance with this pattern that helps

support the entity of his being, he develops not piecemeal but as a whole even though some aspects of his growth are more pronounced at some stages of his development than others. Emotional development, for example, takes place at the same time that physical, social, and intellectual development occurs even though at certain periods of the life of an individual there are spurts in one or more of these aspects and seeming lags in others.

How then can awareness of this essential unity of the developing organism, this "wholeness" of the learner, affect the work of the teacher of the language arts? Let us note a few of these ways.

1. Whenever the teacher is guiding the child in language development, the teacher should proceed so as not to interfere, in any phase of the child's growth, with his optimum development. For example, if the child shows signs of nervousness when he is giving a talk, the teacher should try to determine the cause of this undesirable reaction and then either not ask the child to give another talk until he has acquired a more stable reaction to the activity or make changes in the learning situation that will, hopefully, enable the child to give a talk without an undesirable effect on his emotional development.

2. When the teacher is guiding the child in language development, he should strive to teach so that he will help the learner grow in other respects also. For example, at the same time the pupil is learning to write a friendly letter, he can be encouraged, in many instances, to have a greater awareness of his responsibility to others, manifested through consideration of others shown in the letter. He can be taught courtesy as a listener when a classmate gives a report or tells a story.

3. The teacher should not try to force learning in the language arts at the expense of other phases of the development of the child. It is possible for a teacher to overstress the importance of language arts activities at the expense of other areas of the curriculum and of the child's all-around development, emotionally, socially, intellectually.

The Design for the Individual

Each individual, even before birth, is influenced greatly in his development through an inner design in accordance with which, to a considerable extent, he unfolds. This design is set in part through the very incidence of his being human. Normal human organisms, just because they are fashioned on the design of human beings, have many similar characteristics of growth. Not only the nature of the traits but also the order of the appearance and development of traits in an individual is greatly affected by the fact that he is a human being. It is because of likenesses in this design that characteristic growth trends can be established.

The concept of the unfolding design is of great importance to the teacher of the language arts since, through knowledge about it, he can expect certain similarities as well as many dissimilarities among the boys and girls whom he teaches. He can anticipate, for example, that listening will precede speaking, that speaking will precede reading, that reading will precede writing. By means of the characteristics—emotional, social, intellectual, and physical—that have been identified as growth norms, the teacher can obtain a clearer picture of the level of a child at any one time than he could without such information. For example, when dealing with six-year-olds, through information from growth studies he can note that it is normal for boys and girls of that age to be lacking in disposition to do much planning in a large group of their peers. At the same time, however, because of the factors of individual differences, he cannot expect any one child to follow details of norms established by Arnold Gesell and others even though they are based on study of large representative samplings.

Variations in Growth Patterns

The sequence of the appearance in the developing child of many phases of growth shows relatively little variation from individual to individual. It is fairly constant in various language activities as well as in overall physical development. First the infant engages in what have been called prelinguistic activities, as he cries or coos. When older be begins to babble, using some of the sounds that show some correspondence to those he will need later in talking. His first use of the language of the environment in which he is living is usually in the form of single words. Thereupon he gradually expresses himself in sentences—first in abbreviated sentences, then in simple but complete sentences, and later in more complex sentences of all types—declarative, imperative, interrogative, and exclamatory.

Though the sequence in which the child learns to communicate shows relatively little variation from one child to another, there is great variation among boys and girls in the timing of the appearance of these characteristics and activities. There are also deviations in the depth of growth possible manifested by various individuals. The complexity of sentences, for example, in which one child expresses himself often differs markedly from that of another boy or girl. The need for a teacher to take account of individual differences in language development is thus evident.

Maturation and Environmental Stimulation

The unfolding of the individual according to his design for living (nature) and the stimulation from the environment (nurture) are important determinants of his growth and development. The inborn design can be af-

fected adversely or favorably by environment. Provision of an environment that affords above average opportunity can, within limits, stimulate development beyond that possible under average conditions.

A few significant implications for the teacher who is guiding the language development of boys and girls are as follows:

1. In an environment unfavorable to language development, an individual is not likely to develop in communication skills to the extent that he might if he were growing up under more promising conditions.

2. In an environment highly favorable to language development for a child of given potentialities, he will probably develop in communication skills beyond the point likely to be achieved by another child with equal potentialities but with only the usual degree of favorableness of environment.

3. There is a point beyond which an especially favorable environment for a child cannot stimulate further development that can be maintained even if temporary gains are made.

4. Immediate gains made because of an unusually favorable environment often are lost when excessive stimulation is removed unless the stimulation followed a period of deprivation of proper environmental circumstances.

5. Without maturation adequate for development of a given language skill unless undue pressure is applied, it is unwise to try to force the growing individual to develop the skill. Persistence by the adult may lead to an unfavorable attitude on the part of the learner to the development of the skill and it may "block" him in other respects.

Readiness for Learning

Readiness for a given task may be thought of as the "teachable moment," which Robert Havighurst defines thus:

When the body is ripe, and society requires, and the self is ready to achieve a certain task, the teachable moment has come.[1]

While Havighurst's statement is a sound generalization, there remain the questions, when making application of it, "When is the body ripe?" and "When is the self ready to achieve a certain task?" There may also be the question, "When does 'society require'?"

A point of view expressed by Jerome S. Bruner that has bearing on readiness has been receiving considerable attention in the teaching of the social studies.[2] His claim

1. Robert Havighurst, *Developmental Tasks and Education.* (London: Longmans, Green and Company, 1952), p. 5.
2. Jerome S. Bruner, *The Process of Education.* (Cambridge, Massachusetts: Harvard University Press, 1960), p. 33.

Figure 1.1.

Photo by Carlton Rust

is that any subject can be taught successfully to any child of school age in an "intellectually honest" manner. If this hypothesis proves to be true, there may well be in it significant implications in terms of the best time for teaching various phases of the work in the area of the language arts. For example, there might then be increased attention given to the study of the science of the language, linguistics, even in the lower grades of the elementary school.

The claim by Jean Piaget that the child goes through somewhat discrete, though overlapping, stages in developing in power to think, too, has been attracting attention, more of late in this country than in earlier decades. [3] Since Piaget is considered by many one of the most outstanding child psychologists, it behooves persons in the field of child growth and development and those in the area of the psychology of learning, as well as specialists in the area of the language arts, to weigh his claims in terms of the teaching of the language arts. (See page 19 for statements concerning Piaget's theory of the development of the intellect.)

In spite of many unsettled questions concerning readiness for learning in any area, there are points, such as the following, which the elementary school teacher can accept with confidence.

1. Readiness for an activity implies that the child is sufficiently mature so that under favorable environmental conditions he can learn the activity with success and without undesirable effects upon him in other respects that would counterbalance or outweigh the gain made through acquisition of the skill.

2. Into activities such as "learning to walk" a child cannot be forced. Readiness for walking, like that for many other activities, is primarily a matter of the "unfolding of the design" of the individual. Barring highly unfavorable environmental influences, the child will acquire such a skill in its rudimentary form almost by himself. For the initial acquisition of such skills there is not much that the adult can do to facilitate learning other than provide a background that is not inimical to acquiring them. What is usually referred to as "teaching" is, in such cases, of little or no avail.

3. In the acquisition of many types of skills there is not merely one stage of readiness, namely that for the initial learning of the skill. There also is need for readiness for later stages in learning of the skill. For example, there is not only a necessity for readiness at the beginning stage of reading instruction but also at later stages that include the development of skills such as learning to use the dictionary.

4. Frequently "readiness" for one of the noninitial stages of acquiring a skill is chiefly excellent performance in the preceding stage in the development of the skill. For example, probably the most desirable way of getting ready to learn to arrange words in alphabetical order is to have proficiency in the preceding stage of knowing the letters in alphabetical order.

5. Because frequently the best evidence of "readiness" for one of the noninitial stages of acquiring a skill is excellent performance in the preceding stage, it is important that the teacher should recognize the desired sequence of stages in the development of the skill. This sequence should be in optimum psychological order of learning, not in logical sequence if there is a discrepancy between the two.

6. Frequently all pupils in one classroom are not ready for acquiring a new skill at the same time. Consequently careful diagnosis of the needs and abilities of boys and girls is of paramount importance, and provisions for adapting instruction to individual differences are necessary.

7. Whether or not a child is ready to begin to learn in a given area is dependent to a considerable extent on the methods and materials used in the teaching. Care should, therefore, be taken to try to select methods and materials suitable for each child.

Here are listed a few illustrations from the field of the language arts, to make clear the general concept of readiness for language arts activities.

1. *Listening.* Even the very young child is "ready" to listen to some types of sounds. He is not "ready" in infancy, however, to make, for example, the differentiation in sounds that he can make at a later period.

2. *Speaking.* Before the child is ready to say his first word, little, if anything, can be done to encourage him to talk, other than to supply an environment in which he hears words spoken frequently to him. Then when he does learn to talk, he is not ready to make the fine differentiations in speech that he may be able to make in adulthood. Furthermore, in order to make the progression from the first of these stages to the latter, he will usually be benefited greatly by considerable help from competent adults.

3. *Reading.* Although a child may be able to learn to read even in preschool days, he is not considered ready to learn to read at that time if he needs to put forth undue effort in the process. On the other hand, if, when he is ready to read, physically, mentally, emotionally, and intellectually, he is not given suitable reading materials and usually if he is not helped in learning to read, he does not acquire that skill at that time.

4. *Writing.* The infant is not able to make the marks with a pencil or crayon that are typical of the nursery school age child. From complete inability to com-

3. Bärbel Inhelder and Jean Piaget, *The Early Growth of Logic in the Child,* translated from the French by E.A. Lunzer and D. Papert (New York: Harper & Row, 1964).

municate through written symbols he may proceed later to large random movements with a drawing or writing instrument till he can write worthwhile compositions of his own creation in words that are spelled correctly and in letters that are easily read and artistically formed.

Goals for Learning

It is deplorable that in some classrooms the teacher alone seems to have educational objectives in mind (and sometimes even his are not worthy of pursuit, as, when, for example, his aim is no more than "to cover the work in the textbook"). Children in some classrooms do much of their work merely because, in their vernacular, they "have to." If force is the compelling purpose for learning, a poor situation exists.

Some pupils work primarily to please the teacher or parent, an aim probably justifiable at times with the very young child for whom in some instances aims more intrinsic to the learning situation are difficult to find, even for significant learning experiences. However, gaining the approval of an adult is not the sole objective on which the work of the elementary school should be based; children should as soon as possible, without haste or hurry, be helped to establish aims for study that will last a lifetime.

Specialists in child development will attest what even casual observation confirms, that many of the goals for the young child, if they are to be genuinely his, must be of value to him at the present or in the near future. To be sure, by the time a child is six he should be able to work for worthy goals more than a few minutes removed from the present. A still older pupil should find as stimulus to action incentives that are realized considerably farther in the future. In fact, one of the tasks to be accomplished during the elementary schooling is to become able to accept, as reason for effort, various goals farther and farther removed from the present.

What then are some of the aims that may be real for the elementary school age child as he is guided in development of the skills of communication? Statements such as these may incorporate reasons for action for some children: (1) Read this story to find out how a dog saved the children of Nome. (2) Let us plan now how we can give good book reports for our assembly program. (3) Some of you have trouble using the words *ran* and *run* correctly. I will help you find out how you can decide which word you need. Goals such as these are more likely to evoke the best efforts of the learner than substitutes such as: (1) Read the story beginning on page 25. (2) Read page 12 in your textbook to find out the rules for giving a good book report. (3) Today we will find out the difference in the use of *ran* and *run*.

At times the question is asked, "By whom should the goal be stated, by the pupils or by the teacher?" Some insist that it should be by the former. Since the general problem of pupil planning is taken up in the next paragraphs, suffice it here to say that probably often it makes little difference whether the teacher or a pupil initially states the aim; what matters is that the children should wholeheartedly accept it as their goal.

Pupil-Participation in Planning

Since boys and girls often learn more effectively when they have a part in planning their activities, a few pointers on pupil-participation in planning are listed here. Additional suggestions are given under "Teacher-Pupil Planning." (See page 36.)

1. The pupils should frequently share in the responsibility of planning. The extent of the responsibility that the pupils should assume is to be determined in part by the maturity, age, and experience of the boys and girls, as well as by the type of situation confronting them.

2. When the final choice does not lie with the boys and girls, they should know before they reach a decision that their recommendation must be one that the teacher considers acceptable if it is to be acted upon.

3. Boys and girls should be held to the choice of procedure once it has been approved by the teacher unless there is adequate reason for altering plans. The pupils should, when planning, be encouraged to do it carefully so that later they will not be likely to regret their decisions. Half-finished work or easy discontinuance of one procedure to follow another should be discouraged. On the other hand, the boys and girls should learn, in theory and in practice, that to persist doggedly with an activity just because it has been chosen may be folly if it becomes clear that it is not one that will best accomplish the objective. When a change in procedure is indicated, however, the boys and girls should be helped to note the waste that frequently accompanies alteration of plans.

4. When children are given a part in choosing a procedure, the choice of a few should not be mistaken for that of all. In some classrooms the most vociferous pupils determine the goals to be sought and the procedures to be followed. The other boys and girls, without expressed objection, often assent because they have no other suggestions or because the teacher directly or indirectly lets it be known that the suggested choice is one that he will accept.

5. With the guidance of the teacher, the boys and girls should plan means for evaluating the success of their procedures in accomplishing the desired results. (For a discussion of "Evaluation and Diagnosis" see page 42.)

Creativity as an Aid to Learning

The use in this book of the term *creativity* is not confined to the work of the artist who produces a masterpiece. It is not even limited to activities such as writing original stories or poetry. Whatever an individual does that in some constructive way expresses his own feelings or preferences for action is considered in this book a creative act. It may be merely a word chosen happily by the pupil as he states his own reaction, a letter that in one or more sentences shows his own convictions, or a message that illustrates his personal way of communicating an idea, for in method of work as well as in results creativity may be shown. If a child finds a way of working that suits him better than one followed by some of the others and he, nevertheless, attains the desired results, he is working creatively. In fact, even failure to obtain the wanted results does not necessarily prevent an activity from being creative. Nor does the fact that someone else, unknown to the child, has already done something in the same way he is doing it, bar the performance of the activity from being a creative one.

Some teachers seem to have the mistaken idea that all they need to do to help pupils be creative is to abstain from giving detailed instructions. The quality of the learning thus is often impaired more than if such instructions were given. In order to thrive, creativity needs more than a vacuum. In various ways, some of which will be pointed out in later pages of this book, the teacher can encourage boys and girls to be creative. When a child has expressed himself through the felicitous choice of a word, the teacher may comment on the selection. When the teacher at times uses methods that are original and reflects the satisfaction that comes from such abandon of routine procedures, the pupils may be able to sense the joy resulting from doing work to express one's own ideas. Sometimes the teacher can encourage creativity as he explains to the children that although he has shown them one way in which they can attack a given assignment, they are free to try others. Occasionally some of the boys and girls may be asked to explain their procedures after an introduction such as this: "Dick has figured out an excellent way to. . . . I think you would like to have him tell you about it."

Self-Confidence as an Aid to Learning

Probably in no other area is the effect of self-confidence on learning shown more than in that of the language arts. Anxiety about success has blocked the way to learning to read for many a child. Lack of self-confidence can unnerve even scholars as they give talks.

There is no intention here of encouraging a "know-it-all" attitude. Self-confidence must be based on fact. To make a child feel self-confident when he is doomed to fail is very likely to have a detrimental effect on future learning. To make a child believe, for example, that he can give an excellent talk with the result that he will at-

tempt to give one in a situation that makes greater demands than he can meet may practically lame him for future activity of a similar type.

Here are a few ways in which the teacher can, in the area of the language arts, encourage reasonable self-confidence in the learner.

1. If a pupil's contribution has been good, the teacher can tell him so.
2. If a pupil has shown improvement in giving a talk, the teacher can praise him.
3. If a pupil is fearful of his ability to give a talk, the teacher can help him to analyze the difficulties involved and possibly to overcome them, at least in part, before he gives his talk.
4. If a pupil who is to take part in a play is afraid that he will not be able to perform in a satisfactory manner, the teacher can point out to him that there is no one set way of interpreting the part and he can help him experiment with various interpretations until he may be able to find one that satisfies him.
5. If a child has many words wrong in an assigned spelling list, the teacher can help remedy the situation through trying to determine the cause of the failure. He may find that the child is using a defective method in studying the spelling of words. In that case the teacher should help him develop a better means of approach. The teacher may discover that the spelling list is too long for the child; then, of course, he can shorten the list for that pupil.

Effects of Attitude toward Others on Learning

In all situations what an individual thinks of his fellowmen can affect his learning. The person suspicious of others or hateful toward them is likely to be poisoned by his own thought. Energy that could be used constructively for learning purposes is then consumed in devastating emotions. This generalization is strikingly true in the area of communication. Incentive for development of skills of communication may be lacking in persons to whom their fellowmen seem unworthy. There are wrongly, of course, exceptions to this rule, for fear or hate impels some to read, to write, to speak, and to listen.

What then is the teacher's role here?

1. The teacher can help the child attain self-respect. Self-respect can breed respect for others.
2. The teacher can work toward creating a climate of goodwill in the classroom.
3. The teacher can help the boys and girls learn to give criticism constructively. While some teachers may believe that the pupils should not be asked to evaluate the work of their peers, for fear of destructive criticism that might be made, much is lost if there is no evaluation by classmates.

4. The teacher can help boys and girls learn to take suggestions from others—their peers, the teacher, and other individuals. In a world in which not all suggestions are given in a kind and helpful manner, he can help the boys and girls not to become upset by unfair criticism. He can help them see that if criticism is unjust, there is often not much to be concerned about. He can help them realize that an individual needs to be concerned about eradication of the cause of the criticism that is justifiable. Suggestions for finding out how to make use of such criticism should be the responsibility of the pupil whose work is being evaluated, of his classmates, and of the teacher.

EFFECT OF LEARNING THE LANGUAGE ARTS ON THE DEVELOPMENT OF THE CHILD

So far we have directed our attention primarily to guidelines from the field of human growth and development, application of which can help the child learn the language arts better. Now let us take note of how adequate guidance in the language arts can affect the developing child.

Probability of Beneficial Effect

Normally as the child begins successively to listen, speak, read, and write, a new world is opened for him. As he improves in these skills that world often gradually, though sometimes suddenly, expands for him. This broadening of horizons can be the means of helping him achieve development in personality and character.

Let us note, for example, what may happen as Susie learns a new word, a word new to her understanding vocabulary, the word *independence*. As she acquires the word under the guidance of an alert teacher, she may add to her understanding of the word from time to time in such a manner that eventually she will take increased pride in doing things independently. But such growth is often not accidental or even incidental; nor is it to be expected that Susie will feel the full import of the experience immediately. It may take years after the introduction of the word to Susie until she appreciates the fact that independence must not be confused with license; that independence may not be desirable at all times; that independence for self is not enough, but that the goal should be to help others to become independent also; that with independence comes responsibility; that the spirit can be free and independent even if the body is in shackles. But when, in the course of years and perhaps of decades, Susie has learned to comprehend points such as these through reflection and/or actual experience, something beneficial, something broadening may have happened to Susie. She may become a person with a more comprehensive outlook as she learns the meaning of *independence* and of many other words.

A caution must be expressed here. If conditions under which the pupil learns language skills or develops in them are inimical to the best in personality and character development, then the process of learning to communicate may have a decidedly detrimental effect upon him. For example, if when a child is introduced to reading, he develops an anxiety complex because of parents or teachers who are overanxious to have him succeed, that state of mind on the part of the learner may not only interfere seriously with his learning to read but may also do temporary or even permanent damage to him as an individual.

Comparative Importance of Effect on the Development of the Child and on Acquisition of Skills

If the choice needs to be made, it is more important that the child develop into a fine person than that he gain great facility in the use of communication skills. Happily, however, the two types of development are not mutually exclusive. One frequently supplements or complements the other. The boy or girl who is guided effectively in learning the language arts can be helped thereby in the development not only of language skills but also of social, moral, and spiritual qualities. The child who is assisted in such a manner that he develops into a wholesome personality by that very act of guidance will probably become more receptive to learning the language arts. For example, as he becomes poised, speaking will be less of an effort than if he were "knotted up" inside.

Here are a few ways in which the teacher can assist the child in the development of his personality and character as he is learning the language arts.

1. The teacher encourages the child who through real effort has made improvement even if the end result is not up to standard for the grade.

2. The teacher finds reading material for the child that not only makes it possible for him to improve in reading skill but also helps him build up new worthwhile

Figure 1.2. Self-Expression through Art.

Courtesy of the Boston Public Schools.

Figure 1.3. Satisfaction through Learning.

interests or develop old ones resulting in enrichment of his life.

3. The teacher adapts his teaching to the varying needs of the individuals whom he is teaching.

4. The teacher discourages the cheap and the tawdry in all facets of communication.

It must not be concluded that insistence on standards in the language arts is inimical to the development of the individual. In fact, lack of standards may be instrumental in developing an irresponsible individual, unwilling to comply with the many restrictions encountered throughout life, violation of which may have disastrous results. There must be standards. What standards there are and how they are enforced make the difference.

Unfortunately there are some ways, the following among them, by which the teacher can, unwittingly, teach the language arts so that the child is harmed.

1. The teacher makes a chart, available for all in the room to see, to show the test results achieved by each pupil in some phase of the language arts. The child whose marks are habitually low, if he gets teased and possibly tormented by others because of his marks, is likely to suffer more than a poor mark in the language arts.

2. The teacher allows uncontrolled criticism by a pupil's peers after he has given a talk and thus may cause a child to wish that he would never have to give another talk.

3. The teacher is not censorous of the quality of the reading the boys and girls do in that he does not discourage the reading of trash nor encourage the reading of elevating materials and thus he neglects one of his finest opportunities.

Provisions for Interpersonal Relationships

As the child is guided in the acquisition of communication skills, there is much chance for desirable development through provisions for rich interpersonal relationships. Much opportunity, with wise guidance, should be given for informal conversation among boys and girls. Committee work, discussion, speaking to an audience—all are important.

Following are a few points, in accordance with which the teacher should plan for improvement of interpersonal relationships among his pupils, as he guides them in development of skill in communication.

1. Unless consistent guidance is provided, boys and girls may develop unsatisfactory rather than satisfactory interpersonal relations. Care needs to be exercised by the teacher so that, for example, as his pupils communicate with one another they become more understanding of one another, more thoughtful of the wishes and needs of their associates.

2. Boys and girls should not be allowed more freedom in their interpersonal relations than that for which they can assume responsibility. However, the teacher should aim to develop among the boys and girls an ever-increasing capacity to assume responsibility and then provide freedom commensurate with the execution of it.

3. In committee work the line between license and liberty should be drawn, and the pupils should be helped to make the differentiation. As a boy or girl develops in social, emotional and intellectual maturity, he can learn to become more and more cognizant of the fact that others have a claim to liberty equal to his own and that consequently his freedom of action must not interfere with a similar degree of freedom of others. Some pupils need, for example, to learn the limitations of self-expression to honor when engaged in committee work.

4. While committee work and other group activities can be highly desirable, there should be much opportunity for the individual to work alone. It is, to be sure, difficult to draw a line of division showing with exactitude

Courtesy of the St. Louis, Missouri Public Schools.

Figure 1.4. Provisions for Interpersonal Relationships.

when in the best interests of the group of the individual there should be committee endeavor and when individual performance in a nongroup situation. Nevertheless variation is valuable so that the pupils acquire skill in both types of activities.

5. The child should be guided so that he does not assume that group standards are necessarily correct. He should be helped to realize that he is responsible for his action even when he is in a group. Furthermore, he should receive guidance so that he will not use the group as his standard of conduct when the group is in the wrong.

6. The child should be helped to realize his responsibility to make a group of which he is a member a better one than it would have been without his presence in it. He should be guided so that he recognizes ways in which he can be an asset to it and so that he will want to be a worthy member—an individual interested in helping the group achieve desirable objectives and in being instrumental in improving group behavior if it is such that betterment is important.

7. Through effective communication with persons who are different in race, in socioeconomic background, in intelligence, and in other respects, the pupil can learn to appreciate more and more those unlike him, to recognize the fact that to be different does not mean to be inferior. The teacher can help establish or maintain an atmosphere of mutual respect on the part of all members of a class to one another by: (a) showing a

deep-seated interest in each pupil, (b) encouraging all boys and girls to make worthwhile contributions, and (c) discussing with the pupils in connection with various learning activities in social studies or literature classes, the contribution of various races and nationalities.

FOR STUDY AND DISCUSSION

1. Cite instances in which a teacher's method of dealing with a problem situation would have been different had he made wise application of the principle "Behavior is caused."

2. Of what import to the teacher of remedial work should knowledge of the following statement be; "Immediate gains made because of an unusually favorable environment often are lost when the excessive stimulation is removed unless the stimulation followed a period of deprivation of proper environmental circumstances"?

3. Name ways in which creativity in the language arts can be evident on the part of a primary-grade pupil; an intermediate-grade pupil.

4. In this chapter are named several ways in which the teacher can, in teaching the language arts, encourage self-confidence in the learner. Name additional ways in which he can affect the personality of the child favorably, with likelihood of resulting improvement in language arts skills and abilities.

5. Read a chapter in a book dealing at least in part with child growth and development. What ways are mentioned, in addition to those given in this chapter, in which knowledge of child development may affect personality development that in turn may have a favorable effect on a child's language development?

6. It has been said that readiness for an activity, such as learning to read, is not determined exclusively by the ability or the intelligence of the learner but also in part by the materials of instruction to be used and the methods to be employed in teaching. What, then, should the first-grade teacher consider, on the basis of a reading readiness test, before he decides that a child is not ready at that time to learn to read?

7. Name some language arts goals that are likely to be not too far in the future for serving as real motivation for a first-grade child. In addition name some that would be likely to be far removed from the present to serve as true motivating forces for him.

8. If Jerome S. Bruner's claim, to which reference is made on page 8, is used as basis for planning a language arts curriculum, what effect might it have on current practice in teaching the language arts?

9. Name ways in which learning in the area of the language arts can affect favorably the spiritual development of a child.

REFERENCES

Almy, Millie. *Young Children's Thinking.* New York: Teachers College Press, 1966.

Boyd, Gertrude A. *Teaching Communication Skills in the Elementary School.* New York: Van Nostrand Reinhold Company, 1970.

Bruner, Jerome S. *The Process of Education.* Cambridge, Mass: Harvard University Press, 1960.

Burns, Paul C; Broman, Betty L.; and Wantling, Alberta L. Lowe. *The Language Arts in Childhood Education,* 2d ed. Chicago: Rand McNally & Company, 1971.

Burns, Paul C., and Schell, Leo M. *Elementary Language Arts Readings.* Chicago; Rand McNally & Company, 1969.

Donoghue, Milred R. *The Child and the English Language Arts,* 2d ed. Dubuque, Iowa; Wm. C. Brown Company Publishers, 1975.

Gardner, D. Bruce. *Development in Early Childhood: The Preschool Years.* New York: Harper & Row, 1964.

Gelfand, Donna M. ed. *Social Learning in Childhood: Readings in Theory and Application.* Belmont, Calif.: Wadsworth Publishing Company, Inc. 1969.

Inhelder, Bärbel, and Piaget, Jean. *The Early Growth of Logic in the Child.* Translated from the French by E.A. Lunzer and D. Papert. New York: Harper & Row, 1964.

Lamb, Pose, ed. *Guiding Children's Language Learning,* 2d ed. Dubuque, Iowa: Wm. C. Brown Company Publishers, 1970.

Lowenfeld, Viktor, and Brittain, Lambert W. *Creative and Mental Growth,* 5th ed. New York: The Macmillan Company, 1970.

Piaget, Jean. *The Language and Thought of the Child.* New York: Harcourt Brace Jovanovich, 1926.

Rebelsky, Freda, and Dorman, Lynn, eds. *Child Development and Behavior: Readings.* New York: Random House, Inc., 1970.

Shuster, Albert, and Ploghoft, Milton. *The Emerging Elementary Curriculum,* 2d ed. Columbus, Ohio: Charles E. Merrill Publishing Company, 1970.

Smith, James A. *Adventures in Communication: Language Arts Methods.* Boston: Allyn and Bacon, 1972.

Snadowsky, Alvin M., ed. *Child and Adolescent Development: Laboratory and Field Relationships.* New York; The Free Press: A Division of the Macmillan Company, 1973.

Stone, L. Joseph, and Church, Joseph. *Childhood and Adolescence: A Psychology of the Growing Person.* New York: Random house, Inc., 1970.

Torrance, E. Paul, and Myers, R.E. *Creative Learning and Teaching.* New York; Random House, Inc., 1970.

Weber, Evelyn, *Early Childhood Education: Perspectives on Change.* Worthington, Ohio; Charles A. Jones Publishing Company, 1970.

2

Developmental Patterns

One of the most productive activities of specialists in child development has been study to determine characteristics of children—physical, emotional, social, and intellectual—at various stages of development. Since knowledge of these characteristics, coupled with information on the patterns of language development, is fundamental to the construction of effective programs of language instruction, this chapter is devoted to a summary of those findings.

METHODS OF STUDY OF CHARACTERISTICS OF CHILDREN

In order to know what weight to place on data on characteristics of children, it is of value to know how the data are gathered and what the strengths as well as the weaknesses of available methods are.

For a long time the predominant method employed in collecting information on the stages of development of children was the cross-sectional method. Through use of it large numbers of boys and girls at a given age can be studied and then the average characteristics of that level, with notations on variations, can be ascertained. For example, when by this method the heights of groups of boys six, seven, and eight years of age are studied, the average heights, with variations also indicated, are reported. This is a relatively quick method of gathering information, for the data on six-year-olds, seven-year-olds, and eight-year-olds can be collected simultaneously.

Since by means of the cross-sectional method none of the children on whom data were collected is studied individually during succeeding years, to offset this shortcoming there has become popular in the field of child development a method designated as the longitudinal method. By means of it, to use the illustration to which reference is made in the preceding paragraph, Johnny's height would be recorded at six, at seven, and again at eight, to provide data for careful study of the variations in height through which Johnny, not a mythical average child, has gone from six to eight years of age. But study of Johnny alone in this manner, to be sure, does not give much helpful information to the field of human development. However, when many boys and girls are similarly studied individually over a period of years, generalizations of validity, made cautiously, can be of vital significance. Study then can reveal what happened to the individuals in the group over a period of time. It can, for example, show whether, as a rule, those who were shorter than average at six still at seven and eight maintained the same relative position or whether rapid increments in growth of the short six-year-old, as a rule, resulted in his being closer to the norm at seven and at eight than he had been at the age of six.

The advantage of the longitudinal method is that data useful for comparative and predictive purposes show up the variations in characteristics studied of each individual in a study over the period of time that is being investigated. A difficulty in the use of this type of research is that data must usually be gathered over a relatively long period of time to show changes within an individual, or significant lack of them. The disadvantages of the longitudinal method are offset, in part, by the cross-sectional method. While there are great potentialities in the use of the longitudinal method, the contribution possible from the cross-sectional must not be underestimated. Both can make and have made outstanding contributions to the field of human development, and, consequently, to teaching.

LIMITATIONS OF AVAILABLE DATA

Although much valuable information has been gleaned through studies of the growth patterns of children, available data have certain shortcomings. Of these the teacher should be cognizant in planning a curriculum based in part on the findings of the characteristics of boys and girls at various stages of development. The following are important points in this relationship.

1. Much additional careful, painstaking study is needed either to reinforce or to contradict, if necessary, present-day generalizations on characteristics of children in all phases of their growth.

2. There are so many gaps in the information that has been gathered to date that many points in the planning of any course of study cannot be settled solely in the light of findings in the field of child growth and development. Common sense, informal observation of children, and knowledge of the psychology of learning should help where child specialists cannot supply the answer and should supplement, in general, their findings.

3. Generalizations giving characteristics of children at various stages of development, reached either through cross-sectional or longitudinal studies, cannot be applied with certainty to all children. In fact, the one certainty is that there is always uncertainty in this respect.

4. It is frequently difficult, even often impossible, to ascertain or to predict which children are exceptions to the rules or generalizations that have been formulated.

5. Although the sequence of appearance of a characteristic or trait is in many instances the same from one person to another, the timing of the appearance shows much variation from individual to individual.

GENERAL CHARACTERISTICS OF THE PRIMARY-GRADE CHILD

Keeping in mind the cautions that have been stated about interpretation of data, let us note the characteristics typical of children, six, seven, and eight years of age. Awareness of the physical, emotional, social, and intellectual natures of boys and girls at primary-grade levels will help us guide pupils in the first three years of school in their development of skills of communication.

Physical Development

The physical development of the child from six through eight is characteristically as follows:

1. Boys and girls increase considerably in size during this period, as a rule two or three inches a year in height and three to six pounds in weight, and the growth is at a steadier rate than in the preschool years.

2. The average girl at six is more advanced than the average boy of that age in general development, including skeletal structure, and she maintains this superiority throughout the usual span of ages of the primary grades. In both height and weight, as well as in other aspects of size, the average boy surpasses the average girl.

3. There is considerable increase in length of legs during this period. The chest becomes broader and the heart increases a good deal in size. However, there is a decrease in the rate of the pulse and of breathing, negative manifestations that are nevertheless signs of development of the organism.

4. The size and general physical well-being of the primary-grade child greatly influence the personality of the growing individual.

5. Boys and girls in the primary grades are by nature so active that it is difficult for them to sit still for a long period of time.

6. The child entering the elementary school is still much more adept in his use of the large muscles than of smaller ones, but during the years in the primary grades he shows considerable growth in coordination of the latter.

7. In spite of relatively slow development of sex organs during the years of six through eight there is an increase in their size, and both boys and girls manifest development in sex feelings although these are much less in-

tense and less obvious than those during later periods of development.

8. Typically the primary-grade child is subject to many colds as well as to childhood diseases and consequently is absent from school rather frequently.

9. Poor posture, as measured by adult standards, is characteristic of the primary-grade child, who is likely to have drooping shoulders and to show lack of strength of the abdominal muscles.

10. Uneven growth of various parts of the skeletal structure is likely, in part, to cause the awkwardness characteristic of the older primary-grade child.

11. The loss of deciduous teeth is one of the striking characteristics of the primary-grade child.

12. As in preschool years, the child in the primary grades continues to be somewhat farsighted. Consequently the length of time for close work and the nature of that work need to be under careful scrutiny by adults. Fusion, as a rule, is better than in earlier years.

Emotional Development

The following are some of the emotional characteristics of the primary-grade child that are of particular significance to the adult guiding the language development of boys and girls of ages six, seven, and eight.

1. One of the outstanding characteristics of the six-year-old is changeableness in level of expression of his emotional responses. He alternates between impulsive reactions characteristic of preceding, less mature stages in his emotional development (like temper tantrums, fighting, lack of intellectual responses) and the more reasoned, deliberate responses characteristic of later stages. The seven-year-old and the eight-year-old typically show less reversion to the impulsive responses of the earlier stages of development.

2. By the time some children reach the second grade they have developed an undesirable self-consciousness which at times results in withdrawal from both adults and peers. Insecurity, often precipitated by làck of felt love and lack of success, is frequently the cause of withdrawal tendencies at this age. In fact, they are also often the reason for self-consciousness.

3. The six-year-old is likely to be self-centered to the extent that characteristics which in adults would be considered extremely selfish are much in evidence. He likes to be first and wants things done his own way. He is often overly aggressive. If he is frustrated he may resort to explosive behavior or to withdrawal. With increasing maturity the primary-grade child becomes less ego-centered and his reaction to not getting what he wants is more likely to be one of withdrawal than of explosiveness. He remains intent on preserving his own personality against all opposition, even though at times a warped being results, partly through lack of intelligent, loving guidance.

4. The primary-grade child is greatly in need of feelings of success, success in work he does at home and school and in his play. Without them disastrous effects on the growing personality may be the result.

5. To love and to be loved is one of the great needs of the human being. Lack of it during childhood is likely to result in a seriously warped personality.

6. Frequently even the well-adjusted primary-grade child shows mannerisms such as biting nails, sucking the thumb, twirling a small piece of material of his wearing apparel, playing with the ears. Pronounced, numerous, or continuing behavior of this type is frequently the result of dangerous tensions that should be relieved in ways other than direct attack upon the offending act.

7. Boys and girls of the primary-grade age levels express their emotional reactions both through words and actions. When the two are at variance, it is probably the action rather than the verbal claim that is the truer index to the feelings of the child. Such a variance is more likely to be pronounced with older children who may wish to hide their true feelings in their oral communication.

8. The primary-grade child is greatly affected by the persons with whom he comes into contact. In general during the primary grades a greater awareness of others develops as the child expands in his social life.

9. The primary-grade child is responsive to guidance in his emotional reactions.

Social Development

The social development of an individual is inextricably knit with his emotional development. How he acts in the presence of others is determined to a large extent by his innermost feelings. This relationship is evident between many of the following points, indicating the social development of the primary-grade child and the emotional characteristics typical of a child of that age level.

1. Probably one of the most outstanding of the social characteristics of primary-grade children is that there is great variation among them in many respects. In spite of the differences, however, there are certain characteristic trends in their social development.

2. Without supervision the play of the six-year-old often degenerates into fighting. Under continuing proper guidance the child in the later primary grades shows less inclination for fighting.

3. Although the typical primary-grade child generally accepts the standards of right and wrong of his parents and teachers, it does not follow that he acts accordingly at all times.

4. The ego-centeredness, characteristic of the child in the early part of the primary-grade levels, while decreasing in strength, is evident in the contacts he has with peers and with adults.

5. The typical child entering first grade without kindergarten experiences is likely to be happier when he is with only one or two or three individuals than when he is a member of a larger group. The child who has attended kindergarten, profiting from the socializing activities of the preceding school year, is usually more accustomed to the larger groups. Both the child with and the one without kindergarten preparation, as they progress through grades one and two and three, become more interested, if the environmental influences are optimum, in associations with larger groups of people and they learn more about how to get along as members of a group.

6. At the beginning of the first grade the child is still greatly interested in associations with adults. Gradually, however, as he associates more with his peers, they begin to count more and he seemingly becomes less dependent upon adults for the satisfaction of his social needs. However, adults continue to be of great importance to him even though they do not pre-empt the center of the expanding stage of the child's life. He needs the security of their affection as he sallies forth into explorations of social living with his age-mates. Even though the child, as he emerges from six-year-oldness through seven-year- and eight-year-oldness often seemingly cares less about adults to whom he previously had ostensibly been clinging, lack of ample evidence of the continuing affection of adults can have devastating results on the child's developing personality.

7. The emotional instability of many boys and girls during part of the period of the primary grades is reflected in their social behavior and at times they tend to be rude and impetuous and stubborn and then again cheerful, cooperative, and generous.

8. As boys and girls progress through the primary grades, they increasingly like to tell others, children and adults, in small and later in large groups, of their experiences.

9. As the child grows from being a six-year-old through being an eight-year-old, he becomes more aware of the need of skill in associations with others. Under appropriate guidance he makes strides in group planning and in executing and evaluating plans. He also becomes more interested in serving occasionally in the capacity of leader. He can learn the difference in leadership and followership roles. He can also comprehend the fact that he should not expect to be leader at all times.

10. During the latter part of the primary grades the child becomes more interested than formerly in the faraway in place and the remote in time. However, these periods and places must be made quite concrete to him if they are to get his prolonged interest and he is to profit from them. Abstractions still are frequently beyond his comprehension.

11. The primary-grade child continues to learn the customs and the prejudices of the culture of which he is a part. Nevertheless, social rank usually means little to him.

Intellectual Development

There are no sudden cataclysmic changes in intellectual development of the child between the time when he is of preschool age and the time when he enters fourth grade. Yet the intellectual development of the child as he leaves the third grade of the elementary school is strikingly different from that of the same child three years before.

These are some of the usual characteristics of the intellectual growth of the primary-grade child that should have considerable bearing on methods of guiding him in his development of communication skills.

1. One of the outstanding characteristics of the intellectual development of the primary-grade child is that there are striking individual differences. These are due in part to hereditary factors, which set the upper limit of intellectual achievement for a given individual. In fact, the range of intelligence is so great that no uniform curriculum can satisfy the varying needs of all children.

2. The intellectual activity of the first-grade child is to a considerable extent determined by factors that have direct influence upon him. He is too ego-centered to care much about many matters not pertaining to him. His intellectual curiosity is greater, as a rule, in regard to the near in time and space than in the distant. However, as he continues on the path to adult intellectual development, he becomes increasingly interested also in matters that have less direct and obvious bearing upon his own self and more in those that are distant in time and space.

3. The difference between reality and fantasy is not always clear to the beginner in the primary grades, but usually by the end of the third grade differentiation is no problem. Even when the child knows the difference, however, he likes to engage in highly imaginative incidents, especially in the first grade. These are enjoyed vicariously and in dramatic play.

4. Interest in immediate goals rather than remote, which is highly characteristic of the child when he begins his years in the elementary school, gives way in part, under wise guidance, to interest in less immediate goals.

5. During the typical three years of the primary grades the child develops more objectivity in his intellectual considerations. At six his judgments are likely to be highly subjective and often inaccurate, and even by the time he becomes nine, subjectivity and inaccuracy are still characteristic, though less so.

6. Interest in the concrete rather than the abstract, in fact, frequent failure to comprehend the abstract, is an outstanding quality of the six-year-old. Even at nine, though abstractions can be understood better than earlier, interest in and comprehension of the concrete are still predominant.

7. The primary-grade child develops markedly in an environment rich in stimulating experiences. However, contrary to the belief of many adults, the child even in preschool years is far from lacking in his power to use higher thought processes.

8. Because of paucity of experience and inability to profit from many types of experiences, the six-year-old has a relatively small number of concepts. However, during the first three years of his elementary school education, under desirable environmental conditions, growth in this respect is phenomenal.

9. The attention span of the six-year-old is brief but under appropriate guidance it can be greatly increased by the time he completes the primary grades.

10. Purpose continues to serve as a significant factor in the persistence with which the learner performs. That purpose needs, however, to be the learner's purpose, not merely that of an adult.

11. The primary-grade child likes to put thought into action. The need for doing and making is characteristic of the intellectual development of the child of that age range.

12. At the beginning of the first grade the child has difficulty in following directions other than very simple ones. Marked development, however, takes place during the course of the next few years.

In chapter 1 (see page 8) it is indicated that claims by Jerome S. Bruner and those by Jean Piaget concerning the developing cognitive powers of the child, if accepted by persons in the area of the language arts, may in time have a marked effect upon the teaching of the language arts. Hilda Taba thus ably summarizes the developmental stages that Piaget identifies:

....He (Piaget) suggests a progressive revolutionary sequence in the development of cognitive abilities. The first stage consists of differentiating, coordinating, and generalizing of the sensory motor schemata. During the earliest years of his life the child is establishing a relationship between experience and action and developing certain fixed habits.
The second stage is that of concrete operations. Ordinarily by about five years of age the child is developing, through manipulation of objects, certain generalizations about reality, and forming simple concepts which represent groupings of objects and events into classes.
The stage of formal thought is reached when the individual is capable of manipulating symbols instead of objects. This form of reasoning no longer depends only on raw reality or descriptive and discrete events and facts. The individual is no longer limited by what is before him. He can deal with hypothetical possibilities.... He can deal with classes of events and objects and can construct relationships between abstract generalizations.[1]

The third stage of logic Piaget believes is typically reached by the age of eleven.

The following paragraph by Hilda Taba presents, in summary, the three stages of intellectual growth that Jerome S. Bruner recognizes.

Bruner postulates a somewhat similar sequence of three stages in representation of the world. The first mode of representation is the inactive, in which events are represented through appropriate motor responses, such as navigating among familiar objects without tripping over them. The second mode, the iconic, organizes events in perceptual images. These images "stand" for events just as a picture of a house "stands" for the real house. The third mode of representation is through symbols, or words.[2]

Significantly Hilda Taba adds:

The important question for educators is how the transitions are made from one stage to another, for in the dynamic of these transitions is the clue to how education can influence the maturation of cognitive processes.[3]

GENERAL CHARACTERISTICS OF THE INTERMEDIATE-GRADE CHILD

Upon entrance to the fourth grade the typical child has changed considerably in physical, emotional, social, and intellectual development from the time three years before when he started in the first grade. These changes have not been cataclysmic, but in their steady development, have nevertheless been certain and significant. They continue in the next three years, during the period of time usually spent in the intermediate grades (grades four, five, and six).

Physical Development

The following points explain characteristics of boys and girls in the period of middle childhood. They all have bearing on guidance in the development of communication skills that normally a child of that period can acquire.

1. Throughout middle childhood the typical girl continues to be at least one year more advanced in physiological development than the typical boy of the same chronological age.

1. Jean Fair and Fannie R. Shaftel (editors), *Effective Thinking in the Social Studies*. The 37th Yearbook of the National Council for the Social Studies. Hilda Taba, "Implementing Thinking as an Objective in Social Studies," National Council for the Social Studies, A Department of the National Education Association, p. 29.
2. Ibid., pp. 29-30.
3. Ibid., p. 30.

2. For both boys and girls in the period immediately preceding the spurt of preadolescence, there is for a short time almost a seeming cessation of physical growth.

3. Girls make their greatest gain in height during the last year of the intermediate grades and during the first of the junior high school. The rapid increase in height of boys usually takes place two years later. Much of the gain is in length of legs.

4. Middle childhood marks a period with fewer illnesses than there were during early childhood, resulting in more regular attendance at school.

5. Development in coordination continues during the period of middle childhood. However, a relatively small number of pupils in the sixth grade are awkward in movements. These tend to be girls who are approaching early adolescence. Their awkwardness is due, in part, to uneven skeletal development and to emotional changes of that period.

6. Posture continues to be relatively poor for many during this period.

7. Middle childhood is a time of much physical endurance and great energy.

8. During the period of middle childhood organs of circulation, respiration, and digestion approach those of adulthood in size.

Emotional Development

To probe into the inner world of human beings is, at best, a difficult task. During the years of middle childhood it is probably more baffling than during some other stages of development.

What the individual reports about his feelings gives one index of his emotional life. But often the child is not accurate in his responses, made either casually or in more formal set-ups as in questionnaires or interviews. At times this lack of accuracy is undoubtedly the result of willful evasion of facts. In many other instances the response is unreliable because the child is unaware of his true feeling. Since he often has more difficulty in understanding himself during the intermediate-grade years than he has during some other periods of life, his own confusion about himself leads to reports about his feelings that are likely, in many instances, to be incorrect.

A second method of gathering data on the emotions is by studying actions. But middle childhood is a period when there is much contradictory behavior—one minute reversion to earlier immature stages and another progression to more adult standards. Furthermore, the intermediate-grade child has "learned" more successfully than when he was in the primary grades to camouflage his true feelings at times by not revealing them through behavior. Consequently, gaining insight into the inner world of the intermediate-grade child

through his actions as well as through his reports is a process subject to many errors.

In spite of the problems involved in ascertaining characteristic feelings of the intermediate-grade child, however, we do have access to valuable though incomplete information. When coupled with common sense, a love for children, and a desire to observe them, the available information can make a great difference in the skill and artistry with which teachers guide boys and girls in their language development. A few comments on the trends of emotional development of the intermediate-grade child are listed here.

1. One of the characteristic patterns of the typical intermediate-grade child is lack of consistency in his actions, which frequently vary between rather adult responses and immature behavior. Often this outward state indicates an inner emotional condition that fluctuates between the impulsive expression of emotions of early childhood and the more intellectual responses of the adult. It would seem that the variation frequently is in the emotion itself, not only in its expression.

2. Both boys and girls continue to care more and more about what their peers think and correspondingly less about what adults want. In fact, there is a growing rejection of adult standards of conduct. Nevertheless, the children of this stage typically still accept the correctness of many of the moral standards that their parents taught them, even though, unfortunately, they do not necessarily live up to the rules they consider right.

3. Boys and girls in the intermediate grades continue to need love and affection from both adults and peers. Behind the seeming indifference to adults there is a deep craving for their affection which, if not satisfied, is likely to have damaging effects upon the child. To be thought of highly by the peer group is, however. also necessary to the emotional well-being of the child in fourth, fifth, and sixth grades; in fact, the peer group counts much more during this period than it did in preceding stages. Middle childhood is a time when the child feels real need of a chum with whom he can share intimately his joys and sorrows, his shortcomings and his assets.

4. The intermediate-grade child becomes more and more aware of himself as an individual. Together with this growth in self-awareness come self-analysis and self-criticism. When kept within the bounds of normalcy, such analysis and criticism of self are healthy. That it is a time of self-awareness and self-criticism is not strange in the case of boys and girls approaching adolescence, for there often are many inner confusions resulting in part from lack of understanding of the new role to be played.

5. To please the parent or the teacher in most cases is no longer sufficient incentive for perseverance in work. Other objectives often supplement or substitute for this

goal that was often a driving purpose in the early primary grades.

6. As boys and girls approach adolescence, they become increasingly conscious of the opposite sex and in time increasingly interested in it; the girls, as a rule, clearly manifest such interest earlier than the boys.

7. Boys and girls are responsive to the idealism of heroes in life and in story.

8. Boys and girls are often greatly concerned in this period of growth about what their conscience dictates to them. When kept within proper limits, this concern is highly desirable. However, at times they become too involved in decisions of conscience and develop so-called "guilt complexes." They are too immature during middle childhood to carry the burden of making many decisions, the solution to which might bother them a great deal. Adults do the child a favor when they decide many matters for him and thus save him the need of making certain emotional involvements, even if the child does not like the decision. However, unless the boy and girl increasingly are given freedom to make their own decisions and to assume responsibility for them, they are likely to be stunted in at least one phase of their development.

9. It is very important to the intermediate-grade child that he be successful in some activities significant to him and that other people consider him capable. Without the satisfaction of success the child's emotional responses may not develop normally. Sometimes under such circumstances he becomes introverted, developing an "I don't care" attitude. At other times he may try so hard to succeed that his disappointment at failure can be highly detrimental to him, or undue concentration on certain activities, for which success is greatly coveted, may make him one-sided.

10. As the intermediate-grade child approaches adolescence, he frequently feels more keenly than before the joy and the pain that typically accompany many phases of development.

Social Development

Below are indicated characteristics in social development of the intermediate-grade child.

1. In the emotions of the intermediate-grade pupil as well as in his actions, unpredictability is one of the most outstanding characteristics during the period of middle childhood. One minute the reaction in a social situation involving one or more people may be that expected during earlier stages of development. The next time, shortly thereafter, it may be on a much more adult level.

2. The typical middle-grade child no longer cares to do as many things alone as he did in earlier years. He seeks the company of others.

3. The company that the intermediate-grade pupil

desires increasingly becomes that of his peers rather than that of adults, with whom he had contentedly spent much time in earlier stages. There is such a pronounced change in this respect that the "poor parent" who formerly had been enthroned by his child now thinks he is "deserted" for members of the child's peer group. But the parent should not be disconsolate, for, first of all, he is not really "deserted" since the child still depends on him for warmth, security, and love although his actions at times seem to belie this fact. Second, this emergence from the close parent-child relationship of earlier days is part of the development from the "dependency of infancy to the independency of adulthood" which every thinking parent desires for his child, painful for the parent though this process often may be.

4. The intermediate-grade child likes to have a close pal, but he is also interested in groups, small groups as well as groups larger than those he chose to join in early childhood. Frequently "secret societies," often harmless in nature, take on greater importance as well as greater complexity.

5. The groups to which intermediate-grade boys and girls belong are more highly structured than were the informal groups of former years.

6. Increasingly boys and girls prefer to be with members of their own sex, a preference that changes somewhat during adolescence.

7. Children of this stage of development often adopt as their own the mannerisms or other actions of those persons who to them are heroes; some are flesh-and-blood persons whom they have met while others are characters from fiction or biography.

8. Problems of juvenile delinquency frequently show up for the first time during middle childhood.

9. The intermediate-grade child is likely to be greatly concerned that his wearing apparel and other possessions should be similar to those of his best friends.

10. As the child progresses through the period of middle childhood, increasingly he becomes more interested in group rather than individual play activities, and he concentrates his interests in a few, not many, types of play.

Intellectual Development

In planning the program in the language arts, the intermediate-grade teacher should be conscious of the relationship between intellectual characteristics of the pupil and the procedures to be employed in guiding the child to optimum language development, some of which are suggested following.

1. The range in intellectual capacity among intermediate-grade pupils within a class is usually greater than that in any one of the preceeding grades. This increase in variation is due, in part, to the fact that the

child with above-normal intelligence continues to grow intellectually each year more than does the average child of the same chronological age, while the child with below-normal intelligence continues to develop less each year than does the average child.

2. Variations in the use made of the potentialities with which an individual was endowed are greater by the time a pupil has reached the intermediate grades than formerly, and consequently there is even greater difference in ability.

3. These are some of the ways in which the intellectual development of the typical intermediate-grade child are manifested:

He is more interested than formerly in the remote in time and space.

He is keenly interested in the world in which he lives so that questions of *how* and *why* are asked frequently.

He is greatly interested in making classifications so that his ever-expanding world can be arranged in his mind into some kind of order.

He is more understanding than formerly of cause-effect and other logical relationships. Under wise guidance he is able to make generalizations on a fairly difficult level.

He has increased in ability to comprehend numerous abstractions but he continues to be in need of many concrete experiences.

He can concentrate for a longer period of time than formerly.

He can follow directions better for he can put into action more complex directions than earlier.

In general, by the time he leaves the intermediate grades he has developed a great deal in understanding truth and various abstractions of goodness.

The intermediate-grade boy is considerably less interested than formerly in fantasy, but some girls very much enjoy reading poetry and prose that give free sway to the imagination.

The reader is referred to the claims of Jean Piaget and Jerome Bruner as given in the discussion of the intellectual development of the primary-grade child (see page 19). The stages there outlined include not only the years typically spent in the primary grades but also those in the intermediate grades.

LANGUAGE DEVELOPMENT OF THE ELEMENTARY SCHOOL CHILD

We have now observed some phases of the general development of the child as he passes through the primary and intermediate grades that have particular implications for the guidance of growth in language abilities. Let us next note the chief characteristics of the elementary-school child as far as growth in language is concerned.

1. Basic to the understanding of growth in the language arts—in listening, speaking, reading, and writing—is the fact that they are inextricably interrelated. Even in the early stages of speaking it is plainly evident that this facet of the language arts is greatly influenced by the listening that the child does—by what he hears of the many sounds in his environment. His background for learning to read is conditioned to a considerable extent by what he has heard and how he has conversed previously. Further development in reading is affected similarly. The child's writing is also influenced by what he has spoken and by what he has read. Thus many skills affect more than one facet of the language arts program. For example, skill in sentence structure is very important in speaking, reading, and writing activities. Some of the skills needed in paragraph structure, such as having a good beginning, keeping to the topic, and having a good ending, are important to both oral and written communication.

2. At the time the child enters the first grade most of the physical organs needed for performing functions in communication are mature enough not to furnish reason for delay in development of the skills. In fact, from early infancy the child's hearing apparatus is mature enough to enable him to pick up sounds in the world around him. Similarly, the speech organs are well developed even at the time of birth. In spite of the fact that the organs are physiologically mature enough to serve functions of speaking and listening well, the elementary school child often needs assistance in developing clearer speech and greater auditory awareness.

There is a difference of opinion as to whether the eye is mature enough by the time the child enters first grade for that to be the desirable time for beginning to learn to read. At that time the child is still inclined toward farsightedness. However, long postponement of learning to read is not urged on these grounds by most specialists in the field. Rather than waiting a few years after the child enters school, until he is no longer likely to be farsighted, they recommend that care be taken that reading materials appropriate in size and clarity of type be used, and that the amount and time spent on close eye work be regulated in the interest of the hygiene of the eye.

By the time the child has come to the first grade his physiological setup for muscular coordinations has been greatly developed although it still is easier for him at that time to make large-muscle rather than small-muscle coordinations—a fact of great importance for consideration in planning a program in handwriting.

3. The broad outline of the sequence of the pattern of the development of the communication skills is essentially the same for all normal human beings. However, the details of language development as they affect the time for taking up various topics in the program of oral communication, for example, have not been established.

4. Although the sequence in the development of communication skills in broad terms is approximately the same for all normal human beings, the timing of the ap-

pearance of various phases in this sequence varies greatly from one individual to another.

5. By the time the child enters first grade he has had almost six years of very fruitful practice in listening and about five in speaking. Typically before entrance to kindergarten the child has acquired skill in the use of many of the essential elements of the English language. Trauger summarizes these acquisitions thus:

By the time they enter kindergarten, children are quite experienced in combining words into statements. In infancy, before starting to put words together, they listened to other people's sentences. Also they babbled a wide variety of sounds, emitting them in an appreciable range of intonations. Gradually they sorted out such sounds and intonations as they heard used in speech and began using words and sequences of words meaningfully. They developed a fair mastery of the English structure pattern. In the earliest grades pupils know the sound system of the language, the subject-verb-object sequence of statement sentences, the inverted sequence and sustained intonation of questions, the patterns of command and exclamation, the placement of the adjective before the noun, the forms signaling tense, singular and plural number, possession, and such vocal signals as pitch, stress, volume, pauses, and tempo. So well developed is this knowledge that a child in the earliest grades generates sentences to meet all his needs. He has yet to master the more complicated patterns of sentences.

The implications of word position are known, too. Statements like "The dog bit the raccoon" and "The raccoon bit the dog" stand in contrasted meanings for any pupil.

There is also a feel for the several classes of words or parts of speech. Before the age of five, and in some cases a year or two earlier, children sense the "nounness" of nouns and the "verbness" of verbs in sentences. A basis exists likewise for an understanding of adjectives, adverbs, conjunctions, and prepositions.[4]

In vocabulary development the first-grade child has made tremendous strides during preceding years of his life, much greater than he is likely to make after entering school or any time thereafter. The problem in his vocabulary development during his early school years lies not so much in the small number of words that he uses as in the limited or erroneous meanings that he associates with some of them.

6. Although there is a close relationship between language ability and intelligence, intelligence is only one factor that helps determine language development. As set by the innate pattern of the individual, intelligence marks the limit of the development that is possible—determines the potentialities for growth. However, environment has a significant part in determining to what extent those potentialities will be realized and in what manner they will be developed.

7. As the child progresses through the elementary school, there is rather steady growth in language abilities and skills rather than development characterized by sudden spurts.

8. As the child advances from six years to thirteen years of age, he shows marked gain in ability to use language skills effectively in group situations involving planning, executing, and evaluating.

9. The following statements indicate some environmental influences that affect language development.

A favorable socioeconomic background seems to be beneficial to the child in the development of language skills. This relationship is probably due in part to the fact that the child brought up in a favorable socioeconomic environment is more likely to have the assurance needed for satisfactory language development. Furthermore, he often has more opportunity to engage in desirable types of communication.

The extent of a child's experience, firsthand and vicarious, and the richness of it determines in part the development of his skill in communication.

The "only child" is likely to be more advanced in language development than the child who has brothers and sisters, probably due to the closer, more exclusive contact with adults with greater language facility than sisters and brothers.

Twins are inclined to be less advanced in language development than other children during their early years partly because much of their association usually is with one another, not with adults.

The quality of the language of the adults with whom the child comes into contact, both at school and at home, greatly affects his power of communication. "Baby talk" by parents when speaking to a child is likely to have an unfavorable effect upon the child's growth in language.

In homes where a language other than English is spoken, the child upon entrance to school is likely to be handicapped in his ability to communicate in English, regardless of advantages in other respects that may accrue for him because of his knowledge of two languages.

In general, girls excel boys in various language abilities. However, boys have been found, too, in many instances to excel girls. The superiority of some boys in this respect may be due in part to the fact that fewer boys than girls seem to be shy in asking questions and in other aspects of communication affected adversely by shyness.

The opportunity the child has to use communication skills helps determine the extent of his language development.

A critical attitude toward the child's language development frequently affects communication skills unfavorably. This statement is not to be interpreted, however, as an argument against wisely given constructive criticism.

If a pupil upon entry to school speaks a dialect unlike that used in school, grave problems are likely to exist for him unless his teacher is skillful in preventing them. Lack of acceptance of the child's dialect, regardless of the part of the country in which he lives, may cause damage to the child's concept of himself and of the rest of his family. Such an attitude on the part of the teacher can be disastrous because the language a child speaks, including his dialect, is such an integral part of him that

4. Wilmer K. Trauger, *Language Arts in Elementary Schools* (New York: McGraw-Hill Book Company, 1963), pp. 140-41. Used by permission of McGraw-Hill Book Company.

nonacceptance of it by the teacher may spell a lack of acceptance of himself and of his family for a sensitive child. The wise teacher accepts the child's dialect while at the same time helping him acquire the dialect spoken in school.

FOR STUDY AND DISCUSSION

1. In what ways is information about the physical development of an elementary school child of particular significance to the teacher in the program of the language arts?

2. How can the teacher relate the program in the language arts to the fact that boys and girls in the intermediate grades are greatly influenced by the sanctions of the peer group?

3. How can the teacher through the language arts help boys and girls learn to distinguish more clearly between reality and fantasy?

4. On page 20 these two statements occur: "The intermediate-grade child becomes more and more aware of himself as an individual. Together with this growth in self-awareness come self-analysis and self-criticism." Cite ways in which the teacher can gear the language arts program so that the boys and girls develop mentally healthy practices in self-analysis and self-criticism.

5. On page 22 it is stated that when the child enters first grade "most of the physical organs needed for performing functions in communication are mature enough not to furnish reason for delay in development of the skills." What then are reasons that in your estimation may serve as cause for delay in teaching some boys and girls to read shortly after they start first grade?

6. How can the teacher help the elementary school child to attain optimum physical maturity as he develops from early childhood to adolescence?

7. Describe an elementary school child whom you know as to his physical, emotional, social, and intellectual characteristics. Include in your description comparisons with the characteristics discussed in this chapter.

8. If Jean Piaget's three stages in the development of cognitive powers (see page 19) are correct, what changes in the language arts program as you know it would it seem important to make?

9. Read again the paragraph on page 19 in which Hilda Taba summarizes the three stages of intellectual growth that Jerome S. Bruner recognizes and note the statement in which she adds: "The important question for educators is how the transitions are made from one stage to another, for in the dynamic of these transitions is the clue to how education can influence the maturation of cognitive processes." What suggestions do you have as to ways in which transition can be brought about successfully?

10. Indicate ways in which the teacher can show acceptance if the child speaks a different dialect than the one used in the school. Can you suggest ways in which the teacher might inadvertently cause the child with a different dialect to feel rejected?

11. In what ways can the school profitably make use of the language arts experiences of the child in his home?

REFERENCES

Boyd, Gertrude A. *Teaching Communication Skills in the Elementary School.* New York: Van Nostrand Reinhold Company, 1970.

Bruner, Jerome S. *The Process of Education.* Cambridge, Mass.: Harvard University Press, 1960.

Burns, Paul C.; Broman, Betty L.; and Wantling, Alberta L. Lowe. *The Language Arts in Childhood Education.* 2d ed. Chicago: Rand McNally & Company, 1971.

Cleland, Donald L., ed. *Reading and the Related Arts.* A Report of the Twenty-first Annual Conference and Course on Reading, University of Pittsburgh. "Developmental Language Patterns of Children" by Dora V. Smith, pp. 19-28. University of Pittsburgh, 1965.

Dallmann, Martha; Rouch, Roger L.; Chang, Lynette Y.; and De Boer, John J. *The Teaching of Reading.* 4th ed. New York: Holt, Rinehart and Winston, 1974.

Donoghue, Mildred R. *The Child and the English Language Arts.* Dubuque, Iowa; Wm. C. Brown Company Publishers, 1975.

Gardner, D. Bruce. *Development in Early Childhood.* New York: Harper & Row, Publishers, 1964.

Harding, Lowry W. *Arithmetic for Child Development.* Dubuque, Iowa: Wm. C. Brown Company Publishers, 1964.

Havighurst, Robert J. *Developmental Tasks in Education.* New York: David McKay Company, Inc., 1952.

Inhelder, Barbel, and Piaget, Jean. *The Early Growth of Logic in the Child.* Translated from the French by E. A. Lunzer and D. Papert. New York: Harper & Row, Publishers, 1964.

Lamb, Pose, ed. *Guiding Children's Language Learning.* Dubuque, Iowa: Wm. C. Brown Company Publishers, 1967.

Olson, Willard. *Child Development.* Lexington, Mass.: D.C. Heath and Company, 1959.

Piaget, Jean. *The Language and Thought of the Child.* New York: Humanities Press, 1959.

Rebelsky, Freda, and Dorman, Lynn, eds. *Child Development and Behavior.* New York: Random House, Inc., 1970.

Ruddell, Robert B. *Reading-language Instruction: Innovative Practices.* Englewood Cliffs, N.J.: Prentice-Hall, Inc., 1974.

Smith, E. Brooks; Goodman, Kenneth S.; and Meredith, Robert. *Language and Thinking in the Elementary School.* New York: Holt, Rinehart and Winston, 1970.

Smith, James A. *Adventures in Communication: Language Arts Methods.* Boston: Allyn & Bacon, 1972.

Strickland, Ruth G. *The Language Arts in the Elementary School.* 3rd ed. Lexington, Mass.: D.C. Heath and Company, 1969.

2

DEVELOPMENTAL PROCEDURES
IN GUIDING GROWTH
IN COMMUNICATION SKILLS

3

Common Problems in Teaching the Language Arts

In spite of the close interrelatedness of the various aspects of the language arts that must be respected in teaching if maximum results are to be attained, a consideration of the methods of teaching each of these phases is important. It is impossible to give concise suggestions for teaching, which this book presents, without somewhere dealing specifically with each of the major components. It is for this reason that in Part Two of this book, which deals primarily with methods of teaching, the suggestions are classified as indicated in the following chapter headings:

    Guiding Growth in Oral Communication
    Guiding Growth in Written Expression
    Guiding Growth in Skills Common to Oral and Written Communication
    Guiding Growth in Handwriting
    Guiding Growth in Spelling
    Guiding Growth in Reading Skills Closely Related to the Other Language Arts
    Guiding Growth in Independent Reading.

Although in succeeding chapters attention is paid separately to each of the foregoing phases of the language arts, nevertheless in this chapter there are discussed some of the problems common to two or more aspects of the language arts. This plan of organization is followed in order to prevent needless repetition.

PURPOSE OF THE LANGUAGE ARTS PROGRAM

What are we aiming to accomplish through the teaching of the language arts? That is, indeed, an important question for teachers to attempt to answer as they plan their work.

General Objectives

There are various degrees of specificity with which the objectives can be expressed. They can, for example, be given in such general terms as in the statement that the teaching of the language arts should help the learner to lead a more "personally satisfying and socially useful life than he would be likely to have without the guidance he gets in the area.

General objectives in the language arts can also be stated in terms of the often-cited facets of the language arts in this manner:

1. To help the learner express himself better orally
2. To help the learner to be a more attentive listener and increase in ability to comprehend better what he hears
3. To help the learner comprehend better the meaning of the written word
4. To help the learner express himself better in writing.

Specific Objectives

For the day-in, day-out work in the classroom specific goals are a requirement for maximum effectiveness. They should spell out in more usable terms the general objectives. In this book specific objectives are considered in connection with various phases of the language arts that are taken up in the chapters to follow.

Enumeration of objectives in the different aspects of the language arts program should not be interpreted as a recommendation to teach them independently of one another. Specific attention to the various parts is given in this book in order to add clarity to general suggestions that are made. In all teaching the interrelatedness should be recognized even though at times it is important to place primary emphasis on one phase, or even on a small segment of it, before it is integrated into the total program.

IMPORTANCE OF THE LANGUAGE ARTS PROGRAM

The significance of the role that development in the language arts can play in the growth of the individual and in turn in the improvement of society has already been pointed out in part in the statement of general objectives. The following list of statements highlights some of the points made and adds others.

1. Through development in the language arts the learner can increase his ability to think.
2. Through language development the individual can increase his power to affect the behavior of others.
3. Through language development the learner can increase his skill in the various fields of human learning.
4. Through guidance in the language arts the learner cannot only increase his skills and abilities, but also improve his attitudes and develop his understandings.
5. Through an individual's effectiveness in the language arts the choice and success of his vocation or profession can be greatly influenced.

INCIDENTAL VERSUS SYSTEMATIC INSTRUCTION

One of the most debated questions in the teaching of the language arts in the elementary school centers around the place of incidental versus systematic instruction. Lack of agreement on the meaning of the terms causes some of the argument. Usually *systematic instruction* in the language arts refers to a program in which the skills are taught according to a systematically thought-out plan. On the contrary *incidental instruction* indicates a program of instruction by means of which the pupils acquire the communication skills incidentally as need for their use arises within lifelike situations that confront the learner.

Most persons favoring systematic instruction do not ignore the opportunities for the development of language skills through lifelike situations. Rather, their argument is that total dependence on such situations as the only means of developing desirable skills does not guarantee that all needed skills will be taught adequately. They do insist upon systematic instruction in addition to the incidental.

Adherents to the claim that the rule should be incidental instruction seldom go as far as to exclude all systematic work. In many cases they insist only that most of the learning be done in bona fide situations in which the child recognizes the need of the skills. There are some teachers who favor only incidental instruction in speaking, writing, and listening phases of the language arts while they want systematic instruction in reading. Others also may agree to systematic instruction in spelling though they object to it in handwriting. Thus the difference between those favoring incidental and those arguing for systematic instruction is frequently one of the extent to which each of these two means should be used.

Arguments Advanced for Incidental Instruction

Some of the commonly advanced arguments for incidental rather than systematic instruction in the language arts are as follows:

1. Learning in the language arts takes place in a program in which the pupils use the skills in communication in a challenging environment.
2. Learning language skills in lifelike situations assists the learner in recognizing the value of the skills he is acquiring and consequently motivates him to try to become proficient in them.
3. Learning communication skills in lifelike situations is likely to provide the learner with the opportunity to practice various language arts skills in the same situation.
4. Learning communication skills in lifelike situations places emphasis on application of what is learned to

other situations, while frequently practice in more formal setups does not carry over into later use to the extent desired.

Arguments Favoring Systematic Instruction

The following are some of the arguments given in favor of systematic instruction:

1. The reaction against systematic instruction set in at a time when much meaningless drill served as the chief means of teaching the language arts. The criticism should be against almost exclusive use of ineffective drill, not against well-planned systematic instruction.

2. Incidental instruction is often accidental instruction, with learning left to chance.

3. In incidental instruction more time than necessary is spent on some skills.

4. Unless there is systematic instruction, some important skills will not be learned at all, while others will not receive the attention needed for the desired degree of mastery.

5. Economy of learning some skills requires that special emphasis be placed on teaching them and that a planned program of practice on them be followed.

6. In nonsystematic programs of language instruction the chief emphasis is usually placed on something other than the skills of language. For example, when the language work is correlated with the social studies to the exclusion of separate work on the development of communication skills, the major attention is often on the subject matter of the social studies rather than on the development of communication skills.

7. Use of a systematic program of instruction in the language arts does not preclude incidental instruction. Consequently the advantages of incidental instruction, without its disadvantages, can be achieved in a program in which systematic instruction takes care of those learnings that are not adequately and economically acquired through incidental instruction.

Point of View Emphasized in This Book

While the writer realizes the importance of the use of lifelike situations for learning in the language arts, she nevertheless believes that there should be a planned program richly supplemented by one in which such situations are used. She believes that many pupils need considerable practice in the perfection of many of the skills required for efficiency—more than can frequently be relied upon to be provided by incidental means only. However, the writer emphasizes the fact that pupils should be helped to find purpose for learning such skills by recognizing their significance in true-to-life situations and that they should be assisted in making application of what they are learning through systematic practice in such situations. To the writer the problems connected

with systematic and incidental instruction do not appear as an either/or proposition. Many of the specific suggestions for teaching given in this book reflect this point of view.

SELECTION OF CONTENT

What is taught in the language arts is important. There is so much information that could be acquired and so many skills that could be developed that selectivity is essential. How then can the content of the program in the language arts in the elementary school be determined wisely? Here are some guiding principles.

1. The language arts are primarily tools of communication rather than subject matter to be learned. It should, however, be remembered that many persons recommending the linguistic approach to the language arts emphasize the importance of teaching phases of the language as subject matter. (See page 40.) Even when this emphasis is stressed application should, nevertheless, be made of the learnings acquired in such a way as to insure an improved use, by the boys and girls, of the English language.

2. Application should be made of what has been established by research in the field of child growth and development so that the curriculum in the language arts is planned in accordance with, not contrary to, what is known about maturation of the child, in terms of abilities, interests, and needs.

3. The content of the language arts program should be selected in terms of the objectives that have been accepted.

4. The content of the language arts curriculum should be determined in part by the ongoing activities of the classroom in other areas and, at the same time, the ongoing classroom activities in other areas should be chosen in part in terms of the needs and interests of the child in his language development. An example of the language arts curriculum determined by the activities in other areas is as follows: When pupils are preparing talks in connection with their work in the social studies, emphasis can and should be placed not only on the acquisition of the subject matter presented in these talks but also on the development of skill in giving talks. On the other hand, when, for example, one of the objectives to be stressed in the language arts program is to acquire a larger and more expressive vocabulary, emphasis on vocabulary may consciously be directed to the acquisition of knowledge and use of "new words" studied in an area of learning in science.

5. The content of the language arts curriculum should not be limited to the needs of the pupil at the time; attention should be given to future needs also. Fortunately, present and future needs of boys and girls are often the

same. Regardless of whether the content serves immediate or future needs, care should be taken that the pupil recognizes the usefulness of the activity.

6. In the selection of content, provision needs to be made for individual differences.

7. When selecting content, the teacher needs to begin where the child is, not where he thinks the learner ought to be.

8. The selection of the content for the elementary school curriculum should be a cooperative enterprise in which teachers on all levels have an opportunity to contribute their knowledge. When this guideline is followed gaps in the learnings in the language arts can be avoided in part, and repetitions can be consciously planned when and as needed rather than usually included haphazardly.

9. Each teacher, sometimes with assistance of pupils, should have freedom in determining details of content within the framework of the program planned for the school.

SEQUENCE AND GRADE PLACEMENT

After the content of the curriculum in the language arts has been determined, it is necessary to decide on sequence and grade placement. To the general pattern of growth we have already referred earlier in this book.

Unfortunately there is a great deficit in available information as to desirable sequence and grade placement of content and activites. The curriculum maker cannot state with confidence that any particular order is the most advantageous. However, even now there need not be groping in total darkness when deciding upon sequence and grade placement. Guidelines such as the following can be of service.

1. From the field of human growth and development help should be utilized from data, such as those presented in chapter 2, which indicate in general terms the sequence in the development of communication skills in the normal individual.

2. From the field of human growth and development data should be utilized that show the most likely times of appearance of particular abilities and skills. As these data are considered it should, however, be borne in mind that there is more variation in time of occurrence than in sequence in appearance of many language abilities.

3. Psychological rather than logical factors should be the determinants of sequence and grade placement whenever there is a conflict between the two types of factors. For example, while logically parts of a sentence might be studied before complete sentences, the psychological order might be the reverse.

4. The abilities, needs, and interests of boys and girls should play important parts in determining sequence and placement.

5. Emphasis should be placed on what Robert Havighurst calls the "teachable moment" when the learner is ready to learn what will be taught.(See page 6.)

6. While the needs of children at any given stage of development should be an important criterion for determining curricular content, the likely needs of boys and girls when they become adults should also be considered.

7. There should be flexibility within the framework of the curriculum so that within it each teacher has leeway in terms of sequence to be followed.

8. The curriculum for any one grade should make provision for the wide range of abilities within the grade.

9. The difficulty of learning an activity or acquiring information should determine in part the sequence and placement.

10. The grade placement of a topic or an activity should be determined in part by the number of other activities or topics already allocated to a grade.

11. There should be a balance of types of subject matter or activities allocated to any one grade. A teacher who overemphasizes, for example, the use of puppetry in developing self-expression may do so to the neglect of the development of self-expression through poetry.

12. The content of the language arts curriculum for any one grade should be chosen in relation to that of other grades.

13. The textbook should by no means be the sole determinant of sequence and grade placement.

14. Provision should be made for review and application of learnings acquired in preceding grades.

PROBLEM SOLVING

Contrary to popular opinion even very young children engage in problem-solving activities. Teacher guidance can be valuable in assisting boys and girls in solving problems more effectively than they would unaided. The teacher can surround the boys and girls with an environment conducive to the solution of problems and can help them in the various steps.

Steps in Problem Solving

The steps in problem solving have been identified in various ways. Here is one simple listing:

1. Sensing the problem
2. Defining the problem
3. Making hypotheses as to how the problem may be solved
4. Deciding on a likely hypothesis (to try first)
5. Testing the hypothesis
6. If the hypothesis does not stand the test, deciding on another hypothesis and testing it and then proceeding in this manner until a hypothesis that works is found.

Arriving at Generalizations

One type of problem solving takes place through arriving at generalizations inductively. Unfortunately too often the teaching-learning process takes place primarily by means of the predominant use of the deductive rather than the inductive method. When the deductive method is used the learner typically makes use of a principle enunciated by the teacher or another individual or one stated in a book. When the inductive method is used, the child learns the principle, by noting differences and/or likenesses through the observation or study of a number of situations on the basis of which he can come to a conclusion. The deductive method is used, for example, when the teacher tells the boys and girls what characteristics of a good ending for a report are, such as avoiding such expressions as "That's all I know on the subject" or "I guess my time is up." The inductive method would be used if the teacher, after presenting to the boys and girls a series of written reports, some of which have satisfactory and some of which have unsatisfactory endings, asks the pupils which ones have a good ending. Then, to continue in the development of a generalization, he could ask the pupils to see if they can make a list of some characteristics of good endings and possibly poor endings for a report. If, following the making of a generalization about what characterizes a good ending, the pupils determine which additional reports, of which they have been given copies, have good endings or if they give examples of appropriate endings, a combination of the inductive-deductive method is used. As a rule, inductive learning, culminating in the making of a generalization, should be followed by use of the deductive method, as the pupils make immediate application of the rule or generalization that has been discovered by means of the inductive method. If this procedure is used, the method is referred to as the inductive-deductive method.

Let us clarify what is meant by inductive-deductive teaching by another example. In order to help the boys and girls learn the correct use of *sang* and *sung*, the teacher might have on the chalkboard several sentences, possibly four or five, in some of which *sang* is used correctly while *sung* is used correctly in the others. The teacher might then ask the pupils whether they can figure out when *sang* is used correctly and when *sung* is the right form. Or he might help the boys and girls by asking questions such as these about each of the sentences: (1) Is there a helping word (assuming the pupils have learned what is meant by a *helping work*) in this sentence? (2) Which word, *sang* or *sung*, is used in this sentence? The teacher can write on the chalkboard, as the pupils answer the question about each of the sentences, a summary such as this, if *sang* is used in the first and third sentences and *sung* in the others:

With a helping word

2. sung
4. sung
5. sung

Without a helping word

1. sang
3. sang

Thereupon the teacher might ask the pupils whether they can tell when *sang* is used and when *sung* is correct. After the generalization has been formulated that *sang* was used without a helping word and *sung* with one, the teacher can tell the class that this is a rule that generally applies. From this generalization, formed by the pupils through use of the inductive method, they are then ready to make application (deductive method) of the generalization. Thus the method of discovery (inductive method) is used in the first part of the learning and the application of that discovery (deductive method) in the last part of the learning situation.

A Suggested Procedure for Arriving at Generalizations

Below is a summary of a suggested procedure that the teacher may wish to follow as he guides boys and girls in the development of a generalization:

1. Have clearly in mind the generalization to be developed
2. Make certain that the boys and girls have had the needed background for learning a given generalization by the inductive-deductive method
3. Present to the class situations that, through questioning, will help the pupils to arrive at the generalization
4. Have a pupil summarize the points that have been stressed in the presentation to which reference is made in step 3 above
5. Reword the summary in the form of a generalization while explaining the extent of universality of the summary
6. Give the pupils the opportunity to give the generalization, either by questioning them or by asking them to state the generalization.

Making Application of a Generalization

Unless boys and girls can make application of a generalization they have learned, it is doubtful whether much learning has taken place. For a generalization to be of value to a child, he must be able to apply what he has learned. The following are some of the ways in which the teacher can help boys and girls make suitable application of a generalization:

1. Asking the pupils to give examples of situations to which the generalization is applicable

2. Presenting to the pupils some situations to which the generalization can be applied and asking them to make the application

3. Having the pupils determine to which of a group of problem situations that the teacher presents the generalization applies

4. Pointing out to the pupils from time to time situations that come up in the ongoing school program to which the generalization can be applied.

Advantages of the Inductive-Deductive Learning Process

Among the advantages of using the inductive-deductive method in teaching-learning situations are these:

1. The pupil is likely to understand a principle better through inductive learning than through being told the rule or generalization.

2. The pupil is likely to remember the generalization better if he has helped in the discovery of it.

3. The pupil is probably more likely to make use of a generalization which he has derived from experience.

4. Frequent use of the inductive-deductive method may help a child to make application of the method in other situations, in school and out of school.

5. Interest in learning can be increased in many instances by use of this method.

Illustrative Generalizations in the Area of the Language Arts

The following are a few examples of generalizations in the language arts.

1. The first word in a sentence should begin with a capital letter.

2. *Rung* usually needs a helping word but no helping word should be used with *rang*.

3. When the word *yes* or *no* is used as part of a sentence in answer to a question, a comma should be used to separate it from the rest of the sentence.

4. Rose Fyleman often writes about fairies.

The reader is referred to page 149 for further suggestions as to how the teacher might proceed in helping boys and girls develop generalizations and make application of them.

LEARNING THROUGH INQUIRY AND DISCOVERY

With the explosion of knowledge it is probably even more important than in the past that boys and girls be encouraged to utilize the methods of inquiry and discovery in some of their learning. The teacher will want to encourage the pupils to use these methods on their own in school and out, both now and in the future. The person who has not learned the value and joy of finding answers to his inquiries and of discovering that which to him previously has been unknown and who has not developed skill in learning through inquiry and discovery may fail to be alert to some possible learnings after he is no longer receiving formal education. And even while he is in school, without the ability to learn through inquiry and discovery, his education will be sorely lacking.

Relationship Between Learning Through Inquiry and Discovery and Problem Solving

Problem solving through use of the inductive method of arriving at generalizations, according to the steps outlined on page 32, can be one method of learning through inquiry and discovery. Care should be taken that the finding of a generalization through the use of the inductive method is of interest and significance to the learner if many of the benefits from problem solving are to be achieved. But not all learning through inquiry and discovery needs to be acquired through use of the procedure outlined on page 32.

Further Considerations

The teacher should be conscious of the fact that there is danger in attempting to have boys and girls rely for all of learning on inquiry or discovery or any form of problem solving. Many a problem is so complex that children could not possibly be expected to solve it. Oversimplification of the process of problem solving, of learning through discovery or of getting answers in other ways through the method of inquiry, may lead to a false assurance or to a neglect of other important ways of acquiring learning. However, it must be added that in most classrooms the concern need not be about overuse of techniques for problem solving for arriving at generalizations or of other methods of inquiry and discovery. Rather, in most schoolrooms lack of sufficient use of such procedures should be the concern.

Learning through procedures of inquiry can be achieved in many ways; for example, through conversation, listening to speakers, reading, studying pictures, or examining realia.

The teacher can encourage discovery on the part of his pupils by providing a climate for learning—in which there is respect for pupils and their findings, in which permissiveness, but not license, prevails rather than authoritarian conformity, in which pupils have access to materials that challenge search for knowledge.

Illustrative Situations

Boys and girls can learn through inquiry in the area of language arts by trying to find the answer to questions such as these: (1) What characteristics of Laura Ingalls Wilder's writing make them beloved by many boys and girls? (2) Which letters in the Initial Teaching Alphabet are the same as those in the usually used alphabet? (3) In what different ways can your dictionary be of help to you?

As boys and girls search for answers to questions such as those listed in the preceding paragraph—as they use the method of inquiry—they may discover, as mentioned previously, important learnings. But they can make a discovery without setting out to make one—without utilizing the method of inquiry. Some of the points in the area of the language arts that a pupil might, under certain circumstances, discover without planning to find out something, are as follows: (1) They could discover that not all letters in cursive writing are the same in the various systems of handwriting. (2) They could discover some of the exceptions to generalizations such as to the one concerning "*i* before *e* except after *c*." (3) They could happen upon the learning that giving a puppet heavy dark eyebrows helps make the puppet look like a villain.

REINFORCEMENT OF LEARNING

Provisions need to be made for reinforcement of learning since, as a rule, skills are not perfected through one exposure. To be sure, much needed practice can be provided by the ongoing classroom activities. Furthermore, some class projects, such as writing a class paper or putting on a puppet show, can be designed primarily to give pupils needed practice in writing or in appearing in front of an audience. However, use of all these kinds of activities frequently does not give opportunity for the desirable amount and type of repetition for perfecting skills.

Guidelines for Providing Meaningful Repetition

These are some of the guidelines that the teacher should keep in mind when it is necessary to isolate somewhat for practice certain elements of a learning situation.

1. Practice should not be "busy work."

2. The purpose of practice work as a rule should be clear not only to the teacher but also to the learner and the boys and girls should be helped, if necessary, to recognize the purpose as significant.

3. Frequently the purpose of practice work can be made clear to boys and girls if they see its relationship to what they are doing in major classroom activities or in important out-of-school activities. For example, if boys and girls are planning to write a class paper, special practice in writing paragraphs in order to have a good paper is likely to be more meaningful than work on topic sentences taken up merely because paragraphing is the next topic in the textbook.

4. Practice is likely to be more effective if boys and

girls have a standard they wish to attain through practice. For example, when practicing oral reading, a set of standards for oral reading worked out by the class with the guidance of the teacher can be valuable.

5. The pupils should have a chance to participate in the evaluation of the success of their practice. At times charts or graphs kept individually, not for purposes of class competition, form significant evaluative devices providing considerable incentive for further improvement.

6. As a rule a pupil should be provided with practice only on those points with which he is likely to have difficulty if such practice were not given.

7. There should be variety in types of practice work. This guideline is important for several reasons, among them these: (a) The work may become monotonous if the same procedure is followed uninterruptedly. (b) Variety in type of exercise is likely to be of value in emphasizing more than one angle of strength desirable in perfecting a skill.

8. Pupils' difficulties in relation to a given skill for which practice is provided should be carefully analyzed and the children, if possible, should help in the analysis. Provisions should then be made as specifically as possible to overcome the shortcomings.

9. As a pupil is perfecting his skill in a given language arts activity, he should be provided with opportunity to apply the ability in lifelike situations.

10. Practice should be spaced in harmony with the findings of educational psychologists, with short intervals between early practice periods and longer intervals between later ones.

11. The practice provided should have considerable likeness to the situations in which the skill will later be exercised.

Games in the Language Arts

Occasional games, when well chosen and well conducted, can provide meaningful practice. Following are given a few shortcomings of many games as language arts exercises, as well as criteria for their selection. For further information on the topic the reader is referred to pages 261-262.

Shortcomings of Many Games. Many games planned as activities to increase language skills can be criticized because of the following reasons.

1. Frequently the child who makes an error is eliminated from the game even though he might be the one who most needs the practice.

2. Often the length of time spent on a game is not commensurate with the amount of helpful practice provided.

3. At times, the pupils become so interested in a game that instead of its serving as a motivation for other

language arts activities, the other activities seem less rather than more desirable after the children have taken part in the game.

4. In many games little, if any, opportunity is given to help the person who made an error know the cause of the error and to assist him in correcting it.

Criteria for the Selection of Games. Some of the points the teacher should bear in mind when selecting games for the language arts are implied in the above list of "Short-comings of Many Games." Here are some additional criteria.

1. As a rule, the pupils should be able to recognize the purpose of the game in terms of language arts learnings.

2. The game should be on the interest level of the players.

3. If there is competition, it should be primarily with self, not with others.

TEACHER-PUPIL PLANNING

Teacher-pupil planning can be done on various levels. Overall planning for the year is one important kind, as the pupils help in determining some of the goals for the year and give suggestions for attaining these objectives. Planning for a single unit of work can also be done with pupil participation. Furthermore, there is frequently much opportunity for desirable planning by boys and girls when an activity like putting on a dramatization or giving a program of choral readings is contemplated. Even in the day-by-day work, such as writing a letter to thank the principal for his help in providing the room with a portable bulletin board, the pupils can assist in planning what is to be included in the letter, on what type of paper it should be written, who should write it, and how it should be sent. For guidelines to effective pupil participation in planning the reader is referred to page 9.

When pupils are participating in planning for an activity or a series of activities in which they will be engaging for a rather long period of time, these are some of the steps that it may be profitable for the teacher and pupils to follow.

1. Decide on the major goal or goals for the activity, regardless of whether it was originally teacher- or pupil-selected. Although frequently problems for study may advisedly be chosen by the pupils themselves, selection by them, rather than by the teacher, is not essential. The important requirement in this respect is that regardless of who suggests the problem, the pupils wholeheartedly accept it as a significant activity and that they set or help in setting steps for the attainment of it.

2. Define the scope of the problem, if necessary, in rather general terms with the possibility of redefinement later.

3. Determine some of the means by which the goals may be reached.

4. List materials that will be helpful in the attainment of the goals and, if necessary, suggest means of making these available.

5. Try to determine what are some of the difficulties that are likely to be encountered in the course of the work on the problem and study means of overcoming these hurdles to success.

6. Strive to make assignments for work to each person in the group in harmony with his needs for optimum development.

7. Plan a time schedule which can be altered, if advisable, as the work progresses.

8. Plan for continuous evaluation while the work is in progress as well as for a final evaluation.

9. Help the pupils set standards for their conduct while working on the problem.

MAKING APPLICATION OF LINGUISTICS TO THE TEACHING OF THE LANGUAGE ARTS

In recent years one of the major concerns of the elementary school teacher has been the problem as to what the relationship should be between linguistics and the teaching of the language arts. Some schools have gone "all-out" for a program of language development that is linguistically oriented; others have almost as categorically denied their connection with such orientation—if not in words then in action. It should, however, be noted that all study of language—in the elementary school and elsewhere—is, in a sense linguistically based, if we accept the definition of linguistics that it is the science of the study of language. Thus one of the questions to which many teachers seek an answer really is: "Should the language arts program in the elementary school be strongly linguistically oriented?" For those who would answer the question in the affirmative (and there are many who would) this question, too, is of paramount importance: "How can effective application of linguistics be made to the teaching of the language arts?"

To give a comprehensive description of the theories espoused by leading linguists and subsequently to outline in detail one or more programs in which application of these theories is made are beyond the province of this book. For such a study the reader is referred to extensive treatment of the subject in books and periodicals.

References

Below is given a list of some of the books that deal exclusively with linguistics in relation to the teaching of the language arts. For titles of additional books the reader is referred to pages 238 and 336. It should be noted that information on linguistics as it refers to the language arts program of the elementary school is also given in most of the recent books on the teaching of the language arts. Many articles on the topic can be found in professional magazines.

Dechant, Emerald. *Linguistics, Phonics and the Teaching of Reading.* Springfield, Ill.: Charles C. Thomas, Publishers, 1969.

DeLancey, Robert W. *Linguistics and Teaching.* Rochester, N.Y.: New York State English Council, 1965.

Durkin, Dolores. *Phonics, Linguistics and Reading.* New York: Teachers College Press, 1972.

Fries, Charles C. *Linguistics and Reading.* New York: Holt, Rinehart and Winston, Inc., 1963.

Goodman, Kenneth S., and Fleming, J.T., eds. *Psycholinguistics and the Teaching of Reading.* Newark, Del.: International Reading Association, 1969.

Lamb, Pose. *Linguistics in Proper Perspective.* Columbus, Ohio: Charles E. Merrill Publishing Company, 1967.

Lefevre, Carl A. *Linguistics, English, and the Language Arts.* Boston: Allyn & Bacon, Inc., 1970.

Wardbaugh, Ronald. *Reading: A Linguistic Perspective.* New York: Harcourt Brace Jovanovich, 1969.

What Is Linguistics?

Although linguistics is not a new science, there have been in this area outstandingly many and significant developments during the past few decades. Furthermore, not until relatively recent years have there been many attempts made to put on a practical basis—practical for the elementary school teacher—findings of linguists as they might have significance for the elementary school curriculum. Consequently many teachers in the elementary school and prospective teachers have through the years had but limited familiarity with the term *linguistics.* The following statements by Charles C. Fries may, therefore, be of value to many readers of this book. Fries defines linguistics thus:

....a body of knowledge and understanding concerning the nature and functioning of human language, built up out of information about the structure, the operation, and the history of a wide range of very diverse human languages by means of those techniques and procedures that have proved most successful in establishing verifiable generalizations concerning relationships among linguistic phenomena.[1]

Linguists differ in the phase of linguistics they study. The historical linguist is primarily concerned with the history of the development of language and languages,

while the *comparative* linguist makes comparisons between various languages. The *descriptive* linguist carefully studies the characteristics of people's languages in certain districts or areas. For a description of *structural* linguistics and *transformational* linguistics the reader is referred to page 138 under "Linguistics and Sentence Structure." Obviously, there is overlapping of interests between different types of linguists; the difference lies in point of emphasis.

As Pose Lamb states, linguists of various schools of thought "may concentrate on the sounds of language (phonology), the origins and changing meaning of words (etymology and semantics), or the arrangements of words in meaningful context in different languages (syntax-structural or transformational grammar).[2]

The Characteristics of Language

How do linguists regard language? *Language* has been defined in various ways. One definition to which Pose Lamb draws attention that is, in essence, in harmony with the meaning that many linguists would be willing to give to the term is stated by Michael Girsdansky, who writes:

Language is a set of arbitrary symbols (words) which are placed in orderly relationship with one another according to conventions accepted and understood by the speakers, for the transmission of messages.[3]

There also seems to be general agreement among linguists that "language is *speech* and language is *systematic*...language is *symbolic,* language is *arbitrary,* and the symbolism of any language is *complete.*"[4] Let us now briefly examine each of these characteristics in terms of the meaning that linguists apply to them.

Language Is Speech. Linguists, for the most part, place much stress on the primacy of speech. They emphasize that writing is secondary, a form of expression derived from speech. They point out that the language of

1. Charles C. Fries, *Linguistics and Reading* (New York: Holt, Rinehart and Winston, 1963). Used by permission of Holt, Rinehart and Winston.

2. Pose Lamb, *Linguistics in Proper Perspective* (Charles E. Merrill Publishing Company, 1967), p. 4. Used by permission of the Charles E. Merrill Publishing Company.

3. From the Book, *The Adventure of Language* by Michael Girdansky © 1963 by Prentice-Hall, Inc. Published by Prentice-Hall, Inc., Englewood Cliffs, New Jersey.

4. George D. Owen, "Linguistics: An Overview." Contribution #11 in Part II, pp. 96-102, in *Elementary School Language Arts: Selected Readings* by Paul C. Burns and Leo M. Schell (eds.). Chicago, Illinois: Rand McNally & Co., 1969, p. 98. The article originally appeared in *Elementary English,* 39 (May, 1962) pp. 421-25.

a people is better represented by the spoken word than the written. To obtain insights into the language of a group, therefore, they study more carefully the speech patterns than the patterns of expression shown in their writing.

Language Is Systematic. There is system to a language, though this system differs somewhat from one language to another. Even the exceptions to the usual form of expression in a given language can often be generalized, and consequently even in the exceptions to broad generalizations there may be a system.

Language Is Symbolic. The words in the language, though entities in their own right, are *symbols* of that which they represent—not that which they represent. The word *man,* for example, is the word that symbolizes, for purposes of communication, the adult male human being. The word *love* symbolizes a state of emotional regard.

Language Is Arbitrary. To be sure, some words in a language were agreed upon as symbols because the sounds of the words have similarity with the sounds produced by the objects they represent. Onomatopeia as a reason for the selection of a word to represent an object with some likeness in sound between the word and the object represented, can still be thought of as arbitrary since, after all, the selection of that word to express that which it symbolizes was arbitrary. Some other word would have been satisfactory, too.

One might ask, "Why is a chair called a chair?" The answer, in terms of the arbitrary nature of the language, is that some people had agreed upon the word *chair* to serve as symbol for the object we now know by that name and that other people accepted that symbol.

The arbitrary nature of language also allows flexibility. A different symbol may come to be used for an object and, in time, the old symbol may no longer be utilized.

Language Is Complete. The claim, in support of this statement, is that the language of a person is sufficient for his needs, that if he needs to have a symbol to express an idea, he will, if necessary, "invent" one. The completeness of language, as the term *complete* is here used, is questioned by some people, whose argument is that for lack of words (symbols) an individual may be unable to express adequately some ideas that he may have.

Explanation of Terms

Although there is not complete agreement among linguists as to some of the terms, there is general acceptance of the explanations of the frequently used terms given below.

Phoneme. A phoneme is the smallest unit of speech by which different meanings can be designated. For example, the ending *ed* in the word *walked* and the *s* in the word *walks* are phonemes, by means of which the difference between the two words can be distinguished.

Morpheme. A morpheme is the smallest unit that bears meaning. There are two types of morphemes, bound-form and free-form morphemes. The latter type can stand alone, while the former cannot. An example of a word consisting of two morphemes is the word *walked. Walk* is a free-form morpheme; *ed* is a bound-form morpheme.

Grapheme. A grapheme is the written symbol of a sound. It may be a letter of the alphabet or it may be a word.

Grapheme-Phoneme Relationship and Phoneme-Grapheme Relationship. The grapheme-phoneme relationship refers to the relationship between the written symbol and the oral. When referring to the relationship between the written word *to* and the sound of the word *to,* we are making reference to the grapheme-phoneme relationship. The phoneme-grapheme relationship refers to that between the sound symbol and the written symbol, for example, between the sound of the word *to* and the written form of that word. It should be noted that frequently the terms *grapheme-phoneme* and *phoneme-grapheme* are used interchangeably. Strictly speaking, however, we should use the former term when equating the written symbol with the spoken (as in reading), and we should use the latter term when equating the spoken with the written symbol (as in writing).

Decoding and Encoding. The process of substituting the phoneme for its equivalent grapheme, as in reading, is known as decoding; the process of substituting the grapheme for its equivalent phoneme, as in writing, is known as encoding.

Attitude of Linguists Toward Phonics

As the reader notes the above explanation of the phoneme-grapheme and the grapheme-phoneme relationships, he may wrongly come to the conclusion that linguists openly endorse a phonic approach to the teaching of reading and spelling. However, such is not the case. The following summarization of the point of view held by a large number of linguists is quoted from *The Teaching of Reading.*[5]

Many linguists are united in their highly critical attitude toward phonics teaching. They condemn it on the

5. Martha Dallmann, et al. *The Teaching of Reading,* 4th ed. (New York: Holt, Rinehart and Winston, Inc., 1973), pp. 502-03. Used by permission of Holt, Rinehart and Winston.

allegation that the study in our schools typically proceeds from the sound to the word (synthetic approach) rather than from the word to the sound (analytic approach). They believe that in the synthetic approach untrue sounds are produced as, for example, when the child sounds the *h* in *hat* as *huh.* So they propose that the learner be introduced, for example, to the grapheme *h,* with its corresponding phoneme, by his attention being drawn to the *h* in a large number of words of the same spelling pattern beginning with the letter *h,* such as *hat, ham, had, has.* However, Emans[6] points out that linguists when criticizing the teaching of phonics are unaware of the fact that phonics is typically taught in the schools of today by analysis of the sounds in words rather than by a synthesis of them. Emans also draws attention to the fact that while linguists in general are highly critical of a phonics approach they seem to be unaware of his contention that a linguistic approach to reading instruction is a phonics (sound) approach, since emphasis is placed on the identification of sounds, though it is in spelling patterns.

Another criticism by linguists is that the teaching of phonics, as it is done in many of our schools, is poorly organized, with gaps in learnings to be acquired and with a defective sequence in the development of the desired learnings. They are also in general agreement in their opposition to much use of the sight method (the whole-word method). (For a discussion of the sight method or whole-word method the reader is referred to page 238.) They claim that the method encourages guessing, requires every word learned by that method to be memorized, and may result in word-by-word reading. It is interesting, in the light of this objection, to note that the child is, after all, learning by the whole-word method, even when he learns words, as recommended by linguists, consistent in spelling patterns, as he names words, such as *hen, den, men, ten,* and possibly including nonsense words such as *gen, ren, jen.* . . .

Should the Language Arts Program Be Strongly Linguistically Oriented?

It is important that the elementary school teacher come to a conclusion, temporary though it may be, in regard to the question, "Should the language arts program be strongly linguistically oriented?" In spite of the fact that some might argue that the elementary school teacher should wait with making a decision on this matter until linguists are more in agreement than they currently are on various theories of linguistics, it is an issue decision on which postponement cannot be made. The teacher must face it as he helps in curriculum-building activities, as he selects materials for his classroom, as he does his day-in, day-out teaching.

As the author states her reactions to the question "Should the language arts program be strongly linguistically oriented?" she is fully aware of the fact that teachers answer the question for themselves. The following comments relevant to the question indicate the author's point of view, one that is reflected in the discussion of linguistics in relation to various phases of the language arts in later chapters of this book.

1. The elementary school teacher should try to take cognizance of all disciplines that might affect the teaching of the language arts. Since linguistics is the science of the study of the language, surely the teacher should learn from the linguist more about the language that he uses and teaches. Since the average elementary school teacher has in the past had little exposure to the findings of linguists and the theories advocated by them, the teacher does well to acquaint himself with them.

2. As the teacher is familiarizing himself with findings in the field of linguistics and theories of linguistics, he will do well not to ignore them in his teaching. He may not accept some of the theories. He may decide not to follow some of the recommendations—and they are, indeed, diverse—made for a language arts program. However, it is difficult for the author to imagine that any teacher studying references such as those given in this book (see pages 37, 238, and 336) would not find means of improving his language arts program through application of some of the knowledge acquired through the efforts of linguists. The author, therefore recommends that the language arts program should, to some extent, be linguistically oriented. How it should reflect such orientation and the extent to which it should be so oriented in any school system she is not recommending in this book.

3. Although the teacher should, in the opinion of the writer, familiarize himself with the basic claims of linguists, he should not try to teach all that he knows about the science of linguistics to the boys and girls in his class.

Guidelines for the Teacher

How then should the teacher proceed in determining the extent to which and the manner in which the language arts program should be linguistically slanted? From the point of view of the author, the linguist is not the person who should tell the teacher how to make the orientation. The linguist is in his proper role when he furnishes background data through the knowledge of which the teacher makes whatever application he considers desirable. As the teacher gains insights from the knowledge of the science of language, with this increased perspective, he should be in a better position to teach the language arts effectively. He should make the decision, however, not alone in terms of the information he has acquired through the findings and theories of linguists. When coming to conclusions concerning the language

6. Robert Emans, "Linguistics and Phonics," *The Reading Teacher,* volume 26: (February 1973), pp. 477-82.

arts program, the teacher should weigh them in relation to his knowledge of child growth and development and of learning theory. He should decide in terms of his situation what application he will try to make of linguistics. Some of the factors in terms of his classroom situation that he will consider are: (1) his own ability, (2) the total school curriculum in all areas, both as it applies to his own classes and to the entire school system, and (3) the strengths and weaknesses of the boys and girls in his charge.

Some additional guidelines that the teacher might follow when deciding upon the ways in which he will profit, in his language arts program, from knowledge of the science of linguistics are here suggested.

1. The teacher should observe the interrelatedness of oral and written communication, noting the primacy of the oral over the written but not neglecting the latter.

2. The teacher should help the boys and girls realize, as they learn about some of the information obtained from linguists, that the study of language can be fascinating. Emphasis on points such as these can be of vital interest to the boys and girls: (a) Who decides on the "correctness" of expression? (b) How does language change? (c) Is nonstandard English incorrect? (d) What does a person's speech reveal about him? (e) To what extent are different levels of language acceptable under varying situations? (f) In what ways is our language a code? (g) What are some of the differences in word order and in idiomatic expression in languages of which you have some knowledge?

3. The teacher should have an appreciative attitude—more tolerant than many teachers have—toward so-called "nonstandard" dialects which are reflected in the speech and written expression of the boys and girls. He should recognize the fact that it can lead to many difficulties if one language or dialect is considered inferior to others. He should be cognizant of the fact that all Americans who speak English speak a dialect.

4. The teacher should try to motivate his pupils so that they will desire to improve their command of standard ways of expression. While the teacher is striving to attain this objective, he should be careful not to make the boys and girls feel inferior because of the language background in which they have grown up.

5. The teacher should recognize the fact that it is difficult to alter language habits. Consequently he should not expect the well-nigh impossible improvement in communication skills in a short period of time.

6. The teacher should check his teaching of the language arts for any deviations that he decides are not justifiable in terms of theories of linguists that he considers acceptable in the light of his knowledge of other disciplines and of learning theory.

7. Before a teacher uses his influence in helping deter-mine what methods and materials should be used in teaching the language arts, he should study various methods and materials carefully. He should bear in mind the fact that not all systems of teaching the language arts that claim to be linguistically oriented are firmly based on frequently accepted linguistic findings. The teacher should try to determine: (a) the linguistic theories on which the material or program claims to be based; (b) the correctness of the claims made in terms of whether or not they are actually a significant part of the program or materials; (c) the desirability of the theories on which the system or the materials are based; (d) the ways in which application of the theories is made; (e) the teacher's judgment of these methods in terms of acceptability in general and in terms of practicality for his teaching situation.

How some of the guidelines listed above and others can be put into practice by the classroom teacher when helping boys and girls with correct usage, grammar and spelling, is indicated in later chapters.

CREATIVITY IN THE LANGUAGE ARTS

Throughout this book emphasis is placed on creative ways of teaching and learning in the language arts. For example, in chapter 5, "Guiding Growth in Written Expression," ways of making oral communication a means of creative expression are presented, and in chapter 10, "Guiding Growth in Independent Reading," many suggestions are given for encouraging art activities with study in the language arts. Chapter 11 is devoted to dramatic expression and choral speaking.

The need for emphasis on creativity is probably greater now than in former eras in American history characterized by rugged individualism. Lest the human spirit become engulfed in the rigidity of a destructive patterned environment, our schools need to encourage self-expression manifested in a manner that proves to be individually beneficial and socially useful. Creativity that is conceived of in this manner can release the creator and spur him on to greater achievement, often in seemingly unrelated areas of his functioning. For example, the very fact that a child has been able to express himself in dramatization may reduce or even overcome antagonism he may have had toward other school activities.

In spite of the high value that should be placed on creativity, our schools, often unwittingly, to be sure, but nevertheless persistently, have frequently not only failed to encourage it but often even stifled it. The rigidity of many a school curriculum, and probably more so that of many a teacher, has repressed creativeness. In fact, studies have confirmed what observation had shown long before statistical evidence was presented, that the creative person is often not the one who is popular with his teacher. He has at times met resistance in classrooms in which a premium has been placed on everyone doing everything in the identical way.

What Is Creativity?

Let us define *creativity* as the term is here used. It is not confined to the field of art or to the writing of poetry or prose. The essence of creativity lies in the fact that an individual performs an activity, physical or mental, that is inspired at least in part by his imagination or by his power of organization or reorganization. It may be shown not only in the results obtained—in the product—but also in the method of procedure that is followed. The child who, for example, in a puppet play on community workmen, manipulates his puppet representing a policeman in a way that he has worked out, shows creativity in method of operating.

Encouragement of Creativity

Creativity can be encouraged by the teacher through observation of guidelines such as the following.

1. *Creativity can be stimulated through a classroom atmosphere that is relaxed and permissive yet orderly and conducive to success in learning activities.* No regimented school program in which decisions are authoritatively made by the teacher furnishes an atmosphere in which creativity of any type is likely to flourish. If respect for the individual's thoughts is not shown throughout the school day, the child is likely to be hampered in expressing his own ideas in any line of art. To be sure, artistic production has pushed itself forth even under adverse conditions. Yet, probably when dealing with no other phase of the curriculum is it as important as it is in creative expression that careful adherence be kept to the suggestions given in chapter 1, "Child Development and the Language Arts." (See page 9.)

A permissive classroom atmosphere that is conducive to development of creativity should not be confused with one in which license rather than liberty is found. In a room in which there is little done to help guide boys and girls to learn the value of authority rightly exercised, of willingness to sacrifice one's own desires for those of others, an atmosphere inimical to true creativity exists. The everybody-do-what-he-wants-to-do type of situation is unlikely to foster an atmosphere in which creativity is encouraged. Consequently the teacher needs to attempt to maintain a room in which he is accepted as the authority, in which orderliness conducive to the best performance of worthwhile work to be done is prevalent, and in which the rights and aptitudes and even harmless personal idiosyncrasies of all individuals are respected.

2. *The physical environment can have an encouraging effect upon creativity.* A barren, untidy, austere classroom is likely to discourage creativity. Through ways like the following the teacher can help furnish a stimulating physical environment:

Displaying pictures that are interesting and stimulating to the child

Having a pet in the classroom

Having a "sharing table," used by pupils and teacher

Encouraging pupils to use a room bulletin board for things they wish to exhibit

Having in the room articles of beauty such as a lovely vase or figurine

Having flowers or plants in the room

Arranging things artistically in the room

Arranging for adequate places for storage purposes

Keeping the room from being cluttered by displaying too many things at any one time

Having an interesting-looking reading corner, with books pleasingly arranged and with an object of interest as centerpiece on a reading table or as ornament on a shelf of a bookcase

Dressing attractively and being well groomed.

The teacher whose classroom is in an old building need not despair of providing a physical environment conducive to creative expression. While he cannot change the walls or ceiling or floor, he can make the room interesting in spite of problems. While surely a new classroom can be an asset to a learning situation, there is also danger in having one. Sometimes teachers who are privileged to teach in a new building may become less ingenious than those who are almost forced into resourcefulness through the very fact that they are in a seemingly discouraging environment. An unimaginative teacher can make a classroom in a new building look sterile and empty, while a teacher with imagination can make an old one into a veritable treasure chest of sources of stimulation.

Equipment can also serve as means of encouraging creativity. Examples of such equipment are slides, filmstrips, motion pictures, projectors, tapes, tape recorders, records, phonographs, radios, television sets. The room can be equipped with work benches, reading tables, bookcases, easily operated duplicators (which some children can learn to use), typewriters. However none of these is essential. Substitutes can be supplied by the wide-awake teacher. Instead of films, filmstrips, and motion pictures, for example, well-selected and attractively mounted still pictures can be used. Field trips can be a substitute for other visual or auditory learning aids. A reading table can be made by pushing together four pupils' desks, and a bookcase can be constructed from bricks for the sides and three or four boards as shelves.

3. *Exposure to many different kinds of worthwhile experiences can be an aid to creativity.* These experiences

can be provided either through first-hand or vicarious means. Some of them, such as field trips, the school can furnish; others the school can encourage parents to provide. Care needs, however, to be taken that the number is not so overwhelming that the result is confusion of spirit, rather than urge to creative activity. Undoubtedly many boys and girls in the upper years of the elementary school have such a crowded schedule of out-of-school activities, valuable though many of them may be, that it would be wise to curtail the number.

EVALUATION AND DIAGNOSIS

Evaluation and diagnosis should be an integral part of the teaching-learning situation, a continuing process in which both teacher and pupils engage. In this book, evaluative and diagnostic procedures specific to the various aspects of the language arts are suggested in chapters that follow. In this current chapter we will take note of some of the points of significance that bear on the topic as they apply to the total program in the language arts.

Basic Considerations When Making Evaluations and Diagnoses

Let us first of all consider these three questions: (1) What are the major purposes of evaluation? (2) What kinds of attainment should be appraised? (3) What are the steps involved in evaluation and diagnosis?

Major Purposes. The possibilities for use of evaluative processes and results for the improvement of instruction are many. Several of the more important functions as they have been identified by Lowry W. Harding[7] are here given. (For various parts of the discussion on evaluation the writer has leaned heavily on the general contributions to the topic of evaluation made by Dr. Harding in *Arithmetic for Child Development.*)

1. Selection and clarification of the goals of instruction, to serve as guides in choosing curricular content
2. Determination of the adequacy of methods and materials of instruction for the needs, interests, and ability of the pupils
3. Identification of rates of pupil growth and progress toward accepted goals
4. Diagnosis of specific difficulties
5. Provision of appropriate practice material for individual pupils
6. Motivation and guidance of learning, especially through self-appraisal by pupils of their own behavior and achievement
7. Establishment of a basis for assignment of achievement marks to pupils
8. Maintenance of efficient planning of work
9. Improvement of curriculum materials of instruction and teaching procedures
10. Provision of a sound basis for public relations, by means of improving reports of pupil progress to parents.

Kinds of Attainments to Be Appraised. All too frequently the emphasis on appraisal in schools is directed toward one or two of the desired outcomes of learning experiences—namely on the skills acquired or facts learned—often to the almost total neglect of some of the others, such as understandings, attitudes, and methods of study. This emphasis persists in many schools in spite of the fact that other desired values are at least as important, if not more so. In written communication, for example, frequently more attention is paid to checking on the mechanical skill that a pupil has developed in terms of sentence and paragraph structure and of capitalization and punctuation than on the attitudes he has acquired toward writing or the growth he has made in expressing thoughts that reveal developing insights. In spelling, often the emphasis is placed almost exclusively on ascertaining the number of words spelled correctly rather than on developing spelling consciousness.

One reason why the major stress is at times placed on the measurement of skills acquired or facts learned is that in many classrooms the chief aim of the teacher has been to teach facts and to help the children acquire skills. Another reason is that even when broader objectives are emphasized, teachers at times fail to attempt to appraise systematically the extent to which they are achieved because they cannot measure them with the accuracy that the extent of the acquisition of facts or skills can usually be determined. However, the fact that these outcomes are partly, with our present means of evaluation, intangible should not deter the teacher from making use of what data he can collect toward the practical appraisal of such results.

Steps Involved in Evaluation and Diagnosis. The major phases in the evaluation of educational outcomes, as far as the teacher's work is concerned, may be identified in terms of the following eight steps, designated by quotation marks, that are listed by Lowry Harding in the book *Arithmetic for Child Development.*

"1. Decide on the objectives and list them."

"2. Define objectives in terms of the content involved and the pupil behavior desired." For example, in the objective "ability to give a book report," the desired behavior is *ability* to give a report. Thus the teacher does not want the pupil merely to memorize what points are essential to a good book report, but to be able to give a good report.

"3. For each objective, list situations in which the behavior can be shown and sampled." For checking on some of the objectives of the language arts program, written tests are appropriate; in other situations other means are more suitable.

Here are a few examples of how the work can be evaluated in language arts situations without written tests: (a) In relation to the development of independence of attack in word recognition, the teacher may ask the child to explain the steps through which he goes as he tries to decide on the "names" of given "new" words by means of verbal context clues. (b) If the

7. Lowry W. Harding, *Arithmetic for Child Development* (Dubuque, Iowa: Wm. C. Brown Company Publishers, 1964), p. 332. Used with the permission of the author.

teacher is trying to find out whether the objective "increasing interest in reading poetry" is achieved, he can take mental note of the frequency with which a child examines suitable and worthwhile poems placed on a library table, before and after the teacher has through various means tried to help him grow in power to appreciate good poetry. The teacher can also ask others, parents or librarians, to report on the child's "behavior" in this respect. Furthermore, he can ask the pupil directly about his interest in poetry, with emphasis, if the objective is the measurement of growth, on growth.

"4. Select specific procedures for getting evidence." It is recommended that the teacher acquaint himself with the available standarized tests. To get a quick overview of the tests on the market, the teacher can consult the most recent edition of the reference book *Tests in Print* published by different publishers different years but often by the Gryphon Press. For the measurement of the results sought in quite a number of the objectives in teaching the language arts, fairly good instruments can be found. For evaluating the accomplishment of other objectives, it may be necessary for the teacher to construct tests or check lists of his own.

"5. Use the procedures and collect the evidence."

"6. Organize and summarize the various types of evidence." Careful attention should be paid to explicit designation as to what items summarized indicate. Often in summarizing evaluative data the report should give background for use in later diagnosis. For example, instead of summarizing a child's ability in reading by one score, it would be much more helpful to have a summary that indicates a score in word recognition, one or preferably more than one in comprehension, scores showing reading rates, and the like.

"7. Check on conclusions and apply them to improvement of the teaching-learning situation." The rechecking can be done, in the case of standardized tests, by using a second form. When data have been gathered through observation, further observation by the same evaluator may be made at a future time or another evaluator may make an appraisal of the same persons who were earlier checked. Application of results is essential. Unless use is made of the findings toward the improvement of instruction, but little is gained.

"8. Encourage the pupils to self-evaluation." As Harding explains, however, self-evaluation "does not necessarily mean a do-it-yourself project." For example, if a person has a pain, his self-appraisal may mean the obtaining of assistance from a physician. In school self-appraisal we need to consider how well the pupil can evaluate at any stage of his development and also what matters it is appropriate for him to "attempt to" evaluate.[8]

Evaluative Techniques

The following list of evaluative techniques, again to quote Lowry Harding in *Arithmetic for Child Development*, page 337 to 338, shows some of the many means of evaluation that can be used.

Activity records
Adjustment inventories
Anecdotal records
Autobiographies
Case studies

Checklists
Collections and scrapbooks
Cumulative records

Dramatic play
Diaries

Essays, themes, and poems
Flow charts, of play, discussion, etc.
Group discussions
Health and medical histories
Interviews

Intelligence tests
Inventories—of interest, attitudes, etc.
Logs of periods or events
Neighborhood studies
Observation: directed, time-sampling, and informal

Oral reports
Parent conferences
Peer-group studies
Personality inventories
Photographs

Questionnaires
Rating scales
Readiness tests
Recordings and films
Sociograms and other projective techniques

Standardized achievement tests
Teacher-made achievement tests
Teacher-pupil constructed tests
Work samples....

Standardized Achievement Tests. Since with standardized tests there are available scores or norms based on extensive sampling, use of them enables the teacher to compare his pupils with many others. Scores are often expressed in terms of grade levels. For example, if a third-grade pupil at the beginning of October receives a score of 3.1 (representing 3.1 years of school), it means that he has achieved as well as the average third-grade pupil who has completed one-tenth of the third grade; if he receives a score of 4.0, it means that he is .9 of a grade in advance in October of the average third-grade pupil on whom the test was standardized.

To get a quick overview of tests on the market the reader can consult the most recent edition of *Tests in Print* edited by Oscar K. Buros and published by the Gryphon Press. Furthermore, he is referred to chapter 13 where names of distributors are given with titles. For a nominal price, some companies provide specimens of their evaluative instruments. Names of some of the language arts tests are given in chapter 13, beginning on page 345.

Teacher-Made Tests. Standardized tests have several advantages over teacher-constructed tests, in addition to the point emphasized in the preceding paragraph that they provide a basis of comparison with pupils in other

8. Ibid., 333-36.

schools. They are, in many instances, constructed by specialists in the field. Usually much more time is spent in construction than that practical for a classroom teacher to use in devising a test.

The advantages, however, are not all on one side. The teacher-made test is often superior to a standardized test in that the former can be constructed in terms of the objectives and learning procedures of a given classroom. The teacher-made test thus may well be more valid for a given group of boys and girls. A safe rule to follow may be to use a standardized test when a suitable one is available and to supplement information gained from it by that obtained from teacher-constructed tests and other means of evaluation.

Forms of Paper-and-Pencil Test Items. Commonly used types of paper- and-pencil test items are essay questions, simple recall questions, completion statements, yes-no (or true-false) statements, multiple-choice statements, and matching items. All of these can be used in teacher-made or standardized tests. Seldom, however, are essay questions used in the latter type. Following are one or more examples of test items for each of the foregoing types in the area of the language arts.

1. Essay questions
   (a) Explain what to do when trying to figure out an unknown word in a sentence.
   (b) Why is it important to know how to outline?

2. Simple recall question
   In which part of a book is the table of contents found?

3. Completion statement
   An adjective modifies a _____ or _____ .

4. Yes-no or true-false items
   (a) Should a comma be used at the end of the greeting of a friendly letter? (Yes, No)
   (b) A comma should be used at the end of the greeting of a friendly letter. (True, False)

5. Multiple-choice statement
   The main character of the book is (jovial, pessimistic, unselfish, quarrelsome).

6. Matching items
   (a) On the line to the left of each item in Column A write the letter of the item in Column B with which it is associated

Column A	*Column B*
____ a possessive pronoun	____ a. children's
____ a proper noun	____ b. man's
____ a singular possessive noun	____ c. Washington
____ a plural possessive noun	____ d. its
	____ e. it's

   (b) Draw a line from the prefix in Column A to the word in Column B with which it can be used.

Column A	*Column B*
____ dis	____ possible
____ im	____ responsible
____ ir	____ connect

OTHER PROBLEMS

Only a few of the common problems in teaching the language arts are discussed in this chapter. Others are taken up in various places in subsequent chapters. Chapter 6 deals with additional problems that present themselves in both oral and written expression. In fact, even though one or more separate chapters are devoted primarily to each of the various facets of the language arts, throughout the book the commonality of many of the problems presented is emphasized and means of correlating and integrating language arts activities are frequently suggested. The reader is encouraged at all times to recognize the interrelatedness of the language arts and to proceed accordingly when teaching.

FOR STUDY AND DISCUSSION

1. **On page 31 this statement is made:** "The content of the language arts curriculum should be determined in part by the ongoing activities of the classroom in other areas and, at the same time, the ongoing classroom activities in other areas should be chosen in part in terms of the needs and interests of the child in his language development." Give illustrations as to how the ongoing classroom activities in areas other than the language arts can be chosen in terms of the needs and interests of the child in his language development.

2. It is agreed that meaningless drill is undesirable. Describe a possible "drill situation" in connection with the development of one or more language arts skills that would be meaningful and in other ways desirable as means of reinforcement of learning.

3. Examine one or more recently published language arts books for use by boys and girls in the elementary school to note to what extent the books are linguistically oriented. If they are, make a study of how linguistics is applied in those books.

4. What are ways in which the teacher can encourage

boys and girls to make use of methods of discovery in the language arts program? How can teachers use strategies encouraging inquiry on the part of the boys and girls?

5. In this chapter (see page 39) some guidelines for use in a linguistically oriented language arts program are listed. What others can you suggest?

6. What are some of the points to observe when determining the place of incidental versus planned learning situations?

7. Suggest ways in which a teacher can stimulate creativity in the language arts program in the upper-elementary grades.

8. If you have the opportunity to examine some standardized language arts tests, it is suggested that you evaluate them in terms of your present knowledge of teaching in language arts in the elementary school.

REFERENCES

Boyd, Gertrude. *Teaching Communication Skills in the Elementary School.* New York: Van Nostrand Reinhold Company, 1970.

Bruner, Jerome S. *The Process of Education.* Cambridge, Mass.: Harvard University Press, 1964.

Burns, Paul C.; Broman, Betty L.; and Lowe Wantling, Alberta L. *The Language Arts in Childhood Education,* 2d ed. Chicago: Rand McNally & Company, 1971.

Donoghue, Mildred R. *The Child and the English Language Arts.* Dubuque, Iowa: Wm. C. Brown Company Publishers, 1971.

Lamb, Pose, ed. *Guiding Children's Language Learning.* Dubuque, Iowa: Wm. C. Brown Company Publishers, 1967.

Moffett, James. *A Student-Centered Language Arts Curriculum, Grades K-6: A Handbook for Teachers.* Boston: Houghton Mifflin Company, 1968.

Ruddell, Robert B. *Reading-Language Instruction: Innovative Practices.* Englewood Cliffs, N.J.: Prentice-Hall, Inc., 1974.

Strickland, Ruth G. *The Language Arts in the Elementary School,* 3rd ed. Lexington, Mass.: D.C. Heath and Company, 1969.

For references on linguistics the reader is referred to page 336, for books on diagnosis and remediation to page 336, and for references on creative expression to page 335. For lists of tests he is referred to page 345.

4

Guiding Growth in Oral Communication

Being able to speak well, according to the needs of a situation, and knowing how to listen effectively are requirements for effective participation in our society. Throughout life oral expression with its complement, listening, is one of the chief means of keeping in touch with the outside world. Thus it behooves the school to emphasize the development of skill in oral communication.

The school has a firm foundation on which to build its program of oral expression. Almost all children before they enter school have already acquired, in the course of normal growth, considerable skill in speaking and listening. Linguists have drawn our attention to the fact that the development in the ability to communicate orally that the child has made from his first cry to the competency he possesses when he enters first grade, has, in fact, been phenomenal. It has been claimed that the achievement the child has made in speech development during the first few years of his life is greater than any that he will ever again make in any area of learning in a similar

length of time. He comes to school with a vocabulary sufficient for the expression of many of his ideas and needs. He knows the basic structure of the language, without ever having had a lesson in grammar! Furthermore, his ability to obtain meaning through listening is, at least, comparable with his ability to express himself.

Though the child comes to school equipped with a surprising degree of competency in oral communication, there is still need for much improvement. It is the province of the school to be influential in stimulating development from the level of speech and listening ability on which the child is toward the level of excellence that will be most beneficial to him in later life.

THE SCOPE OF THE PROGRAM

What then is the scope of the program in oral communication? In answering this question, let us consider the following topics: (1) general objectives, (2) needed skills, (3) types of activities, and (4) grade placement.

General Objectives

The elementary school teacher will want to help the boys and girls to:

1. Develop skills and abilities essential to effective speaking and listening

2. Become more closely knit members of social groups, such as the classroom group and the family, of which they are a part

3. Express their thoughts and emotions better and thereby achieve the self-expression important to mental health and maximum contribution to others

4. Become increasingly thoughtful of the persons with whom or to whom they are talking or to whom they are listening, and give evidence of the improved attitude

5. Appreciate the complexities and usefulness of their language and to interest them in learning more about it

6. Develop and/or maintain a respect for languages and dialects unlike their own.

Needed Skills

Listed below are skills important in various types of speaking situations:

1. Speaking in a clear, pleasant voice
2. Pronouncing words correctly
3. Enunciating distinctly
4. Having good posture
5. Having a pleasant manner
6. Using words that express the intended meaning accurately
7. Using sentences effectively (when it is desirable to express thoughts in sentences)
8. Organizing thoughts well
9. Knowing when to speak and when to listen and acting accordingly
10. Speaking tactfully and listening politely.

Types of Activities

On various levels of the elementary school, boys and girls should be given help in the following types of activities involving oral expression:

1. Taking part in converstion and discussion
2. Giving talks and reports
3. Telling stories
4. Making explanations and giving directions
5. Making announcements
6. Asking riddles
7. Telling jokes
8. Showing courtesies demanded in social situations of various types.

Somewhere in the elementary school the pupils should receive help in learning how to observe the accepted procedures and civilities in social or business situations, such as the following:

1. Telephoning
2. Making and acknowledging introductions
3. Being interviewed
4. Greeting callers and guests
5. Participating in a program
6. Serving as member or leader of a club or committee.

Grade Placement

If the teacher endeavors to adapt his instruction to the needs of the boys and girls in his charge, he will not follow a rigid pattern in determining matters of grade placement. He can be guided in his choice by suggestions given under "Sequence and Grade Placement" (see page 32) and by the objectives, needed skills, and types of language arts activities that are listed in the preceding paragraphs under "The Scope of the Program." Growth toward achievement of these goals should be taking place without interruption throughout the years the pupil spends in the elementary school. More definite applications of the general principles relating to grade placement are given later in this book when the activities involving oral communication are considered.

GUIDELINES

In chapter 3 reference is made to some points that the teacher should keep in mind when teaching any of the language arts. Let us now consider some of those that have special bearing on teaching various phases of oral communication.

The teacher should recognize the primacy of oral communication as compared with written. Skill in the former should serve as a basis for development of ability in the latter. This point and several that follow are being stressed by linguists.

The teacher should credit the child with the skill he has developed in oral communication, much of it during preschool days. The teacher should ascertain the nature and extent of the child's background and then, starting where the child is, help him improve his speech.

The teacher should be cognizant of the difficulties in oral communication of the child from a non-English-speaking home or from an economically or culturally disadvantaged home. In the case of classrooms where most of the children have acquired considerable proficiency in oral expression in the dialect used in the school, it is especially important that the teacher not forget the needs of those whose language background deviates from that of the other boys and girls in the room. For a discussion of this point the reader is referred to chapter 12, "Adapting Instruction to Individual Differences." (See page 326 on "Working with the Culturally and Economically Disadvantaged Child" and page 328 on "Working with the Child from the Non-English-Speaking Home and with the bi-Lingual Child.")

The teacher should carefully guard against doing anything to cause a child to feel inferior to others because of his language. He should make the child feel that he is accepted for what he is and that differences in language do not spell inferiority. (For further discussion of this point see page 327 and page 328 of chapter 12.)

Even when the emphasis is on oral communication, the teacher should be aware of the close interrelatedness of the language arts. For example, when he helps the boys and girls give better talks, he should recognize the fact that skill in reporting on events in the order of their occurrence often is needed in both oral and written communication. Furthermore, knowledge of this fact should be reflected in his teaching, so that the boys and girls, too, see the interrelation and apply learnings in one facet of the language arts to the others.

The teacher should encourage effective speaking and listening habits not only during periods devoted primarily to the improvement of oral expression and listening, but also at many other times. For many boys and girls the teacher should provide direct help in improvement of skills in oral communication. For example, after the teacher has, in a meaningful situation, developed with the pupils the importance of having an interesting beginning for a talk, he may find it desirable later to have definite periods of practice on giving talks with interesting beginnings when the pupils might perform activities such as these:

1. Examine records of oral reports to determine which have good beginning sentences.
2. Decide which of a list of sentences would make good beginning sentences.
3. Give sentences of their own that would serve as good beginning sentences. Attention to the use of beginning sentences, for example, should not, however, be confined to a period of development or of specific practice on that point or not even to language arts classes. The teacher should hold the pupils up to the same standards for talks regardless of whether they are given in language classes or at other times.

The teacher should acquaint the pupils with his goals for the oral communication program and he should encourage them to participate in determining their own goals. If the pupils have a part in setting goals and/or if they are aware of goals held by the teacher and accept the teacher's goals as worthwhile, the learning is likely to be superior to that which takes place when the learners are not conscious of worthy objectives. The objectives should be achievable in the fairly near future if they are to prove of maximum incentive for learning. Immediacy of possible accomplishment is important, especially for the very young child.

The teacher should encourage the pupils to develop a varied background of worthwhile experiences, through *either firsthand or vicarious participation.* Paucity of experience is one reason for lack of effectiveness of expression. The child with a wide background of experience has something to talk about. He is also more likely to be interested in what others are saying than is the pupil with a more restricted background.

The following will suggest ways in which the teacher can encourage the pupils in the development of a wider background of experience:

1. Having exhibits in the room, such as "show-and-tell tables" and exhibits of articles pertaining to science, social studies, health, or other areas of human interest
2. Displaying pictures
3. Displaying books
4. Taking the children on field trips
5. Encouraging parents to take the boys and girls to places of interest and significance
6. Telling pupils points of interest in a variety of areas and doing it in such a manner that they will want to gain more information
7. Providing time for pupils to listen to one another
8. Engaging speakers to talk to the boys and girls
9. Encouraging reading.

The teacher should help the boys and girls understand the importance of telling interesting and significant points in acceptable form. There should not be a question as to whether content *or* form is important. Emphasis should be on both for the two are not mutually exclusive but can add value to each other. Content in poor form is undesirable; form without content is intolerable.

The teacher can help the boys and girls recognize the importance of good form in oral expression by:

1. Discussing with the pupils the importance of good form
2. Having the children listen to two talks identical in content but with extremes of form—desirable and undesirable—and then having them tell which is more interesting to hear
3. Having an employer tell the class the importance of good form in speech when applying for work and having other adults tell the class of the significance they attach to good form in expression
4. Discussing with boys and girls the fact that content and form are not mutually exclusive
5. Stressing both content and form in the various language arts activities in which the boys and girls engage.

The teacher should help the boys and girls to be considerate of others in oral communication. Courtesy should be an aim both in speaking and in listening.

These are points that should be considered and emphasized:

1. When to speak and when to be silent
2. What types of topics are acceptable in oral expression under various circumstances
3. How, through demeanor, to show courtesy to listeners
4. What voice qualities to develop.

The teacher should provide for many opportunities for oral expression. Improvement in oral communication is brought about primarily through participation in speaking and listening. There should be an abundance of situations in which language can be used functionally. Definite provisions should be made in the ongoing program of the room for many activities that involve speaking and listening. Provisions should be made, however, for somewhat structured situations involving oral communication as the pupils give reports, tell stories, participate in dramatization, and take part in choral speaking.

The teacher should strive to help create a classroom atmosphere that is conducive to self-expression through oral communication. In a regimented classroom optimum development of this type is not encouraged. A free and informal spirit should prevail in the room. On the other hand the maximum benefit from participation in activities involving oral communication is not likely to be obtained in a room where license is confused with liberty and where confusion reigns rather than the considerate give-and-take of an orderly classroom.

Here are other points of importance in creating and maintaining an atmosphere in the classroom in which self-expression through oral-language activities is likely to be fostered.

1. Every pupil should feel fairly relaxed much of the time.
2. The relationship between the teacher and the pupils should be one of mutual respect and goodwill.
3. The relationship among the boys and girls should, as a rule, be such that everyone feels accepted by his peers.
4. The arrangement of the pupils' seats should contribute to the desired atmosphere, by being informal rather than a straight-row lineup.

The teacher should serve as a model in oral communication. The importance of this point needs to be emphasized. Whether he is taking part in coversation or discussion, giving a report, making an explanation, or participating in oral communication in any other way, he should observe the specifications for excellence that he expects the pupils to observe (and many more!).

TAKING PART IN CONVERSATION AND DISCUSSION

Of the situations calling for oral communication, none, other than listening, occurs more frequently than that involving participation in conversation and informal discussion. It is also one of the types of speaking situation that is most neglected in terms of the amount of specific help given to boys and girls.

Let us now define terms. *Conversation,* as used here, refers to the free, easy-flowing exchange of ideas in an informal setting where, usually without previous planning, individuals express their ideas or make other comments or ask questions without holding themselves very long to any one topic. In *discussion,* on the other hand, attention is typically concentrated on one or a series of topics. To be sure, conversation often involves discussion. Discussion is part of conversation whenever in the exchange of ideas one topic is considered for a longer time than is characteristic of conversation without discussion. Discussion, like conversation, is usually informal. It can be structured, however, as it is, for example, in the panel discussion—a topic discussed later in this chapter (see page 53)—or in the even more complex situation involving debate.

Because there are many likenesses between conversation and informal discussion, the suggestions as to how to develop abilities in each of these topics are combined in this part of the chapter, even though at times one is specifically discussed and at other times the other.

It should be noted that the structured phase of the school program offers but limited opportunities, in most cases, for conversation. Conversation does not lend itself readily to a group of twenty or more individuals. "Conversation periods," in which a class is divided into groups and given a topic to talk about, are often ineffective. Stiltedness is likely to characterize such attempts at conversation. Frequently, too, such periods become discussion, not conversation, periods. The time before and after school and "free periods" during the school day afford opportunities for conversation.

Appropriate Topics for Conversation

As boys and girls progress through the elementary school and later, they should be learning increasingly to make finer lines of distinction between topics that are and those that are not desirable for conversation.

Criteria for Judging Suitability. The pupils should learn to check the appropriateness of conversation by noting whether the topic is:

1. Of interest to the group
2. Not embarrassing to anyone in the group
3. Not gossip

4. Entertaining, informative, or inspirational
5. Not cheap, tawdry, or vulgar.

List of Appropriate Topics. From time to time through discussion, explanation, or suggestion, boys and girls can be helped in determining what types of topics are suitable for conversation in harmony with the criteria listed. Some topics that may be considered are as follows:

Hobbies
Summer trips
School events
Sunday school
Clubs
Content of any school subject
Current events
Books
Motion pictures
TV programs
Exhibits
Something unusual that happened
Pets.

Methods of Helping Pupils Select Appropriate Topics. Methods such as the following can be utilized to help boys and girls develop in ability to talk only on appropriate topics when they engage in conversation or informal discussion.

1. Explaining, by the teacher, of what constitutes appropriate and inappropriate topics
2. Reading materials in a textbook or on duplicated sheets in which are discussed what constitutes appropriate topics
3. Making a list of some appropriate topics of conversation and naming some inappropriate ones
4. Making a bulletin board drawing attention to the choice of topics for conversation
5. Giving a dramatization demonstrating use of appropriate and of inappropriate topics
6. Recording and illustrating, in a section of a class or individual language arts notebook, learnings on the choice of topics for conversation.

Means of Acquiring Background Information

One of the requirements of an effective conversationalist is that he have something of significance or of interest to tell. Many persons seem to need to make no special effort to attain and utilize an experience background that is adequate for participation in conversation. However, others do not achieve such a background or, if they have it, do not utilize it, without guidance. For the latter group suggestions as to sources such as the following can be of value in improving the quality of their contribution to a conversation:

(1) through reading, (2) through listening, (3) through observing, and (4) through participating in activities.

In the following ways pupils might be helped to obtain the desired assistance from sources named above.

1. The teacher might comment on how he learned some interesting contribution that he made to a conversation.
2. The pupils could be asked rather frequently for the source of their information, especially when they contribute well to a conversation or an informal discussion.
3. The boys and girls could be asked to read a given selection in order to locate points that they would like to discuss with the group.

Inappropriate Times and Places for Conversation

In many instances, it is important to help boys and girls become aware of when it is improper or impolite to carry on conversation.

List of Inappropriate Situations. The pupils should learn to recognize the fact that, as a rule, conversation in situations such as the following is either entirely inappropriate or improper, or is inappropriate or improper when carried on for any length of time or in other than in a very subdued voice;

1. While in church
2. While at a funeral
3. While at a program
4. While seeing a motion picture
5. When someone is talking
6. When someone is studying
7. When someone is sleeping who would be disturbed by conversation
8. When someone listening to a program would be disturbed by conversation
9. When someone is saying his prayers.

Methods of Helping Pupils Decide upon Appropriate Times for Conversation. The following means can be used to help boys and girls decide when it is inappropriate to talk or when only a few remarks should be made in a subdued voice:

1. Making a list of places or situations in which, as a rule, it is inappropriate to talk
2. Discussing situations in which members of the class have noticed someone talking when quiet should have been observed (without mentioning names)
3. Checking a series of written descriptions of situations to indicate in which of them it would be improper to carry on conversation
4. Making a bulletin board that draws attention to the

appropriateness or inappropriateness of conversing under indicated circumstances

5. Recording and illustrating, in a section of a class or individual language arts notebook, learnings in regard to situations in which it is inappropriate to talk.

Introducing or Changing a Topic of Conversation

Some pupils may need help in developing skill in introducing a topic and in changing a topic of conversation. Procedures such as the following may be used:

1. Listing types of situations in which it is important for someone to change a topic of conversation

2. Making a list of polite expressions that may be used when changing a topic of conversation

3. Checking a series of written descriptions of desirable and undesirable means of changing a topic of conversation

4. Giving a dramatization to illustrate polite and impolite methods of changing a topic of conversation

5. Making a bulletin board that draws attention to something learned about introducing or changing a topic of conversation

6. Recording and illustrating, in a section of a class or individual language arts notebook, learnings in regard to introducing or changing a topic of conversation.

Expressing an Opinion

Some important points that elementary school children should keep in mind about expressing an opinion have been discussed on preceding pages. They should also remember that; (1) All opinions that people express as their own should honestly be theirs. (2) At times it is kinder not to express than to express an opinion. (3) As people express their own opinions, they should also be willing to listen to those of others on the same subject. (4) At times it is important to substantiate opinion with facts. (5) When older people have expressed their opinions, boys and girls should take special care before they express a contradictory opinion. (6) People should recognize times when it is essential to express an opinion. (7) If people have been wrong in an opinion they have expressed, they should, if possible, admit their error.

Listed here are some procedures by means of which pupils can improve skills in expressing their ideas in conversation or informal discussion.

1. Discussing the importance of expressing an opinion politely and otherwise properly

2. Listening to explanation by the teacher as to important points concerning how and when to express an opinion

3. Reading information in a textbook or on duplicated sheets as to how to express an opinion

4. Listing criteria to observe when expressing an opinion

5. Discussing times when it is essential for a person to express his opinion even though he would prefer to be silent

6. Discussing the importance of expressing opinions that are "honestly theirs"

7. Making a list of polite expressions to use when about to state a contradictory opinion

8. Checking a series of written reports that illustrate desirable and undesirable means of expressing an opinion

9. Demonstrating ways in which an opinion can be substantiated

10. Dramatizing situations in which opinions are expressed politely and otherwise properly and situations in which they are expressed impolitely and otherwise improperly

11. Making a bulletin board that draws attention to something learned about how to express an opinion

12. Recording and illustrating, in a section of a class or individual language arts notebook, what has been learned about expressing an opinion.

Developing and Maintaining a Voice Suitable for Conversation

The pupils should be helped to act in accordance with points such as these when engaging in conversation or informal discussion; (1) The participant in a conversation should speak so that everyone in the group can hear him without strain. (2) The participant in conversation should guard against talking unnecessarily loud. (3) A pleasant voice should be maintained at all times. (4) No person in a small group should whisper to another.

Some of the ways in which boys and girls may be helped in developing or maintaining a voice effective in conversation are:

1. By discussing and listing the characteristics of a voice desirable for conversation

2. By taking part or observing a dramatization of a conversation in which undesirable and one in which desirable characteristics of a voice are illustrated

3. By making recordings of conversations and then evaluating the voices in terms of criteria that have been accepted

4. By making a bulletin board that draws attention to something learned concerning a desirable voice in conversation

5. By making a "movie" that points out in word and picture some important learnings about the use of the voice in conversation or discussion

6. By recording and illustrating, in a section of a class

or individual language arts notebook, learnings about a desirable voice in conversation and discussion.

General Procedures

Guidance in achieving greater ability in participating in conversation and informal discussion can be given through use of informal conversation situations and through planned lessons.

Use of informal situations. Development in conversation skills can be encouraged through many informal situations in which conversation and discussion occur. The period on the playground or in the gymnasium, the free periods before school in the classroom, and the time devoted to the various planned school activities afford excellent opportunity.

It is not enough that pupils have adequate opportunity to engage in conversation. While practice is essential, it does not provide a guarantee that it will not be practice in error. Consequently the teacher should help the pupils develop higher standards even on those occasions where learning to converse better with others is not the reason for the activity, or at least not as far as the boys and girls know.

1. Informal conversation during "free periods." These are some ways in which guidance can be provided during "free periods":

The teacher can remind the boys and girls of the importance of only one person talking at a time.

The teacher can draw into the conversation or discussion those pupils who have not been participating by asking them questions and by suggesting that everyone be given an opportunity to express himself.

The teacher can illustrate how to make a person who has just joined a conversation group feel at ease in the group (1) by telling him about what the group is conversing, (2) by drawing attention to the importance of doing what he did to help the newcomer become part of the group, and (3) by encouraging the pupils to do likewise at other times.

The teacher can comment from time to time on the observance of any of the points about conversation that have been emphasized in developmental lessons for improving conversation and discussion and he can give the pupils opportunity to do likewise.

The teacher can provide many "conversation pieces," and encourage the pupils to do likewise, for display on bulletin boards, on shelves, and on tables.

2. Informal conversation during ongoing activities. The suggestions for guidance given in the preceding paragraph hold, for the most part, not only for "free periods" but also for times of planned work in the ongoing activities of the classroom. Such guidance can also be given in situations such as the following in which:

The boys and girls plan the work for activities, of short or long duration, discussing questions such as "How can we do our finger painting so that everyone has a chance?" or "In what different types of activities might we engage in order to find an answer to our problem?"

The pupils discuss questions that have been raised dealing with the subject matter they are studying, such as "Why has Mexico been called a beggar sitting on a bag of gold?" or "How should we show our visitors what safety rules we try to observe?"

The pupils discuss what should be included in a concluding activity for a unit on which they are working in the social studies or in science or in some other content area.

The pupils tell about additional points that they have learned about a topic that they are studying, such as what the Eskimos eat or how the people of West Germany have been rebuilding their country.

The pupils evaluate their work in response to questions such as "Which of these points do you think we observed particularly well?" or "On which of these points do we need much improvement?"

Use of Planned Lessons. For some boys and girls the incidental work on development of skills in conversation and discussion afforded by situations that can be utilized during "free periods" or during the course of ongoing activities is not enough to insure efficiency in these ways of oral expression. Consequently planned lessons, designed particularly to help the pupils in the development and maintenance of skills, are advisable. These lessons are of two types, developmental and maintenance. The term *developmental lesson* refers to one in which a new learning is developed, while the term *maintenance lesson* designates one in which a learning acquired earlier in part is reinforced.

1. Developmental lessons. When to introduce a new consideration for attaining proficiency in conversation through informal situations and when to do so through a class period specifically set aside to be devoted, at least in part, to the development of a skill cannot be spelled out with specificity. (For suggestions on teaching a developmental lesson see page 56.) In general, when a point is easy to grasp, possibly such as the importance of not putting one's hand in front of one's mouth when speaking, it might well be developed in an informal situation. A point of greater complexity, such as the following, may often better be taken up for the first time in a developmental lesson; (a) when and when not to interrupt and how to interrupt when necessary, (b) helping others take part in conversation, (c) suitable topics

for conversation, (d) appropriate and inappropriate times and places for conversation, (e) changing the topic of conversation, and (f) disagreeing with others in conversation.

2. Maintenance lessons. Developmental lessons often need to be supplemented by maintenance lessons. Presentation of a point at one sitting and making application of it at that time usually does not suffice in learning a generalization of considerable complexity or in establishing a habit. For many boys and girls it often is important to provide at intervals considerable opportunity for further application of what has been developed. At times it is sufficient to provide such practice incidentally; however, in many cases, such reinforcement is not enough. Incidental practice then needs to be supplemented by planned lessons in which the pupils have the opportunity to make secure their earlier learnings. At such times strategies such as these might be employed:

The teacher redevelops, with shortcuts in procedure, a point taught earlier.

The pupils summarize their learnings on the topic.

A demonstration or dramatization is put on, emphasizing the point.

The pupils read recorded conversations, indicate orally or in writing, which are correct and which are incorrect, and state how the errors could be corrected.

In small groups the boys and girls practice roleplaying as they observe conditions decided upon earlier. For example, a group might be given a slip of paper stating, "Dramatize a conversation in which one person interrupts someone politely at a time when an interruption is necessary."

The pupils tell about situations in which, since their last study of the point, they had made suitable application of their learnings.

The pupils ask questions about application of previous learnings in terms of situations with which they were confronted.

Methods. In both developmental and maintenance lesson procedures such as these can be utilized: teacher explanation, pupil explanation, silent reading, oral reading, discussion, summarization, written work, question-and-answer procedure, demonstration, dramatization, evaluation.

Suggestions for utilization of the methods listed are given at various places in this and other chapters. Description of procedure, therefore, of only one—namely dramatization—is given here.

Dramatization is of special value in the work on oral expression because dramatization itself is a means of oral communication. To help boys and girls see the need of learning when and when not to interrupt, as well as how to interrupt when necessary, for example, the teacher

could ask several pupils to plan with him beforehand a skit in which they include several rude and untimely interruptions and one in which interruptions are made politely. The teacher can then during class time announce that two or more pupils have prepared two skits, one in which they are going to demonstrate how interruptions should not be made and another in which they illustrate how they can be made politely. The pupils in the audience can then be asked to watch the demonstration in order to find out what rules they can make to guide them on that point. After the skits have been presented, the discussion can follow on what was done properly and what improperly and a list can be made on the chalkboard of rules to observe concerning interruptions during conversation.

Similarly dramatizations of rules can be given during phases of lessons in which the pupils are provided with opportunity to apply what they have been taught in the presentation part of a lesson. For example, the class could be divided into several groups, with each group given a slip of paper indicating what the members of the group are to dramatize later while the rest of the class are spectators. Each group should probably have a different set of directions. Examples of such statements follow.

1. While the boys and girls are having an interesting conversation, one pupil interrupts to remind the group that it is time to do a task that their teacher had asked them to begin at that time. The interruption is made politely.

2. Someone in a group brings into the conversation a pupil who has not been taking part.

A few general suggestions to bear in mind when planning dramatizations of the types described are: (1) The directions should be simple enough that the pupils can follow them with success. (2) The directions should allow for some ingenuity. (3) The skit should be brief. (4) While some of the skits might advisedly demonstrate what not to do, the emphasis, in general, should be on portrayal of correct procedures. (5) Provisions should be made for all pupils to take part in skits, even though the participation may be spread over a period considerably longer than one day. (6) Care should be taken that the skits are on a refined plane of expression, without vulgarity, even those in which incorrect procedures are demonstrated.

Development of Skills in Special Types of Situations

Many of the suggestions in the preceding pages have been limited to those that apply to almost all types of situations involving conversation or discussion. Next are given suggestions for somewhat specialized types of conversation or discussion, namely "sharing time," panel discussions, and conversation at mealtime.

Sharing Time. Sharing Time, as the term is here used, refers to the time of the school day set aside for boys and girls to report to their peers events or other points of interest to them. Because frequently the participants illustrate what they tell by showing objects, at times this period is called the "show-and-tell" time. Although it is used more frequently in the primary than in later grades, it need not be restricted to the former. However, when it is used effectively in the intermediate grades, the structure should be more complex than in lower grades.

Sharing Time is considered by some educators to be one of the most useful periods of the school day, one in which pupils have the opportunity to express themselves informally. For others, however this period is the butt of critical remarks. Evaluation of the Sharing Time results in the conclusion that both praise and criticism of it are well deserved. Which should be given depends upon how the period is conducted.

1. Values. When used wisely, the Sharing Time can make contributions to learning such as these listed below:

The shy pupils can get a sense of importance as they show or tell something in which their peers are interested and thus they may lose some of their shyness.

The talkative pupils can learn to take their turns in expressing themselves.

Sharing Time can present an excellent opportunity for improvement in habits of listening.

The boys and girls can learn to do cooperative planning as they help plan standards to observe and procedures to follow during Sharing Time.

The boys and girls can get practice during Sharing Time in the various methods they use for communicating their ideas, such as talking, dramatization, demonstration, oral reading.

Through Sharing Time the boys and girls may become more interested in what they can observe in the classroom, on the playground, at home, and in other places.

As the boys and girls gather information to present during Sharing Time, they can develop in skill in doing research.

2. Procedures. Some of the means by which a presentation can be made are: telling, demonstration, puppetry, skits, other methods of dramatization, book reports, reading poetry or prose, make-believe radio or television programs, showing objects, picture, or diagrams. Additional suggestions for procedure are as follows:

At times the Sharing Time can advisedly be divided into two phases. During one part of the period anyone could briefly contribute who has something of special importance to tell that he *just must* tell that day (like getting a new pet for his birthday). During the other part of the period a planned program for the day could be presented, possibly one in which various children selected beforehand make their contributions individually on whatever topic they have chosen. For the nonplanned part of the period those pupils could be called upon who before class had told the teacher or a pupil chairman of something they want very much to tell the class that day. During the more structured phase of Sharing Time the pupils who are on the program for the day could plan ahead of time how they could make an effective presentation. Care should be taken that, as a rule, no child is on the program for this part of the period a second time before each one has been on it once. A chart can be posted on which each pupil signs up for the day he will appear on the program.

During Sharing Time there can be informal discussion of some important topic of the day, such as Washington's birthday or an eclipse of the sun.

In the intermediate grades there may be worked out a schedule of the type of contribution to be made on a given day of the week. For instance, Monday may be designated as a day for reports on science, Tuesday as a day devoted to books, Wednesday as a day for reports in the area of social studies.

A class newsletter or magazine could make frequent reference to points brought out in Sharing Time. Or a magazine or booklet could be devoted exclusively to what was done or learned during that period. In such a booklet there might be an introductory part describing Sharing Time in the room, a list of values of Sharing Time, a list of criteria to observe, and reports on interesting information gained.

Evaluation of contributions should be made. Questions such as these may be asked: "What was particularly fine about our contributions today?" or "How could our audience make it easier for a person to talk to the group?"

When standards have been worked out by the group and possibly posted, occasionally there could be a checkup by an individual or by the group as to how they are being observed. At times special practice might be provided to improve upon one that needs special attention.

Panel Discussions. Although the term *panel discussion* to many teachers suggests a type of procedure so complex in nature that it is reserved for pupils beyond the elementary school, some types of discussion that can be designated as such are so lacking in complexity of structure that they can be used even in lower grades. As the term is used in this book, it is applied to any discussion by a group of persons with an audience who listens to it. A description of how such panel discussions might be conducted is given later in this chapter. (See page 57.)

1. Values. Some of the values that can be attained through panel discussions, either by the participants or the audience or by both are given below.

The use of panel discussions provides desirable variation in classroom procedure.

In some phases of a panel discussion the participant is provided with practice in thinking and expressing himself on the spur of the moment in front of an audience.

Purpose for doing research is given by means of some panel discussions.

In panel discussions practical opportunity is provided for putting into functional use what has been learned about participating in discussion and about listening.

2. Guidelines. To help boys and girls attain maximum values from participation in or from listening to panel discussions, here are two guidelines that the teacher should follow.

From the continuum of very simple to rather complex procedures that can characterize a panel discussion, choice of method should be made in harmony with the abilities of the pupils, as influenced by age, mentality, grade level, and environmental factors.

Participation in a panel discussion should, as a rule, not be limited over a period of weeks or months, to only some of the pupils in the class.

3. Topics for panel discussion. Here are some topics in the areas indicated that are suitable for panel discussions.

Social studies; (a) How is the life of children in Switzerland like and how is it unlike that of boys and girls in our country? (b) How can we help community workers?

Science: (a) wild flowers in our neighborhood, (b) ecology.

Physical education or health: (a) how to take care of our teeth, (b) games around the world, (c) how to keep our bodies clean.

Language arts: (a) what to do during Sharing Time, (b) what to remember about conversation at the dinner table, (c) books you may wish to read.

Conversation at Mealtime. If we judge by some reports of remarks made at mealtime at school and at home, it seems important that boys and girls in the elementary school should get help in learning significant points about conversation at the table and that they should be stimulated so they will want to observe them.

1. Points to be stressed. Although many of the points that pertain to all types of conversation may need to be stressed in connection with conversation at mealtime, the following probably need special emphasis: (a) Conversation at mealtime should be pleasant. (b) Matters of sickness or accident should not be discussed. (c) Nothing should be said that will be embarrassing or upsetting to anyone at the table. (d) There should be no criticism of food. (e) A person should feel responsible for entering into conversation at the table.

2. List of procedures. Many of the learnings that are needed concerning conversation at mealtime can be acquired through incidental means such as participation in school parties and eating lunch at school. However, for some pupils special emphasis is needed in situations specifically planned to help them with table conversation. Some possible procedures are here indicated:

Discussing the importance of appropriate conversation at mealtime

Participating in skits that demonstrate desirable and undesirable conversation at mealtime

Reading descriptions of reports of desirable and undesirable table conversation and noting each type

Drawing up rules for conversation at the table

Discussing the importance of being polite to any individual who disobeys the rules about conversation at mealtime

Making a booklet on what has been learned about conversation at mealtime

Drawing cartoons illustrating desirable and undesirable comments at mealtime.

Illustrative Teaching Situations

In planning a developmental lesson in almost any phase of the language arts these phases usually should be included as parts of the lesson: motivation, presentation of the new learning, and application of it. (See page 53.)

The purpose of the motivation is to interest the boys and girls in learning about the topic or in some cases to help them recognize need for study. Sometimes the motivation may consist merely of a statement by the teacher, in which he explains the lack that he has observed in pupils' conversation. If so, the teacher can tell the class that he will try to help them improve in that respect. At other times the motivation may really be an integral part of the presentation as, for example, when in order to show pupils what to do when two persons start talking at the same time, one skit is presented to illustrate how the problem is handled poorly and another how it is taken care of properly.

During the presentation the points to be learned during the lesson are emphasized. Often it is preferable to make the presentation through inductive procedures, as, for example, when the pupils are studying the importance of talking only about topics that are not embarrassing to anyone in the group. In such a situation the boys and girls may read two recorded conversations and decide what makes one better than the other. Or, as already suggested, the points of significance may be brought out through two skits a few pupils have prepared before class with the help of the teacher.

After the new point of the lesson has been developed, it is well for either the teacher or a pupil, preferably the latter, as a rule, to state in a sentence or more what has been learned.

During the application phase of the lesson, which should usually occur not only during the developmental lesson but also at later times, the pupil has an opportunity to use what he has learned. Small conversation groups may be established in which the pupils talk with one another according to the specifications that the teacher may have recorded for them on slips of paper handed to the chairman of each group, or the pupils may judge one sample conversation presented by a small group of boys and girls for the benefit of the rest of the class. In the application of the lesson the pupils should be encouraged to try to apply what they have learned at all times when they engage in conversation.

Panel Discussions. As the teacher plans or helps the pupils plan a panel discussion, he will want to keep in mind guidelines such as those stated on the preceding page, as well as points such as the following: (a) Topics should be selected in terms of suitability as to the ability of the boys and girls, their interests, and the value of the topic to them. (b) The teacher should guard against over-use of the panel discussion, to prevent boredom and to provide desirable variety. (c) Considerable guidance in planning and presenting panel discussion should be given, at least occasionally. (d) The audience should frequently be checked on its learnings from panel discussions by means of discussion, oral questions and answers, and written responses. (See also page 55.)

The following descriptions of possible procedures in a panel discussion indicate, roughly in order of complexity, some of the ways they can be conducted in the elementary school.

In the first grade a group of boys and girls, three to five in number, appear in front of their classmates with pictures they have drawn on some topic such as "My Pet." As each pupil shows his picture, he makes one or more comments about it. When all have shown theirs, the teacher, serving as chairman, opens the rest of the period to questions and comments about the pictures or the explanations, first to pupils on the panel and then to the audience. The teacher also may wish to make comments or ask questions. At the close of the discussion there can well be an evaluation of the discussion by the members of the panel, the audience, or the teacher. Questions such as these may be asked in evaluation: (a) Could you hear us? (b) Could you see our pictures? (c) Did we have good posture?

After some of the pupils in a third grade have been reading about the food of the Eskimos, they can participate in a panel discussion. A chairman, either the teacher or a pupil, can ask each participant to report on what he learned on the topic, perhaps as each makes several comments. The chairman can then summarize what has been said and ask for additional points or for questions, first from members of the panel and then from the audience. The teacher may wish to contribute also. An evaluation of the discussion can follow.

After the pupils in a fifth-grade room have been studying about how to develop skill in conversation, some of the members may take part in a panel discussion on the topic. They can meet beforehand with the teacher to decide what points to discuss in order to be able to help the audience remember what to do to be an effective participant in conversation and to put their knowledge into practice. They may decide upon points such as these: (a) importance of being effective in conversation, (b) helping others take part in conversation, (c) interruptions in conversation, (d) situations in which conversation is out of order.

Next, each participant can be assigned a topic. After each member of the panel has thought for a few minutes about points he plans to stress, he can outline his plans for the panel and ask for suggestions. When suggestions have been made, time can be allowed for the pupils to plan their reports alone. The group may also have a voice in deciding on the pattern of procedure during the time of the panel, which may be as follows: (a) A pupil chairman gives the purpose of the panel and outlines the procedure. (b) All the topics are presented by panel members. (c) Questions and comments are given by the panel members when all reports have been completed. (d) Questions and comments are given by the audience. (e) A summary is given by the chairman. (f) Evaluation of the panel follows by the members of the panel, the audience, and the teacher. After making plans for procedure, the panel is ready to begin its presentation.

Conversation at Mealtime. The following are a few suggestions for procedure that can be followed in a plan for a day in order to help boys and girls in the upper-primary or lower-intermediate grades to improve upon their conversation at mealtime. The suggestions might be followed in the order given or variations might be made in the sequence of using some of them, in omission of others, and in addition of still others.

The teacher refers to a desirable discussion during a mealtime and asks pupils to name some points that made it desirable.

Pupils name other points that should be observed during conversation at mealtime.

The pupils refer to some ways in which mealtime could be made unpleasant through undesirable types of conversation.

The class draws up a list of guidelines for conversation at mealtime.

The pupils state why it is important to observe these guidelines.

The class reads an account of a conversation at an imaginary mealtime to determine which parts were suitable and which unsuitable and then they discuss their decisions.

A few pupils put on impromptu skits, one illustrating desirable and the other undesirable conversation at mealtime.

The teacher suggests that each pupil think of some ways in which he can contribute through his conversation to a happy mealtime at school, at home, or elsewhere.

The teacher asks for suggestions as to what should be an individual's reaction at mealtime if someone else violates a principle of good conversation.

DEVELOPMENT IN ABILITY TO GIVE TALKS AND REPORTS

The following topics are used in this section as consideration is given to talks by children about their own experiences and to reports: (1) values, (2) guidelines for teaching, (3) topics and titles, (4) methods, (5) book reports.

Values

In order that giving talks may be made a highly worthwhile activity, it is well for the teacher to have in mind the values that can be derived from this experience.

1. Learning to give talks is of value to boys and girls as they give the many talks that should be given in relation to various ongoing activities in school.

2. Through guidance in giving talks the quality of those that children and adults need to give outside of school, at club meetings, political gatherings or church meetings, can be affected favorably.

3. Through the opportunity to give talks the pupils' fund of information can be extended, both as they prepare their own talks and as they listen to those of others.

4. Through giving talks about their own experiences the boys and girls can be helped to see the worth of common everyday happenings.

5. Opportunity is provided, by means of an effective

program in giving talks, for development in the art of listening.

6. As the boys and girls learn to give talks, they can make functional use of many important skills of oral expression on which they need practice, such as talking in sentences and speaking with a pleasing and effective voice.

Guidelines

The following are helpful guidelines for a program in the improvement of ability to give talks:

1. There should be a reason for giving a talk, one recognized as worthwhile by the pupils.

2. The total program should be well planned.

3. The program should include talks the pupils give in connection with work in the content areas as well as on personal experiences.

4. Included in the program should be developmental lessons in which there is presentation of skills to be attained or knowledge to be acquired in relation to giving talks.

5. For some pupils the program should include practice-type lessons in which major emphasis is placed on the practice of a skill rather than on the subject matter of the talk. For example, pupils might give only the opening sentences for a talk if emphasis is on giving a good beginning for a talk. Similarly they might give talks at times in which, while the subject matter is of importance, they try to see if they can give the talks without using unnecessary *and's.*

6. The pupils and the teacher should frequently make evaluations of talks given and of the total program for the development in ability to give talks. (See page 79.)

7. Means of expression such as demonstrating, illustrating, or dramatizing should at times be used to supplement the statements by the speaker. For example, when a pupil gives a talk on one of his hobbies, he might have pictures to show illustrating it, or, in the case of some hobbies, he might show what he has made. Through the help of some of a pupil's peers, a dramatization—a very short one—might be put on in connection with a talk on schools in colonial New England.

Topics and Titles

Many of the topics for talks would advisedly be selected by the pupils, with the teacher as final judge of the acceptability of the proposed titles or topics. At other times the teacher might be the one to suggest the topics. In either case, it is important that the children talk on topics with which they have familiarity. At times they gain familiarity through research as in the case of topics dealing with the social studies or science; at other times they may speak on firsthand experiences. The latter type, while particularly valuable for younger children, should not be neglected even with older boys and girls.

Many of the topics and titles on which pupils will talk can be determined by the activities significant in the ongoing school program involving the social studies, science, health, literature, and even modern mathematics. However, since the more or less incidental selection of topics does not supply all the guidance that some pupils need in learning to select topics or titles for talks, it may be of value for the teacher to suggest a few suitable ones.

List of Topics and Titles. What then are some of the topics and titles which boys and girls can use for talks? The following topics, with suggested titles, are merely illustrative of many others:

1. Pets: (a) Tricks I have taught my dog, (b) My pet crow hides things.
2. Hobbies: (a) My vegetable garden, (b) Trees are my hobby.
3. Trips: (a) An exciting moment on our trip, (b) We rediscovered the source of the Mississippi.
4. People: (a) A real friend, (b) My unforgettable character.
5. Personal experiences: (a) Something funny, (b) It happened to me.
6. Learnings in the language arts: (a) Using the telephone, (b) How to give a good book report.
7. Special days: (a) It was a Christmas present, (b) Christmas at our home.
8. School: (a) My first day at school, (b) Going to a new school.
9. Social studies: (a) How the Indians told time, (b) The boyhood of Columbus, (c) From tree to tire.
10. Hygiene: (a) How to catch a cold, (b) How not to catch a cold.
11. Current events: (a) A modern explorer, (b) It happened yesterday.
12. Science: (a) Discoveries in space, (b) The next eclipse.
13. School projects: (a) Being a good school citizen, (b) Improving our lunchroom.
14. Home: (a) That is my chore, (b) A pleasant winter evening at home.

Selections of Topics and Titles. The boys and girls may be helped in choosing appropriate topics and titles for talks as they:

1. Discuss topics from other curricular areas on which they can give talks that would help others get worthwhile information.
2. Look at pictures on a topic, such as pets or funny experiences or vacation experiences, to see if they would like to report on an event suggested by one of the pictures.

3. Bring things for a "show-and-tell" table and then decide whether an explanation of an object they brought would constitute a good topic for a talk.
4. Suggest topics on personal experiences on which they would like to hear reports.
5. Place in a box, possibly called "Our Idea Box," suggestions for topics or titles.
6. Suggest attention-getting titles that may be used for a talk on a given topic.

Methods

Listed here are activities in which the pupils can engage to improve in ability to give talks. It should be kept in mind, however, that the chief method by which one learns an activity is usually by performing it, rather than by reading or talking about it, till the skill is mastered to the extent that mastery is the objective. In other words, there needs to be much opportunity afforded to give talks.

Some of the suggestions listed below are possible means of evaluation. The reader is referred for more information on evaluation to page 42 and to page 79.

Although the following suggested activities are listed as activities for boys and girls, teacher guidance is important in all of them.

1. Deciding on questions they would like answered if someone else talked on the subject and then answering these questions in their talks
2. Studying the beginning sentences of recorded reports and deciding which are interest-arousing
3. Choosing from a list of beginning sentences for reports those that would make them want to hear reports beginning with those sentences
4. Giving reports with good beginning sentences
5. Listening to evaluation by their peers or by the teacher of the beginning sentences of their reports
6. Studying the ending sentences of recorded reports and deciding which are good endings
7. Giving reports with good ending sentences
8. Listening to evaluation by their peers or by the teacher of the ending sentences of their reports
9. Indicating which sentences in a series of recorded talks do not keep to the topic
10. Listening to evaluation as to whether any of their sentences did not keep to the topic by their peers or by the teacher
11. Indicating which of a series of pictures on a topic are not arranged in the order in which the events they represent are given in a written paragraph illustrated by the pictures, and then arranging the pictures in the right sequence
12. Indicating which sentences in a series of recorded talks are not given in the right order and then rearranging them

Figure 4.1. Pictorial Illustration as a Means of Appraisal.

13. Listening to evaluation by their peers or by the teacher as to whether any of their sentences were out of order

14. Evaluating the posture of speakers

15. Making a list of requirements for a good talk such as an interesting topic, a good beginning, keeping to the topic, arranging points in the correct order, good posture, good audience contact, freedom from mannerisms, good sentences, correct pronunciation, clear enunciation, a good ending. (The reader is referred to figure 4.2.)

16. Rehearsing their talks to someone at home or to one or more of their classmates or to the teacher

17. Evaluating their own reports in terms of chief difficulties, deciding on means of overcoming major problems, and then giving talks in which each pupil tries hard to eliminate a problem with which he requests the help of his classmates and the teacher

18. Evaluating their own talks by means of tape recordings

19. Keeping a card on which, with the help of the teacher, each pupil checks his strengths and weaknesses on each talk as he uses the criteria that have been worked out by the class

20. Participating in programs in which talks are given, some perhaps as "mock" radio or television programs

21. Participating in radio programs

22. Showing ways in which talks can be vitalized through illustrations, demonstration, and the like.

Figure 4.2. A Checklist for Self-Evaluation

Book Reports

A special type of report that pupils in the elementary school, even in the primary grades, can give is the book report. In general the suggestions that are given in the preceding pages for reports of various types apply to book reports also. Following are given additional points, which are supplemented by others on written reports in chapter 5, "Guiding Growth in Written Expression." (See page 104.) Chapter 10, "Guiding Growth in Independent Reading," also contains suggestions on giving book reports.

Guidelines. The following are some guidelines which the teacher may find helpful:

1. Oral book reports by boys and girls should be of value in that they serve two major purposes, namely, to interest the pupils in doing more worthwhile reading and to help them learn to better perform various skills in the language arts in a functional situation.

2. The quality of books reported upon, though on the pupils' level of appreciation, should be high. There is no place for trash in the book report program. Consequently, the teacher should be the final judge as to the books on which reports should be given to the class.

3. The boys and girls should be encouraged to report

only on books that they enjoy. However, the caution given in the preceding item should nevertheless be observed.

4. The boys and girls should be given guidance in learning how to prepare book reports. If a pupil does not know how to proceed to plan a report, he is likely to dislike the process and then giving reports may discourage further reading. Likewise listening to poorly given reports is not likely to be incentive for reading. Help can be given in these ways:

A good model of a book report can be supplied. The teacher or the librarian might give a sample of an oral report. This technique is more likely to be successful if the boys and girls are told that the person reporting is trying to illustrate the type of report they themselves could give.

The pupils, with the help of the teacher, could draw up standards for reports after having heard one or more good reports or after having read and discussed some that are poor and some that are good.

The class could make a list of points that should be included in a book report. Among items on such a list might be: name of the author, title of the book, interesting or significant content, the opinion of the reviewer.

The class could work out a list of ways in which illustrative materials can be used with book reports.

The teacher and pupils could evaluate reports given by the pupils. Great care needs, however, be taken that criticism does not leave a sting. Often it is better to name only strong points of a report after a pupil has given one. Then, after a series of book reports have been given, the class could, without mentioning names, indicate some points on which the group might work to give better reports.

5. Care should be taken to have reports given in a functional setting, at least part of the time. Books on the social studies, for example, that fit in with a topic currently being studied in that area, could be reported upon at the appropriate time in connection with that work. Book clubs, too, furnish an interesting setting for giving book reports.

6. Giving book reports should be adapted to individual differences. Some ways in which this guideline can be observed are: (a) The teacher helps pupils who are likely to have difficulty in giving book reports to select books that will be relatively simple for them to review. (b) The teacher gives extra assistance to the pupils who, seemingly, without this help could not give successful reports—successful from the point of view of the reporter and of the audience. (c) Extra book reports are given by brighter children as one means of providing worthwhile additional activities.

Points to Remember When Showing a Book to an Audience. Here are a few directions the boys and girls might follow, with benefit, as they show a book to their audience.

1. Show the book so that everyone can see it.

2. If you show pictures in the book, make certain that everyone can see them well enough to profit from the showing.

3. If not all the pupils could see the pictures in a book that you want to show them, do not show them at the time of your report but tell the class where you will place the book so that everyone can look at the illustrations at a later time. You might write on the board a list of pages at which you suggest the class look.

Other Means of Vitalizing a Book Report. With the guidance of the teacher the class could draw up a list of additional means of vitalizing the giving of a book report. Included in such a listing might be points such as the following.

1. Drawing an illustration of a scene or character of the book.

2. Dramatizing a scene from the book. One or more pupils, under the direction of the reporter, might plan beforehand the dramatization of an interesting scene, to be presented, possibly as a surprise, at the time when the report is given.

3. Showing the class a map, possibly from the book, indicating the setting of the book.

4. Making a poster to interest the pupils in the book. This poster might be displayed a day or longer before the report is given.

5. Pantomiming part of the book. The reporter may need the assistance of one or more of his classmates for this activity.

6. Constructing a time line picturing events in the book. Such a time line is especially worthwhile when the book reported on has a historical background.

7. Putting on a puppet show to illustrate part of the book. (For suggestions on puppetry see page 308.)

8. Making an accordionlike folder of pictures illustrating main events of the book. (For an illustration of an accordianlike folder see page 265.)

9. Making a "movie" illustrating the book. (For an illustration of a "movie" see page 246.)

10. Constructing a mobile illustrating characters or scenes of a book. (For an illustration of a mobile see page 264.)

11. Dressing in simple costume while giving a report in first person. For example, a paper hat resembling that worn by Doctor Dolittle may be enough to add color if the book to be reviewed is *The Story of Doctor Dolittle* by Hugh Lofting.

DEVELOPMENT IN ABILITY TO TELL STORIES

Since telling of personal experiences is discussed on preceding pages of this chapter, in this part such ac-

Figure 4.3. A "Movie Theater" for Use in Illustrating Books.

counts are not included. Here are given suggestions for reproducing stories that have been heard or read and for telling original stories. The differentiation observed between the stories and the accounts of experiences is that the latter are factual without necessarily involving a plot. In the story, plot is essential. To be sure, the line of demarcation between the two types is not always a clear one and for practical classroom purposes does not need to be.

Values of Storytelling

Storytelling, which no longer is done as much in the home as it was before the time of extensive mass communication and mechanization, is an art that our civilization can ill afford to lose. Let us note some of the values that the child can derive from listening to stories and/or telling them. He can:

1. Become more familiar with the culture of the race
2. Learn some of the values that are permanent in society
3. Develop appreciation of literature
4. Improve his vocabulary
5. Get functional, meaningful practice in many skills of oral expression such as talking in a pleasing voice, being considerate of the audience, speaking in correct sentences, organizing the thoughts to be expressed, and using good English
6. Become emotionally involved in such a way that the involvement adds to his mental health
7. Get a closer grip on things of the spirit. (Bible stories are very valuable in this respect.)
8. Add to his fund of information and gain vicarious experiences
9. Develop his imagination
10. Derive pleasure and give it to his audience
11. Increase his interest in reading

Guidelines

Guidelines are listed here on which to base a program in storytelling.

1. No pupil should be required to tell a story that he does not like.
2. As a rule, a pupil should not tell a story to a group unless he has made preparation for telling it.
3. Storytelling should take place in a relaxed atmosphere. (If feasible, the audience should be arranged in a compact but informal group around the storyteller, who, as a rule, should be seated.)
4. Standards for storytelling should be worked out by the class with the help of the teacher.
5. Evaluation of storytelling should take place in such a manner as to encourage future interest in telling stories.
6. The teacher should encourage individuality of expression and of manner in the storyteller.
7. The storyteller should show enthusiasm appropriate to the story he is telling.

Choosing Stories to Tell

Among the guidelines in the preceding paragraph one important principle in the selection of stories to be retold has been stated, namely "No pupil should be required to tell a story that he does not like." Following are additional suggestions.

1. Only worthwhile stories should be retold.
2. With the help of the teacher the pupils should draw up standards for the selection of stories to be retold.
3. The pupils should have an important part in the selection of stories for retelling.
4. The pupils should have readily available many sources of fine stories of the type that they would be able to retell.

5. The storyteller should select a story that he thinks his audience will enjoy hearing.

6. During the course of the school year a variety of types of stories should be told to the class. (Some may be folk tales of long ago, some modern folk tales, and still others, stories about present-day adventures and other happenings.)

7. Each child, when of an age and maturity to retell stories, should be encouraged to learn to tell more than one type.

Choosing Topics and Titles for Original Stories

It may be that many boys and girls who could get great satisfaction out of telling or writing original stories do not do so because they do not know what to tell or write.

Aids in Choosing Topics and Titles. One of the most important points for the teacher to remember as he guides boys and girls in the selection of topics or titles for original stories is that the same topic, especially if it is a quite restricted one, is not likely to appeal to all children in a room even if it is one that seems just right for some in the class. Following are enumerated a few ways in which the pupils can be assisted in deciding upon topics or titles for original stories.

1. The teacher can tell or read to the pupils or suggest that the pupils read myths, fables, and other fanciful tales, and then the teacher can ask for suggestions for topics or titles of myths and other fanciful tales that the pupils can tell after the characteristics of such stories have been discussed.

2. The pupils can be encouraged to post on the bulletin board pictures that they think may suggest titles for stories to others in the room. (As caption on the bulletin board might be the question, "What Titles for Stories Do These Pictures Suggest?")

3. The teacher may discuss with the boys and girls the importance of having "catching titles" for their stories.

4. The pupils may check a list of possible titles for stories to indicate which sound particularly interesting. In the list might be titles such as these: (a) An Adventure, (b) Thanksgiving Day, (c) A Turkey's Thanksgiving, (d) Alone in the Dark Forest.

5. The pupils may make a composite list of interest-catching titles that they made up or that they have heard or read.

List of Topics and Titles. The list that is given here contains both topics and titles. No attempt has been made to separate the two, for sometimes what constitutes a topic for one person's story might be a title for that of another. For example, "My Pet" might be either topic or title, or the title on the topic "My Pet" might be "Peter, the Crow."

The topics or titles in the following list are not some on which necessarily each pupil in a room can develop or wants to develop an original story. It may even be that for some boys and girls not one of these is suitable. However, it is hoped that the list may suggest to the teacher others which he may in turn propose, directly or indirectly, to a pupil.

Peter Groundhog's Shadow
Doctor Dolittle Goes into Orbit.
"Do Not Cry Over Spilled Milk."
"Cast Your Bread Upon the Waters."
The Life History of a Frog
We Entertained a Pilgrim Girl at Thanksgiving.
Hungry on Christmas Eve
If Houses Could Talk
With Christopher Robin
Make Way for Puppies
The Discontented Princess
Thanksgiving in Animal Land
Brooms for Witches

Methods. Some of the methods that may be used in helping pupils tell stories are suggested under "Guidelines" on page 62. Others follow.

1. After the teacher has read or told a story to the class, the pupils discuss characteristics that make that story a good one.

2. The pupils analyze some of the stories they have read in terms of characteristics that make those stories good.

3. The class draws up a list of characteristics of a good story. In lower grades the pupils may name criteria such as these: (a) Is it interesting? (b) Does it have a surprise? In intermediate grades analysis might be more detailed, on points such as these: (a) Does it have a good beginning? (b) Does it have action? (c) Do interesting things happen? (d) Is it given in descriptive language? (e) Does it have a suitable ending?

4. The teacher gives a make-believe story or retells one of the complexity the pupils will be able to give, and then the class may name characteristics of his method of telling the story that showed skill as storyteller. The list may include points such as these, in addition to those already mentioned in the preceding paragraph: (a) good sentences, (b) pleasant voice, (c) telling events in order, (d) use of conversation, (e) correct pronunciation and clear enunciation, (f) freedom from interfering mannerisms, (g) correct use of words, (h) use of interesting and descriptive words, (i) telling the story without notes, (j) desirable length, (k) evidence of enthusiasm.

5. In the lower grades the pupils give their stories to small groups.

6. The teacher gives the beginning of an original story and then asks the pupils to plan a continuation of it.

7. The teacher (a) displays a series of pictures on a bulletin board to illustrate a story, (b) has the pupils discuss what they think is happening in the pictures, and (c) suggests that some may like to plan a story of their own about the pictures.

8. Although in the first grade storytelling may be confined primarily to telling original stories, pupils should not be discouraged from retelling stories if there is a point in doing so or if both the teller and the audience will enjoy the activity.

9. At times there will probably be need for practice lessons in which the chief objective is not enjoyment but improvement in the art of storytelling. At such times the pupils may discuss the points on which they need help. Each storyteller may announce to the audience what his chief problem is and ask the class to see whether he has shown growth and to give him suggestions for further improvement.

10. Children in one room invite others to hear stories. For example, Christmas stories can be practiced and then shortly before the holidays another class be invited to sing Christmas carols and to listen to stories as they gather around the Christmas tree.

11. The class has a period during the day or week set aside for storytelling. However, storytelling should not be confined to such times only. For example, the time when the boys and girls are studying about Indians in the social studies may be appropriate for telling an Indian "why" story.

12. The class listens to some records of stories well told or to stories told on the radio or television and evaluates them in terms of the criteria that they have set up for storytelling.

13. The pupils rewrite a brief story in which the events have been listed in scrambled order.

14. The pupils study stories to note interesting endings.

15. The pupils tell stories as tape recordings are made. These recordings can be used for programs and for purposes of evaluation.

16. Some or all of the pupils form a story club, the purpose of which is to hear stories and to develop skill in telling stories.

Storytelling by the Teacher

As is suggested in preceding pages of this chapter, the teacher can help boys and girls in storytelling by telling stories to them. Through his selection he can stimulate in his listeners an appreciation of "the good, the beautiful, the true." He can also aim to serve as a model for the boys and girls in storytelling. In fact, whether or not he

Figure 4.4. A Setting for Storytelling.

wishes to be a model, he is. Whether the teacher will be a good or poor one, however, lies in part within his power to determine.

By following the suggestions given in this chapter for storytelling by boys and girls, the teacher can set goals for himself. For further help he is referred to discussion of the art of storytelling in books listed in chapter 13, "Resources for the Language Arts."

Two points should, however, probably be emphasized here. Contrary to the suggestions of some writers, the teacher should probably not limit his repertoire of stories to just a very few that he has memorized or almost memorized. The joy and satisfaction that boys and girls get from listening even to stories that have imperfections in delivery is ample proof that even lesser efforts than those resulting in perfection on the part of the storyteller are often highly rewarding. In the writer's opinion, it is much better for the teacher to have a fairly large number of stories, of considerable variety, ready for telling, without memorizing them, than to limit himself unnecessarily by memorization or near-memorization of a few. In fact, an argument can be advanced against memorization not only because of the limitations it may put on the number the teacher can tell but also because of the artificiality that is often characteristic when stories are reproduced verbatim by someone other than an artist. It is, however, important that the teacher should know the story so well that he is not handicapped by trying to remember it when he should be concentrating on interpretation. In his preparation he will need to become so familiar with the story that he sees clearly in his mind's eye the characters whom he will interpret and the events that he will relate.

Another point to be considered at this time is the answer to the question, "When should stories be told and

Figure 4.5. Illustrations as Aids to Storytelling.

when read?" There is no one ready answer to this question, but a few pointers may be given. How many stories the teacher will tell and how many he will read will depend in part on the amount of time he feels justified in devoting to learning to tell stories. In general it can be recommended that those stories be read in which it is essential that that the exact words of the recorded story be used much of the time, unless, of course, the storyteller plans to memorize the story in entirety or in large part. Furthermore, picture books with text usually are better read than told. For many stories, however, the close personal relationship that can be achieved through telling, rather than reading, argues for the former method.

DEVELOPMENT IN ABILITY TO MAKE EXPLANATIONS AND GIVE DIRECTIONS

What adult among us has not at times been puzzled when others have given explanations or directions in such a manner that they were incomprehensible? And who among us has not at times himself given them so poorly that his listeners have been in a similar predicament!

Guidelines

Some basic points to observe in helping boys and girls develop in ability to make explanations and give directions are listed following.

1. *Boys and girls should be helped to see the need for giving clear explanations and directions.* The resulting understanding can give them purpose for attention to correct ways of proceeding when, in informal situations, the need arises for giving explanations and directions. Similarly it can give the children incentive for engaging

in learning situations in which special emphasis is placed on how to perform these activities.

2. *The work in each grade should be introduced in a bona fide situation.* In the modern elementary school there are many opportunities for giving explanations and directions. They should be utilized by introducing the work for a grade in a functional setting. For example, as a pupil explains how he made his model airplane, help can be given to him and the rest of the class in learning how to give clear-cut explanations. As a pupil explains to the class how to get to a place showing the undesirable effects of erosion, for example, the situation can be utilized for learning how to give directions well.

3. *The boys and girls should be given a part in developing standards.* Points such as these, with wording to suit the grade level, could be listed:

Include all essentials.
Omit all nonessentials.
Decide on good sequence.
Choose words well.
Suit the explanation to the audience.
Make use of illustrative material when helpful.

4. *Some boys and girls should be given more help in learning how to make explanations and give directions clearly than is afforded by the situations arising in the ongoing program of the school.* As in the case of the development of many other language arts skills, special practice lessons may need at times to be set up to provide the desirable amount of explanation and practice. However, there must be in the mind of the pupil a clear relationship between such lessons and the value of application of what is learned to life situations requiring the use of the skill.

Situations Requiring Explanations or Directions

Boys and girls may find themselves in situations in which needs for explanations or directions such as the following occur.

1. How bread is made; why the colonists objected to taxation by England; why the Indians fought the white men

2. How heat travels; what is meant by the water cycle; how we can tell time by the Big Dipper; why we have time belts; why we always see the same face of the moon

3. How to make things, such as candles, butter, puppets, puppet stages, costumes, paper-sculptured articles, dioramas, panoramas, Christmas decorations, May baskets, gifts

4. How to play a game, arrange a bulletin board, plant a vegetable

5. How to administer various types of first aid

6. How to take care of a pet

7. How to get from one place to another

Methods

Here are some suggestions as to how pupils can be aided in the acquisition of skills important for giving explanations and directions.

1. Make a chart or have some pupils make one listing the points that have been decided upon as standards.

2. Suggest to pupils in the primary grades the possibility of using a series of pictures as "notes" when giving directions for making something. For example, a pupil might explain how to make a mask out of a paper bag while showing illustrations of these steps:

Get a bag.   Cut.   Color.   Paste.

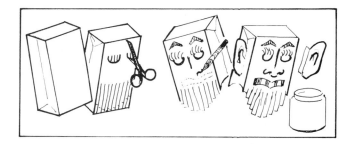

Figure 4.6. Illustrations as an Aid in Giving a Report.

3. Give the boys and girls copies of different explanations or directions written on various levels of understanding and ask them to decide for which grade level each is suitable.

4. Provide the pupils with copies of explanations or directions in which one or more points are included that are not important to the topic and have them indicate which points are superfluous.

5. Give the pupils copies of explanations or directions in which one or more points are out of the right order and ask them to arrange the sentences correctly.

6. Through skits, help the pupils show the difference in effectiveness if an explanation or directions are given at a proper tempo rather than too fast or too slowly.

7. Through skits, help the boys and girls show effective and ineffective ways in which visual aids can be used when giving explanations or directions.

8. Assist the class in listing types of visual aids that can be utilized in some instances to make clearer an explanation or a set of directions and have the pupils demonstrate how some of these (such as maps, diagrams, materials needed in construction) can be used effectively.

9. Discuss with the class *do's* and *don'ts* about responding to questions on explanations or directions asked by the audience when stressing points such as the following: (a) Be courteous. (b) If you do not know the answer, say so. If possible, suggest ways in which the questioner can find the answer or tell him that you will try to find it for him. (c) Answer to the point.

10. Through skits, help some pupils show how the question-and-answer period following the giving of an explanation or of directions can be conducted according to accepted standards and how it sometimes is conducted in violation of them.

11. Interest one or more pupils in making a poster to emphasize how to give explanations or directions.

12. Provide practice in giving directions and then check the effectiveness by having one or more persons in the audience follow them.

13. Have pupils give directions necessary to proceed from one place to another in the neighborhood or some other known territory.

14. Emphasize the importance of including in directions for going to another place the location of easily recognized buildings or other things in the environment that will help the person follow the directions.

15. Have pupils give orally a set of directions that indicates how to go from one place to another as outlined on a map of the city or of the neighborhood.

DEVELOPMENT IN ABILITY TO MAKE ANNOUNCEMENTS

Closely akin to the ability to make explanations is the ability to make announcements. This is important to the elementary school pupil. It is an ability amenable to teaching.

Guidelines

The guidelines for development of skill in making announcements are similar to those for development of skill in giving explanations and directions. A few are given here.

1. Boys and girls should be helped to see the need for learning to make announcements.

2. As a rule the help that boys and girls receive in making announcements should be provided at times when bona fide announcements are necessary.

3. Some boys and girls might be given more help in learning how to make announcements than is afforded by the situations arising in the ongoing program of the school.

Language Arts Skills and Abilities That Can Be Developed

Making announcements effectively can help the boys and girls in acquiring many different language arts abilities, the following among them:

1. Ability to arrange thoughts in logical order
2. Ability to speak concisely

3. Ability to appreciate the level of understanding and interest of the listeners

4. Skill in speaking in sentences

5. Skill in choosing exact words to give intended meaning.

Situations Involving the Need for Announcements

Below are listed some examples of situations that arise in the modern elementary school in which announcements might advisedly be made by boys and girls.

1. A boy or girl in the first grade might make an announcement to pupils in a different reading group than the one of which he is a member, as he tells them that they are invited to a "movie" that his group has made after reading a story in their reader.

2. A second-grade child might announce to boys and girls in another room that he has lost an article and describe it to the group.

3. A third-grade pupil might invite the boys and girls in another room to an assembly program that his grade will be giving.

4. A fourth-grade pupil who is the chairman of a committee might announce to the room the plans for making the school and the playground safer.

5. A fifth-grade pupil might make an announcement at a P.T.A. meeting inviting the parents to a program that his class will give as concluding activity after completing the study of a unit in the social studies.

6. A sixth-grade pupil might extend to the boys and girls in the preceding grade an invitation to a science fair that the sixth grade is putting on.

Methods

There are many ways in which the teacher can help the boys and girls learn to make announcements. It is hoped that those listed below will be suggestive to the teacher of others that he might utilize—some particularly applicable for use with the boys and girls in his charge.

1. Help draw up a list of standards for making announcements.

2. Read in their language arts books or on duplicated copies of materials that the teacher has written what some of the important points are that should be watched when making announcements.

3. Make posters emphasizing one or more points of importance when making announcements.

4. Discuss when it is of value to use visual aids while making announcements.

5. Draw up a list of criteria to observe when showing visual aids while making an announcement.

6. Criticize written reports of announcements, some of which include all essential points while others are lacking some.

7. Put on skits to illustrate desirable and undesirable ways of making announcements, for discussion by the class.

8. Summarize, verbally and pictorially, in a language arts notebook the essential points learned about making announcements.

9. Restate some announcements made to primary-grade children so that they would be suitable to make to intermediate-grade pupils and vice versa.

DEVELOPMENT IN ABILITY TO ASK RIDDLES AND TELL JOKES

It is worthwhile to guide boys and girls in development of ability to ask riddles and tell jokes for several reasons, these among them: (1) Riddles and jokes are frequently told by children and adults and at times so inadequately that special attention should be directed toward improvement. (2) Through attention to asking riddles and telling jokes a functional setting can be provided for practice on various language arts skills of value in other types of situations. For example, practice can be given in choice of words, in speaking with poise, and in use of good sentences.

Cautions

Some cautions to observe when helping boys and girls learn to give riddles and jokes are as follows.

1. Guard against having the pupils give riddles or jokes that are in any way "shady." (It may be necessary for the teacher to be informed beforehand about the joke a pupil plans to tell.)

2. Try to prevent the pupils from telling jokes that may hurt someone's feelings.

3. Help the pupils to avoid the common errors of telling so much when asking a riddle that the point is given away in the mere statement of the riddle or of telling so little that the riddle is incomplete.

Methods

Listed following are some suggestions for guiding boys and girls in development of ability in asking riddles and telling jokes. The pupils may:

1. Discuss criteria for desirable riddles and jokes.

2. Read riddles and jokes and evaluate them in terms of established criteria.

3. Tell riddles and jokes that they have heard or read, at times primarily for the enjoyment of the audience and at other times partly for evaluation by their peers of the method of telling the riddles or jokes.

4. Make up riddles and ask them of the class. (The

Who Am I riddle is one on the level of children even in the primary grades when it is on a topic such as (a) objects with which the pupils play, (b) means of transportation (c) animals. An example of a very simple *Who Am I* riddle is: I have long ears. I am a big animal. I have a trunk.)

5. Make a collection of riddles and jokes, including some original ones, and exhibit them on a bulletin board or in a booklet with a title such as "Smile a While."

6. Examine a list of jokes in some of which the point is brought out well and in others of which it is given poorly, to determine which jokes are well stated.

DEVELOPMENT OF SOCIAL COURTESIES

Increased attention is being given to helping boys and girls gain skill and poise in observation of social courtesies in activities such as telephoning, making and acknowledging introductions, interviewing, and greeting callers. Consequently emphasis is being placed on having pupils learn what social courtesy demands, on stimulating them to want to meet the demands, and on giving them help in acting in accordance with them.

Telephoning

Since even the preschool child at times uses the telephone, the first grade is not too early to begin providing guidance in its use. Furthermore, even by the time the pupil is in the sixth grade he still has need, in many instances, of help in the proper use of this means of communication.

What Should Be Learned. Some of the learnings to be acquired in the use of the telephone are listed below.

> How to hold the telephone
> What kind of voice to use when telephoning
> What to say when answering the telephone
> When to phone
> How to dial a number
> What to say first when calling a person by telephone
> What topics are appropriate and what inappropriate for telephone conversation
> The importance of courtesy
> What determines the suitable length of a telephone conversation
> Who should end a telephone conversation
> How to take a message for someone else
> How to make long distance calls
> How to call in case of emergency
> How to get the operator

Methods. Following are listed a few suggestions for procedure.

1. Explanation by the teacher. The teacher can ex-
plain to the pupils some of the important points to observe and give reason for observing them.

2. Reading on the topic. The pupils can read parts in a textbook or material on duplicated sheets that give suggestions on telephoning and show the importance of good telephone manners.

3. Discussion by the class. The boys and girls can discuss what they have learned about good manners in telephoning and help make a composite list of points to observe. The list can serve for purposes of appraisal. Items listed in the preceding section on "What Should Be Learned" can be changed to statements of rules.

4. Putting on skits. The pupils can participate in putting on skits or in observing them and in evaluating them. They can be used to introduce the work on telephoning in a grade by having two persons demonstrate first good and then poor telephone manners so that the class can later discuss rules governing telephone courtesy. Skits can be used in later stages of work on telephoning when the boys and girls apply in a "functional setting" what they have learned. Slips of paper can be handed to pairs of children with directions such as this one indicating what they should do for later evaluation by the group:

> Dramatize a telephone conversation in which someone responds correctly when a person asks to speak to an individual who is not at home. Then present another skit to show an incorrect way of answering the telephone when someone asks for a person who is not at home.

5. Making a poster illustrating rules for telephoning.

6. Making displays for a bulletin board. On a poster entitled "What's Wrong Here?" can be depicted a scene in which two children are talking over the telephone,

Figure 4.7. An Illustrated Checklist.

with evidence such as the following of violations of rules for courtesy as revealed either through the illustrations or through the remarks on the poster: (a) having the mouth too far from the mouthpiece, (b) calling at mealtime, (c) asking the other person to guess who is speaking.

7. Making an illustrated booklet on how to use the telephone.

8. Studying written records of telephone conversations to determine which rules for telephoning are followed and which violated.

9. Practicing various points about telephoning, such as distance of the mouth from the mouthpiece and suitable voice, with a toy telephone.

10. Giving a demonstration as to how to dial a number.

11. Making a telephone directory of names and telephone numbers that each child may want.

12. Checking a list of times when it is appropriate or inappropriate to call, such as: mealtime; after school; at six o'clock in the morning; at eleven o'clock at night; at half-past seven in the evening.

13. Checking a list of remarks to indicate which are appropriate and which inappropriate, such as: (a) Get your mouth closer to the telephone. (b) I can't hear a word you are trying to say. (c) Do you like Susy? (d) I hope you can come to my party. (e) My mother bought me a new dress. (f) Why doesn't your mother get you a new dress?

14. Using a "Teletrainer" for practicing correct means of handling a telephone. The "Teletrainer," a device loaned without charge to schools by many of the Bell Telephone offices, consists of a central control box and two telephones on fairly long cords.

Illustrative Teaching Situation. Below are listed suggestions for a possible plan for a class period emphasizing correct use of the telephone. Although the points are listed in a sequence that might be followed by a teacher in the upper-primary or lower-intermediate grades, the teacher may wish to change the order. Furthermore, he may wish to omit some and add others to adapt the suggestions for procedure to the needs of the class he is teaching.

Several pupils put on two skits, practiced before class, one as illustration of correct use of the telephone, the other of incorrect use of it.

The audience enumerates points of correctness in the one skit and of incorrectness in the other.

The pupils give additional suggestions, supplemented by some from the teacher, of the *do's* and *don't's* in the use of the telephone.

The class, with the teacher as "scribe" in writing on the chalkboard, draws up a list of *do's* and *don'ts.*

The pupils check telephone conversations, given to

them in written form, in terms of the criteria they have developed.

The pupils indicate which in a list of possible comments during a telephone conversation are desirable and which undesirable, and they give reasons for their decisions.

The pupils are paired and then plan a telephone conversation, some emphasizing strong and others poor points in the use of a telephone.

Some of the pupils will present their planned telephone conversation to the group and then lead in a discussion as to poor and good points in the dramatization.

Pupils individually, without reporting, decide on points they need to watch particularly when telephoning.

The class discusses the importance of being critical of one's self when phoning but not of others.

Introductions

Making and acknowledging introductions are activities that fall within the realm of the elementary school child. Besides learning how to acknowledge introductions, elementary school children may learn how to make introductions under circumstances such as the following: (1) introducing a speaker, (2) introducing a younger person to an older person of the same sex, (3) introducing a boy to a girl or to a woman, (4) introducing a man to a woman, (5) introducing a girl to a man, (6) introducing two persons of about the same age and the same sex, (7) introducing a new child or a visitor to the class.

Knowledges and Skills to Be Acquired. These are some points that children should learn and be able to put into practice when introducing a person to one or several individuals.

1. The name of the person being introduced should be given distinctly.

2. The persons being introduced should acknowledge each other by giving an appropriate greeting and by repeating the name of the other person.

3. Something should be told about each person that will make each interested in the other or that will facilitate conversation.

4. The introduction should be brief.

5. The persons introduced should engage in conversation with one another if there is opportunity to do so.

Methods. The following methods can be used to help boys and girls acquire needed learnings.

1. The teacher can serve as model as he makes and acknowledges introductions within the hearing of the children.

2. The boys and girls can read about how to make and acknowledge introductions through the use of textbooks or duplicated sheets.

3. With the guidance of the teacher, the class can discuss points essential in making and acknowledging introductions.

4. The pupils can make a check list of points for evaluating the making and the acknowledging of introductions.

5. The pupils can participate in or observe skits in which, for the pupils' evaluation, correct and incorrect procedures are used. Slips of paper can be distributed to groups of pupils with specifications for skits such as: (a) Introduce a classmate to your mother correctly and then tell the class what rules you observed. (b) Introduce a boy to a girl incorrectly and ask a classmate to explain what was wrong.

6. The pupils can check a list of written records of introductions and indicate which are done properly and which improperly. In the case of those not done correctly, they should state which rules were not observed.

7. The boys and girls can indicate which of a list of remarks for use in an introduction are undesirable, such as: (a) I heard your team was really defeated. (b) So you are from California. That is one state I do not care to see. (c) I hope you will enjoy our schoolroom. We do many interesting things.

8. The pupils can make a poster showing a correct way of introducing two persons, through picture and words.

9. The pupils can check *true* or *false* a list of statements about introductions such as these: (a) A girl should be introduced to a boy. (b) A man should be introduced to a woman. (c) It is all right to say something uncomplimentary about the town from which the person to whom you are being introduced comes if the statement you make is true.

10. The pupils can make an accordionlike folder illustrating a point of importance.

11. A tape recording can be made of an introduction for later evaluation.

Interviewing

Boys and girls in the modern elementary school encounter real situations that require interviewing. As they are working on a unit on the growth of their town, for example, they may find it important to obtain information from an old-time resident of the community. Or as they try to improve the lunchroom in their school, they may find interviews the means of obtaining valuable suggestions from school personnel and from their classmates.

What Should Be Learned About Interviewing. Here are some of the learnings that should be acquired and put into practice.

1. Before a person decides to ask someone for an interview, he should have clearly in mind a purpose for it.

2. The interviewer should plan carefully what he will ask the person to be interviewed.

3. The interviewer should inquire courteously of the person to be interviewed whether he is willing to be interviewed for the stated purpose.

4. The interviewer should try to conduct the interview at a time convenient for the person whom he is interviewing.

5. The interviewer should, in many instances, take notes during the interview.

Figure 4.8. An Accordionlike Folder Emphasizing Sequence in Making Introductions.

6. The interviewer should try to take as little time as possible for the interview while still obtaining needed information.

7. The interviewer should thank the person being interviewed at the close of the interview and often later, sometimes by letter.

Methods. The procedures that can be used to help boys and girls acquire skill in interviewing are, in general, similar to those described for telephoning. (See page 68.) Here are some pertinent ones.

1. Reading about how to interview
2. Listening to explanations by the teacher about interviewing
3. Discussing types of situations for which interviews are valuable
4. Making a check list for evaluating interviews
5. Checking records of desirable and undesirable interviews
6. Checking as true or false a series of sentences about interviewing
7. Participating in or observing role-playing and then evaluating the procedure followed in the skit
8. Making posters illustrating desirable and/or undesirable features of an interview
9. Interviewing classmates or others on a matter of importance
10. Discussing how to make use of data collected
11. Making a summary of data collected in a poll taken by the class
12. Reporting or having someone in the class report on an interview that he had with someone who gave him information of significance to the class
13. Writing a thank-you letter to a person interviewed or evaluating some letters written by others.

Greeting Callers

Following are a few suggestions for receiving callers, the need for which frequently occurs in the life of an elementary school child. Boys and girls should learn:

1. To greet a person who comes to the door politely
2. Not to let a person they do not know enter the home
3. To invite a person they know into the home if he has come to call on a person who is at home
4. To go to the person who has a caller in order to tell him of his caller if he is in another room, not to shout for him
5. To take careful note of the name of a person who called on someone not at home and later to report the name to the person for whom the call had been intended.

How to receive callers can be learned through these and other methods: reading, discussing, listing criteria, making or studying posters, presenting skits, indicating which statements about the proper way to receive callers are true and which false, having a host or hostess in the classroom to receive callers.

DEVELOPMENT OF EFFECTIVE LISTENING

Development of skill in listening has probably been more neglected than any of the other three main facets of the language arts—more than skill in speaking, reading, or writing.

Facts about Listening

Although there is a scarcity of conclusive research on methods of improving skill in listening, attention to facts such as the following, it is generally agreed, can bring about development in that skill.

1. *Physical factors affect listening.* Relative quiet seems to be one of the factors that is conducive to listening and to development in ability to listen. However, while it is desirable that when boys and girls are being helped to become better listeners there should be a fairly quiet environment, it would be undesirable to depend on almost total quiet for the development of skill in listening. Children, especially in this age of mass communication, need to develop in ability to listen even if complete silence does not characterize the background for a listening situation. However, at first when concentration is placed on improvement in listening, it is particularly important to provide a background free from many distracting sounds.

A fairly comfortable position for the listener also seems to be a valuable factor in improvement. A person who is in physical discomfort, for example, one who stands through a lecture, probably misses some of the points that he would get if he were seated fairly comfortably. For some levels of listening, however, where active rather than passive attention is demanded, it is possible for the listener to sit on a chair so comfortable that he fails to be as alert as he would if he were on one less conducive to lounging.

Temperature also seems to affect the ability to do prolonged listening on a high level of concentration. Either too cold or too warm temperature seems to have an adverse effect.

2. *Health affects listening.* While many persons in poor health undoubtedly are excellent listeners, it seems that, other things being equal, the person in good health has the better chance of effective listening, especially on the levels of listening requiring considerable concentration and the exercise of the higher thought processes. Some interfering factors in the physical health of children in attendance at school are colds, headaches, and fatigue.

3. *A stable emotional state of mind is conducive to listening.* Perhaps the relationship between the emotions and listening can be stated more accurately if it is given in negative terms in a statement such as this one: "An unstable emotional state of mind is detrimental to listening." Fear, anger, jealousy, resentment, insecurity, and other destructive emotional states can cause a person to be unable to comprehend well what he hears. Even extremes of joy and happy excitement seem to interfere with the best concentration. A state of emotional equilibrium or one approaching it in which a peaceful, contented state of mind prevails is likely to be accompanied by better powers of listening than one of imbalance.

4. *An atmosphere of goodwill in a classroom, in which the pupils feel they are liked by the teacher and by their own peers, is background in which skill in listening is more likely to develop than in one that lacks this feeling of warmth of personal relationships.* Unless a person feels kindly toward those who are speaking, he is not, under many circumstances, as likely to pay undivided attention as when he knows he is listening to a friend. Furthermore, in an atmosphere in which the child does not feel accepted, he is less likely to participate constructively in the give-and-take of speaking and listening.

5. *A classroom in which there are many opportunities for communication through oral and written means is a factor in the development of skill in listening.* It is not enough to emphasize the importance of opportunities chiefly for listening purposes. Instead the emphasis should be placed on all the facets of the language arts—reading, writing, speaking, and listening. Without emphasis on the various communication skills, the program in the language arts can easily become unbalanced. There is danger of spending so much time on listening that the school program is somewhat deplete of other activities, activities that by themselves are needed for the well-rounded development of the individual.

6. *There are various levels of listening to be recognized by the teacher.* These range in the elementary school from the fleeting, almost momentary attention that may be given to sounds to the type of listening characterized by concentration and critical analysis, as well as other kinds of personal reactions requiring higher thought processes. Intermediate levels, between which there is overlapping, when compared with the lower range of attention identified above, are characterized by growth in attention that:

Is of longer duration
Is more active than passive
Is less wavering
Recognizes the speaker's plan of organization
Produces associations in the mind of the listener.

Courtesy of the Boston Public Schools

Figure 4.9. Listening Levels May Differ.

7. *Recognition of desirable purposes for listening can be of help in growth of skill in listening.* One way in which the purposes of listening can be classified is: (a) listening to get information and (b) listening for enjoyment. In listening for either of these purposes the whole gamut of complexity of listening can be included. For example, to obtain information a person can pay but a passive attention to something he hears, maybe getting only a point here and there from a radio program while, much of the time, he busies himself with other thoughts; or he can follow carefully, with many personal reactions through association, the complex organization and difficult-to-comprehend statements of some speakers.

When listening for enjoyment he can merely tap his foot as he pays secondary attention to a jazz program on the radio while he is doing a social studies assignment or he can be "lost to the world" around him while he listens to a symphony orchestra. The pupil who recognizes a purpose for listening is more likely to profit from the experience than the one who does not. Boys and girls, therefore, should often be given reason for listening. It is not enough, as a rule, to tell the pupils to listen to a report on a given topic. They are likely to gain more in power to listen and in the acquisition of information if they are asked, for example, to listen to find out how the schools of the children of Japan differ from those of boys and girls in the United States or why irrigation is not carried on more extensively in a territory under consideration.

8. *Interest is a significant factor in listening.* Interest can be aroused through the selection of a topic of appeal to the boys and girls. It can be stimulated through questions that the teacher may point out would be answered in a report, especially if the questions asked seem worthwhile to the children. It can be aroused by giving the pupils a background for the topic to be presented. For example, after the teacher has told the boys and girls an interesting incident in the life of Benjamin Franklin, he may announce that a child will give a report telling about other occurrences in Franklin's life he thinks they will enjoy hearing.

9. *Participation in drawing up standards for listening is conducive to better listening, especially when these same standards are used for evaluative purposes.* Standards can be drawn up by the class after participating in activities such as reading selections on how to listen; listening to the teacher talk about important points to observe when listening; observing some people as they listen attentively; discussing the characteristics of a good listener; watching a skit in which attention and inattention are demonstrated. For a list of standards the reader is referred to page 81.

10. *Children vary greatly in ability to listen even within a grade.* Because of this fact the teacher should try to ascertain the listening levels under various types of situations and provide needed individual attention. Such differentiation is important not only in free conversation and in listening to speakers but also in listening for enjoyment. One pupil may, for example, need different help in learning to listen appreciatively to a musical selection than others require.

11. *Special help in listening under selected types of situations can be of value.* For example, since listening to a speaker involves some skills that listening to a person with whom one is conversing does not, improvement in these two types of listening situations may require different methods of procedure. Some of the types of situations under which listening may need to be improved are shown by the listing given on page 74.

Courtesy of the Cleveland Public Schools.

Figure 4.10. Recognizing a Purpose for Listening.

Listening to a record
Listening to television
Listening to the teacher
Listening to a person who is talking with one
Listening when in a small group
Listening to directions and explanations
Listening to a play or a story
Listening to a tape recording
Listening to a speaker
Listening to poetry
Listening to sounds around one
Listening to the conversation of others
Listening to announcements
Listening to choral speaking
Listening to panel discussions
Listening when being introduced.

12. *The length of time during which pupils can listen effectively varies.* No exact number of minutes can be cited for the attention span of listening of any type. Variation is caused by factors such as previous listening habits, interests in what is being heard, difficulty of comprehension of what is being heard, purpose for listening. While care should be taken that no attempt is made to try to force the child to extend his span of attention beyond that which he can attain without undue strain, efforts should be made steadily to increase it by exposing him to longer and longer periods of listening and by aiding him in holding his attention throughout that time.

13. *Taste in listening can be developed.* Boys and girls can be guided to higher levels of appreciation in music and in other types of listening. No effort, however, should be made to try to force a child whose highest level of appreciation is wildest of the Wild West music to appreciate, without intermediate steps, a Bach recording.

14. *Skill in listening is frequently affected by vocabulary, and vocabulary can be affected by listening.* In the vocabulary used by a speaker or by a storyteller there may be so many unfamiliar words that the listener's comprehension is affected adversely and that consequently he may lose interest in listening. On the other hand, if a limited number of words above the child's level of understanding is used, his vocabulary can be increased. This improvement in vocabulary is possible especially when meanings of "new words" are built into that which is being said. For instance, if the pupil does not know the word *burrow,* the use of the word in a comment such as the following may help him figure out the meaning and make it easier for him the next time he meets the word to understand it even if its use is not made clear through the context:

The mother rabbit had dug a hole for the new home in the **bushes near the palace.** The little rabbit had watched her **make the burrow.**

15. *Skill in listening is affected by experience, and listening extends experience.* The child lacking in experience background is not likely to be greatly interested in a large variety of listening experiences. The pupil who has been to Quebec will probably be more alert when hearing about that city than the one who has not been there. Happily, too, experience can be extended vicariously through listening.

Do's and Don'ts for the Teacher

1. Speak in a pleasant voice, one to which the pupils can enjoy listening.

2. Build upon the listening experiences that the child has had at home and/or in earlier years at school.

3. Remember that listening is more than hearing, and help the boys and girls to recognize the fact that attention to a speaker's words often requires thinking.

4. Encourage the listener not to be so absorbed in his own ideas about a point the speaker has mentioned during the course of his talk that he will not note subsequent points the speaker makes in the rest of his talk.

5. Be a good listener yourself. When a pupil or other person is speaking, show by your behavior that you are listening to the speaker. Some teachers spend much of the time that they should spend in listening by watching members of the audience. This is bad practice because boys and girls may develop the habit of not listening as they note the teacher's inattentive manner.

6. Guard against giving instructions such as "Let's all pay attention." Rather, indicate for what the pupils should be listening.

7. Avoid the practice, in which some teachers engage, of repeating directions or explanations unnecessarily. Otherwise the pupils may develop poor habits of listening, as they realize the teacher will most likely make his explanation more than once. Or the pupil may be bored by that which the teacher repeats. However, the teacher should be careful that he makes his points clear. At times, for example, after the teacher has given a direction of more than one step, a pupil may be asked to make application of it for demonstration purposes, to insure that the point is made clear to those who are listening.

8. Discourage interruptions of the speaker, even if he makes an error in speech or in facts presented or in deductions from facts he presents.

9. Don't encourage fake attention. The teacher might lead a discussion on the fact that merely looking intently at the speaker does not guarantee good listening. He can help the pupils to understand that a person looking intently at the speaker may sometimes feel justified in letting his mind wander rather than concentrating on what the speaker is saying.

Methods

Since there are many different types of listening situations as well as varying purposes and levels, it is important that teaching procedures should be varied. To improve in power to listen, boys and girls can:

1. Listen to sounds of farm animals or to sounds around them of which recordings have been made on records available commercially.

2. Play games in which they identify sounds they hear when they are blindfolded such as beating a drum, playing notes on the piano, tapping a pencil on a table.

3. Make a list of happy sounds such as a mother singing a lullaby or children laughing, and of weird sounds such as the hooting of an owl or the blowing of a fog horn on a dark windy night.

4. Give rhyming words.

5. Say the rhyming words in couplets or short selections from poems that the teacher reads or tell which of a series of three or more words written on the chalkboard finish the rhyme scheme of an incomplete rhyme that the teacher reads such as:

I hear in the chamber above me
　The patter of little feet,
The sound of a door that is opened,
　And voices soft and (clear, sweet, dear). [1]

6. Listen to someone read a poem or play a recording of one in order to comprehend the story, to "see" the pictures that it brings to mind, to tell how they like it, to note how it is being read without undesirable singsong, to decide whether it is suitable for inclusion in a program, to answer a question that has been asked by the teacher.

7. Listen to a story to see if they will like it, to decide whether it is suitable for reading for a program or for dramatization, to compare it with another version of the same story.

8. Draw up criteria for telling stories and then listen to recordings of stories or to stories told over television or radio to note how the criteria are met.

9. Listen to the recording of an individual's reading of a poem or story or of a talk by him in order to apply criteria worked out by the class, with the view to possible improvement.

10. Discuss when it is important to give entire attention to something being heard and when it is enough to give only secondary or no attention to it. (For example, when one group is reading with the teacher in one part of the room, the boys and girls working elsewhere should learn not to pay attention, as a rule, to the teacher unless he addresses a remark to them.)

11. Compile a list of action words that describe sounds, such as *tapping, thumping, rattling, barking, shouting, squeaking,* and then identify each sound.

12. Discuss which radio and television programs are suitable for children and then give exact information about when these can be heard or viewed.

13. Draw up a list of points made in a talk which are controversial or which state opinions, and make a similar list of statements contained in a record of a talk.

14. Discuss the importance of looking at a speaker while he is talking and observing other niceties such as not playing with something, not talking, not interrupting unnecessarily.

15. Discuss the responsibility of the speaker to make his remarks worthy of being heard.

16. Listen to a talk of which the pupils have been given an outline so that they learn to follow the plan of organization of a speaker and then listen to other talks to decide upon the outline followed.

17. View a sound "movie" after the teacher has prepared the pupils for it through activities such as: (a) presenting background data; (b) giving them an outline of the main parts of the "movie"; (c) listing on the chalkboard questions that will be answered in the "movie" and asking them to read them before they see the "movie."

18. Give a summary of something the pupils have heard such as a story or a television program.

19. Participate in putting on a skit or observe it as different types of listening (secondary, fairly attentive, and very attentive) are demonstrated and then discuss the points brought out in the skit in regard to learning to become better listeners.

20. Listen to directions for games and then play them.

21. Make a poster showing through words and picture some *do's* and *don'ts* about listening.

22. Arrange in order of occurrence the events of a story that has been told by unscrambling a list of sentences in which those events are given in mixed-up order.

23. Take a listening test, one that checks the listener's ability to answer questions based on what was said.

24. Make an ending to a story, the first part of which has been read or told to the class.

25. Evaluate a point of view expressed by a speaker, in terms of previous learnings.

26. Have practice in selecting the main idea of a talk they hear or of a selection read to them and in naming details that support that main idea.

27. Look for clues, such as *first, second, third* or *furthermore, however, nevertheless, but,* that help in following the outline of the speaker of a selection that is being read.

28. Make an outline of a talk. Before the teacher asks the pupils to make an outline, he must be certain that the speaker follows an outline, for many do not.

1. Henry Wadsworth Longfellow, "The Children's Hour."

29. Evaluate recordings or television programs. The teacher's purpose in such listening may at times be to help the boys and girls improve their tastes in listening. At other times he may ask the boys and girls to take note of qualities of speech, such as pitch, tone, and rapidity of speech.

30. Listen to answers to questions asked of the speaker. Observance of this point will prevent a child from engaging in the habit that many people have, of not refraining from talking while their questions are being answered.

31. Mark *True* or *False* a list of statements about listening such as: (a) It is important to listen carefully to everything. (b) If a speaker makes a statement during his talk to a small group; anyone who disagrees with him has a right to interrupt him immediately even if the speaker has not asked for interruptions. (c) Even if a talk is uninteresting, the audience should be polite to the speaker.

32. Make a check list individually of points each pupil thinks he needs to observe in particular as he tries to become a better listener.

OPPORTUNITIES FOR GROWTH THROUGH SPECIAL ACTIVITIES

The modern elementary school provides many rich opportunities for development of oral communication in meaningful settings. To many of these reference has been made in preceding pages of this chapter. Two are discussed here, namely (1) planning and participating in programs and (2) being a member or leader of a club. Chapter 11, "Creativity through Dramatic Expression and Choral Speaking," discusses two more areas of oral communication, as indicated by the title of the chapter.

Planning and Participating in Programs

Programs can be planned for presentation to pupils in other groups in the same classroom, to pupils in other rooms, to parents, or to the general public. They can deal with a large variety of subjects as indicated by the following types: Christmas programs, Thanksgiving programs, Mother's Day programs, Lincoln's and Washington's birthday programs, and programs consisting of the culmination of a unit the children have been studying, such as on safety, China, or conserving energy.

Programs suitable for the elementary school can also be classified as to method of presentation. A program may consist of any one of the following types or of a combination of them: a dramatization, a puppet show, a pageant, folk dances, a pupil-made "movie," a make-believe radio or television performance, a panel discussion, an exhibit with explanations.

Guidelines. A few helpful guidelines follow.

1. *The program should be of educational value to the participants.* While there is nothing wrong in having as one of the purposes in putting on an occasional program that of maintaining or developing school-home cooperation, the children should not be used merely as agents for public relations. Benefits should accrue for the participants in the form of acquisition of learnings or practice in skills or abilities and attitudes connected with appearing in front of an audience, such as proper use of voice, poise, consideration for others.

2. *The audience should be able to accomplish a worthwhile objective through attending the program.* It is of particular importance that the time be well spent when the audience consists of boys and girls excused from other school activities. To be sure, to have fun when watching a program can be a desirable objective. However, usually the objective should be more than entertainment. Part of the program can be in terms of observing how a program can be put on effectively. To accomplish this goal attention can be directed to the speech, manner, and preparation of the participants. As a rule, the subject matter of the program should be such that the pupils in the audience can acquire useful learnings.

When inviting pupils to a program care should be taken that the subject matter or method of presentation is neither below nor beyond the level of the audience. The range in grades for which most programs are suitable is not as inclusive as from grade one through grade six. Usually a program of real value to a first-grade audience is too juvenile for sixth-grade boys and girls.

Even parents or the general public should not be invited to a program unless through it they can learn something. The objective should not be to see one's child "show off" in public. Frequently in the case of an audience made up of adults, the main educational accomplishment might well be finding out more about what the boys and girls are learning.

3. *Throughout the time of preparation for a program, methods should be used that will make the work of educational value.* The goal should not be merely a good performance. For example, the boys and girls should be given an opportunity to help plan a program partly because such thinking through of what is to be included and of what the procedure should be will, if the planning is well done, help the pupils plan better in the future.

4. *There should be wide participation by pupils in programs.* It is not to be expected in short programs which one group gives for another in the same room, or even always in short ones given for another grade, that at all times all pupils will take part. Over a period of time

when several programs are given by a group or grade, however, each pupil should have the chance to participate. When programs are presented to parents or to the general public or when they are given to another grade as culmination of a unit of work, every child should have a part. Unless there are children of such exceedingly low mentality as are seldom found in other than special rooms in the public elementary schools or children with physical defects that would prohibit their taking a regular part in the program, each child should be given a responsibility that is of educational value to him and one that is recognized by his peers and the audience as having such merit. To let a pupil do nothing repeatedly in programs other than work such as passing out the songbooks, straightening the chairs, or distributing the programs is likely not to help him as much as he could be benefited through such programs. Furthermore, if parents are invited to the program, it is likely to be embarrassing to his family and him if his part is always limited to that type of participation.

5. *There should be a high standard of performance.* How high it should be will vary with the situation. A program for another group in the room probably will not need to be as finished as one to which the public is invited. The purpose for the program will determine in part the quality of the end-product desired. There is no situation, however, when a slipshod performance is excusable.

6. *Care should be taken not to invite another class very often.* Each group has certain educational objectives and each teacher should try to make optimum use of the time of his pupils toward the achievement of these goals. Frequent attendance at programs put on by other classes may well interfere with making the best use of the time of the children in accomplishing the aims set for their own class.

7. *There should be evaluation of the program.* Self-evaluation by the participants is very important. At times, however, help in appraisal can be obtained from the pupils in the audience. For example, if intermediate-grade pupils served as audience, they might be asked to mark a check list similar to the following:

Evaluating Our Program

We tried to observe these points in our program:

____1. Talking so all could hear us

____2. Having an interesting program

____3. Helping our audience learn something

____4. Being well prepared.

Put a check to the left of each point that you think we accomplished.

Suggestions for Programs. Below are a few suggestions for programs boys and girls can put on either as assembly programs or as programs given in their own homeroom.

1. Boys and girls could put on a make-believe radio or television program. A pupil-constructed microphone or illustration of the front side of a radio can be used to add to the presentation as the pupils in the audience "pretend" they are listening to a commercial program.

2. The pupils could put on a program on "Christmas in Other Lands." Talks, songs, and dramatization—through puppetry, pantomime, or plays—could be used to present the message.

3. As culminating activity for a unit in the social studies a program similar to this one could be planned in connection with a unit on "What We Owe to Ancient Greece and Rome":

An explanation of work on the unit

A demonstration of phases of Olympic games

A debate between an Athenian and a Spartan about their way of living

A skit showing a day in the life of a patrician family

Interpretive dancing

An explanation of exhibits displayed in the room where the program is being given.

4. Following the study of "Our European Background" intermediate-grade boys and girls could include in a program some of the following:

An introductory talk

The life of Verdi (report)

Playing "The Nutcracker Suite" (part of it)

"The Child Handel" (report on picture)

Galileo and the Telescope (report)

Slides of European buildings

Costumes of Europe (report)

European customs (report)

Telling stories

Motion picture on Sweden

Explanation of our exhibit.

Being a Member or Leader of a Club

In the primary- and lower-intermediate grades, it is preferable not to try to organize formal clubs in which many rules of parliamentary procedure are followed. Informal club meetings will suffice there; in fact, they may be the only type to be held even by some boys and girls in the upper-intermediate grades. At these informal meetings boys and girls might present programs or discuss matters of significance to the class. Either the teacher or a pupil can serve as chairman. Such meetings can be held either regularly—possibly weekly, every two weeks, or monthly—or irregularly.

The older boys and girls—probably those in the upper-intermediate grades—can profit by organizing a club in which somewhat formal procedures are followed. Consequently some suggestions on parliamentary procedure are included in the discussion.

Objectives. The objectives that can be attained through organization of a club vary from situation to situation. These are among those that might be achieved:

1. A club serves as an integrating point of reference for many school activities, such as giving book reports, plays, readings.

2. Through club membership a unity among the boys and girls is developed.

3. Membership in a club adds to the interest boys and girls will have in school.

4. The boys and girls become acquainted with some points in parliamentary procedure.

5. The class gains understanding of some phases of voting procedures as officers are elected and issues are determined by vote.

Kinds of Clubs. Two kinds of clubs can be found in the elementary school—room clubs and special-interest clubs. All members of a classroom are automatically members of a room club. Typically and advisedly it meets during schooltime. The concern of the group may be a variety of topics. At times the club may deal with special problems of the class, such as "How to Make Our Lunchroom More Attractive" or "How We Can Make Visitors to Our Room Know They Are Welcome." But concentration need not be only in such areas. At times the programs might consist of book reviews, plays, choral readings, or similar types of activities. In some instances, however, the room club may, throughout the year, have one particular theme. It might, for example, be a book club or a "Better Citizenship Club."

Clubs that can be designated as "special-interest clubs" are those whose membership includes only those pupils who select the club as one to which they wish to belong. In such cases, we may find several special-interest clubs within one classroom. For example, there may be a book club, a science club, a crafts club, a writing club. It is recommended that it be made possible for each child to join one of the groups. When that is the case, the meetings can be held during schooltime, with the various club meetings held concurrently. The teacher may find it important to meet with the various chairpersons of the groups before each meeting in order to assure desirable programs and procedures. Furthermore, during the club meetings the teacher should be present at times with one group, at times with another, to give guidance and counsel. Occasionaly all groups might meet together, possibly in order to receive instruction in parliamentary procedure or to discuss other methods of improving the organization and procedures of all of the clubs. At other times the purpose for a joint meeting might be to provide opportunity for one or more of the clubs to present a program to the group.

Parliamentary Procedure. As indicated earlier, clubs in the intermediate grades present an opportunity for boys and girls to learn and practice the rudiments of parliamentary procedure. During the organizational meeting, the teacher may find it advisable to serve as temporary chairperson. At such a meeting some or all of these points might be included in the protocol:

Discussion of the purpose of the club to be organized

Enumeration of officers needed or desired

Listing of major responsibilities of each of the officers

Discussion of qualifications desired in the case of each officer

Determination of method of selection of officers

Election of officers.

Other points that may be stressed either at the first meeting or other meetings of the club are:

General procedure to be followed during meetings
Order of business
Place and time of meeting
How to make a motion
How to vote on a motion
Taking minutes of a meeting
How to adjourn a meeting
How to appoint or elect committees
Responsibilities of committees
How to give committee reports and what to do about them.

Other Suggestions. The following listing includes a few suggestions for guidance of clubs in the elementary school.

1. Every child should be given an opportunity to belong to a club. If the club has a room club, every one, is mentioned earlier, should be included in the membership.

2. Although the meeting time for clubs should ordinarily be during schooltime, when not all members of a class are attending a special-interest club meeting, it may be necessary for such clubs to meet during out-of-school hours.

3. As a rule no fees should be charged by the club, either as membership dues or as levies for special activities.

4. Officers should be changed frequently enough so that many boys and girls have an opportunity to profit from assuming the responsibilities incumbent upon an officer, but not so often that they do not have a chance to

learn to perform satisfactorily the duties involved in an office. Rather than having officers elected for the full school year, it might be wise to consider the possibility of having a change every three months or so.

5. All boys and girls should have responsibilities within a club organization. In fact, at times each child should be given a leadership role. This does not mean that each pupil should at some time or other be an officer. Leadership as committee chairperson, as an individual designated to head a certain endeavor, as the person to make an evaluation of an activity—these are among leadership responsibilities that can be distributed among the members of a club.

5. Boys and girls should be helped to realize the importance not only of leadership roles but also of being constructive "followers."

6. Club activities should be enjoyable to the group. A club should be considered by the boys and girls as a "special" of the school program.

EVALUATION OF ORAL COMMUNICATION

Some of the suggestions given for development of skill in oral communication that have been stated earlier in this chapter can also be utilized as means for evaluating it. Means for evaluating oral communication that are indicated below should be applied in terms of some of the ideas given under "Evaluation and Diagnosis" on pages 42 to 44 of chapter 3, "Common Problems in Teaching the Language Arts."

Charts may be made to emphasize points that should be observed during all types of oral communication. The possible content of one for primary and of one for intermediate grades is listed below.

When We Talk We

1. Speak plainly.
2. Look at our listeners.
3. Express ourselves clearly.
4. Say something worthwhile or interesting.

Points to Watch When We Talk

1. Enunciation
2. Pronunciation
3. Voice
4. Manner
5. Sentence structure
6. English
7. Looking at the listeners

As a variation from the charts suggested here, a chart illustrated with one or more pictures can be made. Additional standards can be recorded on charts for each type of oral-communication skill such as skill in discussing, taking part in conversation, telling stories.

Taking Part in Conversation and Discussion

The following suggestions indicate some ways in which participation in conversation and discussion can be evaluated.

1. With the help of the teacher, boys and girls can draw up a check list for appraisal of the selection of topics for conversation. Points in such a list, depending somewhat upon the age and ability of the boys and girls, may include these among others: (a) The topic should be of interest to most or all of the listeners. (b) The topic should not be one that will be embarrassing to anyone in the group. (c) The topic should not be one that will be likely to induce gossip. (d) The topic should be one that is not likely to encourage unkind comments about other people.

2. A check on the suitability of a pupil's voice can be made through use of a tape recorder. The pupil can then engage in self-evaluation of his voice. In the appraisal questions such as these may be asked: (a) Can I be heard distinctly without running words together? (b) Do I talk fast enough? (c) Is my voice pleasant? (d) Do I show variety in my voice? (e) Does my voice express my attitude toward the topic about which I am talking?

3. Pupils can check hypothetical items of conversation in terms of appropriateness for mealtime conversation by indicating which of a list such as the following constitute desirable and undesirable conversation.

____ I wish you would make potato salad the way Aunt Mary makes it. I don't like the way you fix it, Mother.

____ I learned some interesting facts about planets today.

____ I saw a horrible accident on my way home from school today.

____ Good, Mother! I am so glad we have chocolate pudding tonight!

Giving Talks

Application of some of the suggestions given in preceding paragraphs can be made to giving talks and reports. Additional suggestions given below can serve as checklists and other means of appraisal as they apply to talks or reports the boys and girls give.

This procedure may be followed in working out a check list, possibly at the beginning of the school year, shortly before the boys and girls give their first talks: (a) The teacher tries to interest the boys and girls in the topic or topics about which they will talk. (b) The pupils are helped to realize the need of speaking as well as they can. (c) The pupils name the points that they think they should watch when giving their talks while the teacher lists them, with modifications if necessary, on the chalkboard. (d) The group gives suggestions for observing each of the criteria on the list.

While by no means exhaustive, the following check list can serve as a desirable instrument for the teacher as he helps the boys and girls set standards for the class. It is recommended that not nearly all the items be included in any one list. The wording given here need not necessarily be used.

1. Is my topic interesting to my listeners?
2. Do I know enough about my topic to make my talk worthwhile for my listeners?
3. Do I have a strong beginning?
4. Do I have a strong ending?
5. Do I keep to the topic?
6. Do I tell points in sequence?
7. Do I stand straight?
8. Do I look at my audience?
9. Am I free of mannerisms that may interfere with my talk?
10. Is my voice pleasant?
11. Can I be heard easily without strain or effort on the part of my listeners?
12. Do I pronounce words correctly?
13. Do I enunciate well?
14. Do I show refinement in what I include in my talk?
15. Do I show refinement in my expressions?
16. Do I use one or more special means of getting and keeping the interest of my listeners (such as giving a demonstration or showing a picture)?
17. Do I give my report without reading it?
18. Do I give my report without using notes?

Though the points for observation drawn up for reports in general also apply to oral book reports, additional specifications may be made for book reports. Points such as these may be listed for evaluation of a book report: (1) title of the book, (2) name of the author, (3) a brief summary of the book, (4) interesting incidents or important information, (5) how I like the book, (6) where the book can be found. (See also page 105.)

An individual record might be kept on a three-inch by five-inch card on which are listed the same points for each pupil that are given in a chart publicly displayed. Whenever a pupil gives a talk the teacher, with or without a conference with the child, can put on this card a check in the appropriate column to indicate which points the speaker observed. The date can be recorded at the top of the column.

Telling Stories

Check lists for storytelling may be drawn up by the class. Such a listing can be made after listening to a good storyteller, after reading points about storytelling discussed in a language arts book, or after thinking of what points one would like to have a storyteller observe.

Observing Social Courtesies

Testing techniques similar to the one suggested following for use of the telephone can be worked out for other situations involving courtesies, such as making introductions, acknowledging introductions, being interviewed, receiving callers. In a list such as the one given, the pupils can be asked to check those remarks which show courtesy in the use of the telephone.

____ Hello, there! Who's speaking?
____ I know it's past your bedtime, but I wanted to ask you a question before I go to bed.
____ No, Mother is not in. Is there a message for her?

Making Announcements

Some of the standards for taking part in communication of various types, listed earlier, also apply to making announcements. There are some, however, that apply especially to making announcements. Some of particular importance when making announcements are listed here in question form.

1. Have I included all needed information?
2. Did I omit all information that is not needed?
3. Did I tell points in the right order?
4. Did I make my announcement to suit the age level of my audience?
5. Did I talk slowly enough so that everybody could grasp what I was saying?
6. Did I use a visual aid if one would have been helpful?
7. Was I courteous?

Some standards that apply particularly to announcements in the form of invitations are also important for the boys and girls to observe. The following are pertinent when giving announcements to invite a group: (1) The invitation should tell clearly to what the group is invited. (2) The invitation should be definite so that there will be no question in the minds of the audience as to whether or not they are invited. (3) The invitation should tell when and where the event will take place. (4) The invitation should make reference to the fact that the announcer or those for whom he is extending it hope that the members of the audience will be able to accept it.

Listening

If standards are drawn up for the evaluation of listening, they should vary with age level. If the points in the evaluation are specific items, they may also vary according to purpose in listening. These are points that may be included in some form in standards set for active listening to a speaker in order to gain information.

1. Looking at the speaker
2. Not playing with anything while someone is speaking
3. Not talking, reading, or doing anything else, as a rule, (other than possibly taking notes) while someone is speaking
4. Noting the speaker's plan of organization
5. Listening with the intent to learn
6. Evaluating what is said, including thinking of points to accept or reject
7. Trying to remember important points made
8. Waiting to make additions or corrections or ask questions until the speaker has finished unless he has specifically indicated that interruptions are all right.

Figure 4.11. A Check on Listening.

In any evaluation of listening it is important to remember that it defies exact measurement. No instrument has been devised by which the profound changes that can often result from listening can be appraised accurately. Despite this difficulty, appraisal that is of value can be made. Through noting the expression on the faces of individuals while they are hearing something, the teacher can get a clue as to how long comprehension continues. The response or lack of it after listening is another index of what has been going on in the mind of the listener. Immediate or delayed questions testing recall can also throw light on the subject. How well children listen to directions or explanations can frequently be ascertained by their ability to follow directions or apply the explanations.

The teacher should not confine his attempts to evaluate to times when the boys and girls are listening to a person speaking to a group. As he talks with a pupil individually and as he observes him in his free conversation with others, during schooltime, before school, or during intermissions, the teacher can obtain information concerning skill in listening. The child who interrupts, who is disinterested unless he himself is speaking or unless the conversation is about him, who unnecessarily leaves the group when someone else is talking, or whose remarks show that he has not been listening—all these actions give the teacher a clue as to how well he is succeeding in helping his pupils become better listeners.

FOR STUDY AND DISCUSSION

1. Name ways in which a teacher of any grade (designating the grade level) can help create a classroom atmosphere that serves as useful background for the development of skills of oral communication.

2. Examine some language arts books for use in the elementary school in order to ascertain to what extent and how some of the claims made by linguists discussed in chapter 3 (see page 36) are applied in the suggestions for teaching of oral communication? What is your evaluation of the suggestions?

3. What precautions can a teacher take, after the class has studied matters of social courtesy in telephoning, in conversation at mealtime, and in making or acknowledging introductions, so that pupils whose parents do not observe the dictates of social custom will not look down upon their parents?

4. Design a bulletin board to be used in connection with work on development in ability (a) to participate in conversation, (b) to give interesting talks, or (c) to give clear directions or explanations. Designate the grade level for which the bulletin board is intended.

5. In chapter 3 suggestions are given for teaching by the discovery method (see page 34). Write a teaching plan for any grade level (but designate the grade level for which you are planning it) showing how the discovery method can be used in teaching an important point in oral communication.

6. Study parts on oral communication given in one or more of the books listed in the *References* section of this chapter to discover additional ideas on the teaching of oral communication. Your teacher may wish to have you report some of your findings to the class and to discuss them.

7. Write the words for a skit of the type that pupils can present (designating the grade level for which it is intended) highlighting a language arts learning. It may be on a topic such as (a) telephoning, (b) engaging in conversation, or (c) greeting callers.

8. Plan somewhat in detail an assembly program that can be presented by any one grade (designating the grade level). Your description should be of a program that is of decided value from the language arts point of view.

9. It may be of value to you to note any jokes that you may hear speakers use and to decide which of them were relevant and which irrelevant to the topic on which the speech was given. Also note the effect upon the audience.

10. Prepare a story suitable for telling to an age level of children with whom you are particularly interested in working. If possible, tell the story to your classmates and ask for their suggestions.

REFERENCES

Boyd, Gertrude. *Teaching Communication Skills in the Elementary School.* New York: Van Nostrand Reinhold Company, 1970.

Burns, Paul C.; Broman, Betty L., and Wantling, Alberta L. Lowe. *The Language Arts in Childhood Education,* 2d ed. Chicago: Rand McNally & Company, 1971.

Burns, Paul C., and Schell, Leo M., eds. *Elementary School Language Arts: Selected Readings.* Chicago: Rand McNally & Company, 1969.

Eisenson, Jon, and Ogilvie, Mardell. *Speech Correction in the Schools.* New York: The Macmillan Company, 1963.

Lamb, Pose, ed. *Guiding Children's Language Learnings.* Dubuque, Iowa: Wm. C. Brown Company Publishers, 1967.

Possien, Wilma M. *They All Need to Talk.* New York: Appleton-Century-Crofts, 1969.

Ruddell, Robert B. *Reading-Language Instruction: Innovative Practices.* Englewood Cliffs, N.J.; Prentice-Hall, Inc., 1974.

Strickland, Ruth. *The Language Arts in the Elementary School.* Lexington, Mass.: D.C. Heath and Company, 1969.

5

Guiding Growth in Written Expression

Before entering elementary school, the child has made much progress in ability to communicate orally. In contrast, in many cases he has done no writing other than possibly his name. It does not follow, however, that he has not had significant preparation for development in this means of communication even though crude drawings and unintelligible scribblings may be the extent of objective evidence.

In preparation for more or less formal experiences in writing, the children assembling in September in a first-grade room show many differences. Some have backgrounds of rich experiences so full of interest that it will not be difficult to guide them in wanting to share them with others, both orally and later more permanently in writing; others come with very limited backgrounds. Some come from homes where parents have taken time to let the children dictate to them brief messages, maybe a sentence or two to include in a letter to a grandmother or grandfather; others come from an environment devoid of such experiences. Some have been drawing pictures as

gifts for their parents, with or without dictation of what the pictures mean; others have not been given the satisfaction of realizing that the pictures they produce or even the scribbling that they do, with proper interpretation by an older person, form a way of expressing their thoughts and a means of giving pleasure to others. Some have received letters which were read to them by grownups; others have had no correspondence addressed to them. Some have observed the satisfaction that older persons in the family receive from expressing their thoughts in writing; others have witnessed writing by others only as drudgery. Some have come to school with anticipation because older brothers and sisters have told them that they will learn to write; others have been discouraged by their peers concerning all school activities, including writing. Some have attended excellent kindergartens where writing readiness has been developed, often seemingly incidentally; others have not.

With such variations in preparation, highlighted by differences in native ability, the children come to school ready or not ready to begin work in written expression. As the teacher in the first grade and those in subsequent grades ask themselves the question, "How can I best assist this child in acquiring or developing ability in the various types of writing that will help him express himself?" they should have in mind points such as the following:

1. The child has need to express himself adequately in writing in order to meet various requirements of the typical school.

2. Writing is important to the individual for utilitarian purposes in his adult life.

3. Writing is a means of self-expression that may be of therapeutic value to an individual, both as a child and as an adult.

4. Although the limits as to how far a person can progress in writing are set by his capacity as determined by his heredity, there is wide latitude in achievement for most individuals. In fact, most persons do not nearly approach their maximum possibilities that under proper guidance they could achieve in this and other areas.

5. Each child should find satisfaction in writing effectively so that he will develop the desire to continue to write and to improve in writing throughout his school years and later.

THE SCOPE OF THE PROGRAM

The two facets of the language arts that constitute written communication are reading and writing. This chapter deals with reading only insofar as the relationship between the two needs to be made clear when considering methods of teaching written expression. The development of some skills common to both oral and written communication, such as correct usage, are studied in chapter 6. Chapter 7 is devoted to the teaching of handwriting and chapter 8 to spelling. In this chapter are given suggestions for helping children do the following: (1) write paragraphs; (2) write letters and reports; (3) do other types of practical writing (such as writing lists, filling in blanks, keeping records); (4) develop skill in using capital letters and punctuation marks; (5) do creative writing; and (6) grow in writing through participating in special activities. The chapter ends with a discussion of "Evaluation of Written Communication."

General Objectives

The teacher should help the boys and girls to do the following:

1. Develop greater efficiency in all types of written expression that are on the level of the elementary school child

2. Attain proficiency in use of capital letters and punctuation marks

3. Become effective in taking part in activities such as helping write a class or school paper or magazine or writing an original "book," either as a group or individual project

4. Maintain or develop interest in writing and in writing well

5. Develop those skills in written expression that are needed for effective participation in other areas of the curriculum

6. Become increasingly considerate of the persons to or for whom they are writing.

It is not sufficient that the teacher alone should have in mind sound objectives for the teaching of written expression. If the program is to be successful, it is essential that the boys and girls themselves also recognize the worthwhileness of attaining proficiency in this facet of communication. Furthermore, the objectives for the accomplishment of which the typical elementary school pupil is likely to subscribe wholeheartedly are, in part, immediate gains, such as the joy of seeing his paper displayed under a caption of "Neat Papers" or the satisfaction of receiving a letter in response to one he had written. Dreams of achievement in a remote future do not, as a rule, furnish incentive for everyday writing experiences.

Grade Placement

Boys and girls who enter the elementary school with prior kindergarten experiences typically have had some writing experiences even if not much more, in some cases, than to write their names. Special attention needs to be paid to the introduction of handwriting to those first-grade pupils who have not previously attended school. Since many of them come the first day of school with the idea that they will immediately learn to read and also write, it probably is wise not to disappoint them by failing to provide some opportunity to write. To give the pupils a satisfying though very elementary start in learning to communicate through written symbols is doubly important because in some instances a child may at the end of the school day be asked, jokingly as far as the parents are concerned but seriously as far as the child knows, "Have you learned to write?" If first-grade teachers have children who have not previously learned to write their names, they may want to have copies ready of each pupil's name, written in manuscript on cards, for distribution to every boy and girl in the room. Then, for example, when the children have drawn a picture, each pupil can write his name on his picture as he reproduces the copy given him. In many instances the teacher may need to have other means of identification, for the writing done by the child may not be legible enough to be read by the teacher.

From the first grade to the end of the elementary school, the child should be helped to achieve the goals established for the program in written expression. He should be guided to attain them as rapidly as he can but without "haste or hurry" and without neglecting other phases of the total curriculum. He will start work on some of the skills in the first grade and on others in subsequent grades.

After work on any skill has once begun, the skill should be further emphasized as the child progresses through the elementary school. This additional attention to it may be in terms of review as is the case, for example, if the child has learned to use a capital letter at the beginning of a sentence. To help the pupils make consistent use of what they have learned about capitalizing the first letter of the first word of a sentence, spaced practice is needed in many instances. In the case of many writing skills or abilities it is necessary, after a beginning that paid attention to only the rudimentary elements of a skill, to help the boys and girls acquire proficiency in the use of its other elements. For example, letter writing in its simplest form can be started in the first grade as the boys and girls dictate the message for a letter to the teacher, who writes the letter in three parts. Later additional features of letter writing can be added to the agenda of work to be learned in each of the succeeding grades.

Additional suggestions for grade placement are given later in this book in connection with some of the specific types of written expression, such as letter writing, writing reports, and doing creative writing. However, no matter what gradation of skills is made in any allocation of their study to grades, it should be observed in practice only to the extent that it is fitted to the individual differences among the boys and girls. Those variations are marked and, with good teaching, increase, rather than decrease, as the pupil progresses through the elementary school.

Suggestions for sequence, on which grade placement can, in part, be based, are given under "Gradations in Development of Growth in Written Expression." (See page 87.)

Guidelines

The following are helpful guidelines for developing skill in written expression.

1. *The teacher should recognize the close interrelatedness of written expression with other facets of the language arts.* The relationship between oral and written expression is, indeed, strong. Linguists have emphasized points of likeness, as well as of differences. For comments of some of the claims of linguists on this point that have bearing on the teaching of written expression the reader is referred to page 37.

Some ways in which a teacher can put to use his knowledge of the interrelatedness of the language arts, as he guides the growth of boys and girls in written expression, are indicated here. The teacher can:

Provide an environment where there are many points of significance or interest to be heard or otherwise experienced.

Discuss with the boys and girls ideas that they received through listening to others and show how ideas gained in this manner can be used in written work.

Discuss with the pupils ideas that they gained through reading and show how these ideas can be used in written work.

Help boys and girls write more effectively by providing them with the opportunity to discuss orally, before they write, some of the ideas that they plan to put into writing.

Help boys and girls realize that learning to write in an organized manner can help them speak with improved organization and to recognize better the thought expressed by others both in writing and in speech.

Be of assistance to boys and girls by showing them how the acquiring of an expressive vocabulary through listening and reading and by using it in their speech, can help them improve upon the effectiveness of words they utilize in written expression.

Provide boys and girls with the opportunity to learn to use correct sentences in oral and written expression and to help them realize the possible carry-over from one of these aspects of the language arts to the other.

Help boys and girls recognize the fact that through recording their own ideas they may be able at times to assist those who read what they have written, to improve upon their powers of communication.

2. *Both content and form should be emphasized in written expression.* As in the case of oral expression, there needs to be no question as to which is important. Both are. In fact, correct emphasis on these two aspects of written work can cause the two to reinforce each other. The person who, for example, can spell the words he needs to use and who is proficient in the use of punctuation marks and capital letters is freer to turn his attention to the content of what he is recording than the person who has difficulty in these respects. Conversely, the pupil who has significant content that he wishes to record can frequently be stimulated to want to learn to write in correct form.

3. *The boys and girls should have a purpose for any writing that they do.* The importance of this guideline is emphasized under "Objectives," on page 84. At times the purpose for writing might be in terms of the fun that

the pupil gets from the writing. At other times the purpose might be to write a story for inclusion in the class paper. Or it might be to write a report for a class book.

4. *The work in written expression should be closely correlated and frequently integrated with other school activities.* One way in which boys and girls can see purpose for writing is by doing it in connection with work in the content areas and in relation to so-called extracurricular activities. Making a file of reports on books dealing with life in the Scandinavian countries makes sense to a group of fourth- or fifth-grade pupils if the reports are to serve as a contribution for pupils who will succeed them in their room the following school year. Helping dictate to the teacher and then copying a letter to be sent to parents inviting them to a school program on Workers in Our Community provides a meaningful opportunity for writing, to a first- or second-grade pupil.

Even when, as is the case frequently, there is a period in the daily program specifically set aside for language arts experiences, much emphasis should be placed on writing done at other times of the school day. There should not be one standard for it during language period and a lower one during other times of the school day.

5. *There is a place for lessons that help boys and girls concentrate on how to improve upon their written expression.* While many of the learnings in written communication should be acquired through planned incidental means, as the children are recording their thoughts in writing for a useful purpose, many pupils can also greatly profit from definite periods set aside to help them learn to write better. In this category of learning experiences fall the activities of those class periods devoted to presentation lessons in which boys and girls are introduced to a new type of writing or to an additional element with which they already have some acquaintance. Examples of these types of situations are:

Introducing a new type of writing: First lesson in writing a book report

Introducing an additional element in writing: Writing a business letter ordering something, after some other types of business letters have been studied

Learning a new skill: Learning how to write a singular possessive noun.

Presentation lessons may, at spaced intervals, need to be followed, in the development of some skills, with practice lessons devoted to the reinforcement of learnings acquired in part at an earlier time.

In both the presentation lessons and the practice lessons the purpose should be made clear to the boys and girls so that they realize their value. With proper motivation during class periods of these types, used wisely in conjunction with a program rich in planned incidental writing experiences, boys and girls can be helped to proceed with genuine eagerness to learn.

6. *The boys and girls should be helped to learn the qualities of effective writing.* These are some of the ways in which boys and girls can be given such assistance.

By comparing written work that incorporates some of the desirable qualities with work in which these same characteristics are lacking

By finding examples of written work that illustrate the qualities of excellence that they have been studying or are about to study

By reading in a textbook or from duplicated sheets some of the characteristics of good writing

By discussing some of the characteristics of effective writing

By assisting in the compilation of a list of qualities of effective writing, such as: conciseness, clarity, interest, significance, good beginning, strong ending, use of correct English, proper use of capital letters and punctuation marks, neatness, acceptable form for writing on paper, courtesy to the reader, appropriateness of choice of words and expressions, suitability of writing in terms of the probable reader(s).

7. *The boys and girls should be provided with considerable opportunity for doing various types of writing.* There can be no specific statement as to how much writing boys and girls should do to attain maximum efficiency. The optimum amount has not even been estimated. It will vary according to age, interests, intelligence, needs, and many other factors. However, no child is likely to learn to write well without considerable practice. The program in the language arts should include a fair proportion of various types of writing, such as creative writing, letter writing, writing reviews or reports, writing answers to questions, making written explanations, writing announcements, and outlining.

8. *Forms used for certain aspects of written work should be uniform throughout the school year.* Some points on which there might well be uniformity within a grade are: width of margins, method of folding papers, symbols used by the teacher for indicating need of corrections (such as *sp* for spelling), block or slant form for friendly letters.

9. *The pupils should be helped to recognize the style of writing, including vocabulary, which is suitable under various writing situations.* The boys and girls should be helped to realize that, just as in oral expression there are times when dignified terms should be used and when a rather formal demeanor is desirable, so at times in written expression formality should characterize the writing, as, for example, in some types of business letters. They should, if necessary, be guided in noting that at other times less dignified language is not only suitable but also desirable, such as, for example, that used in a personal letter to a classmate. Boys and girls should be

aided, however, in understanding that incorrect English or cheap or tawdry expressions are never acceptable.

10. *Pupils should not be expected to write on topics about which they know little.* In order to write well on a subject it is often necessary to know much more about it than one will write. Selection of points that are particularly significant cannot, as a rule, be made by the writer who knows but little on his topic. One of the ways in which boys and girls can be stimulated to do better writing is by helping them broaden their experience background. In fact, frequently when remedial work in written expression is indicated, a considerable part of the problem may lie in the lack of something to write about, rather than in the failure to make application of acceptable standards in the mechanics of writing. It is because of the importance of knowing well the topic about which one will write that often children do their best writing when they report on experiences that they have had.

11. *Boys and girls should understand policies followed in the evaluation and correction of written work.* Unless the pupils are conscious of the general procedures followed in the evaluation and correction of written work, they may fail to benefit from this phase of the instructional program. (See suggestions on evaluation under "Evaluation and Diagnosis" beginning on page 42.)

GRADATIONS IN DEVELOPMENT OF GROWTH IN WRITTEN EXPRESSION

From the time a child enters until he finishes the elementary school, he typically progresses from a stage where he is unable to write, to one where he can record his thoughts fairly well and often independently. The stages through which he passes may be identified thus: (1) readiness for writing, (2) dictation, (3) copying, and (4) writing by the pupil, developing from decided dependence to considerable independence.

As each of the gradations listed in the preceding paragraph is here described, the reader should bear in mind this point: The steps do not consist of stages in the sense that the first one needs to be completed before the second is begun or the second finished before the third is started or the third no longer used when the pupil has begun to do the semi-independent or independent writing of the last of the four categories here named. There should be much overlapping between the various stages.

Readiness for Writing

Just as there is, for many boys and girls, a stage in the development of skill in reading when readiness to comprehend the thought from the written page needs to be given special attention, so there is a stage in learning to express one's self in writing when readiness for that process needs to be developed with some of the boys and girls. Furthermore, as in the case of learning to read, there is need of attention to readiness for adequate performance on each successive stage in learning to communicate in writing.

The teacher can be of aid to the child as he becomes ready for the initial experiences in expressing himself through writing by: (1) making him feel secure in his classroom, (2) helping him achieve an attention span favorable for writing, (3) helping him realize some of the values to be obtained through writing, (4) broadening his experience background, and (5) providing him with many opportunities for oral communication.

Developing a Sense of Security. The child who is not assured of the goodwill and confidence of his peers and his teacher is not as likely to want to write as the one who feels secure. He will frequently be so tense that he cannot free himself of his feelings of insecurity long enough to concentrate on writing.

Below are stated some ways in which the teacher can help boys and girls achieve a feeling of security.

Providing an atmosphere of friendliness and cooperation in the classroom

Seating the insecure child near pupils who are thoughtful and not domineering

Encouraging the children to share their experiences orally with others in the class

Pointing out contributions that are made by pupils for the welfare of others

Treating with respect the attempts of writing made by boys and girls.

Achieving a Lengthened Attention Span. Since writing usually requires concentrated work, especially for the beginner, some boys and girls seem to be unable to write well in part because of the brevity of their attention span. As their minds flit from one thought to another, often wholly unrelated to the writing that they presumably are doing, the writing either stops entirely or ceases to be effective. Furthermore, because of lack of desirable results from such attempts, the pupil is likely to develop an aversion to writing that will increase his difficulties in concentrating on it at future times.

What can the first-grade teacher do to help the child increase his attention span? Here are a few suggestions:

1. Compliment a child when he has shown perseverance in a task.

2. Discuss with a child from time to time the importance of attending to one thing at a time.

3. Provide an environment for writing that is free from a large number of overstimulating and distracting factors.

4. Have work requiring concentration come when the child is not fatigued.

5. Do not expect the child to engage in an activity longer than he is likely to be able to pay the needed attention.

6. In harmony with the child's maturity, continue to increase the length of time when he is engaged in various activities requiring considerable concentration.

Realization of Values Attainable. Since one of the best ways to prepare boys and girls for writing experiences is to interest them in writing, anything done to help them realize the values they can acquire through writing can serve as means for developing readiness for it. Some of the ways in which beginning first-grade children can learn to see reasons for expressing themselves through written symbols are:

1. Telling what they think may be the writing under a picture in a book that the teacher is reading to them and then being told what it is

2. Taking home to their parents duplicated lists of things needed or some other message that the boys and girls recognize as important for their parents

3. Noting the many types of written materials in the room and their use on bulletin boards and on tables in the form of labels, pictures with brief explanations, posters with captions, magazines, and books

4. Discussing why it would be convenient to know how to record one's thoughts.

Broadening the Experience Background. To help the boys and girls improve in ability to express themselves orally and in writing, the teacher will want to capitalize upon the learners' experiences. Furthermore, he will try to broaden the pupils' backgrounds of experience so that they have a greater fund of knowledge from which to draw in oral and written communication. The first-grade teacher can help his pupils extend their experiences so that they will be more ready for writing by:

1. Providing many interesting and informative pictures and discussing them with the children

2. Having a "sharing" table on which the boys and girls display objects of interest

3. Having exhibits for which the teacher himself provides the materials

4. Taking the children on field trips of various types

5. Having speakers come to the room to talk

6. Showing films and filmstrips

7. Making available good television programs

8. Telling or reading stories to the children.

Oral Communication as an Aid to Written Communication. Because of the close interrelationship between oral communication and written expression, much can be done by the teacher of pupils in the first grade, through providing opportunities for oral communication and in fostering readiness for giving expression to their thoughts. Some means are as follows:

1. Maintaining a classroom atmosphere in which talking at appropriate times is encouraged

2. Providing children with much opportunity for listening to worthwhile and interesting oral means of communication

3. Letting boys and girls meet in small groups for discussion purposes

4. Providing time for unstructured dramatic experiences

5. Encouraging boys and girls to dramatize stories

6. Having a "telling" or "sharing" time (See page 55.)

Dictation to the Teacher

After the pupils have attained reasonable readiness to start expressing themselves through the written symbols, they are prepared to dictate their thoughts, individually or in a group, to their teacher. Dictation of this type is a helpful first step in written expression at a time when boys and girls have not achieved writing skills needed for recording their own ideas. It should be noted, however, that even with boys and girls who could do the writing alone, it will at times be expedient for the teacher to let them dictate to him so that the pupils will not be handicapped by producing a wide gap between their ideas and the written expressions that might be created at a time when writing is still a somewhat cumbersome activity for them.

Occasions for Dictating. The school day affords many occasions for pupils to dictate their thoughts. Here are only a few:

1. Telling a "make-up" story

2. Making plans for the day's activities

3. Listing articles needed for a project

4. Listing plans for a project

5. Listing questions to ask a person who will speak to the group or who will show them something (as, for example, the farmer whose farm is to be visited or the policeman who will talk about how he can help boys and girls and how they can help him in his work)

6. Giving information about the work of one's father for a class booklet

7. Making statements about what has been learned on a given topic

8. Reporting on an experience

9. Dictating a letter (possibly to a sick child or to someone who had assisted the class in a project)

10. Dictating riddles to be guessed by others in the room

11. Dictating "What is . . . Stories," describing, for ex-

ample, winter, a good time, snow, Christmas. An illustration of such a "story" dictated to the teacher might be:

Winter is making snowballs.
Winter is riding on our sleds.
Winter is wearing warm clothes.
Winter is Christmas.

"Color stories" such as this one can be used as theme for dictation to the teacher:

White is new snow.
White is a clean sheet of paper.
White is a pretty dress.

Definitions such as these can be assembled to form a chart or a notebook and illustrated by the children.

Sequence in Method of Dictation. When the child first starts dictating to the teacher, it is desirable to have only brief records made. He may help compose a list of articles that he needs to bring from home or a one-sentence note to take home, or he may give a name to a picture he has drawn, which the teacher writes below it. He may dictate a sentence for the teacher to write about his picture, such as "Father gave my dog Toy to me for my birthday."

When the child starts giving dictation of more than a list of items or of more than one sentence, the teacher may want to record verbatim what the child is saying without stopping him to improve upon points such as sentence structure, sequence, or vocabulary. Through interruptions for errors in form during the early stages of dictation, the teacher may make the child lose desired spontaneity of expression as he might then be concentrating on how he says something rather than on what he is saying. After the teacher has recorded all the pupil wishes to say, the teacher can do the necessary editorial work as he rewrites the material. He should be careful not to make so many changes that the thoughts are chiefly the teacher's rather than the child's.

A more advanced step in dictation is reached when the pupil is able to take responsibility for improvement of parts of what he is dictating or to note corrections by the teacher before the latter makes a record of some points the child has named. For example, when the child gives a statement out of order, the teacher may ask, "But what is the next thing that happened?" or when the child uses *ran* instead of *run*, he may say, "Let's say, 'Toy had *run* home.'" Prompting the child by asking, "What do we want to say next in our report?" also may help the learner to do more organized thinking. When the first draft has been written, it is suggested that the teacher read it to the child to see if he has any suggestions for improvement. It is at this time that the teacher may wish to recommend further changes, possibly through questioning the child.

When a group of boys and girls rather than only one child dictates to the teacher, a similar sequence of procedure from less to more complex planning is recommended.

Since necessarily the time the teacher has for recording what individual children dictate to him is greatly limited, in some schools a teacher of older boys and girls in the elementary school might initiate a service project in which some of the members of his class take dictation from the younger children. Such a plan might be of mutual benefit to both the ones dictating and to those doing the recording.

Materials for Recording. The teacher might make a record of the child's dictation with an ordinary pencil or a thick first-grade pencil or a felt-tip pen, on small sheets of paper. Or he might, if a typewriter with primary-size type is available, use the typewriter. The chalkboard is used by many teachers, while others use large sheets of paper, such as newsprint, on which they write with magic markers. At times tagboard or mounting board is used.

No specific guidelines can be drawn up as to the type of materials most suitable in various types of situations. However, the following statements may be of some help on this question.

1. When working with only one child small sheets of paper are very convenient to use. When the first draft is not viewed by the child, it matters not what type of pencil is used nor whether a pen is used. If the pupil helps in the correcting of the first draft, use of a primary-grade pencil or a primary-grade-size typewriter is recommended rather than the ordinary pencil, pen, or typewriter.

2. Recording the first draft on the chalkboard, and even the final draft if no permanent record is wanted, is a means of saving paper. Furthermore, changes can readily be made through erasures.

3. Use of newsprint or other large inexpensive sheets of paper has some advantage over use of the chalkboard. It is good when a somewhat permanent record is wanted. It can be moved from place to place.

4. Some teachers like to make the first draft on the chalkboard and the final one on newsprint or other paper.

5. Tagboard or mounting board can be used. However, both, especially mounting board, are so expensive that, unless it is desirable to keep the record for a long time or for a special purpose, it is not recommended for frequent use.

The Language Experience Chart. The experience chart typically is a record of an experience that the pupils in a class have had, are having, or are planning to have. The content is determined by the pupils with guidance from the teacher, and it is recorded by the teacher. However, making an experience chart is not necessarily a group undertaking. The chart may be planned by one pupil, with the assistance of the teacher. For example, each member of a group might individually plan a chart on the work of his father or mother, on a happy time he has had, or on a pet. As in a group experience chart, the teacher serves as scribe. The completed chart can be presented to the class by the individual who planned it and then put into a large notebook made available to the class or it can be posted in the room. Construction of an individual-experience chart can provide the teacher with an excellent opportunity to note the strengths and weaknesses of the pupil planning it. Thus, it can make the teacher aware of the type of help each child should be given in improving his skills in various phases of the language arts. It can also reveal to the teacher, in many instances, emotional needs of the child.

Experience charts can be classified not only as individual or group charts, but they can also be referred to as either reading experience charts or language arts experience charts. The difference is primarily one of purpose. Important in the planning of a reading experience chart is the fact that boys and girls will get practice in "reading" the material they have dictated. This type of chart constitutes an important element of the reading-readiness program in many first-grade rooms. The language arts chart is not designed chiefly for use in progress in reading but is made primarily for a record of the content and for experience in language activities other than reading.

For a rather detailed description of the reading-experience chart the reader is referred to page 233. In addition to the difference in purpose, the language arts experience chart differs from the reading chart primarily in the following respects:

1. Less attention needs to be paid in the language arts chart to keeping the vocabulary restricted.

2. Less practice is usually required on "reading" by the pupils of the language arts chart than on "reading" the reading experience chart since mastery of a reading vocabulary is not one of the major purposes for which the former is constructed.

3. More emphasis is often placed by the teacher in the language arts chart than in the reading experience chart on the development of such abilities as choice of vocabulary for enrichment of the child's means of expressing his thoughts, development of organizational skills, use of capital letters to begin sentences, and use of proper punctuation marks for ending sentences.

Additional Suggestions. Here are a few further points to note in connection with dictation by boys and girls as the teacher serves as recorder. They are of significance regardless of whether or not the dictation is made in order to produce an experience chart.

1. The boys and girls should recognize a worthwhile purpose for the writing.

2. When a group plans what is to be recorded by the teacher, the final draft should be written in conformity with the rules of good English, in correct sentences if sentences are required, and according to other standards of expression acceptable for the level and purpose. When the written work is planned by only one child, under the guidance of the teacher, this suggestion may not always apply. Generally the suggestion should be applied when the product—the written work—is to be shown to other boys and girls. When the end result is not to be viewed by other pupils, there are times when the teacher may wish to record a child's suggestions exactly as he dictates them. Such practice can provide the teacher with an excellent record of a child's level of achievement in the type of oral skill measurable through such dictation. Furthermore, it can provide the child with greater faith in his ability to express himself than he would be likely to receive if all of his suggestion for written record were subject to suggested revisions.

3. When the dictation is a group, rather than an individual, project, participation should be distributed among the members of the group.

4. Reference has already been made in connection with the discussion of language arts experience charts to the fact that various language arts skills can probably be developed through the construction of these charts, such as enrichment of vocabulary, development of organizational skills, and emphasis on how to begin and end sentences. These skills can be developed not only in constructing experience charts but also in other dictating the pupils do to the teacher. Such matters as placement on paper, neatness, and sentence structure can also be stressed. The teacher can help the pupils develop language arts skills as he refers to where on the chalkboard or paper he starts writing, to the margins he leaves, to where he begins a new sentence, to the capital letter he uses at the beginning of a sentence or for the word *I* or with the name of a person, place, or thing, and to simple uses of punctuation marks. He can do so by the comments he makes, such as, "I am writing *Mary* with a capital letter because it is the name of a person" or by questions he asks, such as, "What mark should I place at the end of this question?"

5. Frequently the written material can be incorporated into booklets, by individuals or the group, or into a class newspaper. For example, stories written about the farm might be placed into a big illustrated book with a simple table of contents, to be kept on the reading table. Or a record could be kept of important happenings during the year and placed into a notebook to be donated to the boys and girls who will be in the same classroom the following year. The record might in-

clude reports on topics such as a visit to a farm, the Christmas party, safety rules on which the group might agree, a program that the class gave. An individual book might contain stories a child dictated to be given as a gift to Father or Mother.

6. Even after boys and girls have started to do semi-independent or independent work, they should at times be allowed to dictate to the teacher what they wish to have expressed in written form. As the children dictate to the teacher, they can concentrate on what they wish to report without being responsible for the mechanics of writing. Unless such opportunity is provided, they may lose for later independent writing some of the freshness and imaginativeness that they experienced in the earlier stage of dictating. Furthermore, because of the effort expended in writing, the boys and girls may keep their own written expression so brief that their message is too elementary for expression of their thought. However, there is also danger of the teacher serving as secretary for too long a time. When a child should begin recording his thoughts will vary from individual to individual.

Copying

Copying, in one sense, is not a stage distinct from dictating. In fact, it can be thought of as an act that at times accompanies the dictating to the teacher by the boys and girls.

At first when children dictate material to the teacher, they may have no part in the actual writing. At such times the final draft may be in the form of a teacher-written chart, a chalkboard record, or a copy typewritten or written in manuscript on a piece of paper or it may be a duplicated copy of what the teacher has written. A step toward pupil participation in writing may be the actual copying of the message by them from the copy that the teacher made. It is difficult for beginners to copy from a large piece of paper posted on the wall or from the chalkboard because of the distance between them and the copy and because of the difference in size between the original and the copy they are making. It, therefore, is advisable that in the early stages of copying the child have a copy of the writing on a sheet of paper on his table. This could be in the teacher's own manuscript writing. Incentive for copying may result from mention of the fact that the child's parents would enjoy receiving a note in his own writing or would like to read, in the child's handwriting, the story that he has dictated.

Greater independence in copying may be achieved as the child copies a report, story, or letter written only in part by the teacher and then adds a sentence or two of his own, with help from the teacher. At times all but the ending of a story or letter could be duplicated. This would allow each child to make up his own ending. The following are some cautions to be observed in connection with copying by the boys and girls.

1. The length of the selection to be copied should be such that the child does not become too fatigued in copying it and yet it should be long enough at times that his capacity to copy in terms of length of selection is steadily being increased.

2. Copying short notes, maybe one sentence in length, many teachers might argue, can be done before the child has learned the names and formations of various letters. The act can be just pure copying. Longer selections should not be copied until the child has learned to identify letters and has had some specific help in the formation of letters, spacing, alignment, and the like. It needs to be mentioned here, however, that some teachers may believe that boys and girls should be discouraged from doing any copying other than their own names before they have had systematic work on writing the letters of the alphabet used in material they are copying.

3. As boys and girls copy what the teacher has written, their attention should frequently be directed toward such matters as capitalization, punctuation, and placement on paper.

4. Neat copying should be encouraged. Of course, the standard of neatness should be set in relation to the abilities of the child.

Writing by the Pupils

The final stage in learning to write is the semi-independent or independent writing by the child. The pupil is not ready for this stage until he can write the letters that he knows he needs for the words he will record and until he has acquired some skill in spelling some of the words that he will want to use in written expression.

Sufficient experience background and opportunity for discussion preceding the writing are of particular importance for the child who is a novice at writing. Frequently such a child may be given the chance to talk on the topic on which he will later write. In this way at a time when the act of writing is still accompanied by need of much attention to the mechanics of writing, the child is not also burdened while writing by trying at the same time to decide what he wants to write.

When the pupil first begins writing without a copy, the teacher should be readily available for help. Some teachers may want only a relatively small proportion of the class to write at one time so that they can give much individual help to these pupils while the others are engaged in activities that do not require supervision. Teachers can handle the problem of words that the writers cannot spell in various ways. Here are some suggestions.

1. Before the boys and girls begin writing, the pupils can think through what they wish to write and then ask

for the spelling of words with which they think they may have trouble. The teacher can write these words on the chalkboard.

2. If all the boys and girls are writing on the same topic, such as "A Christmas Dream," the teacher may write on the chalkboard words that are later likely to be used by many—words that might, without help available, cause difficulties in spelling, such as *dream, Christmas, Santa Claus, gift, present.*

3. When the pupils come to a word in their writing that they cannot spell, they may leave a blank space on their paper and continue writing until the teacher has time to help them as he progresses around the group. The teacher can then write on a slip of paper the word or words that the pupil requests. Or he may encourage the pupil to write the word as he thinks it might be spelled on scratch paper, waiting to write it on his best copy until the teacher has verified the spelling with him. Or, in some cases, the teacher may suggest that he write, before he can help him, words of which he is in doubt, only the first letters of the words as he thinks they should begin.

4. Each child can develop a small file of spelling words, arranged according to the first letter of a word, which he can use when writing.

5. As soon as a pupil has developed skill in looking up the spelling of a word in a dictionary, he should be encouraged to make use of that tool.

DEVELOPMENT IN ABILITY TO WRITE PARAGRAPHS

Basic to much work in written communication is the ability to write in paragraphs. How the pupils can be guided in the development of skill in constructing paragraphs is discussed below as these points are stressed: (1) objectives, (2) guidelines, and (3) methods.

Objectives

As the teacher helps boys and girls in the development of ability to write paragraphs, these are points of information or skill that he should aim to have the children acquire somewhere in their elementary school education:

1. Knowledge of what a paragraph is
2. Knowledge of characteristics of a good paragraph
3. Knowledge of the importance of the use of good paragraphs
4. Skill in the use of topic sentences
5. Skill in making all sentences in a paragraph contribute to its central thought
6. Skill in relating points in the correct order
7. Skill in using good beginning sentences
8. Skill in using good ending sentences

9. Skill in making transitions from one paragraph to another. (This objective might be emphasized with only the more able boys and girls.)

Guidelines

Points such as the following serve as guidelines in helping boys and girls acquire the information and the skills listed in the preceding paragraph.

1. *Work on paragraph development should continue throughout the elementary school education.* It can begin in the first grade when the teacher writes, first, one-sentence paragraphs and later longer ones, at the pupils' dictation. In every grade thereafter there should be emphasis on paragraph structure until by the end of the sixth grade the boys and girls have attained considerable knowledge about the types of information listed under "Objectives" and until they have developed to a considerable extent the skills named under the same topic. While many boys and girls in the first six grades probably should not often be encouraged to write reports or stories of more than one paragraph, others can successfully develop skill in multiparagraph reports or stories.

2. *Much of the work on paragraphing can be done through incidental means.* As the boys and girls are writing paragraphs as part of the ongoing school program, real purpose for good paragraph structure can be demonstrated. Social studies, science, health, and literature all lend themselves readily to such work and even physical education, the arts, and mathematics can afford opportunities for producing good paragraphs.

3. *As a rule, incidental means of teaching paragraph structure need to be supplemented by lessons of which the chief aim is to help boys and girls develop skill in paragraph structuring.* These lessons can be both presentation lessons, where points new to the children about paragraphing are developed, and practice lessons, through which at well-spaced intervals the pupils can consolidate their learnings. In both types it is important that the boys and girls realize the significance and worthwhileness of the work.

4. *It should be recognized that the paragraphs in books for children often do not serve as models in paragraphing.* In due time boys and girls should be familiarized with the fact that this shortcoming exists. If the teacher helps them, they will probably not be as inclined as they might be if they made the discovery themselves, to think that it is not important to have good organized paragraphs found in print could serve as an organized paragraphs found in print should serve as an opportunity to impress boys and girls with the fact that not nearly everything that appears in print is well written.

Methods

Here are some means by which boys and girls may be able to attain the needed knowledge and skills.

1. Knowledge of what a paragraph is through:

Hearing the teacher use the term *paragraph* during the beginning stages of somewhat incidental learning about paragraphs even though the boys and girls will not be expected at that time to use the term. References can be made to it as the teacher mentions to the class when he writes a paragraph of more than one sentence that he is writing the sentences in one paragraph because they are all on the same topic

Hearing an explanation by the teacher, with samples of paragraphs, as to what is meant by a paragraph

Following directions given by the teacher, such as "Read the first two paragraphs on page 31 to find out what Bobby wanted to get for his mother" or "Read the paragraph orally that tells us what Bobby's mother said she would like for her birthday."

2. Knowledge of characteristics of a good paragraph through:

Participating in a series of developmental lessons in which each of the following characteristics of a good paragraph is studied: (a) keeping to the topic, (b) giving points in correct sequence, (c) having a good beginning sentence, (d) having a good ending sentence, (e) beginning a paragraph on a new line, and (f) indenting the first word of a paragraph (unless the block form of paragraphing is used) to a desired extent.

Making a chart in which the characteristics of a good paragraph are listed

Finding paragraphs that do and some that do not possess the characteristics of a good paragraph and giving reason for the classification made

Participating in a developmental lesson in which the use of paragraphs in direct quotations is made clear

Giving reasons for division into paragraphs of direct quotations in a series in which different people are quoted

Dividing into paragraphs a written record of conversation involving direct quotations in which the division into paragraphs had not been made

Constructing good paragraphs.

3. Knowledge of the importance of using good paragraphs through:

Participating in class discussion of the importance of good paragraphs

Listening to explanation by the teacher

Noting the difference in desirability between a series of poorly written and a series of well-constructed paragraphs

Rewriting a poorly constructed paragraph into a well-constructed paragraph.

4. Skill in the use of topic sentences through:

Finding in a series of paragraphs the sentence around which the rest of a paragraph is built and then being told by the teacher that such sentences are called topic sentences

Selecting the topic sentence in a series of paragraphs

Changing paragraphs that do not contain topic sentences into some that do

Building a paragraph around a sentence such as "Our room contains many interesting things" to be used as topic sentence

Determining (a) which paragraphs of a series contain topic sentences and (b) which do not contain topic sentences.

5. Skill in making all sentences in a paragraph contribute to the central thought of the paragraph through:

Telling what each sentence in a given well-organized paragraph, relating to an indident, tells about the incident

Stating which sentences in a poorly constructed paragraph do not contribute to the central thought of the paragraph

Writing paragraphs in which all sentences contribute to the central thought

Taking part in a discussion, while examining paragraphs that bring out the fact that in well-organized paragraphs some sentences contain main points bearing on the topic, others give details, and still others give illustrative or background material

Checking paragraphs to find out which type of contribution, if any, each sentence in each of the paragraphs presented makes to the central thought, namely: (a) contains main point bearing on the topic, (b) gives details, (c) illustrates a point, (d) gives background data, (e) serves another useful purpose.

6. Skill in relating points in a correct order through:

Arranging in order a series of pictures illustrating a paragraph or series of paragraphs

Finding the sentences that are out of order in paragraphs not in acceptable sequence

Putting in order scrambled sentences that when arranged correctly constitute a good paragraph

Rewriting paragraphs in which thoughts are expressed out of order when more than a rearrangement of the sequence of the sentences is needed to produce a good paragraph.

7. Skill in using good beginning sentences through:

Examining a series of paragraphs to note which have beginning sentences that indicate what the paragraph is about and that interest one in the rest of the paragraph

Planning improved beginning sentences for paragraphs that do not have a good beginning and stating why the revision is an improvement.

Writing paragraphs that have a good beginning sentence.

8. Skill in using good ending sentences through:

Examining a series of paragraphs to note whether or not the ending sentence of each contributes to the rest of the paragraph

Examining a series of sentences each of which would make a good ending sentence and another series which would not

Making a list of sentences that would not make a good ending sentence such as: (a) That's all that I know about this topic. (b) I hope I have not bored you.

Planning improved ending sentences for paragraphs that have poor endings.

9. Skill in making a transition from one paragraph to another through:

Noting paragraphs in which a satisfactory transition is made and explaining how it is made

Discussing the need of having sentences that show transitions between paragraphs

Listing sentences that show how a transition can be made from one paragraph to another

Writing sets of two or more paragraphs in which a good transition is made.

DEVELOPMENT IN ABILITY TO WRITE LETTERS

With the possible exception of note-taking, none of the types of written expression is employed more frequently than letter writing. Because teachers recognize the importance of providing help in letter writing, the subject has been included in the curriculum throughout the elementary school, in many instances starting even in kindergarten and continuing in high school. In spite of all the attention that has been afforded the topic, the letters written by many adults are woefully lacking in both form and content. Furthermore, for a variety of reasons many letters that should be written never materialize.

With facts such as these in mind, teachers need to know, "What can we do to make the work on letter writing more effective?" This section of this chapter gives a partial answer to the elementary school teacher by means of consideration of these questions: (1) What do

boys and girls need to learn about letter writing? (2) In what sequence and on what grade levels should guidance in meeting these needs be provided? (3) What guidelines should the teacher observe when teaching letter writing? (4) What methods can be used for teaching both personal and business letters? (5) What additional suggestions are valuable in teaching the writing of personal letters? (6) What additional suggestions are valuable in teaching the writing of business letters?

Learnings to Be Acquired

The learnings to be acquired in relation to letter writing can be divided as to knowledge, abilities, and attitudes. It is according to this classification that they are here discussed.

Knowledge to Be Acquired. Instruction in the elementary school should be geared so that the child acquires the following knowledge about letter writing:

1. The type of paper that is acceptable for writing letters for various purposes

2. The medium—pen, pencil, or typewriter—appropriate for writing various types of letters under differing circumstances

3. The color of ink to be used when a letter is written in ink

4. The parts of a letter, personal and business, and the reason for each part

5. The points to be included in the heading, inside address (in case of a business letter), salutation, complimentary close, and signature

6. The placement of the items in the various parts of a letter in relation to the page and to one another

7. The capitalization and punctuation of the parts of a letter

8. The points of importance to note in relation to the body or message of various types of letters

9. Acceptable methods of folding a letter

10. The points to be included in the send and return addresses on an envelope

11. The placement of the various items of the send and return addresses on an envelope in relation to the envelope and to one another

12. The placement of the postage stamp

13. Methods of determining how much postage is required.

Abilities to Be Developed. Acquisition of the knowledge needed concerning letter writing is not enough. Knowledge does not insure ability. The teacher thus will want to make certain that the boys and girls will make use of the various items of knowledge listed in the preceding paragraph.

Figure 5.1. A Chart to Emphasize How Addresses Should Be Written on Envelopes.

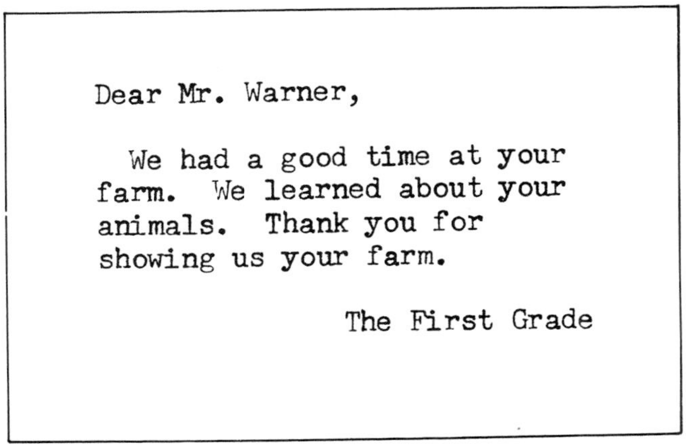

Dear Mr. Warner,

    We had a good time at your farm. We learned about your animals. Thank you for showing us your farm.

              The First Grade

Figure 5.2. Letter Writing. A Cooperative Venture in the First Grade.

Attitudes to Be Developed. How a child feels about letter writing is going to determine to a considerable extent his effectiveness in it while he is in school and when he is on his own. Indicated below are some of the attitudes the teacher will want to try to help boys and girls develop.

1. The pupils should want to be careful that their letters will seem courteous to the recipient.

2. The boys and girls should understand that when they receive letters that seemingly are lacking in courtesy the writer may not have intended to be discourteous.

3. The pupils should desire to be as prompt in writing letters as the situations demand.

4. The boys and girls should want to be prompt in mailing letters that they have written.

5. The pupils should be tolerant of the errors of others but critical of their own.

6. The pupils should be interested in putting into effect everything they know about letter writing.

Sequence and Grade Placement

In what order should the various learnings be acquired and on what grade levels? Courses of study and expert opinion expressed in other ways show lack of uniformity. Furthermore, research does not provide us with the answer. However, the following points indicate some points on which quite a number of teachers might agree.

1. The three-part letter (greeting, body, and signature) is usually used in the kindergarten and in lower-primary grades; later the five-part friendly letter (heading, greeting, body, closing, signature) takes its place.

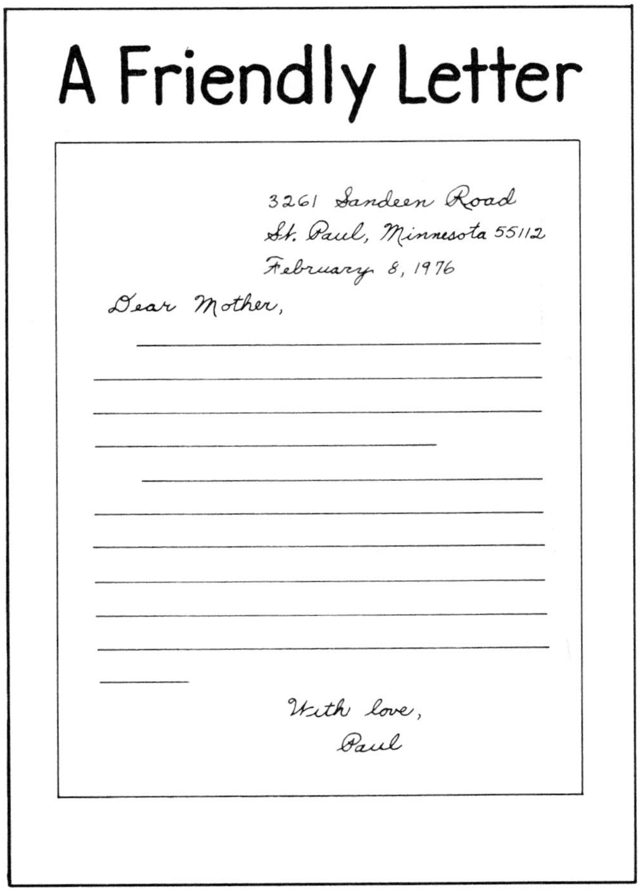

A Friendly Letter

3261 Sandeen Road
St. Paul, Minnesota 55112
February 8, 1976

Dear Mother,

_____
_____
_____
_____
_____
_____
_____
_____
_____
_____

With love,
Paul

Figure 5.3. The Five-Part Letter.

2. An introduction to letter writing might be the simple, brief note, possibly addressed to parents of the boys and girls. The teacher could duplicate a copy for each pupil on which only the greeting and the body of the letter written by the teacher occur. The signature is provided by each pupil. Sometimes the content is determined by the teacher and read to or by the group before the signatures are attached to the individual copies. At other times, it can be recorded on the chalkboard or on a large sheet of paper as the pupils suggest what is to be included in the letter. Copies of such a letter can then be duplicated by the teacher, or, when the children are able to do so, copied by each child and then signed by him. At times, as the boys and girls develop in writing skills, space can be provided on a duplicated copy of a letter for each pupil to add a sentence or two of his own before he signs the letter.

While some letters can advisedly be produced as composite letters by the group even in the upper grades of the elementary school, the individually written letter, often with the guidance of the teacher, can in many instances be introduced toward the end of the first grade or beginning of the second.

3. Work on business letters is usually not introduced until the pupils have had considerable experience writing friendly letters. However, simple business letters, for example, to order something or to request materials, can be written even by boys and girls in the upper-primary grades.

Guidelines

Some guidelines are suggested in the preceding comments on teaching letter writing. Additional ones, such as the following, may help the teacher in deciding upon points of procedure.

1. *Much of the work in letter writing should consist of writing bona fide letters.* Writing letters to imaginary people or to historical characters long dead is usually not a very desirable practice. The letters that boys and girls write, as a rule, are letters that should be sent.

2. *In addition to writing meaningful letters that are to be sent, provisions should be made for lessons devoted primarily to helping boys and girls master the skills of letter writing.* Some of these lessons should be presentation lessons, in which new learnings are acquired, such as how to write the inside address of a business letter. Others, at properly spaced intervals, should provide for any reinforcement needed beyond that effected by the writing of letters that are to be mailed or otherwise delivered. For example, at times a series of practice exercises might be helpful which call for supplying missing punctuation marks for the parts of a letter other than the body of the letter. It is important that the boys and girls be helped to recognize the value of such exercises so that they do not think of them merely as "busy work."

3. *The pupils should be allowed to write some of their own letters at school, aside from any school assignment.* These could be written during free periods or as substitutes for some types of work in handwriting. The pupils should be free to ask the teacher for help. However, they should feel no obligation to show these letters to him.

Methods

Suggested following are procedures applicable to both personal and business letters. Those that pertain only to letters of one of these two categories are given in the next two sections of this chapter, where special consideration is given to each of these two types. In connection with either personal or business letters the pupils may do the following:

1. Examine letters that have been posted on a bulletin board.

2. Examine a bulletin board on which is posted a chart showing a neat letter written in ink and on proper writing materials as well as a letter in sharp contrast with it. A question like "Which Kind of Letter Do You Write?" can be posted near the illustrations on the bulletin board.

3. Make or help make a chart on which lines are drawn showing where various parts of a letter should be written.

Dear Bob,

When can you visit me?

This is a picture

of my pet crow.

His name is Peter.

Jim

Figure 5.4. A Three-Part Letter.

4. Participate in discussion on various phases of letter writing.

5. Assist in making a checklist for evaluating letters.

6. Make a list of different types of situations for which boys and girls on their grade level might need to write letters.

7. Participate in a skit or observe one which shows the reactions of recipients of well-written and poorly written letters.

8. Make or contribute to making a booklet on letter writing. Such a booklet may contain samples of well-written letters of all types studied; poorly written letters with comments as to how the letters can be improved; explanations of the purpose of various parts of letters; rules for writing various types of letters; an explanation as to how courtesy can be shown in letter writing; examples of envelopes written in block and slant style (if both are taught); an article on "The Story of a Letter"; and a report on the history of written communication.

9. Do exercises similar to those to which reference is made under "Illustrative Practice Exercises." (See page 102.)

Additional Suggestions Concerning Personal Letters

As indicated earlier, the comments about letter writing in the preceding pages are applicable to both personal and business letters. Let us now consider some additional points about personal letters.

Types of Personal Letters. The following types of personal letters advisedly may be studied somewhere in the elementary school program; the usual so-called friendly letter, the letter of congratulation or praise, the letter expressing sympathy, the letter of invitation, the letter of acceptance of an invitation, the letter of regrets in answer to an invitation, the letter of apology, the letter of complaint, and the thank-you letter.

1. The usual friendly letter. The following are some of the learnings about the usual friendly letter that boys and girls should acquire:

The content should be of interest to the person to whom the letter is written.

Questions should be asked or comments made about the welfare or other concerns of the person to whom the letter is written.

The writer should, as a rule, avoid brief reference to many topics, since more detailed treatment of fewer is more interesting.

The style should be appropriate to communication with the person to whom the letter is written. (The tone of a letter addressed to Grandmother should be more dignified than one written to a classmate.)

The letter should be friendly. (There is no place in it for anger, discourtesy, or irritation.)

The letter should express opinions of the writer.

The letter should be free of trite statements such as "I have wanted to write to you for a long time but. . ." or "I better quit or you will be too tired to finish reading this."

2. The letter of congratulation. Boys and girls have opportunity to write letters of congratulation when friends have achieved an honor or have done something praiseworthy without recognition for it. These are a few specific situations that may call for a letter of congratulation or praise from a pupil in the elementary school: (a) A classmate has received a medal at a pet show. (b) A friend has been chosen to represent the Brownies at a district camp. (c) A friend has shown bravery in a situation.

A few points to be noted about writing letters of congratulation or praise are as follows:

The letter should make clear for what event or achievement the person to whom the letter is written is being complimented or congratulated.

The expression of congratulation or praise must be sincere.

The wording should be such as to convey real appreciation without showing exaggeration.

The letter should not include any statements that may detract from the expression of congratulation or praise. For example, the following would violate this requirement: (a) I want to congratulate you on having won second place in the pet show. Isn't it too bad that you didn't get first place? (b) I want to congratulate you on having won second place in the pet show. I know it is the first time that you have won a place in the pet show. My sister won second place two years and first place one year.

3. The letter of sympathy. Even boys and girls in the elementary school have occasion to write letters of sympathy. Sympathy can be expressed by them to a sick friend, to a person who has been in an accident, or to someone whose relative has died.

Expression of sympathy can be included in the usual friendly letter or in a letter in which nothing else is discussed. If sympathy is expressed in the usual friendly letter, the tone of the rest of the letter must be in harmony with the expression of sympathy. Nothing should be included in it that would be likely to make the recipient more unhappy than he probably is. For example, in a letter to a boy who has broken his leg, inclusion of a part such as this would show poor judgment: "I know you hate to miss the baseball game this Friday afternoon. Why did you have to break your leg just at this time? I surely am thankful that I don't have a broken leg and have to miss that game."

4. The letter of invitation, the letter of acceptance, and the letter of regret. Boys and girls may have occasion to write letters inviting (a) their parents to school, (b) the principal to see an exhibit in their room, (c) the pupils of another room to come to a program they are giving, (d) a person who helped them with a study of a unit of work in science or the social studies to come to their culminating activity for that unit.

Elementary school pupils at times have need for writing invitations outside of school when, for example, they invite someone to a party or to be a week-end guest.

For both school and out-of-school use pupils will need

to know how to answer invitations and how to accept them or send their regrets. They should learn what points should be included in a letter of invitation, namely: (a) a clear statement as to the event to which the person is being invited, (b) the exact time of the event, and (c) the place where the event is to take place. Sometimes additional information is necessary. For example, if the party is a birthday party, it may be advisable to make clear whether or not presents are intended. At times it is desirable to let the person to whom the invitation is extended know the length of time of the event. If there is to be an admission charge to an event, the amount of admission should be stated in the invitation.

Boys and girls should be taught the following:

That every letter of invitation should say something that makes the person invited feel he is really wanted

That courtesy, as a rule, demands an answer to invitations either in the form of acceptance or regrets. The pupils could also be helped to understand when responses are not mandatory, as, for example, when all the boys and girls in a school are invited to an ice-cream social for which there is a charge

That when an invitation is extended in writing, it usually should be answered in writing

That regardless of whether or not an invitation is accepted, in replying the person invited should thank the sender of the invitation

That in a letter of acceptance it is important to restate the time and place of the event for which an invitation has been extended, since such a statement can help clear up any misunderstanding as to time or place

That preferably in a letter of regret the writer should, as a rule, possibly in general terms, indicate why he cannot accept the invitation.

5. The letter of apology. One of the ways boys and girls can express their regret about their wrongdoings or unintentional inconveniencing, harming, or saddening of others is through the letter of apology. The following situations are typical of some of the times when letters of apology by elementary school children may be in order: (a) when a boy or girl has unintentionally run over and broken a plant that his neighbor, who is out of town, has in his yard; (b) when a person is sorry for an unkind remark he has made; (c) when children playing ball have broken a window in the home of a neighbor who is out of town; (d) when a discourtesy has been shown to a speaker or visitor in a classroom.

These are some of the points that boys and girls should be taught about writing letters of apology:

That it is usually better to apologize in person than by letter if the individual is within reasonable distance from the one to whom an apology is due

That at times, even after one has apologized in person, it is also courteous and thoughtful to write a letter of apology

That if a person has unintentionally acted in such a manner as to make necessary an apology, it is often advisable to explain how he happened to act as he did

That if an individual has done something to require an apology, he should make it clear that he is genuinely sorry for his action. (An apology that is not genuine should not be written.)

That if a person can make amends for what he has done, it is important to state what he will do or to ask what he can do to try to make up, at least in part, for his actions

That if a letter of apology is desirable, it should be sent promptly

That if a person receives an apology, he should be forgiving and let the person who apologized know that he holds no grudge.

6. The letter of complaint. Boys and girls may send a letter of complaint, other than in business situations, on occasions such as the following: (a) if an exhibit that a class has put in the hall is being molested by pupils from another room; (b) if a speaker who has been engaged by a class to speak at a program to which pupils from another room have been invited is not treated with politeness by the visitors.

These are some of the points about personal letters of complaint that boys and girls should learn:

That it is often better to state a complaint orally rather than in writing

That the writer should be careful not to attach wrong motives to the person to whom he is complaining. It is well to assume that the possible offender may be innocent in this respect unless he has been proved guilty.

That a letter of complaint should be written with great courtesy.

7. The thank-you letter. Pupils can write letters thanking: (a) boys and girls from another room who have invited them to a program or an exhibit; (b) pupils in an upper grade who have done something for the room, such as making a pen for a pet rabbit belonging to first-grade pupils; (c) a person who has served as speaker or who has allowed them to visit a farm, bakery, fire station, or other place on a field trip; (d) parents when pupils are away from home.

Some points about writing thank-you letters that children should learn are:

The importance of writing thank-you letters promptly

The fact that frequently even if one has thanked a person orally it is also desirable to send him a thank-you letter

The desirability of saying something about a gift for which one is thanking the giver

The importance of trying to write a letter of thank-you in such a manner that the recipient will be convinced of one's gratitude.

Methods. Below are several suggestions for methods of procedure that apply in particular to writing of personal letters.

1. The boys and girls can evaluate a group of statements by writing *Yes* on the line to the left of a statement if it is a desirable statement to include in a thank-you letter and by writing *No* if it is undesirable. Statements such as these may be listed:

_____Thank you for the gift that you sent me even though I wish you had sent me money instead.

_____It was kind of you to send me a pencil with my name on it. I wish you could see some of the presents that I received. Some are very expensive. My aunt sent me a transistor radio.

_____Thank you for sending me a pencil with my name on it. Since I often do not know which pencil is mine, this pencil is very welcome.

_____Thank you for the pretty scarf that you sent me. How could you know that I wanted a green scarf to go with the new winter coat that my mother bought me!

2. The boys and girls can indicate by writing *Yes* or *No* which statements of a list are suitable for inclusion in the usual friendly letter and in some of the various special types of personal letters such as those of complaint, of invitation (as well as acceptance or regret), of apology, of sympathy, or of congratulation or praise.

3. Some of the pupils can put on a skit in which they illustrate the right and wrong way of writing a letter of complaint. One part of the skit can show what effect a letter written by a person who was angry may have upon the recipient. In the other part there can be shown how a letter of complaint was written in such a way that it had no undesirable effect upon the receiver. Others in the class could then discuss points that were observed and those that were violated in the skit. Scenes portraying the effect of other types of personal letters could similarly be shown.

4. The group could draw up a checklist of points by means of which to appraise each of the various types of personal letters. In this list could be included only those points that are not already stated on a general checklist worked out for all types of personal letters.

Additional Suggestions Concerning Business Letters

Here are a few additional points that should be emphasized in writing all types of business letters.

1. Only one side of the paper should be used in a business letter.

2. A business letter should have an inside address.

3. Some salutations and complimentary closings that are appropriate for personal letters are inappropriate for business letters and vice versa. The following illustrate some desirable salutations for business letters:

> Dear Sir   Dear Madam
>
> Dear Mr. . .   Dear Mrs. . .

The following are among acceptable complimentary closings for business letters:

> Sincerely yours   Yours truly

4. The final mark of the salutation of a business letter is the colon.

5. The business letter should without fail contain all needed information but none that is unnecessary.

6. The signature of a business letter should give the first and last names of the sender, with or without the second name or its initial, or it should give the initials of the first or of the first and second names of the sender and the last name as, for example: *John Carlson, John Robert Carlson, John R. Carlson, J. Carlson,* or *J.R. Carlson.* It should be written in longhand even if the rest of the letter is typed. However, in a typed letter it is customary to have the name in type, either with or without a line above it, directly below the signature in longhand, as, for example:

John R. Carlson   or   John R. Carlson

Figure 5.5. Form of a Business Letter.

If the name is not typed below the longhand signature, it is important that the signature be written very plainly.

7. Some types of stationery suitable for personal letters are inappropriate for business letters. The business letter should be written on white, slightly off-white, or delicately tinted paper, such as a very light brown or tan. The usual size of paper used in a business letter is 8 1/2 by 11 inches. However, for a very brief message it is proper to use a smaller sheet of paper.

8. If there is an enclosure with the letter, mention should be made of it in the letter. This is an example of such a reference:

> I am enclosing a self-addressed stamped envelope.

Types of Business Letters. Boys and girls in the elementary school may have occasion to write business letters of the following types, either as class projects or as individual writing: (1) letters ordering things, (2) requests for free materials, (3) requests for services and responses to answers received, (4) letters of complaint, and even (5) letters of application.

1. *Letters ordering things.* At times pupils order books by mail. They also order other articles such as model airplane kits, small rock exhibits, pets (such as hamsters), or shell exhibits. Some learnings that boys and girls should acquire about writing letters ordering things are:

> The need of checking on the reliability of a firm
>
> An evaluation of the true worth of an article they wish to order
>
> A careful decision as to whether the article will most likely meet their needs
>
> Knowledge of items to include in a letter ordering things and of the method in which they should be included in a business letter, such as: the title and author of a book; the catalog number of an article other than a book, with exact specifications as to size, color, etc.; a statement as to how the article will be paid for; inclusion of a check or money order unless the thing ordered is to be sent COD; the correct way of writing dollars and cents in a business letter.
>
> The need of keeping a copy of the letter sent. So that the pupil can check whether his order has been filled properly, it is desirable for him to keep a copy of the letter ordering something.

2. *Requests for free materials.* Both in and out of school boys and girls write letters requesting free materials from travel agencies, chambers of commerce, publishing companies (copies of catalogs, for example), manufacturing companies, consuls, state departments, as well as other sources. (Since companies have been bombarded with letters asking for free materials, it is important that boys and girls learn to judge when it is right and when it is not right for them to request meterials.)

Here are a few additional learnings that boys and girls should acquire concerning the writing of letters asking for free materials.

> The writer should state clearly why he wants the materials that he requests. In one instance when a person wrote for free materials for use at school, a representative of a travel company came from another town to see the writer of the letter. His company had wrongly assumed that the writer was contemplating a trip to the land about which material had been requested. It should be noted that many companies are pleased to send material to boys and girls when they have reason to think that good use will be made of it.
>
> As many specifications as are valuable to insure getting only what is useful should be stated. For example, if a fourth-grade pupil is requesting material on England, he should indicate his grade level. If he observes this suggestion the travel bureau or other agency need not waste its money sending him folders useful only for adults.
>
> When a letter asking for free material is composed as a class project, only one copy of the letter should be mailed so that unnecessary time is not spent by the recipient of the request in reading many letters making the same request.
>
> An expression of thanks should be included in every letter requesting free materials.
>
> If a person receiving valuable free material for which he has written finds it is not suitable for his purposes or if he has finished using it, he should try to give it to someone who may be able to make use of it.

3. *Requests for services and responses to answers received.* The following are examples of situations in which pupils find reasons for writing business letters requesting the services of others.

> The class wants permission to take a field trip to a bakery, post office, fire station, telephone office, or telegraph office.
>
> The class would like to have someone talk to them on a specified subject.
>
> One or more pupils would like to have the opportunity to interview someone about a matter of significance to the class.

The following are points for boys and girls to note when writing letters requesting services.

> The letter should include information such as: (a)

what services are wanted; (b) by whom the services are wanted; (c) for what purpose they are wanted; (d) when they are wanted; (e) who the writer of the letter is.

The letter should be businesslike in wording.

The letter should show appreciation for consideration of the request.

The letter might indicate possible times when the writer, at the convenience of the recipient, might go to the latter for an interview about the subject of the letter or it might ask the recipient to indicate when it would be convenient for him to see the writer, should he prefer the latter type of arrangement.

A self-addressed stamped envelope should, under many circumstances, be enclosed.

Regardless of whether or not the person whose services are requested gives his consent in person or by a letter, it will at times save possible misunderstanding if the class or a member of the class writes a letter confirming the arrangements. The message on such a letter of confirmation might be similar to the following:

Thank you for being willing to talk to our class about your trip to Hawaii. We will expect you in Room 115 of the Washington School on Friday, June 14 by 11:15 A.M. We agreed you would talk to us for forty-five minutes.

We are looking forward to hearing your talk.

4. *Letters of complaint.* Business letters of complaint are still another type of letter that boys and girls may need to write in situations such as these: (a) when an article that has been ordered is not satisfactory; (b) when material that has been ordered has not been delivered.

Some of the points suggested for the personal letter of complaint (nonbusiness letter) in a preceding part of this chapter apply also to business letters of the same type. In the case of an article that has been ordered which proves unsatisfactory, the letter should indicate when the article was ordered and explain what is wrong with it. Inquiry may also be made as to which of several possible procedures could be followed in making up for the deficiency.

5. *Letters of application.* Although most applications for work made by boys and girls (for example, work as lawn boy, errand boy, newspaper carrier, or babysitter) should be made in person, there are times when a written application seems preferable. When writing a letter of application the writer should remember that:

It is important to make the letter as nearly perfect as possible since the applicant will probably be judged in part by the letter.

The letter should ask that the writer be considered for the work, give his age and grade level,

describe his business experience (if any), supply the employer with names and addresses of persons (other than relatives) who will serve as references, and express appreciation for the consideration that may be given the application.

If an applicant does not know that a vacancy exists, he might begin his letter with a statement somewhat like this: "If you need a boy to distribute your papers on a route in the south end of town, I would like to apply for the position."

6. *Other business letters.* Occasionally boys and girls will find need for writing thank-you letters that are also business letters. They may, for instance, thank a travel bureau for a generous supply of free materials of use in a unit in the social studies or they may write a letter of thanks to the city council for having taken measures to insure greater safety around the school.

There may be occasion when business letters of apology need to be written by elementary school pupils. One such situation might arise when a class had previously sent a letter of complaint stating that an article ordered had not been received, only to find out that it had reached the school promptly but, through no fault of the sender, had not been delivered to the right persons.

Methods. On pages 96 and 97 are listed methods that apply to both personal and business letters. The statements that follow indicate additional points of procedure for helping boys and girls write effective business letters.

1. On the bulletin board may be exhibited various types of business letters, some well and others poorly written, for evaluation by the boys and girls.

2. The pupils may check a series of statements, some well and some poorly expressed, in a business letter of complaint.

3. A businessman may talk to the class about desirable and undesirable features in business letters that he and others in his company receive.

4. The pupils should realize the desirability of proofreading all their letters, both business and friendly. They should check for accuracy in all parts of their letters. To help them proofread letters, they may at times be given copies of letters which contain some errors that they would be able to detect on the basis of knowledge they have acquired. Or such letters can be written on the chalkboard so that together the group can do the correcting. If procedures such as these are followed, the teacher should try to help the pupils see the value of proofreading their own letters.

5. A committee of the class might make a collection of business letters written on different colors of paper. After

they have been placed on a bulletin board or otherwise displayed, the class could discuss which stationery was appropriate for use in writing business letters.

Illustrative Practice Exercises

To help the pupils learn to write letters, exercises such as the following may be used to supplement suggestions given earlier in this chapter. It is hoped that the ones given here will suggest other types to the teacher, to fit in with the needs of his particular group of boys and girls.

Exercise 1. The pupils can be asked to write headings such as the following, as they should appear in a letter:

3101 stevens street madison wisconsin 53705 january 1 1976

Exercise 2. The pupils can be asked to indicate, by *yes* or *no,* which items, such as the following, are appropriate greetings for a friendly letter: *Dear Sir; Dear Madam; Dear Sally; Dear Mother.*

Exercise 3. The pupils can be asked to indicate, by *yes* or *no,* which of a series of closings, such as the following, are appropriate for a business letter: *Yours truly; Respectfully yours; With kindest wishes.*

DEVELOPMENT IN ABILITY TO WRITE REPORTS

It should be noted that many of the suggestions given in chapter 4 in relation to oral reports (beginning on page 58) also apply to written reports.

Guidelines

Helpful guidelines for the teacher when assisting pupils in development of ability to write reports are as follows.

1. *The boys and girls should have a real purpose for writing.* It is not enough that the teacher have in mind sound objectives that may be achieved. The boys and girls, too, should feel that something can be accomplished through writing every report that they produce.

2. *At times the purpose the pupils have for writing reports may be, at least in part, that of perfecting language arts skills important in writing reports.* Usually, to be sure, the purpose of the boys and girls should consist primarily of recording information for the writer's use or for the benefit of others who may read the reports. However, there are times when it is appropriate to have lessons in which primary emphasis is not on recording information that will be useful, but chiefly either on learning how good reports should be written or on practicing what they have learned. An example of part of a presentation lesson in writing reports is one in which the boys and girls learn about the importance of having a proper sequence of events recorded in a report. An example of a practice lesson is one in which the boys and girls receive practice in arranging events in a report in proper order, by means of procedures such as these:

Numbering in correct order sentences of a report that are in scrambled order

Reading orally the rearranged sentences of a paragraph that had been recorded in scrambled order

Rewriting a paragraph of a report in which the sentences are in mixed-up order.

3. *The person making a written report should know well the topic on which he writes.* If he is reporting on a personal experience, he should have it well in mind. If he plans to report on information that he has acquired through reading and listening, he should know so much about his topic that he is in a position to select that which is most significant for his report. Wide acquaintance with such a topic is also important because it will help prevent inaccuracies of statement often made by persons with limited knowledge on a topic. The remark by George Palmer, "I cannot teach up to the edge of my knowledge without danger of falling off," can be paraphrased for report writing.

4. *Oral work should frequently precede the writing of reports.* Especially in the practice stages of writing reports, boys and girls should often be given an opportunity of discussing with one another or with the teacher some of the information on the topic on which they plan to report. Through this interchange of ideas the pupils' background can be broadened and through comments by the teacher and at times by pupils the person to do the writing can also get ideas for the organization of his material.

5. *When writing reports boys and girls should try to make application of everything they have learned about writing regardless of whether the reports are for a language arts class, for one in the social studies, or for any other area.* All the learnings in the language arts and all the skills acquired in written and oral communication—in vocabulary, sentence structure, organization, correct usage, spelling, handwriting, capitalization, and punctuation—should be transferrable.

6. *Boys and girls should be encouraged to show originality of expression.* To be sure, reports need to be true to facts. Nevertheless, there is much opportunity for individuality even in report writing.

Methods

Suggested procedures for guiding growth in writing reports are as follows:

1. In the lower-primary grades the pupils may as a group make an experience chart as described earlier. (See page 89.)

2. Even in the intermediate grades the pupils may at times work as a group on a brief report. The procedure can be that of the class first discussing what may be included in the report and then giving sentence after sentence as the teacher writes them on the chalkboard.

The pupils then can read the report and decide upon improvements to be made.

3. For longer reports suggestions can be given by the group as to the type of information that should be included. For example, if a committee had decided to write a report on Christopher Columbus for reading to others in the room on October 12, they may first of all make an outline similar to the following, which can be recorded on the chalkboard:

> Early life
> Plans
> Search for aid
> First voyage
> **Later voyages.**

Next, the pupils can suggest different points that should be included under the various parts of the outline. A note written under "Early life" might be "place and date of birth"; under "Plans" a note might state "different from what others believed." After the note-writing has been completed, individual pupils may be assigned various parts to write, with the understanding that they can later get help from others in revising their reports.

4. The boys and girls can make a notebook on the topics of various units in the social studies or science in which reports are included. Each pupil may make a notebook of his own or contribute to a class notebook.

5. Accordionlike illustrated folders can be made by individuals or groups of pupils. To these folders, made of heavy paper such as mounting board, can be attached illustrations of steps in a process with a brief explanation of each step written on the part of the folder immediately preceding or following the illustration. On such a folder, for example, the steps in mailing a letter or in making applesauce can be indicated.

6. While working on a unit in science on "The Sky above Us" the boys and girls can put on an imitation broadcast in which they read reports some of them have written. In some communities opportunity may be given for actual broadcasts on a radio station of reports written by pupils on topics of general interest to the public. In schools with a public address system the boys and girls can broadcast on a topic of interest to the school audience.

7. The pupils may make an illustrated report on something they have studied by drawing a mural, supplemented by a booklet in which are given reports explaining the illustrations. For example, they may illustrate life in Colonial times and write reports to accompany the mural on topics such as "The First Permanent English Settlement in America," "The Year 1619 in the Virginia Colony," or "Life in Old Plymouth." The booklet can be made available for reading by visitors to the room.

8. The boys and girls may make a "movie" showing the chief events in the life of a person such as Thomas Edison, Abraham Lincoln, or Marian Anderson, and write a booklet containing reports on various events of importance in the life of the person depicted. In lower grades a "movie" may be made on "Our Community Workers" with possibly only a sentence or two explaining the work of each person pictured.

9. Logs or diaries form another type of report writing. The diaries or logs may be kept on the pupil's own activities or on those of the class. In some cases, in connection with work in the social studies, the boys and girls may like to write imaginary diaries of persons, real or fictitious, of long ago. To make such diaries worthwhile it is important that the writers be well acquainted with the life of the times about which they are writing.

10. Class books and class papers furnish excellent incentive for report writing. (For discussion of the latter, the reader is referred to page 126.)

11. Reading of material on report writing and then discussing it can be a worthwhile activity for pupils.

Figure 5.6. A Mural to Accompany Written Reports.

12. Comparing the qualities of well and of poorly written reports can serve useful purposes.

13. Posting well-written reports can serve as incentive for writing some of similar quality.

A Teaching Plan

The following teaching plan, an adaptation of one written by two former college students, Sally Atkinson Hudnutt and Elva Pickwick Dunham, indicates one procedure that may be followed as boys and girls write a report on a personal experience.

Explanation of Background: We are assuming that third- or fourth-grade boys and girls are writing a series of reports, autobiographical in nature, and then putting them into a booklet for which they will make a table of contents. Some of the topics or titles that may be included in the booklet are "My First Day in School," "A Book I Like," "My Pet," "Something Funny that Happened to Me," "My Family," or "My Hobby." In no case will anyone be required to write on a specified topic; he can always choose some other one. Before the children write on a topic, some of the pupils will give talks on it. We are assuming that some pupils have given talks on the topic selected for this plan, "Something Funny that Happened to Me," and that all have prepared oral reports on the topic on which they will write.

A. *Aim:* To write as good reports as possible for inclusion in our booklets

B. *Materials:*
1. Standards for written reports, given on a chart
2. Sentences for capitalization on the chalkboard
   a. My first day at school was september 6, 1966.
   b. The first school that I attended was the washington school in winona, minnesota.
   c. My teacher's name was mrs. johnson.
   d. On the first friday we had a party.
   e. after we had had our refreshments, we played ball.
3. Miscellaneous
   a. Pens
   b. Pencil (if needed)
   c. Ink paper
   d. Scratch paper

C. *Outline of Procedure:*
1. Introduction
   a. The teacher states that today the pupils will be given the opportunity to write on the topic of the talks they have prepared.
   b. The teacher encourages the pupils to write as good reports as possible for inclusion in their booklets.

2. Study of points to watch while writing reports
   a. Reading silently the points on the chart (See *B-1*.)
   b. Work on one point on chart (under *B-1*), "Capitalization"
      (1) The teacher explains that the sentences under *B-2* contain errors made in their last papers.
      (2) Pupils name rules for capitalization they have learned. (It is assumed that the pupils have learned to capitalize the following: (a) the first word of a sentence, (b) the name of a person, (c) the name of a place, (d) the names of the days of the week, (e) the names of the months of the year, (f) the abbreviations Mr. and Mrs. and the word Miss as in Miss Brown.)
      (3) The class corrects errors in sentences under *B-2*.
         (a) Pupils read the first sentence silently.
         (b) A pupil indicates the error in capitalization in the first sentence.
         (c) A pupil makes the correction on the chalkboard.
         (d) The same procedure as given under (a) through (c) is followed for the rest of the sentences.

3. *Writing the report*

   If a pupil needs to find out the spelling of a word, he leaves a space on his paper for it until the teacher, who circulates around the room, comes to his desk and writes on scratch paper the word(s) he wants spelled.

4. *Forward look*

   The teacher makes arrangement for a time when pupils who have not finished their papers can complete them.

Book Reports

As is true of oral book reports, written reports on books can be a means of discouraging, rather than encouraging, interest in reading. But such need not be the case. Many of the suggestions given on oral book reports (see page 60) also have some bearing on written reports. In this section we will consider some ways to make functional the written book report and to make writing book reports interesting to the boys and girls. For additional suggestions that may be of value, the reader is referred to chapter 10, "Guiding Growth in Independent Reading."

Guidelines. The following points can serve as general suggestions to the teacher.

1. *Frequently oral reports should precede written.* However, it is not necessary that all reports given orally should later be written or vice versa.

2. *The boys and girls should recognize a real purpose for the reports they write.* They may write to keep a record of their reading for their own future reference or for the benefit of others.

3. *When writing book reports the pupils should be encouraged to make application of what they have learned about writing other types of reports.*

4. *The skills acquired in writing book reports should be of value in other written work.* Not only can and should skills learned in other writing be applied to the writing of book reports; additional skills acquired while writing book reports can also be made to serve in improving other writing boys and girls do. Thus a reciprocal relationship should exist in the application of skills acquired in the two types of writing. Among such skills are: writing good paragraphs, using vocabulary expressively, writing neat papers, writing legibly, and spelling words correctly.

Excellent opportunity for work on capitalization and punctuation, as well as alphabetical order, can be provided in connection with written reports on books. The boys and girls can be taught how to write the names of authors with titles of books in alphabetical order. Functional use of this ability can be made, for example, as pupils prepare a list or an index of books to read for a class magazine.

5. *Long reports on books should be discouraged.* A well-written report of no more than two or three paragraphs is to be desired, in most cases, from elementary school pupils, over longer ones.

6. *The form of written reports can be worked out by the group.* This suggestion is of special value if the reports are to be used in a common file or in a class notebook of book reports. Points such as the following may be included in the lower grades:

> Author
> Title
> What the book is about
> More about the book
> Name of the writer of the report
> Date of writing the report.

For intermediate-grade pupils items such as these may be suggested or required:

> Bibliographical data (author, title, publisher, address of publisher, and date of publication)
> Summary of the book (in one or a few sentences)
> Interesting incidents or significant information
> Writer's opinion of the book

> Signature of the person making the report
> Date of writing the report.

7. *Even if a form is worked out by the class for use in most written reports, originality on the part of boys and girls in writing book reports should be encouraged.* The pupils can be helped to understand how, even when following a form that has been agreed upon, they can show originality in their comments summarizing a book, in describing one or more incidents, in stating significant information, or in expressing their opinion of the book. At times, too, they may want to write some of their reports without following the form decided upon for most reports.

8. *Boys and girls should have the opportunity to study well-written book reports.* Some of these might be found in a textbook while others might be written by the teacher or some of the boys and girls.

9. *Book reports should, in many instances, be corrected.* If the first draft of a book report is not without error, in terms of knowledge the writer has acquired, it should be corrected and, under some circumstances, the report should be rewritten, especially if others are to have access to it.

10. *The boys and girls should have opportunity to evaluate book reports.* A score sheet against which the pupils can judge written reports could be constructed by the group. Points to be included could be related to both content and to form.

Procedures. Some suggestions for procedure have been given in the preceding paragraphs. A few additional ideas are given below.

1. A simple file of cards on books read by the boys and girls, including among other points the reader's reaction to the book, can be kept.

2. A class notebook can be made in which on each right-hand page the name of the author and the title of the book are given. Below the author and the title every pupil, after he has read a given book, can write a brief comment on it and sign his name to his statement(s).

3. A class or individual loose-leaf notebook can be kept in which are filed alphabetically, a sheet per book, brief written reports on books read, possibly illustrated.

4. Reports may take the form of an imaginary diary of a character in a book, of an imaginary letter written by one book character to another, or of an imaginary conversation between characters of different books.

5. Each pupil may make a two-page booklet on a book he likes. It could be made from a large sheet of construction paper that has been folded. The title, name of the author, and possibly an illustration could appear on the cover. On the second page of the inside of the folder, a review written on white lined paper could be pasted and

opposite it an illustration could be drawn or quotations from the book cited. These reports could be placed on the library table for all to read.

6. So-called "category notebooks," utilizing loose-leaf filing, could be made by organizing the books being read into groups such as mysteries, historical fiction, fables, and myths. One might be called "This and That," under which could be included the reports that do not fall under the other categories upon which the class decides. As a pupil finishes reading a book, he can sign his name to the page on which the title of the book he read appears.

DEVELOPMENT IN ABILITY IN OTHER TYPES OF PRACTICAL WRITTEN EXPRESSION

In addition to writing letters and reports elementary school pupils have need for learning how to do the following types of practical writing: (1) writing lists, (2) filling in blanks, (3) writing announcements and directions, (4) keeping records, and (5) recording bibliographical data.

Writing Lists

Even before the beginner in the elementary school can make his own lists, there often are many opportunities for him to participate in helping with lists which the teacher records on the chalkboard or on large sheets of paper. Even beginning some time in the first grade the pupils copy some of these cooperatively constructed lists and later boys and girls may have frequent occasion to make lists of their own.

Types of Lists. Some of the types of lists that the elementary school child can make or participate in making are:

1. Names of pupils who are absent

2. Names of boys and girls who want milk or juice for lunch

3. Names of pupils who have been assigned special duties such as watering flowers, arranging books on the library shelf, and passing the wastepaper basket

4. Names of persons who have made a contribution to a given cause

5. Names of persons who have not returned permission slips

6. Names of important people studied in a unit of work

7. Materials needed for a proposed project or experiment

8. Questions or topics to be studied in a proposed unit of work

OUR QUESTIONS ABOUT THE
DUTCH IN AMERICA

1. Why did the Dutch come to America?
2. When did they come to America?
3. Where did they settle?
4. What work did they do?
5. Who were the leaders?
6. What were their schools like?
7. What were their churches like?
8. Did they have any interesting customs?
9. Why did the English take the land away from the Dutch?
10. What did the Dutch do after the English took their land away from them?

Figure 5.7. Questions as a Means of Giving Direction in the Study of a Unit.

WHAT WE WANT TO STUDY ABOUT
THE NEW ENGLAND STATES

1. Location and size
2. Surface and climate
3. History
4. Occupations
5. Schools
6. Cities
7. Other places of interest

Figure 5.8. A List of Topics as a Means of Giving Direction in the Study of a Unit.

WHAT WE WILL DO WHEN WE WORK
ON OUR UNIT

1. Read
2. Draw pictures
3. Give talks
4. Write reports
5. Study pictures
6. See a "movie"
7. Make things
8. Draw maps
9. Give a play

Figure 5.9. A List as Record of Plans for Work on a Unit.

9. Activities in which to engage while working on a unit
10. "New words"
11. Minimum essentials to be learned
12. Names of flowers, birds, or trees.

Points to Learn. Boys and girls should, if necessary, be helped so that they will know points such as the following and so that they will put into use their knowledge of them:

1. When it is of value to keep lists
2. In what form to write lists (sometimes horizontally across the page and other times vertically)
3. How to classify points in a list
4. How to punctuate items
5. What media to use when making lists for various purposes (pen, pencil, or crayon)
6. How to use various types of lists effectively (by checking off items, for example).

Methods. The pupils can acquire information, skills, and attitudes about keeping lists by:

1. Watching the teacher make lists
2. Assisting in compiling lists as they dictate points for the teacher to record
3. Making lists, many of which can be evaluated by the class or by the teacher
4. Listening to the teacher's explanation as to capitalization and punctuation of points in a list and answering questions as to how the teacher should capitalize or punctuate items to be recorded
5. Arranging points in order
6. Classifying items in a list. For example, when the questions for a proposed unit of study have been recorded on the chalkboard, the pupils can help in classifying the questions by placing together all questions that deal with climate, with occupations, with history, and the like. Or they can make an outline of points to be studied, through the use of a system of topics and subtopics.
7. Examining and evaluating tidy and untidy lists that have been posted on a bulletin board for appraisal.

Filling in Blanks

It may be that one reason why filling in blanks, especially in long questionnaires, is distasteful to many adults is that they have not had adequate training in so doing.

Types of Blanks. A few of the many types of blanks that elementary school pupils can profitably learn to fill in are as follows:

1. Blanks for enrollment in school
2. Applications for library cards
3. Cards for withdrawing books from a library

4. Applications for membership in groups
5. Blanks as a means of obtaining free materials
6. Blanks on standardized tests
7. Deposit and withdrawal slips for school banking.

Learnings to Be Acquired. The following are points to be learned about filling in blanks:

1. When to use pen and when pencil
2. How to spell words often needed in filling in blanks (such as the father's name or his occupation)
3. Why it is important to try to write within the space provided
4. How to proceed in trying to write in the space provided
5. Why it is important to fill in all applicable parts of a blank that ask information suitable for recording
6. Why accuracy is important in filling in blanks
7. What to do when an item of a blank does not apply
8. What types of information to be willing to supply
9. Why it is important to write the name and address very distinctly
10. Why it is important not to sign a paper unless one is certain what one is signing.

Methods. The following types of activities can be used in helping pupils develop ability to fill in blanks:

1. Discussion of many of the points listed in the preceding paragraph
2. Practice in filling in blanks
3. Skits indicating circumstances under which it is wise and others under which it is unwise to sign one's name
4. Examination of types of blanks posted on a bulletin board.

Writing Announcements and Directions

Although much of the work in the elementary school in making announcements and giving directions is likely to be oral, there is also a place for writing announcements and directions.

Types of Situations. The following suggest some of the meaningful ways in which boys and girls in the elementary school can write announcements and directions:

1. A poster or a written statement on the bulletin board or chalkboard announcing an event such as a program or the coming of a dental clinic
2. A notice of a coming event in the school paper or the community newspaper
3. A list of directions as to how to do things, such as making a bird feeder, a Christmas ornament, or a May basket
4. A record for a card file for use by the teacher and others as to how to get to the home of a pupil

5. A card for a file giving directions as to how to get to various places of interest in the community

6. A chart giving directions for writing a good paragraph

7. A chart giving a list of directions for operating a filmstrip projector or other equipment that the pupils can operate.

Points to Learn. Following are listed some of the topics on which information concerning writing announcements or directions may be helpful to boys and girls:

1. Brevity and conciseness needed in making announcements and giving directions

2. Circumstances under which it is proper and improper to post announcements

3. Physical appearance of written announcements

4. Rules for making attractive posters, including attention to balance, proportion, color harmony, emphasis, and mounting

5. Items to include when making announcements of various types

6. Importance of stating points in correct order when giving directions

7. Value in checking written announcements or directions before making them available to others

8. Value of diagrams with some written directions

9. Value, at times, in itemizing the parts of a direction.

Methods. Boys and girls can be helped in writing announcements and directions by:

1. Being provided with practice in giving announcements and directions orally.

2. Making a list of suggestions to keep in mind when giving directions such as: (a) Have clearly in mind what the directions are. (b) Determine the best order for giving the various points in the directions. (c) Check against the inclusion of unnecessary details. (d) Check the directions to make certain that all necessary points have been given correctly. (e) Draw a diagram if you think it will be of value in making the directions clear.

3. Judging which of a series of directions presented in written form are clear and which are not clear and then indicating what is wrong with those that are inadequate.

4. Checking a written list of descriptions of situations in which it would be proper or improper to post announcements such as: (a) posting an announcement about an event in the classroom in the principal's office without having obtained permission from him; (b) posting an announcement about an event in the classroom on newspaper print that has become torn through poor or extended storing.

5. Making a list of situations in which it would be improper to post announcements.

6. Arranging in sequence a set of directions in which the steps of the directions have been written in scrambled order.

7. Writing directions for getting from one place to another as indicated on diagrams on the chalkboard or on duplicated sheets of paper.

Return of Our Birds		
	Date	Pupil
ROBIN	Apr. 2	Maria
BLUEBIRD	Apr. 5	Dan
MARTIN		
GOLDFINCH		
WREN	May 7	Sara
ORIOLE		
BLACKBIRD	Apr. 6	Jody

Figure 5.10. A Chart for Record Keeping.

Keeping Records

In the modern elementary school the ongoing program of the school affords many opportunities for keeping records.

Opportunities for Keeping Records. Some of the opportunities for keeping records are indicated in the following list:

1. Keeping a record of the temperature or other phases of the weather such as sunshine, precipitation, wind velocity, and humidity

2. Making a chart showing the return of birds to the vicinity

3. Keeping an attendance record

4. Making a class notebook in which are recorded important events of the year

5. Making a time line showing important events that took place in the classroom

6. Keeping a record of books read.

Points to Learn. Some of the points boys and girls should know about keeping records are:

1. The importance of accuracy

2. The need of promptness

Figure 5.11. A Time Line to Show Important Events in a Classroom.

Our Weather Chart

Date					
Time					
Temperature					
Barometer					
Humidity					
Rainfall					
Wind direction					
Wind speed					
Sky					
Clouds					
Forecast					

Figure 5.12. Keeping Record of the Weather.

3. The value of neatness
4. Types of records it is important to keep
5. Uses to be made of records
6. Means of storing records
7. The private nature of some records.

Methods. Suggested methods for helping pupils grow in ability to keep records are given following.

1. The pupils can observe the teacher as he keeps a record, possibly of class attendance, while they note the care with which he checks the data, the promptness with which he records them, the neatness of his record, and the safety of the place in which he stores the record.

2. The pupils can observe or participate in a skit in which some of the important points to learn about record keeping are portrayed.

3. The boys and girls can check a list of items such as the following to show which are desirable places for storage of the indicated records:

_____The bulletin board for posting a chart showing the return of birds to the vicinity.

_____The library table in the classroom, for placement

of an individual's record of the money he has deposited in the school bank.

_____The drawer of the teacher's desk in which he keeps the attendance record.

4. The boys and girls can check as true or false a list of points about record keeping, such as the following:

_____Records should be made promptly.

_____Everyone in the room should be allowed to read all records of deposit made in a school bank.

_____It is proper to ask one's friend to see his record of height and weight.

5. The class can make a notebook in which they record and, in some instances, illustrate the points they have learned about keeping records.

Recording Bibliographical Data

Bibliographical data written by boys and girls in the lower grades usually consist of only the author and title. In the intermediate grades author, title, name of publisher, address of publisher, and date of publication can advisedly be included. In these grades some boys and girls might also learn how to record needed data on stories or articles in magazines, pamphlets, or children's encyclopedias.

Situations for Recording Bibliographical Data. Some of the reasons why pupils in the elementary school record bibliographical data are to:

1. Introduce others to a book by means of a poster giving an illustration and the title and author of the book

2. Identify the book on which a report for either a class or individual card file or notebook is being made

3. Keep a list of books, stories, or articles helpful for work on a given unit of study

4. Keep a record of recommended books

5. Make an inventory of books in the room library

6. Make a list of books wanted from the public library

7. Compile a list of books that might be ordered for the room library.

Points to Learn. So that pupils will not be confused, it is recommended there be agreement among the teachers of a school on the form to be used for recording bibliographical data. With such a uniform method of recording in mind, the teacher should help them learn:

1. The reason for inclusion of all the items listed as bibliographical data

2. The order in which bibliographical data should be written in an entry

3. The capitalization, punctuation, and underlining of parts of bibliographical entries

4. The placement of bibliographical data on a sheet or card.

Methods. Listed here are suggestions that may help pupils acquire needed information and skills and desired attitudes concerning the recording of bibliographical data that can be utilized as the boys and girls:

1. Engage in discussion led by the teacher and listen to his explanation as to the reason for inclusion of each point in a record of bibliographical data

2. Engage in discussion led by the teacher and listen to his explanation as to capitalization, punctuation, and underlining used with bibliographical entries

3. Make corrections on sheets containing bibliographical data in which errors have been made

4. Arrange in desirable order a list of references to books and articles in magazines, children's encyclopedias, or pamphlets pertaining to a given topic.

DEVELOPMENT OF SKILL IN CAPITALIZATION AND PUNCTUATION

Even though considerable time and energy are spent in the elementary school and in high school in helping boys and girls learn to capitalize and punctuate correctly, the written work of high school and college students and of adults shows many errors in capitalization and punctuation. Furthermore, many of the mistakes occur on points to which much attention has been directed in the elementary school and in later schooling.

Guidelines

What are the reasons for the ineffectiveness of the program of instruction in capitalization and punctuation? One of them probably lies in the teacher's lack of knowledge, understanding, or application of guidelines such as these:

1. *Work on capitalization and punctuation should be carried on in such a way that the pupils sense the worthwhileness of capitalizing and punctuating correctly.* Violation of this principle is probably one of the chief reasons for many errors. The boys and girls, as well as older people, are often not impressed with the need of capitalizing and punctuating carefully. Somehow, we as teachers have failed to make correctness of capitalization and punctuation seem important enough—important enough so that the great majority of people will try to put into practice what they know.

2. *The teacher should be careful not to assume that pupils already have information that they lack.* Many teachers fail to present carefully points on which practice is being given because they assume that the pupil knows what should be done, in terms of capitalization and punctuation. For example, a sixth-grade teacher may

assume that in regard to a point of punctuation, such as using commas to separate words or groups of words in a series, the pupil needs only more practice when in reality he needs a review of the work taken up on that point in the preceding grade or grades, involving further explanation, demonstration, or development.

3. *The boys and girls should be given many opportunities to apply in writing situations what they are learning about capitalization and punctuation.* Too frequently the major emphasis in terms of application of what is being learned is a series of practice exercises, without emphasis on application of generalizations developed inductively—or through the method of discovery—and without sufficient opportunity to use the newly acquired learnings in meaningful situations.

4. *Incidental learning situations do not provide all the practice that many boys and girls need on points to be learned and skills to be acquired in capitalization and punctuation.* Many boys and girls need reinforcement in the form of exercises or possibly games, to help them master the skills being taught. Care needs to be taken, however, that such practice is not given on points that the boys and girls can acquire economically through more functional learning situations. Furthermore, boys and girls should recognize the value of such work so that they approach it wholeheartedly, with the desire to learn.

5. *The teacher should try to ascertain the needs and capacities of each learner.* Tests serve as one source of information on the abilities of various pupils. Although the better standardized tests in the area of the language arts give a fairly accurate general survey of the abilities of the person tested, they are not diagnostic enough to indicate with the desired accuracy the status of the individual's ability in all the important skills to be acquired. Consequently homemade tests that provide enough different testing situations on various points to make them truly diagnostic are of value. (For samples of test items, the reader is referred to page 44.)

The teacher can also, of course, note the strengths and weaknesses of a pupil in skills in capitalization and punctuation by study of his written work. Diagnosis of what he does on practice exercises frequently indicates whether or not he needs additional help or practice on certain points. Examination of the pupil's writing, other than in situations involving practice exercises, is also a fairly good index of the pupil's needs. The teacher can examine the work when the pupil is not present or he can go over it with him and thus attempt to find out whether the errors are due to carelessness, lack of knowledge, or failure to recognize the desirability of doing his best when writing.

6. *The work on capitalization and punctuation should be adapted to individual differences.* This statement is to be interpreted as meaning that even though group in-

struction is utilized, after the needs of individuals have been ascertained, attention should be paid to individual differences in various ways, such as these: (a) excusing a pupil from presentation lessons on given skills; (b) not requiring a pupil who does not seem to need further practice as provided by practice exercises, to do the work; and (c) providing additional meaningful instruction for boys and girls who can profit from it.

7. *Only useful skills should be taught.* It is doubtful whether elementary school pupils should be taught generalizations about capitalization and punctuation unless there is a functional need to apply the generalization. If the boys and girls do not recognize a need for what they are taught, they are not apt to learn or to apply what they learn. Furthermore, there are so many skills in the language arts that are of vital significance to the child in his everyday writing that it is usually poor selection of content to teach those items that the pupil cannot use at the time or in the fairly near future.

The Program in Capitalization

The results of studies as to what should be learned in the elementary school are inconclusive. Consequently any suggested lists lack authenticity.

Points to be taken up in the elementary school undoubtedly should be determined to a considerable extent by the needs of the pupils. Those that are used most should be given priority provided they are simple enough for the child to learn.

By the time boys and girls have completed the elementary school, those of average ability should probably have learned the following uses of capital letters:

1. The first word in a sentence
2. The word *I*
3. Names of persons, initials, polite titles, races, nationalities
4. The first word, the last word, and every so-called "important word" in a title and in the name of a company, firm, special product, television program, and radio program. (Children should learn that words such as *a, an, and, at, from, in, into, on, or, the, to, with* are not considered "important words" in titles.)
5. The first word and each "important word" in the name of a city, state, school, club, building, geographical feature such as *valleys, mountains, oceans, rivers,* and *continents*
6. Proper adjectives such as *Bostonian, American, Japanese*
7. The first word of a direct quotation
8. The first word and every "important word" in a salutation of a letter and the first word of the closing of a letter
9. Many abbreviations. (Although pupils should learn

that many abbreviations are capitalized, they should be expected to learn the abbreviations of only a few frequently used ones such as *Mr., Mrs., Dr., R.R.* and *P.O.*)
10. The word *God* and other words for the Deity
11. The word *Bible* and other titles of writings sacred to a religion
12. Words such as *Father, Mother, Aunt, Uncle, Sister, Brother* when they are used as a name
13. Words such as *North, Southwest, Far East* when they refer to a part of the country or of the world.

The Program in Punctuation

By the time pupils leave the elementary school, those of average ability should probably have learned the following uses of these punctuation marks.

The Period

1. At the end of a declarative and an imperative sentence (although the terms *declarative* and *imperative* might not be taught)
2. After abbreviations
3. After initials
4. With numbers or letters preceding a list in outlines
5. With numbers or letters to help indicate items in a list of words, sentences, or longer thought units even if the items are not included in an outline

The Comma

1. After the greeting in a personal letter and after the closing in a personal or business letter
2. Between the date of a month and the year (as a rule)
3. Between the name of a city and state when written on the same line
4. With words or groups of words in a series
5. After *yes* or *no* when used in a sentence as part of an answer
6. With a direct quotation that forms part of a sentence, to separate it from the rest of the sentence unless a question mark or exclamation point is needed to make the separation
7. After a word or group of words, other than a sentence, which shows some, but not much, surprise or expresses moderately strong feeling
8. After the name of a person addressed
9. With appositives
10. After the last name of a person if it is written before the first name, as in an alphabetically arranged list

The Question Mark

1. After an interrogative sentence (although the term *interrogative* may not be taught)
2. After a direct quotation in question form

The Quotation Marks

1. In a direct quotation, to set off the exact words of the speaker
2. Around the title of a story or of an article, but not of a book

The Exclamation Point

1. At the end of an exclamatory sentence (although the term *exclamatory* might not be taught)
2. After a single word or group of words that expresses strong feeling

The Apostrophe

1. In a contraction
2. In a possessive noun

The Hyphen

1. Between syllables if a word is divided at the end of the line so that one or more syllables occur at the end of one line and the remaining syllable(s) at the beginning of the next
2. In a compound word, including compound nouns, compound adjectives, compound adverbs, and compound numbers

The Colon

1. In the salutation in a business letter
2. Between the hour and minutes when expressing the time of day, as in 9:30 P.M.

Grade Placement

The needs of the pupils as they participate in a rich, comprehensive program in the language arts should probably be the chief determinant of grade placement. However, only those skills should be taught that are on a difficulty level within the ability of the boys and girls to acquire without undue stress. The following illustrations may be of value in allocating topics to various grade levels.

1. When the first-grade teacher is reading to the boys and girls material from the chalkboard or from a chart as he points to what he is reading—sweeping the hand or a pointer or ruler below the writing while the children watch as they listen—he may at times make reference to the fact that he stops when he sees the period in the sentences on the board. Care should be taken, however, that the boys and girls do not think of all periods as stop signs.

As the boys and girls in the first grade and often in the first half of the second grade dictate stories to the teacher, the teacher frequently supplies whatever punctuation marks or capital letters are needed as, at times, he comments on the forms to which he wishes to draw attention. Occasionally he may ask the class what mark of punctuation to use and why, or where and why to use a capital letter. Since the pupils' sentences ordinarily will be lacking in complexity, only simple uses of capital letters and punctuation marks will be necessary. If some more difficult uses are needed, it is recommended that the teacher supply them without making special reference to them.

In the first grade the child usually is ready to acquire some information as to why capital letters and punctuation marks are used (as *stop* and *go* signs) and as to what are the name and form of the comma, the period, and the question mark. First-grade pupils may be ready to learn these uses of the capital letter:

At the beginning of the sentence
In names of persons, their town or city, the days of the week, and the months
With the word *I*.

Some first-grade pupils can advisedly be helped to learn to use capital letters in writing the name of the avenue or street on which they live as they write their own addresses. Capitalization of names of holidays or other special days can also be noted by first-grade children.

The first-grade pupil usually is ready to learn that a sentence that tells something needs a period at the end while one that asks a question calls for a question mark. At times in this grade boys and girls can well be taught to put periods after figures given in lists when they write lists of words.

2. In the second and third grades it is important to review points taken up in first grade that have not been mastered. Additional points of capitalization that many boys and girls are ready to learn in those grades are the capitalization of:

The names of towns and cities
The first word in the salutation of a letter
Titles like *Mr., Mrs., Dr.*
Initials
Names of countries and states as well as of rivers, lakes, and other geographical terms that they will use in their writing
The first and last words and all "important words" in a title
Words such as *Father, Mother, Sister, Brother Aunt, Uncle* when they are used as names.

The following uses of punctuation marks may be stressed with boys and girls in the second and third grades:

The period with abbreviations and initials and after letters or figures given in outlines
The comma after the greeting in a personal letter; after the closing in a letter; between the date of a month and the year (as a rule); after the name of a city

or town when it is written directly to the left of the name of the state

The exclamation point at the end of an exclamatory sentence and after a single word or group of words not constituting a sentence if it expresses surprise or strong feeling

The apostrophe in a contraction.

As some boys and girls write book reports, they might learn that titles of books when written in longhand or typed should have underlines if they are included in sentences.

3. In grades four, five, and six there should be review of all points that have been studied and not mastered in earlier grades. Sometimes review requires reteaching as well as further practice in making application of what is in the process of being learned. Additional points under "The Program in Capitalization" (page 111) and "The Program in Punctuation" (see page 111), not already introduced in the primary grades, can constitute the new work of these grades.

Methods

The following list of ideas as to methods of teaching needed skills in capitalization and punctuation may suggest others to the reader.

1. The teacher can discuss with the boys and girls the fact that capital letters and punctuation marks are used in order to make it easier for the reader to comprehend what the writer wants to communicate.

2. The teacher or the boys and girls can make a chart showing the chief functions of punctuation marks.

3. In the intermediate grades the teacher can help pupils note how at times punctuation makes a decided difference in the meaning of sentences. He can give illustrations such as the following for discussion as to meaning and he can encourage the boys and girls to make up other sentences for presentation to the class.

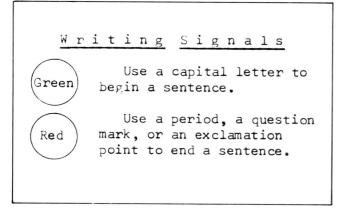

Figure 5.13. Writing Signals for the Lower Grades.

My brother who is away at college will not be able to come home for Mother's Day.

My brother, who is away at college, will not be able to come home for Mother's Day.

Susan said, "My brother is sick."

"Susan," said my brother, "is sick."

4. The class can make a handbook of rules for capitalization and punctuation that they have learned.

5. As the pupils in the lower-primary grades dictate stories or reports to the teacher while he supplies the needed capitalization and punctuation, the teacher can at times comment on his use of capital letters or ask questions concerning the need for capitalization. As he uses punctuation marks he can similarly ask questions and make comments.

6. Under the guidance of the teacher the pupils can examine books to note certain uses of capital letters and punctuation marks.

7. As boys and girls begin doing their own recording of their thoughts (rather than dictating them to the teacher), the teacher can make himself available to answer questions about capitalization and punctuation as well as about other points about which boys and girls may wish to ask him. He can also help the children individually as they examine their stories or reports for possible errors, those in capitalization and punctuation included.

8. For correction by the class the teacher can copy on the chalkboard sentences containing errors in capitalization and punctuation taken from a set of papers written by the boys and girls in the class.

9. The pupils can give reasons for use of capital letters and punctuation marks in sentences, stories, reports, or letters in textbooks. Only those uses of capital letters and punctuation marks that the boys and girls have studied should be discussed unless a pupil volunteers or asks for information on others.

10. The pupils can read about the uses of capital letters and of various marks of punctuation recorded in their textbooks or on duplicated sheets of paper. Discussion and application of what was read should follow.

11. The boys and girls can be guided so as to "discover" some of the uses of punctuation marks. For example, the teacher might have on a chart, on the chalkboard, or on duplicated sheets of paper, a series of sentences illustrating the uses of the comma with words of address. Sentences such as these might be used, illustrating a comma after the name of the person addressed, a comma before the name of the person addressed, and a comma before and after the name:

Dave, where are you going?

Where are you going, Dave?

Where, Dave, are you going?

If several sentences illustrating each of these three ways

of punctuating the name of the person addressed are included in the list, the boys and girls could be encouraged to see if they can "discover" how to punctuate sentences in which the name of a person addressed is used.

12. The pupils can take responsibility for helping one another in proofreading. However, it is recommended that, as a rule, the writer himself proofread his work before he asks someone else to help him in the task.

13. Pupils who need practice on some uses of capital letters or punctuation marks, beyond that furnished by their own writing, can do exercises in textbooks or on duplicated sheets.

A Teaching Plan

The following plan, slightly modified, was written by a former college student Judith Huehl Scholtz. It shows methods that can be used to teach, through a combination of the inductive and deductive methods, how to punctuate telling and asking sentences. The writer of the plan assumed that the boys and girls, with whom the plan might be followed, are in the second year of elementary school and that they have had work on the difference between sentences and sentence fragments and between telling and asking sentences.

A. *Pupils Aim:* To find out what mark of punctuation to use at the end of a telling and of an asking sentence

B. *Materials:*
   1. Board work
      a. Exercise I (Sentences to illustrate telling and asking sentences)
         (1) Where is John?
         (2) My dog is big.
         (3) What is in this box?
         (4) Jack is in the house.
      b. Diagram in which to record punctuation marks in the development of the generalization

Telling	Asking

      c. Exercise II (Sentences for oral practice in which the punctuation is already given)
         (1) My mittens are red.
         (2) What is your name?
         (3) I like to play in the snow.
         (4) Can you swim?
         (5) Will you come to my party?
         (6) I live near a lake.
         (7) Jim lives near a river.
         (8) What did Anne draw?
         (9) When is your birthday?
         (10) Bob wrote a story about dogs.

      d. Exercise III (Sentences for group practice in which pupils need to supply the end punctuation marks)
         (1) Did you see my shoes
         (2) The girls sang two songs
         (3) We wrote letters today
         (4) Where were you
         (5) I helped make lunch
         (6) Can you help me
         (7) What should I do
         (8) Sally painted this picture
         (9) Who made this puppet
         (10) Did you make it
      e. Directions for Exercise III
         (1) Read the sentence orally.
         (2) Tell what kind of sentence it is.
         (3) Tell what punctuation mark is needed.
         (4) Place the punctuation mark at the end of the sentence.
   2. Duplicated copies of sentences for Exercise IV, numbered, for written practice in which pupils supply the end punctuation marks

Jim runs to school	(telling, asking)
Is it raining now	(telling, asking)
Are you going for a walk	(telling, asking)
Mary likes to play ball	(telling, asking)
What is your dog's name	(telling, asking)
I went swimming today	(telling, asking)
My book is at school	(telling, asking)
Where do you live	(telling, asking)
I saw your mother	(telling, asking)
Did you see her	(telling, asking)

C. *Procedure:*
   1. Introduction
      a. The teacher explains that some boys and girls have had difficulty knowing what punctuation mark to use at the end of a telling sentence and at the end of an asking sentence.
      b. The teacher states that today he is going to help them find out what punctuation mark to use at the end of a telling and of an asking sentence.
      c. The teacher tells the class that at the end of the class period he will give each pupil a list of sentences for which he hopes everyone will be able to give the correct ending punctuation mark. (See Exercise IV, C-2.)
   2. Preparation
      a. The teacher states that the class will now review when a sentence is a telling sentence and when it is an asking sentence.
      b. The pupils tell whether the sentences on the

chalkboard in Exercise I are telling sentences or asking sentences. (See *B-l-a.*)

(1) Report on the first sentence
  (a) A pupil reads the sentence orally.
  (b) The pupil tells whether it is a telling or an asking sentence.

(2) Report on sentences 2 through 4
  The pupils follow a procedure like that of (*l*) above.

3. Development of the generalization
  a. Study of sentences in Exercise I (see *B-l-a*) in order to fill out the diagram (see *B-l-b.*)
    (1) Work on first sentence
      (a) A pupil again tells what kind of sentence it is—telling or asking.
      (b) Another pupil tells what mark of punctuation is given at the end of the sentence.
      (c) The teacher records in the diagram under *Asking,* the number of the sentence (namely *l*) and places a question mark to the right of the number.
    (2) Work on sentences 2 through 4
      The class follows a procedure like that for (*l*) above.
  b. Summarizing the work on the exercise
    (1) A pupil tells, as the teacher points to the diagram, what mark of punctuation was used to end each telling sentence in the exercise.
    (2) A pupil tells, as the teacher points to the diagram, what mark of punctuation was used to end each asking sentence in the exercise.
  c. Stating the generalization
    (1) By the teacher
      (a) The teacher states that a period is usually used to end a telling sentence.
      (b) The teacher states that a question mark is used to end an asking sentence.
    (2) By the pupils
      Several pupils state the generalization.

4. Group work on Exercise II (see *B-l-c*) and Exercise III (*B-l-d.*)
  a. Work on Exercise II
    (l) Work on the first sentence
      (a) A pupil reads the sentence orally.
      (b) The pupil tells whether the sentence is a telling or asking sentence.
      (c) The pupil tells why the punctuation mark that was used, was needed.

(2) Work on sentences 2 through 10
  Pupils follow a procedure like that for (*l*) above.
  b. Work on Exercise III (see *B-l-d.*)
    (1) Work on the first sentence
      (a) A pupil reads the sentence orally.
      (b) The pupil tells whether the sentence is a telling or an asking sentence.
      (c) The pupil tells what mark of punctuation is needed to end the sentence.
      (d) The pupil places the punctuation mark at the end of the sentence.
    (2) Work on sentences 2 through 10
      The pupils read the directions to be followed (see *B-l-e*) and then follow them.

5. Written work using Exercise IV (see *B-2.*)
  a. The teacher states that the pupils will read each sentence silently, draw a line under the word *telling* or *asking* to show what type of sentence it is, and place the needed punctuation mark where it belongs.
  b. The class together do the first sentence.
    (1) The pupils read the sentence silently.
    (2) The pupils draw a circle around the correct word in parentheses that shows what kind of sentence it is.
    (3) One pupil tells around which word, *telling* or *asking,* he drew a circle.
    (4) The pupils place the correct punctuation mark at the end of the sentence.
    (5) One pupil tells what punctuation mark he placed at the end of the sentence.
  c. All pupils do the second sentence on their paper.
  d. A pupil tells around which word, *telling* or *asking,* he drew a circle in the second sentence and what punctuation mark he placed at the end of the sentence.
  e. The pupils complete the exercise individually, excepting as the teacher helps those pupils who he decided might need more help.
  f. The class checks the papers.

6. Forward look
  The teacher suggests that the pupils check all telling and asking sentences that they write to make certain they are using the correct punctuation marks.

CREATIVE WRITING

What is creative writing? If we define creative writing as any writing that shows originality of thought, expression, or organization, much so-called practical writing can be considered, in part, creative. Obviously there is then a great range in what can be classified as creative writing. A letter, for example, which is usually thought of as an example of practical writing, is not necessarily devoid of characteristics of creative writing if we specify originality as criterion for creative writing. In a sense, one well-chosen word that truly reveals a sincere inner thought from the writer is evidence of creativity. Thus, although in this book, for purposes of clarity of presentation, a division has been made into practical and creative writing—designating as creative the writing that is not primarily for practical purposes—it should be borne in mind that no clear line of demarcation can be drawn to establish a discrete dichotomy. (The reader is referred to a discussion on "Creativity in the Language Arts," which begins on page 40.)

Courtesy of the Harris Elementary School, Austin, Texas.

Figure 5.14. Creative Writing Can Be Stimulated.

Values to Be Derived from Creative Writing

Some of the values of creative writing are the same as those that can be suggested for all constructive types of creativity for boys and girls. Important among the significant purposes that creative writing can serve are the following:

1. It can be a means of self-expression, with the accompanying release to the writers.

2. It can help in meeting some of the other innate needs of the boys and girls (in addition to that of self-expression).

3. It can prove to be a happy leisure-time activity.

4. It can give a start to boys and girls who have literary talent that should be developed.

5. It can serve as motivation for reading worthwhile material.

6. It can furnish practice in applying and therefore enforcing language arts skills (even though that should not be a major purpose for creative writing.)

7. It may serve as a means by which the teacher can get insight into the joys, the sorrows, the hopes, and the fears of some of his pupils.

8. It can make school seem and be more worthwhile to some of the boys and girls.

Guidelines

In our discussion of "Encouragement of Creativity" (see page 41) we have already given consideration to several points that apply to all types of creativity—not only to creative writing. Let us now turn our attention to points that apply specifically to creativity in writing.

When the reader studies the points in the paragraphs to follow, he should bear in mind that many of the suggestions given have not been established by research. In the field of the arts it is difficult to come to scientific evaluation of many of the questions of procedure. But in practice the teacher cannot wait to have many points established scientifically. He must proceed according to his weighted decisions in the light of the best evidence available. It is from this point of view that he should read the following discussion.

1. *Exposure to good literature can serve as a means of stimulating interest in and development of ability in doing creative writing.* Telling and reading stories of literary merit but yet on the level of the children's comprehension and appreciation can arouse an interest in the pupils to write their own stories and poems or even their own "books." Ways of stimulating a child in this manner are discussed under "Writing Prose" beginning on page 119, and suggestions for interesting him in writing poetry are recorded under "Writing Poetry" beginning on page 120.

2. *Boys and girls can be stimulated to creative writing through exposure to writing done by their peers.* Such exposure can be made through: (a) reading by the teacher to the class poetry or prose written by some of the pupils; (b) reading by boys and girls to their peers some of their creative work; (c) reading to the class by the teacher poetry or prose written by pupils in other schools; (d) posting on the bulletin board or placing in a notebook stories or poems written by members of the class or by boys and girls in other schools.

3. *A pupil's creative work should not be made available to others without his full consent.* Before a teacher reads to the rest of the class or makes available the copy of a pupil's creative writing, he should make certain that the writer has no objection. Furthermore, he should not

make the child feel that he ought to read his own work to his classmates unless he wants to do so. His writing should not be published in a school or community publication or in a magazine without the writer's consent. However, at times the teacher can influence a reticent pupil whose original reaction was against sharing his writing so that he is willing to have it shown if the teacher explains to him that he believes others will enjoy it. But the final decision must come from the child. Before using a story or poem for a children's magazine published commercially, the consent of one of the parents should also be secured.

4. *There are advantages and disadvantages in displaying a pupil's creative writing even when the child is willing, in fact, even if he is pleased, to make his writing available to others.* Advantages are rather evident. Such practice may encourage the child who lacks confidence, may give others needed exposure to writing by peers, may encourage the writer to write more stories or poems, and may stimulate others to write. However, the advantages need to be carefully weighed with possible disadvantages such as the following: (a) The writer may develop a tendency to become set at his present level of writing if considerable attention is given to something that he has written. (b) When the writer is not given similar publicity at other times, he may become discouraged. (c) The writer may get more joy from the publicity than from the expression of creativity he has experienced. (d) The writer may become more interested in writing for the honor than for the sake of expressing his thoughts. (e) It may be discouraging to others in the room if their writing does not receive publicity, especially when there may develop a tendency to put emphasis on "publication" rather than on expression of what one thinks.

5. *Boys and girls should not be forced to do creative writing.* The arts do not flourish at command. However, the child can often be guided gently so that he will want to participate in creative writing. No assignment should be made requiring every boy and girl to write a story or poem. After careful motivation for creative writing, the children who want to write a story or poem may be invited to go to one part of the room while others are allowed to perform other activities that will not interfere with the writers. Hopefully boys and girls who at first were not in the writers' group may, of their own free will, ask if they may join it.

6. *The main emphasis in the first draft of creative writing should be on content rather than form.* Observance of this guideline is particularly important in the early stages of learning to write when much emphasis on form can easily interfere with needed attention to ideas. When making his first draft the child should feel free to record his thoughts as they come to him, without stopping to look up a word in a dictionary or ask for the spelling of it. If he plans to read a story or poem to others, however, he should check his first draft in order to note whether he has expressed himself as best he can. Furthermore, if he intends to have others read his story, he should also do editing for capitalization, punctuation, handwriting, spelling, and desired neatness of paper. In most cases such editing will probably require rewriting the paper before it is shown to others.

While needed emphasis on perfecting a pupil's form in writing should be placed on that skill when the child does practical writing and when he makes a second draft of creative writing, there is probably also a relationship that should be noted between form and content even in the first draft of creative writing. While a pupil should not be restricted in his first draft through overattention to form, he can nevertheless be encouraged even then to write as best he can without undue concentration on form. There is no virtue but there is possible harm in jotting down points in the first draft, for example, without spelling words to the best of the pupil's ability.

7. *Evaluation of creative writing should be done with care.* Here are a few points to observe in terms of evaluation of creative writing.

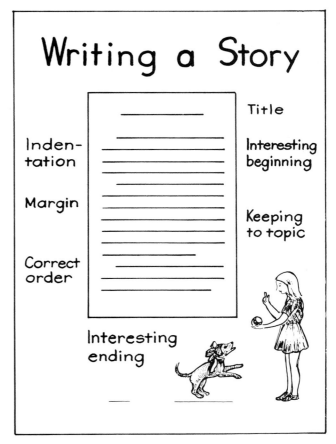

Figure 5.15. Illustrated Checklist Serving as Means of Evaluation.

The teacher should not insist on reading all creative writing done by the boys and girls. If a child does not want to show his writing to the teacher, his wishes should be respected.

Frequently if a story or poem is to be shown to others at the discretion of the writer, the teacher may help the pupil correct his writing after he has made all corrections that he can without assistance.

Making many revisions of creative writing usually is not as profitable as spending time that might be used for such rewriting, on further writing in which the child tries to improve upon former writing.

The teacher should be very tactful in criticisms that he makes on any creative writing.

There are dangers involved in criticisms by peers— sometimes more serious than when given by the teacher. Consequently criticism by classmates should be used with caution.

The teacher should guard against high praise for any piece of creative writing. If too much praise is given, the child may feel, by contrast, discouraged at times when he does not receive it. Furthermore, there is always danger that he may then begin writing for recognition rather than for self-expression.

8. *There is probably a close relationship between creative writing and creativity in other areas.* While many people can not express themselves with satisfaction in various forms of art, it would seem that participation, either vicariously or firsthand, in some creative activities other than writing may serve as means of stimulating growth in writing. This relationship may be due, in part, to the release of tension afforded by any form of self-expression, which in turn may affect happily further self-expression.

9. *Through guidance in becoming more observant boys and girls can develop in ability to do creative writing.* Their attention may be drawn to things of beauty such as a sunrise or sunset, a snowflake, the patter of rain, the designs of Jack Frost, the murmur of a stream, the strength of massive machinery, or the majesty of the mountains. In fact, the pupils may to advantage be helped to become more aware of all types of environmental factors, including the concrete and the abstract, the feelings of people, the cause and effect of various circumstances.

10. *Boys and girls who are helped to express themselves more clearly are likely to make progress in creative writing.* One reason for lack of a high level of creativity undoubtedly is the paucity of thoughts to be expressed. Another is scarcity of words at the command of the pupils with which to express adequately the thoughts that they have.

11. *Frequently boys and girls reveal their inner lives through writing.* This revelation can be made, of course,

in part through direct statement of their feelings as they write on topics such as "The Subject I Like Best" or "An Embarrassing Moment." In many instances the affective nature of an individual is shown more clearly through writing that is not on the surface as self-revealing as it gives the impression of being. As boys and girls write about others, often in fanciful tales, the problems and difficulties they themselves experience are, at times, indicated. Frequently, conditions the opposite of those bothering a child are pictured in his writing. The child who is being wounded by lack of love from his parents may reveal his soul by means of a heroine who is showered profusely with love not only from her parents but also from others. The writer may express his hunger for love in his own thwarted life, with its almost inevitable accompaniment of animosity, by picturing a child-dominated situation. In cases in which the creative writing taps the often hidden consistent desires of a child it may give him some release and help him solve his problem in part. Furthermore, through wise guidance the child can at times be helped to overcome some feelings of "hurt" that he harbors. While therapy in circumstances such as this when poorly done can do more harm than good, nevertheless, as in the case of bibliotherapy and other types of therapy for healing personalities, when approached cautiously and with understanding, it can be truly therapeutic.

12. *The optimum method of motivation for creative writing varies greatly from one individual to another.* One person may be stimulated to write a poem because the teacher read one to the class. Another may get the idea for his writing from a casually made remark. Still another may be inspired to write following a class discussion of the plight of wild geese that on their southward migration were deterred for hours when confused by the bright lights of a city over which their flight had been "scheduled."

13. *Patience is a requisite for guiding boys and girls in the development of abilities in creative writing.* Often the beginning of true creativity in writing seems slow. The results at first may seem, to the casual eye, less desirable than the concise statements written by boys and girls who are doing not much more than following directions as they write on topics such as "How I Spent My Vacation." Growth that is inner often does not show up outwardly for a long time. Impatience on the part of the teacher may block a child's flow of free expression possibly forever.

14. *Thinking is an integral part of creative writing.* If the teacher wishes to help children grow in ability to do creative writing, he should stimulate their thinking. However, no time should be set aside for stimulation of thought; a "thinking period" would further add to the clutter of periods found in the daily schedule of some

classrooms. Boys and girls, instead, should be helped to think through real problems arising during the school day.

15. *The teacher who wishes to help boys and girls in creative work should expose himself to conditions that make him more creative.* In order to guide boys and girls in creative work, it is not enough for the teacher to have knowledge of and apply methods for guiding them in doing creative writing. If he will write some poetry or do some creative writing in prose form (maybe for inspection by no one else), he may be better able to understand the trials, tribulations, and joys that boys and girls experience when they write. Should the teacher, however, decide not to try creative writing, at least he should read good literature so that he can develop a deeper appreciation of it, which in turn should make him better able to guide boys and girls in creative writing.

Writing Prose

The guidelines stated on the preceding pages apply equally to writing poetry and prose. Let us now pay special attention to means of guiding growth, first in writing prose and then in writing poetry. As the reader examines the suggestions, he should keep in mind that there is disagreement among educators as to the best means of cultivating creativity in writing. Consequently he will need to exercise discrimination in his observance of the points suggested below.

1. The pupils may note interesting legends for bulletin boards or captions for pictures, discuss them, and then make up and evaluate some for other bulletin boards on which pictures are posted.

2. The class and the teacher may discuss differences and likenesses between creative and practical writing.

3. The children can select from various types of practical writing some sentences or groups of sentences that make that part of the writing creative because it expresses the writer's own feelings or thoughts.

4. The pupils may copy words or groups of words in selections of practical writing that show various signs of creativity for inclusion in a notebook or for posting on a bulletin board.

5. The class may listen to and read myths and then draw up, with the help of the teacher, characteristics of the myth. Next they may suggest topics for original myths such as "What Happened to the Rabbit's Tail."

Courtesy of (Educational Communications Department) Prince George's County Public Schools, Prince George's County, Maryland.

Figure 5.16. Aids to Creativity.

Thereupon some boys and girls may write myths and then be willing to read their production to the class. The original myths can be placed in a class notebook on fanciful tales, or can be included in each writer's own collection of original writings.

6. The class may listen to and read fables and then decide on differentiating characteristics of the fable.

7. Some of the children may write fables and then read them to the class or use them for inclusion in a class notebook on fables or in an individual notebook on creative writing.

8. The members of the class may compile a list of proverbs and then read them to each other, with possible discussion of some.

9. The boys and girls may make up stories about pictures that suggest topics for good stories. Near a picture posted on a bulletin board may be stimulating questions such as: (a) Why do you think Jack looks worried? (b) What do you think his sister will suggest that he do? Or the caption above a group of pictures may be "What Stories Do You See in These Pictures?"

Figure 5.17. Pictures as Motivation for Creative Writing.

10. After the boys and girls have read a series of "tall tales" and have discussed outstanding characteristics of the "tall tale," they may like to make a list of topics about which "tall tales" can be written, such as "Paul Bunyan's Dressmaker" or "Porky the Porcupine Tells a 'Tall Tale.' "

11. After reading and hearing some puzzles or riddles, the boys and girls can be helped to draw up a list of

criteria for judging them. Among these might be cleverness, appropriateness (excluding the cheap), brevity, and plausibility of the answer. Then the pupils may make up puzzles and riddles of their own. An interesting bulletin board can be made with a legend such as "Who Knows the Answer?" An illustration of a boy or girl scratching her head could be given near the list of riddles or puzzles. Provision should be made for supplying the readers with the answers, probably on a separate sheet of paper. A collection properly edited could be sent to a member of the class absent because of illness.

12. Boys and girls can show originality in writing various types of greeting cards—for Thanksgiving, Christmas, Easter, Mother's Day, and Father's Day.

13. Occasionally the teacher may announce to the class that he is going to tell a story he made up. Sometimes he may stop at a crucial point and let the boys and girls suggest different endings. He may write the part of the story he told and then, with possible endings recorded by boys and girls, place it on the reading table in a folder on which are written the words, "Which Ending Do You Prefer?"

14. The boys and girls may draw up a list of points to observe when writing stories such as: (a) Decide what you want to write about, about whom your story will be, where it will take place, how you will start it, what interesting or exciting things will happen, how you will end it. (b) Put your thoughts into writing. (c) Read the story silently (or if possible, orally to yourself) to see whether you have told it in the best way you can. (d) If you plan to let others read your story or if you intend to keep it, correct it for any errors in writing and in many cases rewrite it. (e) If you wish ask your readers or listeners for suggestions for improvement.

15. In the lower grades the teacher may record the "make-up stories" suggested by boys and girls. A child should feel free to ask his teacher to serve as his scribe. With the young child or the one who has no more skill in storytelling than the young child, the teacher may wish to take down verbatim what he says without asking him to make any improvements before the teacher makes a record of his thoughts. Then the teacher may himself edit the work or he may have the child help in improving it as the teacher reads it. The pupil may also be asked to help with capitalization and punctuation as the teacher asks questions such as this: "Why did I put a question mark after the sentence 'Would you like to go with me?' "

16. At times the teacher may find it wise to record the endings for stories at the dictation of boys and girls. For example, when a pupil who is still finding it difficult to manipulate the mechanics of writing has written the first part of his story and then is too tired to finish it or finds it too exacting to complete it alone, the teacher may offer to serve as scribe for the rest of his story. By so doing, the

teacher may keep the child from writing an ending that is so abrupt that it displeases the child and may cause him to lose interest in future creative writing.

17. Diaries can serve as expression of creativity. To be sure, diaries can also be thought of as practical writing. However, when they show originality, they can well be classified as creative writing. The boys and girls may read selections from diaries and discuss with the teacher the important characteristics of well-kept diaries. They should be helped to see the importance of dating the entries. They should recognize the fact that unless a diary is about interesting or significant points or serves as an interpretation of the writer's feelings or thoughts, it is often not worth keeping. Boys and girls may wish to write diaries of their own or, as a class project, want to keep a diary of important happenings in the room, or decide to write diaries of people such as: (a) a girl who came with the Pilgrims to Plymouth in 1620 or (b) a child who is taking an imaginary trip through a country about which the boys and girls are studying. If the diary deals with a period of history or a far-off land, the boys and girls should have enough background for writing so that the diary does not help make permanent the erroneous conceptions the writer may otherwise have.

18. Sometimes after boys and girls have shown great enjoyment of a story character such as Doctor Dolittle, Winnie the Pooh, Mole (in *The Wind in the Willows*), or Miss Hickory, they might suggest additional experiences that such characters might have and write stories reporting on these adventures.

19. The teacher may encourage the pupils to report when they have written a story they would like to share with the class. Such stories might be submitted for consideration for reading by being placed in a box entitled "Our Very Own Stories."

20. Sometimes boys and girls who do not do creative writing alone are encouraged if for a while they can have a partner in their writing. Some types of writing lend themselves better to such cooperation than others. An imaginary diary of a young page during the feudal ages is one example. Before the partners start writing, they should have acquired considerable information about that period of history; they should have discussed important points they wish to include in the diary and the moods that they wish to portray; they should have an outline; and they should have decided who will write the various entries. After each child has done his individual writing, the two should read the entire diary carefully to determine needed changes.

Writing Poetry

The reader is referred to page 116 for guidelines for helping children write both prose and poetry, since the suggestions that follow are supplementary to those given there. Furthermore, a number of the ideas presented under "Writing Prose" (see page 119) can also, with or without modification, be applied to writing poetry. To them, too, the attention of the reader is directed.

Methods. In connection with the following suggestions for the teacher, of methods for guiding children's growth in writing poetry, it must be remembered that the teacher should not try to force his pupils to write poetry.

1. Introduce the boys and girls to writing poetry by reading it to them frequently.

2. Provide the boys and girls with opportunity to read poetry orally to themselves and their classmates.

3. Before reading a poem to the class, as a rule, prepare the audience for appreciation of it.

4. After a poem has been read to the class, frequently give the audience opportunity to read it themselves, possibly to find lines that they may like particularly well, to note how the poet states a certain point, or to find out to what he compares something. Sometimes the teacher may wish to have the boys and girls read orally the lines that appeal to them in particular.

5. Encourage the boys and girls to look for words or groups of words in poems they read by themselves that are particularly expressive, picturesque, beautiful, or imaginative. The teacher may give them the opportunity at times to show or read these selections to the class. The pupils may want to keep the quotations as a class or individual collection.

6. After reading limericks to the class and showing them copies of some, help the pupils work out the pattern and rhyme scheme of the limerick. The pupils may either as a class or individually make endings for a limerick of which they are given the first two lines. Some might be encouraged to try to write limericks of their own.

7. While the pupils are on a walk to see different signs of fall, encourage them to speak of what they are seeing. Then when they return to the classroom, they may be given a chance to continue their conversation and the teacher may record some of the words used in describing signs of fall. As the teacher is writing on the chalkboard or on a piece of newsprint, the pupils could be encouraged to give not only expressions that they had already used in their conversation but also additional interesting ones that tell how they feel. Thereupon the teacher might tell the class that he plans to use some of their expressions in a poem that he will write. Possibly the following day the teacher will want to read the poem to the class and give each child a copy on which are underlined all the expressions received from the class. The next time when boys and girls have an experience to which they wish to react poetically, such as a walk through newly-fallen snow, they can again dictate to the teacher ex-

pressions that are symbolic of a suggested mood or idea. The children who wish to write a poem on the experience may be invited to use any of these expressions in their poems.

8. Give the boys and girls suggestions such as these as to steps in writing a poem by themselves: (a) Think of some idea or act or feeling about which you would like to write a poem. (b) Think of what you would like to say about the topic. (c) Jot down your thoughts in note form without paying any attention to rhyme. (d) Revamp what you have recorded so that it is in poetry form, either rhyming or not rhyming.

9. Discuss with the class characteristics of a fine poem. The pupils then can note how these characteristics are exemplified in various poems.

10. When in free play or other spontaneous activities you find that a child starts singing, making up words to accompany his actions, jot down at times the words he is saying. The teacher may show the song to the composer and at times, if he readily consents, to the rest of the class.

11. Provide various rhythmic experiences for boys and girls such as being in a band or listening to one, so as to develop their natural sense of rhythm. However, the teacher should guard against beginning experiences in poetry writing by beating out the rhythm of poems for fear that the result would be a set of stilted jingles in which the emotional quality is lacking. When boys and girls have had considerable experience in writing poetry without special attention to rhythmic pattern, they can at times profit from explanation and demonstration of various rhythmic designs. They can then discuss the importance of suiting the pattern of rhythm to the mood to be portrayed.

12. Introduce the boys and girls to simple rhyme schemes—the couplet, the triplet, and the quatrain— and help them discover which lines rhyme. In some instances the teacher may wish to introduce older boys and girls to some types of poetry forms that do not rhyme such as the Japanese haiku, tanku, and senryu described by Nina Willis Walter in her delightful and informative book *Let Them Write Poetry.*

13. Help boys and girls realize the economical manner in which words are used in poetry by asking them to express in prose some thoughts given in poetry and to state in poetry some recorded as prose.

14. Help boys and girls determine which of a group of poems written by persons whom they do not know, either children or adults, merely give an image and which go farther in that they also tell how the writer feels concerning that about which he is writing.

15. Encourage the pupils to look for beauty. They can discuss things of beauty in the room, using as appropriate words to describe them as they can. They can

also report on beauty they have experienced outside of school. The boys and girls can be encouraged to go beyond the concrete in their appreciation as they note circumstances such as these: (a) an older sister tenderly helping a young child after his tumble, (b) a mother singing a lullaby to her baby.

16. Encourage the pupils to collect pictures or objects of beauty that may inspire someone to write a poem. A brief discussion of a few possibilities for stimulating poetic expression, such as a shell or a picture of the starry heavens, may at times be appropriate.

17. Encourage the children who would like to illustrate a poem that they have heard or read to do so. Those who wish may first draw a picture of how they feel about something and then "draw" that picture in the words of poetry.

18. Discuss points such as these with older boys and girls: (a) the importance of selecting words that state the thought concisely; (b) the fact that a poet needs to show originality either in the topic selected or in handling an old topic in a new way; (c) the undesirability of awkwardness in sentence structure; (d) the desirability of avoiding the use of overworked expressions or slang (unless the slang is used in a direct quotation); (e) the fact that all poetry does not rhyme.

19. Through explanation, class discussion, study of models, and copying of poems by the pupils, help them acquire knowledge of these points concerning the appearance of poetry on paper: (a) Free verse is often not indented. (b) Indentation in poems that rhyme is not required. (c) Lines that rhyme should have the same margin.

20. Help the pupils acquire inductively generalizations such as these about rhyming, listed in *Let Them Write Poetry* by Nina Willis Walter.

> Except in a tercet, do not have more than two successive lines rhyming.
>
> Avoid near rhymes, such as *home* and *alone,* and rhymes identical in sound, such as *see* and *sea.*
>
> Rhymes should not be more than two lines apart.
>
> Do not use the same rhyme more than once in a short poem, unless the poem has a refrain.
>
> Do not use forced rhymes, twisting words out of their meaning for the sake of rhyme or saying things awkwardly in order to make the rhymes come out right.[1]

21. Encourage the boys and girls to memorize poetry. Some poems can well be memorized by the entire class as a group project. Others, selected by an individual as

---

1. Nina Willis Walter, *Let Them Write Poetry.* (Holt, Rinehart and Winston, Inc., 1962), pp. 122-29, and pp. 139-140. Used by permission of Holt, Rinehart and Winston.

some that he would like in this repertoire, could be studied without participation by the rest of the group in the memorization process. Regardless of whether the memorization of poetry is a group or individual undertaking, certain specifications or regulations should be kept in mind, among them the following:

Memorization of poetry should not be looked upon as a chore, but as a pleasurable activity.

Boys and girls should be helped to realize the value of having "at their fingertips," stored in memory, some poems of beauty and strength.

Poems memorized by the group as a whole should be of appeal to the class and they should be worth memorizing.

Through class memorization of a poem, boys and girls should get suggestions for possible economical procedure in memorizing poetry on their own. As a rule, the procedure for studying the poem is first to look at the work as a whole, then pay attention to parts of it, and finally study it again as a whole. It is a method recommended by those favoring the whole-part-whole method of learning, which many would claim more economical than the part method. The fact that there are individual differences among boys and girls in optimum methods of study should, however, be recognized. A further complication in making use of the whole-part-whole procedure is that the length of a selection that may be a "whole" or a "part" to one child may not be that for another.

22. Give the boys and girls opportunity to do choral speaking of poetry. (For a discussion of choral speaking, the reader is referred to page 310.)

Exhibit of Poetry. One way in which boys and girls can be encouraged to write poetry is by suitable display of poems written by the pupils or by others. Care should be taken that pupils are not strongly urged and never forced to share their original writing with others. Care also needs to be taken to avoid dangers in exhibiting children's poetry even when the writers are willing to share their poems with others.

Here are some suggestions for display of poems.

1. Have in the room interesting-looking books of poetry with, at times, one or more on special display.

2. Post poems, sometimes groups of poems, on a bulletin board. There may be a picture to illustrate the poetry, drawn by the pupil or otherwise obtained, together with a challenging legend written on the bulletin board.

3. Copy a poem, if it is short, on the chalkboard, possibly in a section entitled "Our Poems" or "Do You Like This Poem?" The latter caption should not be used when the poem was written by someone in the class.

4. On the first "page" of an accordionlike folder post a poem and on the succeeding "pages" let the pupils illustrate parts of the poem. The words illustrating a picture could be written near it.

5. Encourage pupils to make individual collections of their poetry and possibly to illustrate it. The collection could be kept in a notebook or in a card file.

6. If you have a class or school paper, consider some of the poems for inclusion in it.

7. Help the class compile a notebook for display on the reading table containing a favorite poem by each pupil in the room. Children are interested in having the name of the person who chose each poem indicated in writing.

8. Help the class keep a notebook in which they record interesting expressions of poetic quality said or written by boys and girls in the room.

9. Make or help one or more pupils construct a poster on which a poem is written, with illustrations to accompany some of the lines of the poem. The lines illustrated could be rewritten near each picture.

10. Encourage the pupils to write poems for their father or mother for Christmas, Easter, Mother's Day, Father's Day, their mother's birthday, or their father's birthday.

11. Help the boys and girls in making a class book, even possibly for publication.

Illustrative Situations for Encouraging Creative Writing

The descriptions of illustrative teaching-learning situations given below supplement suggestions given earlier in this chapter.

Making a Class Book of Creative Writings. A very interesting and worthwhile project in which a class could engage is that of making an illustrated book of creative writings. Any teacher planning to guide his pupils in making one is advised to examine that gem of children's writing, the book entitled *Children's Voices* by Bertha Roberts and A.T. Beckman, published by Silver Burdett Company. It is valuable for the teacher not only because it gives excellent samples of children's writings but also because it indicates procedures followed by the authors in stimulating their pupils to creative endeavor.

Content of a book. A class book on children's creative expression could be made on any grade level, first through sixth, and beyond. It could contain:

1. Original stories

2. Original poems

3. Expressive sentences a pupil has given orally or in written form, recorded as a child talked or copied from his written work

4. Picturesque or otherwise expressive groups of

words, similes among them, that a pupil has used orally or in writing

5. Illustrations, including pictures children have drawn or painted or photographs of sculpture made by the children correlating with their written expression

6. Notes for music that pupils have composed representative of various moods, some possibly to accompany poems or illustrations

7. An introduction in which the pupils summarize their creative activities

8. An essay or several in which children express some of their ideas on creative writing.

Motivation. To interest boys and girls in making a book of their creative writings the teacher may wish to use one or more of the following ideas:

1. He may save some of the pupils' writings before he approaches the class with the thought that they may wish to put their writings into book form. When he has made a small collection of their writings, he may present the idea of a class book to the boys and girls. The enthusiasm of a good teacher will probably be enough to generate it on the part of the pupils.

2. He may read to the class poems written by boys and girls in other schools and then suggest that they may wish to keep a record of their creative work.

3. He may tell the boys and girls about the book *Children's Voices,* to which reference is made earlier in this section, and state that he thinks the class could write a good book, too.

4. He may discuss with the pupils purposes that can be served by a class book containing their creative work such as: (a) getting enjoyment out of it themselves; (b) giving pleasure to their parents when they have a chance to read the book; (c) leaving the book for the pupils who will be in their room the following year.

Suggestions for procedure. Here are a few additional ideas:

1. Since a class book that contained all the creative writings of all the pupils in a classroom would probably be too voluminous and too lacking in selectivity to accomplish its purpose, each pupil might make an individual notebook patterned after that of the class book. In it he could keep all of his creative writing and illustrations that he wants to save, including copies of any of his that are part of the class book.

2. The boys and girls can make a table of contents for the class book and the individual books.

3. All written work should be carefully proofread before copied for inclusion in the books.

4. The books should be neatly and attractively done so that they are a joy to behold.

5. A looseleaf notebook arrangement of some type is the best unless writing of the final copy and making the

illustrations are not begun until all the material has been submitted and the sequence of the contents of the book has been determined.

6. While a desirable ground rule is that each pupil's work should be represented in the book, nothing should be included in the book that the writer or illustrator does not want in it.

Writing an Autobiography. Some of the fifth-grade classes with which the author of this book has worked have responded with marked enthusiasm to the idea of writing their autobiographies. Before anything is said about writing their own biographies, the pupils can write a report on topics such as "My Pet" or "A Joke on Me." Then the idea can be suggested, by the teacher, of writing a collection of reports that with the one already written could be included in the booklet. The pupils can help select topics for subsequent writing. Topics such as these can be suggested: (a) My Family, (b) My First Day at School, (c) An Exciting Day, or (d) A Book I Like. While topics can be suggested by the group, each pupil can be encouraged to select his own titles—titles less prosaic than the wording of the topics. When quite a number of reports have been written, proofread, and, if necessary to maintain a high standard, rewritten, each pupil can arrange his in suitable order, write a table of contents for his booklet, and make the covers for it. On the front cover the pupils can write the title of the book, such as *About Me* or *The Story of My Life.* Pupils can illustrate their reports with pictures they draw, appropriate pictures from magazines, or snapshots (but, let us hope, not their mother's treasured mementos of early childhood days of the young writer!) Great pride was taken by some of the pupils in the author's classes in their booklets and pleasure was given to other members of the class as they read avidly the productions of their classmates.

Developing a Writing Center. The value of having a part of the elementary school classroom attractively and appropriately equipped as a writing center is increasingly being recognized. Its value can be enhanced if the boys and girls are given an opportunity to participate in planning it and, later, in maintaining it as an attractive and useful portion of the room. While, of course, there is no one set of procedures that needs to be followed in the establishment of a writing center, below are listed some ideas which, it is hoped, will suggest to the teacher others particularly applicable to his classroom.

Motivation. In order to help boys and girls in the development of ability to express themselves in written form, the teacher may, from time to time have a few pupils—possibly as many as three or four at a time—sit near him so he can give them individual attention. The

Figure 5.18. A Writing Center.

teacher may have these pupils gather around him in a corner of the room at a table, possibly improvised by pushing together some of the children's desks. After the teacher has helped some of the pupils several times, under circumstances similar to those described above, he may wish to draw to the attention of the class the inadequacy of the arrangements for help made thus far and present to them the possibility of creating a writing center. The teacher can then briefly describe a writing center, giving but few details so that the pupils can use their imagination in planning their own. Thereupon he can lead a discussion during which the class designates some of the values of a writing center.

Planning the physical aspects of a writing center. Under the guidance of the teacher the boys and girls could then decide on matters such as these: (1) where they should have their writing center, (2) what furnishings they might be able to use, (3) what supplies they would like, and (4) how to make the center attractive. They could also decide on what books it would be valuable to have in the center. Next the class, either through the work of committees or through participation by the entire group, could draw diagrams showing proposed arrangements of the planned center.

Here are suggestions for a center on which the group might agree. It could be separated from the rest of the room by a screen extending over part of two sides of the area. It could be painted on one or both sides by the pupils depicting, for example, a scene conducive to the play of the imagination, such as a fairyland scene or one showing the majesty of the peace of nature. Or one side of the screen, the one facing the corner, could be made of cork or some other material that would serve as a bulletin board. To this bulletin board or to one placed elsewhere in the writing area could be attached lists of ideas for story titles or story themes, poems written by members of the class or by other boys and girls or by adults, or short literary prose selections. Pictures—some of which could

be drawn by the pupils—to stimulate them to use their imagination which might result in creative writing are also recommended for interesting display. A table of a comfortable height for the boys and girls when writing, or a substitute, is a requirement. On the table could be placed an interesting object, possibly with a piece of construction paper of appropriate color and size as "base" or "doily" for it. Or a plant or some flowers in an attractive vase—not in a milk bottle or jelly jar—could serve as centerpiece. A supply of pencils, pens, and paper, as well as paper clips, a stapler, crayons, and paints can be arranged in orderly fashion. A wastepaper basket must be considered an essential. For those boys and girls who like more privacy when writing than is supplied when several write at one table, a few armchairs or separate desks could be included in the corner. A rocking chair might encourage a relaxed mood. A bookcase with books attractively displayed—books on various subjects and on differing levels of difficulty—can also add substantially to the value of the corner. A dictionary is a "must" for older boys and girls. A globe can also be an asset. Of possible advantage could be a file with pictures that might suggest to some a story or poem to be written.

Creating a writing center. After a diagram for the planned center has been accepted, with the suggestions from the whole class, a committee, working with the teacher and the rest of the class could be in charge of setting up the center. Maximum participation by pupils is usually desirable.

Drawing up specifications for use of the writing center. Regulations governing points such as these can be drawn up by the group: (1) when the center can be used, (2) how many can use it at a time, (3) what conduct would be desirable, and (4) what provisions should be made for keeping the center attractive and useful. Point 4 may involve setting up a "governing committee" responsible for carrying out the plans that have been accepted.

Evaluation. Following use of the writing center, from time to time, there can be class evaluation of the effectiveness of the center. Notes placed by the children into a "suggestion box" might serve as nucleus for the appraisal. Following the evaluation, plans for improvement can often be made.

Expansion of the center. The writing center can be expanded into a creative-expression center with needed materials for painting, sculpturing, dramatic activities, musical activities included in the equipment for the area. In fact, from the very beginning of work on the center, the desirability of having a part of the classroom set aside for a variety of creative expression might be emphasized and even the original plans include reference to various means of creative expression. On the other hand, for many classrooms it may be simpler to begin with the idea of a writing center and then later to enlarge upon the function of the area.

OPPORTUNITIES FOR GROWTH THROUGH SPECIAL ACTIVITIES

The program in written expression should be closely interrelated with the ongoing activities of the classroom in the various curricular areas and in activities and projects that cut across the boundaries of the separate subjects.

"Publication" of a Paper

One special activity that can be stimulating, that can be fun, that can help in work in various areas, and that can serve as means of developing skills in writing in a meaningful background is the "publication" of a paper by the pupils.

Kinds. Below are listed kinds of "publications" produced in elementary schools.

1. *The news sheet.* The news sheet, often used in the first grade, can consist of a large sheet of newsprint on which the teacher writes the news items that the boys and girls planned. In place of this on a large sheet of paper can be attached small pieces of paper on which are written the news stories the boys and girls have helped compose. Some rooms have daily news sheets. These can be saved in a portfolio to become a record of some of the year's activities. Duplicate copies can be made of some or all of the editions, one for each child.

2. *The class "newspaper."* Commonly a class "newspaper," written by a class in the intermediate grades, consists of several sheets of paper stapled together, with enough copies so that each child can have his own. Sometimes this paper deals with a variety of happenings in the room that publishes the paper but it may also contain notes, written by pupils in the grade producing the paper, on what is happening in other rooms. Sometimes each issue is devoted chiefly to one topic such as a unit in the social studies or a science project. The "newspaper" with emphasis on happenings in a room is probably the more common of the two types.

3. *The school paper.* In some elementary schools the entire school cooperates in "publishing" a school paper. In such cases the main responsibility for the paper often rests with the fifth or sixth grade. An editor-in-chief is selected from the room that has the major responsibility for the paper. A room editor might represent each grade cooperating with the room issuing the paper. He could be charged with the responsibility of acting as liaison person between the room for which he was chosen as representative and the room that is putting out the paper. The editor might explain to him the types of contributions wanted, the general rules to be observed, and any other matters that might help make the contributions from the other grades valuable.

Figure 5.19. A News Sheet.

4. *The department paper.* Sometimes the pupils of grades four, five, and six together write a school paper. Such a paper follows the general plan described for the school paper excepting that the paper tells primarily or exclusively about the work of the three intermediate grades.

5. *The room magazine, the department magazine, or the school magazine.* Instead of writing a "newspaper," the class, department, or school might "publish" a magazine, possibly two or three times a year.

6. *The column in the community paper.* Although columns in community papers are more likely to contain articles by or about the high school than the elementary school, there is no reason why steps may not be taken by the principal in small communities to encourage the inclusion of a column in the town paper that would be devoted, at least in part, to happenings in the elementary school, some or all of which are reported on by pupils. Special care needs to be taken that such a column will

serve as an aid, not as a hindrance, to the establishment, maintenance, or development of good public relations. It is desirable that before an article is submitted to the local paper, it be shown to the principal for any objection he might have. Parents' permission may also be important in many instances.

Suggestions for the Class "Newspaper." Although the following suggestions are given primarily for writing a class "newspaper," as that term is used in the preceding listing, some of them—in some cases with adaptation—can be observed in connection with one or more of the other types of "publications" that have been mentioned.

1. Unless the pupils are interested in writing a class "newspaper," it is doubtful whether one should be written. This statement is based on the belief that one of the main purposes for teaching language arts skills through participation in writing a "newspaper" is that the class will have an interesting setting in which they can be taught.

2. There are various ways in which boys and girls can become interested in writing a class "newspaper." When the incentive to write one does not spontaneously come from the boys and girls, the teacher may be able to interest them in having a paper by: (a) showing the boys and girls some papers written by other pupils, either in their own school or in other schools; (b) suggesting, in connection with some activity about which the pupils show enthusiasm, that if the class had a "newspaper" it could be a means of reporting on the activity to others; (c) explaining to the boys and girls some of the other values in having a class "newspaper" and giving them opportunity to suggest some.

3. Before a class begins work on a "newspaper," they would find it helpful to decide upon points such as these: purpose of the paper, general content and format or form of the paper, approximate length, and the need or lack of need of an editor and an assistant editor.

4. These are some decisions concerning content that may be made previous to the writing: (a) whether the paper should deal only with activities of the classroom writing the paper or whether there should also be reports on the activities of other classes in the building; (b) in what ways the content can be presented (as, for example, through reports, stories, poems, or illustrations); (c) whether all of the contributions to the paper should be made by members of the class. (It is recommended that the teacher help the boys and girls recognize the value of original content. The teacher may give as a guideline for the paper that all contributions are to be by members of the class. He or the pupils can give reason, for instance, why all poems that are included should be written by pupils in the room, why all illustrations should be

original, and why, if jokes are included, they, too, should not be some from other sources. One of the possible exceptions to limiting the content of contributions to members of the class is that a brief report in the paper by the teacher, principal, or other staff member may, in some instances, be desirable.)

5. A special warning about jokes for the paper may be needed by the group. The importance of the quality of the jokes in terms of wholesomeness should be recognized. Furthermore, the boys and girls should be helped to understand why jokes, included in the paper should not be ones that might hurt the feelings of any individual.

6. When considering the form or format of the paper, points such as these might be given attention: (a) how to present the "heading" of the paper (giving such information as name of school and date of publication) concisely and in interesting form; (b) ways in which each page of the paper can be kept from looking monotonous (such as enclosing the caption of one of the contributions in a rectangular frame, including illustrations, providing a variation between poetry and prose, including listings); (c) whether the names of the contributors should appear in the paper.

7. Every pupil in the room should contribute to the paper. Furthermore, these student-contributions should not consist only in services such as duplicating or assembling the paper, but they should, other than for the editors, be written contributions or illustrations. Some of the reports or other articles might be the product of a group of pupils, as, for example, when three members of the class write a report together.

8. If the decision is made to have an editor and an assistant editor, points to be considered are: (a) Should they be appointed or selected? (b) What should be the qualifications of the editors? (c) What duties and responsibilities should the editors assume?

9. It is usually wise when first planning for a class "newspaper" to keep the commitments simple. For example, decision to have several papers during the school year should probably not be made before one has been produced, for then the desirability of having more than the one can be judged better than it can be determined before even one edition has been "published." It is recommended that, as a rule, the paper be kept fairly short—maybe consisting of no more than three or four pages.

10. Emphasis should not only be on format and content, but also on the quality of the English. Such points as correct sentence form, good paragraph structure, and correct spelling should be stressed. Indeed, one of the values in having a class paper is that practice in improv-

ing such skills can be provided in a meaningful situation.

WRITING HAIKU AND TANKA

In recent years there has been a decided increase on the part of boys and girls in using a Japanese poetry form known as haiku. It is a seventeen-syllable poem, with five syllables in the first line, seven in the second, and five in the third. Nina Willis Walter[3] describes the haiku as:

> . . . It may be as delicately charming as a dragonfly's wing or as deep-toned as a temple bell. But whatever its mood, it must fulfill certain requirements if it is to be a true *haiku.*
>
> To begin with, it must have poetic significance. Any seventeen-syllable statement of fact, or of thought based upon observation or philosophical perception, may be divided into three lines of 5-7-5 syllables. But only those statements that suggest more than they say, that record inspired moments in clear-cut pictures, that present an emotion symbolically in a frame of beauty definitely calculated to arouse an emotional response in the reader are true poetry.

Other characteristics of the haiku are brought out in the quoted description a few paragraphs hence.

Similar in many respects to the haiku is the tanka, a form that boys and girls, too, use. The syllable count in the tanka is 5-7-5-7-7.

How one former student teacher[4] vitalized her teaching is here explained in her words.

> The writing of *haiku* and *tanka* proved to vitalize both the social studies and English. This activity was completed in English class as a creative writing experience and was correlated with a unit on Japan. The writing of *haiku* and *tanka* took place on two successive days. On the first day a discussion of the play *Lute Song,* seen the day before, lead to the study of Oriental art forms. A few *haiku* were read, some written by the masters Basho, Issa, and Buson, and others written by children their own age. At this time a report prepared ahead of time was given on the origin of *haiku.*
>
> The subject about which a *haiku* is written was studied next. The children were asked what they thought a Japanese person living about 712 [the year attributed to the writing of the first *haiku*] would write about. They correctly suggested such things as crickets, butterflies, frogs, stars, flowers, wind insects, and other things found in nature. . . The children then gave phrases which referred both directly and indirectly to nature and the seasons. Next attention was turned to the chalkboard, on which was written the form of a *haiku*: first line, five syllables; second line, seven syllables; and third line, five syllables. Another

haiku was read and several children told what it meant to them. The idea was stressed that the writer and the reader are co-creators of the *haiku* or *tanka* and the poem derives its meaning from both parties.

> The children were then ready to write a *haiku* as a class. Subjects were suggested and . . . [a topic chosen]. The three lines were [then] composed . . . After the haiku was completed, it was copied on paper and mounted on the bulletin board.
>
> The following day the children wrote *haiku* and *tanka* individually. After reviewing the form and subjects of *haiku,* it was explained that a *tanka* is . . . [like] a *haiku* to which two seven-syllable lines are added. The children began . . . choosing the form they preferred. Many had time to write both forms.

Figure 5.21 illustrates how an attractive mobile can be made by mounting copies of haiku on pieces of paper that children can make to resemble Japanese fans. Figure 5.22 shows how illustrated copies of pupils' haiku can be mounted on a bulletin board. This figure is also suggestive of how other poems written and illustrated by the boys and girls can be displayed.

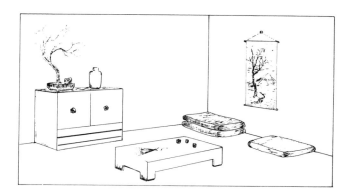

Figure 5.20. Background for Study of Haiku.

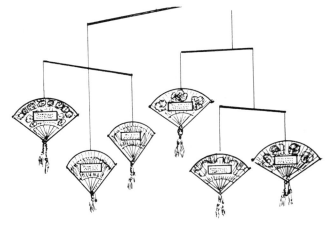

Figure 5.21. Mounting Haiku on Pupil-Made Fans.

3. Ibid, pp. 122-130.
4. **From an unpublished paper by Pamela Blazer.**

Figure 5.22. Haiku Mounted on Bulletin Board.

Other Special Activities

Following are listed a few of many interesting and significant school activities that involve much writing:

1. Writing the script for a puppet show, play, or pageant. (See page 308.)

2. Making class books on special activities in which the group has participated during the course of the school year.

3. Making a booklet on a unit of work such as "The Clothes We Wear" or "News from Space."

EVALUATION OF WRITTEN COMMUNICATION

In schoolrooms where there is much opportunity for written expression, it is not essential that the teacher evaluate every piece of written work. Careful appraisal of everything written, if enough is being done, would take too much of the teacher's time. The boys and girls may at times write a paragraph demonstrating the suggestions they have just discussed and illustrated without even handing their papers in to the teacher. The evaluation in such instances may consist of each pupil checking individually how well he observed the standards for a good paragraph composed by the group. The pupils may practice daily or several times a week writing for a few minutes in a notebook. They may have the understanding that the teacher will not collect the notebooks daily—perhaps not until a pupil has written into his booklet five, six, or seven times. Then the teacher will select for detailed analysis one of the reports that the pupil has written since the last time the notebooks were collected. Suggestions to the pupil concerning the one chosen for appraisal should often be in writing so that the next time the child's writings are examined the teacher can check how much the pupil was able to profit from earlier com-

ments by the teacher. When possible, oral conferences with the pupil should supplement the written remarks.

Additional suggestions for means of evaluating written communication follow.

1. Checklists for skills in written reports can be devised similar in form to the ones described on page 79 for oral communication. These points may be listed on a three-inch by five-inch card: (a) neatness, (b) sentence structure, (c) punctuation, (d) capitalization, (e) beginning, (f) interestingness, and (g) ending.

2. A neatness scale can be constructed against which points such as these may be checked: (a) placement of writing on paper, (b) freedom from recognizable erasures and from parts crossed out, (c) clean appearance of paper.

3. Pupils can be tested on capitalization and punctuation through exercises such as the following.

Directions. Place a question mark, period, or exclamation point at the end of each sentence.

Did you know that we have a pet in our room
Bobby brought a hamster to school

Directions. Write these sentences. Use capital letters where they are needed.

We wrote a letter to mr. smith.
he is a farmer.

Directions. Write the possessive form of each of the following groups of words:

the books belonging to the boy
the books belonging to the boys
the books belonging to the children
the toys belonging to the babies.

FOR STUDY AND DISCUSSION

1. Explain why the vocabulary for the language experience chart does not need to be as carefully controlled as that for the reading experience chart.

2. Outline a procedure that can be followed in a presentation lesson on writing a thank-you letter in a third-grade classroom.

3. Write a plan for teaching some phase of capitalization or punctuation other than any considered somewhat in detail in this chapter. You may wish to model your plan on the form of the one on the use of final marks of punctuation given on page 114. However, do not feel restricted to that form.

4. Under the heading "Other Special Activities" (see page 129 are listed some interesting and significant activities, not developed in this chapter, that involve considerable writing. What activities of that type can you add to the list given?

5. Examine papers written by elementary school pupils, noting the excellences of the writing and the problems that are revealed. What suggestions do you have for helping the writer of each paper?

6. How can some of the claims made by linguists that are discussed in chapter 3 (see page 36) be applied to the guidance of growth in written expression?

7. Examine language arts textbooks for the elementary school as to the treatment of written expression. What suggestions for teaching written expression beyond those given in this chapter do you find? Evaluate those suggestions as to suitability and usefulness.

8. Draw a diagram of a hypothetical classroom, choosing any one of the first six grades, in which the physical equipment is such that it would encourage creativity in written communication. Label the equipment and designate the grade level. Also write a brief paper explaining the diagram.

9. Think of ways in which you as teacher could show your creativity in helping pupils initiate and bring to fruition the plans for a creative writing project. Write a description of your proposed procedures.

10. In various professional books and magazines examples of creative writing done by boys and girls are given. You may also have access to one or more other sources of such writing. Evaluate the writing in terms of criteria mentioned in this chapter.

11. Study one or more of the references for teachers given at the end of this chapter to find ideas on teaching written expression that are not presented in this chapter. Evaluate them in terms of their possible usefulness in the elementary school.

REFERENCES

Applegate, Mauree. *When the Teacher Says. "Write a Poem."* New York: Harper & Row, Publishers, 1965.

Applegate, Mauree *Freeing Children to Write.* New York: Harper & Row, Publishers, 1963.

Burns, Paul C.; Broman, Betty L.; and Wantling, Alberta Lowe. *The Language Arts in Childhood Education,* 2nd ed. Chicago: Rand McNally & Company, 1971.

Burrows, Alvina Treut; Jackson, Doris C.; and Saunders, Dorothy O. *They All Want to Write.* New York: Holt, Rinehart and Winston, Inc., 1964.

Donoghue, Mildred R. *The Child and the English Language Arts.* Dubuque, Iowa: Wm. C. Brown Company Publishers, 1975.

Lamb, Pose, ed. *Guiding Children's Language Learnings.* Wm. C. Brown Company Publishers, 1967.

Lefevre, Carl A. *Linguistics. English. and the Language Arts.* Allyn and Bacon, Inc., 1967.

Moffett, James. *A Student-Centered Language Arts Curriculum. Grades K-6: A Handbook for Teachers.* Boston: Houghton Mifflin Company, 1968.

Roberts, Bertha, and Beckman, A.T. *Children's Voices.* Morristown: Silver Burdett Company (General Learning Corporation), 1939.

Strickland, Ruth. *The Language Arts in the Elementary School.* Lexington, Mass.: D.C. Heath and Company, 1969.

Taylor, Elvin. *A New Approach to Language Arts in the Elementary School.* West Nyack, N.Y.: Parker Publishing Company, 1970.

Tidyman, Willard F.; Smith, Charlene; and Butterfield, Marguerite. *Teaching the Language Arts.* New York: McGraw-Hill Book Company, 1969.

Walter, Nina Willis. *Let Them Write Poetry.* New York: Holt, Rinehart and Winston, 1962.

6

Guiding Growth in Skills Common to Oral and Written Communication

Because of the close interrelationship among the various facets of the language arts, they have many skills of value in common. The skills needed for both oral and written communication discussed in this chapter are those pertaining to (1) vocabulary, (2) sentence structure, (3) note-taking, (4) outlining, and (5) grammar and correct usage.

VOCABULARY

Words are the basis of much of listening, speaking, reading, and writing. Without suitable command of words, the individual is likely to be unable to speak or write interestingly and concisely, to listen intelligently, and to comprehend written material that with a larger vocabulary he might understand. As a result of these shortcomings, he will be handicapped in various activities in school. A poor vocabulary may well be the cause of personality defects, for the person who cannot express himself adequately may become shy and in time he may even become a recluse. The professions and many

other vocational pursuits lean so heavily upon vocabulary that the individual with a deficiency in this respect is likely to be heavily penalized. Without an adequate vocabulary a person is not likely to be able to use his leisure time for much worthwhile reading nor for listening to some of the excellent programs on the radio or television nor for participating in stimulating conversation. Furthermore, vocabulary and thinking are so closely related that thinking is hampered by an inadequate vocabulary.

Kinds of Vocabulary

An individual has several kinds of vocabularies. Commonly they are classified as (1) the listening or hearing vocabulary, (2) the speaking vocabulary, (3) the reading vocabulary, and (4) the writing vocabulary. When categorizing vocabulary into these types, it should be borne in mind that there is a close relationship between them. Consequently efforts to improve any one of them can have a salutary effect on the other kinds. The teacher should plan his program of vocabulary development in such a manner that the maximum transfer from one type to one or more of the other types takes place.

Listening or Hearing Vocabulary. An individual's listening vocabulary consists of the words he can comprehend when he hears them in oral expression. The listener may understand one meaning of a word but be ignorant of others. Furthermore, there are differences in comprehension of even the same meaning of a word. For example, a person hearing the word *love* may understand that it refers to the state of being liked very much, but he may have no idea of the depth of feeling that is associated with the word if the speaker is talking about love that expresses itself in sacrifice.

The young child's listening vocabulary typically surpasses in number of words his other types of vocabulary. He can, as a rule, understand more words as he listens than he uses in his own speech and more than he can comprehend in his reading or uses in his writing.

Speaking Vocabulary. The child should have a sizeable speaking vocabulary before he starts to learn to read or write. Ordinarily, the speaking vocabulary continues larger than the reading vocabulary well through the primary and often fairly long into the lower-intermediate grades. However, by the time the pupil leaves the elementary school, he generally does not use nearly as many words in his speech as he can comprehend with some degree of interpretation when he meets them in print.

Reading Vocabulary. In the early stages of learning to read, the child's reading vocabulary remains small chiefly because he cannot recognize many words in print, not because he does not know the meaning of many. In fact, reading material for beginners is usually planned so that the words the children encounter are those whose meaning they know. It is only as the pupil progresses into later stages of learning to read that he is likely to find many words he does not understand. (Very little is said in this chapter about the development of the reading vocabulary since the topic is taken up in chapter

Writing Vocabulary. The last of the four types of vocabulary that the child acquires is the writing vocabulary. Even after a child has been writing for several years, his writing vocabulary lags behind his speaking vocabulary. Some adults, however, have a larger writing than speaking vocabulary. Research has not established where the reversal in size of the two typically occurs in individuals in which it does take place.

Guidelines

Following are listed helpful guidelines.

1. *There is a marked correlation between intelligence and vocabulary.* Many intelligence tests for use in the elementary school recognize this closeness by devoting a

part of the tests to appraisal of the vocabulary of the learner.

2. *Environment is also a powerful determinant of the size and nature of an individual's vocabulary.* Even though intelligence can be thought of as setting the limits of possible vocabulary development, rarely, if ever, does an individual make use of all leeway in growth possible for him. In fact, the person with an intelligence quotient slightly above normal who has grown up in an environment favorable to language development may have a more effective vocabulary than the one with an intelligence quotient somewhat higher than normal who has been reared in surroundings, in school or out of school, that are inimical to optimum vocabulary development. Because of the influence of environment on vocabulary, care needs to be taken in interpreting intelligence tests that consist in part of a vocabulary test.

3. *The vocabulary of the home and the playground greatly affects the program in vocabulary development of the school.* Even before the pupil enters first grade, he has had several years during which he has been speaking and listening. After he has enrolled in school, he continues to spend most of his waking hours outside of school in such activities. Consequently, if the type of vocabulary the child uses outside of school is meager or otherwise unsatisfactory, it may offset in part efforts by the teacher to help him improve his vocabulary. Furthermore, any attitude in the home that reflects lack of interest in, or even possibly disdain of, vocabulary growth, may affect adversely what the teacher is trying to encourage in this respect.

While the teacher's attitude must be one of understanding, it should not be one of hopelessness nor of giving up. If there are unfavorable outside-of-school influences on the child's vocabulary, the teacher should try to counterbalance them while being cognizant of the fact that habits are often difficult to break, especially when there are, during the time when attempts are made at a change, lapses into the patterns to be eliminated. Sympathetic understanding of the child's dilemma should characterize the actions of the teacher as, patiently but consistently, he not only tries to help the child break undesirable means of expression but at the same time attempts to obtain his full cooperation in the venture. Care needs to be taken that in no way will the child develop a feeling of shame about his home because it is lacking in high standards in choice of vocabulary. However, vulgarity of speech should not be tolerated.

One of the environmental factors that has considerable bearing on the size and quality of the vocabulary of an elementary school child is his socioeconomic background. Quality of vocabulary, as the term *quality* is here used, refers to the extent to which the individual's vocabulary corresponds to that in which the instruction of the school is given and, therefore, to the standards expected in many schools. (The reader is referred to chapter 12, "Adapting Instruction to Individual Differences," in which attention is paid to this complicated factor: see page 326.)

4. *One of the best ways of helping boys and girls in vocabulary development is to furnish them with a variety of rich, meaningful experiences and opportunities to discuss them.* Types of situations that encourage such incidental development of the child's vocabulary are listed in the next part of this chapter. (See page 134.)

It is especially important for those pupils who fall behind their peers in vocabulary development to be provided with many meaningful experiences. Erroneously, some teachers believe that the best remedy for this deficiency is to provide the child with more and more practice exercises or to use other direct means of improving his vocabulary. Usually it is wiser to spend part of the effort in vocabulary improvement in providing the child with many experiences that will give him real reason for using an improved vocabulary. Means of encouraging him to develop through provision of opportunity for such experiences may seem incidental to the child but to the teacher they may often represent carefully thought-out methods of procedure.

5. *In the lower-primary grades increase in the pupil's meaning vocabulary is obtained primarily through oral means of expression.* The words that the pupil reads in suitably graded reading material in the lower grades are selected, in part, in terms of words that have meaning for him. It is in these grades that much emphasis, therefore, needs to be placed on vocabulary improvement through oral communication. As the pupil progresses through the upper-primary and the intermediate grades, he will have increasing opportunity to improve his vocabulary through words that he reads. Throughout the elementary school, however, oral communication should be utilized in furnishing the child with greater word power.

6. *At times indirect or incidental methods of teaching vocabulary development should be supplemented by direct methods.* While vocabulary development is stimulated through an environment rich in meaningful experiences in which vocabulary seemingly receives but incidental attention, such an environment for many boys and girls needs to be supplemented by situations set up primarily in order to help them grow in word power.

7. *When direct methods of increasing word power are used, the pupils should be convinced of the worthwhileness of the activities.* "Busy work" is inexcusable because it is wasteful. For good results not only the teacher but also the pupils should realize the worth of what they are doing. Motivation for practice exercises, for example, on the use of *threw* and *thrown*, might be in the form of convincing statements by the teacher that he will try to help them in that lesson to overcome an error that some or many of them are making.

8. *Recognition should be given to the fact that the words an individual uses differ somewhat in formal and in informal speaking and writing situations.* In informal conversation, such as that in which the pupil engages when he converses with members of his family or friends, he is likely to use words that he would not use in more formal situations. Furthermore, in the informal writing of personal letters or personal memoranda, he will probably use some words that he would not use in more formal business letters or in report writing. The child should be helped to recognize these facts and to learn some types of words appropriate for one kind of situation but not for the other. This differentiation in type of vocabulary should not be made, however, in such a manner that the child thinks words that are cheap, vulgar, or incorrect are permissible in informal speech or written expression.

9. *Boys and girls frequently experience difficulty because of the fact that many words have a variety of meanings.* The teacher should realize that the child with limited experience with a given word is likely to interpret it incorrectly when it appears in a setting in which it has a different meaning from the one that he has been attaching to the word. The teacher needs to bear in mind that the meaning an individual associates with a word is often determined by his experiences with that word. To the child of a miner living in the area of the Mesabi Range in northern Minnesota the *range* is likely to evoke a different association than to the boy who has been saturated with stories of cowboys on the ranges of the West.

10. *Many children need to be helped to appreciate the value of an effective vocabulary.* This point needs particular note when the pupil comes from an environment in which the value of attention to vocabulary is not emphasized. However, regardless of background, boys and girls should be aided in recognizing the importance of making independent efforts to improve their vocabulary.

11. *Boys and girls need to learn that some words are used primarily to give information and others chiefly to produce a certain emotional effect.* The concept of "loaded words" may need explanation as the child learns to recognize such words as *native land* (rather than the name of the country) and *loved ones* (rather than *relatives*) as emotive words. The pupils should be helped to understand that even though it is proper to use words that reveal one's emotions or that are likely to produce a certain emotional effect on the listener or reader, emotive words are often dangerously used by persons who wish to influence others unduly.

12. *As boys and girls read materials in the content areas, including the social studies, science, mathematics, and health, they need special help meeting various vocabulary problems.* One problem lies in the fact that many words of which they already know one meaning

have a different meaning as part of the more specialized vocabulary of a given field of knowledge. The child who has long used the word *mouth*, for example, may be confused when he hears or reads about the mouth of a river. A further problem lies in the fact that a large number of new words is introduced per given number of running words. In the reading material in the content subjects the vocabulary burden usually is not as carefully determined as in the reading textbooks to which the child has been accustomed. The problem of meaning is increased by the fact that the pupil frequently does not have the concepts, for example, of words such as *liberty*, that the writer of the material may assume he has.

13. *The teacher's attitude toward vocabulary improvement, his own vocabulary included, is likely to affect that of boys and girls.* Through precept and example the teacher can help pupils realize that acquiring more power over words can be fun as well as useful.

Situations that Encourage Vocabulary Development

Probably the chief means of encouraging growth in the vocabularies of boys and girls is to provide them with many meaningful experiences such as:

1. Talking with one another, with the teacher, and with visitors
2. Listening to stories told by the teacher, the librarian, and other boys and girls
3. Listening to directions and explanations and giving them
4. Listening to poems read or given by other boys and girls, the teacher, or the librarian
5. Reading, telling, or listening to stories
6. Reading poems silently and orally
7. Discussing poems and stories
8. Looking at or drawing pictures to illustrate words

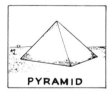

Figure 6.1. Illustrations of Words.

9. Drawing pictures and deciding on captions for them
10. Making posters or other displays for bulletin boards
11. Making a mural or a "movie"
12. Seeing a "movie"
13. Listening to a radio or television program
14. Planning work activities and evaluating them
15. Reporting on events that have taken place

16. Looking at material on exhibit
17. Watching the bulletin boards
18. Making a class book or a book by a committee or by individual pupils
19. Planning and giving a party
20. Planning and giving a puppet show, a play, or a pageant
21. Giving, writing, and listening to book reports
22. Writing a news sheet or a class or school newspaper or magazine
23. Singing or composing songs
24. Participating in choral reading
25. Planning and putting on a book fair or a school exhibit
26. Planning a class or school program
27. Playing games
28. Doing creative writing
29. Writing letters, reports, and announcements
30. Reporting on things that have happened
31. Having a school or class garden
32. Taking care of a pet
33. Participating in construction activities
34. Listening to recordings, including tape recordings, of the pupil's own speech.

Methods

With the stress that many linguists have placed on the study of the structure of a language, there may be on the part of some teachers fear that the power emphasis on vocabulary may remain unrecognized. Such neglect is not a necessary concomitant of the application of linguistic principles to the teaching of the language arts. Care should, however, be taken that time that should be spent on vocabulary development is not relegated to other emphases on growth in self-expression. Important though structure in sentences and in longer units of thought is, it must not be developed at the expense of inadequate attention to the formation on the part of the learner of a rich and appropriately used vocabulary.

The following are some of the procedures that may be used to help boys and girls grow in power to understand and use words. Some of the suggestions are usable in connection with situations in the ongoing program of the school. Others are adaptable when a more direct approach to the problem of development in vocabulary seems indicated. One method of helping boys and girls with specific instruction in vocabulary is the dictionary. (Suggestions for helping the pupils use the dictionary to gain in knowledge of the meaning of words are given together with ideas for developing other dictionary skills in chapter 9; see page 250.) Other suggestions for methods that might be used for vocabulary development are given following.

1. Draw attention to words that are used in oral com-

munication. Some ways in which the attention of the pupils can be drawn to words are as follows:

As the teacher uses a new word in a sentence when he is talking to the class, he writes the word on the chalkboard and explains what it means in the context in which it is used.

The teacher, as he talks with the class, includes "built-in" definitions or words. For example, as he writes the word *burrow* on the chalkboard, he might say, "The rabbit ran to his *burrow*, his home among the roots of the old oak tree." Then he might proceed by asking the children a question such as this, using the word *burrow*, "How many of you have heard of a rabbit's burrow?" If a child, in his responses, uses the word *burrow*, the teacher might draw attention to the fact that he used that word.

Comments can be made on the appropriateness or descriptiveness of words that pupils use in their speech.

Before the teacher reads a selection to a class, he writes on the chalkboard one or more difficult words that the pupils will hear and he then questions them about these words or makes comments on them.

2. Have the boys and girls make lists of types of words such as the following:

Of synonyms and antonyms of specified words
Of homonyms, with sentences containing them
Of descriptive action words (verbs)
Of descriptive name words (nouns)
Of descriptive words that tell how, where, and why (adverbs)
Of words that describe name words (adjectives)

Figure 6.2. Means of Motivating Work on Antonyms.

Of words that describe a sound or a smell
Of the special vocabulary encountered in a unit of study
Of substitutes for overworked words such as *nice, lovely, terrible, exquisite, marvelous*
Of words with prefixes and suffixes
Of compound words.

3. Write a story or duplicate one for the class, omitting many of the descriptive words. Then have the pupils supply words that would fit in the blanks left in the story.

4. Ask the pupils to determine which words in a group give the more precise meaning. Examples of such groups are: *walked, sauntered; spoke, whispered.*

5. Encourage the pupils to make charts, possibly illustrated, giving the new words encountered in connection with an area of study or with a unit in that area such as a chart with new words used in a unit on Switzerland as, for example, *glacier, chalet, alp, attitude, inn.*

6. Have the pupils keep individual notebooks or a file system of words the meanings of which they are learning. The pupils might be encouraged to write each word, tell what it means, use it in a sentence and, if possible and helpful, draw an illustration of it.

7. Develop with the pupils the meaning of commonly used prefixes and suffixes. Thereupon they can identify the prefixes and suffixes in words presented to them and show how the meaning of the root is affected by the affix.

8. Have the pupils form derivatives from root words such as *happy, unhappy; wrap, wrapped, unwrap, wrapping.*

9. Give the pupils crossword puzzles based on knowledge of words and encourage them to make or help make some. For example, in the lower grades a simple puzzle using questions such as these can be constructed:

What word means the opposite of *short*?
From what smaller word is *running* made?
What word means more than one boy?
What is a baby cat called?

10. Discuss with the boys and girls the importance of expressing themselves well, bringing out points such as these:

The relationship to clarity and interestingness
The value at school in various subject areas
The value when looking for work or working
The importance in terms of showing refinement
The use of slang.

11. Have the pupils read material in their textbooks or on duplicated sheets of paper discussing the importance of choosing words well.

12. Encourage the pupils to make cartoons or other illustrations showing the importance of careful choice of words.

13. Help the boys and girls figure out the meaning of a word in context by: (a) asking them what meaning(s) would fit into a sentence containing a blank space for a word; (b) having them tell what an underlined word in a sentence might mean judging from the rest of the sentence and then check the word in the dictionary; (c) asking which possible meaning of a word fits into the context of a given sentence.

14. Guide pupils in putting on a skit showing the value of choosing words well.

15. Ask the pupils to restate in a more interesting manner underlined words or expressions used in sentences.

16. Have the pupils dramatize the meaning of specified words that are used in sentences such as "The child *sauntered* home from school."

17. Provide time and assistance for the pupils to improve some of their written work by substituting words with meanings that express more exactly what they wish to say than those they have used.

18. Help boys and girls to note the change in meaning of a sentence when verbs such as these are used: *crept, stalked, rushed, ran, walked,* or *tiptoed.*

19. Give the pupils practice exercises of the types suggested under "Illustrative Practice Exercises." (See page 137.)

Concept Development

Throughout the discussion on vocabulary we have noted the importance of the child acquiring the meaning of words he hears, uses, reads, and writes.

In the development of concepts, thinking is involved. The ability of the child to think, including his level of cognitive learning, is, therefore an important consideration for the teacher in his attempts to help the child develop in conceptual ability. Through experiences that the child has, either firsthand or vicarious, if they are on the level of his comprehension, he learns to acquire the meaning of words heard or read.

The child will learn many concepts by himself without assistance from others. However, frequently through help from his peers or from adults, he achieves a clearer concept of a word and achieves it more quickly than he would without it. Sometimes through lack of guidance he may arrive at an erroneous idea of that which he conceptualizes. For example, let us take a young child living in the city. When he sees a cow for the first time or a picture of a cow, if he is merely told that that is a cow, he may falsely generalize that all big four-footed animals are cows and so when he sees a horse, he may call it a cow. With help from others he may, when introduced to the term *cow,* be guided in noting the characteristics of an animal called a cow, so that he develops a correct concept. Through such help in forming a generalization, after seeing more cows, he can differentiate, let us say,

between a cow and a horse. Thus the child develops a concept through a process of generalization and differentiation, through the inductive-deductive method of learning.

Acquiring a correct concept of a concrete object is a relatively simple matter when compared to that of conceptualizing noncrete terms, such as *beautiful, small, thoughtful.* The meaning of such words can be developed, however, through the same process, by making a generalization of what the word stands for based on the use of the term in various situations and by then differentiating between situations or objects that possess and those that do not possess that characteristic.

Additional points that may help the teacher in assisting boys and girls in increasing the number and quality of concepts are:

1. *He should provide wide experience for the child, on the basis of which he can form concepts.*

2. *He should help the learner in the development of concepts of the concrete not only through providing or utilizing firsthand experiences but also through vicarious or secondhand experiences.* For example, a child may gain a clear concept of what a sheep is without seeing one at the time when he forms the concept. Through pictures of sheep and descriptions of sheep he may be able to form a correct concept of what a sheep is. Or, in case he has seen one sheep and noted some of its characteristics, through pictures of sheep, he may be helped to arrive at a correct generalization.

3. *He should recognize the fact that, especially in connection with the development of a concept of the nonconcrete kind, the child frequently may not be able to attach to a word all the meanings that a word has.* This consideration should not, however, keep the teacher from helping the child to learn one or more meanings of the term. For example, it may rightly take years for the child to progress to an understanding of the word *generous.* In early childhood it may refer only to a person who gives something to him. In the course of time the child may add to the concept that generosity also refers to kindness shown to other people, not only through giving things, but also through helping others. Still later he may note that generosity deals not only with actions but also with thoughts, as he begins to understand how a person may have either a generous or a selfish thought. Thus the teacher should realize that it takes on his part, time and patience as well as knowledge of child growth and development.

4. *He should recognize that not all development of concepts should be by the inductive process.* Deductive teaching also has its role when, for example, the teacher tells the child what a word means or when the pupil looks up a word in the dictionary. Opportunity at times to make application of a learning in such a manner is prob-

ably just as important, if not more, than making provision for the application of what is learned through inductive teaching.

5. *He should guide the learner so that the pupil recognizes the danger of generalizing on the basis of too few examples.* When the boys and girls realize this fact they are more likely, when making generalizations about words without the help of others, to postpone generalization of the meaning of a word until they have examined more than one situation of the type on which they will build a generalization.

Illustrative Practice Exercises

Below are given suggestions for a few of the many types of practice exercises that may be of value to some pupils.

Exercise 1. As oral and/or written work the boys and girls may substitute one of a list of synonyms for a specified word such as *said,* in sentences, such as these: (a) Tom *said,* "What a beautiful day!" (b) Evelyn *said,* "It is a beautiful day!"

Exercise 2. The boys and girls may match words, given in two columns, that are similar in meaning, such as, for example those in the following lists:

_____ abundant	1. believing
_____ trusting	2. quiet
_____ silent	3. helpful
_____ kind	4. bravery
_____ courage	5. wisdom
	6. plentiful.

Exercise 3. The boys and girls may substitute "loaded words" for informative words, such as those indicated in these sentences: (a) The speaker told the audience about their *relatives* in that far-off country. (loved ones) (b) They sang songs of their *country.* (native land)

Exercise 4. The boys and girls may substitute underlined words in a group of sentences for words that mean about the opposite, as, for example, the word *departed* in place of *arrived* in a sentence such as "The train *arrived* on time."

SENTENCE STRUCTURE

To be unable to talk in good sentences presents a problem in the clarity and interestingness of oral expression. Furthermore, lack of sentence sense can interfere with comprehension of what is read, especially when the sentences are long and involved. Similarly, written expression and ability to comprehend what is communicated orally may be affected adversely by lack of sentence sense.

Results, as revealed in the speaking and writing of boys and girls leaving the elementary school and their written and oral expression during later years, seem to indicate that either not enough emphasis has been placed on improvement of sentence structure or the teaching has not proceeded in accordance with well-known principles. Noting the emphasis placed on sentence structure by many elementary school teachers and the space devoted to that topic in textbooks, one is inclined to conclude that much of the inadequacy in the recognition and use of good sentences may be due to inadequate teaching procedures.

In the discussion of sentence structure that follows, these points are taken up: (1) objectives, (2) guidelines, (3) linguistics and sentence structure, and (4) methods.

Objectives

The teacher will want to have the pupils become able during the course of the elementary school education to understand or do the following:

1. Know the value of good sentence structure
2. Recognize sentences
3. Know the kinds of sentences (declarative, interrogative, exclamatory, and imperative)
4. Begin a sentence with a capital letter and end it with the proper punctuation mark
5. Write and speak in clear-cut sentences
6. Know under what circumstances it is important to use complete sentences and to use them at such times
7. Avoid run-on sentences
8. Avoid many short, choppy sentences
9. Have variety in sentence structure
10. Comprehend rather long and involved sentences in oral and written communication.

Guidelines

Important guidelines are as follows:

1. *The emphasis in teaching sentence sense or sentence structure should be placed on helping boys and girls express themselves clearly, concisely, and interestingly, not primarily on teaching them the mechanics of saying, writing, or recognizing sentences.* Boys and girls who have interesting and significant comments to make are more likely to talk and write in correct sentences than those who lack background experience and who do not really want to communicate their thoughts. The pupils should be helped in becoming conscious of the fact that an important goal is to speak and write in such a way that others can comprehend the material fairly readily.

2. *Growth in ability to use sentences is to a considerable extent a matter of maturation.* As in other areas of human achievement, the limits for development are set for the individual by his inheritance. Further-

more, unless interrupted there is a sequence in sentence development that seems to be part of the pattern of inner unfolding of the indivudual. First the child talks in words or in substitutes for words. Next he talks in words that form the skeleton of a sentence. Then follow complete sentences, simple in form. Sentences more involved and longer come next. Consequently environmental factors need to be selected to "go with the current" of the pattern of growth, not against it.

3. *There is a close relationship between thinking and sentence sense.* When the pupil is helped to clearer thinking, he may be directly or indirectly given assistance in expressing himself in sentences.

4. *Criticism of the child's sentences at times when he speaks in somewhat formal situations other than those specifically designated for purposes of improving in sentence structure may have a detrimental effect upon his spontaneity of expression.* If he is interrupted other than in training situations or corrected after he has finished speaking, he may become shy about expressing himself in the future or he may pay so much attention to the mechanics of speaking that he neglects suitable concentration on what he is saying. On the other hand, if the child is never helped to improve his speech through appraisal of the sentences that he uses when his purpose is to tell a story, give a report, or engage in conversation, there is danger that he will use one set of standards for sentences when he is given specific help in talking in sentences and a set of lower standards at other times. Such a lack of carry-over from the former to the latter type would, indeed, be unfortunate and the value of the whole program in the improvement of sentence structure would be greatly jeopardized.

5. *There is a place for lessons definitely planned with the objective of helping boys and girls develop a better sentence sense and of helping them talk and write in effective sentences and comprehend such sentences in both oral and written communication.* Some such lessons should be devoted to introducing boys and girls to various phases of the problem of developing effectiveness in relation to sentence structure. Others should be used for practice purposes at well-spaced intervals. If lessons of this type are to be effective, not only the teacher but also the pupils should be convinced of the worthwhileness of the work.

6. *The fact that as pupils are enrolled in the intermediate grades they may sometimes make more errors in sentence structure and have additional difficulty in comprehending what they hear or read, due to problems related to sentence structure, than they did in the years immediately preceding, is not necessarily reason for discouragement or alarm.* The increase may be accounted for in some instances by the fact that boys and girls typically speak and write in more involved and longer sentences and listen to and read sentences of that nature when they are in the intermediate grades than when they were younger. Furthermore, the ideas to be expressed are more advanced and consequently harder to put into words than those of earlier days. The lag may thus be only apparent, not real.

7. *There is a close relationship between use of sentences in oral and in written expression.* Attention to sentence structure in oral situations can often be given in such a manner that value will also be accrued in written communication and vice versa. However, it must not be assumed that because there is a relationship, the skills required in oral and written expression are identical. Because of the greater difficulty pupils often have in written expression, it is frequently desirable to have the work on various phases of development of sentence skill begin with emphasis on oral communication.

Linguistics and Sentence Structure

Linguists have much to say about sentence structure. In fact, one of the basic interests of both structural linguists and transformational grammarians is the emphasis placed on structure, structure of sentences included among other concerns. The structural linguist, as far as sentence structure is concerned, primarily tries to describe the structure. The transformational grammarian places much emphasis on what he often refers to as kernel sentences—of which there are but a relatively small number—and transformed sentences formed from the kernel sentences.

Both structural and transformational linguists will reject the definition of a sentence as a group of words expressing a complete thought. They point out the inadequacy of such a definition in terms of its meaninglessness when application of it is attempted. It has been claimed that boys and girls who have been taught such a definition, if they have learned to recognize sentences, have done so in spite of, rather than by means of, the definition.

Linguistics offers no easy substitute for the long-used definition of what a sentence is. Nor does it attempt to do so. The point of view is that a language that lends itself to expression in so many types of *utterances*—a term used frequently by linguists to designate *sentences*—as English does, cannot be expected to be subject to a simple definition as to what constitutes a sentence. What most linguists try to do, rather than to define a sentence, is to give descriptions of various types.

Linguists differ in their identification of types of sentences. The transformational linguists frequently refer to two, the kernel sentence and the transformed sentence. They believe that there is a quite limited number of types of basic or kernel sentences, from which various transformations can be made. According to such analysis an example of a kernel sentence is: *Boys play ball.* Or the kernel sentence could be written as *The boys play ball,* with the addition of what is referred to as the determiner *the.* Among the transformations that can be made from this kernel sentence are:

Are the boys playing ball?
Is ball being played by the boys?
Ball is being played by the boys.
The boys do not play ball.
Don't the boys play ball?
Were the boys playing ball?
The boys do play ball.
The boys will play ball.

Transformations of the kernel sentence *The boys play ball,* can thus be made through additions and through changes in voice and tense, by means of changes from positive nonemphatic statements to negative emphatic statements, and transformation of statements to questions. The kernel sentence can also be transformed by means of additions, such as these:

Some of the boys play ball.
The boys in the second grade play ball.
The boys and girls play ball while their parents watch them.
The boys and girls who finished their school work play ball on the south side of the playground.

Linguists will admit that typically boys and girls entering first grade have at their command use of basic forms of the structure of the language. They already talk in a variety of sentence forms. Educators who favor study of the structure of the language by elementary school pupils will justify that study—even of those parts of which the child has considerable control in his speech—on the basis that through conscious study of the utterances that boys and girls are already able to make correctly and through study of additional possible types, the children's command of the language and appreciation of it can be increased. It should be noted that many educators, however, have not accepted such claims concerning procedures for teaching sentence structure, nor, for that matter many other claims by linguists or by teachers enthusiastically making application of some tenets of linguists to the teaching of the language arts in the elementary school.

In the next paragraphs, under "Methods," among the suggested procedures for helping boys and girls become more proficient in using and interpreting sentences, there are included some that incorporate the recommendations of those who believe application of claims of linguists will help boys and girls to approach the desired proficiency. However, there are many more recommendations as to procedure of which the teacher should know who wishes to make full use of the findings of linguists and of the recommendations of educators based on a study of linguistics. For additional information on this topic the reader is referred to books on linguistics listed in chapter 13 (see page 366) and to many of the general-professional books on the teaching of language that consider the topic of linguistics. The teacher or prospective teacher may also wish to refer to the elementary school language arts textbooks that are linguistically oriented—some more, others less. One series that has a decided linguistic orientation is *The Roberts English Series: A Linguistic Program* by Paul Roberts, published by Harcourt Brace Jovanovich. The work in this series shows many ways in which boys and girls can be helped through a linguistic approach in matters pertaining to sentence structure.

Methods

In harmony with the guidelines given (see page 137) and some of the comments made under "Linguistics and Sentence Structure," (see page 138) methods for helping boys and girls in matters pertaining to sentence structure are here suggested.

1. The teacher discusses with the pupils why it is usually desirable to talk and write in sentences.

2. The pupils are guided to note why it is usually desirable to talk and write in sentences as they compare two paragraphs written on the chalkboard, the first in sentence fragments so that it is difficult to comprehend the meaning and the second in sentences in which the first paragraph was rewritten.

3. Provisions are made for first-grade children to dictate sentences to the teacher. As the teacher serves as recorder, at times, he comments on the capital letter at the beginning of a sentence and on the terminal punctuation mark. For example, he may say, "I will use a capital letter here because it begins our second sentence." Or he may ask, "Since this is a question, what punctuation mark should we place at the end?"

4. The teacher makes incidental reference to sentences in connection with what the pupils read when, for example, he gives directions such as: (a) Read the next sentence in order to find out. . . . (b) Read the sentence that tells us why Susan wanted an apple.

5. The teacher explains to the pupils what constitutes a declarative, an interrogative, an exclamatory, and an imperative sentence as the pupils note sentences on the chalkboard or as the teacher records on the chalkboard sentences of the various types that the boys and girls give orally.

6. The teacher explains to the boys and girls that some groups of words look like sentences but are not. He asks the boys and girls to select those in a list of groups of words (some of which are sentences and others sentence

fragments) which are not sentences and then to change them to sentences.

7. The pupils match a group of sentence fragments such as the following as they comply with the direction given.

Direction. On the line to the left of each group of words in the first column, write the number of the group of words in the second column that finishes the sentence.

_____ Stephen had found   1. a broken leg.

_____ The crow had   2. Stephen's pet.

_____ Stephen took   3. a crow.

_____ The crow became   4. the crow home with him.

8. The boys and girls state what kind of sentence each of a series is, though written without final marks of punctuation, and then supply the needed punctuation in sentences such as the following:

Where are you going with that crow

I am taking the crow home with me

9. The pupils finish a sentence by selecting the ending word from a list and then supply the final mark of punctuation.

I will show my crow to (school, Mother, garage)

10. The pupils write in sentences series of words that are listed in scrambled order.

crow a has pet Jim

Jim has a pet crow.

Figure 6.3. Arrangement of Words into Correct Sequence.

11. The boys and girls finish sentences of which only the first few words are given.

I like

My crow never

12. The children rewrite sentences in which no capital letter nor final mark of punctuation is given.

13. The teacher asks the pupils to observe how the voice is inflected at the end of a question. He then tells them that while in oral expression raising the voice helps a person to know that a question is asked, in writing a question mark helps identify it.

14. The teacher puts on the chalkboard some poorly expressed sentences written by boys and girls possibly in paragraph form, and asks the class to plan ways of improving them.

15. The teacher writes on the chalkboard sentences that are confusing because they contain irrelevant material and then asks the pupils to decide what should be deleted. Sentences such as the following might be recorded:

As I ran to school today with my little rat terrier that Father gave me for my last birthday, when I was nine years old, I lost my tablet.

16. The teacher helps the boys and girls express themselves in better sentences by suggesting that when they want to say something that is rather difficult to explain, they might first ask themselves the question that they want the explanation to answer.

17. The teacher helps the pupils recognize the fact that it is not always important, not even desirable, to talk in complete sentences as, for example, he draws attention to complete and incomplete sentences such as the following that he has recorded on the chalkboard:

How much is the bus fare? Fifteen cents.

Who is with you? My sister.

18. The teacher emphasizes the fact that at times *and's* are desirable as they combine groups of words, closely related in thought, that could form independent sentences such as the following:

I put my books in the house and then I quickly hurried out to see the fire.

The pupils can be given practice in deciding in which instances, in relation to sentences on the chalkboard, it is desirable and in which it is undesirable to use *and's* to connect groups of words that could, with the omission of the *and*, be written as separate sentences.

19. The teacher writes on the chalkboard a series of sentences in which words such as *when*, *while*, *since* are used instead of *and* to connect two parts of a sentence, each of which could form a separate sentence, as, for example, the following:

It was very cold *and* I wore my winter coat.

Since it was very cold, I wore my winter coat.

The pupils can then be asked to rewrite other sentences containing unnecessary *and's* by using connectives such as *when, while, since, because, after.*

20. The class discusses reasons why many people run sentences together when speaking. Some reasons that may be mentioned are: (a) Since the speaker is not certain of what he wants to say next, he tries to give himself time to think by including an unnecessary connective. (b) The speaker has formed a habit of using unnecessary connectives. (c) The speaker does not know that use of words such as *since, because, while* can keep sentences without unnecessary *and's* from being short and choppy.

21. The pupils indicate what connectives can be used in cases such as the following to combine two thoughts into one sentence:

My coat is blue.   Mary's is red.

22. The pupils note the contrast between a written report in which all the sentences begin in the same way and one in which some of the sentences have been changed so they have different beginnings. They then decide which makes the more interesting report.

23. The boys and girls note different ways in which a sentence can be structured as they read sentences such as these that the teacher has written on the chalkboard:

When I came home late last evening, I was very tired.
I was very tired when I came home late last evening.
Last evening, when I came home late, I was very tired.

24. The pupils combine two sentences by compounding the subjects of sentences such as:

The boys played ball.
The girls played ball.

25. The pupils combine two sentences by compounding the predicates of sentences such as:

The boys played baseball.
The boys took a swim.

26. The pupils use relative pronouns to combine sentences such as:

The girls were making puppets.
We watched the girls.

27. The pupils make transformations from kernel sentences such as *The children were playing*. Samples of a few possible transformations are:

The girls were playing with their dolls.
The girls in the first grade were playing with their dolls.
Were the girls playing with their dolls?

28. The boys and girls change the order of words in sentences such as the following so that the subject begins the sentence:

Into the room the dog ran.
Quickly the boys caught him.

29. The boys and girls change the order of words in sentences such as the following so that the subject does not begin the sentence:

The children played out of doors after the storm.
The girls attended a party in the afternoon.

30. The boys and girls check on variety of sentence structure by listening to a recording of a talk they have given.

Illustrative Practice Exercises

Below are a few samples of parts of practice exercises that some teachers may find useful with their pupils. It is also hoped that these illustrations may suggest to the teacher others that would be particularly helpful to the boys and girls in his class.

Exercise 1. Build a longer sentence to answer each of the following questions, beginning the sentence with the words *I played ball*. Write your answer on the line provided below each question.

a. When?

_____

b. With whom?

_____

c. Where?

_____

d. How long?

_____

Exercise 2. Some run-on sentences are given below. Form one correct sentence from each of the groups of run-on sentences. Write your sentence on the blanks provided.

a. It was a warm day and we went swimming.

_____

b. We went to the skating rink and the warming house was locked.

_____

NOTE TAKING

Notes can be useful for talks boys and girls give as well as for papers they write either about their own experiences or on data that they have acquired through reading, talking with others, or other activities.

There is real need for helping elementary school pupils learn how to record notes effectively and how to use them. Efficiency in writing and using notes can help them in self-expression. It can be of value to them in that it provides them with a form for recording information basic to improved thinking and greater efficiency. If desirable learning experiences are provided, the elementary school boy or girl can be helped to acquire a skill that many persons who have completed the first six grades have not developed satisfactorily for their needs. The significance of this statement can be realized as one thinks of the poor note-taking habits, including the use made of notes, of many high school and college students as well as of adults outside of school.

Guidelines

Important points to note in helping boys and girls develop skill in taking notes and using them are as follows.

1. *Emphasis should be placed on skill in note taking throughout the elementary school.* Drawings may, at times, serve as notes. By the time a pupil leaves the elementary school he will, it is hoped, have learned to take notes on a topic by consulting various sources.

2. *The boys and girls should be helped to see the value of taking notes.* Probably the best ways in which the pupils can learn to recognize the value of taking notes are by taking them for purposes that to them serve a real need and by being helped to take them and use them effectively.

3. *Help should be given in the development of various types of note-taking skills.* It should not be assumed, for example, if a pupil has learned to take effective notes for organizing a talk based on personal experiences or on what he has heard one or more persons say, that he will also be able to write useful notes for organizing a paper on information he has gathered through reading books on a given topic.

4. *The boys and girls should be helped in locating information in books and other written materials.* Discussion of how such help can be provided is given in chapter 9.

Methods

The teacher can guide boys and girls by doing the following in order to help them in recording and using notes.

1. In recording notes through:

Using, as the teacher tells a story, illustrations he has drawn or secured which follow the sequence of the story and letting the boys and girls see the picture as he tells the story

Guiding the pupils in drawing pictures to illustrate a story that the teacher has told or read to them so they can tell it

Guiding the children in drawing illustrations of a personal experience that later they can tell the class or dictate to the teacher or they themselves record in writing

Using and showing to the class sketches the teacher has drawn or has otherwise obtained of steps in a process he is explaining

Guiding the boys and girls in making sketches of the steps in a process the teacher or the pupils are explaining or about which they are reading

Showing the pupils two sets of notes taken on a given selection from an encyclopedia in order to find the answer to a specified question and then asking the pupils to decide which is the better set and to tell why. One of the sets of notes might: (a) contain irrelevant material, (b) be so sketchy that it is almost meaningless, (c) omit some important points. The contrasting set of notes should be without these shortcomings.

Showing the pupils a set of notes that the teacher took on a question on which they may want information as he draws attention to points such as these: (a) the inclusion of the title of the book and author from which the notes were obtained; (b) the pages in the book on which the information was found; (c) the use of quotation marks when the exact words of the writer were recorded; (d) the fullness of the notes; (e) the brevity of expression used without sacrifice of clarity; (g) the relevancy of the notes. The group can then give reasons for the desirability of observing in note writing each of the points noted.

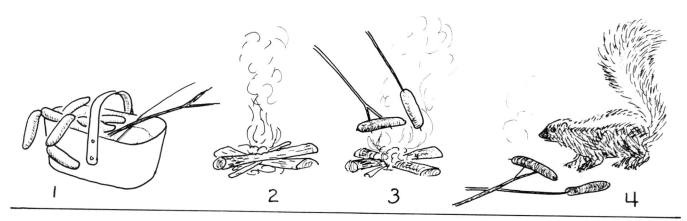

Figure 6.4. Illustrations as "Notes" for Reports on Personal Experiences.

Making a chart headed with a question such as "What are *YOUR* Notes Like?" on which are posted an excellent set of notes as to form and content and one poor in both respects

Helping the class decide on subtopics on which they would like information on a topic such as hamsters (in case the boys and girls are planning to get a hamster as a pet) and then having the group divide into committees to find information on each of the subtopics such as: (a) what a hamster looks like, (b) food, (c) shelter, (d) value, (e) habits

Having the pupils decide on a topic on which they want information and after they have gathered the information and recorded it, giving them an opportunity to have their notes evaluated

Guiding the boys and girls in looking up information on a topic when they do not know on what subtopics they will need or find information. If a pupil were planning a talk on a topic about which he does not know much, he might be advised not to try to decide on subtopics until he has read for a while on the general topic.

Helping the pupils select from a series of statements about a general topic those about which one wishes to talk when reporting on a stated specific phase of that topic

Giving the pupils a list of sentences on a topic which they are to organize in terms of subtopics (either stated by the teacher or by the class or decided upon by each pupil individually)

Giving the class an opportunity to discuss the importance of taking accurate notes

Providing the pupils with an opportunity to think of an interesting experience they have had as the teacher jots down notes while they organize the material for a talk or a written report

After giving a talk or having a pupil give a talk or after reading to the boys and girls or after having provided them with the opportunity of listening to a radio or television program or a recording, having them check which of a series of points, listed on a sheet of paper, were brought out in the talk or reading

Discussing with the boys and girls points to observe when taking notes on a talk, possibly heard over the radio or on television, such as: (a) Do not concentrate so much on your note taking that you fail to comprehend much of what the speaker is saying. (b) While you listen to the opening sentences, try to get your clue as to the outline the speaker will follow. (c) In some instances, to get the full value of your notes, rewrite them more fully shortly after the talk has been given.

Discussing with the pupils the fact that some people like to keep notes on a topic in which they are especially interested and to add to the notes over a long span of time. For example, a person whose hobby is trees might want to keep a classified file of information on trees.

Discussing with the pupils suitable forms for keeping more or less permanent notes and showing them samples of some

Helping the pupils take notes as they carry on experiments or take field trips

Having the pupils take notes on instructions as to how to do something such as making a papier-mache head for a puppet.

2. In using notes through:

Discussing with the class the importance of not always following the organization given in their source(s) when using the notes for a paper or talk and explaining to the class if the same organization is followed in many instances credit should be given to the source

Discussing the importance of using quotation marks and at times indicating the source whenever in a paper the exact words of the speaker or writer are given

Discussing with the class how to use notes in a talk if it seems desirable to use them

Having some of the pupils put on skits as they demonstrate correct and incorrect methods of using notes when giving a talk

Providing the pupils with practice in writing a paper or giving a talk after taking notes on a topic.

OUTLINING

Outlining can help boys and girls in listening, speaking, reading, and writing. More specifically, these are some of the chief ways in which outlining can serve the elementary school child:

1. As an aid to recall of what he reads, hears, or otherwise experiences
2. As a study aid, if he is furnished an outline of what he is studying
3. As a guide for talks that he will give or of papers he will write
4. As an aid in planning dramatizations.

Skill in outlining can be acquired by the average pupil during the course of his years in the elementary school if he is given adequate guidance. Some teachers, unfortunately, have assumed that pupils need only spasmodic help in learning to write outlines and in using them. Putting this theory into practice in many schoolrooms has resulted in a large number of boys and girls leaving the elementary school and even high school who have not learned how to make effective outlines and how to make good use of them.

Guidelines

Following are points on which a sound program of guiding boys and girls in acquiring skills related to outlining should be based.

1. *Outlining is one means of organizing material.* Consequently, experiences of value to the child in growth in skill in organizing are likely to assist him in becoming more adept at outlining.

2. *Outlining, like other means of organizing materials, is closely interwoven with thinking.* Even after the pupil has comprehended what he has read, heard, or otherwise experienced, he needs to think as he tries to decide upon the main points. He needs to think as he tries to select less major points (subtopics) that support the main points. He needs to think as he figures out the interrelationship between subtopics and supporting details.

3. *Outlining should be taught in such a way that boys and girls see the usefulness of the learning.* Outlining or any activity preliminary to learning how to outline, such as learning to organize materials not in outline form, should frequently be taught in situations in which the pupils readily recognize the value. Such situations include many that can easily be identified by the teacher within the scope of the ongoing activities of a modern elementary school. For example, one is classifying a rock collection for display on an exhibit table.

4. *So-called incidental training in outlining is not enough for many boys and girls.* In addition to the opportunities afforded by incidental learning, for a large number of pupils lessons need to be provided in which new learnings about organizing material the pupils need to acquire are developed, such as the identification of the details to serve as subpoints for subtopics in an outline or the form to be followed in outlining. Furthermore, from time to time lessons need to be set up to supplement the incidental work and the development lessons so that well-spaced practice will be provided.

5. *The teacher should, in part, plan the program in outlining in harmony with the sequence of steps arranged as to difficulty.* In the primary grades much of the work is usually preliminary to actual outlining. There the chief emphasis in this respect can be on organizing material without putting it into outline form. For example, boys and girls may help decide what event should come first in a play, what books should be placed in a space marked "Books on Nature," or what should be the order of events in a program that they are planning. In the fourth grade, considerable attention may well be paid to the organization of the paragraph in terms of (a) selection of the topic of the paragraph, (b) identification of the topic sentence if there is one, (c) decision as to whether only relevant points are made, (d) consideration of the desirability of the sequence in which points are given,

and (e) study of the appropriateness of the beginning and ending sentences. In the fifth grade, if not before, boys and girls may be prepared to outline two or more consecutive related paragraphs. Work on the form of outlining is often begun in the later primary grades and continued in the intermediate grades with attention to increasing complexity of form, often through subpoints supporting subtopics.

Methods

In the listing of methods that follows, suggestions for organizing material are given that are considered of either preliminary or supplementary help in the actual teaching of outlining.

Methods for Organizing Material for Help in Outlining. The teacher can list on the chalkboard items that the pupils dictate to him, such as articles needed for a field trip or what was seen on a field trip and then have the pupils work out a classification of the points.

CHIEF PRODUCTS		
Farm Products	Manufactured Products	Minerals
wheat	watches	coal
corn	silverware	iron
oats	gloves	copper
beans	machinery	

Figure 6.5. Classification That Can Be Worked Out by Class.

The teacher can write on the chalkboard at the pupils' dictation a list of words (such as a list telling what signs of fall they saw on a walk) and then classify them according to the pupils' directions, possibly under captions such as *birds, animals, flowers, other plants, other signs of fall.*

The pupils can make a classified list of products found in a country that they are studying.

The teacher can point out to the pupils the fact that words such as *first, second,* and *third* when used in context, frequently give a clue to part of the structure of the paragraph or a group of paragraphs in which they are used. He could next emphasize how the use of those words in the pupils' sentences help make clear the structure. The pupils could compare a written paragraph containing those words with the same paragraph in which these words are not used and note the difference in clarity.

The pupils can draw a series of pictures illustrating in sequence events in a story.

The boys and girls can make a list of questions or topics on which they want to obtain information when studying a unit and then they can list the questions or topics under different headings.

The pupils can arrange in correct order a series of paragraphs on a topic in which the sentences are presented to them in scrambled order.

The boys and girls can study the table of contents of a book to note its organization. The teacher can ask questions such as: (a) Which story do you think is about a pet? (b) How many stories are given in the section about "Animal Friends"?

The boys and girls can read a story to plan the scenes they want to include in a dramatization. After the scenes have been listed on the chalkboard, the pupils can check to see whether they are arranged in the right order and, if they are not, arrange them correctly.

Methods for Outlining (Beyond Those Dealing with Organization in General). Before the teacher gives a short report, he can place on the chalkboard an outline, with the main topics only, of the talk and tell the class that he will follow that outline as he gives a talk. Later on when the boys and girls are ready for learning the use of subtopics and subpoints of subtopics, the teacher can place on the chalkboard before he gives a talk, a more complete outline of it.

As the boys and girls make plans for an exhibit the room is presenting, the teacher may ask them to name articles they wish to include in the exhibit and then to classify them. After the pupils have made the classification, the teacher may write it in outline form as the pupils state points to be recorded. The class can then use the outline as they plan how they will secure each article and where they will display it.

In outlines that the teacher places on the chalkboard, attention may be drawn to the lettering and numbering of the main points, the subtopics and the subpoints, as well as to the use of capital letters, punctuation marks, and indentation.

As the teacher is working out the points of an outline with the boys and girls, he can have them take responsibility for telling where the various points should be placed in the outline, what numerals and letters should be used, and where capital letters and punctuation marks are needed.

The pupils can supply the numerals and letters, with needed periods following them, of an outline that is correct excepting for the omission of those parts.

The pupils can be given a paragraph and told that it deals, for example, with four points, one of which is already recorded on the chalkboard. Then the pupils can be asked to find the other three points and name them

for the teacher to write on the chalkboard. A paragraph on "Clothes of the Indians" may be duplicated and part of an outline on it, in a form such as the following, written on the chalkboard for the pupils to complete:

Clothes of the Indians

  I. What the men wore
 II. _____
III. _____
IV. _____

The pupils can be given a series of consecutive paragraphs on a topic along with a partial outline of those paragraphs, with possibly only the first main topic and the first subtopic of that main topic listed, in addition to the numerals and letters for the other parts. For example, with paragraphs on "The Work of Boys and Girls in Switzerland" a partial outline such as the one that follows might be recorded on the chalkboard or duplicated on sheets of paper.

The Work of Boys and Girls in Switzerland

  I. The work of boys in summer
   A. They watch the cattle.
   B._____

 II. _____
   A. _____
   B._____
   C._____

III. _____
   A. _____
   B._____

IV. _____
   A. _____
   B._____

The pupils can be asked to complete the outline as they study the paragraphs.

The pupils can place a series of statements, that might represent notes taken by boys and girls, under the correct topics, the names of which are given to the class. For example, the pupils can be asked to arrange a series of notes given in mixed-up order, under the correct main points as listed in a partial outline, such as the one here given.

The Story of the Pilgrims

  I. Why the Pilgrims left England to go to Holland
 II. Why the Pilgrims left Holland
III. The voyage to America

IV.   The first hard winter in America
V.   The first Thanksgiving in Plymouth
VI.   Later days in Plymouth

Statements such as these might be listed for classification under the above-indicated topics:

The boys and girls were learning to speak Dutch.
The Mayflower set sail from Plymouth, England.
The Pilgrims invited the Indians for the feast.

Older boys and girls might change the sentences to phrases as they write information such as that listed above, as main points and subtopics of the outline.

The teacher can give the pupils a written report and an outline of it in which some of the subtopics are in incorrect order, with the direction that they rearrange them correctly.

The boys and girls are helped in learning the terminology of outlining, such as *main points* and *subtopics,* first by seemingly incidental reference to them by the teacher. Later the teacher may write the words on the chalkboard and after explaining what parts each designates, the pupils may be encouraged to use those terms in their discussion and explanation.

To give the pupils practice in writing the form of an outline correctly, the teacher may give them an outline correct in content but poor in form in that periods, capital letters, and numerals and letters for lists are omitted or used incorrectly.

The teacher can give the boys and girls an outline of a reading assignment and suggest ways in which they can use it as they are studying.

The pupils can, first with the aid of the teacher and later individually, make an outline of points on a topic on which they would like information. Then they can look up that topic in one or more encyclopedias for children or young people to see if they can obtain the information on each of the subtopics and to see if there are additional topics or subtopics that should be included in the outline. They can then change the outline if they find they cannot get information on some points but can find it on others that are not included in the draft of the outline that they used as they began their search for information.

The teacher can give the pupils an outline form with the name of the subject as in the following case:

Old and New Ways of Communication

I.   _____
    A.   _____
        1.   _____
        2.   _____
    B.   _____
II.   _____
    A.   _____

B.   _____
C.   _____

With an outline form such as the foregoing the boys and girls may be given a list of topics to serve as main topics, subtopics, and subpoints to subtopics, with the direction that they should fit them into the outline form.

The pupils can be helped in learning that the divisions of the same order in an outline must be "mutually exclusive and collectively exhaustive" by: (a) showing them some outlines in which the principle is observed; (b) showing them some outlines in which it is not observed; and (c) having them write an outline in which it is observed, which they can discuss with the class in terms of the principle.

The pupils can be given help in keeping points under a given division or subdivision in an outline parallel in structure so that if *I* is given in sentence form, *II* and *III* are also so listed or that if *A* under *I* is in phrase form, *B* and *C* are also given as phrases. They can be helped to understand this point by the teacher doing the following: (a) emphasizing the point as models are studied; (b) helping them observe the point as an outline is being worked out by the class as a whole; (c) providing them with opportunity to check outlines that they write to note whether or not they observed the point.

GRAMMAR AND CORRECT USAGE

There has long been controversy as to whether the work on correct usage in the elementary school should include grammar and, if it should, what grammar should be taught and how. Part of the controversy is due to fundamental differences of opinion. At one extreme are those who believe in formal grammar; at the other are those who contend that all work on correct usage in the elementary school should be incidental study, without any attempt at helping the pupil arrive at rules or generalizations or names of the parts of speech, the parts of sentences, and other so-called grammatical terms. Between these two extremes are various shades of opinion.

Part of the controversy is due to lack of definition of the term *grammar*. If grammar is thought of as the formal study of rules governing the structure of the words and groups of words within a sentence, to be applied in practice situations without close relationship to meaningful experiences involving true communication, then many teachers are definitely opposed to teaching grammar in the elementary school. However, if grammar is thought of as the study of words or groups of words within a sentence in such a way that the sentences an individual uses will therefore tend to be structurally correct (whether or not such study involves arriving at some generalizations that are meaningful to the learner), then many teachers favor teaching grammar in the elementary school. Unless terms have been clarified in any argument on the subject the possibility of misunderstandings due to lack of clarity must be recognized.

Guidelines

In the writer's opinion the following points can be used as guidelines.

1. *In the elementary school curriculum there is no place for formal grammar which deals primarily with the study of rules.* Memorizing many rules of grammar seems to have little effect on the English an individual uses. Persons who know many rules often fail to apply them. Individuals who use good English do not necessarily have knowledge of the rules of grammar. However, the foregoing statements should not be interpreted as meaning that no rules or generalizations should be learned. The writer of this book believes that there are generalizations regarding correct usage that boys and girls should know. We do not hesitate to help them develop generalizations in the natural world of science, for example, for we know that they can be of real value to them as they make application of them to various situations. Similarly we should not deprive them of tying together points being learned out of fear of teaching formal grammar. Nevertheless, it is questionable whether any generalizations about correct usage should, as a rule, be developed through formal study in the lower-primary grades. Rarely do boys and girls on this level of the educational ladder have the ability to arrive satisfactorily at generalizations through such study or to make application of them, without the need of too much time being spent on their development and use. With the younger and more immature pupils the teacher may advisedly at times explain to a child who says, for example, "I taked it home to my mother," that a preferred way of expressing the same thought is to say, "I took it home to my mother."

2. *The content of the program in correct usage should be determined in terms of the curriculum, the needs of the pupils, and their ability to learn.* Through study of the curricular requirements the teacher can ascertain what learnings in the area are recommended for his pupils and which were designated for learning in a preceding school year. The specifications for the grade level of his pupils can serve as checklist against the needs of the boys and girls in his charge. The teacher must not assume that they have mastered all points of correct usage designated for previous years. He can check the pupils by means of observing their speech, by studying their written productions, and by testing through commercially produced or teacher constructed materials.

3. *In the elementary school much emphasis should be placed on learning correct English through teaching-*

learning situations that to the learner seem incidental. Since an individual is greatly influenced in his speech and in his written expression by the type of English he hears, the importance of the example the teacher sets in his speech is of vital concern. Furthermore, with due consideration of the laws of habit formation, the teacher needs to provide the learner with many opportunities for speech in informal as well as in more or less formal speaking situations.

4. *Incidental teaching of correct usage, through the ongoing classroom activities, does not constitute an adequate program for many pupils.* Direct attention to matters of correct usage, beyond that which is given through more or less incidental attention to them, should, as a rule, be given in the intermediate grades.

5. *The language of the child in the early years of his elementary school education greatly reflects the language of his home.* Ordinarily the language equipment with which he comes to school has served his purposes quite adequately even if it may differ markedly from the language usually considered acceptable in the school.

6. *In trying to help the child develop in ability to use standard English, when that spoken in his home deviates markedly from it, the teacher needs to proceed with great tact.* Children may resent insistence by the school on a level of expression markedly different from that to which they have been accustomed. In fact, the child whose family background of oral expression is directly or indirectly criticized by the school may develop a feeling of insecurity. The intimate language of his own family is tied up in the child with awareness of belongingness that, if destroyed, may leave the child at loss in a world where he needs all the security he can get in order to develop to the maximum during the critical years of his childhood. On the other hand, unless the English being taught at school is going to be functional outside of school, there is not much chance for marked improvement. Any policy, therefore, on the part of the teacher to encourage the child to think that it is quite all right to speak in whatever way he has been speaking outside of school is also detrimental to progress in English. (See page 326, "Working with the Culturally and Economically Disadvantaged Child.")

7. *Pupils need to be convinced of reasons for improving their English.* Unless boys and girls are truly motivated to change their patterns of expression, attempts by the teacher to alter them may result in resentment. Furthermore, some pupils may try their best at school to speak in accordance with the English usage taught by the school, as a school exercise, but not be interested in the least in improving their use of language in out-of-school situations, thereby possibly nullifying much of the work on correct English.

8. *There are different levels of English.* Although the

teacher will need to be desirous of having the child make application of what he learns at school in regard to correct English, he should keep in mind that the same speech pattern recommended for use in school is not always appropriate for all other situations. The informality of speech, for example, that is perfectly acceptable for communication on the playground often is not satisfactory in somewhat more formal classroom and in some other out-of-school situations.

9. *When direct instruction in the use of correct English is given, the inductive-deductive method of teaching generalizations is often superior to the deductive method used alone—in which the learner is told the rule and then asked to apply it.* It is generally conceded that boys and girls seem to understand generalizations better if they have helped in their development. Furthermore, the children seem to make more intelligent and immediate application of them under those circumstances. It also seems that they remember better, for a longer time, those generalizations which they have helped formulate. (For suggestions concerning learning generalizations see pages 33 and 34. An example of a teaching plan is presented later in this chapter; see page 156.)

10. *Much of the work on the improvement of English in terms of correct usage should be oral rather than written.* One reason for this preference for the oral over the written when concerned with matters of correct usage common to both methods of expression is that many more such errors are made in oral expression. Many a pupil who is not likely to write *it don't* may, in speaking, when he has less time to think as he is expressing himself, make that error. Since many of the incorrect expressions have been heard rather than read, it seems reasonable to attack the difficulty in the type of situation in which the errors have become somewhat ingrained in the individual.

11. *As a rule, it is undesirable to interrupt a child while he is speaking, in order to correct his English.* If a child is corrected while speaking, especially when he is giving a talk, he will probably be embarrassed. He can easily then lose the train of the easy flow of his thought and in the future may be paying more attention to the form of his speech than to the content. There are times, however, when the agreement might be—when the class has been working on the overcoming of a specific type of error (let us say, the use of the unnecessary *and*)—that a child should be stopped when he makes the error. In such cases the value of the interruption should be clearly recognized by the boys and girls.

12. *There are times when the pupils should have responsibility for correcting the English of their peers.* Some teachers shy away from this practice for fear that an individual may be hurt if he is criticized by his classmates. They know that it is often harder to take even just criticism from one's equals than from one's superiors. They also realize that at times boys and girls may be criticized by their peers in an unfriendly manner. However, the values that can be attained through evaluation by classmates are so great that use of this important source of help should not be neglected in a classroom in which the teacher has been able to help the pupils establish an atmosphere usually characterized by mutual trust, good will, and helpfulness. Nor should pupil appraisal of each other be limited to noting points of strength. Such evaluation would be weak and often insincere.

13. *Language games should be used rather sparingly.* Frequently the amount of time spent on games in the language arts program is not in proportion to the learning acquired by the boys and girls who engage in them. However, teachers can rightly argue that at times the use of a game, though not justifiable in terms of the learnings acquired in proportion to the time spent on the activity, can be justified because of the interest in the language arts that the game may arouse. Nevertheless, teachers should ask themselves, in relation to a game they plan to use, whether it would arouse greater interest in language games rather than in language learnings. They should bear in mind that the excitement of a game may even have a detrimental effect on language learnings since, after participating in a game, the boys and girls may find the activities not involving games to be boring.

14. *Since many errors in the use of English may have become a habit for a pupil, they usually cannot be eradicated at once.* The teacher should make provision for repeated emphasis on points that have been studied. Patience is required by the teacher when he wishes to help a child break a habit and acquire a new one.

Inductive-Deductive Teaching of Generalizations

Suggestions for teaching generalizations by means of the inductive-deductive method are given at various places in this book. (See pages 33 to 34 as well as item number 9 in the preceding discussion. Additional points for developing generalizations are among the recommendations given below.)

1. *Only a limited number of generalizations should be taught in any one grade.* The number will depend upon the ability and needs of the boys and girls as well as upon the requirements of the school curriculum. To be able to make application of a relatively small number of generalizations is much to be preferred to a partial understanding and consequent faulty application of many.

2. *The fact that not all boys and girls within a class will be likely to need the same help with all generaliza-*

tions should be reflected in the teaching. Some of the pupils may already know the generalizations that are to be taught to others. Furthermore, not all will require the same amount of application made in class situations, of generalizations that are being presented.

3. *The teacher should be aware of the difficulties pupils encounter in regard to a given form of English and then should plan his teaching accordingly.* For example, boys and girls are likely to make more errors when they use the past form of the verb *see*—by using *seen* for *saw* than by substituting *saw* for *seen.* In practice exercises on the use of *saw* and *seen,* therefore, it is usually desirable to have more sentences in which the word *seen,* rather than *saw,* is the correct form.

4. *Steps for teaching and helping boys and girls make application of generalizations concerning correct usage should be clearly formulated in the teacher's mind.* For steps that can be followed the reader is referred to "A Suggested Procedure for Arriving at Generalizations" given on page 33. His attention is also drawn to the teaching plan on *saw* and *seen.* (See page 156.)

5. *The teacher should guard against faulty generalizations.* There is special danger of overgeneralization. For example, when differentiating between the use of *wrote* and *written,* some pupils might erroneously deduct that *written* is never correctly used with a helping word. The generalization is that *wrote* is never used correctly with a helping word and that *written* usually requires one. An illustration of a sentence in which the word *written* is used correctly without a helper is: "This report, *written* by a first-grade pupil, was the one we chose for posting."

6. *Though care should be taken not to teach anything that is faulty, it is not necessary—in fact, it is often undesirable—to introduce in initial lessons on a point, all the ramifications that application of a generalization can have.* For instance, when helping boys and girls discover that *is* is used correctly with a singular subject and *are* with a plural subject, it will most likely be enough with younger boys and girls to use simple constructions exemplifying the generalization—examples in which the simple subject consists of only one word. It may not be until a later time that the teacher will want to help his pupils to recognize the fact that *are* should be used when two singular nouns in the subject are connected by the word *and.*

7. *It seems advisable to have, at times, a written selection for practice purposes in the form of a story or description, rather than in isolated sentences without bearing on one another.* For example, in an exercise on *ran* and *run* (with the latter word as part of a past perfect or pluperfect verb phrase), it would seem less monotonous to younger boys and girls if the words were to be supplied in a series of sentences about an incident when children played hide-and-go-seek. In content of this type, sentences such as the following might appear:

> When we played hide-and-go-seek, Mark _____ the farthest.

> I could not tell where Sue had _____ .

The teacher should guard against using practice work as "busy work." Both the teacher and the pupil should be able to recognize purpose for an exercise.

Bearing of Linguistics on the Teaching of Grammar and Correct Usage

This section on the bearing of linguistics on the teaching of grammar and correct usage in the elementary school will not include a discussion of some of the differing points of view held by various groups of linguists, such as the structural linguists, the transformational, or the generative-transformational. For a treatment of these and for other points the reader is referred to pages 37 and 138 and to professional books dealing somewhat in detail with linguistics, some of which are mentioned in various parts of this book, including chapter 13. (See page 336.) Rather, in this section are indicated a few points that, regardless of the differentiating and contradictory claims of various schools of linguists, a sizable number of educators believe should be considered when planning an elementary school language arts program. Following a brief discussion of these points, attention is paid to the divergence among teachers as to the extent to which they make application of these guidelines proposed by those who favor a language arts curriculum that is strongly oriented to claims of linguists.

Claims of Linguists. Some of the points of view or procedures bearing on grammar and correct usage, that many linguists hold or follow are indicated here.

1. Linguists study the English language as it is spoken by English people and describe their findings. Their procedure is in contrast with that used by traditional grammarians as they attempted to outline the grammar of the English language in terms of Latin grammar even though English is primarily a Germanic, not a Latinate, language.

2. Like the makers of formal English grammar, linguists formulate generalizations. But their generalizations are based on how a language is actually used, not on any idea of how it should be used.

3. Linguists do not try to make judgments about the correctness of language. To persons with a linguistically oriented interpretation of language, correctness of speech is not a logical consideration but a sociological one. That language, so linguists point out, which is considered correct by a group of people is the language

spoken by those whose language they approve as desirable. "Standard English" as judged by educated people is that English which educated people speak. But to less schooled people or people living in unfavorable socioeconomic areas the standard English of the educated is not the accepted standard English. Furthermore, in different parts of our country different expressions and modes of speaking in general are accepted by the educationally elite as standard.

4. Linguists assert that a given individual is likely to speak or write on different levels on different occasions. They might point out, for example, that the language considered suitable on a football field is not that which is desirable in a report given in school; that the language appropriately used by a child in a letter written to his pal may not be appropriate in a letter he would write to his grandparents.

5. Linguists emphasize the fact that no living language is static. They accept change, without any quarrel with it. They merely describe it, without passing judgment on it. They will call attention, for example, to some of the trends in the changes taking place in a language. For instance, they point out that regularizing irregular expressions is a centuries-old trend in the English language. (This regularization process is the one that the preschool child follows when he says, "I ringed the bell" or "I taked it home." He uses the form for the past tense of *ring* and *take* that regular verbs use, namely that of adding *ed* or *d* to the infinitive form of the verb.)

6. Linguists emphasize the fact that the language of a people gives insight into the users of the language. This observation holds true whether the reference is to various languages, to dialects within a language, or to one person's use of the language. An individual's speech can reveal much about him.

7. Linguists hold that many of the definitions presented in traditional grammar are inadequate. They point out that they are often not specific enough to be helpful and that, in some cases, they are oversimplified. For example, criticism of the definition of a noun as the name of a person, place, or thing is that the definition by itself could hardly lead a learner to decide that a word like *happiness, kindness,* or *poverty* belongs in that classification. Linguists get around the difficulty of definition by describing various characteristics of nouns, such as these: (a) A noun can fit into given slots in sentences. (For example, only nouns would correctly fit into the blanks of this sentence: The _____ left his _____ at my_____.) (b) Determiners such as *a, an,* and *the* can be used with nouns.

Variations among Teachers in Application of Linguistic Principles and Procedures. When teaching the language arts, elementary school teachers differ greatly in the extent to which they make application of principles and procedures followed by linguists. This divergence is due in part to the variation in knowledge that a teacher has of the field of linguistics and its possible implications for the teaching of grammar and correct usage in the elementary school. Because of the paucity of information many teachers possess in this respect, it is not strange that they frequently prefer to teach in the area of the language arts without paying attention to the claims and methods of linguists. However, lack of familiarity with the field is not the only reason why some teachers do not attempt to incorporate in their teaching alleged implications of the claims of linguists. There is honest difference of opinion as to various points about the teaching according to such principles even among teachers fairly well versed in the teachings of linguists. One classification that highlights such differences in teaching the language arts according to the applications of linguistics that some educators consider desirable is outlined in the threefold one given below.

1. Some teachers wish to go "all out" in making use of the principles suggested by linguistics that seem to have some application to the teaching of grammar and correct usage in the elementary school. Such teachers may usually find that they are well advised to follow the program as advocated in a desirable language arts book for boys and girls, one with strong linguistic orientation. The great majority of elementary school teachers, at the present time, have not had enough preparation in the area of linguistics to teach the language arts with heavy linguistic slantings without recourse to a textbook that will provide considerable assistance. They are also advised, even though they may follow the program in the textbook for children, to study professional books dealing with the teaching of the language arts that have such orientation—books such as those to which reference is made at various places in this book.

2. There are some teachers who do not favor teaching grammar and correct usage in the elementary school in the general pattern suggested by those educators who are trying to apply linguistic principles to the teaching of these areas. Some of these teachers believe that grammar and correct usage can be taught more effectively in the elementary school by following the procedures advocated by more traditional grammarians. Others who do not accept the suggestions made by educators favoring a linguistic orientation do not do so because they are opposed to teaching grammar in the elementary school.

3. Some teachers believe that only a quite limited application of the claims of linguists should be made when teaching the language arts in the elementary school. They may devote time in their language arts program to topics such as these that are not necessarily related to the teaching of grammar: (a) the changing

nature of a language, (b) what constitutes accepted speech in a given area among a given group of people in a given type of situation; (c) the development of language, (d) differences in the structure of some languages, (e) etymology. Or when teaching only the rudiments of grammar in the elementary school, as they base their work primarily on that of the traditional grammarians, they nevertheless wish to incorporate some of the ideas of linguistically oriented programs. For example, as they deal with nouns and other parts of speech—to which linguists refer as *class forms* rather than parts of speech—they may try to help the boys and girls by explaining to them some of the characteristics of the various parts of speech emphasized by linguists. Or even if the teachers are not affected by the claims of linguists, in their choice of subject matter taught nor in the generalizations to be learned by the pupils, they may still wish to employ the teaching procedure recommended by writers of linguistically oriented textbooks for children. It is by means of this method that boys and girls may learn to develop generalizations and then apply them, rather than to memorize rules given to them with the expectation that they then will make use of them.

What Should Be Taught

There has long been lack of agreement on what should be taught in the American elementary school as far as grammar and correct usage are concerned. The difference of opinion has not diminished with the introduction of questions concerning what, if any, claims of linguists should influence the teaching of the language arts and how, if accepted as significant for the program, application should be made of these tenets. In fact, it would seem as if there now is less uniformity of practice than several decades ago.

Some of the criteria to be applied in determining in part what should be taught are discussed on preceding pages of this chapter. Need, level of difficulty, and importance are mentioned. In the application of these criteria to the selection of points in grammar and correct usage there are real difficulties. No study has as yet ascertained with certainty what topics should be taken up in the elementary school. However, there have been comprised some lists that can serve as checks when drawing up a program for guidance in correct usage. One such study is that by Robert C. Pooley.[1] Another is that by Paul McKee.[2] Still another is a listing given by Ruth Hochstetler,[3] under the topic "Grade-Placement Practices," which appears in the book *Guiding Children's Language Learning,* edited by Pose Lamb. For additional suggestions beyond the three to which reference is here made and of which a copy is given following, the reader is referred to language arts textbooks for boys and girls.

1. Robert Pooley's list entitled "Errors to Be Attacked for Elimination in the Elementary School" included the following:

ain't for *hain't*
hair *are*
a orange
have *ate*
he *begun*
was *broke*
he *brung*
climb (short *i*)
clumb
he *come*
have did
he, she, it *don't*
I *drunk*
didn't, hadn't ought
was *froze*
he *give*
I *got* for *I've got*
my brother, *he* (and other double subjects)
her, him and *me* went
hisself
there *is, was* four
knowed, growed, etc.
learn me a song
leave me go
me and Mary went
haven't *no,* haven't *nothing*
he *run*
have *saw*
I *says*
he *seen*
them books
theirselves
this here
that there
us boys *went*
we, you, they *was*
with *we* girls
have *went*
have *wrote*
it is *yourn, hern, ourn, theirn*

While Pooley does not object to the items on the list that follows to be emphasized with individual pupils who

1. Robert C. Pooley, *Teaching English Usage,* English Monograph No. 16 (New York: Appleton-Century-Crofts, 1946), p. 180-81.
2. Paul McKee, *Language Arts in the Elementary School* (New York: Houghton Mifflin Company, 1939), p. 292-94.
3. Ruth Hochstetler, "Facets of Language—Grammar and Usage" in *Guiding Children's Language Learning,* 2d ed. Pose Lamb, ed. (Dubuque, Iowa: Wm. C. Brown Company Publishers, 1971), p. 312-13.

are ready for work on the elimination of some of these errors, he does not recommend them for study by an entire elementary school class. He refers to the list as "Points to Receive No Class Instruction in the Elementary School"

None of us *are, were* there.
Can I go?
Do the work *good.*
I haven't got a pencil.
I couldn't *hardly* do the work.
She gave it to John and *I.*
He *lays* down every day, is *laying* down, *laid* down, has *laid* down, etc.
Do it *like* Ido.
He acts *like* he is cold.
It is *me, him, her, them.*
Everybody, everyone said that *they.* . . .
Who did you choose?
If I *was* you, I'd play ball. I wish I *was* you.
Who are you waiting for?
I *will* probably be late.
One of my brothers *were* here.

2. Paul McKee's list. After careful consideration of studies on correct usage, Paul McKee has worked out the following list about which he says (page 292): "This list includes those items which various studies have shown to possess high frequency and persistency of difficulty."

I. Verbs.
1. *Come* for *came.*
2. *Give* for *gave.*
3. *Ain't* for *isn't.*
4. *Is* for *are,* and *are* for *is.*
5. *Knowed* for *knew.*
6. *Can* for *may.*
7. *Throwed* for *threw.*
8. *Run* for *ran.*
9. We *was* for *we were.*
10. *Has went* for *has gone.*
11. *Has took* for *has taken.*
12. *Saw* for *seen.*
13. *You was* for *you were.*
14. *Learn* for *teach.*
15. *Done* for *did.*
16. *Have did* for *have done.*
17. *Rung* for *rang.*
18. *Set* for *sit.*
19. *Sit* for *sat.*
20. *Lay* for *lie.*
21. *Rung* for *rang.*
22. *Seen* for *saw.*
23. *Ask* for *asked.*
24. *Git* for *get.*
25. *Et* for *ate.*
26. *Guess* for *think.*
27. *They was* for *they were.*
28. *Don't* for *doesn't.*
29. *There is* for *there are.*
30. *If there was* for *if there were.*
31. *Have got* for *have.*
32. *Hadn't ought* for *ought not.*

II. Pronouns.
1. *Them* for *those.*
2. *I and you* for *you and me.*
3. *Me and you* for *you and me.*
4. *Me and him* for *him and me.*
5. *It was me* for *it was I.*
6. *Hisself* for *himself.*
7. With John and *I* for John and *me.*
8. It was *her* for it was *she.*
9. *Those* kind for *this* kind or *that* kind.
10. It was *him* for it was *he.*
11. *Him* and *I* for *him* and *me.*
12. *Theirselves* for *themselves.*
13. *Us* boys (nominative).
14. *Them* girls for *those* girls.
15. *Each* does *their.* . . . for *each* does *his.*

III. Double negatives.
1. *Haven't got any* for *haven't any.*
2. *Haven't no* for *have no.*
3. *Don't know nothing* for *don't know anything* or *doesn't know anything.*

IV. Redundancy.
1. *This here, that there* for *this, that.*
2. *Where is it at?* for *Where is it?*
3. *John he* for *John.*
4. *He went and threw it* for *he threw it.*
5. *Go get it* for *get it.*

V. Adjectives.
1. Incorrect comparison of simple adjectives such as *bad, good, little, much, honest, far, comfortable, patient, useful,* etc. Examine lists of common words to discover adjectives actually used by people in the various degrees.

VI. Adverbs.
1. *Good* for *well.*
2. Correct use of simple adverbs such as *carefully, slowly, rapidly, nicely, surely, quickly, closely, fairly.* Examine lists of common words to discover adverbs actually used.

VII. Miscellaneous.
1. *Of* for *have.*
2. *Like* for *as though.*
3. *Are* for *our.*
4. *Their* for *there* and vice versa.
5. *An* for *and.*
6. *Where* for *were.*
7. Introductory words, *well, why, listen.*
8. The "loose" *and.*

9. Confusion of *in* and *into*.
10. Confusion of *of* and *off*.
11. Confusion of *a* and *an*.

3. Ruth Hochstetler's listing. Under "Grade Placement," Ruth Hochstetler introduces the listing with the words:

> Many textbooks in language concentrate on the same types of learning for any one grade level. More recent textbooks concentrate on oral language and on much more absorbing content. The following seem to be the points of grammar, usage, and other material that are considered important, however. These are stated in behavioral terms insofar as it is possible.[4]

Her listing is as follows:

First Grade

Eliminate gross examples of nonstandard usage
(ain't and hain't, brung, growed, knowed)
Recognize a sentence in manuscript
Express ideas so that the audience will listen

Second Grade

Eliminate additional examples of nonstandard usage
(hisself, theirselves, them books, this here)
Put self last
Learn that a sentence tells or asks
Express ideas so that others understand

Third Grade

Learn standard usage
(see, do, go, run, come, bring, and burst
has for *has got* and *have* for *have got*)
Put self last
Use those and them correctly
Make sentences complete thoughts
See need for statements, questions, and commands
Try to eliminate run-on sentences and use of "and"
  between sentences
Use well-made and original sentences
Use name, describing, and action words
Understand word order and how it functions in gram-
  mar
Construct sentence patterns
Recognize nouns, noun markers, and pronouns and
  their functions
Understand what verbs are

Fourth Grade

Master the standard forms of common verbs
Understand the terms noun and verb
Understand singular possessive noun—'s
Understand the subject, predicate, and word order
Begin to understand coordination and subordination
Understand the noun phrases, nouns with noun
  markers

Understand the verbs and verb markers
Understand the adjectives and their inflections
Understand the adverbs of place, time, and manner

Fifth Grade

Use verbs
(begin, blow, break, fly, give, and so on)
Use a and an correctly
Understand:

  the function of a noun
  common and proper nouns
  singular and plural nouns
  singular and plural possessive nouns

Understand:

  present and past tense of verbs
  subject and predicate
  different kinds of predicates
  double negatives
  the function of conjunctions—coordination
Know basic sentence patterns
Know about inflection, derivation, and functional
  shift

Sixth Grade

Use standard forms
Use standard prepositions
(at—to; in—into; among—between)
Use adverbs and adjectives correctly
Choose correct forms of pronouns
Understand the function of prepositions and conjunc-
  tions—subordination
Understand the agreement of subject and verb

Figure 6.6. Comparison of Adjectives.

4. Ibid.

Use grammatical terms functionally
Use a variety of sentence patterns
Understand what a morpheme is
Understand a transformation
Use transformations to produce compound and complex sentences
Use negative, interrogative, negative-interrogative, and passive transformations
Understand relationship between intonation patterns and meaning and intonation patterns and punctuation

Methods

Some suggestions for teaching boys and girls to recognize sentences and to express themselves adequately through sentences are given on preceding pages of this chapter. (See "Sentence Structure," page 137.) Below some additional methods are given under the headings "Suggestions Relating to the Subject and Predicate" and "Other Suggestions."

Suggestions Relating to the Subject and Predicate. Here only those points regarding procedures related to the subject and predicate are emphasized. Knowing these points may help in the identification of these parts of the sentence and, hopefully, lead to improved oral and written expression. It is also hoped that in the listing a few of the suggestions relating to the subject and predicate can provide ideas for teaching other points related to grammar and usage. However, as explained earlier, the reader who wishes to follow a program in teaching the language arts that has a strong linguistic orientation as far as teaching grammar is concerned, will, in addition to considering the points that follow, want to study carefully books dealing with the teaching of grammar according to such orientation as well as pupils' textbooks in the language arts similarly slanted in emphasis. Likewise, the reader who desires detailed guidance in teaching according to suggestions from more traditional grammarians is advised to read professional books and children's textbooks that emphasize that approach to grammar and correct usage.

The teacher can help the boys and girls with the subject and predicate of sentences by:

1. Writing on the chalkboard a list of simply constructed declarative sentences and then asking the class about what each of the sentences tells as he underlines the complete subject of each sentence

2. Telling the boys and girls that the part of the sentence that tells what the sentence is about is the subject of the sentence

3. Asking the pupils to name the subject of declarative sentences written on the chalkboard or on paper and to give the reason for their selection

4. Asking the pupils to form sentences in each of which one of a specified group of words is used as the subject, for example: (a) the boys, (b) some men

5. Having the boys and girls select the subject and predicate in each of a list of declarative sentences

6. Asking the pupils to find the subject of an interrogative sentence. The teacher may help the pupils find the subject after he has changed the question to declarative order as in:

Interrogative form: What are you doing?
Declarative form: You are doing what?

Then the teacher may point out to the pupils that when they try to find the subject of an interrogative sentence, they may find it of help to change the question to declarative order.

7. Pointing out to the class that when they try to find the subject of an exclamatory sentence not in the same order as the usual declarative sentence, it may help them to change the exclamation to declarative form.

8. Helping boys and girls recognize the complete subject and complete predicate by transforming simple sentences, such as "The boys are playing" to longer sentences. After they have pointed out the subject and predicate in that sentence, for example, they could be asked to add words to the subject and to the predicate and then name the complete subject and complete predicate of the sentences they have formed, such as:

The boys are playing ball.
The older boys are playing ball.
The older boys are playing ball on the schoolgrounds.

9. Asking the pupils to rewrite sentences so that the subject of each, which, if necessary, the teacher can underline, is found in different parts of sentences, as in this sample:

The boys and girls went to the museum yesterday.
Yesterday *the boys and girls* went to the museum.

10. Having the boys and girls act out a sentence to help them in determining the subject and predicate

11. After the boys and girls have selected the complete subject of a sentence in which the subject consists of more than one word, asking them to name the most important word in the subject—the one word that names what the sentence tells about. After they have selected the most important word in the subject of each of several sentences, the teacher may tell the class that such a word is called the *simple subject*. Thereupon the pupils may be asked to select the simple and the complete subjects of several sentences. Work on the simple and complete predicates can be done similarly.

12. After the boys and girls have selected the complete predicate of sentences in which the predicate consists of more than the verb or verb phrase, asking them to name the most important word or group of words in the pred-

icate, the word or group of words that tells what is being told about the subject. After the pupils have thus selected the most important word or group of words in the predicate in several sentences, the teacher can tell the class that the most important word or group of words in the predicate of a sentence is called the *simple predicate*. Thereupon the pupils could be asked to select the complete and the simple predicates of several sentences.

13. Helping the boys and girls with simple forms of diagramming in which they place on one line the simple subject (marked *s*) and the simple predicate (marked *p*) and on a line or lines below each the rest of the subject and predicate. One simple form that can be used with a sentence containing a subject, with modifier, and a predicate, with modifier, is the following:

s	*p*
girls	played
The little	with their dolls.

For sentences containing a subject, verb, and complement and for other forms of sentence structure, different schemes for diagramming can be worked out.

14. Encouraging the pupils to make a poster that will remind them how to find the subject and the predicate of a sentence.

15. Asking the pupils to find the subject and predicate of each of two short sentences that can be combined into one sentence with a compound subject such as:

The boys went on a picnic.
The girls went on a picnic.

Then the teacher may have the pupils find the subject of the sentence "The boys and girls went on a picnic," as well as of other sentences with a compound subject. He can next tell them that subjects connected by *and, or*, or *nor* are called compound subjects. Work on compound predicates can be done similarly.

16. Asking the pupils to find in a paragraph (a) a sentence with a compound subject, (b) a sentence with a compound predicate, and (c) a sentence with both a compound subject and a compound predicate

17. Providing the boys and girls with practice in forming sentences with compound subjects and sentences with compound predicates out of short groups of sentences that can be combined in that manner

18. Helping the pupils find the subject and predicate of declarative sentences in which the subject is not at the beginning of the sentence, such as "Early in the morning they left for home."

19. Asking the boys and girls to match the subjects in one column with the predicates in an exercise such as the following:

The rain	went to the bakery.
The book	will make the grass green.
We	are blooming.
The flowers	contains many interesting stories.

Additional Suggestions. The teacher can help the boys and girls in learning more about grammar, including correct usage, by procedures such as those here listed:

1. Providing the boys and girls with the opportunity to decide under what circumstances samples of varying levels of written or oral expression are suitable. Reference could be made to a classification of levels such as that worked out by Robert C. Pooley,[5] who classifies levels as to: the illiterate, the homely, the informal standard, the formal standard, the literary, and the technical levels. Or the classification frequently used dividing the levels of usage into three levels, the standard, substandard, and slang, could be utilized. The teacher might present a list of such samples, have the pupils indicate in writing the level on which or the circumstances under which each would be acceptable, and then orally give reasons for their responses.

2. Sponsoring the making of a mural summarizing learnings the class has acquired on the history or development of communication. Illustrations might include signalling, carving on stone (as on the Rosetti Stone), the invention of the printing press, the Morse code.

3. Encouraging children who know a language other than English to report on differences in the language they know and English. Some pupils might discover points such as this one:

There is a difference in word order in some languages. (For example, "Ich fühle jetzt besser" would have as literal translation "I feel now better.")

4. Helping boys and girls learn about language by encouraging them to be on the lookout for facts about it. Some pupils might report on points such as these that for them constitute discoveries even though they have been known by others for a long time:

Babies first talk in single words, not in sentences.
Correction of an individual's speech by others, unless tactfully done, can cause embarrassment.

5. Discussing with the pupils helpful, polite ways in which they can assist one another in improvement of their oral and written expression

6. Encouraging boys and girls to be helpful to people with language disorders, such as stammering or stuttering, and having them discuss ways in which they can render such assistance

7. Suggesting that boys and girls note differences in speech in people from various parts of the country and helping them to recognize the fact that standards for correctness of expression differ from place to place

8. Motivating the boys and girls so that they want to be able to speak in "standard English." Any discussions

5. Robert C. Pooley, "The Levels of Language," *Educational Method*, 16 (March 1937): 290.

of the value of being able to communicate in "standard English" should be carried on in such a manner that the boys and girls do not get the impression that persons not speaking "standard English" are inferior.

9. Helping the boys and girls put on a skit in which the value of "good English" is demonstrated

10. Teaching the boys and girls which verb form to use as the teacher helps them develop generalizations such as the following:

> *Done* is usually used with a helping word.
> It is never correct to use *did* with a helping word.

11. Having the pupils make application of their learning by filling blanks in sentences, by choosing the correct form in statements of the multiple-choice type, and by using sentences of their own illustrating the correct response

12. Helping the pupils make crossword puzzles that are based on knowledge of correct usage.

13. Discussing with the boys and girls the importance of avoiding repetition of incorrect forms when they are trying to break the habit of using them. How wrong habits can be broken and right ones established can profitably be discussed with many boys and girls.

14. Having the pupils make posters or cartoons that will serve to remind them and others of the correct forms they have been studying.

15. Encouraging the pupils to make a handbook on correct usage. Such a notebook could list the various forms of correct usage upon which the class has been concentrating. On separate pages generalizations that have been developed might be stated. In addition, each pupil might make a list of those forms that he uses incorrectly at times. The teacher may wish to keep a file of exercises on the various items of correct usage studied during the year. A pupil can then choose from the file those that deal with the correction of his own problems in the usage of words.

16. Providing programmed material on correct usage. Such material can be especially beneficial for use with the slow learner. One advantage is that the steps in carefully constructed programmed lessons are usually small enough so that a pupil can readily grasp each point. The self-checking nature of the materials saves the teacher time that might be used in checking some other types of materials. The interest factor, especially when machines are used, is another important advantage of such materials. (See "Programmed instruction," page 321.)

A Teaching Plan

The following plan is an adaptation of one written by a former college student, Carole Stoffer Luce. It may be suitable for use with alterations, in a third or fourth grade. By means of a developmental lesson, such as the one outlined here, using steps like the following the teacher can assist boys and girls to discover a generalization and make application of it by: (1) helping the pupils realize the need for the learning, (2) drawing the pupils' attention to specific points (through questioning and comment) in illustrative sentences, (3) having pupils summarize their findings, (4) stating the generalization, and (5) providing for application of the generalization.

Background Information. It is assumed that boys and girls have studied the words *sang, sung, rang, rung,* and *threw, thrown* and that they are familiar with the terms *helping words* and *helper* as used in this plan.

A. *Pupils' Aim:* To learn how to use *saw* and *seen* correctly

B. *Materials:*
   1. Board work
      a. Sentences to develop the generalization
         (1) We *saw* four huge fire engines at the station.
         (2) Some of us have *seen* fire engines before.
         (3) The fire chief has *seen* many burning buildings.
         (4) All of us *saw* big ladders.
      b. Sentences for oral practice in which *saw* and *seen* are already included in the sentences

Crossword puzzle:

¹r	a	n	²g		³s	
			⁴o	n	e	
⁵w			n		t	
⁶e	a	⁷t	e	n		
r		a			⁸a	
e		u			t	
		⁹g	i	v	e	n
		h				
		¹⁰t	a	k	e	n

Across:
1. The fire-alarm (rang, rung).
4. Jim lost (won, one) of his balls.
6. The boys had (ate, eaten) their lunch.
9. Dick has (gave, given) me this bat.
10. Jim had (taken, took) the apples home.

Down:
2. The children had (went, gone) home.
3. He had (set, sat) the basket on the chair.
5. The children (was, were) at home.
7. Mr. Smith (teached, taught) our class today.
8. Who (ate, et) the candy?

(1) I have *seen* an elephant at a parade.

(2) I *saw* an elephant at the circus.

(3) My mother said she has *seen* my mittens.

(4) She *saw* them under my coat.

(5) My sister *saw* the package first.

(6) We had *seen* many people.

(7) We *saw* some people whom we knew.

(8) Our teacher said, "I have *seen* Fred."

c. Sentences for oral practice for which pupils need to choose correct word forms

(1) She has (saw, seen) my report card.

(2) I (saw, seen) her leave the house.

(3) We have (saw, seen) that movie.

(4) Tom and I (saw, seen) the team practice.

(5) We had (saw, seen) the ducks fly south.

(6) He has (saw, seen) our new neighbors.

(7) Jane (saw, seen) my ruler.

(8) I (saw, seen) him on TV.

Figure 6.7. Illustration to Emphasize Correct Usage.

2. Poster illustrating independence of *saw* and dependence of *seen* on helping words such as *has, have, had*

3. Duplicated copies of sentences for written practice, for which the pupils are to supply the correct form *saw* or *seen*, with directions

a. We _____ the new bus today.

b. Have you _____ it?

c. I _____ it last week.

d. Mary _____ it first.

e. I _____ a bigger bus last summer.

f. Tom had _____ a bus like it last year.

g. We _____ the plane land.

h. She has _____ the answer.

i. I _____ what I wanted.

j. Suzanne had _____ the birthday presents.

k. You _____ what happened.

l. They have _____ our house.

m. We _____ them too late to stop them.

n. Dotty _____ a yellow bird in the tree.

o. Mother has _____ the bird.

C. *Outline of Procedure:*

1. Introduction

a. The teacher tells the pupils that boys, girls, and adults often misuse the words *saw* and *seen*.

b. The teacher tells the class that he has noticed that some of the pupils at times misused *saw* and *seen*.

c. The teacher tells the class that this day he is going to help them learn the correct use of these words.

2. Development of the generalization

a. Initial study of the first sentence under *B-1-a*

(1) A pupil reads the sentence orally.

(2) A pupil tells what word is underlined in the sentence and tells whether or not the word is used with a helping word such as *has, have,* or *had.*

(3) The teacher writes the following on the chalkboard as the first entry under the caption "No Helper":

1. saw.

b. Initial study of sentences *2, 3, and 4, under B-1-a*

(1) The teacher asks the pupils to do the following when he calls on them for the remaining sentences under *B-1-a:* (a) Read the sentence orally. (b) Name the underlined word. (c) Tell whether or not a helper is used with the underlined word.

(2) The teacher writes the responses on the chalkboard according to the reference made under (1) *above* so that the following appears on the chalkboard:

Helper	*No Helper*
2. seen	1. saw
3. seen	4. saw.

c. Giving of summary statement

The teacher refers to the listing given under *C-2-b-(2)* and asks the class which of the words, *saw* or *seen,* is used without a helper and which is used with a helper in those sentences.

d. Giving of generalization

(1) By the teacher
  (a) The teacher says that *saw* should never be used with a helping word and that *seen* usually needs a helping word.
  (b) The teacher writes the generalization on the chalkboard.
(2) By the pupils
  Several pupils state the generalization.
  e. Reference to the poster (See Figure 6.7.)
    The teacher explains that *in sentences the pupils are likely to use* the first six words listed need a helper.
3. Oral work on sentences on the chalkboard
  a. Work on sentences under *B-1-b*
    Pupils follow this procedure with each of the sentences:
    (1) They read the sentence orally.
    (2) They tell why the word underlined is used, naming the helper if *seen* is used.
  b. Work on sentences under *B-1-c*
    (1) Pupils work on the first sentence.
      (a) The pupils read the sentence silently.
      (b) A pupil tells which word in parentheses should be used.
      (c) A pupil tells why he chose the word he selected.
      (d) A pupil reads the sentence orally.
    (2) Pupils work on sentences 2 through 8, using the same procedure outlined under (1).
4. Written work (See *B-3*.)
  a. The pupils read the directions silently.
  b. The teacher asks the children to refer to the rule on the chalkboard and the poster if necessary.
  c. The teacher states that pupils who finish early should write sentences of their own using *saw* and *seen*.
5. Correcting papers
  The pupils follow this procedure as the teacher gives the number of each succeeding sentence:
  a. A pupil tells what word he chose.
  b. The pupil gives the reason for his choice.
  c. The pupil reads the entire sentence orally inserting the correct answer.
6. Forward look
  a. The teacher encourages the pupils to use words correctly at all times.
  b. The teacher asks the pupils to think of words other than *saw* and *seen* which usually need "helpers" and to name other forms of the

same words that should not be used with "helping words."

EVALUATION

Some of the means of evaluating factors common to both oral and written communication are illustrated following.

Vocabulary

Exercises such as the following can test the pupils' knowledge of the meaning of words.

1. *Directions.* On each line below write the word in that row which means about the same as the word in dark print.

  small: large, tired, little _____

  over-statement: exaggeration, paucity, elite _____

  _____

2. *Directions.* On each line below write the word in that row which means about the opposite of the word in dark print.

  dark: wet, bright, stupid _____

  alert: disgruntled, inattentive, antagonistic _____

  _____

3. *Directions.* Cross out the overworked words given in parentheses in the sentences below. Write a word to take the place of each word you crossed out.

  We had a (wonderful) _____ time at the park.

  It was a (gorgeous) _____ day.

4. Draw a diagram illustrating each of the following terms: *fall line, isthmus, gulf, portage.*

Sentence Structure

Here are a few ways in which evaluation can be made of the pupils' knowledge of sentences and of their use of them.

1. The boys and girls can indicate which from a series of sentences and sentence fragments are sentences and which are not sentences.

2. The pupils can give sentences of the various types they have studied, such as declarative, interrogative, exclamatory, and imperative sentences.

3. The boys and girls can be asked to change two or more short, choppy sentences into a longer sentence.

4. The pupils can write a sentence in a different way, as shown in the following example: (a) The children went on the trip on a cold, rainy day. (b) On a cold, rainy day the children went on the trip.

5. The pupils can expand basic sentences (kernel sentences) as is indicated on page 159.

Kernel sentence: Men are working.

Many men are working on our road.
Many young men are working on our new road.

FOR STUDY AND DISCUSSION

1. Name meaningful situations, in addition to those listed earlier in this chapter, through which vocabulary development can be encouraged in the elementary school.

2. Devise a practice exercise to help boys and girls in any one of the intermediate grades improve in some phase of sentence structure.

3. In what ways could a teacher help boys and girls recognize the importance of learning how to outline?

4. To apply some points on outlining stressed in this chapter, write the outline for this chapter using letters and numerals to indicate the various parts in the manner in which they are used in this chapter in the outlines presented.

5. What cautions would you want to bear in mind as you plan to have boys and girls help one another in the program of correct usage?

6. Name ways in which growth in the correct use of words (correct usage) can be stimulated in the elementary school.

7. Devise diagrams of bulletin boards that can be used to encourage and to help boys and girls with correct word usage. On what grade level(s) might each of your suggested bulletin boards be of value?

8. Examine two recent language arts series for use by elementary school pupils—one that is strongly linguistically oriented and a second that is not. Note what items of grammar or correct usage are taught and the grade level at which each is presented. Also note procedures used in the teaching. At the present time what is your reaction to the way in which correct usage and/or grammar is treated in the two textbook series?

9. Study a recent course of study for the elementary school and note carefully the parts dealing with the topics discussed in this chapter, namely: (a) vocabulary, (b) sentence structure, (c) note taking, (d) outlining, and (e) correct usage and grammar. What are some significant points that came to your mind as you were studying the course of study?

10. To what extent do you think the language arts program should be linguistically oriented? Give reasons for your suggestions.

11. Give suggestions for helping a child who speaks on the illiterate level acquire the desire to learn to speak standard English. What precautions would you take so that he would not be likely to feel that he and his family are inferior to people who speak a standard English?

12. Examine one or more professional books on the teaching of the language arts to note suggestions given for teaching the topics discussed in this chapter. If you find points of disagreement between this book and the one(s) you examine, what is your reaction to the points of controversy? Note the important points made that are not made in your own textbook. Be able to discuss these additional points.

REFERENCES

For references for this chapter the reader is referred to those given at the end of chapter 4, chapter 5, and chapter 13.

7

Guiding Growth in Handwriting

Regardless of whether or not there is justification for the complaint that handwriting has deteriorated, it must be acceded that the quality of the handwriting of the American people is on a much lower level than it could be expected to be in a nation that has been and is giving unparalleled attention in terms of time, money, and man power to providing educational opportunities for its citizenry.

What are the evidences of the inadequacy of writing ability in school and out of school? Research has given partial answers; however, no scientific study is necessary to establish convincing proof. Facts such as the following provide evidence.

1. Addresses on so many letters are illegible or almost unreadable that some of the large post offices have individuals on their staff whose responsibility it is to try to decipher such addresses.

2. Many of the letters received at the Dead Letter Office are referred to it because the handwriting could not be figured out by the personnel in the post office. Many of the letters relegated to that office never reach their destination because even experts in that office are not able to determine to what addresses they are to be sent.

3. Business yearly loses large amounts of money because of errors and wasted time caused by illegibility of writing on sales slips or checks and in letters ordering things.

4. Many businesses, such as telephone companies, gas companies, and insurance companies, enclose self-addressed envelopes with their statements or bills, probably partly because of the illegibility of the handwriting of many people.

5. It is undoubtedly true that some students receive lower marks than they otherwise might on examinations and on other handwritten papers because their handwriting is such that the teacher cannot readily comprehend the meaning that the writers are attempting to convey.

6. Recipients of friendly letters have difficulty in figuring out the meaning that their correspondents are

attempting to express and at times are unable to ascertain it even after considerable attention has been given to trying to decipher it.

7. The character of much writing, even when legible, is so inartistic that the reader is deprived of a certain aesthetic satisfaction that can result from viewing something well done.

8. Many persons, it seems, refrain from writing because they know they are inefficient in that skill in terms of effort required and of the results they achieve.

BASIC CONSIDERATIONS IN TEACHING HANDWRITING

Before turning to a study of specific procedures for guiding growth in handwriting, let us give attention to certain important general considerations.

Causes of Neglect of Handwriting

Light may be thrown on how to guide growth in handwriting by inquiring as to the reasons for the partial neglect in the past, by many teachers, of the development of skill in handwriting. The following are among contributing causes.

1. There has been, on the part of many teachers, a lack of knowledge of the psychology of handwriting in that (a) they do not recognize the skill aspects of written communication and (b) they do not understand the principles underlying the teaching of skills.

2. There has been a tendency in some schools to emphasize incidental learning rather than an efficient combination of systematic instruction with the incidental.

3. The disappearance of the penmanship supervisor was not followed, as a rule, by steps to give the classroom teacher adequate preparation for the teaching of handwriting, which was delegated to him.

4. The alleged claim, prevalent in and out of school, that excellence in handwriting is no longer very important in the modern world of the typewriter and other machines used for communication purposes, has taken away part of the motive for effective teaching and learning of how to write.

5. Recognition of the shortcomings of writing practices that had been popularly followed caused many persons to revolt against systematic practice of any kind.

Shortcomings of Earlier Practices

No attempt is made here to disparage en toto some of the programs of handwriting in vogue several decades ago. They had their strengths as well as their weaknesses, and they played, it seems, a significant role in bringing about progress in the teaching of handwriting. However points in some of the programs of the early decades of the century to which considerable objection was and is being raised, and rightly so, by teachers during more recent years are listed here.

1. An overemphasis was often placed on handwriting as a skill.

2. Undue attention was frequently paid to the mechanics of handwriting.

3. There was at times excessive emphasis on formal, isolated drill.

4. Much drill was of a mechanistic type.

5. There was little correlation made, on the part of some teachers, between drill on handwriting and the work in the content subjects.

6. Skills acquired during the writing period often did not carry over into writing done by boys and girls outside of school.

7. There was in some schools a great preponderance of group instruction to the almost total neglect of individualized instruction.

8. Uniformity of style was stressed by many teachers at the expense of acceptable originality in handwriting.

Goals of Instruction

A sound program of instruction cannot be planned merely through an avoidance of past teaching errors. A constructive program must (a) be determined by worthy goals of instruction and (b) be in harmony with sound principles of teaching.

General Objectives. Simply stated, the aim of handwriting instruction is to help boys and girls learn to write legibly and neatly at a commendable rate, without undue strain.

The desired goals to be achieved by the pupil by the time he leaves the elementary school can be summarized thus:

1. The pupil should be able to write legibly, with the quality that is acceptable in adult handwriting. Since in the majority of schools handwriting is not given much emphasis as a developmental subject of the curriculum beyond the sixth grade, it is recommended that by the end of the sixth grade the child be able to do writing of the quality represented by a score of 60 on the Ayres's Handwriting Scale.

2. The pupil should be able to write at a fairly rapid rate, with speed dependent, in part, on the purpose for which the writing is being done.

3. The pupil should be able to produce a neat paper, written without smudges, signs of erasures, or crossing out what had been recorded. He should use a format suitable to the material and the purposes for which the writing is being done.

4. The pupil should acquire the ability to write for a rather long time without undue strain.

Another way in which the objectives of the handwriting program might be defined in rather general terms is by stating that the program during the course of the work in the elementary school, should help boys and girls to do the following:

1. To become ready to learn to write
2. To learn to do manuscript writing
3. To make the transition from manuscript to cursive writing
4. To learn to do cursive writing

Specific Goals. Whether or not a teacher uses a commercially produced handwriting series, the programs suggested by the better series may be of help to him in determining the specific aims he wishes to accomplish. The goals as recorded for grades one and six in *I Learn to Write* by E. C. Seale and Company[1] follow. For statements of the objectives of that program for grades two, three, four, and five, the reader is referred to the teacher's editions of the books for those grades.

The objectives for boys and girls of grade one are listed as follows:

1. To enjoy writing
2. To become interested in improving their writing
3. To develop the ability to evaluate their writing and to improve it
4. To develop a writing style that is easy to read
5. To make each letter clearly and correctly so that it cannot be confused with any other letter
6. To write words so that each is easily recognized as it stands alone
7. To write stories of two or more sentences
8. To make progress in the different technical phases of writing

The goals for the sixth-grade program are given in the following manner in the teacher's edition for that grade:

1. To improve upon the writing skill developed during previous years
2. To increase ability to express thought in clear, correct language
3. To organize material in such a way that it makes a neat, attractive page
4. To be aware of the personal responsibility for legible writing in all social and business situations
5. To maintain skills in manuscript writing.

Guidelines

The relationship between the selection of goals and the formulation of guidelines, such as the following, should be two-way. The goals should in part determine the guidelines, and the guidelines should be useful in arriving at the goals.

1. Readiness for writing and for the various stages in learning to write should be determined and, if necessary, developed.

2. Since handwriting is a phase of the language arts, it should be taught as part of the total language arts program, in which one facet of the language arts reinforces the others and is, in turn, reinforced by them. This statement should not, however, be interpreted as meaning that systematic instruction in handwriting is unnecessary.

3. Handwriting should be correlated with work in other areas, including not only the other language arts activities but also other phases of the school curriculum and out-of-school activities.

4. Since handwriting is in part a neural-muscular skill, the laws governing economic development of skills should be observed in the teaching.

5. Since handwriting is in part a neural-muscular skill, the teacher should base instruction—especially the beginning phases—on knowledge of the neural-muscular development as indicated by specialists in the area of child growth and development.

6. Since not only correct but also incorrect practice can become a habit, it is important that boys and girls receive guidance in an activity before they have established incorrect writing habits.

7. Boys and girls should be helped to discern the need for correct finger movement and to practice it, for good handwriting requires not only arm and wrist but also finger movement.

8. Practice conditions should approximate as much as possible those under which a skill will be required in non-practice situations.

9. Since handwriting is more than a skill—also a means of self-expression—more than the drill aspects should be emphasized.

10. Since example is important in learning, the teacher's handwriting should serve as a model of what he wants to teach. While a quality of 60 on the Ayres's Handwriting Scale is considered by many to be a satisfactory standard for adults, it has been suggested that the teacher's handwriting should be comparable to that of 70 on that scale.

11. Since handwriting is a communication tool, considerable uniformity should be achieved but not to the exclusion of the possibility of some individuality.

12. A pupil in the elementary school should learn to write so well that in his written communication he can, in time, be able to give almost complete attention to the ideas he wishes to express rather than to the phases of the writing act.

1. The material is used with the permission of the Bobbs-Merrill Company, Indianapolis, Indiana, publishers of *I Learn to Write* series.

13. Systematic instruction should be paralleled with much opportunity for incidental learning.

14. Attention should not only be paid to legibility but also to the ease and speed with which writing is done and the attitude of the writer toward it.

15. Emphasis should not be placed primarily on letter strokes or letter forms but on thought units of expression—on words, sentences, paragraphs, and longer forms of written communication.

16. There should be emphasis on the attainment of good posture, rhythmic movement, and other mechanical features of good handwriting; but the learner should be helped to realize that these aspects of the handwriting program receive their significance primarily through their relationship to the final outcomes as shown in improved handwriting.

17. Individual differences should be recognized and the program planned to meet them adequately. (The reader is referred to chapter 12.)

18. Standards of good handwriting against which the learner can compare his own writing should be made available to him, and he should be given needed help in making self-evaluations.

19. Pupils should not only be cognizant of sound goals for the handwriting program as a whole but should also have specific goals in mind for each day's work on improvement in ability to write.

20. The value of rewards should be recognized, with major emphasis on the intrinsic value that knowledge of progress offers. Praise, when well deserved, can prove to be a valuable incentive. Only limited use, if any, should be made of such signs of accomplishment as awards, buttons, or badges.

21. There should be a working atmosphere in the classroom that can greatly contribute to the probable effectiveness of learning—characterized by pupils happily busy with an activity they consider worthwhile and an orderliness which prevents undue interference with anyone's success by others in the room.

ORGANIZATION

In spite of the time, energy, and money that has been spent on research aiming to determine the optimum classroom organization and procedures for the teaching of elementary school subjects, including handwriting, no final answer, convincing to all educators, has been formulated to the question: "How can the classroom best be organized for providing an effective program of instruction in handwriting?" The answers to questions such as the following, to which attention is subsequently given, indicate points of controversy: (1) Should there be a planned systematic procedure for teaching handwriting or should it be taught only incidentally? (2) If time is set aside in the school program for systematic instruction in

handwriting, how often should such writing classes meet and what should be the length of the periods? (3) If class periods are set aside for teaching handwriting, what should be the objective of the handwriting period and what should be the aim, as far as handwriting is concerned, of other periods of the school day when pupils write? (4) If class periods are devoted to teaching handwriting, should they be used for group or individualized instruction or a combination of the two?

Incidental versus Systematic Instruction

The chief point of argument in the debate seems to deal with whether the most effective organization is to have class periods set aside for teaching handwriting or whether the instruction should be given incidentally in other than handwriting periods. Let us examine arguments for and against the use of class periods set aside for that purpose.

Arguments Advanced Against Periods for Teaching Handwriting. Arguments such as the following are at times given against separate periods for handwriting instruction.

1. There is danger of lack of carry-over from separate periods for writing practice to ordinary writing situations.

2. Boys and girls find more purpose in writing that is done as part of the ongoing activities of the school program than in that done during periods set aside specifically for learning to write.

3. There are so many individual differences among boys and girls, as reflected in the type of help they should be given in handwriting, that large-group instruction is impractical.

4. It is a waste of time for many pupils to have regular class work for the improvement of handwriting.

5. Organization of the school program into a fairly large number of separate class periods is likely to result in one that is too segmented for effective attention to the whole child.

Arguments Favoring Periods for Teaching Handwriting. Following are listed not only arguments advanced in refutation of some of those enumerated but also additional ones in favor of setting aside periods in the school program for teaching handwriting.

1. Handwriting is too complex a skill to be trusted for proper development to only incidental methods of procedure.

2. Without systematic instruction boys and girls are likely to develop poor habits of writing that need to be broken because the learner is left "on his own" at crucial stages in the development of handwriting habits.

3. When separate periods are used for instruction in handwriting, it is possible to develop a program in which

the pupil is helped to progress from easier to more difficult phases in learning to write more effectively than in incidental programs.

4. Primary focus on a skill to be developed, at a time when other considerations are secondary, is frequently characteristic of a more effective teaching procedure than a less direct attack on a problem.

5. Systematic instruction can provide the learner with the practice needed at well distributed intervals.

6. Even in handwriting classes much attention can advisedly be paid not only to the skills but also to other essentials for effective handwriting in meaningful situations.

7. Even in a program in which a separate period is used for handwriting, much attention can and should be paid to it in writing activities in which the pupil engages. The learning to be achieved during the writing period as well as application of what is taught at such times unifies the writing during the handwriting period and the writing done at other times.

8. Often fundamental skills and basic habits can be developed more economically through group rather than individual instruction.

9. The handwriting class can and should be taught in such a way that not all instruction is given as a group process but that work is individualized as needed.

```
10:20 - 10:25   Presentation of new
                work to class
10:25 - 10:32   Work on practice ex-
                ercise on new work
                by class as group
10:32 - 10:45   Application of new
                learning to activ-
                ities requiring
                writing by various
                individuals, with
                teacher guidance
```

Figure 7.1. Illustration of a Plan for Group and Individual Help during Handwriting Class.

10. Pupils who require less time for the development of writing skills and habits—less than others in the class—can and should be excused from class whenever attendance seems not to be indicated for them.

Nature of the Handwriting Period

Surveys indicate that the predominant practice in the schools of the country seems to be to set aside a period in the school program for the teaching of handwriting.

Frequency and Length of Writing Periods. There is, as might well be expected, considerable variation in the frequency and length of periods for handwriting. In some school systems systematic instruction in handwriting ceases at the end of the sixth grade while other schools continue the program through grade eight. In many schools provision is made for a handwriting class daily, while in others handwriting is taught fewer than five days a week. Especially in the upper-intermediate grades is there more likely not to be found a daily period for handwriting instruction. From fifteen to twenty minutes is often the length of the period, but in the lower grades periods of only ten minutes are also found in some schedules.

The Writing Period as Part of a Language Arts Block. A practice followed with success in a considerable number of schools is that of providing for systematic instruction in handwriting by means of a block of time set aside for all the language arts other than reading. In such a block, for example, twenty minutes may be used daily for spelling class, twenty minutes on some days for handwriting class, and twenty minutes or more for other language arts activities. In place of this, separate classes in handwriting may be held within that hour only two or three times a week, varying from week to week. During these periods special emphasis can be given to the development of basic habits and skills of handwriting and on individual diagnosis followed by appropriate remediation. On the other days of the week the only writing done during the language arts period is in connection with the writing in spelling class and in other language arts activities, such as writing a report or a

```
Plan for Oct. 1.
   1:00 - 1:20   Spelling: presenta-
                 tion of words for
                 week
   1:20 - 2:00   Language: writing
                 stories

Plan for Oct. 2.
   1:00 - 1:20   Spelling: oral and
                 written work
   1:20 - 1:40   Handwriting: develop-
                 mental lesson
   1:40 - 2:00   Language: oral work
                 on correct usage

Plan for Oct. 3.
   1:00 - 1:20   Spelling: trial test
   1:20 - 2:00   Language: planning a
                 puppet play
```

Figure 7.2. Illustration of a Language Arts Block.

poem. The teacher might advisedly vary the days of the week when the more formal work on handwriting would be done, depending on the activities that the boys and girls would be doing that day during the rest of the time set aside for language arts. For example, on a day when the pupils would be spending much of twenty minutes writing the spelling words or when they would be writing a report during the remainder of the language arts period, no special writing class might be scheduled for that day.

Relationship Between Activities During Handwriting Period and Other Writing. When separate periods, within or outside of a language arts block, are set up for systematic instruction in handwriting, it is important that the relationships named below exist between writing done in and out of writing class:

1. The boys and girls recognize that the purpose of the activities during the handwriting period grows out of their needs for written communication.

2. Application is made in all writing activities of the habits and skills acquired or in the process of being acquired during the handwriting period.

3. Frequently during writing classes boys and girls write material with content value, even though time often needs to be set aside for practice procedures where the only utilitarian value of the reinforcement lies not in the subject matter but in the practice that it provides for acquiring or perfecting a skill.

Group Versus Individual Instruction During Handwriting Period. Some of the opponents of systematic instruction in writing classes base their stand, at least in part, on the fact that individuals differ so much in their handwriting needs that group instruction is impractical. While, undoubtedly, all too frequently in writing classes there is too little individualized instruction, that shortcoming is not inherent in the set-up. Some ways in which both group and individualized instruction can be carried on effectively in handwriting periods are indicated below.

1. Frequently group instruction is valuable when a new skill or habit is to be developed if it is one that should be presented to everyone in class.

2. At a stage in work on reinforcement of a skill when all the pupils still need further development of a skill, it is often economical to give class instruction.

3. At times when techniques of diagnosis are being demonstrated and studied, group instruction is recommended because of economy of time effected and because of the beneficial result of having some discussion of errors carried on that is not directed at those of a given named individual.

4. Group instruction is superior to individual teaching when the child can learn through the give-and-take of discussion of topics dealing with handwriting.

5. Individualization of instruction is desirable when some pupils have achieved a given skill to the extent that it is not most profitable for them at times to continue work toward its perfection.

6. At times some pupils might advisedly be excused from all work on the improvement of handwriting during a given class period and be free to work on some other phase of the school curriculum.

7. Even at times when all children are working toward the acquisition of the same skill, individual instruction might be given as the teacher helps one child after another with his problem.

8. At times, during the first few minutes of a period, group instruction might be given, to be followed by each pupil individually working on that phase of the problem on which he needs to improve.

9. After a pupil has had group instruction in basic skills for a considerable length of time, a greater and greater proportion of the time for handwriting class can often be spent on individualized instruction in which each pupil tries to put into practice what he has learned through group instruction.

10. When two or more pupils, but not the entire class, require help on the same point, those with the same need may temporarily be grouped for instruction. This grouping may continue for only part of a class period or may be in effect for a week or longer. Furthermore, some pupils may leave the group before it is discontinued.

MATERIALS OF INSTRUCTION

One way in which the teacher can obtain a good idea of the materials available for teaching handwriting is to examine the catalogs of leading publishers.

Materials Distributed by One Company

The following are among the many handwriting materials distributed by the Zaner-Bloser Company, publishers of *Creative Growth with Handwriting* by Walter B. Barbe, Virginia H. Lucas, Clinton S. Hackney, and Constance McAllister.

1. Recorders, in which the pupils write
2. Teachers' editions of the pupils' recorders
3. Other books for teachers, among them *Writing on the Board* and *The Whys and Hows of Teaching Handwriting* by Emma Myers
4. "Alphabet Guide Charts," illustrating the formation of letters and numerals
5. Wall strips in both manuscript and cursive writing
6. Scales for evaluating pupils' handwriting, with a scale for manuscript writing for each of grades one, two, and three, and a scale for cursive writing for each grade from two through nine
7. Various aids to correct letter formation

8. A variety of lined and unlined writing paper with a range in the distance between the rulings

9. Pencils, penholders, and pen points.

Selection of Materials

In choosing suitable materials for the various age or grade levels, the teacher may be guided by points such as these:

1. For beginners in handwriting primary-size pencils are preferred by many teachers.

2. Many teachers favor introduction of the pen in the fourth grade or later.

3. There was a time when it was standard practice that the pen used during handwriting class should be a wooden penholder with a steel pen point. However, more and more teachers have come to believe that boys and girls should be given help in using the type of pen that they use when "on their own." For a time, therefore, practice was given in the use of a fountain pen. Since the ball-point pen is used more now than either the steel-point pen or the fountain pen, there seems to be little justification for refusing to let pupils get their practice in handwriting with good pens of this type.

4. In the very first stage of learning to write, unlined paper seems to be advantageous. When primary-grade children begin to use lined paper, the rulings should be quite far apart, with possibly one inch between the top line and baseline. A midline on the paper, between the top and baseline, is also desirable for boys and girls in the lower grades.

MANUSCRIPT VERSUS CURSIVE WRITING

A very radical change in the style of handwriting was introduced into the American schools in the 1930s when manuscript writing began to be taught in quite a number of primary grades. (For an illustration of a manuscript alphabet, see figure 7.4. For illustrations of cursive writing, see figures 7.15 and 7.16.) The method quickly spread from school system to school system. Because of differences in samplings and in sampling techniques, investigations vary in their findings as to the extent to which manuscript writing is now being taught in the elementary schools of our country. A conservative estimate is that it is used in at least 85 percent of the schoolrooms of the nation as a beginning method of instruction. Research has established that in the greater number of schools in which manuscript writing is used as the beginning method of handwriting a change is made to cursive writing after one or more years of manuscript writing.

Arguments Advanced for Manuscript Writing in Lower Grades

Reasons such as the following seem to have convinced the vast majority of educators that as an introductory system of handwriting manuscript is superior to cursive writing.

1. Because of the muscular immaturity of the beginner it is easier for him to write manuscript than cursive. In manuscript writing, which consists of straight lines, circles, and parts of circles, he has chance for more periods of rest since he lifts his crayon or pencil more frequently—typically at the end of every stroke of a letter—than in cursive writing. In the case of many words in cursive writing, the writer lifts his tool only after he has completed the entire word.

2. For a beginner, because of his muscular immaturity and his comparatively low mental age, it is easier to master the three separate strokes of manuscript writing—the straight line, the circle, and the part of a circle—than it is to gain facility in making the larger number of strokes in cursive writing.

3. Since manuscript writing resembles more closely than cursive the print which the pupil finds in the books he reads, use of manuscript may reinforce his learning to read rather than confuse him.

4. In the early stages of manuscript writing the child can write meaningful messages sooner than if he were learning cursive writing.

5. Manuscript writing is more legible than cursive.

6. Manuscript writing takes less time than cursive.

Arguments Advanced Against Manuscript Writing in Lower Grades

Even though manuscript writing is used almost universally in our schools as a beginning method, there are some persons who question its use. Arguments advanced against the use of manuscript writing, such as those given following, should be considered because there has been no absolute scientific proof to establish the superiority of one system over the other. Popularity of a method must not be confused with excellence.

1. It is poor policy to have boys and girls learn two systems of handwriting.

2. There is considerable difference even between manuscript writing and print—a difference that many teachers of beginning reading do not seem to take into account and consequently do not give the pupils the needed guidance in either reading or writing.

3. With manuscript writing it is not possible to use the rhythm and the arm movement attained in cursive writing that are seemingly essentials for minimum fatigue in writing situations of considerable duration.

Consideration of Arguments

In connection with some of the arguments given for or against the use of manuscript writing these points should be kept in mind.

1. There is no conclusive evidence that either manuscript or cursive writing is the more legible if conditions of practice and other factors are kept constant.

2. There is no proof that either manuscript or cursive writing can be executed with greater speed if conditions of practice and other factors are kept equal.

3. When the boys and girls make the transition from manuscript to cursive writing they are spending time and energy trying to learn two systems of handwriting rather than using them to learn one well.

4. Many teachers seem to incorrectly assume that the child who knows manuscript writing can automatically read print. It is true, however, that manuscript writing more closely resembles print than does cursive.

5. The argument that it is necessarily easier to achieve suitable rhythm and arm movement in cursive than in manuscript writing has not been established by scientific investigation.

A Dual System of Handwriting

Probably the most convincing of the arguments advanced against the use of manuscript writing lies in the fact that in most of today's schools there is a subsequent changeover to cursive writing. Responses such as the following, some of which are not accepted by those who oppose a dual system, are possible objections to manuscript writing on the basis that a dual system is uneconomical of time and energy.

1. Under good guidance boys and girls can accomplish the changeover from manuscript to cursive writing without much difficulty providing the transition is made at the most felicitous time and in the best manner.

2. Learnings from the manuscript writing period can be utilized when learning to do cursive writing.

3. The advantages of using manuscript writing as the initial means of written expression outweigh the disadvantages of the need of a changeover.

4. Since or if the disadvantages of a dual system of handwriting are serious, it does not necessarily follow that the one style of writing that should be taught is manuscript. It might be more desirable to teach only cursive writing.

**Objections to Manuscript Writing
as the One Style of Handwriting**

Whenever the desirability of teaching only manuscript writing is suggested, a storm of protest can be expected, not only from the relatively small number of persons opposed to teaching it as a beginning method but also from many who are ardent defenders of the present plan, in operation in most schools, of teaching manuscript writing to beginners and then later making the transition

to cursive writing. Several of these objections, with responses given to each, may be summarized thus:

1. Manuscript writing of signatures is not accepted by banks. (Yet in *Readings in the Language Arts* this information is given:

Vergil Herrick observed that most banks will accept a manuscript written signature if it is the writer's regular signature. Part of the confusion over this issue lies in the fact that officials may not distinguish between "printing" one's name, that is, the use of all capitals by a person unaccustomed to writing this way and the long-practiced hand of the manuscript writer.[2])

2. Manuscript writing for many persons is synonymous with the immature writing of young children. (If a large number of adults would be taught only manuscript writing, this objection would soon lose weight.)

3. Children like to learn to write like adults. (Again, as in the case of the preceding argument, this statement would hold little weight after the change to a single system of handwriting—the manuscript style—had been in effect for a decade or so.)

4. Cursive writing is more legible and can be executed with greater speed and with less accompanying fatigue than manuscript. (These claims have not been scientifically established. Furthermore, the fact that many businesses request that their clients write addresses in manuscript rather than cursive writing would indicate that these companies consider manuscript writing more legible than cursive.)

5. Teachers in the upper grades are not adequately prepared to teach manuscript writing. (Were it determined that it is desirable to have a single style of handwriting taught and that the style should be manuscript, provisions could be made for preservice and in-service education of teachers to overcome this handicap in a relatively short time.)

READINESS FOR WRITING

The importance of readiness for learning to perform an academic activity is not limited to reading and arithmetic, two subject areas in which there has been quite universal recognition of its significance. It needs to be given due attention in relation to beginning writing instruction. Trying to teach a child to write before he is ready for the activity may have detrimental effects on the development of the child in general. More specifically, it may adversely affect his handwriting and his attitude toward it.

2. Verna D. Anderson, Paul S. Anderson, Francis Ballantine, and Virgil M. Howes, *Readings in the Language Arts* (The Macmillan Company, 1964), p. 163. Used with the permission of the Macmillan Company.

Appraisal of Readiness for Writing

To the question "Is this child ready to learn to write?" no one quick answer can be given. No tests have been developed that give a scientifically definitive response to that inquiry. Furthermore, the inability to accurately check readiness is due in part to the fact that a child may be ready for the program of beginning writing instruction of one teacher but not of another. Even for the same program of writing instruction there are varying degrees of readiness, all of which may be sufficient for the beginner if due attention is paid to individual differences.

Points to Note When Appraising Readiness. Even though research has not provided us with a reliable gauge for measuring readiness for handwriting, there are some fairly helpful observations that can point to whether or not a child is ready to begin to write. Following are some of the factors so closely related to success in handwriting that they should be noted in an attempt to determine readiness.

1. *Muscular coordination.* The extent of a child's neural-muscular coordination is of great importance. In the developmental process coordination of the arm muscles precedes the finer coordination of the wrist and finger muscles. The chief question that arises in this connection with the child entering the elementary school is whether he has developed sufficient functioning of the wrist and finger muscles, harmonizing with his neural and visual activity, to give reason for encouraging handwriting activities of the type usually engaged in in beginning handwriting programs. If a child lacks ability to perform, without undue strain, that which is required for legibility in handwriting, he is at a disadvantage when confronted with the demands of many teachers. If he needs to exert himself greatly in order to achieve the muscular coordination needed in writing, he may overstrain himself and may consequently develop an antagonistic attitude or something akin to fear toward handwriting.

2. *Visual acuity.* For writing the child needs sufficient visual acuity to recognize what is to be written (if he is copying) and to be able to see what he has written. Fortunately upon entrance to the elementary school most boys and girls possess sufficient visual ability to perform satisfactorily, without eyestrain, the demands of the usual program of handwriting instruction. Even children with quite poor eyesight can be ready for writing with proper visual corrections when supplied with suitable writing and reading conditions and appropriate materials.

3. *Visual discrimination.* The child must have not only the necessary eyesight but also ability to make visual discriminations, an ability amenable to training. He needs to be able to recognize differentiating features of letters, words, and other points of importance in handwriting. He must be able to get a clear image of the *b* or the *d*, for example, and to take mental note of the difference in the visual image on his retina.

4. *Reading ability.* To be sure, boys and girls can engage in some writing activities before they have learned to read in the sense in which we ordinarily use the word *read* when referring to the reading activities of first-grade pupils. They may, for example, copy a note they have dictated to the teacher who has written it on the chalkboard inviting their parents to visit the classroom. Though the very first stages of learning to write may not include recognition of any of the letters of a word, very early in the program of writing instruction it seems highly desirable that a pupil be able to identify the letters he writes if he is to get the maximum help from the instruction. In general the procedure, maybe almost universally followed, of having systematic instruction in reading begin before systematic instruction in handwriting is started seems justifiable.

5. *Ability to spell.* There is a relationship between writing and spelling that is close, indeed. The child who knows the spelling of a word he is about to copy, for example, is freed from the necessity of concentrating on the sequence of the letters. It is impractical at all times to insist that a child learn to spell a word before he writes it, however, since through writing it he can also acquire the ability to spell it.

6. *Ability to differentiate between right and left.* When group instruction is given in handwriting, as is commonly the practice in the primary grades, it may be important that the child should be able to differentiate between his right and left hand.

7. *Attention span.* To be ready to receive systematic instruction in handwriting, the pupil needs an attention span that will enable him to pay attention to one activity long enough to participate successfully in the various learning activities required in the program.

8. *Ability to follow directions.* Since a program in systematic instruction in handwriting involves following directions, the child who has difficulty in following simple directions is at a disadvantage. Furthermore, since most handwriting instruction in our schools depends heavily on group methods of teaching, the child who is ready to learn to write should be able to profit from instruction given not only individually but also in a group situation.

9. *Interest in writing.* Interest in an activity is one of the valuable aids to learning. Handwriting is no exception to this rule.

Methods of Appraisal. One of the factors related to writing readiness mentioned in the preceding paragraphs, visual acuity, can be ascertained by tests of vision, even some, if necessary, given by a specialist when

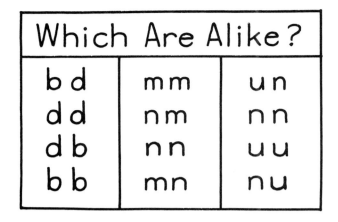

Figure 7.3. Test or Exercise to Appraise or Develop Visual Discrimination.

there is reason for suspecting poor vision. The ability to make visual discriminations can be tested by parts of many reading-readiness tests. It can also be evaluated through teacher-made exercises, of which one type is illustrated by figure 7.3. Such exercises can be used both for testing visual discrimination as well as for developing it.

Factors other than those pertaining to vision can be noted through observation or teacher-planned testing situations. For example, a child's muscular coordination can be checked by noting how well he handles objects, whether he seems to be free of undue tension when engaged in motor activities, and how well he can draw. Ability to follow directions can be observed as the pupil takes part in the ongoing activities of the classroom or as the teacher administers a test that he has constructed, with directions similar to this one: "On the first line draw a circle and on the second line draw a straight line." Interest in writing can be indicated by questions that the child asks the teacher about writing when he sees the teacher write or about his own "scribbling" attempts at writing.

Development of Readiness

The adult who wishes to see the child become ready to write should not merely wait for him to acquire so-called "writing readiness." There are ways in which readiness for writing can be encouraged and developed.

Guidelines. First of all, let us note some of the principles that can serve as guidelines in attempts to help the child develop readiness for writing.

1. Boys and girls should be encouraged to participate in the ongoing activities of the home and the school that help in the development of readiness for handwriting.

2. For some children activities should be provided by the teacher specifically with the intention of developing

writing readiness. Some of these activities may advisedly be in the form of practice exercises.

3. Care should be taken that the pupils enjoy participating in writing-readiness activities, so that the similarity of the activities to those used later in writing will in some cases interest them in writing and never prejudice them against it.

4. Tools for written expression should be made readily available to the child.

Ongoing Activities in the Home. Encouragement of participation in many of the activities that take place in the home can help the child become ready for handwriting. A few of these are:

1. Listening to interesting material that someone has written or read to the child such as a letter from an absent member of the family

2. Attempting to "write" a letter to an absent member of the family or other friend

3. Dictating to an older person a message to be sent to a friend

4. Drawing or painting

5. Cutting or pasting, which can help develop muscular coordination

6. Playing with blocks or toys, which can help develop muscular coordination

7. Observing others in the family receive satisfaction out of writing

8. Modeling with clay

9. Participating in games that require the identification of the right and left hands.

Ongoing Activities in the School. Many activities in the regular school program can be utilized for the development of writing readiness, the following among them:

1. Dictating to the teacher "stories" for an experience chart, lists of materials needed, thank-you notes, and rules to observe

2. Participating in activities that develop hand-eye coordination such as painting, drawing, clay modeling, cutting, and pasting

3. Engaging in activities that develop coordination of the larger muscles, including skipping games, playing with toys and blocks, taking responsibility for a pet, caring for plants, and keeping books and classroom equipment properly arranged

4. Making use of the chalkboard through "writing" or drawing on it

5. Listening to directions and then following them

6. Taking part in some activity such as listening to a story for an increasing length of time, thereby lengthening the attention span

7. Telling where on a large chart the teacher should start writing as the boys and girls dictate to him

8. Engaging in activities such as lacing shoes, using rhythm instruments, doing finger painting.

Other Activities. Activities such as the following can be specifically designed to guide some or all of the pupils in the development of readiness for writing.

1. Arranging pictures in a left-to-right and a top-to-bottom sequence

2. Discriminating between pictures, words, and letters that are arranged on the chalkboard or on paper, or discriminating between objects that are quite similar

3. Practicing how to hold chalk, crayons, or pencils for effective drawing or "writing"

4. Drawing circles in the air, on the chalkboard, or on paper to the rhythm of some action games such as "Farmer in the Dell" or "Here We Go"

5. Drawing circles and straight lines on large sheets of paper or on the chalkboard, at times according to directions as to size and placement

6. Copying their own names for purposes such as identification of drawings they make and some of their other possessions. Signature of duplicated notes to parents or others is another use that the pupils can appreciate as of significance if well presented by the teacher. While in a sense, of course, writing of the child's name is writing, not readiness for writing, in another sense it can be thought of as a "prewriting activity" when the writing is being taught merely as copying, not as study of the various letter forms constituting the name.

DEVELOPING SKILL IN MANUSCRIPT WRITING

After some or all the boys and girls in a first-grade room have acquired a desirable degree of writing readiness, questions such as the following need to be answered by the teacher: (1) What constitutes acceptable form in manuscript writing? (2) What basic writing habits should be developed? (3) What are "first steps" in teaching handwriting? (4) How can the teacher proceed by means of systematic instruction to give boys and girls the needed guidance? (5) How can manuscript writing be used functionally?

Form of Manuscript Writing

For effective teaching of any skill the teacher should have clearly in mind what constitutes the desired outcome. In handwriting that goal can be partly defined in terms of the form of the writing.

The Alphabet of Manuscript Writing. It is important that the child be taught the form of the letters according to one of the systems of handwriting. Although there is relatively little difference in the forms of manuscript letters as recommended by various commercial systems, not to guide the child to adhere to one system is to invite possible confusion in letter formation. Figure 7.4 gives the alphabet in manuscript form and the figures used by the Zaner-Bloser Company, with letters in the proportion that the company advocates for beginners.

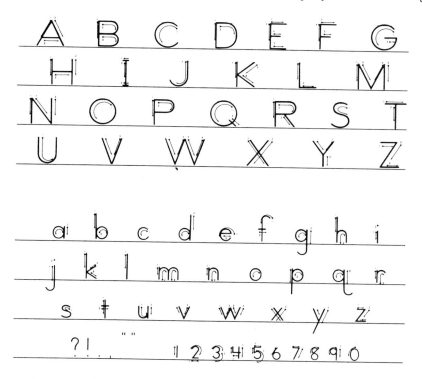

Figure 7.4. Manuscript Alphabet and Numerals for Beginners.

To encourage uniformity of letters, it is helpful for the manuscript alphabet of one company, both capital letters and lower-case, to be displayed, probably in the form of the wall charts available from publishing companies.

The Strokes of Manuscript Writing. One of the reasons why manuscript writing is relatively easy for beginners is that essentially the letter forms are three in number: (1) the straight line (vertical, horizontal, and slant); (2) the circle, and (3) the part of a circle.

Adding further to the simplicity of the writing is the fact that in order to secure the best form, the writer lifts his writing instrument at the end of every straight line and of every circle, and at times after a part of a circle. For example, in writing the word *runs* in manuscript, the writing instrument is lifted seven times at the places indicated below.

Figure 7.5. [3]

The sequence in the formation of strokes in the case of most letters is from left to right and from top to bottom. For example, in the letter *b* the left-hand stroke, namely the straight line, is made first, from top to bottom. In the letter *a* the circle (or part of a circle) is made before the straight line. The capital *M* is one of the exceptions to the rule, as illustrated below!

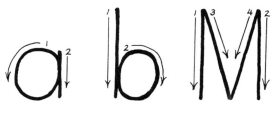

Figure 7.6.

Further information about strokes is given in the following quotation from Frank N. Freeman's *Reference Manual for Teachers,* [4] prepared for the Zaner-Bloser Company.

To make the letters correctly the child should be able to make both clockwise and counter-clockwise circles. Letters *a, c, d, e, g, o,* and *q* are made with counter-clockwise circles. The circle parts of *b* and *q* are made in the clockwise direction, the same direction that is used in making the curves of *h, m, n, r,* and *j;* and the curves on figures *2, 3,* and *5.* In making letters with curved parts such as the tails of *g, j,* and *q,* the top of *f,* the humps on *h, m, n,* and *r,* and the bottom turn on *u,* the curved stroke should be almost a half circle and equal in degree to the curve of the *o.*

Other Matters of Form. Also important in the consideration of the form of manuscript writing are matters of size and proportion, color or shading, slant, alignment, and space between letters and words.

1. Size and proportion. The following quotation from Emma Harrison Myers [5] indicates guidelines for both size and proportion of letters.

. . . There should be a gradual reduction in the size of the writing as the child's coordinations develop. Freeman recommends that paper with lines one inch apart be used in grade one. In grade two he reduces to three-quarter inch ruling. In each case he recommends a guide line at the halfway mark to develop the proper relationship in size between minimum letters and tall letters, i.e., the minimum letters are one-half the size of the tall letters and capitals for manuscript writing. By grade three he reduces the ruling another quarter-inch to one-half inch ruling, still keeping the same proportion of minimum letters to tall letters. In manuscript writing the tall letters are *l, b, h, k, f,* and *d.* All of the other lower-case letters, except *t,* are made one-half the size of these tall letters. Tail letters go below the line one-half space. Capital letters are made the same size as the tall letters. The letter *t* is midway between the minimum and tall letters in size.

In some handwriting manuals a deviation from the foregoing recommendation is suggested. The capital letters and the tall lower-case letters are slightly less than double the height of the small letters when using paper with guidelines that divide the space for each line of writing into two equal parts. (See figure 7.7.) The top of the capital letters and of the tall lower-case letters is slightly below the top of the upper half of the space reserved for a line of writing. This deviation from the rule is made to give a paper a less crowded appearance by keeping the lines of writing a little farther apart. For the same reason the strokes that fall below a line are, on ruled paper, often made a little less than half as long as the minimum letters are tall. The desirability of not having the tall letters reach the baseline of the preceding line of writing and of having the below-the-line strokes slightly less than half a space below the line can readily be envisioned by noting the height and the below-the-line length of the letters in figure 7.7.

2. Color. The color of writing may be too dark, too light, irregular, or correct. The writing instrument in part determines the color. However, pressure on the writing tool also plays an important part in determining color.

---

3. This figure and several others are made similar to parts of illustrations of publications of the Zaner-Bloser Company.

4. Frank N. Freeman, *Reference Manual for Teachers.* Grades One through Four for *Guiding Growth in Handwriting.* The Zaner-Bloser Company, 1959, page 31. Courtesy of the Zaner-Bloser Company, Columbus, Ohio.

5. Emma Harrison Myers, *The Whys and Hows of Teaching Handwriting.* The Zaner-Bloser Company, 1963, page 51. Courtesy of the Zaner-Bloser Company, Columbus, Ohio.

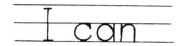

Figure 7.7.

3. Slant. The basic slant in manuscript writing is "straight up and down." It is achieved rather readily for the right-handed child if the paper is parallel to the top of the desk or table and if the writer is in correct position for writing, as illustrated in figure 7.11. So that the part of the line on which the writing is being done at any time is directly or almost directly in front of the eyes, the paper should be moved towards the left as the child writes a line, with a recommended shift of paper about two or three times per line. The child can be taught to check his slant by drawing dotted lines through the vertical lines of slant in words he has written as shown in the accompanying diagram, figure 7.8.

Figure 7.8.

If a pupil is having special difficulty in keeping the slant correct in manuscript writing, the teacher may wish to rule the paper with parallel vertical lines, indicated by dots or by broken lines, as shown in figure 7.9.

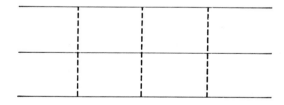

Figure 7.9.

Even though the basic slant in manuscript writing is "straight up and down," many letters have other lines of slant. Some slant to the right and others to the left, as, for example, the second and third strokes of both the upper- and the lower-case letter in figure 7.10.

4. Alignment. Some writers do not stay on the line. They may begin a word on the baseline, but then swing upward or downward in their writing. Still others have ir-

Figure 7.10.

regular alignment with part of the writing above the line, part of it on the line, and part of it below the line.

5. Spacing. The space that should be left between the letters of a word and between words cannot be stipulated in terms of fractional parts of an inch, for it should be proportionate to the size of the writing. The suggestion is sometimes made to first-grade children that they leave enough space between letters for the forefinger to be placed there and that they double that space between words. If this suggestion is made, the boys and girls should be discouraged from frequent use of their fingers to measure spacing. Probably a better practice is to provide boys and girls guides in the form of copies of manuscript written the size that they are writing in which the spacing is correct. Attention of even fairly young writers should be drawn to the fact that the spacing between letters in manuscript writing differs with the width and form of the letters. For example, after wide letters such as the capital *M* and the capital *W* less space should be left than between two narrow letters such as the *l* and the *t*.

Basic Writing Habits

Some of the pointers given here concerning basic writing habits apply to both manuscript and cursive writing; others apply to manuscript writing only. In the section in this chapter that deals with developing skill in cursive writing, attention is paid to variations from those given in this part on manuscript writing.

Posture of the Writer in Manuscript Writing. Not all teachers will agree on stipulations concerning the writer's posture. However, there seems to be no argument that the position should be one that will be comfortable for the writer. There seems to be general acceptance, too, that the feet should be flat on the floor and that the writer should directly face the table or desk on which he is writing. The seat should be high enough so that the writer's knees do not touch the desk and low enough so that his feet rest comfortably on the floor.

Position of Paper, Hand, and Writing Tool in Manuscript Writing. For the right-handed writer the paper in manuscript writing should, according to Emma Harrison Myers, be "placed squarely on the desk. The writing hand is placed directly in front of the center of the body. The right hander pulls vertical lines toward the center of the body. The crayon points toward the right shoulder."[6] According to the same authority, the left-handed child doing manuscript writing should have the paper "slanted so that vertical lines are pulled toward his left elbow. The crayon points toward the left elbow."[6]

Directions applying to both the right-handed and the left-handed child who is doing manuscript writing are

6. Ibid., p.v.

Figure 7.11. A Recommended Position for Manuscript Writing for the Right- and Left-Handed Pupil.

given in these words in the teacher's edition of the *Expressional Growth Through Handwriting* series: "Rest the writing hand on the tips of the last two fingers with the palm down. Hold the crayon loosely between the thumb and first two fingers. (The crayons should be placed just forward of the big knuckle on the first finger.) Bend the thumb slightly." [7]

Placement of Auxiliary Materials. Attention must be paid not only to the placement of the paper on which the pupil writes but also to any other materials, such as books or paper, which he needs to use while writing either for copy purposes or other reference. However, teachers should encourage boys and girls to remove all materials not needed for writing from their desks so that ample space can be provided for freedom of movement. The pupils should be helped to form the habit of placing needed auxiliary materials to the left of the writing paper if they write with the right and to the right of the writing paper if they are left-handed. They should be asked to place the reference material at the angle that is most convenient for reading purposes.

Movement and Rhythm. Arm movement is important for excellence in writing. Finger movement should, however, not be barred but, if necessary, encouraged. The arm muscles should be used for the general left-to-right progression in writing while finger movement should be utilized for the production of smaller strokes that require greater care in performance. Even wrist movement has a legitimate place.

It is important that the movement should be rhythmic to avoid undue strain when writing for a rather extended time and to produce better-looking copy. Especially with the beginner it is valuable to stress rhythmic movement so that a habit of writing with jerky movement can be prevented.

"First Steps" in Manuscript Writing

An exact line of demarcation between readiness for manuscript writing, suggestions for which are given on

preceding pages of this chapter, and the "first steps" in manuscript writing would be difficult to draw. With clear recognition of that fact, some suggestions for "first steps" are here given.

Guidelines. The following general suggestions are for application in the early stages of teaching manuscript writing.

1. The chalkboard should be used freely by both teacher and pupils, with the pupils' first writing experiences on the chalkboard on a space without lines but with later writing on a ruled chalkboard with lines probably not closer than four inches apart.

2. Large sheets of unlined paper, possibly news print—may be folded to make the sheet of manageable size—can be used at first while later ruled paper with lines about four inches apart and still later with less space between lines is appropriate. (In time, even as little as one-inch lined paper, with two spaces used for capital letters and other tall letters, should be used.)

3. Crayons should probably be used at first with many children, and in many cases later the so-called "primary pencil," with thick lead and a larger circumference than the regular pencil is often recommended.

4. Even though there needs to be emphasis on letter forms in early handwriting instruction as well as later, from the very beginning the work on letter formation should be made functional through use of the letters in meaningful units—words and larger thought units.

5. The words or groups of words written by the pupils should frequently serve a purpose, such as writing one's name to identify possessions, writing words for a picture dictionary, or writing a letter to take home.

6. Copying, rather than tracing, should be encouraged and later reliance should be placed at least in part on visual memory of letters and word forms.

7. Attention should be paid even in the early stages of handwriting instruction to the formation of proper habits of position, sequence, and direction in letter formation.

Suggested Activities. Application can be made of the guidelines given in the preceding paragraphs and of others by means of activities such as those described following.

1. On the first day of school or thereafter the teacher may give to each pupil a small piece of tagboard with ruled lines, on which the teacher has written the child's name in the size that is suitable for a beginning writer. From this card each pupil can copy his name to identify his drawings and other possessions.

2. If pupils have difficulty in knowing where to begin tall and small letters, the teacher can give each pupil a piece of paper, with baselines and guidelines, on which

7. Ibid., page v.

he has written a vertical line double space in height and below it a vertical line of single-space height. He may explain that on the first line he has a stroke for a tall letter and then he may ask the pupils to make a stroke of similar height to the right of it (after they have pointed out the place where they will begin the stroke). Next the pupils can proceed similarly with the line representing the beginning stroke of a small letter. After they have finished both lines by writing strokes of required height, they can write a line of vertical strokes, at the direction of the teacher, some the height of small letters and the others of tall letters. (Emphasis throughout this exercise should be placed on the fact that the vertical lines are made from the top down.) A similar exercise can be done with large and small circles. With the circles, too, care should be taken that they are the right height and that the direction of the stroke is the desired one.

3. The teacher writes on the chalkboard something of value to the boys and girls as they watch. On a space ruled with baselines and guidelines, he may write the sentence

Today is Monday.

As he writes it, he may make comments such as these: "I am going to write 'Today is Monday.' I start near the left of the line. I make my letters from the top down. I move my chalk from left to right as I write. This is the word *Today*. I am leaving quite a wide space after *Today* because now I am beginning a new word. The word is *is*. Now I leave another wide space for I am beginning another word, the word *Monday*."

The next day the teacher may say, as he writes while the pupils are watching, "I am going to write 'Today is Tuesday.' I am going to ask someone to show us where I should begin the first word, at this side of the line (as he points near the left side of the space) or at this side of the line (as he points near the right side of the space). Show us where I should start our first word, the word *Today*." Then the teacher can proceed: "I start the word *Today* up high because the letter is a tall letter. The next letter is not tall. So I start it here (as he points to the correct place on the guide line). The last letter of this word I will start at this line (pointing at the guide line), but I will end it below the line. Now I have finished writing a word. Before I write the next letter I am going to leave a wide space. Why am I going to leave a wide space?" In a similar manner the teacher may continue writing and commenting or asking questions concerning the rest of the sentence.

Possibly the third day one or more pupils will be ready to copy the first two words of "Today is Wednesday" on the chalkboard directly below the words written by the teacher.

4. The teacher provides a lined space on the chalkboard (permanently lined if the school authorities approve) where the children can write during free time. Every day he may write at the top of the space a word or group of words, which he reads to the class. Some of the boys and girls then can copy it in the space below the teacher's writing. When the teacher has time, he can guide the child who is practicing. At other times a team of two pupils may help each other in evaluation of the writing as first one and then the other writes.

Figure 7.12. Use of a Model in Chalkboard Writing.

5. Before handwriting class the teacher may write on five different areas of the chalkboard the letters, words, or groups of words on which there will be practice that day. After he has helped the group during the introduction of the work for the period, five or six pupils can go to the chalkboard for practice in writing a copy of what the teacher has written. As the pupils are writing, the teacher may go around to the different pupils and help them as needed. At the same time the other boys and girls can be writing the same material at their seats, from duplicated copies the teacher has given them or from copies in their writing recorders. During handwriting class on succeeding days another group of five or six pupils can also do work on the chalkboard while the others write at their seats, until all have had a chance at chalkboard writing.

Guidelines for Practice in Development of Skills in Manuscript Writing

Systematic instruction in handwriting may be divided into (1) those class periods or parts of periods in which new points are presented (referred to here as *developmental procedures*) and (2) those in which the pupils practice skills presented earlier. Suggestions for both these types have been presented earlier in this chapter and more are given under "Other Considerations," see page 185. Let us note the following guidelines for providing the pupils with practice on points that have been presented.

1. Some practice on a skill being presented is important in the class period when a new point is being developed. Furthermore, in many writing lessons no new point should be presented but the entire class period should be devoted to strengthening a skill presented.

2. The boys and girls should clearly know the purpose of the practice work and the purpose should be specific.

3. The pupils should be guided so that they will accept a worthy purpose for the practice.

4. The pupils should be encouraged to compare their product at the beginning of a practice period with one later in the period.

5. The boys and girls should be helped to understand that they need not be discouraged if every attempt at improvement does not result in advancement.

6. A practice period should not be so long that it exceeds the attention span of the boys and girls for the type of activity.

7. Much practice in handwriting should be provided in classes other than handwriting classes, as the boys and girls make functional use of writing.

Functional Uses of Writing in Lower Grades

A few of the many ways in which boys and girls can engage in writing activities meaningful to the primary-grade child are as follows:

1. Writing their names for identification of their possessions and for other utilitarian purposes, such as listing who wants milk, who will serve on a committee, or who is to be on a given team

2. Writing their names, addresses, and telephone numbers

3. Writing the day and date on a daily newsletter posted in the room or written on the chalkboard

4. Writing the date on a large calendar

5. Writing captions for pictures or objects

6. Making a picture dictionary or a picture-word file

7. Writing letters. In the lower-primary grades the class letter dictated to the teacher may be the preferable procedure. All pupils may copy the letter, but only one usually should be sent to any one individual. The other boys and girls may keep copies of their letters in folders of their own in which they save samples of their work.

8. Using workbooks for reading, spelling, or handwriting. Boys and girls may be motivated to do their best writing in their workbooks if they know that these will be on exhibit at parents' night or if they know that they will have an opportunity to take them home at regular intervals to show their parents.

9. Making a bird book. Below pictures of birds the name of each bird can be written and with older children one or more interesting statements about each.

10. Making books for Mother's Day

11. Making booklets for units of study

12. Making an accordionlike folder on which pictures are drawn and on which comments by the pupils about the pictures are written.

THE TRANSITION FROM MANUSCRIPT TO CURSIVE WRITING

Surveys differ in the details of the findings reported as to when the transition is made from manuscript to cursive writing. This variation undoubtedly is due to a large extent to the variety of the samplings used. However, a study of the reports indicates that while in a few schools the changeover is made as late as in the fourth grade, it often occurs in the last part of the second or in the third grade.

Here are guidelines that can be followed when trying to determine the optimum time for the transition.

1. The best time differs from class to class and even from pupil to pupil.

2. The methods used during the period of transition should help determine when the changeover should be made.

3. Care should be taken that pupils are not asked to learn a second system of handwriting until they have acquired the ability to express themselves with some efficiency and satisfaction in one.

4. The pupils should not be encouraged to discontinue all manuscript writing, either during the period of transition to cursive writing or later.

The following factors should be given serious attention in deciding when to begin encouraging a child to make the transition from manuscript to cursive writing:

1. Muscular coordination sufficient to do a good quality of manuscript writing. Cursive writing calls for use of smaller muscles than manuscript writing, coordination of which is developed later than that of the larger muscles.

2. Ability to do manuscript writing with correct body, paper, and pencil position.

3. Ability to do manuscript writing with rhythmic movement and with well-formed letters.

4. Interest in making the transition.

5. Ability to read cursive writing.

Developing Readiness

Although the factors contributing to readiness for writing or for readiness for phases of writing are influenced in part by maturation, they are also amenable to training and education. Consequently the teacher should not merely wait for the appearance of signs of readiness but should strive to help the child reach the stage of development in which he can advisedly learn to do cursive writing (if a transition to cursive writing is made in a school system).

Here are guidelines that the teacher may wish to follow in helping boys and girls make the transition.

1. It is unwise to hurry the pupil into making the transition. If the transition is made early in the second grade, it may occur at the time when the child is just beginning to do some independent writing. A change in handwriting at such a strategic time may unduly arrest the child's development in independent writing.

2. The best preparation for readiness to make the transition is doing manuscript writing well—with good movement, with correct position of body, paper, pencil, and in well-formed letters and correctly spaced letters and words.

3. The teacher can help develop interest in making the changeover in a variety of ways. He can emphasize the fact that after making the transition the pupils will be able to write in two different ways, not in only one. Although the point may be made that when the boys and girls are able to do cursive writing they will be able to write like grown-ups, care needs to be taken not to overemphasize it. Otherwise it may lead to a disdain of manuscript writing and cause the pupil to lose desire to continue to do any manuscript writing after he has acquired skill in cursive writing.

4. Unless a pupil is fairly efficient in reading cursive writing, he will be likely to have considerable difficulty in learning to write it.

5. Cursive writing is decidedly different from manuscript. It should not be assumed that the latter is merely an adaptation of the former, the transition to which a pupil can easily make without guidance from the teacher. Among the points of difference are: position of the paper, slant, formation of letters, and connecting strokes.

Position of Paper

Although the correct body position of the writer is the same for manuscript as for cursive writing, the placement of the paper is different.

The Zaner-Bloser Company recommends that in manuscript writing the right-handed writer place his paper so that the upper and lower edges are parallel to the lower edge of the desk and that in cursive writing he have it at an angle of approximately thirty degrees to the lower edge of the desk. This company recommends that in both manuscript and cursive writing the left-handed writer tilt his paper, in the case of most writers, at an angle between thirty-five and forty-five degrees in cursive writing and at a larger angle in manuscript writing.

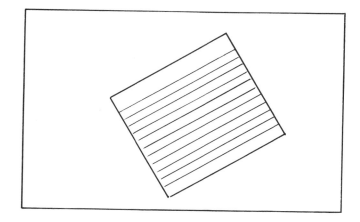

Figure 7.13. Position of Paper in Cursive Writing for the Right-Handed.

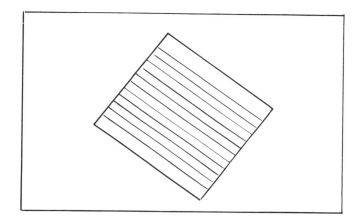

Figure 7.14. Position of Paper in Cursive Writing for the Left-Handed.

The Alphabet of Cursive Writing

There are variations, though relatively few and slight, in the forms of accepted alphabets of cursive writing. Two alphabets are reproduced here as figures 7.15 and 7.16.

New Points to Be Taught

The following is a list[8] of new points to be taught in cursive writing, when the transition is being made from manuscript to cursive writing and/or in later stages of learning to write.

1. Slanting position of paper.
2. Slant in writing.

8. Frank N. Freeman and the Zaner-Bloser Company, *Handwriting Aid for Primary Teachers*. Zaner-Bloser Company, 1948, page 95. Reprinted by permission of Zaner-Bloser Company.

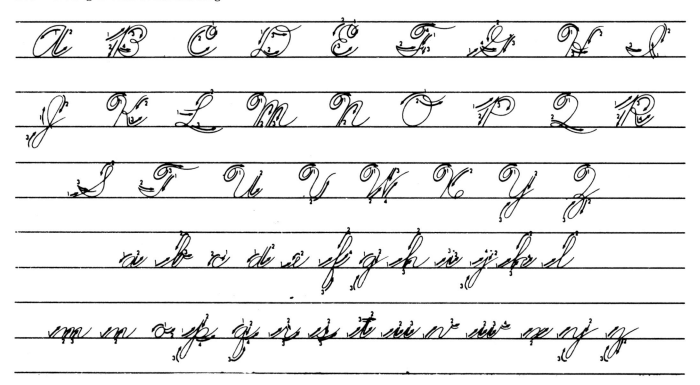

Figure 7.15. Reproduction from the Zaner-Bloser *Creative Growth with Handwriting Series.* Used with the permission of the Zaner-Bloser Company.

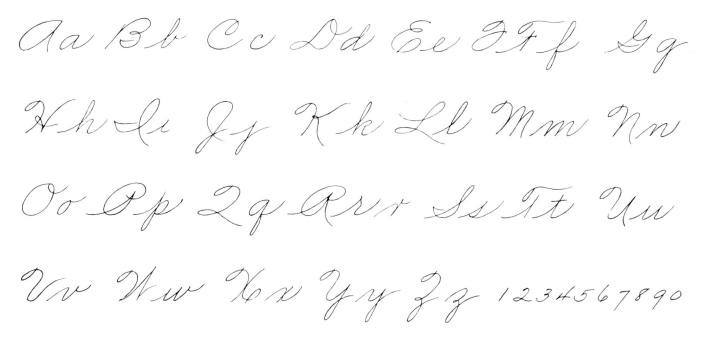

Figure 7.16. Reproduction from *My Progress Book, Cursive Writing the Easy Way*, published by The A.N. Palmer Company. Used with the permission of the A.N. Palmer Company.

3. Connecting strokes between letters.
4. Loops on letters to form upper and lowercase letters.
5. Completely new form of letter—*b e f k r s z.*
6. Finish stroke on letters.
7. The initial strokes—undercurve and overcurve.
8. Close spacing between words.
9. Increase in speed.
10. New Capital Letter forms.
11. Correct number of letters per line.
12. Dotting of *i* and crossing of *t* after word is finished.
13. Retraced letters *b u r s w.*
14. Relative heights of letters *p d t.*
15. Lighter quality of line.

Classification of Handwriting Strokes

The following classification is from the teacher's edition of the *Expressional Growth Through Handwriting* series by the Zaner-Bloser Company.

Beginning Strokes of Lowercase Letters. Almost all lowercase letters in cursive writing begin at the baseline. They begin with (1) the undercurve (like the *b, e, f,* for example) or (2) with the overcurve (as, for example, the *m, n, v.*) The letters *a, c, d, g, o, q* at the beginning of a word start with the downcurve.

Ending Strokes of Lowercase Letters. Ending strokes can be identified, as the Zaner-Bloser Company does, as (1) the undercurve ending (in letters such as the *e, i, u*), (2) the overcurve ending (as, for example, in the *g, j, y*), and (3) the check-stroke ending (as in the *o, b, v,* and *w*).

Connecting Strokes of Lowercase Letters. The Zaner-Bloser Company classifies connecting strokes of lowercase letters thus on page v of *A New Universe:*

1. "From an undercurve ending to an under curve beginning as in: *hi, ru, fl, st, ap,* and *ph.*
2. From an overcurve ending to an overcurve or downcurve beginning as in: *ya, gy, jo,* and *zz.*
3. From undercurve to overcurve as in: *rn, ev, ay,* and *lx.*
4. From overcurve to undercurve as in: *al, gh, gr,* and *je.*
5. From check-stroke to undercurve as in: *ow, br, wi, ve, wr,* and *bl.*
6. From check-stroke to overcurve and downcurve as in: *oa, on, bo, by,* and *wa.*"

Capital Letters. The classification of uppercase letters used in Zaner-Bloser materials is as follows: (1) letters beginning with the ⟨ stroke (*H, K, M, N, W, Z, U, V,*

Y, X); (2) letters beginning with a loop (*S, G, L, I, J*); (3) letters that have a cap (*T, F*); (4) oval-shaped letters (*O, D, C, A, E, P, B, R*).

"First Steps" in Making the Transition

There is no one best way for making the transition from manuscript to cursive writing. However, here are some points that the teacher may find of value for the changeover.

1. Discuss with the class the fact that there are two commonly used kinds of writing and show the same word or words written in both types.
2. Familiarize the boys and girls with the terms *manuscript* and *cursive.*
3. Have pupils tell where or when they have seen examples of cursive writing.
4. Encourage them to want to learn another way of writing.
5. Help the boys and girls note some of the differences between manuscript and cursive writing, stressing points such as those named under "New Points to Be Taught" beginning on page 177.
6. Check the pupils' ability to read letters and words in cursive writing and provide practice in reading cursive writing.
7. Show the boys and girls how a letter quite alike in the manuscript and in the cursive, the letter *i,* for example, is written in both styles.
8. Present from time to time the various groupings of letters as to beginning and as to ending strokes as well as to other aspects of form.
9. Give the pupils opportunity to use the chalkboard for cursive writing.
10. Have part of the chalkboard reserved for directions and assignments written in cursive writing and give needed help in reading these directions and assignments.

TEACHING CURSIVE WRITING

Many of the suggestions given in the preceding part of this chapter, entitled, "The Transition from Manuscript to Cursive Writing," also apply to the program of cursive writing beyond the transitional stage. Additional suggestions for the handwriting program in its later stages are here given.

Motivation

To offset the drudgery that might otherwise be associated with phases of practice in the development of any skill and the lack of purpose for doing one's best that might characterize the attitude of the writer, the teacher should try to encourage the child to learn to write and to make application of what he has learned. Following are some ways in which the pupils may be stimulated to want to do their best.

1. The teacher shows samples of writing that are difficult to decipher and has the pupils discuss the problem of the reader.

2. The teacher encourages the pupils to set individual goals for themselves by the use of handwriting scales and then from time to time study their progress toward their objectives.

3. During handwriting class the teacher tries to secure a relaxed, happy classroom atmosphere, in which the learner is more likely to enjoy the activity he is doing than he would in one that is tense and unhappy.

4. If a mark in handwriting is given on a report card or by other means of reporting to parents, the teacher makes clear to the boys and girls and to the parents that the mark is based on the writing that the pupil does not only during handwriting class but also at other times.

5. The teacher displays some of the better papers written during classes other than handwriting class.

6. The pupil keeps a folder in which he saves dated samples of his handwriting. These samples may be selected for the folder without previous announcement that the paper will be put into the folder at a given time.

7. The pupils engage in many activities in which they see the importance of good handwriting such as bona fide letter writing, making booklets, and making charts.

8. The pupils participate in the evaluation of their handwriting.

9. The teacher helps the pupils realize that illegible handwriting may be interpreted as errors in spelling.

10. The teacher displays posters in the room, often pupil-made, encouraging the boys and girls to write well.

11. The teacher encourages an atmosphere of work during handwriting period by using the time at the beginning of the period when paper is distributed so as to assure a prompt beginning by: (a) listing on the chalkboard before class the materials needed; (b) writing on the chalkboard before class the directions for the writing activities in which the pupils are to engage that day; and (c) asking questions about handwriting, such as "How far below the line should the below-the-line loops extend?"

Achieving Characteristics of Legible Cursive Writing [9]

Legibility in cursive handwriting is determined by characteristics that can be classified as to: (1) size and proportion, (2) color or shading, (3) slant, (4) letter spacing, (5) beginning strokes, (6) ending strokes, (7) word spacing, (8) alignment, and (9) letter forms.

Size and Proportion. The desired size and proportion of letters vary according to the maturity and skill of the writer. Published handwriting programs give suggestions for the reduction in size from the time the pupil starts cursive writing, when lines, one-half inch apart are recommended, with the small letters about one-half the size of the capital letters (often in the second half of the second grade or in the third grade) until the time (frequently in the fifth or sixth grade) when the pupil is ready to write the size and proportion recommended for the adult.

In general, these recommendations as to size are made for adults when writing on paper on which the lines are 3/8 of an inch apart:

> Capital letters and the loop letters *l, b, h, k,* and *f*: 3/4 space
> The letters *t, d,* and *p*: 1/2 space
> The small lowercase letters: 1/4 space
> The below-line loops: 1/2 space below the line.

Boys and girls should be helped in diagnosing errors in the size of their letters by noting whether they are too large, too small, or irregular. They can be helped in recognizing the following frequent causes of each of these shortcomings and in correcting their errors.

1. Too large writing. Too large writing is often caused by using primarily arm movement rather than a desirable combination of hand and finger movement and by holding the writing instrument too far from the point.

2. Too small writing. Too small writing is often caused by using a disproportionate amount of finger and hand movement rather than sufficient arm movement, and by holding the pen or pencil too close to the point.

3. Irregular size. The cause of irregular size frequently is unsteadiness in writing, resulting from not curving the thumb enough when holding the writing instrument.

Color or Shading. The boys and girls can be given help in understanding that too light or too dark shading may be caused by a too fine or a too heavy pen point. They may need help in recognizing the fact that too heavy writing is also frequently caused by holding the pen too close to the point; in learning that too light writing is frequently caused by holding the pen too far from the point or by turning the pen point (if it is not a ball-point

9. The classification of characteristcs of handwriting is, with but slight alteration, the one followed in the *SELF-CORRECTIVE HANDWRITING CHARTS* by Ellen C. Nystrom, no longer in print. Acknowledgment is also here made of the fact that suggestions from these charts are incorporated in comments as to how to achieve these characteristics.

pen) so that the eye of the pen is not up; and in realizing that heavy downstrokes often result from too much pressure of the forefinger onto the writing tool.

Slant. The relationship of slant to position of the paper and to the pull of the pen or pencil toward the middle of the body needs to be made clear to some boys and girls. A tilt of the paper at an angle of about thirty degrees to the edge of the desk helps secure correct slant. Moving the paper from right to left in case of the right-handed writer, with the left hand several times, maybe three, as the writer progresses across a line of writing can be demonstrated to the child as a means of securing correct slant while failure to do so may cause a problem of slant. (It should be noted, however, that very few adults, even among the good writers, make this adjustment of the paper as they write. Usually those who maintain good slant make up for this lack of motion by a change in the position of the fingers, hand, or arm as they progress from left to right.)

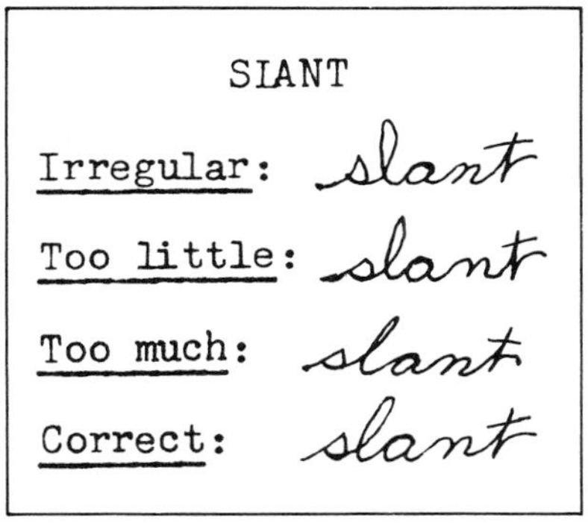

Figure 7.17.

The cause of irregular slant often is failure to shift the paper or failure to make the downstrokes of letters toward the center of the body of the writer. Too slanting writing is frequently the result of tilting the paper more than thirty degrees to the edge of the desk, while lack of slant often results from tilting it less than thirty degrees.

Letter Spacing. Defects of letter spacing consist of: (a) too crowded writing, (b) too scattered writing, and (c) irregular spacing between letters. As a rule, difficulties in letter spacing are closely related to defects of slant. Scattered letter spacing is often caused by too much slant, crowded letter spacing by too little slant, and irregular letter spacing by irregular slant.

Beginning Strokes. Boys and girls should know that the first stroke of the letters *a, c, d, g, o,* and *q* does not begin on the line but starts at or near the top of the letter if the letter is used alone or begins a word. They can check whether they use beginning strokes starting on

the line for letters that need them and do not use them for those that are usually written without them. They can also be helped to note whether the strokes they write for letters beginning on the line are too long, too short, or irregular. They can get suggestions for overcoming shortcomings from knowledge of facts such as these:

1. Irregular beginning strokes are often caused by writing letters that show irregularity of size.

2. Too short strokes of letters beginning on the line are often associated with letters that are too small or with letters of too little slant.

3. Too long strokes that begin on the line are often associated with letters that are too large or that have too much slant.

Ending Strokes. Errors in ending strokes include in addition to those of form of the ending strokes: (a) irregular strokes, (b) too short strokes, and (c) too long strokes. The causes of irregularity of ending strokes, of too short strokes, and of too long strokes are the same as those for beginning strokes (i.e., for those letters beginning on the line) with the corresponding shortcomings. Correct proportion of ending strokes requires that they be the same height as the small lowercase letters. Thus in adult-size writing the ending stroke of a letter should be one-third the height of the capital letter, in other words, the height of the small lowercase letters.

Word Spacing. If the beginning and ending strokes are correct, it is fairly easy for a writer to achieve correct spacing. Scattered word spacing is often caused by too long beginning and ending strokes, crowded word spacing by too short beginning and ending strokes, and irregular word spacing by irregular beginning and ending strokes.

Boys and girls should be helped to note that the space left between the last word of a sentence and the first word of the following sentence should be wider than that between two words within a sentence.

Alignment. By correct alignment is meant writing that rests on the baseline. Irregular alignment is often caused by not placing the paper in the correct position and by not moving it to the right two or three times, at regular intervals, as the writer—the right-handed writer—progresses along a line of writing. As indicated earlier, seldom do persons voluntarily shift the paper several times for each line that they write. The author's observation has been that people are, indeed, not at all likely to make such a shift unless they are writing in handwriting classes. To offset the difficulty in alignment that might be caused by such failure to shift, an adjustment can be made and often is made in the position of the fingers, the hand, and the arm as the writer proceeds in his writing across the writing line.

Letter Forms. Two alphabets, that by The Zaner-Bloser Company and that by the A.N. Palmer Company, are given earlier in this chapter. Although there are but few differences in the various generally accepted alphabets, to avoid confusion and lack of uniformity in the writing of any one individual, it is recommended that the pupils in a school be taught to use one set of letters consistently. A helpful publication in pocket-size form is the one entitled *Points to Remember about Each of the Letters of the Alphabet.*[10] The nature of the booklet is summarized on the first page in these words;

In writing the alphabet, there are many important points for each letter that help both teacher and pupil with letter structure. We are listing here, under each letter, some of the important points to keep in mind: the numerical count for the letters and a descriptive word count.

A page is devoted to each lowercase and each uppercase letter of the alphabet and to each of the figures from 1 through 10.

There are some letters on which many pupils need special practice. Probably more illegibilities in cursive writing result from incorrect writing of the letters *a, e,* and *r* than from poor writing of any other letters. Additional letters frequently written so poorly that they cause spelling problems are *t, s, c, n, d, b, h, c, v,* and the capital *I*. Frequent specific causes of illegibilities are:

1. Not crossing the *t* nor dotting the *i*
2. Leaving letters "open" that should be closed, like the *o,* and the *d* (which are then confused with *cl*), and the *a*
3. Not using loops in loop letters
4. Making loops in some letters that should be written without loops
5. Making straight lines where there should be curved lines
6. Writing an *n* like a *u,* an *r* like an *i,* and a *c* like an *a*.

Development of Appropriate Speed

The two major objectives in teaching handwriting are (1) to write legibly and (2) to write at an appropriate speed. Means of developing legibility are discussed in preceding paragraphs. Let us now note points of value to consider in relation to the development of speed of writing.

1. In the lower grades practically no emphasis should be placed on speed. However, dawdling habits should be discouraged even in those grades.
2. Speed varies, and rightly so, from individual to individual.
3. As a child grows toward maturity, there tends to be a positive relationship between speed of writing and quality of cursive writing.

4. Care should be taken that slowness in writing is not due to the learner's drawing rather than writing the words by means of which he plans to communicate.

Correlation and Integration with Other Subjects

The work in cursive handwriting, as is also the case in manuscript writing, should be closely integrated or correlated with other subjects. In fact, much of the practice in handwriting should be done in connection with the written communication of value in the ongoing school program. Purpose for learning skills of handwriting and means of application of them should be furnished, to a considerable extent, by the content areas.

It is hoped that the ways in which correlation can take place that are listed here will suggest many others to the teacher.

Reading. Handwriting can be correlated with reading through:

1. Making posters, in cursive writing, in which books are recommended to classmates
2. Making a chart showing common sounds of vowels and consonants
3. Writing a bibliography of books that pupils have particularly enjoyed.

Spelling. The following are some ways in which handwriting can be correlated with spelling.

1. Making a card file of a pupil's own word problems
2. Noting words marked wrong in spelling lists because of illegibility
3. Making a chart giving the letters which are frequent cause of illegibility, such as the *n, u,* the *l, e,* the *h, k*
4. Making a chart listing the steps through which pupils might go when studying a new word.

English. Language arts activities other than reading and spelling can be correlated with handwriting in these and many other ways:

1. Giving in good English and in a well-constructed talk the points to observe when performing a skill in handwriting that is being learned
2. Making a chart or poster illustrating the correct usage of some irregular verbs
3. Writing a book of poetry containing favorite poems
4. Writing original poems or stories

10. The Zaner-Bloser Company, *Points to Remember about Each of the Letters of the Cursive Alphabet.* For Upper Grades, The Zaner-Bloser Company, 1963. Courtesy of the Zaner-Bloser Company, Columbus, Ohio.

5. Writing the script for a puppet play
6. Writing bona fide letters
7. Writing articles for a class or school paper or magazine.

Social Studies. Here are a few ways in which handwriting can be correlated with the work in the social studies.

1. Making a time line
2. Making a vocabulary chart of new words learned in the study of a unit or area of study
3. Writing a bibliography of good books on a topic studied
4. Writing a make-believe diary of a person living long ago or far away
5. Making an individual or a class booklet.

Mathematics. Mathematics can be correlated with handwriting, not only by all the usual writing done in mathematics, but also in the following somewhat special ways:

1. Writing a booklet containing interesting facts about the development of numbers
2. Making charts demonstrating processes in mathematics, such as long division
3. Keeping a record of skills acquired in mathematics
4. Keeping a record indicating the uses of mathematics made by the pupils outside of class.

Health and Safety. The following types of work in health and safety can give reason for striving for improvement in handwriting:

1. Making a health or safety booklet, either as a class or as an individual activity
2. Writing a skit for a health play
3. Writing an original story about health or safety
4. Making a list of safety or health rules.

Science. Work in handwriting can be correlated with science by:

1. Making a bird, flower, or tree book
2. Making charts on migration of birds, erosion, the water cycle, the ways in which heat travels, the solar system, and space travel
3. Recording the results of experiments that the class performed
4. Writing original poems about topics of scientific concern and interest.

Music, Art, and Physical Education. Below are listed ways in which the work in music, art, and physical education can be correlated or integrated with handwriting:

1. Writing an original song
2. Making a booklet of songs of a particular kind

3. Making a file of games that the class enjoys playing
4. Making a accordionlike folder giving the stories of famous pictures
5. Writing poems to illustrate pictures or drawing pictures to illustrate poems
6. Writing a booklet of famous composers or artists.

TEACHING THE LEFT-HANDED CHILD

Since studies seem to indicate that on the average two or three pupils in an elementary school classroom can be expected to have a preference for the left hand over the right, the question as to how to teach the left-handed child to write is a problem that almost every elementary school teacher needs to face.

Determining the Hand Dominance

There is disagreement among psychologists and specialists in handwriting as to the cause of left-handedness, right-handedness, and ambidexterity. Some claim that preference of one hand over the other or of no preference is determined by the hereditary pattern of the individual. Others claim that which hand is the dominant one is primarily or solely a matter of early practice or training. The great difficulties often encountered when attempts are made to change the left-handed writer to a right-handed one are frequently used as argument for the former position. However, it is also argued that the tenacity of a once-established habit could account for the difficulty of changeover. Regardless of whether or not hand preference is cheifly an inherited trait or primarily the product of practice, it does seem as if often by the time a child reaches school age, his hand preference is quite firmly established.

In order to deal with the question as to which hand the child should be encouraged to use, it is important to try to determine his hand dominance. Casual observation of the child as he goes about activities in which he uses his hands is one means of giving an answer to the question, "Is this child left-handed?" But such informal observation is hardly enough to try to answer as important and far-reaching a question as that of hand preference. Simple tests, if a variety of them are used, can be given by the classroom teacher as he sets up testing situations in which he takes note in writing of the preferred hand of the child in activities such as these:

1. Picking toys off the floor
2. Handing an article to the observer
3. Taking an article that the observer hands to the pupil
4. Throwing a ball
5. Bouncing a ball
6. Drawing with crayon or pencil or painting

7. Cutting
8. Using a fork or spoon when eating
9. Holding a cup when drinking
10. Pointing at things
11. Washing the face with a washcloth
12. Combing the hair
13. Driving nails
14. Threading a needle
15. Placing pegs into holes
16. Pounding with a hammer.

One test that has been used to try to determine hand dominance is given by placing a pencil directly in front of the child on a table or desk so that the lead points toward the middle of his body and then asking him to pick up the pencil or asking him to draw or write with it.

If a test is made comprising probably five or six of the items suggested and if that test is given to an individual at two or three different times, the percent of times that he uses the right hand rather than the left is a rough index of handedness. If 100 percent of the attempts during the times that the test is given show preference for the right hand, it can be assumed, for practical purposes, that the pupil has a decided right-hand preference. If in no case the child shows a preference for the right hand over the left, it can probably be assumed that his left hand is the dominant one. If the number of times a pupil uses the right hand is the same as the number of times he uses the left hand, then there is indication of possible ambidexterity. If in 75 percent or more of the attempts a pupil shows preference of one hand over the other he might be considered to have a definite, though not perfect, preference for the hand used more frequently.

To Change or Not to Change

"That is the question" that has long puzzled teacher and parents. In spite of much research, agreement has not been reached. There seems, however, to be considerable evidence for the recommendation by the late Frank N. Freeman, psychologist and specialist in the field of the teaching of handwriting, who believed that if a child has a definite perference for the left hand, especially when at the same time he does not follow rather readily the suggestion that he write with his right hand, he should be allowed to write with the left hand. This point is readily accepted by many teachers particularly in the case of the child who has already begun to write with his left hand. It is this recommendation that the writer accepts.

Reasons given for not insisting that the child with decided left-hand dominance or the child, regardless of dominance, who has long written with the left hand should write with his right hand include:

1. The child with left-hand dominance or the one accustomed to writing with the left hand, regardless of dominance in terms of his hereditary pattern, is often able to write more legibly if he is allowed to write with his left hand.

2. Writing with the right hand by a child with left-hand dominance at times seems to cause nervousness. Even though the incidence has not been established as a frequent result, the seriousness of such a possible development makes many teachers and parents unwilling to risk much encouragement for a changeover.

3. Change from left-handedness to right-handedness seems in some instances to bring about speech difficulties. As in the case of nervousness, as a possible effect of the change from left-handedness to right-handedness, so in the case of speech difficulties, the incidence has not been established as being a frequent concomitant or result. But, again as in the case of nervousness, many parents and teachers are unwilling to risk the speech problems that may result even though these undesirable effects that may be brought about have not been established as frequent.

4. Change in handedness may cause reversals in reading and writing.

There are some authorities in the field of the teaching of handwriting who insist rather persistent effort should be made, if necessary, to influence the child to write with his right hand. They argue that the likelihood of resulting nervousness, speech difficulties, or problems of reversal in reading and in writing is so small that the changeover should be made in order to avoid the disadvantages of left-handedness. The claim could be made that the undesirable results from a changeover could possibly be prevented if the transition were made in the best manner feasible.

In general, authorities seem to agree that the child who may, as far as heredity is concerned, be equally able to use both hands but who prefers his left hand, should be encouraged to make the change if he has not at the time rather firmly established the habit of writing with the left hand.

If a change to right-hand writing is attempted, the teacher and parents should explain to the child the advantages and try to obtain his cooperation. They should assure him at the outset that if he finds it very difficult to make the change, it will be all right if, after making an honest attempt, he continues to write with his left hand. Such assurance is of value in keeping the child from being unduly concerned with the matter of success or failure.

Disadvantages of the Left-Handed Writer

The disadvantages of the left-handed writer result to a considerable extent from lack of instruction in correct body and paper position. Without guidance the child may develop a backward writing slant. Furthermore, he may develop an awkward body position as he writes in a so-called "hook position" in an attempt to see what he is writing while he tilts his paper to the left. He may have his paper in that position in accordance with instructions given to the right-handed child because it has not been explained to him that his paper should not be turned in the same way.

Position of Paper and of Body

If the child who writes with his left hand is given early guidance in acquiring and/or maintaining the position of paper and body described earlier in this chapter, the disadvantages of left-handedness can be reduced considerably. (See pages 173 and 177.)

It should be noted that there is no one position of paper that should be insisted upon for all children who are left-handed. Especially important is this precaution in cases where the child has already established a fairly satisfactory handwriting through positioning his paper in some way other than that which has here been recommended. For example, one position that seems to produce satisfactory results is placing the right-hand side of the paper parallel to the desk. Any position, however, that results in the "hooked" hand placement has many serious disadvantages, among them the smeariness of the paper is likely to result.

Other Teaching Suggestions

The following recommendations should be observed when helping the child who writes with his left hand once it has been decided not to try or not to continue to try to have him acquire the habit of writing with his right hand.

1. Help the left-handed child feel that there is nothing wrong or odd in being left-handed.

2. Provide the left-handed child with much practice in doing manuscript writing on the chalkboard during the early stages of learning to write as he stands directly in front of his writing.

3. Let the left-handed writer postpone the changeover from manuscript to cursive writing longer than most of the right-handed children. In fact, arguments against a changeover from manuscript to cursive handwriting are more convincing in case of the left-handed child than in case of the right-handed.

4. Furnish the left-handed pupil with a pencil with hard lead to avoid smudging, and if he uses a ball-point pen, give him one that does not easily smear.

5. Supervise carefully a left-handed pupil's experiences in the early stages of learning to write so that he places his paper correctly, holds his writing instrument properly, sits in good position, and uses correct arm and hand movements.

6. Help the child in the acquisition of suitable slant. There are those among teachers of handwriting who believe that the teacher should not insist on the slant proper for the right-handed writer, but should have the child strive for uniformity of slant even if it deviates from that of the right-handed child by slanting less from right to left, having a straight-up-and-down slant, or even writing with a backward slant.

7. In rooms where chairs with arms as desks for writing are used, give the left-handed child a chair with an arm at the left—not right—side.

8. Recognize the importance of early attention to the left-handed writer since, without special help, he is likely to develop undesirable writing habits.

9. Since many teachers believe that by the time the child who is a left-handed writer has reached the intermediate grades it is too late profitably to encourage him to change to the right hand, at that time put emphasis on helping the child overcome those habits connected with left-handedness that he may have developed, which most seriously interfere with efficient writing.

10. Excuse from much writing, during classes other than handwriting, the pupil who is striving to overcome a serious and rather persistent poor habit in writing. This caution should be observed since the pupil who is trying to overcome such a habit may find that at first his writing under the desired circumstances is less satisfactory than that which he has been accustomed to doing. Consequently he would possibly be tempted to revert to a habit he is trying to break if much writing is required of him when he does not have the time to concentrate on the new habit he is trying to establish.

11. Consider seriously the desirability of teaching the left-handed writer with special problems to type even in the elementary school and investigate the feasibility of such action in a given situation.

OTHER CONSIDERATIONS

In this section attention is given to the following points: (1) the instructional program, (2) writing numerals, (3) use of the chalkboard, and (4) miscellaneous teaching suggestions. The attention of the reader is also drawn to the fact that further consideration is given to individual differences in handwriting in chapter

12, "Adapting Instruction to Individual Differences."
(See page 322.)

The Instructional Program

In most school systems the instructional program in handwriting is based almost entirely upon that advocated by one of the companies publishing handwriting materials such as the A.N. Palmer Company, Bobbs-Merrill Company, or The Zaner-Bloser Company. Pupil's recorders for the various grades are purchased for or by the children. With the help of the teacher's manual and other aids the main structure of the educational program is laid. In other schools the program is determined either without the use of a published program or with relatively little dependence on one.

Planning the Schoolwide Program. Even when much dependence is placed upon a published program in handwriting, the need of schoolwide planning should not be overlooked. If plans for initiating a schoolwide program or for drastically revising one are considered, attention should be paid to: (1) formulation of objectives, including knowledge to be gained, abilities to be acquired, and attitudes to be developed; (2) deciding upon the sequence of the parts of the program; (3) determining, in rather general terms, the grade placement of various abilities or skills to be acquired; (4) listing resources available, including professional books and materials for use by the boys and girls; (5) studying methods of teaching; (6) planning means of evaluation; and (7) considering ways of correlating and integrating handwriting with other parts of the school program.

Frequently as the result of rather intensive study there may be produced a resource unit on handwriting which is written chiefly by members of a committee but to which contributions from the entire staff of the elementary school are solicited. In such a unit there may also be included suggestions as to work that can be done in the secondary school to supplement that begun in the first six grades.

Planning the Program for a Grade. Even if a schoolwide program has been accepted and a commercial program in handwriting is followed to a considerable extent, there is need of planning by each teacher of some of the details of a handwriting program for his grade. However, a good schoolwide program will simplify the work of the teacher as he plans for his room. Similarly many suggestions can be utilized by the teacher from programs worked out by companies that publish the better handwriting materials. After the teacher has studied available guides, he may wish to do the following:

1. Set goals.
2. Determine the scope and sequence of the program.
3. Decide on means of testing the pupils to determine their general level of achievement as well as their strengths and weaknesses, and later on their progress.
4. Decide on general teaching procedures.
5. Make a list of methods and specific techniques to utilize.
6. Keep record of available materials and resources.

Writing Numerals

Boys and girls should be helped to realize the need of paying special attention to accuracy in writing numerals. At times a letter poorly formed can be deciphered through the context of the sentence in which it is found. A figure usually needs to stand on its own, however, for the context is often of no value in supplying the reader with a clue as to what the figure may be. (This difficulty usually does not exist when figures are given in serial order. For example, a poorly written *2* can be recognized as such when written in a *1, 2, 3,* sequence.)

Here are a few suggestions for teaching numerals in addition to those given so far.

1. Draw attention to the fact that the numerals are written the size of the "small small letters."
2. Discuss with the boys and girls which figures are often confused with others when written carelessly such as the *6* and the *0*, the *1* and the *7*, and the *9* and the *7*.
3. Make certain that the boys and girls in the first grade associate each figure with its correct value or order. Pupils may, for example, be asked to draw a line from one figure to an illustration showing the corresponding number of objects. Or opposite a given number of objects they may write the correct figure or may draw the required number of objects opposite a figure.

The Chalkboard as an Aid to Handwriting

It is to be regretted that in many modern elementary school classrooms relatively little chalkboard space is provided. It is hoped that the elementary school teacher will use his influence as new buildings are being constructed, to help those in authority realize the importance of considerable chalkboard space.

Use of the Chalkboard. With the limited chalkboard space in many classrooms it can easily be assumed, though erroneously, that the chalkboard is almost solely for the teacher's writing. However, if its use is reserved almost exclusively for that purpose, some of the most significant possible values of the chalkboard, such as those indicated here, are overlooked.

Figure 7.18. The Chalkboard as an Aid to Handwriting.

1. There is less danger of developing cramped writing if the pupils use the chalkboard frequently, for the movement in chalkboard writing is almost entirely arm and shoulder movement.

2. The larger handwriting on the chalkboard shows up—more readily than writing on paper—the problems and deficiencies in the handwriting of a pupil.

3. The teacher can watch many pupils, perhaps ten or even twelve almost simultaneously as they are writing on the chalkboard.

4. The teacher can guide the child's hand while he is writing at the chalkboard more effectively than when he is writing on paper.

5. The boys and girls enjoy writing on the chalkboard.

Characteristics of Chalkboard Writing. The following points give information that characterizes good writing on the chalkboard.

1. Size. The size of the writing on the chalkboard for primary-grade children should be larger than that for intermediate-grade boys and girls. It is recommended that the size of the board writing be about five times as large as the writing that boys and girls do on paper. For first grade it should be about five inches in height (for capital letters); for grade two, four inches; for grade three, three and one-half inches; and for grades four and above, three inches. However, the desirable size depends not only on the grade level of the child but also on the distance from which the material is to be viewed, the quality of the stroke, and the type of writing surface.

2. Color or shading. The quality of the stroke should be such that the writing can be clearly and readily recognized from the distance from which it is to be read. The writer should press the chalk enough that he obtains a clear, sharp stroke. To maintain such a stroke as the writing proceeds, it is important to turn the chalk in the

hand frequently enough to avoid writing that would result in an uninteresting stroke, lacking in sharpness. The desirable stroke for manuscript writing is broader than that for cursive writing.

3. Slant. It is often less difficult to obtain the slant (or lack of slant) for manuscript writing on the chalkboard than to obtain the proper slant for cursive writing. The latter should be at an angle that deviates somewhere within the range of twenty to thirty degrees from a perpendicular.

4. Beginning and ending strokes. Some of the suggestions for achieving correct beginning and ending strokes for cursive writing on paper that are given earlier in this chapter are also of value in obtaining correct beginning and ending strokes in writing on the chalkboard.

5. Spacing. For correct letter and word spacing in cursive writing on the chalkboard the same proportionate distance should be maintained as in cursive writing on paper.

6. Alignment. Alignment on the chalkboard presents a problem beyond that which the writer meets when he works for correct alignment on paper. While a teacher should try to learn to write straight across an unlined chalkboard, often for demonstration purposes he will want a lined board. If the board is lined the boys and girls can better visualize the alignment as well as the size and proportion of letters as they will want to write them either on the chalkboard or on paper. For the pupil in some of the beginning stages of writing (though not the very first, when he should not be impeded by lines) it is important that a lined surface be provided.

Many teachers like to have a lined chalkboard near the center of the front of the room. Lines should not be cut into that chalkboard (as is sometimes done if it is made of slate). Less permanent lines should be made so that the chalkboard is not marred for other purposes. Felt-tipped pens are used with success, as are tempera paints with some types of chalkboards. With both of these media erasure does not remove the lines, but in time, fortunately, they wear off.

Suggested Procedures. Following are a few suggestions as to methods of procedure in board writing.

1. It is good practice to have pupils who are beginning to learn to write to do much of it on the chalkboard. Sometimes one or more pupils may write on the board while the others are watching. At other times those at the seats may be writing on paper for a short time, maybe for five to ten minutes, while others are at the chalkboard. A system of rotation to give all pupils a chance, though not necessarily daily opportunity, for writing on the chalkboard before any one pupil has had a second chance can be worked out.

2. Even after pupils in the primary grades have learned to write fairly well with the pencil, they should not be deprived of making use of the advantages that board writing offers. Practice on the chalkboard beyond the primary grades is often reserved for those boys and girls who are in need of special help. However, it could also be of much help to others, especially when a skill is being presented in a developmental lesson.

3. The boys and girls should be encouraged to use arm and shoulder movement almost exclusively when writing on the chalkboard.

4. It is good practice to have the pupils whose seats are near the back of the room come forward at times while the teacher is demonstrating at the chalkboard. Similarly those sitting near the sides of the classroom, if the teacher uses a chalkboard area near the middle of the front wall for demonstration purposes, may be invited to come toward a place of better visibility.

5. In a lesson in which the chalkboard is used, after the pupils have seen purpose for the lesson, these steps may be followed: (a) demonstration by the teacher; (b) explanation by the teacher; (c) demonstration by one or more pupils; (d) evaluation of the pupils' demonstrations; (e) practice by the class; (f) comments by the teacher on points of difficulty, with suggestions for correction as he again demonstrates the point; (g) further practice by the boys and girls; and (h) further evaluation.

The Chalkboard and Its Care. Chalkboards made of slate are probably still in existence in some schools, especially older ones. Composition chalkboards have, however, at least to a large extent, replaced the slate boards. In turn, these are giving way in some schools to glass chalkboards.

Listed here are a few suggestions for care of chalkboards made of slate or composition board: (a) Do not use water, for it is likely to wear off the surface of composition boards and to take color out of the slate, graying it so that illegibility may result. (b) Do not use oiled cloths on slate or composition boards. (c) Use clean erasers, supplementing their use with a chamois skin, when cleaning slate boards or composition boards. (d) When erasing the board, start at the top and proceed to the bottom so that the dust falls into the chalk tray. (e) Have clean erasers, clean chamois skin, clean chalk trays, and clean chalkboards.

Miscellaneous Teaching Suggestions

Below are given additional suggestions for teaching handwriting.

1. Visual aids to learning should be used frequently. The importance of the chalkboard and the availability of models of the letters of the alphabet, both in manuscript and cursive writing, and various other commercial aids to better writing have already been indicated in earlier

pages. Bulletin boards can be used effectively for the improvement of writing. They can be constructed either by the teacher, the pupils, or by teacher and pupils together. The often seen alphabet train displayed above the chalkboard or near the top of it is one example of a valuable aid. On each of the cars of the train, made of various colors of construction paper, are written the letters of the alphabet, one for each car, in uppercase and lowercase form. At times the train will display the letters in both manuscript and cursive writing.

When the pupils are making the transition from manuscript to cursive writing, the teacher might display a chart divided vertically through the center. On one side of the chart words could be written in manuscript and on the other the same words in cursive writing. It may be useful for some pupils to have the spelling words currently being studied recorded on this chart or the chalkboard.

The opaque projector can be used successfully in many types of teaching situations. Not only can pages of a book in manuscript or cursive writing or parts of such pages be projected onto the chalkboard, tagboard, poster paper, or screen, but projectors can also be used to project pupils' writings in order to point out excellences and difficulties. For class instructional purposes it is desirable not to identify the pupils whose writing is being criticized; in fact, it is often best not to give the name of the boy or girl whose writing is projected in order to show excellences. Such publicity might discourage the pupil who is not good in writing, and the child whose success is proclaimed publicly might become proud.

Transparencies (made by the teacher or commercially available) can serve as a decided aid in learning. They can be in the form of either "permanent" or nonpermanent transparencies. The writing on the later can later be erased, and the acetate roll or sheet on which the writing had been done can be used repeatedly for other demonstrations. The nonpermanent transparencies are particularly good for showing boys and girls how letters or parts of letters or words are formed since the boys and girls can observe the teacher in the act of writing. Overlays of transparencies can be used to help boys and girls make evaluations of writing on which the overlays are placed.

2. The typewriter is being used increasingly in the elementary school. While there is no justification for saying that because the typewriter is used so much in life outside of school, it is not important to teach boys and girls to write well, nevertheless there is a justifiable role for the typewriter in the elementary school. Theory and practice in the use of the typewriter in the elementary school vary from school to school, even from teacher to teacher. However, the following points are probably acceptable to a large number of teachers:

Allowing boys and girls in the upper-elementary grades to learn to use the typewriter can add to the interest in handwriting but care should be taken that it is not used as a substitute for learning to write well.

Ability to use a typewriter can add to a child's interterest in communicating his thoughts in writing.

It is questionable whether all boys and girls in any grade of the elementary school should be required to learn to type. It can be used as an elective activity. In some schools it may be desirable to make use of it, in part, as an enrichment activity for those boys and girls who have achieved a desired quality of handwriting. If the latter practice is followed, care should, however, be taken that those pupils who most need the advantages that can accrue from learning to type, are not deprived of them.

Unless boys and girls are given help in using the typewriter (i.e., unless they are taught how to type) it is very likely that they will develop many poor habits in typing.

3. The practice of "air writing," which used to be fairly popular, is of doubtful value. We refer here to having pupils move the first finger of the hand or a pen or pencil held in correct position in the air so as to form imaginary letters or strokes of letters or words. Since neither pupil nor teacher can check on the correctness of the "writing" being done, the pupils may unknowingly imitate the strokes incorrectly. Furthermore, the skill being practiced is rather far removed from the skill that is desired, namely correct formation of letters or parts thereof on paper. As in other forms of practice exercises, it holds as general principle that practice in handwriting should be in a situation as nearly comparable to the one in which it is used as is practical. If broad movements of the arms and hands are desired, it is suggested that the pupils practice on the chalkboard or on large sheets of unlined paper, rather than "writing in the air."

4. At times the practice of "each one teach one," so advertised in teaching reading to adults, could be utilized in handwriting. Once in a while the pupils could be paired off so that each person in a couple will help the other evaluate his writing and give suggestions for improvement, possibly illustrating his suggestions. Insofar as is practical, it may be desirable to have the pupils choose their partners.

5. Occasionally the teacher may find it a desirable variation from oral directions, to write directions on the chalkboard—directions such as these that the boys and girls are to follow at the beginning of the handwriting period:

Take out your handwriting materials.

Place your paper in the correct position.

Get into writing position.

Head your paper.

Be ready to listen.

6. The boys and girls could make a loose-leaf, handwriting notebook. Materials such as the following could be included in the notebook: duplicated copies of correct forms of lowercase and uppercase letters, both in manuscript and cursive writing; suggestions worked out by the class for having good writing posture (with the help of the teacher, of course); illustrations as to how the paper should be placed on the desk for manuscript and/or cursive writing; statements as to how to attain correct slant and how to avoid various types of incorrect slant, as well as similar information about other qualities of handwriting including shading, size, beginning and ending strokes, alignment, and spacing.

7. Establishing an exchange system may serve as incentive for the improvement of handwriting. This exchange may be between two classes in the same school system or it may be between children in different parts of the country. It would usually be advisable to have both groups of children follow the same regulations in regard to matters such as whether the copy exchanged is the first copy the child makes of a given selection, whether a copy of the handwriting of each pupil in a room will be submitted, and what month of the year the writing will be done. Display of the writing can be made in the room of the pupils who receive such samples of handwriting. Emphasis on content and form can be combined if the samples of writing are bona fide letters.

EVALUATION OF HANDWRITING

Various publishing companies sell handwriting scales. Some of them, such as the Ayres Scale, range from very poor samples of handwriting to a sample representative of superior handwriting. At least one company has a scale for each grade from one to six, with the one used for grade six also used to measure handwriting of pupils in the upper grades and high school and of adults.

A few samples of commercial materials that can be used for evaluating handwriting follow; all are available through the Zaner-Bloser Company. Other publishers or distributors of handwriting materials also furnish materials that can be used for evaluative purposes.

1. The worksheets for manuscript and cursive handwriting and for the transition period from manuscript to cursive

2. "Body position charts," illustrating correct position for manuscript and for cursive writing for the right-handed writer and some for the left-handed writer, and "hand charts," showing correct position

3. The "C-thru-Ruler."

Periodically, possibly once a month, the pupils may write a sample of their best handwriting on a uniform size of paper. The writing can be timed, though the major emphasis should be on legibility and form of letters not on speed. After the boys and girls have written for a few minutes and time has been called, they can write in column form, below the sentences that they have written—also in their best handwriting—the following words representing qualities of handwriting: *color, size, slant, beginning strokes, ending strokes, letter spacing, alignment, letter formation,* and *rate.* The teacher can write a characterizing word or group of words to the right of each point listed. For example, opposite the word *slant* he may write either *correct, lacking slant, too slanting,* or *irregular slant.* The rate per minute can then be computed and a quality rating, based on the scale for the grade, can be recorded.

Some teachers may like to use papers of boys and girls in the room to form a scale with ratings comparable to those given on some charts. In some cases the teacher himself may need to furnish one or more samples on the scale for which he did not find comparable samples on the pupils' papers. It is best not to reveal the identity of the writer of any of the samples for fear that the poorer writers may be embarrassed.

Pupils' papers from classes other than handwriting should also be evaluated for handwriting. As a means of appraisal of the neatness of the handwriting on arithmetic papers, for example, a chart can be made without names of pupils, giving samples in which the writing is very neat, average in neatness, and lacking in neatness. If marks are given in handwriting on a report card, in calculating the mark the teacher should consider not only the writing in handwriting class but also that done at other times.

Figure 7.19. A Means of Self-Evaluation of Handwriting.

FOR STUDY AND DISCUSSION

1. Suggest methods that you could use for motivating boys and girls in a primary grade room to improve their handwriting; in an intermediate-grade room.

2. How would you answer the question that a pupil in the intermediate grades might ask as to why many successful adults do not write legibly?

3. Write the alphabet in both manuscript and cursive writing, including uppercase and lowercase letters. Then compare your letter formation with those recommended by a good publishing company of handwriting materials. What suggestions for improvement of your own writing can you give?

4. If you are a right-handed writer, how would you try to demonstrate writing to the left-handed writer? If you are a left-handed writer, how would you try to demonstrate it to the right-handed writer?

5. Make a list of ways in which handwriting can be correlated with specific other school subjects in any grade of the elementary school.

6. Make a study of several handwriting scales available commercially and evaluate them.

7. Study the handwriting materials—materials for boys and girls as well as teachers' manuals among them—produced by one or more publishing companies. Note the extent to which suggestions given in this chapter are implemented in those materials. Also note and evaluate any suggestions to the contrary that you may find, as well as additional ideas that you consider useful.

8. Study one or more references on handwriting, possibly of those listed under "References" following. What, if any, ideas contrary to those expressed in this chapter are given? At the present time what is your stand on the points of controversy? What additional valuable suggestions for teaching handwriting do you find in one or more references that you read?

9. You may find it helpful to construct a display for a bulletin board on the teaching of handwriting. If you do not construct it, draw a sketch of such a bulletin board and describe it.

10. If you have the opportunity, observe a left-handed person as he is writing. Also, if possible, consult with his teacher concerning any special problems the child may encounter and as to means by which the teacher is trying to help the pupil meet them.

11. You may be interested in doing some research on the relationship between left-handedness and the following factors: footedness, eyedness, and brain dominance.

12. You may wish to study the history of handwriting. One book that you might like to consult is *The Story of Handwriting* by William and Rhoda Cahn, published by Harvey House (1963). Another is *Painted Rock to Printed Page* by Frances Rogers, published by J.B. Lip-pincott (1960). You may also wish to read the brief resume on "History of Writing" given on pages 39-40 of *Teaching Communication Skills in the Elementary School* by Gertrude Boyd with Van Nostrand Reinhold Company as publishers (1970). Which of the facts you may have gathered might be of interest and/or value to an elementary school child?

13. You may wish to study the topic "Use of the Typewriter in the Elementary School" and then make a report on your findings.

REFERENCES

Anderson, Dan A. "Teaching Handwriting," *What Research Says to the Teacher: Number 4.* Washington, D.C.: National Education Association, 1968.

Boyd, Gertrude A. *Teaching Communication Skills in the Elementary School.* New York: Van Nostrand Reinhold Company, 1970.

Burns, Paul C. *Improving Handwriting Instruction in Elementary Schools.* Minneapolis, Minnesota: Burgess Publishing Company, 1963.

Burns, Paul C.; Broman, Betty L.; and Wantling, Alberta Lowe. *The Language Arts in Childhood Education.* Chicago: Rand McNally & Company, 1969.

Burns, Paul C., and Schell, Leo M., eds. *Elementary School Language Arts: Selected Readings.* Chicago: Rand McNally & Company, 1969.

Donoghue, Mildred R. *The Child and the English Language Arts.* Dubuque, Iowa: Wm. C. Brown Company Publishers, 1975.

Greene, Harry A., and Petty, Walter, T. *Developing Language Skills in the Elementary Schools.* Boston: Allyn and Bacon, Inc., 1967.

Herrick, Virgil, ed. *New Horizons for Research in Handwriting.* Report of the Invitational Conference on Research in Handwriting. Madison, Wis.: University of Wisconsin Press, 1963.

Horn, Thomas D., ed. *Research on Handwriting and Spelling.* Urbana, Illinois: National Council of Teachers of English, 1966.

Lamb, Pose, ed. *Guiding Children's Language Learning.* Dubuque, Iowa: Wm. C. Brown Company Publishers, 1967.

Myers, Emma Harrison. *The Whys and Hows of Teaching Handwriting.* Columbus, Ohio: The Zaner-Bloser Company, 1963.

Petty, Walter T. ed. *Issues and Problems in the Language Arts: A Book of Readings.* Boston: Allyn and Bacon, Inc., 1968.

Smith, James A. *Creative Teaching of the Language Arts in the Elementary School.* Boston: Allyn and Bacon, Inc., 1967.

Strickland, Ruth G. *The Language Arts in the Elementary School.* Lexington, Mass.: D.C. Heath and Company, 1969.

Tidyman, Willard F.; Smith, Charlene; Butterfield, Marguerite. *Teaching the Language Arts.* New York: McGraw-Hill Book Company, 1969.

Zaner-Bloser Company, The. *Writing on the Board.* Columbus, Ohio: The Zaner Bloser Company, 1958.

8

Guiding Growth in Spelling

The history of American public education presents considerable evidence of the great interest that has been given to the importance of spelling and to the methods of teaching it to boys and girls. During the many decades that Noah Webster's "blue-backed speller," officially known as *Webster's Spelling Book,* was the universally used spelling textbook, beginning with its publication in 1783, spelling was emphasized in the schools to the extent that, it would seem, other subjects of the limited curriculum must have suffered. During that period faith was placed on learning a far longer list of words than the most ambitious of modern spelling programs would advocate.

Spelling was the first elementary school subject that was placed under the careful scrutiny of research when James Rice made his classical study on the relationship between the length of the spelling period and the ability of boys and girls to spell.[1] He found lack of a close relationship between the two. Reduction in the length of the spelling period in the typical American school, following Rice's research, did not, however, result in a decrease in the concern about the teaching of spelling. Research and classroom experimentation have continued, with concentration on spelling tests and scales, word lists, study-test and test-study procedures, textbooks, "spelling readiness," and functional spelling instruction.

An area of investigation in the teaching of spelling that is currently claiming the attention of an increasing number of people concerns itself with the relationship between the tenets of linguists and the teaching of spelling. There are individuals, found both among linguists and among leaders in elementary school education, who have faith that by means of linguistically oriented spelling programs there can be greatly reduced the chief reason for difficulty in spelling. The references are to the problem presented by the irregularities of spelling in English orthography, the lack of a one-to-one relationship between phonemes (sounds) and graphemes (written symbols or letters of the alphabet). Although much

1. James M. Rice, "The Futility of the Spelling Grind," *The Forum* 23 (1897): 169-172.

of this chapter is devoted to teaching of spelling without special attention to linguistics, the last part of the chapter deals (1) with claims of linguists, (2) with pertinent research, and (3) with suggestions for implementing the findings. Following these topics is a brief consideration of a linguistically oriented spelling series.

BASIC CONSIDERATIONS IN TEACHING SPELLING

As background for a subsequent emphasis on methods and materials of instruction, the following points are considered in the introductory pages of this chapter: (1) shortcomings of earlier programs, (2) goals of spelling instruction, (3) motivation for spelling, and (4) time allotments.

Shortcomings of Earlier Programs

In order to avoid some of the deficiencies of earlier programs of spelling instruction, let us note what they were.

1. Spelling was frequently introduced earlier in the school program than readiness for spelling seems to have indicated.
2. Emphasis was placed on a very long list of words.
3. Many of the words in spelling lists were more difficult than those included in modern lists.
4. The words in spelling lists were not scientifically selected in terms of utility.
5. The lists were poorly allocated to grade levels since neither usefulness of the words nor difficulty of learning them were established by research.
6. Too great faith was seemingly placed on transfer of learning.
7. There was lack of stress on the relationship between spelling and the other language arts.
8. Little help was given boys and girls in the method of studying words.
9. Inadequate provision was made for systematic review.
10. There was an overemphasis on the value of writing a word—one that had been misspelled—a specified number of times for practice purposes.
11. There was an overemphasis on oral spelling.
12. There was an overemphasis on spelldowns.
13. Inadequate attention was paid to individual differences.
14. Relatively little time was spent on improving the spelling of words not included in spelling lists, words which the boys and girls used in their functional writing.
15. An unnecessarily large amount of time in the school day was often allotted to spelling.

Goals of Spelling Instruction

In the modern elementary school, teachers try to:

1. Help the boys and girls recognize the importance of correct spelling
2. Help the pupils write correctly the words they use in written communication
3. Guide the pupils so they will want to correctly spell the words they use in their writing
4. Develop in the boys and girls independence in spelling so that in time they need not rely on the teacher or a textbook for the spelling of a word
5. Guide the pupils so they will habitually use methods of learning to spell a word that for them are effective.

Motivation for Spelling

The following two aims listed in the preceding paragraph deal with motivation in spelling: (1) to help the boys and girls recognize the importance of correct spelling and (2) to guide the pupils so that they will want to correctly spell the words that they use in their writing.

The Importance of Spelling. The need for uniform spelling can be pointed out to elementary school children by explanation, discussion, and demonstration of the effect on written communication if each person were spelling in whatever way he wished. Furthermore, the teacher can discuss with the boys and girls the fact that when people seeking work make a written application, the employers often judge them in part by any errors of spelling that may appear on their letters of application. The pupils may be told that some employers ask applicants who come to them in person also to write a letter of application so that they can see what type of letter they can write. Boys and girls should be informed that the ability to spell correctly is often considered one of the important qualifications of an applicant even if his work would not involve writing. In fact, it could be pointed out that an applicant might lose the opportunity to obtain a position because of a single misspelled word that may appear in a letter of application or on an application blank.

The fact that many people other than employers judge an individual in part by spelling ability could also be noted. Since it is considered good form to spell correctly, they could be helped to realize that failure to do so in many cases constitutes reason to believe that a person is slow of learning, unschooled, or careless.

Even though boys and girls should be taught to be critical of their own spelling, some may need to be cautioned not to judge others severely by standards of perfection. For instance, it would, indeed, be unfortunate if a child thought the less of his parents because of their lack of ability to spell, possibly through no fault of their parents. At the same time that the teacher tries to instill in boys and girls the desire to be good spellers, with tact and sincerity, he should point out to them that many other characteristics of people are nevertheless much more important than the quality of their spelling.

The Desire to Spell. In a sense the realization of the importance of spelling is merely preliminary to the next step—that of wanting to spell correctly. However, to know the importance of spelling is frequently not sufficient incentive to learn. The child should be guided so that, after recognizing a need for spelling, he wishes to become a good speller. He should be helped, if necessary, to come to the realization that the goal of being a good speller can often be accomplished, at least in part, if he really wants to become one—enough to be willing to follow suggestions for making improvement.

Other Points. As emphasis is being placed on knowledge of the importance of correct spelling and on developing a desire to become a good speller, the following points should be noted.

1. If boys and girls realize that the words they are asked to spell are important to them in their writing, they are more likely to want to learn them.

2. Care should be taken that the means of motivation does not interfere with learning to spell. For example, when words are presented in an interesting context, such as a story, the teacher needs to guard against placing so much emphasis on the context that the pupils have their attention directed chiefly to the theme of the story, rather than to the spelling of the words. In fact, there is real question whether the stories given in some spelling textbooks and workbooks do not serve as a means of diverting the pupils' attention from the real problem, learning to spell, through interesting the boys and girls in the story rather than in learning to spell the words. Similarly some spelling games can be so exciting that they do not interest the pupils in spelling, but in games.

3. Competition with self, rather than with others, should be stressed.

4. It is not necessary, not even desirable, that every day when the boys and girls study spelling the teacher try to motivate them to better spelling. The desirability of the teacher, from time to time, helping the boys and girls see the value of correct spelling, has already been discussed. However, if he tries to urge them to become better spellers every day, his comments may have an effect the opposite of what was intended. Statements such as these, if not used too frequently can, however, be effective in stimulating the child to give his best effort to the task:

Today I am going to help you not to make mistakes in the use of the words *there* and *their*.

I will help you with the plurals of nouns ending in *y* in the singular.

Some spelling words in this unit end in a silent *e*. Let's try to discover what the silent *e* in these words does.

Simple statement of the chief purpose of a lesson is at times important; at other times, when it is quite self-evident, even such attempted motivation can be boring and, therefore, detrimental rather than helpful.

5. Knowledge of results serves as motivation, especially if the results are desired ones. In fact, one of the best ways for interesting a person in striving for further improvement is to show him that he is making progress.

6. Purpose for spelling can be highly meaningful to boys and girls when they engage in bona fide writing situations in which they are truly interested. Consequently, the teacher who provides many occasions such as the following is likely to aid growth in spelling: writing and proofreading articles for a class paper or magazine; writing a letter to a pupil who is absent from school; writing a thank-you letter to an adult who has spoken to the group.

7. The attitude of the teacher toward spelling can serve as a motivating influence. The teacher who shows enthusiasm for teaching spelling is more likely to inspire it in his pupils than the one who gives the impression, though unwittingly, that he thinks of it merely as a task to be performed. His own care in spelling correctly can also motivate the class to pay more attention to spelling, especially if they like him. For example, when he accidentally misspells a word on the chalkboard, as soon as he notes his error, he could say, "I am glad that I caught the mistake."

8. The teacher's skill in spelling can influence the boys and girls in their desire to be good spellers. It is poor advertising if a teacher, who tries to impress the boys and girls with the importance of good spelling, sends home a note to the parents with an error in spelling which, possibly, the parents may draw to the attention of the children.

Time Allotments

What is the optimum length of time to be spent on spelling in the daily or weekly schedule? One reason it is impossible to give an authoritative answer to this question is that the extent to which spelling is given incidental attention during the school day undoubtedly affects the length of time that might advisedly be set aside for learning-to-spell periods. Another reason is that research has not thus far, with surety, pointed to any one length of time as the best. In fact, since so many factors, such as means of using the class period and the number of spelling words studied, have bearing on the desirable length of time, it is doubtful whether research can ever say with conclusiveness that a given number of minutes a week is *the optimum* length of time for spelling classes.

Research, together with expert opinion, has, however, thrown light on the problem of time allotments. It seems to be rather commonly believed that about an hour and fifteen minutes a week spent in spelling classes is somewhere near a desirable length of time. Before deciding on following this rather general practice, the teacher should bear in mind the fact that the length of time he will want to use for spelling class should be determined in part by factors to which reference is made in the preceding paragraph.

How the total number of minutes a week for spelling can best be allocated to the daily schedule has not been determined. Some teachers favor spending fifteen minutes five times a week on spelling. Others favor an unequal division of the time, with limits to be determined in the light of the type of work to be done each day. For example, some teachers who follow the plan of working on a given set of new words for five class periods during the week like to have a longer period of time on the day when they present the words than on other days. The following, or a variation of it, might be their schedule.

First day: 25 minutes
Second day: 15 minutes
Third day: 10 minutes
Fourth day: 10 minutes
Fifth day: 15 minutes

Still other teachers set aside a block of time each day, possibly an hour in length, commonly referred to as the language arts period, during which all the language arts except reading are taught. Thus they do not specify how much of the block should be used daily for spelling, how much for handwriting, and how much for so-called "English." The length of time in such a block that they use for spelling may vary from day to day. Some teachers may decide not to spend time on spelling every day of the week.

READINESS FOR SPELLING

Before regular instruction in spelling begins, the child should be ready for the task. Let us then consider these points about spelling readiness: (1) the need for spelling readiness, (2) prerequisites for spelling, (3) appraisal of spelling readiness, and (4) methods of developing spelling readiness.

The Need for Spelling Readiness

It is now conceded by many specialists that formal instruction in spelling should not take place in the first grade. Some educators may question beginning such teaching even in the second grade. The reason for this delay in teaching the child to spell is concern that he may suffer in the following ways if he is confronted with formal teaching of spelling before he is ready for it.

1. The child may be kept from taking part in activities more important at the time to his total development than spelling.

2. The child may develop an aversion for school activities because of inability to do what is expected of him in spelling.

3. It may become difficult in the future to interest in spelling the child who has been defeated in his early efforts to learn to spell.

4. If the child receives formal spelling instruction at the time he is beginning to learn to read, learning to spell may, depending on the method used, interfere with learning to read.

Prerequisites for Spelling

Whether or not a child is ready to learn to spell will depend to a considerable extent upon the nature of the spelling program to be followed. Some of the other factors that will help determine whether a child is ready are his (1) mental age, (2) ability in visual and auditory discrimination, (3) knowledge of the alphabet, (4) reading ability, (5) knowledge of phonics, (6) ability to write, (7) ability to spell a few words, and (8) interest in learning to spell.

Mental Age. If any one desirable mental age for beginning formal instruction in spelling had to be named, it might be about seven or seven and one-half years. However, as in the case of readiness for reading, no one mental age can be set as the optimum or even the minimum age at which formal spelling instruction should begin. If a child ranks high on the other prerequisites of spelling listed in the preceding paragraph, he may be able to learn to spell before he has attained a given mental age that might ordinarily be considered desirable. For example, a child with considerable skill in visual discrimination, who knows the alphabet, who has a rudimentary knowledge of phonics, and who is highly motivated to learn to spell, even if his mental age is somewhat lower than, say seven years, may have a better chance to succeed in beginning spelling than one who has a higher mental age but who is less able to make visual discriminations, who does not know the entire alphabet, who has less knowledge of phonics, and who is not highly motivated to learn to spell.

If formal spelling instruction is begun in a second grade, as it is in many schools, it is questionable whether, if there are only a few pupils with a mental age of less than seven or seven and one-half in the room, it would be advisable to have such individuals wait with spelling instruction even though they may not possess in more than average measure any of the other prerequisites for beginning spelling of a somewhat formal type. To postpone instruction with a few may be a source of discouragement to them. Frequently the wise plan, when most of the boys and girls are ready to begin work in formal spelling, is to start it with all, but to adapt the work for those with lower mental ages to their capacity, possibly by presenting fewer words or by giving simpler instructions or by providing practice exercises particularly suited to those of lower mental development.

Visual and Auditory Discrimination. The ability to discriminate between symbols for letters and words is essential to success in spelling. The child must be able to differentiate quite readily, for example, between letter forms such as *m* and *n.* He needs to be able to note quickly that the vowel, for example, in *sat* and *sit* is not the same. Auditory discrimination also is an important aspect for readiness for spelling. Many errors in spelling seem to be caused by "hearing" words incorrectly.

Knowledge of the Alphabet. The pupil who does not readily recognize the names of the letters of the alphabet as capital letters and as lowercase letters is likely to be handicapped even in a beginning program of spelling. The recommendation is that in the beginning program in both reading and spelling instruction the words should be written in manuscript.

Reading Ability. The child who has successfully completed the reading of material equivalent in difficulty to that of most first- or beginning second-grade readers seems to be well enough equipped as far as reading ability is concerned for work in a desirable program of beginning spelling instruction.

Knowledge of Phonics. To be successful in learning to spell, the child should have knowledge of the rudiments of phonics. Knowledge of common sounds of the consonants and vowels, in various positions in words, as well as of much-used consonant blends, seems to be a prerequisite. (The relationship of phonics to spelling is explained somewhat in detail later in this chapter. See page 217.)

Ability to Write. Since spelling is useful almost exclusively in writing situations, the ability to do some writing is essential to spelling. A child who cannot write the letters of the alphabet legibly without undue effort is hardly ready to learn to spell the words as he writes them. He should be able to copy not only words that are written in books or on paper at his desk but also those that appear on a chart or on the chalkboard, if either a chart or the chalkboard is used in teaching spelling.

Ability to Spell a Few Words. A desirable prerequisite for anything corresponding to formal spelling instruction is the ability to spell a few words learned in informal situations, possibly without the child's even knowing what the letters are that constitute the words he is writing.

Interest in Learning to Spell. As in all other areas of learning, the interest of the learner is of great significance in the learning process. Some of the ways in which interest can be developed are indicated under "Interest in Learning to Spell" in the following section on "Appraisal of Spelling Readiness" and also in items given under "Methods" in the section following "Appraisal of Spelling Readiness." (See page 198.)

Appraisal of Spelling Readiness

There is no standardized test that the teacher can give to a child to determine with even reasonable surety that he is ready to begin to learn to spell. However, there are suggestions a teacher can follow to help him decide whether or not a boy or girl is ready to begin with a program of spelling instruction and to ascertain what type of instruction he should be given. Some of these have been given in the preceding paragraphs. Others, organized around the listing of prerequisites for spelling readiness given above, are given below.

Mental Age. The best index of mental age that is obtainable for a child is secured through intelligence tests. (The reader is referred to listing of intelligence tests given in chapter 13. See page 345.)

Visual and Auditory Discrimination. It is important that the teacher have the difference between visual acuity and visual discrimination, as well as between auditory acuity and auditory discrimination clearly in mind. A child who has visual acuity—one who can see plainly, for example, the letters *u* and *n*—may not be able to differentiate or discriminate between the two. To test a child's ability to make visual discriminations an exercise with items such as the following can be used as he is asked to cross out the word that is different from the others in the row:

dime   dime   dine   dime   dime.

Or he may be asked to draw a line under the word in a row that is the same as the first word in the row, as in this illustration:

dine   dime   dime   dine   dime.

Since skill in visual discrimination is checked in many reading-readiness tests, teachers may find the level of performance by means of such a test. (See page 228.)

A child who has considerable auditory acuity—that is one who can hear well—may not be able to differentiate, for example, between the sound of the words *bear* and *hair,* a skill important to spelling. (For further discussion on auditory discrimination the reader is referred to page 228 of chapter 9, "Guiding Growth in Reading Skills Closely Related to the Other Language Arts."

Knowledge of the Alphabet. The teacher can ask the

child to read the letters of the aphabet, written in manuscript. The letters should not be given in alphabetical order, for the pupil might be able to identify the letters by their order rather than by their form if they are given in ABC order. It maybe is not essential that a child know each letter of the alphabet. However, if he misses many, he should be given help in learning them either before or shortly after spelling instruction is begun.

Reading Ability. One very simple test for reading ability, if the child was not given a standardized reading test, is to have him read orally to the teacher in the last part of a first-grade reader or the first part of a second-grade reader of the series used in the school. If he can read the material with no more than a few errors per page, he would seem to be ready for spelling instruction as far as level of attainment in reading is concerned.

Knowledge of Phonics. Following are some ways in which a child's knowledge of phonics, important for beginning spelling, can be tested:

The teacher can ask the child to write the letter with which each of a series of words begins as the teacher names them.

The teacher can ask the child to point at the letter *d,* for example, which the teacher has written on the chalkboard, when he names a word beginning with *d.* The child can further be instructed to point at the letter *p,* also written on the chalkboard by the teacher, when the teacher names a word beginning with *p.* Other consonants whose sounds are frequently confused can be identified in a similar manner.

The pupil can be asked to name words that begin with the same sound as one that the teacher names.

The child can be asked to check a series of words that he has learned to read in which, for example, the sound of the *a* as in *cake* occurs.

Ability to Write. The teacher writes on the chalkboard one or a few short sentences that the pupil is able to read, which he is to copy. If the pupil has done the copying so that it is legible and so that there are no more than a few errors in writing the letters (omissions, substitutions, or repetitions), it would seem that the writing ability of the child would be advanced enough that he ought not to be unduly handicapped in beginning spelling because of his handwriting.

Ability to Spell a Few Words. A child's ability to write his own name without a copy is one index of readiness for spelling. If from time to time the teacher has drawn the attention of his class to the spelling of a few words frequently written by pupils, such as *Mother* or *today,* the teacher may ask them to write those words without copy. Failure to write such words correctly should not, however, be interpreted as a serious shortcoming.

Interest in Learning to Spell. One way in which the teacher can appraise the child's interest in learning to spell is by noting his reactions when the teacher informally refers to the spelling of words. For example, he can observe whether the child is interested in responding when the teacher asks questions such as this one as he writes on the chalkboard: "With what letter should I start the word *man*?" Over a period of time as questions of that type are repeated, the teacher may be able to form some idea of the child's attitude toward spelling. Questioning children individually concerning their attitude toward spelling, too, if suitable questions are used, may throw light on their true feelings. Questions such as these might be asked: (a) Why am I careful when I write on the chalkboard that I spell the words correctly? (b) How would it help you if you could spell many words? (c) Would you like to have me help you learn to spell some of the words you need in writing letters?

Methods

The methods used to help boys and girls grow toward readiness for spelling should not be pigeonholed into a period of the day designated for spelling readiness. Rather, means for getting the children ready to learn to spell should be employed throughout the school day, many of them, as far as the children know, incidental in the ongoing program of the room. The following are some of the ways in which the teacher can guide the boys and girls so that they will become ready for systematic instruction in spelling. It will be noted that many of the activities of value in developing "readiness for spelling" are similar to, if not identical with, those that foster "readiness for reading." (See page 229.)

1. Providing the boys and girls with a large number of interesting and worthwhile experiences so that they will have the background for dictating reports or stories which they would like to have in writing

2. Writing at a child's dictation a caption for a picture that he has drawn

3. While writing a story at the dictation of one or more pupils, occasionally making comments or asking questions or giving directions such as these that draw attention to spelling: (a) What is the first letter of the word *mother*? (b) Who can write the letter with which our next word *farmer* begins? (c) The next word for our story is given on this word card. Write it here in our story. (d) Let's spell this word *run* together, for it is a word we often use in writing.

4. Helping the children who are lacking in auditory discrimination by any of the means suggested for development of that ability in chapter 9. (See page 230.)

5. Orientating pupils to the left-to-right and top-to-bottom sequence in writing by: (a) drawing attention to that sequence in reading; (b) showing the child where the teacher starts and how he continues when writing

something on the chalkboard, a chart, or a piece of paper; (c) asking a child occasionally where he (the teacher) should start as he writes at the pupil's dictation and asking him in what direction the writing should progress; (d) having a pupil name the first letter in a word, the next, and the next

6. Helping boys and girls who have difficulty with enunciation

7. Having the pupils copy a story or letter the teacher has written on the chalkboard at the dictation of the class

8. Helping the pupils copy lists they may need such as lists of supplies; names or room duties to be performed and names of those who are to do them; the sequence of activities for the day

9. Having the pupils do semiindependent writing with the teacher available to help in spelling of the words in the simple sentences that the children write

10. Having a pupil who asks for the spelling of a word write the first letter of the word before he is given help by the teacher

11. Providing a series of picture cards which the children are to match with letters of the alphabet

12. Having the pupils give words that start with the letter of the alphabet to which the teacher points

13. Having a "pupil-teacher" point at the letters of the alphabet given on the chalkboard in mixed-up order as others name them

14. Providing the pupils with sheets of paper on each of which are two columns, with capital letters in the first column to be matched with lowercase letters in the second

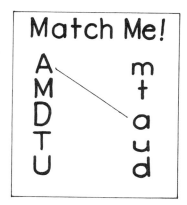

Figure 8.1. An Exercise for Matching Upper- and Lowercase Letters.

15. Providing the boys and girls with picture dictionaries and helping them use these books

16. Helping the pupils make picture dictionaries either as a class or individual project

17. Helping boys and girls learn to write according to suggestions given in chapter 7

18. Helping boys and girls acquire the rudiments of knowledge of phonics and various other skills in reading as suggested in chapter 9

19. Playing a game on the order of Bingo in which letters of the alphabet in mixed-up order are used. The caller can either name the letters to be covered on the cards provided or name words beginning with the letters to be covered.

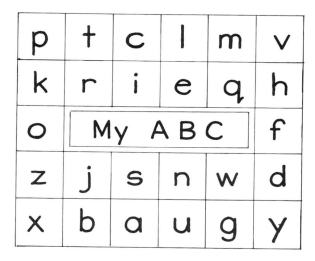

Figure 8.2. A Game for Letter Recognition.

ORGANIZATION FOR SPELLING

Three questions of organization of the spelling program that have far-reaching effects are considered here. They deal with (1) incidental versus systematic procedures, (2) the multiple-day versus the daily plan of procedure, and (3) study-test versus test-study procedures.

Incidental versus Systematic Procedures

The controversy as to whether spelling should be studied only incidentally has been raging in educational circles ever since the early decades of the century. Some of the early studies in spelling seemed to indicate that results from only incidental study were not inferior to those obtained when systematic procedures were followed. However, the validity of those studies has been questioned and evidence has been accumulating that seems to indicate that systematic procedures in teaching spelling are important. While there still is no unanimity of belief on the question, many specialists in the field have the point of view, to which the author subscribes, that usually the best results are obtainable when incidental means of teaching spelling are utilized in the various activities of the school program providing these are supplemented by systematic teaching of spelling in a separate period of the school day or during a part of a block set aside for the language arts.

It should be noted, too, that many pupils learn to spell a large number of words which they have seen in reading material or which they have written, without their attention being directed in particular to the spelling of the words. Other boys and girls seem to learn only a relatively small number of words in this manner.

The Multiple-Day versus
the Daily Plan of Procedure

If a teacher or a school has decided to use a systematic procedure for teaching spelling, supplemented, it is hoped, by many incidental means of learning to spell, the question arises as to the plan of organization. A very popular plan, according to which many of the spelling textbooks in the elementary school are organized, is the five-day plan. It calls for the repeated study for five consecutive school days of a list of words, usually ranging in number from about seven or eight to twenty, with the number varying according to grade level and the spelling series. This plan is sometimes referred to as the weekly plan, with Monday thought of as the first day of the five to be spent on a given list of words, Tuesday as the second, and so on. However, authors of some spelling books and probably some teachers think of it as a five-day plan—not a weekly plan—on which the first work on a list does not necessarily fall on Monday. Some find that designation more convenient because of the fact that vacations of part of a week or other events that may interfere with having spelling every day can throw off the schedule for the weekly plan.

Uniformity of opinion is lacking as to the order in which work on words should be taken up in the five-day plan. However, some time during that period is devoted, according to most plans, to each of the following phases of spelling: presentation of words, testing (both pre-testing and end testing), finding what each child's difficulties are in terms of types of errors, individual study of words including development of study habits, extended activities on some word forms or word building or phonics, and review. Review is not limited to the activities of the five-day unit but usually in published programs provisions are made for systematic rewiew at spaced intervals thereafter.

In contrast to the five-day plan is the one that was used extensively in earlier times and still has not been abandoned. According to it a smaller number of new words is presented than in the five-day plan and new words are studied each day. However, reviews are also provided or can be provided on later days at spaced intervals in the one-day plan.

Not all plans for systematic teaching of spelling are the so-called one-day or five-day plans. Four days or three days for study on a list of spelling words are used by some teachers. However, the most common of the multiple-day plans probably is the five-day plan.

Research on the comparative value of the two types of plans, the multiple-day and the daily plan as those terms are used here, is inconclusive. There is a difference in opinion of writers and of teachers on the question of relative worth, even in regard to the following statements, but it can be said, at least, that no conclusive evidence has been presented that contradicts them.

1. When systematic spelling instruction is first begun in primary grades, it is probably advisable to present a few words several times a week with continued study on succeeding days.

2. Pupils with low intelligence may profit more from only having a few words presented daily, with provisions for adequate review, than from having all words for a given week presented on the first day along with subsequent study of the entire list—or those words a child missed—on all subsequent days of the week.

3. Pupils with many difficulties in spelling, regardless of their grade placement or their intelligence, would probably profit more from a one-day plan of procedure with adequate review than from a multiple-day plan.

4. After pupils of near-average, average, or above-average intelligence who are near-average, average, or above-average spellers are beyond the stage of beginning work in systematic instruction in spelling, the multiple-day plan is probably superior to the one-day plan for them.

Study-Test versus Test-Study Procedures

One question often raised by persons who wish to recommend or use a multiple-day plan of procedure is that of the comparative desirability of study-test and test-study procedures. More specifically, the question is: "Is it better to test the boys and girls on a list of words before they study them or is it more advantageous to have the first testing follow some study of the words?"

To make clearer the two procedures, let us note how they can be used in the five-day plan. If less than five days is spent on a given list of words, the methods used in the five-day period as here outlined can be telescoped into fewer days.

Test-Study Procedures. Although there are many variations of test-study procedures, these steps are somewhat typical of them: (1) Either before the pupils have seen a list of new words or after they have had only a brief approach to the new words, they are given a pretest on the list. (2) Thereafter each pupil studies the words that he missed on the test. (3) Next he is retested. (4) Thereupon every pupil again studies the words that he missed. (5) A so-called final test is then given.

To summarize, the five steps enumerated in the preceding paragraph can be identified as (1) pretesting, (2) studying, (3) testing, (4) studying, and (5) testing. The procedure is sometimes called the test-study-test-study-test procedure. In the five-day plan, in many instances roughly each of these steps constitutes the work for one day. Provisions are made for further study of any words a pupil misses on the final test given on the fifth day, and provisions for systematic spaced review of all words in the weeks and months to follow are made.

Study-Test Procedures. These four steps are typical of those followed in study-test procedures, in which study of words precedes testing: (1) The pupils study the new words rather carefully. (2) The pupils are tested. (3) The pupils study the words missed. (4) The pupils are again tested. When these four steps are followed, the procedure is sometimes called the study-test-study-test procedure. If five days of consecutive study are devoted to a list of words, the first and second days can be spent on study, the third on the trial test, the fourth on more study, and the fifth on the final test. Or, instead, the first day can be devoted to study, the second to a trial test, the third and fourth to further study, and the fifth to the final test. Provisions are made for further study of words that a pupil misses on the final test and for systematically spaced review of words in the weeks and months that follow during the school year.

Relative Value of Test-Study and Study-Test Procedures. Although research has not established which of the two methods is superior, at the present time there is some reason for believing that considerations such as the following should help determine which of the two should be used.

1. An argument against the test-study procedure is that pupils might be discouraged in studying a list of words if they found out in a pretest that they have missed a large percent of the words.

2. Another argument against the test-study procedure is that a pupil might spell a word correctly on a pretest and then miss it in a test given later. For example, when he writes the word *receive* in a pretest, he may be in doubt whether the vowel sound in the second syllable is spelled *ei* or *ie* but, without any surety, he may happen to spell it *ei*. If he gives no further attention to the word before the time of the next test, he may again wonder whether the long *e* sound should be spelled *ei* or *ie* and then by chance happen to write it *ie*. The child studying the word before his first testing will at least have the benefit before the final test of some study of a word that he really does not know.

3. An argument for the test-study procedure is that a pupil who has spelled almost all words correctly is encouraged by knowing he has only a few words to learn.

4. Another argument for the test-study procedure is that a pupil does not waste time studying the spelling of words he already knows. For pupils who do not know how to spell a fairly large proportion of the words on a list, the study-test procedure is probably superior to the test-study plan. For others, the test-study procedure probably is better. To obtain an estimate of whether a given pupil is likely to miss many words on pretests, his achievement on tests given on earlier lists may be considered or he can be given a semester pretest on a sampling of the words for the term.

STEPS IN LEARNING TO SPELL A WORD

Merely to tell a child to study a word or to study it by writing it a specified number of times is no longer considered adequate procedure.

Learning to Spell a Word with Teacher Guidance

Although many teachers as well as writers on the subject of spelling have developed plans for studying the spelling of a word, there is no one system that has been established as superior to all others. Many, however, would agree in general on the following as significant steps in learning to spell a word when a teacher is present to guide the work: (1) pronunciation of the word; (2) clarification, if necessary, of the meaning of the word; (3) getting a clear image of the word; (4) recalling the word; (5) writing the word; (6) checking the writing; and (7) repeating steps three through six, in case of error, until the word is learned.

Figure 8.3. Illustrated Steps in Learning to Spell a Word.

Pronunciation of the Word. While, as a rule, a pupil can recognize in written form, words suitable for his spelling lists, attention, nevertheless, should be paid to pronunciation. Acceptable practice for this step of the procedure varies. Some teachers like to write the list of new words on the chalkboard before class, numbering the words for easy reference. Then at the beginning of the period they pronounce each word as they point at it and have the pupils pronounce it after them in unison. Others prefer to have pupils who do not recognize a word get help in word recognition through other than the sight method, according to which every word is pronounced for them. Consequently, some teachers, referring to the numbered list of words on the chalkboard, ask the pupils to give the number of any word they they cannot pronounce. Then the teacher tries to help the child who has difficulty with the word to decipher it by means of context clues (as the teacher writes a helpful sentence on the chalkboard in which the word is used) or by means of structural analysis (including syllabication or phonetic analysis). If the teacher thinks that someone may not know the pronunciation of a word for which no one has asked, he might call on someone to pronounce it and if he mispronounces it or is unwilling, because of lack of recognition, to try to pronounce it, the teacher helps him in figuring out the word. After each word about which there is considerable likelihood that there may be a problem in pronunciation has been taken up in this or a similar manner, the teacher pronounces the words as he points at each and the pupils say each word in unison after him.

Teacher and pupils should pronounce the words distinctly. It is questionable, however, whether the words should, as a rule, be "over-pronounced." At least the first pronunciation of a word by the teacher should be a normal saying of the word, without undue attention to the separate syllables. If the teacher thinks it helpful to have the pupils, in case of some words, place special emphasis on each syllable, he may either himself do so or ask the class to do so. It is, however, important that the child hears or gives at least once the normal pronunciation without "over-pronunciation."

If necessary, pupils should be cautioned about how to pronounce words in unison. Besides "over-pronunciation" of words, somewhat common shortcomings in concert pronunciation of words are these: (a) The class says the word too loudly. (b) The pupils overemphasize one or more syllables even though they do not "over-pronounce" the whole word. (c) The class does not pronounce a word simultaneously, as one or more pupils produce an "echo effect." The following are ways in which the teacher can help prevent these undesirable practices.

To prevent too loud responses the teacher can tell the pupils that they sound better if they say the words in a soft, pleasant voice. Or he can ask a few pupils to put on a brief role-playing skit, demonstrating too loud and normal saying of words in unison.

To prevent overemphasis on one or more syllables and "over-pronunciation" in general, the teacher can tell the boys and girls why it is undesirable or he can ask the class why. (One reason why the practice is undesirable is that pupils may then later be inclined to mispronounce the words. Another is that pupils may later depend on the clue for spelling furnished by "over-pronunciation.")

To help the class say the words without an "echo," the teacher can point at the words as he says them, tell the pupils how it sounds when not everyone says the words together, have the pupils discuss the matter, or have several pupils put on a skit showing the undesirability of an "echo." If any pupil persists in "echoing," the teacher may give him individual practice outside of class or temporarily ask him to refrain from joining the others in saying the words in unison.

Clarification of Meaning. After the pupils know the pronunciation of the words on a list, attention should be paid, if necessary, to the meaning. An aim of compilers of spelling lists for various grades is to include words boys and girls are likely to be using in writing. Consequently, if the words are well graded, there should not be many words about which there is a question about meaning. Since the pupil's meaning vocabulary exceeds his spelling vocabulary, the emphasis in spelling lists is rightfully placed on words of which they know the meaning, not on those of which they do not know it. Still, since published grade lists are planned for the entire country, there may be on any list some words the meaning of which an individual or even an entire class does not know.

The question of multiple meanings of a word might be raised in connection with this step of the process of learning to spell it. Usually at this point—when the new list of words is being presented—the teacher can be satisfied if the pupil knows one common meaning of a word. Emphasis on multiple meanings can be placed later on during the multiple-day sequence when through extended activities the child is helped to learn more about word meanings and other matters related to spelling.

The following steps may be followed when helping boys and girls acquire the meaning of words in a spelling list being presented if· some of them are not in the understanding and speaking vocabulary of one or more of the pupils.

1. The teacher may ask the boys and girls to name any words on the list of which they do not know the meaning.
2. The teacher can help the pupils who do not know the meaning of a word by: (a) explaining a common

meaning; (b) asking someone who knows the meaning to explain it; (c) using a sentence or having a pupil use one in which the meaning of the words is "built-in" and, thereupon, (d) asking a pupil who did not know the meaning whether he can tell from the sentence what the word means. In some instances a pupil may demonstrate the word (pantomime it) or draw a diagram to illustrate it.

3. A pupil who had not known the meaning of a word can, after suitable help, be asked to use it in a sentence that shows whether he has learned the meaning.

4. If no one asks for the meaning of a word that the teacher thinks some pupils may not know, the teacher can ask a child to use the word in a sentence that indicates its meaning or to explain it. If the child cannot do so, the teacher or another pupil may explain the word, use it in a sentence, demonstrate it, or illustrate it. Subsequently the child who had not been able to show that he knew the word can then explain it or use it in a meaningful sentence.

A few further points to consider when helping boys and girls with the meaning of words in a spelling list are given below.

1. If a homonym is included in a list and there is reason to think that the meaning of the other spelling of the homonym may be known by a pupil, it may be wise to have a child explain the meaning of the word and use it in a sentence. In some instances it may also be desirable to write the homonyms on the chalkboard and then use them in sentences.

2. It is often a waste of time to have the pupils use all the words on a spelling list in oral sentences, because it is likely that everybody knows the meaning of many of the words without such practice.

3. Helpful practice on the meaning of words can be given through the context which many spelling books provide for use when a list of words is presented. The context is often in the form of a story that contains all the words on the spelling list. Some teachers have pupils read the whole story silently in the hope that the use of the words will be made clearer. (The teacher should be cautioned not to have someone read the story orally while the rest read it silently because such practice discourages effective oral reading and encourages slower habits of silent reading for the pupils who can read more rapidly silently than orally.)

Getting a Clear Image of the Word. Even while the child pronounces and/or hears each word pronounced and while he learns the meaning of a word, he should be encouraged to note the spelling of the word. Furthermore, after he has concentrated on the pronunciation and if necessary on the meaning of the word, he should try to form a clear mental image of the word as he looks

at it with the intent of learning the spelling. With some longer words children may profit if the word is written on the chalkboard twice, once without division into syllables and once with it.

At this step some of the distinguishing or irregular features of the spelling of a word can be pointed out. Questions such as these can be asked as the pupils look at a word: (1) What double letter is found in this word? (2) How is the long-*a* sound spelled in this word? In the case of a word that is spelled as it sounds, the teacher may wish to make a comment similar to this: "I believe that you will not have trouble with this word because it is spelled the way we would expect it to be spelled."

Recalling the Word. In this fourth step the learner, without looking at the word, thinks of its spelling. Some teachers ask the pupils to close their eyes to try to "see" the word. Others merely tell them to "say" the letters silently to themselves without looking at the word and without vocalization. The pupils are encouraged to check their recall by again looking at the word.

Writing the Word.. The pupils are then ready to write the word. This writing is frequently done on scratch paper or in the case of a few pupils on the chalkboard.

Checking the Writing. After the pupil has·written the word, he checks it. He can do so by looking at the word, hearing the teacher spell it by syllables, or using both of these methods. As he checks it, if he has made an error he takes special note of his mistake. It may be helpful in the case of an error to draw a circle around the part misspelled or to rewrite the word correctly, drawing a line under the part in which an error was made.

Repeating Steps if Necessary. The last four steps, as listed here, should be repeated until the child has written the word correctly.

Learning Independently to Spell a Word

Any spelling program in which the teacher does not help the boys and girls to form good habits when studying a word without teacher guidance is falling short of accomplishing an important objective that should be attained in guiding growth in spelling. The steps to be recommended for individual study should be similar to those used for group work, though not necessarily identical. The following should prove useful.

1. Look at the word.
2. Say the word softly to yourself.
3. Think of the spelling of the word as you look at it.
4. Without looking at the word "see" it in your mind.
5. Compare your "picture" of the word with the copy.
6. Write the word.
7. Check your writing of the word.
8. Repeat the steps if necessary.

To facilitate memory of the steps they could be abbreviated on a chart in a manner such as this:

1. Look.
2. Say.
3. Think.
4. "See."
5. Compare.
6. Write.
7. Check.
8. Repeat, if necessary.

The children should understand that the steps in learning to spell a word are given to help them. They may be told that many pupils who have followed these or similar steps have improved their spelling. They should also be told that if after a while they can learn to spell well without going through each of these steps, they should omit those that they do not need.

METHODS

The suggestions for methods of procedure given in the preceding pages of this chapter are for the most part somewhat general in nature. In this part specific suggestions are listed. They are discussed under this grouping: (1) studying the meaning of words, (2) formulating generalizations, (3) using phonics as an aid to spelling, (4) studying word forms , (5) spelling games, (6) use of audiovisual aids, (7) other activities, and (8) questionable procedures.

Studying the Meaning of Words

The following suggestions are given to supplement those stated earlier (see page 202) on helping boys and girls acquire the meaning or meanings of words. The pupils can do the following:

1. Write the correct homonym as the teacher reads sentences such as this one:

    Did you *hear* him?

2. Select the correct homonym in a set or sets of homonyms given in parentheses in a sentence and then write the correct one(s) in space provided for that purpose.

    (Their, There) is no reason to think that they will be (hear, here) soon._____,_____

3. Make a list of homonyms and use each in a sentence, orally or in writing, to illustrate the meaning of each word.

4. Match spelling words in one column with the meaning given in a second column. (This suggestion is similar to that given for homonyms in item 7.)

5. Find in a dictionary the meaning that best fits the use of an underlined word in a given sentence.

6. Proofread some material, possibly written by the children, in which there are errors in spelling homonyms or other words they have studied.

What's Wrong Here?

Have you scene hour knew aquarium? I hope you will come too our room this afternoon two sea it. Sum of the boys and girls helped plan it. Miss Hill said that they have put the write plants into it. Did you no that won has to be very careful in choosing the food for an aquarium?

Figure 8.4. An Exercise in Detecting Wrong Homonyms.

7. Match homonyms given in one column with words or groups of words explaining them in a second column, as, for example:

sea	also
two	at this place
too	more than one
here	water
hear	look
see	understand through listening.

8. Read a series of sentences containing various meanings of words of which the boys and girls are studying the spelling and then explain the meaning of the spelling word in each of them.

9. Solve a crossword puzzle in which all the words to be filled in are spelling words.

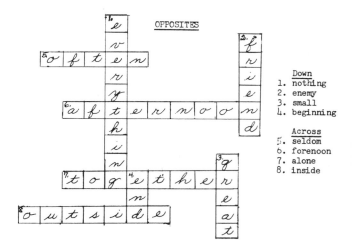

Figure 8.5. A Crossword Puzzle as a Spelling Device.

10. Make a crossword puzzle for others in the class to solve in which all the words to be filled in are spelling words.

11. Study the different uses of a word with multiple meanings as listed in a dictionary, and then use sentences illustrating the meanings within the pupils' comprehension.

12. Give synonyms for words in a list.

13. Substitute synonyms in context for overused words.

Formulating Generalizations

There seems to be general agreement that learning generalizations, when certain guidelines are observed in the process, can be of real value to many boys and girls. (See page 33.) Through knowledge of a few generalizations they do not need to think of every word they learn to spell that can be covered by a generalization, without relationship to others they may have previously learned to spell. It should be noted, however, that pupils with low mental ability may be hindered, rather than helped, as they try to formulate or make application of generalizations. These points should be considered:

1. Only those generalizations should be taught of which the pupils can make fairly wide application to words they need to spell.

2. Only those generalizations should be taught to which there are not many exceptions, especially not among words that the pupils need to spell.

3. Only those generalizations should be taught that are simple enough for the learner to comprehend and remember without undue difficulty.

4. Boys and girls should be helped to develop generalizations rather than to be asked to memorize a set of rules.

5. After formulating a generalization, boys and girls should be given adequate opportunity to apply it.

Generalizations to Be Learned. Even among persons who recommend learning generalizations according to guidelines such as those listed, there is disagreement as to which ones should be taught. Here are some that are frequently considered important for boys and girls to learn in the elementary school, though not necessarily in the language in which they are stated here.

1. When adding a suffix beginning with a vowel to a word ending in a silent *e*, the *e* is usually dropped.

2. When adding a suffix other than one beginning with *i* to a word ending in *y* preceded by a consonant, the *y* is usually changed to *i*.

3. *I* comes before *e*, as a rule, when *ei* or *ie* represents the long *e* sound, excepting after *c*.

4. The final consonant of a word often needs to be doubled when adding a suffix to a word ending in a single consonant preceded by a single vowel. The rule ap-plies in the case of one-syllable words and of words with more than one syllable providing the accent is on the last syllable.

5. The letter *q* in a word is followed by the letter *u*.

6. Plurals of nouns are often formed by adding *s* to the singular.

7. Nouns ending in the *s, sh, ch, x,* or *z* sound in the singular usually form the plural by adding *es* to the singular.

8. Many nouns that end in *f* or *fe* in the singular form the plural by changing the *f* or *fe* to *v* and adding *es*.

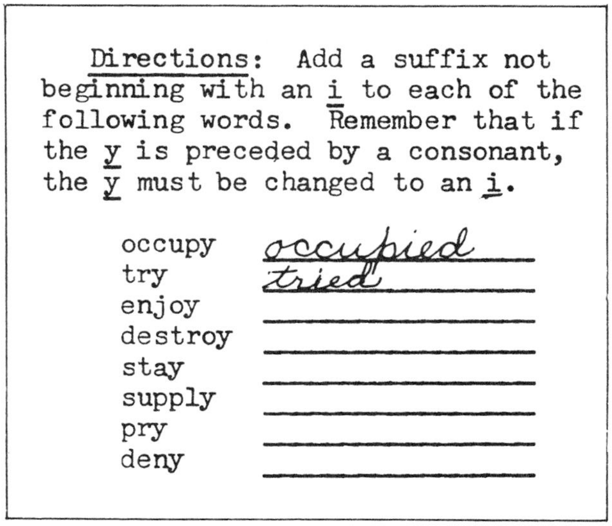

Directions: Add a suffix not beginning with an **i** to each of the following words. Remember that if the **y** is preceded by a consonant, the **y** must be changed to an **i**.

occupy — *occupied*
try — *tried*
enjoy — _____
destroy — _____
stay — _____
supply — _____
pry — _____
deny — _____

Figure 8.6. Application of a Generalization about Adding Suffixes.

9. The *k* sound is usually spelled *c* when it comes before *a, o,* or *u*. When it comes before *e* or *i,* it is usually spelled *k*. After a long vowel sound the *k* sound is usually spelled *k*.

Developing Generalizations. Undoubtedly many boys and girls develop some spelling generalizations by themselves. The teacher's role is to help them formulate more accurate generalizations than many would be likely to form without assistance. The following description illustrates how, through induction, the teacher can help the pupils make the generalization that *i* should usually be written before *e* excepting after *c* when the long sound of *e* is being represented.

The teacher can proceed by having on the chalkboard a few words in which *ei* and *ie* have the sound of the long *e,* such as *believe, piece, conceit, receive, mien.* The pupils may be asked to note that in every one of those words the *ie* and the *ei* have the long sound of *e.* Then they may be helped to observe each of the words as they note what letter precedes the *ie* or *ei.* A listing such as the following may be developed and put on the chalkboard:

Before ei	*Before ie*
c (conceit)	l (be*l*ieve)
c (receive)	p (*p*iece)
	m (*m*ien)

Next the pupils may summarize their finding that *ei* was used when preceded by *c* and that *ie* was used when preceded by a letter other than *c.* The teacher may then state that this finding holds true in other cases, when the *ei* or *ie* has the sound of the long *e.* Thereupon the pupils can note the spelling of other words in which *ie* or *ei* has the long sound of *e* and explain how the generalization applies in each case. When additonal words are studied that are governed by this generalization, the teacher may frequently wish to help the pupils note the application.

**Using Phonics as an Aid
to Spelling**

The recent emphasis on linguistics (see page 238) in the teaching of reading is also currently making a marked impact on the teaching of spelling.

For several decades there had been many teachers who were critical of much use of phonics as an aid to reading and spelling. Their criticism, elicited partly by the sterile, ineffective manner in which phonics had formerly often been taught, was, in many instances, against systematic instruction in phonics. Consequently in a large number of schools, especially in those in which many "progressive" methods were used, phonics was not taught. In these schools the main method by which boys and girls were taught to read was the look-say or sight-word method. (See page 238.)

It is now rather generally conceded that a knowledge of phonics is important in learning to spell. To be sure, some people who are good spellers have not been taught phonics in school—at least not systematically—but have acquired the fundamentals of phonics without such aid. Regardless, however, of how phonics was learned, incidentally by the pupil in or out of school or through a planned program of instruction, it is an essential to good spelling. Without any knowledge of phonics an individual would have to acquire the spelling of each word without much recourse to previous learnings. (To be sure, knowledge of structural analysis or synthesis might be of some value to a person in learning to spell.) For example, the person learning to spell the word *ball,* without any information about phonics, would not be able to expect that the word would begin with the letter *b.* It would be just as logical to him if it began with the letter *c, g, f,* or any other. Thus without phonics he would be confronted with a stupendous task when trying to learn to spell.

Although undoubtedly some persons have learned much of what is important about phonics in spelling without guidance from the school, for most boys and girls learning phonics "on their own" is a highly questionable procedure. It allows for many gaps in learning and for errors in conclusions. Furthermore, more time may be spent in many instances in arriving at generalizations without any aid than would be required if the learner were given help in learning phonics. This statement, must not, however, be taken as argument against teaching a considerable part of important phonics learnings in a functional setting, with the teacher as guide.

Frequently people have argued against teaching phonics as an aid to spelling on the basis that in the English orthography, in the case of many letters or groups of letters, there is a lack of a one-to-one relationship between the letter and its sound. Many letters have more than one sound. For example, the letter *c* has the sound as in *cat* and the sound as in *cent.* Furthermore, many sounds are represented in writing by more than one letter or group of letters. As illustration, the sound of the letter *k* as used in the word *king* can be represented not only by the letter *k* but also by *c, ck, que* (as in unique). Or it can be silent as in the word *knight.* However, in spite of many inconsistencies existing in the English orthography, there is probably not a single word in the language that does not contain at least one phonic element used according to one of the fundamental "rules" of phonics.

In a sense, the role of phonics in reading and in spelling is different. In reading, the person sees the letter or group of letters and from it he needs to determine the sound (providing he approaches the recognition of the word through the use of phonics). In spelling, the order is reversed. He knows the sound but must determine what letter or letters are used in a given word to indicate that sound. It is partly for this reason, to avoid confusing the learner, that it is recommended that systematic work in spelling be delayed until he has had some experience in reading. Many teachers would suggest, therefore, that spelling be taught only incidentally during the first year of the elementary school. Examples of incidental learning—incidental as far as the pupil is concerned—are: (a) The teacher draws attention to the fact that a new word that the class is learning to read, let us say the word *man,* begins with the same sound and letter as a word they can already read, such as *mother.* (2) As the pupils dictate to the teacher the content for an experience chart, before he writes a given word he asks the pupils with what letter they think he should begin the word. (This question should not be asked frequently and, as a rule, only if previously attention has been directed to the letter with which a given word begins.)

If phonics is to be of maximum value in the learning-to-spell process, care must be taken that the elements of phonics to be taught are chosen with discrimination. The selection should take place in terms of the importance of the element insofar as the use the learner can make of it and the difficulty of learning it. Only a limited number of generalizations of value in learning to spell should be developed. Reference to important ones is made earlier in this chapter, along with suggestions as to how to proceed in developing them. (See page 205.)

For further discussion of phonics the reader is referred to the topic "Use of Phonetic Analysis" (see page 241) as it applies to reading, since some of the suggestions given for phonics as an aid to word recognition provide understanding for using phonics in learning to spell.

Studying Word Forms

Suggestions for helping boys and girls study word forms, in addition to those mentioned in connection with other topics in this chapter, are listed below.

1. Have the pupils tell how many pronunciation parts there are in each word that the teacher pronounces from a list.

2. Tell the pupils that each pronunciation part is called a syllable and have them use the term *syllable* as they refer to such a part.

3. Spell the words in syllables as the pupils check their spelling.

4. Have the pupils look up the syllabication of words in a glossary or dictionary.

5. Discuss with the class why division into syllables sometimes helps in spelling a word.

6. Tell the class that words should be divided at the end of a line only between syllables and have them show on the chalkboard how given words would need to be divided.

7. Have the pupils give a list of words, as the teacher writes them on the chalkboard, beginning with the prefix *un,* for example. Then ask them to tell what the prefix does to the meaning of the rest of the word. The pupils can similarly study other common prefixes.

8. Help the boys and girls arrive at the generalizations involving word forms to which reference is previously made in this chapter. (See page 205.)

9. Have the pupils name compound words as the teacher writes them on the chalkboard and have them tell whether they are written (a) as two or more words, (b) as one hyphenated word or (c) as one unhyphenated word. The teacher can then tell the pupils how to find out from a glossary or dictionary how a compound word is written and provide them with practice in finding out how a series of such words, some of which are compound words, is to be written.

10. Introduce the boys and girls to the word *contraction* by showing them, for example, how the words *does* and *not* are combined to form *doesn't.* Then the pupils can state from what words other contractions are formed and match two columns of words, in one of which are given contractions and in the other words from which the contractions are formed. The class also can discuss when it is proper and when improper to use contractions.

11. Provide the boys and girls with practice in building words from root forms by adding prefixes and suffixes such as, for example, *interest, interests, interested, interesting, uninteresting, interestingly.*

12. Have the boys and girls underline the root words in derived forms.

13. Demonstrate to the pupils the fact that when one recognizes a root word that he knows how to spell, it is often not difficult to learn the spelling of forms derived from it.

14. Help the pupils develop the following generalization for forming possessive nouns: (a) Write the name of the owner. (b) Add an apostrophe. (c) Add an *s* if that *s* is pronounced in the possessive form.

15. Have the pupils tell which of a list of words are possessive singular and which are possessive plural.

16. Ask the pupils to use possessive nouns in writing groups of words such as these: (a) the coat belonging to the boy, (b) the coats belonging to the boys, (c) the coats belonging to the lady, (d) the coats belonging to the ladies, (e) the coat belonging to the man, (f) the coats belonging to the men.

Spelling Games

In chapter 3, "Common Problems in Teaching the Language Arts," some guidelines for use of games in the language arts program are given. (See page 35.) The suggestions that are enumerated there should be kept in mind when considering the following and other possible games.

1. "Oral dominoes" can be played in a variety of ways by having the first child spell any word he wishes to spell or one from a given spelling list. The next pupil is to spell a word *beginning with the same letter that ends the word chosen by the first child.* For example, if the first child spells *run,* the second could spell *no.* It would then be the responsibility of the third pupil to spell a word beginning with the letter *o.* In this manner the game would continue.

2. A variation of the Bingo game described on page 199 is one in which new and review words for a week could be tested, with the list possibly including some review words. The child can make a bingo layout by folding a square sheet of paper so that the result is five squares by five squares. Near the left-hand side of each square each pupil writes the first letter of each of the

words to be included in the bingo game. Care should be taken by the pupil that he not write the letters in the order in which the words for which they stand appear in the list. As the teacher dictates the spelling words—also not in the order in which they were originally listed—each pupil writes the words in the appropriate space. The first child who has written five words in a row, vertically or horizontally, calls "Bingo." Not until his paper has been checked for spelling, however, is he proclaimed the winner.

3. Boys and girls can be supplied with pieces of stiff paper—maybe one-half inch by one-half inch—similar to the squares used in playing anagrams. On each square should be written or typed a letter of the alphabet, with probably as many occurrences of the letters in the alphabet as are given in the commercial anagram sets. With these alphabet squares two or more pupils can play anagrams in much the same way as the game is ordinarily played. However, a check on the spelling of the words should be provided after the pupils have used them, probably with the check made by the teacher.

4. Scrambled letters of a word can serve as basis for a game in which the pupils write the word with correct sequence of letters. A time limit might be given for this game, and the pupil having correctly spelled the largest number of words can then be proclaimed winner.

5. Spelling words formed from root words by the addition of prefixes and/or suffixes can be made into a game. The teacher can write on the chalkboard a list of words to each of which a prefix or suffix can be added, such as *walk, ride, slow, possible, turn.* The child who in a stated length of time has formed the largest number of words by the addition of affixes can be proclaimed winner providing each word is spelled correctly.

6. A spelling game can be played as the teacher gives directions or asks questions such as these while the pupils look at the new and review words for the week: (a) Spell a word with a prefix that has the root *important.* (b) The /f/ sound is represented in different ways in this spelling list. Find a word in which the /f/ sound is not represented by the letter *f.* (c) What word rhymes with the word *walk*?

7. For practice on homonyms a list of homonyms, in the pupils' vocabulary, is written on the chalkboard. As the teacher points at a word such as *right, grown, pear, to,* the pupil spells the homonym for the word and uses it in a sentence. Similarly a game could be made through practice on spelling synonyms.

Use of Audiovisual Aids

In many of the preceding suggestions for teaching spelling, reference has been made to the use of visual aids to learning. A few additional ones are suggested below and mention is made of the role that audio aids can play.

1. A large variety of charts can be of value in learning to spell. For example, a chart may list the generalizations that have been developed by the class to aid them in spelling. One or more illustrations, in the form of words governed by the rule, could be written below each generalization.

The trunk and branches, made of brown construction paper, to represent a pear tree might be pasted to a large sheet of tagboard. As boys and girls learn to spell a set of homonyms, the words of that pair could be written on a leaf made of green construction paper, which can then be attached to a branch of the tree. To emphasize the reason for having the tree be indicative of a pear tree, the words *pear, pair, pare* might be included among the homonyms. In fact, the leaf on which these words are recorded could be given a prominent place on the tree.

2. Seasonal displays emphasizing the spelling of words frequently used by boys and girls when writing about Christmas, Easter, Thanksgiving, and Halloween can be made. For example, a simple stand-up of a pumpkin might be constructed, with cards bearing such words as *ghost, Halloween, fun, party.*

3. Words for emphasis in spelling—possibly the word list for a week—can be presented to the class on a transparency. Probably the chief value of a transparency used for this purpose (over words written on the chalkboard) is to add variety and, therefore, interest to the spelling procedures. If a given transparency is used several times—either in the same school year or in subsequent years—the teacher can save time. Furthermore, if the teacher desires to write the words on the transparency as the pupils watch him, he can face the class, rather than have his back to the boys and girls as he would be doing were he writing the words on the chalkboard.

4. Tapes or cassettes can be used with profit either for class or individual instruction. Not only the words to be learned but also directions and suggestions the teacher thinks appropriate can be recorded on tapes or cassettes. The advantage in using such recordings with the whole class may be that they not only add variety to class procedure but also save the teacher from the necessity of teaching, without talking at the time, some phases of the spelling program. The importance of such respite is appreciated by the teacher who realizes how a preplanned and prespoken lesson of this type may add to his poise during periods of less up-to-the-minute participation by him. Cassettes can be used effectively by one or several pupils, especially if earphones and/or learning carrels are available.

Other Activities

The following additional suggestions for activities may prove useful in teaching spelling.

1. The pupils write words that rhyme with given words.

2. The pupils tell which pairs of words named by the teacher rhyme.

3. The boys and girls check which pairs of words given in written form rhyme, such as:

bat, rat; seat, feet; feel, fed;
made, bad; by, lie.

4. The boys and girls draw a line under each of a given series of words that have the same vowel sound found in a word for which an illustration is given. For example, a picture of a ball can be drawn and the words *bat, cat, baby, barn,* and *play* can be written near it. A variation of this is to have a word given in which the letter or letters spelling that sound are underlined and a list of words given in which the pupils are to underline the letters spelling the same sound. For example, one item in such an exercise may be:

*c*ake: made, neighbor, receive, make, sat.

5. The teacher dictates sentences to the boys and girls. At times he may wish to give the pupils a chance to study the sentences before they write them. When dictating a series of sentences, this procedure may be used:

a. Give the number of the sentence.
b. Read the sentence as a whole.
c. Read the sentence in parts as the pupils write the parts.
d. Reread the sentence.

It is probably desirable to mark the entire sentence wrong if any error in spelling, capitalization, or punctuation occurs.

6. The pupils proofread their written work. At times it may be advisable for the teacher to work with each child as he does so.

7. The pupils make a picture dictionary, as an individual or class project, in which words of which the spelling may be needed are written and illustrated.

8. The pupils make files of cards with words that may be needed for spelling. These cards, possibly illustrated, could also contain meaningful sentences in which the words are used.

Figure 8.7. A File for Spelling Words.

9. The pupils make a list of words that have various spelling patterns such as: *eat, meat, seat, beat, heat, neat* (and, with older boys and girls, *wheat, feat, treat* can be included).

10. The pupils make a list of words which illustrate the generalizations about spelling they have helped formulate.

11. The boys and girls list words containing different spellings of the same sounds such as *meet, meat* and *receive, believe.*

12. The pupils underline in a list of words the phonograms common to some of the words in the list, as indicated in figure 8.8.

Draw a line under the letter
or letters that represent the <u>k</u>
sound in these words.

1. wreck   5. cent

2. knit   6. come

3. cat   7. kit

4. lock   8. book

Figure 8.8. An Exercise for Recognizing Phonograms.

13. The pupils match words in two columns so that they form a compound word, as in this example:

grand   ball
base   father
tea   spoon

14. The pupils use the dictionary to find the spelling of words: (a) when one of two spellings of a word (one correct, the other incorrect) is suggested; (b) when a blank is left for a letter or letters in a word, such as *bel......f;* (c) when a word is pronounced by the teacher. For further suggestions for helping pupils develop power in using the dictionary, the reader is referred to chapter 9. (See page 205.)

Questionable Procedures

Two questions that puzzle some teachers are briefly discussed here. They are: (1) Is tracing words good practice? (2) Should homework be assigned in spelling?

Tracing Words. The tracing method as commonly used by teachers for spelling purposes is an adaptation of the Fernald kinesthetic method, which is frequently employed with retarded readers.[2] When used as a spell-

---

2. Grace M. Fernald, *Remedial Techniques in Basic School Subjects.* McGraw-Hill Book Company, 1943.

ing method, the pupil is encouraged to trace with a finger or pencil (or with chalk if the chalkboard is used) a large copy of the word he is trying to learn to spell. After the teacher has pronounced a word, the child pronounces it in parts while he traces the copy of the word supplied to him. When he has traced it, he pronounces the entire word. The pupil repeats this process as long as he thinks he needs the practice before he can write the word from memory. After he has tested himself, if he has not spelled the word correctly, he repeats the procedure until he masters it.

It is highly questionable whether this time-consuming method of learning to spell is to be recommended for most children. It might, however, be tried with boys and girls who are retarded in spelling. It might also be occasionally used with the average or above-average spellers for words that are particularly difficult for them.

Homework in Spelling. If the school provides about an hour and fifteen minutes a week for spelling instruction in addition to time spent on incidental teaching of spelling and if the school makes good use of that time, it would seem that it should be unnecessary, as a rule, for children to take home a spelling assignment. Dawdling habits of work may be developed through such practice. However, the child who has been absent from school for a while may occasionally profit from homework.

TESTING AND REVIEW

One of the features of well-planned test-study and study-test procedures is the emphasis put on test and on reviews.

Provisions for Testing

The following provisions can be made for testing:

1. The pretest given before the boys and girls have studied words in a spelling list

2. The trial test, sometimes given after the pupils have studied the words that they have missed on a pretest and, in many cases, after they have engaged in other activities involving the use of spelling words. This test is frequently given on the third day of a five-day procedure. (It should be noted that sometimes the pretest is also referred to as the trial test.)

3. The final test, given on the last day of the five-day period (or the fourth day if the fifth day is used for review or restudy). Often this test contains not only the words for the week but also review words from earlier weeks.

4. The test on words missed the preceding week. This test can be given individually to each child.

5. A test on words of a few weeks before, possibly three, four, five, or six weeks before. Sometimes one such test on words of a given list is followed by another weeks later.

6. The semester test or the year test on new words or review words studied during the course of the semester or year. A presemester test can also be given in order to find out what procedure for teaching may be the better with a given group or individuals, the test-study or the study-test plan. The presemester test also serves as a means of measuring progress during the semester. For similar reasons a test at the beginning of the year on words to be studied during the course of the year may also be given.

7. The standardized spelling test or the test based on a standardized spelling scale. Some teachers use standardized tests or scales to ascertain a pupil's level in spelling. Others may prefer those that they themselves make from words in the spelling lists. If spelling scales or standardized tests are used, it may be advisable to check the words for frequency of use as established by research unless evidence on the validity of a test or scale for a desired purpose is given, making further checking by the teacher unnecessary. (Some commercial tests and scales are listed in chapter 13; see page 346.)

Suggestions for Testing

A few additional suggestions for testing in spelling are listed here.

1. *In planning a presemester, a semester, a beginning-of-the-year, or an end-of-the-year test, there should be a representative sampling of the words for the semester or school year.* If a test is to serve as an adequate end-test or as an index of the level of the child's ability in spelling, the more difficult or easier words must not be weighted in number. One way in which to avoid such a shortcoming is to select, in terms of placement on lists, the words to be included in the test. For example, after the teacher has decided how many words he wants in a test and knows how many words will be studied during the semester or year, he can divide the number of words to be studied by the number of words he plans for the test. If the answer were about six, he could then decide that he would include every sixth word in the list until he has the desired number for the test.

2. *Pupils should not be given opportunity to study the spelling words immediately before a final test or a review test.* If the boys and girls study the words shortly before they are tested, the test will indicate immediate, not long-term, recall.

3. *In dictating a list of words a procedure such as the following can be used.*

    a. Give the number of the word (so that the pupil will not be likely to omit a word or otherwise become confused in his own numbering).

    b. Pronounce the word distinctly (without "over-pronouncing" it).

c. Use the word in a sentence (so that the pupil can be certain that he heard the word correctly, not with the thought that he writes the entire sentence).

d. Repeat the word.

If this procedure is followed, it is probably advisable to tell the pupils that if the teacher is giving the test too fast for them, they should raise their hands as soon as they have difficulty keeping up. In that case it would be unnecessary after the list has been dictated to repeat all words or to answer questions asked by the pupils as to what various words on the list are.

4. *While most of the words in a test could be written by the pupils in column form, it is at times advisable to have one or more sentences dictated so that the children will write the entire sentence(s).* Each sentence should contain one or more words from the list being studied or from review words. It should contain no words the pupils are not expected to know how to spell unless the teacher has written the unknown words on the chalkboard, from which the boys and girls can copy them.

5. *Words that are not written legibly should be counted wrong.* There should be no question as to each letter of a word if it is to be counted right. However, lack of excellence of the form of a letter should not be reason for counting the word wrong if it is plain what letter is intended.

Figure 8.9.

6. *While no authoritative answer can be given to the question as to whether a word should be counted wrong if it has been crossed out or erased in case the final spelling is correct, there is good argument for counting wrong all words in a spelling test that were not written correctly the first time.* A supporting claim is that if a pupil does not know the spelling of a word well enough so that he can immediately write it correctly, he perhaps has not mastered the word.

7. Some teachers check the spelling of boys and girls by having them supply missing letters—frequently those that are assumed to be the letters within a word most likely to be missed such as the *ie* in the word *believe.* It must be kept in mind that unless the teacher pronounces the word in which one or more letters are omitted in writing, the pupil may at times be unable to recognize what word is wanted. Then, it could be argued, if the teacher names the word anyhow, why not have the pupil

engage in practice by writing the entire word, not merely supplying the missing letters? The question is justified.

Another means of evaluation is to omit one or more letters in a word which the pupil is to supply when with the incomplete word is given a word or group of words that will help identify the word to be completed. The following is an example of such a listing:

the____r: belonging to them
bab____s: more than one baby.

Yet another means, though a questionable one, is that of having pupils detect which words in a list, in a sentence, or in one or more paragraphs are written incorrectly. The danger is that the wrong rather than the right form may be impressed upon the learner's mind.

8. To help in the evaluation of the success of a spelling program questions such as these about the children's spelling and spelling habits can be asked: (a) Are the boys and girls really interested in becoming good spellers? (b) Are they interested in finding their spelling mistakes in the writing they do throughout the school day and at other times? (c) Are they learning means of finding the correct spelling of words with which they need help? (This last question can be asked with profit only after the pupils have learned how to use word lists for that purpose or to look words up in a dictionary even if they do not know the spelling beforehand.)

9. *There is convincing argument that can be advanced for having each pupil correct his own test paper.* Through checking his own paper the pupil is provided with the opportunity to scrutinize carefully his own spelling of a word, an opportunity he does not have, to the same extent, if either the teacher or a classmate checks his paper. If the pupil corrects his own paper, immediately after writing the words—a customary practice—the child has the added advantage of knowing right off what his errors are. This advantage he would not have if the papers were handed to the teacher for future checking.

An argument proposed against the practice of having each pupil correct his own work is that the child may cheat or may have the wrong image of a word so firmly established in his mind that it is difficult for him to recognize his error. As far as cheating is concerned, the teacher should try to educate the boys and girls so that they realize the wrongness of that practice as well as its futility. Furthermore, the teacher should be alert enough to know when there is cheating. To avoid in part the temptation to cheat, the teacher may ask the pupils to correct the papers with a different medium than the one in which they wrote them. If a pencil was used in writing the words, a crayon or a pen may be used when correcting.

Correcting of papers by the pupils should be thought

of primarily in terms of the help to the pupils, not chiefly as saving the teacher's time by his not checking the papers. In fact, as a rule, it may be advisable for the teacher himself to recheck at least the final test. If he follows this suggestion, he is in a position to note carefully the errors and types of errors made by the class in general as well as by each individual. Moreover, the teacher can then ascertain whether or not a pupil has difficulty in checking his own paper. If a pupil has a problem with correcting his papers, the teacher may wish to give him individual practice in checking the spelling of words.

As the boys and girls correct their spelling papers, it is recommended that the teacher spell the words by syllables. After all the words in a list have been spelled orally by the teacher, the pupils may profitably be given the opportunity to refer to a list to note any words that they may wish to recheck.

10. *Graphing the results of a final test is helpful practice.* A pupil can keep a simple graph showing his attainment on each final test. It is best not to have the graphs open to inspection by others. Competition should be with one's own record, not with those of others. Furthermore, if the results on a test are posted, the pupils with lower marks who had worked hard may become discouraged and those who easily get a perfect score may be kept from being humble about their achievement.

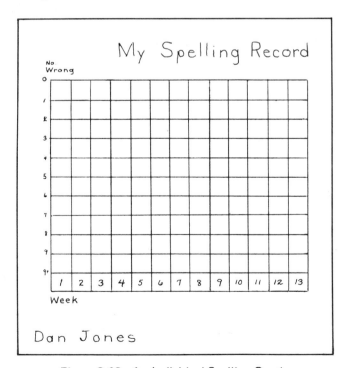

Figure 8.10. An Individual Spelling Graph.

11. *If marks for spelling are recorded on a report card, more than spelling achievement on the words in spelling lists should be taken into consideration.* A pupil who has a perfect score on every final and review test during a marking period should not be given an excellent rating on his report card if he spells poorly on papers written during the school day other than the spelling period. The proposed marking policy, however, needs to be carefully explained to the boys and girls (and in some cases to the parents) if it is contrary to earlier practice with a given class.

Provisions for Review

Ample opportunity should be provided for review. Follow-up on the trial test by study of words missed is not enough. Other opportunities for systematic well-spaced review are indicated here.

1. *Review in the form of restudy of "new words" missed on a final test.* Boys and girls should be asked to keep a list of words that they miss on final tests and then restudy those of the preceding list one or more days after work on a new list has begun. They can then be individually tested on the words they missed.

2. *Review after the final test of some words previously included in spelling tests.* Some teachers habitually include the list of words studied in an earlier week in the spelling activities for the week. For example, a teacher may decide that every fifth day of a five-day plan, he will test the boys and girls not only on the words currently being studied but also on those they concentrated upon four weeks before. It is important when such provisions for testing of review words is made that there is also time provided for the boys and girls to restudy the review words that they missed.

3. *Review of words included in end-of-the-semester or end-of-the-year tests.* Because of the time element review of words missed on a test given at the end of the year is at times not possible. However, it is probably desirable to try to schedule end-tests in the elementary school so that they are not given after all regular classes are over, in order that the pupils will have an opportunity to do necessary review indicated by the testing. It would be advisable to have the end-of-the-year test given a week or more before the close of the school year so that time for review can be provided.

4. *Review of lists of words commonly misspelled.* Some teachers may wish to provide their pupils with copies of frequently misspelled words and make provisions for study as well as for review and testing of these words.

5. *Review of words on individual lists.* If the pupils are keeping lists of words they want to learn to spell other than those given in spelling or class lists, opportunity for systematic review and testing of these words should be provided. For purposes of such testing it may be

desirable to team each pupil with another so that they can dictate the words to one another.

WORD LISTS

One of the questions of great importance in connection with the teaching of spelling is "What words should the child learn to spell?" Those who do not believe in systematic study of spelling may answer the question simply by stating that each pupil should learn to spell the words that he needs in his writing. However, a child in the upper-primary grades and intermediate grades who expresses himself adequately in writing will often use many more words in his written communication than it seems practical for him to learn to spell. Consequently this question also may need to be answered: "What should be the criteria for determining which of the words a pupil uses in his writing should he learn to spell?"

Regardless of whether or not systematic procedures for spelling instruction are followed, these criteria for word selection are considered important: (1) frequency of use of a word in children's writing, (2) likelihood of use of word in adult writing, (3) difficulty of learning a word, and (4) similarity of spelling pattern.

The criterion of "likelihood of use of a word in adult writing" presents a problem. While many words frequently used by children in writing are also much used in adult writing, others are not. Which of the words frequently used by children in writing but not by adults should be included in spelling lists cannot be answered with finality. The problem is further complicated by the fact that by the time boys and girls are adults many of the words they will then use often in their writing may not be the ones now frequently written by adults. In general, perhaps the best procedure is to include in spelling lists those words pupils are likely to use much in their writing. However, regardless of the construction of the lists of spelling words a pupil is studying, it is important to help him acquire a method of learning to spell new words—a method that he can also use, with adaptation, in later years when learning to spell additional words needed as an adult.

Published Lists

Research studies culminating in lists of words for spelling purposes have taken into consideration (1) the words that pupils use frequently in writing, (2) the words that adults use frequently in writing, and (3) the words that are often misspelled. Some of the lists are: Ernest Horn's "A Basic Writing Vocabulary," appearing in the University of Iowa Monographs in Education, First Series, No. 4, Iowa City, Iowa; "The 222 Spelling Demons," listed in a four-page publication by that name by James A. Fitzgerald, published by Bruce Books, 866 Third Avenue, New York, 10022; and Leslie W. John-

son's "One Hundred Words Most Often Misspelled by Children in the Elementary Grades," which appeared in the *Journal of Educational Research,* October, 1950. There is also the much used list based on the writing of boys and girls which was compiled under the direction of H.D. Rinsland.[3]

Class Lists and Individual Lists

Lists of spelling words based on the needs of a given class or individuals in it are often used in schoolrooms in which no standard list of words nor a list in spelling textbooks is employed. However, such lists are also used in many rooms in which pupils study the words of a published list. In fact, a desirable use of a class or individual list is made when it complements a list based on research.

Some teachers suggest that every pupil should keep a notebook or file of the words that he wishes to use in his writing but cannot spell. Other teachers compile a class list of words that the group is likely to need in writing, including many words in the content areas. There are objections to this procedure. One is that the list is likely to become too long, especially for the poor speller who will probably find that he has difficulty in spelling a considerable proportion of the words that he uses in writing—too many for him to try to include in his spelling vocabulary. Another is that many of the words a pupil uses in writing may not be used by him often in the near future. Merely because boys and girls in their writing in connection, for example, with a unit on Alaska may be writing about kayaks is no reason why they need to add the word *kayak* to their spelling vocabulary,

Figure 8.11. A Spelling Notebook.

3. Henry D. Rinsland, *A Basic Writing Vocabulary of Elementary School Children.* The Macmillan Company, 1945.

especially when they may not know how to spell commonly used words such as *their* or *walk.* Maybe all that is needed is to have *kayak,* together with other words used in connection with the study of Alaska, written on a chart headed "New Words" from which boys and girls can copy the word *kayak* when they use it in writing.

Provisions should be made for the study and testing of words on class and individual lists. Words on the former can be added to the regular spelling list for study, testing, and review. For the words on the individual lists, time should be set aside for study. However, since the number of words as well as the words themselves will differ with individuals, it may be desirable that the pupils study them whenever on their daily or weekly schedule they have time to do so, whether during spelling class or at other times. Pupils should be assisted from time to time in determining which words and how many they may find advisable to place on their individual lists for study. A plan might be worked out, as suggested earlier whereby the pupils are paired for work on these lists and maybe once a week or so each pair of pupils meet to dictate the spelling words to one another. Tape recordings of individual or class lists can be used effectively by one or more pupils at a time. It is desirable not only to keep the list of words for class or individual study in notebooks (or on cards) but also to write the tests in notebooks so that a record of the type and frequency of error for each pupil is available for diagnostic purposes.

AN ILLUSTRATIVE TEACHING PLAN

The following plan for teaching spelling in a third-grade class is an adaptation of a weekly plan written by a former college student, Jackie Ford Webster. It is intended for use with a consumable spelling book in which the five-day plan is followed, as described earlier in this chapter. (See page 200.) Naturally many deviations from this plan will be necessary to make it fit the spelling series used if it is not the series on which the plan was based. Changes also will be necessary in terms of the class being taught.

A. *Materials:*

In addition to a copy of the consumable spelling book for each child the following materials will be used.

1. Monday
   a. The list of words (numbered) for the week, written on the chalkboard
   b. A list of words (written on a card for the teacher's use) that may cause difficulties in pronunciation or meaning
   c. A list of words in the story (other than the spelling words) that may cause problems of word recognition (listed on the chalkboard)

2. Tuesday
   Words for special study, written on the chalkboard

3. Wednesday
   Sentences containing words for the week, for use by the teacher when giving the test

4. Thursday
   a. Words missed frequently, written on the chalkboard
   b. Other words needing special attention, written on the chalkboard

5. Friday
   Sentences containing words for the week, for use by the teacher when giving the test

B. *Outline of Procedure:*

1. Monday
   a. The teacher hands back Friday's spelling papers and gives instructions for study of misspelled words.
   b. The pupils look at the picture in the spelling book and talk about it as they get a background for some of the words.
   c. The pupils look at the list of spelling words to see if there are any they cannot pronounce.
   d. If there are questions about pronunciation, the teacher helps the pupils by means of one or more of the following methods: (1) sight, (2) phonetic, and (3) structural analysis (syllabication or root words).
   e. If no one asks for the pronunciation of words that the teacher thinks may be difficult for some, he asks the pupils to pronounce those words. (See *A-1-b.*) If they cannot pronounce them, the teacher helps the pupils by means of one or more of the following methods: (1) sight, (2) phonetics, and (3) structural analysis (syllabication or root words).
   f. The pupils practice the pronunciation.
      (1) The teacher indicates the purpose for reading the story.
      (2) The class says the words after the teacher.
   g. The pupils study the story.
      (1) the teacher indicates the purpose for reading the story.
      (2) The teacher helps the pupils with the pronunciation of any difficult words (See *A-1-c.*)
      (3) The pupils read the story silently.
      (4) The pupils answer questions about the story as the teacher checks comprehension.

h. If there are some words of which one or more pupils do not know the meaning, a pupil or the teacher explains and/or uses each one in a sentence.

i. If no one asks for some of the words that the teacher thinks may cause difficulty, the teacher asks for the meaning. (See *A-1-b.*)

j. The teacher points out special spelling difficulties in some of the words.

k. The pupils begin independent study of the spelling words, using this procedure:
  (1) They look at the word.
  (2) They write the word.
  (3) They check their spelling.
  (4) If wrong, they repeat the first three steps.

2. Tuesday
  a. The pupils note the words which may present special spelling problems.
  b. The teacher helps the class with the directions for one or more exercises in the spelling book and makes provisions for those finishing earlier if the work is to be written.
  c. The pupils do the exercise(s) in the spelling book (for the second day).
  d. The pupils study the words, using this procedure:
    (1) They look at the word.
    (2) They write the word.
    (3) They check their spelling.
    (4) If wrong, they repeat the first three steps.

3. Wednesday
  a. The pupils study the words independently.
  b. The pupils take the trial test, as the teacher follows this procedure:
    (1) He gives the number of the word.
    (2) He pronounces the word.
    (3) He uses the word in a sentence.
    (4) He repeats the word.
  c. The pupils check their papers as the teacher or a pupil reads the words orally and spells them. (If further check is necessary the pupils correct their words from a list on the chalkboard or in their books.)
  d. The pupils write the correct spelling of words they missed on the trial test.
  e. The pupils continue studying the words that they missed on the trial test and on tests of previous weeks, while those who did not miss any words do work provided for them by the teacher.

4. Thursday
  a. The class continues oral study of words with special difficulties in spelling.

b. The teacher helps the class with directions for one or more exercises in the spelling book (for the fourth day) and makes provisions for the pupils finishing earlier if the work is written.

c. Pupils do the exercise(s) in the spelling book.

d. The class independently study the spelling words for the week as they pay special attention to words misspelled on the trial test.

5. Friday
  a. The pupils take the weekly test as the teacher follows this procedure:
    (1) He gives the number of the word.
    (2) He pronounces the word.
    (3) He uses the word in a sentence.
    (4) He repeats the word.
  b. The pupils correct their papers as the teacher or a pupil reads the words orally and spells them. (If further check is necessary, the pupils correct their words from a list on the chalkboard or in their books. The teacher rechecks the words later.)
  c. The pupils are checked on review words.

SPELLING IN VARIOUS CURRICULAR AREAS

Setting aside a period in the school day for spelling does not free the teacher from the responsibility of guiding the pupils' growth in spelling at other times during the school day. A few suggestions for making application of spelling to other curricular areas are given in this part of the chapter.

Spelling and Handwriting

The teacher should bear in mind that:

1. Pupils should be helped to see the importance of legible handwriting to correct spelling.

2. Errors in spelling can be caused by poor handwriting on the part of the teacher.

3. Pupils who write poorly may practice the wrong spelling of a word as they study it from their own copy.

4. Pupils who make errors in spelling because of illegibility of handwriting should be given help in the correct formation of letters.

5. Slowness in handwriting may cause some pupils to make errors in spelling when a list of words or when sentences are dictated.

6. Pupils should not be given credit for the spelling of a word if it is not written so legibly that there is no question as to each letter intended.

7. When pupils make the transition from manuscript to cursive writing, they should, in the early stages of the

transition, be allowed to write their spelling words in manuscript.

Spelling and Written Expression
(Other than Handwriting)

In all types of written expression, whether in language arts classes or in connection with work in the content areas, much opportunity for guiding growth in spelling is afforded. Here are some points in regard to the relationship of spelling to this phase of written communication.

1. The desire to learn to spell can be developed as the child wishes to express himself through written communication.

2. Errors in spelling in written communication should not be emphasized to the extent that the content of what a pupil wishes to express suffers; however, correct spelling can go along with desirable content.

3. As a pupil learns to spell better, he may grow in ability to express himself in writing and as he expresses himself better in writing he may become a better speller.

4. At times before the pupils in a class write on a given topic, the teacher may place on the chalkboard some of the words which the pupils might be unable to spell—words that many of them might want to use in their written work that day. At other times he might ask each pupil to have available a piece of paper on which the teacher can write any words that the pupil wants spelled.

5. The teacher can help a pupil proofread the first draft of what he writes and help him with the spelling of any words he has misspelled.

6. The teacher can encourage the pupil to proofread what he writes for others to read.

7. The pupils can learn to use a picture dictionary and later a regular dictionary, to find the spelling of a word.

Spelling and Oral Communication

The interrelationship between spelling and oral communication lies in part in these facts:

1. Pupils may be able to spell better when they talk about a topic before they write about it. Then the attention of the child while writing may not be needed so much on the thought that he wishes to express, with the consequence that he can then attend more to matters of spelling.

2. Slovenly enunciation can have an undesirable effect on spelling; clear enunciation can have the opposite result.

3. Incorrect pronunciation can have an undesirable effect on spelling, and correct pronunciation can have a desirable one.

4. The teacher should recognize the possible relationship between the divergent dialect a child uses and problems that may arise as the teacher dictates words or sentences in the cultivated speech of the community in which he is teaching.

5. Habits of good listening can help the pupil acquire familiarity with words that will be beneficial to him in spelling.

Spelling and Reading

In the last part of this chapter—the part dealing with "Linguistics and Spelling"—and in chapter 9 "Guiding Growth in Some Reading Skills Closely Related to the Other Language Arts" are given suggestions showing the interrelationship between reading and the other language arts, a relationship that the teacher should have clearly in mind. A few points of importance to the teacher in regard to spelling and reading are given following.

1. There seems to be a positive correlation between skill in reading and ability in spelling. However, a fairly large proportion of good readers are not good spellers. There appear to be, however, relatively few poor readers who are good spellers.

2. Phonics taught in connection with reading can reinforce that needed for spelling though the function of phonics is different in these two facets of the language arts. In reading, the reader needs to decide, from seeing the written symbols, what sounds are represented by those symbols; in spelling he needs to decide what written symbols he should use to represent the sounds he has in mind.

3. The fact that a pupil meets a given word in his reading very frequently is no proof that he will be able to spell it. The very fact that he runs across it frequently in reading might cause him to recognize the word so rapidly that he needs not pay attention to the individual characteristics of the word.

4. Many boys and girls learn to spell a large number of words without direct study of the spelling. However, boys and girls seem to vary greatly in ability to learn to spell words without specific attention to the spelling.

5. The degree to which initial reading instruction is taught chiefly by the sight word method, rather than primarily by phonic methods, may considerably influence the extent to which the learners are likely to learn to spell the words in their reading books, without special attention to the spelling.

6. The reading vocabulary of a pupil is not a safe index of what his spelling vocabulary is. A pupil should not be expected to be able to spell all the words that he learns to read.

7. As boys and girls read material on their level, their vocabulary is likely to expand, especially beyond the in-

itial stage of reading instruction. Such growth in vocabulary would seem to have a beneficial effect on spelling since people possibly have less difficulty in spelling words that they know the meaning of than the words they do not know.

Spelling and the Content Subjects

Various points regarding spelling and the content subjects are scattered among preceding pages of this chapter. Reference to the first two of the following has previously been made.

1. Spelling should be considered important in writing that the pupil does in all subject areas. If marks are given in spelling on a report card, the quality of spelling that he achieves in all of his writing should be taken into consideration.

2. A pupil should not be expected to learn to spell all the special words with which he comes in contact in his content subjects, not even all of those that he may need in his writing. Listing on a chart words the child is likely to use in written communication, without special attention to spelling, frequently suffices for filling the needs of the writer.

3. Interest in the development of language can be indicated as a pupil shows interest in noting differences and likenesses between words in various languages. For example, the spelling of words such as *labor* and *labour* can be pointed out, or the likenesses of the words *Mutter* (German), *mater* (Latin), and *mother* can be discussed.

4. In social studies classes the difference in spelling of English words in colonial times and now can be emphasized.

LINGUISTICS AND SPELLING

Although to date more thought has been given to the role of linguistics in the teaching of reading in the elementary school than in the teaching of spelling, increasingly more attention is being paid to the relationship between linguistics and the teaching of spelling. There are those in the field of linguistics and in education who believe that proper application of findings of linguists to the teaching of spelling can revolutionize instruction. They maintain that as teaching methods change radically to implement into classroom practice the findings of linguists, learning to spell can become a greatly simplified process. Others, however, look questioningly upon many of the linguistically based spelling procedures and programs that have been advocated and upon the materials that have been produced for such programs. Let us, therefore, first of all, examine some of the tenets of linguists as they have or may have bearing upon the teaching of spelling. (See also page 36.)

Claims of Linguists

Linguists, like specialists in many other areas, differ widely in their claims. In fact, the diversity of beliefs held is so great that it might be suggested that education not take them seriously until they have reached greater uniformity. However, to the writer that seems an unwarranted conclusion to reach after examining some of the differences of opinion existing among linguists. Great advances in other sciences or areas of human endeavor have, as a rule, not been made by postponing an application to life's problems until there is agreement among those who have specialized in that area. So why decide to delay action on the educational scene until that time, which will probably never come, when linguists agree on all significant issues—issues that might have important bearing on the teaching and learning of spelling? Rather, let us take note of some of the claims of linguists that may influence the spelling program in our elementary schools.

The "Regularity of the Irregularities" of the Grapheme-Phoneme Relationship. The lack of a one-to-one correspondence in the English language of the written symbols (the graphemes) and the sound symbols (the phonemes) has generally been considered the chief reason why boys and girls and adults have difficulty in spelling. This difficulty can be illustrated by the child who recognizes the *k*-sound (/k/) in a word that he wishes to write but is puzzled whether that phoneme is represented in the given word by a *c*, a *k*, a *ck*, a *qu* (as in *unique*). While linguists readily admit that the grapheme-phoneme correspondence is a complicated one, it is claimed that if one studies the irregularities in their relationship, one can note schemes or patterns into which many or all of them fall.

Recommended Procedure for Teaching Spelling. On the basis of claims such as those described in the preceding paragraph, some linguists recommend that vocabulary study proceed from study of words that are regular as to spelling (that have a close phoneme-grapheme correspondence), through those that are semiregular, to those that are irregular. Some want the progression based on phonemic families, for example, with words such as *at, bat, cat* taught together or in sequence. They point out that if teaching follows this procedure, the child can easily learn many words after he notes the general pattern observed in those spellings. Some linguists recommend that much of the grouping of words for study can advisedly be in terms of contrasts, as, for example, the child notes the effect of the final *e* (the final *e* signal) in *fate* as compared to the word with the same sequence of letters but without the silent final *e*, the word *fat*. It should be noted that the sequence in teaching according to linquists recommending these policies is in terms of the structure or spelling of the word, not in terms of criteria that have been rather commonly accepted in the past, such as frequency of the use of the word, utility of the word to the child, or groupings of words around stories or topics. An example of the latter is a "unit" in a speller in which words such as *glacier, igloo, whale* might be studied after presentation in a brief selection about Eskimo life.

Pertinent Research

A study entitled "Phoneme-Grapheme Relationships Basic to Cues for Improvement of Spelling" has been undertaken at Stanford University with Paul Hanna as director of a project sponsored by the U.S. Office of Education. Analysis is made with the use of computers of 17,000 words. As a result of extensive study Hanna reports that "even a limited knowledge of the phonological relationships between the sounds of letters of the orthography can provide the power to spell literally thousands of words." [4]

It should be pointed out that no matter how statistically reliable the analysis of any research may be, until it has been subjected to experimentation in the classroom, proof of seemingly sound theoretical consideration has not been established for practical purposes.

Implications for the Classroom Teacher

Though scientific proof of the correctness of various linguistically-based procedures for teaching spelling is lacking, the teacher cannot afford to ignore them even if he may not accept some or many of them. It is, therefore, advisable that he familiarize himself with one or more of the books dealing with linguistics and the teaching of the language arts. The following are among books the teacher may wish to consult. Others are listed in chapter 13. (See page 336.)

Anderson, Paul S. *Linguistics in the Elementary School.* New York: The Macmillan Company, 1971.

Lamb, Pose, ed. *Guiding Children's Language Learning.* Dubuque, Iowa: Wm. C. Brown Company, Publishers, 1967.

Savage, John F., ed. *Linguistics for Teachers: Selected Readings.* Chicago: Science Research Associates, 1973.

A book, although it is designed to help adults improve their spelling, can also be an aid to the person concerned with the teaching of spelling to boys and girls. It is *A Programmed Text: Spelling by Principles* by Genevieve Smith, published by Appleton-Century-Crofts, 1966. This book deals in part with principles that throw light on some of the tenets advocated by linguists.

A few points worthy of the teacher's consideration

regarding the relationship between linguistics and the teaching of spelling follow.

1. An essential task of the teacher in a linguistically oriented program of teaching spelling—and to some extent in all spelling programs—is to help the learner differentiate among the common sounds (phonemes) of the language and to learn what letter(s) or combination(s) of letters (graphemes) are commonly used to represent each of these phonemes.

2. It seems futile for today's teacher to spend much time and energy decrying the fact that we do not have a system of orthography in which there is a one-to-one correspondence between phonemes and graphemes. It is the responsibility of the teacher, in spite of this characteristic of the English language, to teach in such a manner that children become good spellers.

3. Hope seems in vain that there will be, within the teaching range of the reader of this book, an overhauling of English orthography to the extent that a spelling system, in which there is a one-to-one phoneme-grapheme correspondence will be widely accepted. Various attempts to instigate simplified spelling systems, intended for universal acceptance in English-speaking countries, have met with failure. There is little reason to expect different results in the foreseeable future. Consequently teachers need to concentrate on how to teach more effectively the system as it is. These statements should not be interpreted as meaning that spelling does not change. However, changes in speech patterns are made more rapidly than those in spelling.

It is interesting to note that if in English a spelling system were universally accepted based on a clear-cut grapheme-phoneme relationship, then spelling would still present some baffling problems. In such a transition this question would naturally need to be solved: "Which dialect should be accepted as the standard one on which a one-to-one grapheme-phoneme correspondence should be based?" With the great differences in enunciation and pronunciation of words in various regions where there are English-speaking people, that which would constitute a phonetically correct spelling of a word for people in one part would not be right for people in another region.

Mention needs to be made here of the Initial Teaching Alphabet (I.T.A.), which is based on a simplification of the sound-letter correspondence. (See page 236 of chapter 9, "Guiding Growth in Reading Skills Closely Related to the Other Language Arts.") Since advocates

---

4. Paul R. Hanna, et al., "Linguistic Cues for Spelling Improvement." Report to U.S. Office of Education on Project Number 1991 for the period of January 2, 1963, to December 31, 1964 (Mimeographed), p. 4. Used with the permission of the U.S. Office of Education.

of the Initial Teaching Alphabet propose that it be used, as the name implies, only in initial reading and writing experiences, there is considerable question related to the possibility of an undesirable effect on spelling when the transition is made from spelling with the I.T.A. orthography to the traditional, as the child changes from writing in an orthography that has a close phoneme-grapheme relationship to one in which for a very large number of words the correspondence is far from perfect. No definitive study has been made on the effect of the changeover.

4. A number of recommendations of linguists have, to some extent, long been followed by many elementary school teachers. For example, teachers have searched for rules or generalizations governing the spelling of words—generalizations that would be on the level of understanding of the pupils and to which there would be but relatively few exceptions. Which of those recommended by some linguists are desirable for teaching on the elementary school level is still an unsettled question. Another point emphasized by linguists, that of the interrelationship between oral and written speech, has been receiving considerable stress in elementary schools for several decades. However, it is fortunate that reinforcement of the needed integration or correlation comes from still another source, in addition to educational philosophy, namely from linguistics.

5. A decision needs to be made as to how the words to be studied for spelling and the sequence in the teaching should be determined. There are several possible ways, these among them: (a) The words could be selected and the sequence determined in relation to the utility in writing of the words for the users. (b) The selection could be made, as linguists recommend, on the basis of the phonemic difficulty of the words, in terms of patterns represented by the spelling. (c) There could be a combination of these two procedures named in the two preceding sentences.

A compromise in harmony with point *c* above has been suggested in the recommendation that the words decided upon by makers of reliable word lists be rearranged and then taught in the order that phonemic groupings would suggest. Even the classroom teacher with limited knowledge of linguistics could decide to teach the words in the spelling book according to some patterns that are recommended. And he could help boys and girls see the relationship between words on lists of individual children and those already studied that follow the same phonemic pattern.

A philosophy of education seems to be at stake in making the decision, as partial settlements are made of the question whether the selection should be in terms of the needs of boys and girls or in terms of the structure of the language. It should be noted that both the "functionalists" in education and the linguistically oriented educators have in mind the same end result, helping boys and girls become good spellers.

CONTENTS

Figure 8.12. Contents from the *Word Book 2* Spelling Program by Ort and Wallace. Copyright © 1976 by Rand McNally and Company; developed by Lyons and Carnahan.

CONTENTS

Figure 8.13. Contents from the *Word Book 6* Spelling Program by Lorrene Ort and Eunice E. Wallace. Copyright © 1976 by Rand McNally and Company; developed by Lyons and Carnahan.

5. There are available on the market an increasing number of spelling series that claim to be linguistically based. As the teacher studies these, he can weigh the suggestions for teaching made by the authors of the series and he can consider for adoption or adaptation any that seem educationally sound for his program for teaching spelling.

A Linguistically Oriented Spelling Series

One spelling series emphasizing some of the recommendations of linguists, that is briefly described here is entitled *Word Book,* authored by Lorrene Love Ort and Eunice E. Wallace and published by Rand McNally & Company in 1976.

Table of Contents. An examination of the reproduction of the table of contents of Book 2 and Book 6 of *Word Book* (figures 8.12 and 8.13) gives some idea from the emphasis placed on teaching together some words that have similar spelling patterns and of making application of other recommendations of linguists. It will be noted that while emphasis is placed on word patterns, the idea long followed of presenting spelling words around a topic is not dropped.

Excerpts from Spelling Units. Following are excerpts from some of the exercise material in the *Word Book* spellers, which show emphasis on word patterns.

From page 73 of *Word Book* 2

Say meat. Hear the vowel sound. In meat, /ē/ is spelled ea.

○ 1. Say meat. Find another Builder Word that has /ē/ spelled ea.

_____

_____

2. You can spell two more words like meat and seat. Look in the dictionary under h and n.

_____

_____

_____

Underline the two letters that spell /ē/ in the words you wrote.

From page 18 of *Word Book* 4

Final *e* pattern. Write the missing words and their roots.
You can follow the example.

1. A brush is for painting; a pen is for _____writing_____ . (_____write_____)
2. A boat is for sailing; a bike is for _____ . (_____)
3. Water in a lake is for
   swimming; ice on a lake is for _____ . (_____)
   When the suffix *-ing* was used with the root
words above, the final *e* of each root word was _____ .

From page 70 of *Word Book* 6

For each line, first write the root of the italicized word. Then add the suffix from the italicized word to the word in parentheses. The first one is done for you.

1. *drummer* _____drum_____ (zip) _____zipper_____

2. *splitting* _____ (wed) _____

3. *saddest* _____ (hot) _____

4. *knitter* _____ (bat) _____

5. *remittance* _____ (admit) _____

FOR STUDY AND DISCUSSION

1. Outline a spelling readiness program for a first grade.

2. Examine carefully several recent spelling series for the elementary school, studying both the pupils' books and the teachers' manuals. What likenesses and what differences do you note among the series? What points of excellence characterize them? What, if any, questionable procedures do you note?

3. Select a five-day spelling list as found in a recent spelling textbook for an elementary school grade. Write a teaching plan based on it, in which you clearly show what class procedures you might follow each of the five days to be devoted to the study of the list. (You may wish to refer to the plan on pages 214 and 215 for some suggestions.)

4. Note what elements of phonics are taught in some of the recent spelling series and pay particular attention to the methods of teaching these elements that are suggested either in the pupils' books or the teachers' manuals.

5. In the newer spelling series that you have an opportunity to examine, what evidence of the influence of linguistics do you find? Is your reaction favorable or unfavorable? Give reasons for your response.

6. When a school is choosing a spelling series for an elementary school, what are some of the criteria that should be considered?

7. Explain how you would develop with fifth-grade boys and girls the generalization "When adding a suffix beginning with a vowel to a word ending in a silent *e,* the *e* is usually dropped." Also show how you might help pupils apply this generalization.

8. What is the difference in the role of teaching phonics as it applies to the teaching of spelling and as it applies to the teaching of reading?

9. What objections do you see to the spelling bee as it it commonly conducted?

10. Examine one or more references dealing with linguistics in relation to possible bearing on the teaching of spelling. You may have an opportunity to report points of special significance to your classmates.

11. What games could be used in teaching spelling? (Suggestions are given in professional books and periodicals and in teachers' manuals accompanying spelling series.)

12. Several spelling lists are named in this chapter. Study professional literature on the teaching of spelling to find information on additional ones.

13. Give suggestions for dealing with a request by a parent that a child be given homework in spelling.

REFERENCES

Boyd, Gertrude A. *Teaching Communication Skills in the Elementary School.* New York: Van Nostrand Reinhold Company, 1970.

Burns, Paul C.; Broman, Betty L.; and Lowe Wantling, Alberta L. *The Language Arts in Childhood Education*, 2nd ed. Chicago: Rand McNally & Company, 1971.

Donoghue, Mildred R. *The Child and the English Language Arts*, 2nd ed. Dubuque, Iowa: Wm. C. Brown Company Publishers, 1975.

Lamb, Pose, ed. *Guiding Children's Language Learning*. Dubuque, Iowa: Wm. C. Brown Company Publishers, 1967.

Smith, Genevieve. *A Programed Text: Spelling by Principles*. New York: Appleton-Century-Crofts, 1966.

Smith, James A. *Adventures in Communication: Language Arts Methods*. Boston: Allyn and Bacon, Inc., 1972.

Strickland, Ruth G. *The Language Arts in the Elementary School*. Lexington, Mass.: D.C. Heath and Company, 1969.

9

Guiding Growth in Reading Skills Closely Related to the Other Language Arts

Emphasis is rightfully being placed in the elementary school on the interrelationship of all four facets of the language arts—listening, speaking, reading, and writing. Without reference to reading none of the other phases of the language arts can be taught adequately. Nor can reading be taught effectively in isolation from the others. However, the teaching of reading is so important an area of the elementary school curriculum that in one book on teaching the language arts in the elementary school, it seems impossible to give adequate treatment to the teaching of that subject. Consequently the parts in this book dealing with the teaching of reading are not to be thought of as a substitute for a book on that subject. This book would, however, be lacking in comprehensiveness and thoroughness if it did not pay some attention to teaching of a selected number of reading skills that are closely related to teaching the other language arts. Consequently in this chapter the following skills are briefly discussed and their relationship to teaching the other language arts is suggested: (1) skills basic to initial reading instruction ("reading readiness" abilities and skills), (2) skills in word recognition, (3) comprehension skills, and (4) skills in locating information and using it.

SKILLS BASIC TO INITIAL READING INSTRUCTION

Probably at no other stage in the development of the ability to read is the recognition by the teacher of the importance of the interrelationship between oral expression and reading as vital for best results as it is during the period before reading instruction begins—during the stage which is often called the "reading readiness period." It is on this period that at the present time one of the controversies in the teaching of reading centers.

When Should Reading Instruction Begin?

Basic to other questions dealing with the period of reading readiness is the question, "When should reading instruction begin?" In terms of the concept of *reading readiness,* the question is "When is the child ready to learn to read?"

For a long time it was generally assumed that the first grade was the optimum time for initial instruction in reading for the majority of boys and girls. Frequently in educational literature recommendations were made, which were put into practice in many schools, that for almost all first-grade entrants reading instruction should not start at the beginning of that school year. Postponement of it for six weeks or more was popular practice. During the time preceding initial instruction in learning to read, the efforts of the teacher in regard to reading were concentrated on how to get the children "ready to read."

To be sure, there had not at any time been complete acceptance of the general policy of not starting reading instruction for most boys and girls until they had been in first grade for a period of weeks or even of months. Just as there were voices raised for postponement until later than that point, there were others arguing that a period of reading readiness was, as a rule, unnecessary in first grade. Some had, right along, even questioned the assumption that had long been made by persons in early childhood education that reading instruction—in fact, even systematic "reading-readiness activities" of a somewhat formal type—had no legitimate place in what was argued should be a highly permissive kindergarten program. Occasionally a daring soul had claimed that many boys and girls could advantageously receive their first instruction in reading in the home, before they entered a school of any type or level.

While in the past the objections to having reading instruction postponed for all till some time in first grade had been voiced by relatively few people, of late a storm of protest on that point has arisen on various fronts. Even by the more conservative, objection to a prolonged period of reading readiness has been made on the grounds that boys and girls, as a rule, do not, at that stage, need it. Argument against such a period in first grade has been based primarily on these facts: (1) Quite a number of boys and girls can do some reading even before they enter first grade. (2) More children attend kindergarten, in which even in those in which there is no formal reading or reading readiness program, they have some experiences that will help them become ready to learn to read. (3) Boys and girls, partly because of the greater mobility of the population and because of the information background they receive through watching television, are less than formally in need of a broader experience background as preparation for reading in first grade.

In increasing numbers experiments have been carried on in pre-first-grade school situations, the results of which give basis for the claim that reading can be taught effectively before boys and girls reach the first grade. The Denver study, [1] conducted under a grant fron the U.S. Office of Education, is only one of those that claim superiority of reading achievement by boys and girls in the primary grades after participating in a reading program in kindergarten. Another study favoring reading instruction before first grade that is frequently quoted to show the effectiveness of early training in reading is the work with Montessori materials at the Whitby School in Whitby, Connecticut, where three- and four-year-old boys and girls are being taught to read.

A book dealing in part with the question as to when to begin reading instruction that has attracted much attention is that by Glenn Doman, Director of the Institutes for the Achievement of Human Potential, Philadelphia. The title of the book is *How to Teach Your Baby to Read.* [2] As a member of a team of specialists in various areas—brain surgery, psychiatry, physical therapy, education, among them—Doman not only found that some of the brain-injured children with whom they worked could be taught to read at an early age but also concluded that such teaching was a factor in their neurological growth. Stimulated by these findings, attention was directed to the learning-to-read process in relation to the child without brain injury. The following quotation from *How to Teach Your Baby to Read* [3] summarizes one of the main points of the book.

Two years of age is the best time to begin if you want to expend the least amount of time and energy in teaching your child to read. (Should you be willing to go to a little trouble you can begin at eighteen months, or if you are very clever, as early as ten months of age.)

In the book, Doman describes in considerable detail procedures he recommends for teaching the young child to read.

Though aware of the fact that a sizeable number of children have been taught to read at early ages, some critics question whether all children who can be taught reading in pre-kindergarten and pre-first-grade years should be taught it at that period of life. It is, of course, to be desired that educators concerned with the question "When should reading instruction begin?" will keep an open mind in regard to the problem as further evidence is being sought and acquired, regardless of what the results of such study would indicate as to best procedure.

Factors Related to Readiness for Reading

The factors that many teachers believe need to be considered in trying to determine whether a child is ready to

1. Joseph E. Brzeinsky, "Beginning Reading in Denver," *The Reading Teacher* 18 (October 1964) p. 16-21.
2. Glenn Doman, *How to Teach Your Baby to Read.* Random House, 1964.
3. Ibid., p. 104.

read can be classified roughly, as they are by various writers, into the following four groups: (1) mental, (2) physical, (3) social and emotional, and (4) educational.

Mental Factors. As is evident from the preceding discussion, there is a difference of opinion as to the optimum mental age for beginning reading. Considerable evidence points to the fact that no one mental age can be considered the most desirable. However, serious consideration needs to be given to the mental capacity of the learner as methods of instruction and materials for beginning reading are being selected.

Physical Factors. Physical factors, too, regardless of the time when reading instruction is begun and regardless of the methods used, are important matters to consider in relation to readiness for reading. The importance of ascertaining the visual efficiency of a pupil when he begins to learn to read has long been known to parents and teachers. When there has been a question about vision of a child, it has been recommended that it be tested. In fact, in a considerable number of schools the vision of boys and girls is being checked before systematic instruction in reading is begun. Increasingly, too, hearing tests are being given to boys and girls upon entrance to school. It is being recognized that, especially when reading is being taught in group situations, lack of hearing efficiency can seriously interfere with learning to read.

Nor are vision and hearing the only physical factors that can have a marked influence on a child's ability to learn to read. Among these others are those suggested later in this chapter under "Evaluating Physical Health." Steps should be taken to try to correct any physical deficiencies that may handicap the child in learning to read (as well as, of course, all other physical problems that can be remedied, regardless of whether they seem to have a direct adverse effect upon beginning reading). If they cannot be corrected, the program of the school should take them into consideration in attempts to adapt instruction to the needs of the individuals. For example, if a child has a hearing problem that cannot be corrected, he should be seated in a place in the schoolroom that is most advantageous for him—where he is in the optimum location for hearing what is being said or what is being read to him.

Social and Emotional Factors. For the child who learns to read in a school situation, social and emotional factors must be carefully noted when determining readiness for reading instruction. Environmental preschool situations as well as the hereditary pattern of a child may have kept him from normal social and emotional development and thus have constituted a negative factor as far as readiness for reading upon entrance to school is concerned. The need of a desirable emotional background for the child who learns to read at home must also be emphasized.

Educational Factors. Among the educational factors that may have a decided effect upon learning to read are matters such as: the desire of the child to learn to read; his ability to discriminate between symbols he sees and between sounds he hears; and the extent of his language development. That these factors are amenable to development through instructional practices makes it all the more important for the teacher to take notice of them.

Determining Readiness for Reading

How then can we determine whether a child is ready to learn to read? Those persons who believe that reading can be taught successfully, without disadvantageous results, to most children long before they begin school will not be likely to concern themselves with all the points mentioned in the preceding paragraphs as criteria for determining when to begin reading instruction. Many teachers, however, believe it is helpful to try to determine readiness in part by such criteria. While directing our attention to each of the group of factors described, let us bear in mind the fact that it is not essential to successful beginning reading that a pupil have a high rating in respect to each one.

Determining the Mental Age. An index of the mental age of an individual can be secured by means of a group or individual intelligence test. However, intelligence has been an elusive characteristic to measure for no test has been devised that is not partly invalid because of the lack of isolation of those test elements that measure the results of environmental factors from others that truly measure native capacity. For example, a child with a broad experience background may register higher on an intelligence test than a child with more limited experiences of the same degree of intelligence.

1. Mental tests. In choosing a standardized intelligence test the teacher or administrator should note not only data on the validity of a test but also other characteristics of good standardized tests such as reliability, availability in more than one form, ease of administration, and cost.

Two well-known individual and probably the most reliable intelligence tests for boys and girls are the "Stanford-Binet Intelligence Scale" revised by Lewis M. Terman and Maud M. Merrill and "The Wechsler Intelligence Scale for Children." The former is published by Houghton Mifflin Company and the latter by the Psychological Corporation. The scores on both of these scales are affected by the language ability of the child, and, therefore, are not equally appropriate for ascertaining the native capacity of an individual with language handicaps and of one not so affected. A nonlanguage individual intelligence test on the market is the "Arthur Point Scale of Performance Tests" published by the

C.H. Stoelting Company of Chicago. Another is the "Peabody Picture Vocabulary Test," available through the American Guidance Service, Circle Pines, Minnesota.

Among much-used group intelligence tests are the "Pintner-Cunningham Primary Test" (Harcourt Brace Jovanovich), "The California Test of Mental Maturity, Pre-Primary Battery (McGraw-Hill), and "The Pintner-Non-Language Primary Mental Test" (Teachers College Press, Columbia University). For information on additional intelligence tests, see page 345 of chapter 13.

2. Other means of determining mental age. Even if the teacher has data on the mental age of a child according to a standardized intelligence test, because of lack of perfection in all intelligence tests, he is advised also to take into account information that can be obtained through means other than mental testing. Observation of the child's intellectual reactions to a variety of situations can give some indication as to whether he seems as bright as others of his chronological age. Furthermore, through study of books on child growth and development the teacher can compare the reactions of the child being observed with those noted for various age groups and can thereby get some insight as to the approximate mental age of the child.

Evaluating Physical Health. Checking with school records if the child has been in kindergarten, consulting with the school health staff, and conferring with parents are often means of securing valuable information on health to supplement that gained through observation.

These are some of the questions to which it will be profitable for the teacher to try to find answers as he attempts to determine a child's readiness for beginning reading as far as health factors are concerned.

Does he frequently complain of being tired?
Does his posture indicate tiredness?
Is his muscular coordination as good as that of the average beginning first-grade child?
Does he have frequent colds?
Does he have a history of poor health?

1. Checking vision. No teacher should consider himself in a position to determine whether a pupil's vision, with or without correction, is sufficient for effective reading without eyestrain or other danger to the eyes. However, through screening tests and through observation of the pupil in nontesting situations the teacher alone or with the help of the school health service can get some clues as to possible vision difficulties of some of the children.

If a test seems to indicate that a pupil's vision is impaired, the school should not make a pronouncement, unless it employs an eye specialist, that the child's vision is unsatisfactory. All the school should do is to recommend to the parents, usually through the school principal, that the child's eyes be examined by a competent doctor.

There is danger of false security if screening tests are used in a school. A pupil may have a serious defect in vision that interferes with effective reading, yet the defect may be undetectable by the test given. Left untreated, it may cause increasingly greater vision problems. Consequently the teacher should be careful not to rule out the possibility of a defect merely because none shows up in the screening test being used.

Cautions such as those mentioned in the preceding paragraph should be kept in mind when the most popular of screening tests used in schools is being interpreted, namely the Snellen Letter chart or the Snellen Symbol E chart. The latter is an adaptation of the regular Snellen chart, for use with boys and girls who do not recognize the letters of the alphabet. Since both of these tests measure vision only at the far-point, not the point at which most reading is being done, a pupil may have serious vision defects interfering with reading at the near-point that do not show up on the test given through use of a Snellen chart. More comprehensive for school use in terms of what is checked are *The Keystone Visual Survey Telebinocular* (Keystone View Division/Mast Development Company) and *The Master Orthorator Visual Efficiency Test* (Bausch and Lomb Optical Company, 635 St. Paul Street, Rochester, New York 14602.

In place of or in addition to giving one or more screening tests, the teacher can note, as he observes each child, whether or not he is often characterized by any of the following, all of which may be indicative of difficulty with his eyes:

Squints
Does not enjoy looking at picture books
Rubs his eyes
Has watery eyes
Can not see pictures at a distance
Has headaches, especially after doing close work
Has inflamed or crusted eyelids
Has sties
Frowns or scowls habitually
Blinks
Holds book too close to or far from eyes.

2. Checking hearing. Many of the larger school systems now have audiometers—machines for testing hearing. Audiometers are of two types, those by means of which one individual at a time is tested and those by which all the pupils in a small class can be tested at the same time. The latter type is not diagnostic as to the type of hearing difficulties that the person tested may have. It is of value in screening those pupils who should be tested later by means of an audiometer designed for individual

testing, preferably by a specialist. Information about audiometers can be secured by writing to the distributors, among them the Otarion Listener Corporation, Ossining, New York, the Beltone Electronics Corporation, 4201 West Victoria Street, Chicago, Illinois, the Sonotone Corporation, Elmsford, New York, and the Zenith Hearing Aid Sales Corporation, 6501 West Grand Avenue, Chicago, Illinois.

Even without the benefit of an audiometer the teacher can try to determine whether his pupils have significant hearing loss, by means of informal tests such as these:

The watch-tick test. The teacher checks the child's acuity of hearing by means of a watch whose tick is plainly audible to a person with good hearing at a distance of a yard or so. It is recommended that the teacher stand behind the child as he tests first one ear and then the other. The child can hold his hand over the ear that is not being tested. The teacher can first stand about four or five feet behind the child, so far away that the examinee cannot hear the watch. The child is instructed to notify the examiner as soon as he can hear the tick while the examiner slowly approaches. This test is more valid when comparative data are obtained on a group of children (not information on only one child) who are tested by the same watch and in the same room. If a child's hearing by this test seems to place him among those in the group with the most acute hearing, there may not be much need of suspicion concerning his general hearing ability unless he shows other signs of a problem. The fact must not be overlooked, however, that a child may not report accurately.

The whisper test. When giving the whisper test, the examiner at first stands far enough from the examinee, perhaps about thirty inches, so that the latter cannot hear him as he names words or figures in a whisper, which the examinee is asked to repeat while he has one ear covered. He should have the other ear turned toward the examiner. To preclude lip reading, the pupil should not be able to see the face of the examiner. The examiner comes closer and closer to the pupil until the latter is able to repeat correctly what the examiner is saying. The test is helpful as a rough screening device if a fairly large number of children, such as an entire class, is examined under the same testing conditions.

The low-voice test. The low-voice test is similar to the whisper test excepting that the examiner talks in a low voice, not in a whisper, and that at first he stands farther away from the examinee, perhaps about twenty feet. It is important that initially the examiner should be so far away from the pupil that the latter cannot hear accurately what is being said.

Even without an audiometer or the use of tests such as those suggested above, the teacher can try to determine whether his pupils have significant hearing loss. He can note points such as the following: ear trouble, frequent need of repetition of questions or comments made by others, tilt of the head, inattention, and listlessness.

Determining Social and Emotional Readiness for Reading. To try to determine to what extent the child possesses social and emotional characteristics that affect readiness for reading, the teacher can observe the child for points suggested by the following questions:

Is he cooperative?
Does he consider the rights of others?
Can he work independently for a while?
Has he many interests?
Is he a good listener?
Does he respect authority?
Is he self-confident (but not overly so)?
Is he able to take criticism?
Does he share materials with others?
Is he willing to wait his turn?
Does he show more than an average degree of daydreaming or emotional upsets?
Is he easily irritated?
Is he afraid?
Is he quarrelsome?

Appraising Educational Factors. Educational factors closely related to readiness for reading can be measured by so-called readiness tests as well as by other less formal means.

1. Reading readiness tests. Although reading readiness tests are not a perfect means for determining whether a child is ready to begin to learn to read as far as educational factors are concerned, they are helpful. By using a reading readiness tests, the teacher can probably find out more within an hour or so than in any other ways during the same length of time about the extent to which a pupil possesses some of the characteristics of educational readiness for beginning reading. However, because of the shortcomings of even the best of readiness tests, other data that the teacher can collect on the child's readiness for reading as far as educational factors are concerned should also be considered with care.

Many reading readiness tests, which are of merit when used in the light of the caution stated in the preceding paragraph, are now on the market. Among others that are widely used are the *Gates Reading Readiness Test* (Teachers College Press, Columbia University), *The Lee-Clark Reading Readiness Test* (California Test Bureau, Los Angeles), and *The Metropolitan Readiness*

Tests (Harcourt Brace Jovanovich). Additional reading readiness are listed in chapter 13; see page 345.

The following are some of the skills and abilities measured by readiness tests, with variation from test to test:

Word meaning
Sentence meaning
Auditory discrimination
Visual discrimination
Following directions
Background of information.

2. Other means of evaluating educational factors. The teacher can obtain much information about so-called educational factors affecting readiness for reading through: (a) less formal observation of the pupils than provided for by reading readiness tests; (b) examination of the school records if the child has attended kindergarten; and (c) conferences with the child and with his parents. A few ways in which the teacher can informally check, without the use of standardized reading readiness tests, are explained or illustrated below.

Testing for auditory discrimination. When checking auditory discrimination the teacher needs to keep clearly in mind that he is not obtaining data on auditory acuity but on auditory discrimination. The two are not the same. Auditory acuity indicates how well the child is able to hear with the hearing apparatus that he has. Auditory discrimination refers to the child's ability to differentiate between sounds. A child may have auditory acuity above the average and yet be low in the ability to discriminate between sounds. He may, even with above average hearing acuity have difficulty, for example, in differentiating between the *b* and the *d* sound, an ability important in learning to read. Fortunately, auditory discrimination is a trait subject to improvement through training.

To check auditory discrimination the teacher may, for example, do the following:

Ask the pupils to tell which groups of words, such as the following, contain words beginning with the same sound: *boy, dog; to, talk; run, rose.*

Ask the pupils to name the groups of words, as the teacher names them, that rhyme. Examples of possible groups to be named are: *same, tame; run, fun; car, cat.*

Have the pupils name words beginning with the same sound as a word the teacher names.

Testing for visual discrimination. The difference between the terms *visual acuity* or *vision* and *visual discrimination* must be kept in mind by the teacher. Visual acuity refers to keenness of vision; visual discrimination refers to the ability to make visual differentiations of that which is being viewed.

To test visual discrimination the teacher may wish to devise test items such as the following:

Test 1. Ask the pupils to draw an *x* through a picture in each row that is not like the others.

Figure 9.1. Which Is Different?

Test 2. Instruct the pupils that some of the words in each row of words, such as the following, are like the first one in the row, while others are not. Ask them to draw a circle around the words that are like the first one in a row.

boy   bag   boy   buy   tag   boy
home   home   home   house   tame   have

Test 3. If two words in a group look alike, instruct the pupils to draw a circle around the group. If two words in a group look different, ask them to draw an *x* through each word in the group.

sing, sing; sun, run; walk, talk; it, it.

Checking the ability to remember words. The teacher can check a pupil's ability to remember words as he orally gives sentences, beginning with short ones and progressing to longer sentences, which the pupil is to repeat verbatim: Examples are: (a) We are going for a walk. (b) This afternoon we will play in our room. (c) Before we go home this afternoon, Miss Peters will tell us a story.

Noting interest in books and stories. The teacher can obtain significant data on a pupil's attitude toward books and stories by:

Noticing the child's reaction when the announcement is made that a story will be told

Noting whether the pupil seems attentive when a story is being told

Observing whether the child looks at picture books placed on the library table

Taking note as to whether the pupil brings books that he likes to school.

Checking method of handling books. Readiness for beginning reading can be checked in part by how a pupil handles books in terms of questions such as these:

> Are his hands clean when he picks up a book?
> Does he turn the pages of a book carefully?
> Does he treat books as if he likes them?

Checking language background. The teacher can check a pupil's language background by:

> Asking him to give the opposite of words such as: *over* (*under*): *big* (*little*); *good* (*bad*); *awake* (*asleep*)
>
> Noting the extent to which he takes part in class discussion
>
> Noting whether he uses words correctly
>
> Checking on the length and structure of the sentences he uses.

Checking other educational factors. Some of the other factors related to reading readiness the teacher can check through informal exercises, questionnaires, and observation are: (a) ability to follow directions; (b) right-to-left and top-to-bottom orientation when "reading" picture books or following the writing in an experience chart; (c) ability to think critically; (d) experience background; (e) knowledge of the alphabet; (f) skill in interpreting pictures.

Developing Readiness for Reading

As the teacher is assessing a child's readiness for beginning to read according to factors such as those considered in the preceding discussion, he will want to use procedures that will help each boy and girl who is not ready for initial reading instruction to become more ready. As the teacher considers guidelines such as those listed here, he should keep in mind the fact that there is no one optimum time for beginning to read, since methods and materials to be used will determine to a large extent whether a given child is ready. Some general suggestions recommended for the teacher's consideration are: (1) *Reading readiness activities should form, to a large extent, an integral part of the regular room program.* Activities such as storytelling, art activities, and dramatics can be engaged in such a manner that they help a pupil become more ready for beginning reading instruction. (2) *Some boys and girls can be benefitted through practice activities in addition to the activities of the ongoing school program.* Exercises in auditory or visual discrimination in following directions and in matching lowercase with uppercase letters, for some pupils, will serve as a helpful adjunct to learnings of this type acquired somewhat incidentally. (3) *No one length*

of time can be considered the optimum for a reading readiness period. The child who has learned to read before he enters first grade should not be given meaningless reading readiness activities but should be given instruction on his level. As stated earlier, methods and materials used in the regular reading program will greatly affect the time when reading activities can or should begin. (4) *Many reading readiness activities can profitably continue into the early phases of the stage of initial reading instruction.* Work on word discrimination is one such activity.

Developing Emotional and Social Readiness. In order to help boys and girls acquire greater emotional and social stability, the teacher needs to provide a school atmosphere in which the following prevail:

1. Respect for each individual in the group
2. A feeling by each child that he is liked by the teacher at all times
3. A feeling on the part of each child that he is accepted by the group as a whole and liked very well by some individuals in it
4. A spirit of cooperation.

Courtesy of West Boulevard Elementary School, Columbia Public Schools, Columbia, Missouri.

Figure 9.2. Games Can Serve as Aids to Readiness for Reading.

One way in which the teacher can help the child develop in social and emotional maturity is to provide him with many worthwhile experiences, such as taking field trips, listening to stories, participating in "sharing times" engaging in dramatic play, playing games, and seeing pictures. Other ways are:

1. Providing the shy child with opportunities to become increasingly involved in activities well graded for him

2. Helping the overly aggressive child take a rightful place in the social scene of the classroom

3. Using praise when deserved but resorting to criticism sparingly

4. Adapting the curriculum to the needs of each child so that he is likely to have a maximum of success experiences and a minimum of frustrations

5. Helping boys and girls appreciate the difference between license and liberty

6. Giving responsibilities to all pupils

7. Helping boys and girls in self-evaluation

8. Helping boys and girls become more self-reliant

9. Avoiding much competition with others

10. Placing a child in a group in which he is likely to be happy

11. Encouraging the child to do without assistance those chores that he can do alone

12. Encouraging every child to develop his special talents.

Helping the Child with Physical Shortcomings. Attention of the teacher to such matters as are suggested in the following paragraphs can be of real value in helping the child become ready to read as well as to develop in many other respects.

1. The teacher can help the pupil who has vision problems by having him sit in the part of the room where he can best see the chalkboard; paying particular attention to the lighting facilities where he is; providing him with printed materials of suitable type; writing large enough on the chalkboard and on materials that are duplicated so that the writing is suited, as well as feasible under the circumstances, to his poor vision; encouraging him to wear glasses if some have been prescribed for him; helping him get emotionally adjusted to glasses if he needs to wear them; developing among the other boys and girls a mentally healthy attitude toward an individual who has problems of vision.

2. The teacher can help the child who has hearing problems by giving him a seat in a part of the room where audibility is excellent; speaking distinctly and loud enough so that he can hear and encouraging all the boys and girls to do likewise; using visual rather than auditory methods of teaching frequently; helping the child realize that a defect is not an excuse for not trying; helping him get emotionally adjusted to his handicap; developing among the other pupils a mentally healthy attitude toward an individual with hearing problems.

3. The teacher can assist the pupil who has health problems other than those associated with vision or hearing by providing rest periods for the fatigued child; alternating periods of concentration with periods of relaxation; trying to provide a room free of drafts; consulting with parents about the child's health habits and needs; encouraging the pupil to eat properly in so far as the food he eats is subject to his choice; emphasizing good posture through precept, example, and opportunity to practice; isolating the child with a cold if it is not necessary to send him home; helping him remedy health handicaps that can be remedied; assisting the child in accepting health handicaps that cannot be overcome; providing proper seating.

Developing Auditory Discrimination. Many of the boys and girls in first grade will probably need no help in auditory discrimination other than that afforded by the ongoing school activities. Others may require help in terms of supplementary practice exercises. The major emphasis should be on the type of discrimination the child will find of value when reading. However, included among the list of activities given below are also some that may be of value to a pupil in becoming ready for making the kind of discrimination that he will need to make when reading. The pupils requiring help in making auditory discriminations could do some of the following activities:

1. Listen for sounds and report on those they heard during a few minutes of silence.

2. Name words that begin with the same sound as one given by the teacher.

3. Make up rhymes and then name the rhyming words.

4. Try to distinguish, with closed eyes, whether the teacher taps on a table, the chalkboard, a glass, or something else.

5. Dramatize stories in which a variation of soft and loud voices is needed, such as "The Three Billy Goats" or "The Three Bears."

6. Tell whether two words named by the teacher begin (or end) with the same sound.

7. Draw a circle around each picture in a group, the name of which begins with the same sound as a specified picture in that group.

8. Draw a circle around each picture in a group, the name of which rhymes with the specified word in that group.

9. Orally match words that the teacher gives with the names of pictures on cards that begin with the same sound.

10. Match pictures in one column with pictures in a second column, the names of which rhyme with those in the first column.

11. Tell in which words named by the teacher (such as *cat, race, name, sat*) there is the sound of the short *a*.

12. Tell whether a given sound, like *p*, comes at the beginning, middle, or end of words containing the sound that are named by the teacher.

13. Collect or draw pictures, the names of which rhyme.

14. Say the name of a picture and place it in a pocket on which there is a picture that has the same beginning sound.

15. Select from a pack of picture cards those that have two pictures the names of whose initial sound is the same.

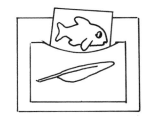

Figure 9.3. Matching Pictures with Same Beginning Sound.

Developing Visual Discrimination. Means through which some pupils can improve in ability to make visual discriminations that will help them get ready for beginning reading are listed below. Some will be of value even after the pupils are in the early stages of learning to read.

1. Checking a series of pictures in each of a group of rows to show which is the largest (or smallest).

2. Telling what is wrong in a series of pictures that have been duplicated, some of which have an incongruity. For example, a picture of a door may be without a knob or both shoes that a child is wearing may be made for the right foot.

3. Solving picture puzzles.

4. Completing one of each of a pair of pictures duplicated on paper so that it looks like the other. For instance, there may be a picture of two pumpkins, one without a stem.

5. Matching the cutoff part of each of a series of pictures with the part of the picture of which it originally formed a part.

Figure 9.4. Matching Parts of Pictures.

6. Sorting cards having pairs of like and unlike pictures into two groups, those that are alike and those that are **different**.

7. Showing the relationship between two sets of pictures, with illustrations for words such as the following:

cow	tomato
school	ball
bat	dress
girl	chalkboard
garden	milk

It is suggested that the pictures be mounted on paper of the same size. If the exercise is to be done independently by one person at a time, it is recommended that the child be enabled to check his own arrangement by means of a code on the back of each mounting.

8. Classifying pictures into categories, such as signs of fall, winter, spring, and summer. The pictures, which for convenience in using and storing should be on mountings of the same size, can be arranged by the pupils under appropriate headings on a bulletin board, on the chalk ledge, in a card holder, or on the chalkboard (with tape attached to the back of the mountings). Smaller pictures can be mounted on uniform-sized paper, which one pupil at a time may arrange in proper categories at his seat or at the reading table. So that the exercise can be self-checking, a key can be given on the back of the mountings.

9. Matching geometric forms of various types, possibly also of different colors, such as blue stars, red **circles, purple rectangles.**

Figure 9.5. Matching Geometric Figures.

10. Arranging cutout words on small cards in the order that they are set up in a model that is given the pupil, possibly written on an envelope in which the cutouts for a given sentence are stored.

11. Arranging in order blocks of similar shapes but of different sizes.

12. Answering questions asked by the teacher, calling for discrimination, such as: (a) How are these two puppets different? (b) How are these two chalk marks different?

13. Answering questions such as: (a) What is different in our room today? (b) What is Sue wearing today that she has never before worn to school?

14. Doing jigsaw puzzles.

15. Guessing what object is described by the teacher. The description may begin with the words "I am thinking of something."

16. Indicating which of a series of letters or words in each row, such as the following, is different from the first one in that row:

run   run   ran   run   run.

17. Indicating which of a series of words in a row begin with the same letter (or end with the same letter)

18. Indicating which of a series of pairs of words, such as those listed following, are alike:

form, from;   pit, tip;   deal, deal;   deal, lead.

Some of the pairs may consist of words that may form a problem in reversals for some children. If a pupil makes reversals, such an exercise may be followed with one in which he points out similar letters in a pair of words as he notes that in words such as *was* and *saw* the placement of the letters *w* and *s* is different.

19. Finding a word card with the same word as a given word on a card holder or on the chalkboard.

20. Crossing out a designated often-repeated word in a group of sentences.

21. Noting similarities in the beginnings of pupils' names.

22. Looking for words on a chart that begin in the same way as a given word.

23. Matching letters or words given in two columns.

24. Drawing a circle around words in a row that begin with one letter (or two) used at the beginning of the first word of a line, such as:

*r*ose   run   fun   robin   sun
*st*art   stone   some   tore   seed

Developing in Ability to Speak. The following are ways in which the teacher can help during the reading readiness period and later not only to keep speech problems from interfering with the pupil's reading but also to make the joy of oral self-expression affect the reading situation favorably:

1. Serving as model of good speech himself.

2. Providing the boys and girls with much opportunity to talk.

3. Providing a classroom atmosphere in which children will want to talk.

4. Making provisions for many interesting activities that will encourage free and informal talk.

5. Providing special practice activities for those pupils who can profit from them, such as: (a) telling which of a series of sentences given by the teacher illustrate good and poor enunciation; (b) playing a game in which each pupil tries to reach the top of a diagram of a ladder on the chalkboard, on the rungs of which are pictures illustrating words for practice in enunciation such as *running, yellow, bus;* (c) having recordings on tape made of the pupil's talks; (d) participating in "sharing time."

Developing the Vocabulary. The understanding and the speaking vocabulary are factors that help determine a child's readiness for reading. Consideration is, therefore, given here not only to the development of a rudimentary reading vocabulary but also to an increase in the child's understanding and speaking vocabulary. The teacher can help the boys and girls in vocabulary development by:

1. Using words in sentences in which the meaning is indicated

2. Providing much opportunity for conversation

3. Reading poetry and prose

4. Making experience charts

5. Providing the pupils with new experiences

6. Asking the pupils to find their names in a list

7. Making "helper" charts

Figure 9.6. Learning to Recognize Names of Pupils.

a favorable effect on the development of readiness for reading and on success during the initial period of reading instruction.

1. The boys and girls can write their own names from name cards written by the teacher.

2. In a picture dictionary made by the class or individuals the pupils can write the word that is illustrated by each of the pictures, below that written by the teacher.

3. The pupils can note where the teacher begins when writing on a chart or on the chalkboard as he asks questions such as: (a) Where should I start my first word? (b) Where should I start the second line?

Developing in Ability to Think Critically. When reading is considered an activity through which thought can be acquired, as it should be, there is a self-evident relationship between ability to think critically and readiness for reading. The teacher can help the boys and girls develop in ability to think critically by doing the following:

1. Asking questions that involve thinking before, during the time, and after he tells or reads stories to the class

2. Asking thought questions of the boys and girls as they plan school activities

3. During "sharing time" (see page 55) asking questions such as these of children who are planning their contributions: (a) Where do you think you should stand when you show your shell? (b) When would it be best to pass around your shell—before you begin talking, while you are talking, or after you have finished?

Developing Other Abilities Important for Reading. Only a few of the abilities important for reading—more specifically for readiness for reading—have been discussed so far. Others to which the teacher will want to pay attention in his efforts to help in the development of reading readiness are the ability (1) to remember, (2) to follow directions, (3) to handle books with skill, and (4) to interpret pictures. The teacher will also want to help boys and girls extend their experience background. Since reading is a process involving thinking, the richer the experiences, regardless of whether they are definitely related to reading, the more likely the child will be able to approach reading with intelligent anticipation of the content. The teacher will also wish to do all that is in his power to develop and help maintain an interest in reading. Many of the activities already suggested as means of guiding growth toward readiness for reading, if they appeal to boys and girls, can be used to stimulate their desire to read.

The Use of Reading Experience Charts

The reading experience chart is one of the widely used means of developing readiness for beginning reading.

Photo by David N. Westlund.

Figure 9.7. Developing Readiness for Readings in the Home.

8. Providing color and number charts

9. Having the pupils use labels for exhibits, for identification of supplies, etc.

Developing Listening Abilities. The relationship between listening abilities and learning to read is especially close when reading is taught primarily in a group situation. However, even when individualized reading programs characterize beginning instruction, there is interrelationship so that development in ability to listen is likely to advantageously affect beginning reading. Through listening the child acquires the vocabulary that will make reading meaningful later. Through listening he can develop sentence sense—an essential for intelligent reading. Through listening activities the foundation is laid on which phonetic analysis is built later in connection with reading. (In chapter 4 there is a discussion of how the listening abilities of boys and girls can be developed, see page 68.)

Learning the Rudiments of Handwriting. Although beginning reading instruction should, as a rule, precede systematic writing instruction, some writing activities or activities related to writing such as the following can have

Some are reports on activities in which the boys and girls have engaged or are engaging in, while others are records of what they plan to do. (See page 89.)

Values. The popularity of the experience chart is undoubtedly due in part to the fact that it can contribute to the accomplishment of many of the objectives of the reading readiness period.

1. It can be the means of extending the pupils's experience background as the class discusses experiences.

2. It can provide experience in democratic living with its contribution to the social and emotional development of the child as he learns to take turns, to respect the ideas of others, to feel the encouragement and satisfaction of a worthwhile contribution, and to work in an orderly manner.

3. It can help interest the child in reading.

4. It can provide orientation in the left-to-right and top-to-bottom directional sequence of reading, especially if the teacher draws attention to it.

5. It can stimulate the development of sentence sense as the teacher uses the term *sentence* when he makes comments or asks questions such as: (a) What shall we have for the next sentence? (b) Where shall I begin the next sentence? (c) Please read the next sentence.

Occasions for Charts. When making an experience chart it is important that the boys and girls recognize a purpose for engaging in the activity. It will be noted that in the following listing the suggested purpose in some cases is not only for making a chart and reading it but also for follow-up activities.

1. The boys and girls can make a series of charts on a trip that they have taken. The purpose may be, as far as the pupils are concerned, to remember important and interesting learnings they acquired.

2. The class can make a series of charts, one on each field trip they have taken during the course of the school year. Their purpose may be similar to the one stated in (*1*) above.

3. The class can make a booklet, after they are able to "read" an experience chart, based on a walk on which they had observed signs of fall (or winter or spring). Every child may be given a duplicated copy of the chart for his notebook. Then he can draw an appropriate cover for his booklet. On one page in the booklet may be the "picture words" the pupils learned while reading the chart, with pictures drawn to illustrate each word learned that can be pictured. After a pupil is able to "read" his booklet (that is, saying it at least in part from memory) he may be allowed to take it home to give to his parents and to "read" it to them.

4. The experience chart can be written on paper that will serve as a page in a large class notebook, in which the pupils can keep an illustrated record of interesting activities of the school year, possibly for turning over to the grade that will follow them in the room the next year.

5. Before Thanksgiving the boys and girls can participate in making an experience chart so that they will be reminded throughout the school year of some of the many reasons they have for feeling grateful.

6. The boys and girls may be stimulated to want to make an experience chart to serve as a written record of plans for an activity they intend to perform.

Planning a Chart. Planning an experience chart usually requires much guidance by the teacher if maximum learning is to result. After the boys and girls have engaged in an activity and have discussed it, the teacher may suggest—if the pupils do not—the desirability of making a record of the experience for a purpose that is meaningful to the boys and girls. (Some desirable objectives for making a chart are indicated in the preceding listing under "Occasions for Charts.") After the class has discussed the general content for the chart, they can proceed with suggestions for sentences to be used, as the teacher, incorporating needed alterations, records them on the chalkboard or on a large sheet of paper. The teacher may then read the chart to the class in order that they may be able to recommend any changes.

Constructing a Chart. Sometimes the form in which the chart is first written suffices. At other times, especially if it is to be kept for future use of the types mentioned earlier, it should probably be rewritten on large sheets of paper, at times illustrated by a picture that a pupil has drawn or by a commercially produced one.

Reading Activities Provided by Experience Charts. Even while the chart is in the planning stage, provision for improvement in reading skills is provided. After it has been constructed, as the teacher reads it to the class, opportunity is given for development of skills important

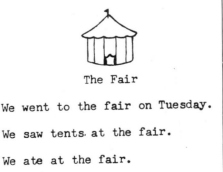

Figure 9.8. An Experience Chart.

to reading. He may ask the boys and girls to say with him the sentences on the chart, to point to sentences that he reads to the class, to note a few words on the chart, and to repeat the sentences without his aid. It will be noted that if an experience chart is used as a reading readiness activity, the boys and girls will ordinarily not be able to read the chart in the sense that the word *read* is usually used. They should not be expected to learn to recognize many of the new words in connection with any one chart—probably no more than three or four. Usually considerable practice on the words selected for study is required.

Points to Remember. Following are additional points for the teacher to keep in mind when he plans, constructs, or uses experience charts for reading readiness purposes.

1. It is important to have wide participation in the planning, so that the chart is not primarily the work of a few pupils and the teacher. If this precaution is not observed, many of the pupils may in time lose interest in the activity. Furthermore, many of the possible benefits will not accrue to all.

2. If the experience chart is to be of maximum value as a reading experience, special attention needs to be paid by the teacher to the selection of some of the words for the chart. It is not recommended that the boys and girls be expected to learn all the new words included in an experience chart. If they learn two, three, or four from each chart, perhaps no more should be expected. If the words to be learned are those that the boys and girls will be likely to use in the near future in their reading, the word study has increased value. The teacher needs to be careful, however, when planning for the inclusion of certain words in the chart not to violate the caution stated in the preceding paragraph.

Figure 9.9. A Folder for Displaying Illustrated Words.

3. The words from a chart that are to be added to the child's sight vocabulary should be used at frequent intervals even after the work on the chart has been discontinued. Without violating the basic principle to which reference is made in the two preceding paragraphs, a teacher can guide the structuring of the story on the chart in such a way that some "review words" are used in subsequent charts. For some pupils direct practice on

those words may be needed. Word cards or picture word cards could be made for practice purposes.

4. Experience charts should not be considered substitutes for early reading in a book. It is not as important now to emphasize this point as it was several decades ago when a substantial number of teachers advocated using experience charts as practically the only reading for boys and girls during the early stages of learning to read. One argument given by some proponents of this practice is that boys and girls enjoy reading more if they have dictated the material to be read. This point is refuted by those who point out that in time it can also become very boring to keep on reading only that material which the reader had helped plan. Other arguments against almost exclusive use of the experience chart as a beginning reading activity are: (a) The pupils are not really reading when they reproduce the sentences they have memorized, since reading is or should be primarily a thought-getting process. (b) The vocabulary is not as controlled as that in textbooks even if the teacher tries, within reason, to have some words used in the charts that will later appear in the child's reading books. (c) Boys and girls find, at times, that reading what someone else has written can be more intriguing than that which they have helped "write."

Interrelationship of Language Arts in the Reading Readiness Program

As mentioned in the opening remarks of this section on "Skills Basic to Initial Reading Instruction," it is highly important that, during the period of a child's life preceding that when he begins to read, the teacher recognizes the interrelationship of the language arts. This point holds whether the child is in his infancy or upon entrance to first grade or later in his school life is first taught to read. Development of skill in listening and growth in ability to express himself orally are important to reading instruction regardless of the age of the learner. Observation of writing, as done by others, can be a practical means of interesting the child in reading.

Linguists, emphasizing the primacy of speech over written means of communication, would stress the significance of having the child before he begins to learn to read and while so doing, develop considerable skill in oral expression. Even teachers whose philosophy of teaching reading is not linguistically oriented would emphasize the importance of having the child able to express himself well orally as one desired prerequisite to reading instruction.

The discussion of procedures for making and using reading experience charts has pointed out, as have other suggestions given in these pages, how children can be helped in laying a foundation for reading instruction through their attention to the writing that the teacher does. It is the wise teacher who recognizes that development in those attributes that help in initial reading instruction can be encouraged through utilization of all facets of the language arts. Because of this interrelationship, this discussion on "Skills Basic to Initial Reading Instruction" is important to the teaching of the language arts other than reading, the major concern of this book.

SKILL IN WORD RECOGNITION

There is much ferment in the field of the teaching of reading about the method or methods to be used in initial instruction in reading. The debate has raged chiefly around the question of how word recognition should be taught. However, no matter which one of several approaches to the teaching of word recognition is followed, success with each method is determined in part by the use made of the other language arts—the language arts other than reading. Furthermore, the impact of the procedure used in teaching word recognition on the other language arts is of vital significance.

The Great Debate

The great debate in teaching word recognition to beginners is well summarized in a book by Jeanne Chall, long a renowned figure in the field of the teaching of reading. The book is entitled *Learning to Read: The Great Debate.*[4] Jeanne Chall has brought to the forefront of educational thinking the question whether a phonic approach to reading instruction is superior to the one referred to as the "look-say" or whole-word or meaning approach, which is the nonphonic approach that had previously been generally recommended by leaders in the field of reading instruction as an initial method. After carrying on an extensive investigation into methods of teaching beginning reading, under a grant from the Carnegie Foundation for the Advancement of Teaching, Miss Chall comes out strongly in favor of what she terms a code-approach method, a phonic method in which the child from the beginning of reading instruction is helped to learn the grapheme-phoneme relationship (the relationship between the alphabet symbols and their sounds). She summarizes her findings thus:

My review of the research from the laboratory, the classroom, and the clinic points to the need for a correction in beginning reading instructional methods. Most school children in the United States are taught to read by what I have termed a meaning-emphasis method. Yet the research from 1912 to 1965 indicates that a code-emphasis method—i.e., one that views beginning reading as essentially different from mature reading and emphasizes learning of the printed code for the spoken language—produces better results, at least up to the point where sufficient evidence seems to be available, the end of the third grade.
The results are better, not only in terms of the mechanical aspects of literacy alone, as was once supposed, but also in terms of the ultimate goals of reading instruction—comprehension and possibly even speed of reading. The long-existing

fear that an initial code emphasis produces readers who do not read for meaning or with enjoyment is unfounded. On the contrary, the evidence indicates that better results in terms of reading for meaning are achieved with the programs that emphasize code at the start than with the programs that stress meaning at the beginning.[5]

Undoubtedly the storm of argument about Miss Chall's book has died down somewhat. However a difference of opinion persists as to the place of phonics in beginning reading instruction. It is questionable whether the controversy will be settled in the foreseeable future, if ever.

Innovative Programs

A major problem in learning to read, as in learning to spell, is caused by the fact that in English orthography a one-to-one correspondence between the graphemes (written representations of sounds, or letters of the alphabet) and the phonemes (the sounds that the graphemes represent) is lacking. That constitutes one reason why a code approach to reading instruction has been frowned upon by many who believe that emphasis during the initial learning-to-read period on as difficult a code as English orthography presents would make the early stage of reading instruction too mechanical, too uninteresting. One major characteristic of recent innovative programs in reading is the attempt that is being made through them to simplify the code, so that there will be less, if any variation, in the correspondence between the sounds of the language and the written symbols for those sounds.

The Initial Teaching Alphabet. The Initial Teaching Alphabet (commonly referred to as *ITA* or *i/t/a*) indicates one means by which allegedly a one-to-one grapheme-phoneme relationship is achieved. In recent years it has been used increasingly, first in schools in Great Britain and later in the United States. Because the English language lacks consistency in representation of sounds by letters or groups of letters, it is rightly claimed, that many a youngster—in fact, many an adult—had difficulty in reading. In an attempt to reduce the problems of the beginner in learning to read, the alphabet for beginning reading shown in figure 9.10 is used in ITA materials.

In the ITA alphabet of forty-four characters it will be noted that twenty-four are found in traditional orthography; some of the others are a combination of letters in the usual English alphabet; several are new characters. Each symbol in the ITA represents one sound and that one sound is represented by no other symbol or combination of symbols. In this respect the

4. Jeanne Chall, *Learning to Read: The Great Debate.* McGraw-Hill Book Company, 1967. pg. 307-8. Used with the permission of the McGraw-Hill Book Company.
5. Ibid., page 307.

Figure 9.10. The Initial Teaching Alphabet.

Initial Teaching Alphabet is in sharp contrast to that ordinarily used when writing English, in which many letters have more than one sound and in which many sounds are represented by different letters or letter combinations.

For information on the ITA and its use in schools the reader is referred, first of all, to the many articles appearing in professional magazines. He is also referred to the book *The Initial Teaching Alphabet*,[6] written by John Downing, the Englishman whose work in the United States has been greatly responsible for developing interest in the alphabet among many teachers in the United States. Suffice it here to note the following statements about ITA.

1. The proponents of ITA emphasize the fact that it is not a method of teaching but a mode of writing. They

stress the point that the alphabet can be used with any method of teaching beginning reading (such as the sight method or the phonic method) the teacher uses, as based on his philosophy of education or upon the procedures by means of which he obtains the best results.

2. John Downing and others point out the fact that use of the Initial Teaching Alphabet should precede use of the traditional alphabet and that it should not be a substitute for it for lifetime reading. *When* the transition should be made from the initial teaching alphabet to the standard one has not been ascertained. Undoubtedly the optimum time for the changeover will depend upon many factors such as the interest, the intelligence, and the skill of the reader, not merely upon chronological age nor upon length of time in school. Some pupils make the transition at various periods during the first school year; others make it later.

3. Since ITA was not used extensively in England before 1961 and not in America before 1963, convincing research on the use of the alphabet, it is claimed by many, is still lacking. This argument is advanced when consideration is given to some of the enthusiastic reports in schools where ITA has been used for a few years.

4. The number of available reading series written in ITA is increasing. Initial Teaching Alphabet Publications, 20 East 46th Street, New York, New York 10017, will furnish on request a list of teaching materials to augment teaching by means of this forty-four character alphabet.

"Words-In-Color"Program. Another approach to minimization of the divergence between the sound and symbols in the English language is the "word-in-color" program, published by Learning Materials, Inc., Encyclopedia Britannica Press. To explain how color is used the publishers in one of their brochures state:

Each of the 47 sounds of English is printed in a distinctive color on wall charts. Alphabet letters or groups of letters (280 signs of English) are colored according to how they sound in a given word. Thus color is used to make English phonetic without in any way changing traditional spellings.

A sound is always represented by *one* color—regardless of its spelling. If it is the short sound of *a*, it is white whether it is in *pat* or *laugh*. Children use these color clues to help them fix the image in their minds.

From the beginning, the pupil writes and reads in *black and white* each colored sign that he is introduced to so that there is immediate and constant transfer. Since he carries the images of these signs in color in his mind, the pupil can evoke and re-evoke the images if he needs them for reading or writing. Thus he is not dependent on printing in color.

Although the words-in-color program has been followed in relatively few schools, it is of importance to note how it is one attempt to obtain a closer relationship between graphemes and phonemes for beginning readers.

6. John Downing, *The Initial Teaching Alphabet*. The Macmillan Company, 1964.

As in the case of ITA the "words-in-color" program has not been used long enough for research to give evidence that many would accept as conclusive, for it was not until 1959 that Caleb Gattegno, the originator of the program, applied to the English language the results of earlier experimentation with the Spanish and Hindi languages.

The Linguistic Approach. In the linguistic approach to reading instruction, no attempt is made to change the symbols of English orthography, either by alterations of the traditional code, as in ITA nor through the use of color, as in the words-in-color program. As indicated in the discussion of "Linguistics and Spelling" (see page 217), the aim is to analyze and classify the problems created by an alphabet lacking a one-to-one correspondence between phonemes and graphemes. Some linguists are attempting to make reading and spelling instruction more effective by locating and classifying the difficulties inherent in the use of the traditional orthography of English and then having their findings incorporated in the reading program. Thus persons favoring a linguistically oriented reading program are interested in presenting a logically justifiable plan of organizing the irregularities of English spelling and reading and of presenting the regularities and irregularities of English orthography in a desirable sequence for learning. Emphasis is placed by them on word patterns and on the progression in teaching from regular, through semiregular, to irregular forms. The attention, thus, is placed on the structure of the word, rather than on the meaning.

Standard Practices

For detailed suggestions on procedures for use with the innovative programs to which reference is made in preceding pages and to other newer programs, the teacher is referred to published materials dealing with the respective programs. For example, if he is interested in the linguistic approach, he may find as excellent introduction to a study of it, one or all of the following books:

Durkin, Dolores. *Phonics, Linguistics and Reading.* New York: Teachers College Press, Columbia University, 1972.

Lamb, Pose. *Linguistics in Proper Perspective.* Columbus, Ohio: Charles E. Merrill Publishing Company, 1967.

Savage, John F., ed. *Linguistics for Teachers: Selected Readings.* Chicago: Science Research Associates, 1973.

Smith, Frank. *Understanding Reading: A Psycholinguistic Analysis of Reading and Learning to Read.* New York: Holt, Rinehart and Winston, Inc., 1971.

Wardbaugh, Ronald. *Reading: A Linguistic Perspective.* New York: Harcourt Brace Jovanovich, 1969.

For names of additional books on linguistics the reader is referred to page 336.

The reader will not want to venture into one of the innovative programs without considerable study of recommended practice. Consequently such suggestions are not given in the short space of this chapter. Those that follow refer to standard practices for developing skill in word recognition.

Use of the Sight Method. As the term *sight method* is here used, it refers to the so-called "look-say" method, where a word is learned without any analysis of it and without any reference to context. The pupil is merely told the word by someone—by the teacher, another adult, or a child. The expression *sight word* is used in this book to designate words that were presented by the sight method. (It should be noted that some writers refer to words as *sight words* when the learner knows the words by sight, regardless of the method by which the word was first presented.)

If the teacher wishes, for example, to present the word *school* as a sight word, he may write it on the chalkboard or show it on a word card as he says to the child, "This word is *school.*" Thereupon the pupil may be asked to repeat *school* and to find the word in a sentence, preferably in one that contains no other word new to the child's reading vocabulary.

It should be noted that a heated controversy has been raging about the use of the sight method. While some teachers recommend that a considerable number of words be taught as sight words during initial reading instruction, others have contended that phonics should be taught from the very beginning so that from the start the reader achieves some independence in word recognition.

Courtesy of the Public Schools, Columbia, Missouri.

Figure 9.11. Reinforcement in Recognizing Words.

The adversaries of the sight method are right in their claim that if all words were learned only by that method, no one could hope to become an efficient reader. Consequently, as is generally agreed now, the sight method, if used, should be supplemented by the phonetic method and other methods.

We may well ask, "Why then, if the sight method is a memory method whereby each word needs to be remembered as such, is it advocated by anyone?" It is recommended by its advocates for use in beginning reading instruction because in a fairly short time, it is claimed, a child can acquire a reading vocabulary sufficient to help him read meaningful material with a limited vocabulary.

Closely allied to the sight method, in fact often part of it, is that of pointing out the general configuration or striking characteristics of a word. The teacher may, for example, when he tells the child the word *book,* point out the fact that there are two circles in the word, or as he presents the word *morning* as a sight word, he may draw attention to the fact that it is a long word. The pattern of words with parts higher than the rest, such as the *f* in *farm,* or with parts below the line, such as the *g* in *go,* may also be emphasized. Since, however, many words have the same general outline, to pay much attention to the general configuration of a word is poor practice.

For many children to hear a word only once during the early stages of reading instruction, does not assure that they will remember it. It is for this reason that publishers of books for beginning instruction have provided considerable subsequent use of a word in context after the initial presentation. Even so, many teachers realize that unless the use of a word in the textbook is supplemented by other opportunities to strengthen the association with a word taught as a sight word, possibly a large number of boys and girls will not remember it on a subsequent day, maybe not even as they find it in the reading for that day.

Some of the procedures suggested here can be employed either at the time of the presentation of a sight word or later, while others are applicable only for practice at the time when a word is presented as a sight word.

1. After the teacher has told the class the name of a word, one pupil or the entire class pronounces it after him.

2. A pupil matches the word on a word card with a word on the chalkboard.

3. A pupil names the words presented as they appear on the chalkboard or on word cards.

4. The teacher names a word that a pupil is to find among the words listed on the chalkboard or on word cards.

5. One pupil points to a word while another names it.

6. A child finds the new words named by the teacher as they occur in a list of sentences that the teacher has written on the chalkboard.

Figure 9.12. "Balloons" Used as Word Cards.

7. The pupils point in their reading book to a word that the teacher names or for which he shows a word card or at which he points as it appears on the chalkboard.

8. After two words similar in general configuration which have been presented as sight words, such as *this* and *that,* have been written on the chalkboard, a pupil encircles the parts that are alike in the two words.

9. One or more pupils indicate which pairs of a series such as the following written on the chalkboard, are alike:

this, that   that, this   that, that
this, this

The reader will find further suggestions that can be applied for reinforcement of association between the written symbol and the name of the word presented by the sight method as he reads the ideas given in subsequent pages of this chapter dealing with means of providing practice on words suggested in connection with other means of word recognition.

Use of Context Clues. Somewhat less dependent than learning words by the sight method is learning them through pictorial or verbal context clues.

1. Picture clues. Obviously not nearly all words can be presented or remembered through picture clues. Nouns

that are names of concrete objects or persons or places, not of ideas or other abstractions, can most readily be recalled in this way. Even with them there may be confusion. For example, if the word *mother* is presented with a picture of a young woman holding a baby, it may not be clear to the beginner whether the word is *mother* or *baby.* Action verbs can be illustrated, but frequently there is no certainty as to what the word is. For example, to illustrate the verb *run,* there may be a picture of a boy running. The reader may, however, be uncertain as to whether the word written below the picture is *boy, run, runs,* or *running.* Some other parts of speech are even more difficult to illustrate pictorially.

To overcome the shortcoming of the picture-clue method, words are often presented in the first grade by a combination of the sight method and the picture-context method. For example, the teacher may show the picture of a boy with the word *boy* written below it and ask the pupils what they think the word is. If they do not suggest the word *boy,* the teacher tells them the word. Then the card can be posted for possible later reference by the pupils.

Following are additional suggestions for using the picture-clue method, either alone or in combination with another word-recognition method, as a means of learning for the first time the word pictured or of reinforcing the original learning.

The boys and girls may have their own sets of picture-word cards, made on a smaller scale than those for class use. It is recommended that in the first grade, in most cases, the teacher do the writing on the cards, for the pupils should have a good model of handwriting when learning to read. To study the word the pupil looks on the side on which both picture and word are given. To test his recall he tries to pronounce the word or recall it without pronouncing it as he looks at the side without a picture. To check his response he can turn the card around to see what picture is given on the reverse side.

Before the pupils are about to read a selection, the teacher may discuss accompanying pictures with them. He may then direct comments and focus his own statements so that the names for the words pictured are the ones to which reference is made in the text. For example, if one of the new words of the story was *apple,* he might ask questions such as these about a picture given on the page: (a) What does Johnnie have in his hand? (b) What do you think he will do with the apple? If the teacher wishes to use a combination of both the picture-context clue and the verbal-context clue methods later on during the lesson, he may tell the pupils, without presenting the word *apple* beforehand, to read a given page. To check word recognition after the pupils have read the page, the

teacher may ask or say: (a) What did Johnnie give his mother? (b) Point to the word on this page that tells us what Johnnie gave his mother.

Sometimes, especially in the intermediate grades, the pupils may find a word that they do not have in their hearing or speaking vocabulary illustrated in a picture. For example, they may be unfamiliar with the word *glacier.* The teacher can then give the necessary background for understanding both the picture and the general meaning of the word as the boys and girls look at the picture. He may even wish to tell children that he believes they will be able to spot the word *glacier* when they run across it in the context. This procedure, of course, is a combination of the picture and verbal context methods.

The boys and girls or the teacher can make a chart of words that can be illustrated—words learned as the class study unit in the content subjects. For example, after studying about Switzerland, the class may use a chart with words such as *alphorn* and *glacier* illustrated.

Figure 9.13. A Picture-Word Booklet for "Circus Words."

The teacher and/or the pupils may make a picture word-card file, to which the pupil can refer when necessary, of words for geographical features such as *equator, isthmus, peninsula.*

2. Verbal context clues. If a reader is helped to determine what a word is by means of the phrase, sentence, or paragraph in which it occurs, he is learning it through a verbal context clue. This method should be used alone

only if the context gives a clue as to what the word may be. For instance, in the sentence "It is a warm day," the child cannot determine by context alone what the word *warm* is, for it could be *hot, cold, mild, rainy, sad,* or one of a large number of other words and still fit in with the rest of the sentence.

Even in beginning reading the method of verbal context clues can be combined with one or more other methods. For instance, if the pupils were given the sentence, "It is a warm day," providing they recognize every word other than *warm,* the teacher may ask what word fits into the sentence that he has written on the chalkboard twice, once with and once without the word *warm,* in this manner:

It is a _____ day.

It is a warm day.

Then after the pupils have named a number of words which the teacher may write in column form on the chalkboard, including the word *warm* (which, if necessary, he himself may name), he can say, while pointing at the second sentence illustrated, "The word that is used in this sentence is warm." If this procedure is followed, a combination of the verbal-content clue method and the sight method is used.

The danger in the use of context clues is that the method is undesirable when used as a guessing procedure. It is for this reason that it should be emphasized that when the pupil is expected to use the verbal context method alone there should be some indication in the phrase or sentence or paragraph as to what the word in question may be. It is also for this reason that it is imperative that not many words are unknown to the reader within a given context—possibly not more than one in any one sentence, especially in the case of beginning readers.

Following are other ways in which intelligent use of context clues, either with or without the use of other word-recognition methods, can be encouraged. Some are for pupils in the initial stage of reading instruction; others are for more advanced readers, while still others can be used advantageously on any level.

Having the pupils tell which of a series of given words fits into a blank for a missing word in a sentence such as:

Winter is my _____ season. (favor, favorite, favorable)

Asking the pupils to draw a line from the blank for a missing word in a sentence to one of a series of pictures indicating the word needed.

Giving pupils practice in choosing the appropriate pronunciation of a word that has two pronunciations by having them read sentences such as the following orally, after silent reading:

I like to *read* stories about the West.

I *read* this book last summer.

Asking pupils to fill the blank in a sentence with a word of which the meaning is built in, in the rest of the sentence, such as:

He was not friendly but very _____.

Use of Phonetic Analysis. The use of phonics discussed here does not describe the program proposed by leading educators who advocate a linguistic approach to beginning reading instruction. As indicated earlier, space in this book does not allow for detailed descriptions of the linguistic approach to reading nor any other of the newer programs. For information on those the reader is referred to the growing literature in the professional field. Suggestions for teachers following rather standard procedures in the use of phonics are given below.

There are those who believe that phonics instruction should be given during the initial stage of reading instruction without being preceded by the sight-word method or emphasis on context clues. Some recommend (1) that pupils follow a planned program according to which many of the sounds of letters or of combinations of letters associated with the proper written symbols are taught before they begin to read consecutive reading material and (2) that the pupils begin reading consecutive material only after they have at their command the phonic elements necessary to an independent or almost independent unlocking of the words they will meet in their reading. According to some of these same advocates of phonics as the means of teaching beginning reading, a sizable number of generalizations pertaining to phonics also need to be taught before regular reading instruction is begun or at least before it is far advanced.

There is also disagreement among teachers as to the subject matter to be taught as well as the teaching procedures to be followed. Before turning our attention to those two questions, let us note the following explanation of commonly used terms.

1. A *digraph* is made up of two letters producing one sound. There are two kinds of digraphs, *consonant digraphs,* such as *th* and *ck,* and vowel digraphs, such as *ei* and *eu.*

2. A *diphthong* represents two vowels that are blended almost to the extent that they produce one sound, such as *oy* and *eu.*

3. A *consonant* blend is a combination of two or three consonants, such as *gr* or *str,* that are blended in such a way that each letter in the combination continues to be heard.

Although, as indicated above, agreement is lacking among educators as to the elements of phonics to be taught in the elementary school, the following points, listed on page 120 of *The Teaching of Reading*,[7] are included as essentials in many programs of reading instruction: "(a) single consonants in monosyllabic and polysyllabic words, found in initial, final, and medial positions of words; (b) consonant blends, such as *st, gr, br, cr, str, pl*; (c) consonant digraphs, such as *ch, th, sh*; (d) single vowels ("short" and "long" vowels, vowels modified when preceding *r*, the *a* when preceding *l* or *w*, and other vowel sounds); (e) vowel digraphs, such as *ea, oa, ai, ay, ee, oo*; (f) diphthongs, such as *oy, oi, ou, ow*; and (g) silent letters."

Also quoted from *The Teaching of Reading* on page 120 is the following listing of generalizations rather commonly recommended for teaching in the elementary school.

A single vowel in a syllable is usually short unless it is the final letter in the syllable. (Example: *bat*).

If a final *e* in a word is preceded by a single consonant, a single vowel preceding the consonant is usually long and the *e* is silent. (Example: *rate*)

The sound of a single vowel preceding an *r* is usually modified by the *r*. (Example: *color*)

The sound of a single *a* preceding an *l* or a *w* is affected by the *l* or *w*. (Examples: *fall; claw*)

A final *y* in words of more than one syllable usually has the long *e* sound. (Example: *frequently*)

A *c* before *e, i,* or *y* has, as a rule, the soft sound. (Example: *city*)

A *g* before *e, i,* or *y* has, as a rule, the soft sound. (Example: *gem*)

Recommendations for teaching procedures involving the use of phonics are listed below.

1. The boys and girls name words that begin with a sound suggested by the teacher. The teacher records these words if the beginning sound in the words is also spelled the same way. It is suggested that at the beginning of the work on phonics practice be limited to those consonants that have the same sound or almost the same sound at all times, namely *b, h, j, l, m, p, t,* and *v*. Later a similar procedure can be used with consonant blends or consonant digraphs and with single consonants other that those that always have the same sound or approximately the same sound.

2. After the boys and girls have learned the hard and the soft sound of the letter *c*, the pupils may tell which of a list of words written on the chalkboard or on paper begin with the soft sound and which with the hard sound. Similarly emphasis can be placed on words beginning with the hard and soft sound of *g* or with the voiced and voiceless sound of *th*. The exercise may further be adapted for use for identification of various sounds of the same letters found in other than the initial positions of a word.

3. A commonly recommended type of exercise on phonetic sounds is the phonic wheel, by means of which the boys and girls can get practice in recognizing words

through emphasis on the beginning consonants, consonant blends, or consonant digraphs.

The wheel can be made in the form of two concentric circles fastened by a brass fastener through a hole punched in the center of the circles. As the pupil rotates the outer circle, he names the words that are formed by a combination of the beginning sound on the smaller wheel and the endings of words on the larger wheel. In the second part of the accompanying illustration is an example of what the writing on the larger circle might be, most of which is hidden from view at any given time.

4. The boys and girls may draw pictures of objects the names of which rhyme, such as *boy, toy*.

5. The pupils can be asked to sort, according to initial

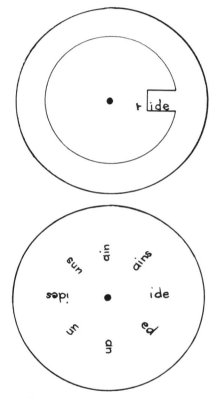

Figure 9.14. A Phonic Wheel.

Figure 9.15. A Variation from the Phonic Wheel; *At* Ending Used with Different Consonants.

7. Martha Dallmann, Roger Rouch, Lynette Chang, and John DeBoer, *The Teaching of Reading*, 4th ed. (New York: Holt, Rinehart and Winston, 1974), p. 120. Used with the permission of Holt, Rinehart and Winston.

consonants or according to rhyme, small pictures pasted on uniform-sized pieces of cardboard.

6. The boys and girls may supply the initial letter of words in a sentence in which the first letter or combination of letters of some words has been omitted.

The _oys and _irls were _aying _all.

7. A chart can be made showing that the silent *e* at the end of a word is important in the pronunciation of the word. Words to illustrate this fact are *rat, rate; rid, ride; hop, hope.*

8. The pupils can find pictures of objects the names of which begin with stated consonant sounds. For example, for the sound of *p* they could find pictures of a pie, a pail, and a party. Each pupil could make his own picture dictionary with these pictures.

9. The teacher, with or without the help of the children, can make a mobile in which each of the illustrations represents a word that begins with the same sound of the same beginning letter.

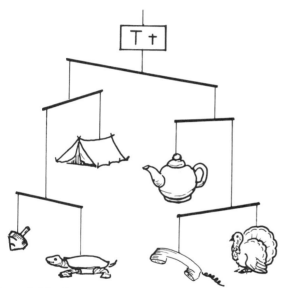

Figure 9.16. A Mobile Illustrating Words Beginning with the Same Sound.

Use of Structural Analysis. So far we have considered three methods of learning to recognize words—the sight method, the use of context clues, and phonetic analysis. Now let us discuss a fourth method—and in some respects the last, for the use of the dictionary is really practical application of the phonic method and of structural analysis—namely that of structural analysis.

When a word is recognized through structual analysis, it is learned through identification of prefixes, suffixes, root words, parts of compound words, syllables, contractions, or form (if the word is possessive, like *father's*). It will be noted that in structural analysis the recognition is through the structure of the word, not in terms of the sound elements of a word as in phonetic analysis.

There is one important caution concerning the use of structural analysis. Pupils should not be encouraged to find "little words in big," as some teachers request, unless the "little words" form the root of the word or unless the word is a compound word. If pupils look, in general, for "little words in big," undesirable habits may result which may cause trouble in word recognition. For example, children encouraged in this practice may well find *moth* or *he* or *her* in *mother* and *so* or *on* in *soon* and thus be misled in attempts at recognition of words.

The work in structural analysis should include: (1) knowledge of syllables, (2) recognition of prefixes and suffixes, (3) recognition of compound words, contractions, and possessive forms of nouns, and (4) knowledge of common rules for forming the plural of nouns.

Teachers' manuals accompanying reading textbook series frequently indicate quite fully the important learnings to be acquired in relation to structural analysis.

The following listing indicates some procedures that can be followed to help boys and girls learn to recognize a word through its structure.

1. The teacher may explain to the class why structural analysis is frequently a quicker method than phonetic analysis and thus have the pupils see reason for recognition of common prefixes and suffixes.

2. A list of common prefixes, suitable for a given group of boys and girls, may be written on the chalkboard as the pupils suggest words that contain these affixes. Discussion may follow on the common meaning(s) of the prefixes. For permanence, information may be recorded on a chart summarizing the important points about prefixes.

3. Older boys and girls may be helped to realize that certain letters and groups of letters sometimes used as suffixes are not always such, as in the case of *ing* in *thing* or *ed* in *fed.* They can be asked to indicate, in a list of words with endings that are often suffixes, in which words they are used as suffixes.

4. The pupils may indicate in which instances in a list of words similar to the following the *s, es,* or *ed* suffix forms a separate syllable and in which it does not. They can then pronounce the words.

drowned	copied	copies	horses
sounded	sounds	washes	bed

5. The boys and girls can be helped to learn the rules for forming singular and plural possessives of nouns and then make application of that knowledge to complete a form such as the following:

Noun	*Possessive Singular*	*Possessive Plural*
boy		
girl		
woman		
baby		

Or the pupils may tell which ones of a series of possessive forms of nouns, such as the following, are singular and which plural: *woman's, women's, babies', man's.*

6. The pupils can be given individual cards on each of which is written a contraction that is pronounced the same or almost the same as a possessive pronoun found on another card, such as: *its, it's; they're, their; there's, theirs.* As the teacher gives orally a sentence containing a word on a card, each pupil holds up the card he thinks is correct.

7. The pupils may be helped to draw up a list of words in which the last letter of a prefix is the same as the first letter of the root of the word, as in *illegal, illegible, irresponsible, irreverent,* or *immobile.*

8. To emphasize the point that care needs to be taken to know which words are hyphenated compound words, which are unhyphenated compound words, and which are not compound words, the pupils can be given guidance in the use of the dictionary to learn how to determine into which of these categories a word or group of words falls. Then, by inserting necessary hyphens or by separating two words in a group by a vertical line, they can complete an exercise with words written in the following manner: grandmother, sisterinlaw, schoolyear.

9. The pupils may find the compound words in a paragraph or story.

10. The boys and girls may be asked to choose the correct ending for words in sentences such as:

She (visited, visits) us yesterday.

11. The boys and girls can indicate the number of syllables in a list of words such as the following:

__unlikely __situation __geography.

Additional Considerations. Before leaving the topic of guiding growth in reading through development of power in word recognition, let us turn our attention to the following questions: (1) What is the role of the textbook in the program of word recognition? (2) How can workbooks contribute to the word-recognition program? (3) What use can be made of games in the program of word recognition? (4) How can picture dictionaries be used to develop skill in word recognition? (5) What is the interrelationship of the language arts in the program of developing skill in word recognition?

1. *What is the role of the textbook in the program of word recognition?* One of the advantages in the use of reading textbook series in the elementary school, especially in the first stages of learning to read, is that the reading vocabulary is controlled. Most publishers and authors take pains to produce basal reading series in which new words are introduced gradually and in which there is enough repetition of the new words that the average child, with proper presentation and later atten-

tion to the words, will be able to develop and maintain a reading vocabulary that includes the words learned through use of the textbooks.

The matter of selection of vocabulary as to the words to be included is also an important consideration of authors and publishers of reading textbooks for the primary grades. Frequently some of the well-established word lists are consulted.

Attention also deserves to be drawn to the excellent contribution made by many publishers of developmental reading textbooks series in the word recognition programs outlined in the teachers' guides accompanying the textbooks.

2. *How can workbooks contribute to the word-recognition program?* Many of the exercises in consumable books, either accompanying textbook series or published separate from any one single basal reading textbook program, are designed to help boys and girls not only learn the vocabulary presented but also develop skill in achieving greater independence in word recognition.

There was a time when there was justifiably much criticism of workbooks. In some instances they possibly did not provide much more than "busy work." However, the quality of many consumable books is now so fine that the teacher using a basal textbook series is well advised to carefully consider the advantages of a good workbook before he decides against using one. Some boys and girls seem to need more practice on words than that afforded in the regular reading books of a series. This practice can be provided through workbooks.

3. *What use can be made of games in the program of word recognition?*
Knowing the power of interest on learning and also recognizing the interest boys and girls have in games, teachers have long turned to reading games in the early stages of reading instruction. Much can be said in favor of wise use of desirable games, but probably just as much or more can be said against some games that are used and against the manner in which some of the desirable ones are misused. Since on page 35 "Games in the Language Arts" is discussed, suffice it here to say that the purpose of a game will determine to a large extent its appropriateness. The teacher should recognize that so-called reading games may serve one of two major purposes, that of helping boys and girls become better readers and that of giving them a recreational activity. When the main purpose is to use the games as a reading exercise, it should not be used unless, to a considerable extent, it is in harmony with the rules of effective practice. If, however, a game is used primarily for the fun that it can provide and only secondarily for its reading value, it may be quite legitimate to use it even if it has doubtful value as a reading exercise. When recreation is

the main objective, the teacher will probably want to use a game during a period for relaxation rather than during a time devoted primarily to learning to read. (The reader is referred to page 36 for a list of publications about games and a list of publishers and distributors of games.)

4. *How can picture dictionaries by used to develop skill in word recognition?* Picture dictionaries are probably of primary value in the reading program because of the help they afford boys and girls in remembering words learned by the sight method. They can also serve as a means of learning new words and as an introduction to later work with nonpicture dictionaries. A list of some commerically available picture dictionaries is given in chapter 13. (See page 342.)

5. *What is the interrelationship of the language arts in the program of developing skill in word recognition?* Regardless of whether a meaning approach or a code approach or a combination of the two is used for word recognition, there should be a close relationship in the teaching of word recognition between reading and the other language arts. In a code approach the relationship between reading and spelling should be highlighted. If the Initial Teaching Alphabet is used in beginning reading instruction, special attention should be paid to any difficulties with spelling that may arise during and following the period of transition in reading to the traditional alphabet—difficulties that arise with some boys and girls. Furthermore, the alleged superiority in creative writing of beginners in reading who use the Initial Teaching Alphabet should, to the extent that it may exist, be capitalized upon.

Another point that needs the careful attention of the teacher in any system of teaching reading or spelling is that, in a sense, the requirement in relation to the phoneme-grapheme correspondence is the opposite in reading and in spelling. In reading the child sees the written symbol and is required to decide on the sound represented by the grapheme. In spelling he knows the sound he wishes to represent and must decide upon the written symbol that represents that sound in a given word. A perplexity is that because of this situation some teachers will claim that a child should have considerable reading ability—possibly the equivalent of that achieved by the average first- or second-grade pupil by the end of the school year; others, for the same reason, chiefly those using a code approach, will argue that the reading and spelling of a word should be taught at the same time even to beginners. Whichever argument is favored, it must be conceded that reading and spelling should reinforce each other regardless of whether the two are taught almost simultaneously or whether teaching the beginner to read precedes teaching him to spell. The latter practice is prevalent in many schools with meaning-approach programs for initial reading instruction, when systematic

work in the teaching of spelling is usually postponed till the pupils have a "head start" in reading sometimes of a year or more.

COMPREHENSION SKILLS

The teaching of many of the comprehension skills should reinforce and be reinforced by the teaching in the areas of the other language arts. In helping boys and girls develop in ability to comprehend what they read and to make application of what they have comprehended, the teacher is advised to proceed according to the guidelines given below.

1. *Guidance in comprehension should not be limited to reading situations.* One way in which help can be given in nonreading situations is this: After a pupil has given a talk, the rest of the class can indicate what points mentioned by him brought out the thought the speaker wishes to present. If any irrelevant facts were mentioned, the classmates can designate them.

2. *Development of skill in comprehending what is being read should help the learner in nonreading activities.* For example, if in reading, emphasis is placed on predicting outcomes, the pupils should be assisted in making application of their learning as they discuss current events. Emphasis on the qualifications of an author in order to judge the probable validity of his claims should carry over as the pupils listen to reports on the radio or television.

Finding the Main Idea

One important comprehension skill, with carryover into all the language arts areas, is that of finding the main idea. Reading for the main idea or ideas often suffices when a child reads a story or an article in a magazine for children or when an adult does leisure-time reading or reads the newspaper. Some ways in which the teacher can help boys and girls develop skill in finding the main idea(s) are by:

1. Letting the boys and girls know the purpose for which they are to read a given selection as the teacher gives directions or makes comments such as "Read the next page to find out how Susie felt when her mother explained what had happened."

2. Having the boys and girls help determine how a certain passage should be read in order to accomplish a given purpose. For example, if the teacher asks the class to read a selection to find out whether Peter got his wish, the class may be asked whether they will need to read the story to get the general idea or to note details in order to be able to answer that question.

3. Asking the boys and girls to record on a card or in a booklet data on each book that they read outside of class. They may be asked to write a one-sentence summary of the book.

4. Helping the boys and girls learn what is meant by a topic sentence and providing them with practice in selecting the topic sentence of paragraphs containing them.

5. Asking the pupils to write a question that a paragraph as a whole answers.

6. Having some pupils draw a series of pictures, each of which summarizes the main action in a series of paragraphs and then having others match the pictures with the paragraphs.

7. Helping the boys and girls plan the topic or themes of each of several scenes thay may enact when dramatizing a story they have heard or read.

8. Asking the pupils to tell what a longer selection is about after they have read only the author's introduction to it, providing the introduction gives the general idea(s) of the selection.

Reading for Details

A pupil reads for details when he looks for data to support a point he plans to make, when he wants to make a costume for a play representative of a period of history, when he plans a report on current events, or when he reads a problem in arithmetic. In helping boys and girls read intelligently for details, the teacher should emphasize the fact that the points to be noted should be pertinent to the objective of the reader. Consequently pupils can advisedly be given help in formulating questions on details that would be of value to them as they read for functional purposes. Emphasis should also be placed on the relationship of details to the central ideas.

Activities such as the following may help the boys and girls in learning to read for significant details:

1. Finding the facts to support a generalization in one or more sources

2. Drawing pictures for a "movie" of a story showing the details brought out in the story

3. Reading to describe how a character of a story should act in a dramatization to be given by the pupils

4. Quoting details in selections read that support the opinions of the readers

5. Drawing pictures to illustrate a character in a story showing many details, and then asking classmates to identify the character or to suggest other details that could have been shown.

Organizing What Is Read

Several types of abilities in addition to that of finding the main ideas and selecting pertinent details are, at least in many instances, important to organizing. They include: (1) arranging events or ideas in a functional sequence, (2) relating details pertinent to the main idea, (3) outlining, (4) taking notes, and (5) summarizing. Suggestions for developing these abilities are given in the following list of activities in which boys and girls may engage.

1. Making a "movie" illustrating a process such as "From Tree to Tire" or "From Ore to Steel"

2. Listening to a story told or read by the teacher as he shows pictures of the scenes and arranges them in view of the children in the sequence of events in the story

3. Making a mural that tells the main events of a story with the needed details to explain these events

4. Arranging in proper sequence the paragraphs of a story which are presented in mixed-up order

5. Making an outline for a report on a personal experience that will be presented to the class

6. Noting the outline that the teacher has written on the chalkboard for a talk that he is giving

7. Completing an outline of which a skeleton such as the following is given:

Caring for Our Teeth

I. Why it is important
  A.
  B.
  C.
II. Steps in brushing the teeth
  A.
  B.
  C.
  D.

Figure 9.17. Part of a "Movie" on the story "Rapunzel" pages 193-201 of *More Roads to Travel* by Helen A. Robinson and others, published by Scott, Foresman and Company, 1965.

8. Participating in making an outline of activities that the class may consider for work on a unit. Part of such an outline for a unit on Alaska may be similar to the following.

I. Reading
   A. Our textbook
   B. Library books
   C. Newspapers and magazines
   D. Travel folders
II. Art work
   A. Making a "movie"
   B. Making an accordionlike picture folder
   C. Making a diorama or panorama
   D. Constructing an Eskimo village
III. Dramatization
   A. Putting on a skit about the discovery of gold
   B. Putting on a play showing life in Alaska

9. Learning the form of an outline by listening to explanation by the teacher

10. Having practice in rewriting an outline or part of an outline that violates the rules of good outlining, such as:

Wrong

I. What we need
   A. Scissors
   B. Thread
II. Pins and needles

11. Before being able to outline, drawing sketches for use as notes when planning a talk or a report on a story. An example of actions of which pupils could draw pictures for such an outline is as follows:

Little Red Riding Hood's mother giving her a basket
Talking with the wolf in the forest
Talking with "grandmother" upon arrival at Grandmother's home
Being saved by the woodcutters.

12. Learning when to use the exact words of a writer for note taking and how to indicate that they are the exact words

13. Dictating to the teacher notes to be used as memoranda for the class.

Critical Reading

The need of critical evaluation of what is read—that is, of examining what is read to ascertain its value—is, indeed, acute in this age of unprecedented use of means of mass communication for educational purposes, for entertainment, for dissemination of propaganda, and for advertising. Following are suggestions as to how the teacher can help boys and girls evaluate what they read as they (1) distinguish between fact and opinion, (2) differentiate between the real and the fanciful, (3) note qualifications of the author, (4) check the accuracy of generalizations, (5) note the up-to-dateness of informa-

tion, (6) decide whether propaganda is being disseminated, (7) discern the attitude of the writer, and (8) predict outcomes.

1. Have the pupils rewrite some statements expressing opinion in such a way that it is clear that they express an opinion. (Fact or opinion)

2. Give the boys and girls an opportunity to make up a fanciful story and have the class tell what their reasons are for considering it fanciful. (Real or fanciful)

3. Have the class compile a list of expressions such as "Once upon a time" that often indicate that a tale is fanciful. (Real or fanciful)

4. Discuss with the class the type of questions that a reader may like to have answered about an author of an article on current-day world affairs in order to know how much faith to have in the article. (Qualifications of the author)

5. Ask the pupils to write paragraphs giving the qualifications of an imaginary author of a selection dealing with a topic such as, for example, "Behind the Iron Curtain." They might write one paragraph that includes insufficient background of the author to write with authority on the topic and another that would seem to show adequate background. (Qualifications of the author)

6. Discuss with the class dangers of overgeneralizations by showing them generalizations that are too broad or that are unwarranted because of lack of data. (Accuracy of generalizations)

7. Ask the pupils to write paragraphs in which facts to support a given generalization such as the following are presented: (a) Air exerts pressure. (b) In the book *Rabbit Hill* the animals in some respects act like human beings. (Accuracy of generalizations)

8. Discuss with the class what types of information need to be kept up-to-date. (Up-to-dateness of information)

9. Discuss with the class the widespread use of propaganda techniques. (Propaganda techniques)

10. Ask the class to rewrite sentences that show an unsympathetic attitude so that they reveal one of sympathy, and also to rewrite sentences that indicate a sympathetic attitude so that they show one lacking in sympathy. (Attitude of the writer)

11. As you read the first part of a sentence, paragraph, or story have the pupils look at a picture that you are displaying, related to the possible ending of the selection and ask the boys and girls to give one or more expected endings. (Predicted outcomes)

Growth in Word Meaning

That there can be a close interrelationship between reading and the other languages in respect to development of a meaning vocabulary is readily recognizable. It is important that the teacher build on this relationship, for the improvement of ability not only in reading but also in the other language arts. A few examples of how he can assist the pupils in this respect are listed following. For a few suggestions as to how the dictionary can be used for increasing the pupil's understanding vocabulary the reader is referred to page 250. (See also "Vocabulary," page 131.)

1. Before the pupils read a given selection, the teacher can assist them with the meaning of some of the words by helping them study pictures given in the book, by providing them with other pictures that illustrate the meaning of one or more of the words, by having a pupil in some instances dramatize a word, or by asking a pupil to use a word in a sentence.

2. Experience can be extended and an emphasis put on vocabulary through field trips, motion pictures, filmstrips, slides, other pictures, talks by pupils and teacher, talks by visitors, book reviews, and wide reading.

3. The pupils may try to see how many different meanings they can think of or find for a word with multiple meanings such as *run, bridge,* or *tide.* Then they can use each in a written sentence. A booklet can be made in which some of the words with a large number of meanings are given in sentences illustrating each of the meanings the class has found. A page can be used for each word.

4. In connection with the study of a unit, the class or a committee can make an illustrated chart listing words learned in the study of that unit. For example, in a unit on the Western States terms such as these may be included: *rodeo, plateau, ore, placer mining.*

5. The pupils may have individual files in which they keep a card for each "new word" they want to remember. They can include on the card the spelling, the phonetic respelling or diacritical markings, the part of speech (if the pupils know the parts of speech), the plural form of a noun, one or more common meanings of the word, and a sentence illustrating each of the recorded meanings.

6. The boys and girls can construct materials to illustrate the meaning of a word such as *lock* (of a canal), *volcano, pueblo, sombrero, drawbridge,* or *portcullis.* Along with the exhibit of this illustrative work, the boys and girls could have brief accounts that they had written of the meaning of each word along with interesting facts about each.

7. At times when there is a built-in definition of a word in the context of which a word is used, the teacher may list it on the chalkboard, within or without the sentence, and tell the class he thinks that as the pupils read the selection they may be able to tell what the word means. After the reading, the check should be made.

8. The pupils may be provided with an exercise consisting of a series of sentences in each of which a word, with multiple meanings that may cause a problem in

comprehension, is underlined. Below each sentence may be written three or more dictionary definitions of the underlined word, of which the pupils are to choose the one that fits into the context of the sentence.

SKILLS IN LOCATING INFORMATION AND USING IT

In listening, speaking, reading, and writing—in all four facets of the language arts—the child can profit from skill in locating information. Furthermore, making use of all these facets can help the child in the development of ability in locating and making use of information. Use of all four of these is illustrated in the suggestions given in this part of the chapter.

Locating Information in Nonreference Materials

Boys and girls should acquire skill in locating materials in nonreference books by familiarity with the

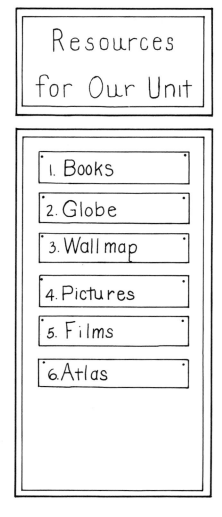

Figure 9.18. Chart of Usable Resources.

use of the title page, the copyright page, the introduction, the table of contents, and the index.

The Title Page. Fairly early in the elementary school the pupils can be referred to the title page in order to note where it is located and what is given on it. Their attention can be drawn to the title, the author, the publisher, and the address of the publisher. In the intermediate grades they may note the designation, if there is one, of the position(s) that the writer(s) hold(s). Information about the title page can often be acquired without much practice through procedures such as the following:

1. The pupils turn to the title page and through questions and comments by the teacher note where the title page is found in the book and what is given on it.

2. The teacher discusses with the class reasons for making information given on a title page accessible to the reader.

3. After the boys and girls have studied several of the parts of the book that help in locating material, they answer a series of questions, some of which deal with the title page. Questions such as these may be included: (a) Where is the title page found in a book? (b) Where do you look to find the name and address of the publisher?

The Copyright Page. Most boys and girls in the primary grades can make but little, if any, use of information given on the copyright page. However, in the last years of the elementary school, the date of copyright of a book can sometimes help the pupils decide upon the value of statements made in it. They can at that time also learn the need for having a system of copyrights and the basic rules concerning copyrights. They can be helped in acquiring these learnings through procedures such as the following.

1. The teacher explains what is meant by a copyright and asks the boys and girls for reasons for copyright laws.

2. The pupils answer questions such as the following: (a) Would a map in a geography book on Europe, with a copyright date of 1940, be a good reference for locating information about the present-day geographic divisions of all European countries? (b) If a book of old folk tales, copyrighted about twenty years ago, were available to you for reading, would it be advisable to look for a collection of the same stories with a more recent copyright date?

The Introduction. Boys and girls in the intermediate grades can be encouraged to read the introduction in books in which the introduction was intended for them and not specifically for the teacher.

The Table of Contents. Among the important learnings that the boys and girls should acquire concerning the table of contents are these: (1) the value of the table of contents, (2) the type of book in which a table of contents is likely to be found, (3) where in a book it is given, (4) the type of information given in a table of contents, and (5) the sequence in which entries are given. To gain these learnings and abilities and to make application of them, procedures such as the following can be used:

1. The boys and girls examine their textbooks to note which ones have a table of contents and how the divisions in each table of contents are arranged.

2. The boys and girls do an exercise in which they are timed as they locate information in a table of contents. Questions such as these may be asked: (a) What is the title of the first story in the last division or part of this book? (b) On what page does [a specified story] begin?

3. The pupils examine the table of contents of a book in order to determine whether or not it is likely to contain information helpful for a given unit of study.

4. The boys and girls make a table of contents for a booklet they are writing such as one on "Our Trips" or "Poems We [or I] Like."

The Index. During the course of the elementary school boys and girls should study the indexes of books in which there are only main entries as well as some in which subdivisions of the main entries are given.

Some of the learnings and/or abilities that boys and girls in the elementary school should acquire about the index of a book are: (1) the value of an index, (2) the type of book in which an index is likely to be found, (3) where in the book it is given, (4) the arrangement of entries in an index, (5) the sequence in which subentries, under main entries, are given (6) the meaning of the various parts of entries as they are found in books the boys and girls use or are likely to use, (7) how to decide under which key word to look to find information on a topic, and (8) how to make use of a reference indicated in the index.

Following are suggestions for developing some of the skills needed in making use of an index.

1. Finding words arranged alphabetically. Basic to skill in using an index is facility in finding words that have been arranged alphabetically. Some ways in which boys and girls can be helped in acquiring skill in finding words that are arranged alphabetically are as follows: (a) The teacher can prominently display the letters of the alphabet in alphabetical order, so that the pupils can read them from their seats. (b) The boys and girls can say the alphabet in concert. (c) The pupils can indicate which of a series of words, either beginning with the same letter or with different letters, are in alphabetical order by writing *yes* on a line if the series is in order and *no* if it is not, such as:

   walk, ring, sing———
   sun, sit, sat ——— .

(d) The pupils may arrange a series of words, such as the following, alphabetically by placing a *1* to the left of the first word in alphabetical order, a *2* to the left of the word that comes second, etc.:

　　____ baby
　　____ apple
　　____ chicken
　　____ fox.

2. Deciding upon key words. Skill in deciding upon key words is needed for finding information efficiently in an index as well as in reference books of many kinds. Here are a few suggestions for helping boys and girls develop skill in determining under what entry words they would be likely to find information they want. (a) If the boys and girls know the term *noun*, it should be explained to them that in indexes and reference books other than the dictionary the main entry words are nouns. (b) The boys and girls can do an exercise in which they indicate which word would be the most valuable entry word in answering a given question. An example of a possible item of such an exercise is: "Were the French or the British victorious at the Battle of Quebec? (French, British, battle, Quebec).

3. Developing other skills. Other skills important for efficient use of the index can be developed through procedures such as these:

After the boys and girls have learned how to use entries other than main entry words in an index, they can be given a timed exercise in which they are instructed to find answers by consulting the index in one of their textbooks. Questions such as these may be included: (a) On what page is a map showing the land included in the Northwest Territory? (b) On how many consecutive pages is information about the Gold Rush of 1849?

The boys and girls can make a chart giving significant information about the index of a book. One point that may be included is the fact that the index is found in the back of a book. Another is that main entries are arranged alphabetically.

The pupils can be given help in understanding the use of the various punctuation marks and abbreviations commonly used in an index.

The boys and girls can make an index for a class or individual notebook they have written or are writing.

Locating Information in the Dictionary

The following are among the learnings and skills that boys and girls should acquire in using a dictionary: (1) finding entry words, (2) making use of the pronunciation aids, (3) knowing how to select the meaning of a word that fits into a given context, (4) using the dictionary to determine the spelling of a word, and (5) being aware of the different types of information given in the front and back parts of the dictionaries they use.

A list of rather specific suggestions to help boys and girls in the use of the dictionary follows.

1. The boys and girls are helped to learn the value of guide words. The teacher may ask them to explain why they think guide words are called that.

2. The pupils indicate which of a series of words would be found on a page in a dictionary in which specified guide words are given. For example, in an exercise such as the following they can write *yes* on the line to the left of a word if they would expect to find it as an entry word between two words named as guide words for a given page and write *no* if it would not be found on that page:

Guide words: *droop, dry*

____drink　　　　　　　　____dull

____drowsy　　　　　　　____drop

3. To impress the boys and girls with the importance of finding the meaning of a word that best fits a sentence in which the word is used, the pupils can be given practice in supplying one of the meanings given in a dictionary as it is needed for each of a series of sentences in an exercise with items such as the following:

"A stitch in time saves nine" is one of the *saws* that we memorized. (*saw*: (a) a tool for cutting; (b) a wise saying.)

4. The pupils can be directed to cross out the incorrect word, after consulting the dictionary if necessary, in sentences such as the following:

The desks in the old schoolroom were (stationary, stationery).

What (advise, advice) did your father give you?

5. The boys and girls may write sentences using each of the different meanings of a word given in their dictionary.

6. The pupils may divide words into syllables and place the accent marks where they belong.

7. The pupils can pronounce a list of words, such as the following, in which the placement of the accent determines a difference in pronunciation and then use the words in sentences given orally: *pro gress', prog'ress; rec'ord, re cord'.*

Locating Information in Encyclopedias

There are several valuable sets of encyclopedias on the market designed, at least in part, for elementary school age boys and girls. They include: *Childcraft* (especially helpful for use with young boys and girls), *Compton's Pictured Encyclopedia, Junior Book of Authors* (with biographical or autobiographical data on famous writers of books for children), *Junior Britannica, Our Wonderful World,* and *The World Book Encyclopedia.* The boys and girls should learn the arrangement of material in

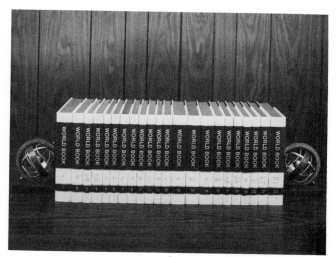

Courtesy of Field Enterprises
Educational Corp., Inc.

Figure 9.19. The Encyclopedia, an Aid to Learning.

each of these encyclopedias that they are using and get practice in finding information in them.

Locating Material in the Library

Boys and girls should become familiar with the arrangement of books in their room, school, and public libraries. In the lower grades they can learn where to look for the picture file, where the picture dictionaries are kept, where *Childcraft* or other reference for their use are shelved, and where nonreference books of interest to them are placed. In the intermediate grades many skills related to locating books in the library should be taught, involving the use of the card catalog and the location of books and magazines in the room or library. One helpful device may be to ask a committee to make a large diagram showing the placement of books in the room or school library or in the children's section of the public library.

WHEN WE GET A BOOK FROM OUR LIBRARY
1. We find the book that we want.
2. We write our name on the card.
3. We hand the book and the card to the librarian in the correct way.
4. We say, "Thank you," when the librarian returns the book to us.

Figure 9.20. A Chart as an Aid in Getting a Book from the Library in Which This Procedure is Followed.

CLASSROOM DIAGNOSIS

As is pointed out in chapter 3, when the teacher attempts to adapt instruction in the language arts to the needs of his group and to the individuals comprising it, he should make careful diagnosis of their abilities and skills pertaining to the language arts. The suggestions given below are to supplement those made under "Evaluation and Diagnosis" given in that chapter on pages 42 to 44. Since problems dealing especially with reading readiness are given on pages 223 to 236, they are not here discussed. Consequently the purpose of the paragraphs that follow is to suggest means of evaluating and diagnosing those phases of the program in the development of reading skills that are closely related to the other facets of the language arts. It should be noted that some of the suggestions regarding exercises for the development of reading skills given earlier in this chapter can also, with or without alteration, be used as means of evaluating and diagnosing the reading accomplishments of the boys and girls.

For a list of some of the standardized reading tests that are on the market, the reader is referred to chapter 13, "Resources for the Language Arts." (See page 346.) The teacher may wish to give one or more of these tests to supplement more informal methods of testing. He may also, through a study of some of the tests, receive suggestions for devising test items for his pupils.

Checking Comprehension

Some educators have been showing considerable interest in what is commonly referred to as the *cloze procedure*. Although cloze exercises are at times used for practice purposes in order to improve skill in some phases of comprehension or for determining the difficulty of a reading selection (its readability level), the chief use made of them thus far seems to be for testing purposes.

When the cloze technique is used, the pupil ordinarily is given one or more sentences or paragraphs in which some words, indicated by spaces left on the copy, have been deleted. He is to supply the missing words. In some instances every tenth word (or any nth word) is omitted from the passage(s), as in the sentence that follows:

Because the pilgrims arrived in America, at the present _____ of Plymouth, Massachusetts, in December, and because they had _____ little food with them, many died of cold or _____ during the first winter.

Sometimes cloze items are constructed with every noun or some other part of speech omitted. The above sentence would be written as follows if every preposition were deleted:

Because the pilgrims arrived _____ America, _____ the present site _____ Plymouth, Massachusetts, in _____ December, and because they had but little food _____ them, many died ____ cold or starvation ____ the first winter.

The assumption when using cloze items for testing comprehension is that the individual who can the better determine from a so-called "mutilated" passage what words have been deleted is the one with greater ability to comprehend what he is reading. It is further claimed by some individuals that this type of exercise can be superior for some testing purposes to a question-and-answer type since it allegedly tests the reader's ability to put together meanings while he is engaged in the act of reading better than the latter.

A few suggestions for checking comprehension through means other than the cloze technique are given following.

The Ability to Comprehend the Main Idea. The boys and girls may be instructed to supply the needed information by following directions such as these:

Put an *x* on the line to the left of the topic in the list below that best expresses the main idea of the following paragraph.

In your own words write a topic that tells what the following paragraph is about.

The Ability to Note Details. The pupils can be asked to comply with directions such as the following in order to give evidence of the extent of their ability to select details.

Below each of the following paragraphs is listed a series of sentences. Some of these sentences contain a detail given in the paragraph. Others give the main idea. Still others give points not mentioned in the paragraph. Put an *x* on the line to the left of each sentence that states a detail mentioned in that paragraph.

In your own words make a list of the details mentioned in each of the following paragraphs that supports the main idea of the paragraph. (The sentence that contains the main idea of the paragraph is mentioned.)

The Ability to Comprehend Directions. The boys and girls may indicate by drawing a diagram how to follow directions for getting from one place to another. They may be asked to arrange in proper sequence a series of statements giving directions to proceed from one place to another or statements giving steps for performing an activity such as making applesauce or a papier-mache figure.

The Ability to Organize. To test the pupils' ability to organize what they have read, the boys and girls may do the following:

Tell which one or more of a series of statements is irrelevant to the other statements in the series.

Arrange a series of points so that they are in suitable sequence.

Fill in the subtopics in an outline on a given selection for which the main topics (written in outline form) are given. The number of subtopics to be given under each main topic may be indicated by the number of figures or letters in the parts of an outline. A sample of part of such an outline is given here.

I.   Causes of the French and Indian War
     A.
     B.
II. Chief Battles of the War
     A.
     B.
     C.

A suggested variation of the work on outlining is to provide the pupil with the subtopics for an outline in scrambled order, and ask him to place them where they belong.

The Ability to Predict Outcomes. Here are ways in which the boys and girls can be tested on ability to predict outcomes.

After the pupils have read part of a selection or after the teacher has read it to them, they can be asked to tell which of several recorded statements gives the probable ending.

After pupils have read part of a story or after the teacher has read it to them, they can write a sentence or more summarizing a possible ending.

The Ability to Evaluate What Is Read. The pupils can be tested on their ability to evaluate what they read by:

Telling which of a group of several persons whose qualifications are enumerated are best qualified to make a given statement that might be considered controversial or questionable in some other way

Deciding whether given statements are statements of fact or opinion

Rewriting statements of opinion so that they clearly reveal to what extent, if at all, they are based on fact and to what extent they represent someone's opinion.

Checking Skill in Locating Information

These are some of the evaluative procedures that can be used to check skill in locating information.

1. The boys and girls can answer questions on various parts of a book such as: (a) In what part of a book is the index found? (b) In what part of a book—the table of contents or the index—are the main entries arranged in alphabetical order?

2. The boys and girls can be timed as they find the beginning page of an entry in the table of contents or as

they find the first page on which reference to an entry in the index is given.

3. The boys and girls can tell which word of a series would be the most likely one under which, in an index or encyclopedia, information to answer a given question would be found.

4. The pupils can be tested on ability to arrange letters and later words in alphabetical order. At first the arrangement of words in alphabetical order might deal only with lists of words in which the first letters are different. Later such lists could include words in which first letters of the words are alike and still later they could also include words in which the first and second, and still later, even subsequent letters are alike. The pupils can rewrite the letters or words in alphabetical order or they can number the words or letters in the right order.

5. The boys and girls can be checked on ability to select the meaning given for a word in a dictionary that fits into the context of the sentence in which the word is used.

FOR STUDY AND DISCUSSION

1. Study reading readiness materials published by commercial companies and evaluate them in terms of the contribution made to the total language arts program.

2. Examine several reading readiness tests that are available to you, as you try to determine which factors relating to readiness for reading each tests. Evaluate them, also, in terms of the quality of the appraisal of these factors that the tests make possible.

3. In what ways, in addition to those suggested under "Determining Readiness for Reading," (see pages 225 to 229) could readiness for reading be appraised?

4. If you have access to instruments for testing vision or hearing, in terms of readiness for reading, become familiar with some of them, noting their purpose, means of administration, and strengths and/or shortcomings. Reference is made here to instruments such as *The Keystone Visual Survey Telebinocular* and *The Spache Binocular Vision Test* (both available through the Keystone View Division/Mast Development Company), the Snellen chart, and audiometers.

5. Write a teaching plan on the construction and use of an experience chart that is suggestive of procedure that could be followed during the early stages of teaching boys and girls to read.

6. Examine several of the newer basal reading series. What provisions are made in the manuals accompanying them, or in the teachers' editions, as to how to interrelate the various language arts when teaching reading?

7. What arguments can you give for or against teaching reading in a separate period of the school day.

REFERENCES

Dallmann, Martha; Rouch, Roger L.; Chang, Lynette Y.C.; and De Boer, John J. *The Teaching of Reading,* 4th. ed. New York: Holt, Rinehart and Winston, 1974.

Durkin, Dolores. *Teaching Them to Read.* Boston: Allyn and Bacon, Inc., 1970.

Hall, Mary Anne. *Teaching Reading as a Language Experience.* Columbus, Ohio: Charles E. Merrill Publishing Company, 1970.

Harris, Albert J., and Sipay, Edward R., eds. *Readings on Reading Instruction,* 2nd ed. New York: David McKay Company, 1972.

Herrick, Virgil E., and Nerbovig, Marcella. *Using Experience Charts with Children.* Columbus, Ohio: Charles E. Merrill Publishing Company, 1964.

Karlin, Robert. *Teaching Elementary Reading.* New York: Harcourt Brace Jovanovich, 1971.

Lee, Dorris M., and Allen, R.V. *Learning to Read through Experiences.* New York: Appleton-Century-Crofts, 1963.

Spache, Evelyn B. *Reading Activities for Child Involvement.* Boston: Allyn and Bacon, Inc., 1972.

Spache, George D., and Spache, Evelyn B. *Reading in the Elementary School.* Boston: Allyn and Bacon, Inc., 1973.

Wilson, Robert M., and Hall, Mary Anne. *Programmed Word Attack for Teachers,* 2nd ed. Columbus, Ohio: Charles E. Merrill Publishing Company, 1974.

Zintz, Miles V. *The Reading Process: The Teacher and the Learner*, 2nd ed. Dubuque, Iowa: Wm. C. Brown Company Publishers, 1975.

10

Guiding Growth in Independent Reading

With the great emphasis again being placed on the development of the skills of reading, it is important that we not neglect giving due guidance to boys and girls in nurturing their independent reading. Happily, increased attention to the skill development program does not, in any way, necessitate lack of concern with the independent reading or literature program.

VALUES OF INDEPENDENT READING

Because of the large variety of materials—poetry, fiction, history, science, for example—that are read independently, many different values can be derived from a strong program of independent reading.

Independent Reading and the Needs of Children

May Hill Arbuthnot and Zena Sutherland classify well the needs of children in their book *Children and Books* [1] in this manner: (1) the need for physical well-being; (2) the need to love and to be loved; (3) the need to

belong; (4) the need to achieve; (5) the need for change; (6) the need to know; and (7) the need for beauty and order.

While, to be sure, books can rarely if ever make up satisfactorily for the neglect a child may have experienced in his environment at home or at school for satisfying his basic needs, books can, in ways suggested here, do much toward supplementing favorable or counteracting undesirable features in the surroundings.

1. *"The need for physical well-being."* If a child is fortunate in the extent to which he feels secure materially, he may be grateful as he reads of how many others need to strive for that which has been given to him without effort or special worth on his part. On the other hand, if he is lacking in a normal amount of material security, there

1. From *Children and Books,* Fourth edition by May Hill Arbuthnot and Zena Sutherland. Copyright © 1947, 1957, 1964, 1972 by Scott, Foresman and Company. Reprinted by permission of the publisher. (Titles on pages 6-15)

are books that may show him that there are other types of security that are more significant than the physical.

2. *"The need to love and to be loved."* Through the right books the child lacking a fair share of love can sometimes vicariously experience a taste of the security resulting from being loved. The child who is loved may develop appreciation of the love bestowed upon him through recognition of the power of love illustrated in books he reads. Both he and his less fortunate classmate who has seemingly been deprived—only temporarily, it is hoped—even of the right to be loving can gain from some books incentive for developing that trait. All, the favored and the neglected, can learn through folklore and other classics of the past as well as through many books of the present era that the power of love will help make life worthwhile. The significance of sound books on religion for boys and girls should be noted in terms of the effect they can have on a child's feeling and knowledge of being loved.

There are, of course, many books for children that deal with the topic of love as demonstrated by that of one person for another, such as *Little Women, Miracles on Maple Hill,* and *The Good Master.* Nor should the fact be overlooked that some of the books about animals, while showing love on a much lower plane, such as *Black Beauty* and *Bambi,* can help boys and girls to fill, though to a very limited extent, the need to love.

3. *"The need to belong."* Many books for children that portray the need for belonging, of being accepted, can give boys and girls a greater appreciation of the security that they may possess, a more profound understanding of the fact that some great individuals have had to struggle to be accepted, and a deeper realization of the importance of their own willingness to accept others. Books dealing with religion may help boys and girls in acceptance of the belongingness, as spiritual beings, that can be theirs.

4. *"The need to achieve."* As the child with unusual problems reads of fictitious or real people who have achieved in spite of difficulties, the lives of such individuals can help the child realize that achievement is by no means confined to those living under favorable conditions.

5. *"The need for change."* Through reading for the pleasure of reading, without any objective akin to work, the child can satisfy in part the "need for change." Such reading can provide for wholesome leisure-time activities.

6. *"The need to know."* With the rapidly expanding field of information accessible in the world, the importance, to a feeling of intellectual security, of learning more and more of the vast store of knowledge has probably greatly increased. To be sure, there are many ways, other than through reading, by which boys and girls can progress towards such security. Radio and television, for example, are powerful media for the dissemination of information. Yet the book has not been replaced by technological media. The child can also, through books, gain insights deeper than those of the intellect only, as a consequence of improved understanding.

7. *"The need for beauty and order."* Through reading about "the good, the beautiful, the right," (in the words of Goethe) and seeing illustrations of beauty, the child can be assisted in having his need for aesthetic satisfaction fulfilled. Better yet, he can derive from reading the ability to differentiate between the uplifting and the cheap, as well as the discrimination to recognize the beautiful around him even when ugliness and disorder sometimes almost hide the truth of beauty.

Other Values of Independent Reading

Other values, in addition to those specifically named in preceding paragraphs, that can be achieved through independent reading are listed here.

1. Independent reading can help boys and girls improve in reading skills. However, a program of reading instruction that is based almost exclusively on the development of the skills of reading can be a very deadly program—one that defeats its very purpose.

2. Through independent reading pupils can grow in language skills other than reading as, for example, in improvement of the listening and speaking vocabulary.

3. Independent reading can be instrumental in helping children establish moral and spiritual values that will endure. Care must, of course, be taken that the materials are such that they will have an uplifting effect upon the reader.

Courtesy of the Dallas Independent School District, Dallas, Texas.

Figure 10.1. Reading for Enjoyment.

4. Independent reading can stimulate children to develop hobbies that will add interest to their lives and those of others.

"THE RIGHT BOOK FOR THE RIGHT CHILD"

To give effective guidance in the independent reading program of a child the teacher needs to introduce him to worthwhile books on his reading level that will be of interest to him.

Courtesy of the Alameda County Schools, California.

Figure 10.2. "The Right Book for the Right Child."

Providing Books on the Child's Reading Level

The reading level of a pupil will determine to a considerable extent what books of quality should be recommended to him. To be sure, to read some books easier than the individual's ability would indicate is not objectionable. Most, if not all, adults occasionally enjoy reading books that are written primarily for persons with less skill in reading than they possess. Boys and girls, too, can, without harm and often with profit, read some books that are very easy for them. However, there is danger that they will not achieve the values they could attain through independent reading if they read such books most of the time. The teacher should guard against that danger.

When the teacher recommends books that are written above the reading level of the child, he runs the risk of lessening the child's desire to read. The same harmful effect may be produced when "on their own" boys or girls select books that are too difficult for them. In fact, a child who starts again and again to read a book that he cannot read without undue problems, may decide that he is not interested in reading and may then do only the reading required of him.

To obtain a measure of a child's reading ability, the teacher can give him one or more standardized reading tests. (See "Reading Tests" on page 346.) Or he can get a rough index of it by constructing a silent reading test based on a selection in a reading textbook designed for the pupil's grade level. If that book proves too difficult, he can test him on a book below his grade level; if it is too easy, he can construct the test on a book above his grade level. Asking the child to read orally a few paragraphs from a reading textbook can also be revealing, especially, in some instances, if he is also asked questions to check

Courtesy of the Dallas Independent School District, Dallas, Texas.

Figure 10.3. Reading for Enjoyment.

his comprehension. Use of book lists organized on grade levels can be used with greater confidence when the approximate level of a child's reading skill is known.

Another index of reading ability, though not always trustworthy, is gained by noting the difficulty of books the child reads when he selects a book without guidance. However, the teacher should remember that the book may be below the child's level, not on it. He should also be aware of the fact that experiments have shown what casual observation, too, has made evident, namely that a pupil can effectively read more difficult materials in areas in which he is greatly interested than in those in which he lacks a propelling motive.

Determining Children's Interests

The teacher can get help in familiarizing himself with reading interests of boys and girls by studying reports on that topic. The reader is referred to a fairly recent report of that type made by Helen Huus,[2] of which the following is an excerpt:

Kindergarten and Grade One. Children of five and six like "pretend" stories, where animals talk and where there is rhythm to the language and where humor consists of exaggeration. Realistic stories of home, little children like themselves, play and daily activities are of interest, and "here and now" stories of cars, trucks, ships (including space ones), and trains are enjoyed.

Second and Third Grades. While seven-year-olds like magic and fairies, the stories have more plot than those that interest the younger children. Eights, too, like complex fairy stories, especially if there is romance as an added attraction. Second graders are interested in all kinds of transportation, in the world and people, while third graders begin to extend their interests and obtain factual information about far away places and events of long ago, though exactly *how* far away or *how* long ago is not yet of great concern.

Fourth Grade. Fourth grade is a transition in many respects: in the amount of textbook reading required of the pupil, in the physical development of the pupil as he approaches preadolescence, and in the increasing separation of the interests of boys and girls.

Boys show interest in action and aggressiveness, in the affairs of the world, and therefore prefer adventure, science, hero stories, biography, history, and tall tales, while girls still cling to the fanciful stories, myths, stories of chivalry and romance, home life, biography, and accounts of everyday life, though not always in that order. Boys will not choose a book ordinarily, that has the name of a girl in the title, but girls will choose a boy's book.

Grades Five and Six. Children in grades five and six continue the interests expressed, with hero worship being accentuated among the boys and romance among the girls. Science and mechanics become more interesting to boys, and girls enjoy lively adventure stories, though they prefer their excitement to be less violent than do boys; hence the popularity of Nancy Drew. Both boys and girls react unfavorably to much description and didacticism. Girls are likely to do more reading than boys, and both of them will read only a limited amount in magazines and newspapers.

Humorous stories and animal stories are liked at any age; in fact, adults, too, still enjoy reading such tales.

For additional reference to children's interests in reading, the reader may wish to consult professional books such as *Children and Books,* fourth edition, by May Hill Arbuthnot and Zena Sutherland, and *Children's Literature in the Elementary School,* second edition, by Charlotte S. Huck and Doris Young Kuhn, as well as books on the teaching of reading and of the other language arts. For information on magazine articles dealing with interests of children, the reader is referred to *The Reader's Guide to Periodical Literature* and *The Education Index.*

Another way in which the teacher can obtain insight into a given child's interests is by having him respond to questions such as: "What do you like to do when you can do what you please?" or "What kinds of stories do you like best?" Casual discussions, without a definite set of questions as in an interview, too, often can be revealing. The teacher also has many opportunities to discover what is of interest to the child as he observes the child throughout the school day. He can note points such as these: (a) in what area or areas of the curriculum the child is greatly interested; (b) what the child does during his "free time"; and (c) on what he reports during "sharing time." Some teachers may find it advisable to keep a written record of such observations rather than exclusively trust their memory.

GUIDELINES FOR DEVELOPMENT OF GROWTH IN INDEPENDENT READING

Several guidelines according to which the teacher should plan the independent reading program have been indicated in the preceding paragraphs. A few more are suggested here.

1. *The boys and girls should be introduced to a variety of books.* While undoubtedly they should not be discouraged from doing extensive reading in an area of major appeal to them, such concentration when done at the expense of most other reading can be narrowing. Consequently the teacher should consciously try to arouse interest in each child in various kinds of books providing, of course, the child is not already reading in a variety of areas. He might discuss the importance of broad reading with the group. A class of older boys and girls might draw up a list of types of books some of them enjoy reading, such as stories about history, frontier days, animals, or geography. Then it might be decided that each pupil will read at least one or two books of each type during the school year and as many more of any kind as he chooses to read. The pupils could be given a form on which they could record under the various classifications the title of each book as they have completed it.

2. *The teacher should encourage boys and girls to read only books of quality.* With the many excellent

---

2. Helen Huus, "Reading Interests," in *Readings on Reading Instruction,* 2nd ed., eds. Albert J. Harris and Edward R. Sipay (David McKay Company, 1972), pp. 311-17. Used with the permission of the author, Helen Huus, and Coleman Morrison, editor of *Problem Areas in Reading, Some Observations and Recommendations,* as part of the Rhode Island Reading Conference Proceedings, Providence, R.I., published by Oxford University Press, 1965, in which the article first appeared.

books for children on the market, there is no excuse for the teacher to allow boys and girls to read trash while in school. Furthermore, he can encourage good reading by having the pupils report only on books that are worthwhile. Fairly "flooding" the room or school library with only good books is another means of stimulating worthwhile reading. A discussion of points that make books worthwhile can serve a useful purpose.

3. *The teacher should use a variety of means of interesting the boys and girls in books.* For further suggestions the reader is referred to the topic "Techniques for Interesting Children in Reading" discussed later in this chapter. (See page 260.)

A PLANNED LITERATURE PROGRAM

Of late, considerable emphasis has been placed on a planned literature program in the elementary school. To be sure, the idea is not a new one. Even a cursory examination of the *McGuffey Readers* will convince one of the fact that they had a decided "literary bent." Reading series such as *Stepping Stones to Literature,* used even in the early decades of the twentieth century, and the Atlantic Readers, of still a later publication date, give evidence of the continuing interest of publishers in providing boys and girls with their literary heritage. In fact, many reading textbooks, in the past and at the present time, devote a considerable number of pages to materials of literary intent—some of proven worth, others of questionable value as literature. Furthermore, quite a number of publishers have marketed literary series as supplements or complements to their basic program of skill development in reading. Others publish series of literature books not designed primarily as supplement to any one series of basal readers, with the intent that they be read along with whatever basal reader is being used or without any basal reader.

The literature program currently advocated by many educators goes beyond those to which reference is made in the preceding paragraph. It does not rely on any one set of readers, either basal or supplementary, though in the program such materials may also be used. Nor is it considered a substitute for the voluntary reading, which should be an integral part of the planned program. The importance of the independent reading program should be increased when provided in the setting of a planned literature curriculum.

The question may well be asked: "Why is a literature program that goes beyond the voluntary independent reading program needed?" In responding to that inquiry one might refer to the teaching of science in the elementary school. Though boys and girls can learn much in that area through incidental means—as they read books, listen to others speak, watch television, make observa-

tions, and experiment—there are relatively few educators, if any, who would argue that such incidental learnings constitute the entirety of exposure that boys and girls should have in that field. The gaps in the acquisition of knowledge would be recognized as one shortcoming of such a procedure. Furthermore, when relying only on incidental learnings, it would be likely that many concepts of significance might not be acquired by boys and girls without systematic instruction. Similarly, as in the area of science, any carefully planned and well-executed literature program should be a means of providing balance, as it purports to introduce the boys and girls to the various types of good literature, to help them in the understanding of it, and to interest them in voluntary reading of a variety of types.

Patterns for Literature Programs

Various patterns for a planned literature program have been worked out. One such, reported in an article entitled "Literature and Creativity—A Systems Approach," is described by the editorial staff of D.O.K. Publishers.[3] Another curriculum design for a literature program, insofar as it deals with human relations, is the well-known and highly regarded one which forms the basis for the book *Reading Ladders for Human Relations,* edited by Virginia M. Reid for the American Council on Education. In the fifth edition, published in 1972, the grouping is around these "ladders":

Ladder 1. Creating a Positive Self-Image
Ladder 2. Living with Others
Ladder 3. Appreciating Different Cultures
Ladder 4. Coping with Change.

A rather detailed curriculum design for a literature program, designed by Charlotte Huck and Doris Kuhn Young, is entitled "A Taxonomy of Literary Understandings and Skills." Of this taxonomy only the main headings and the first-order subdivisions are given below.

Understands Types of Literature
  Differentiates fiction from nonfiction
  Differentiates prose from poetry
  Recognizes folk tale
  Recognizes fable
  Recognizes myth
  Recognizes realistic fiction
  Identifies historical fiction
  Identifies fantasy

Understands Components of Fiction
  Recognizes structure of plot
  Recognizes climax of story
  Recognizes character delineation and development

3. "Literature and Creativity—A Systems Approach," *Elementary English* 49 (May 1972): 676-82.

Recognizes theme of story
Recognizes setting—both time and place
Describes author's style or use of words
Recognizes point of view

Understands Components of Poetry
Interprets meaning
Looks for imagery in poem
Can describe diction (poet's choice of words)
Recognizes sound effects of poetry
Identifies various forms of poetry

Evaluates Literature
Understands authors write to achieve purpose
Evaluates setting
Evaluates plot
Evaluates characterization
Evaluates style of writing
Evaluates point of view
Evaluates theme

Applies Knowledge of Literary Criticism
Uses criteria for type of literature
Asks appropriate questions to analyze writing technique
Sees relationships among literary selections
Recognizes similarities and differences in works of one author or illustrator
Asks appropriate questions for understanding large meanings
Recognizes that literature give insight into human thought and action
Applies insights gained through literature to his own life
Continues to seek new understandings. [4]

Planning a Literature Program

A school that is planning to develop a literature program should recognize the fact that to be most successful it should be worked out on a schoolwide or systemwide basis. Other suggestions for undertaking the organization of a literature curriculum include the following:

1. *Before definite work on planning the program is begun, steps should be taken to interest the teachers in it.* Unless most of the teachers will consider it worthwhile to have such a program, the results are almost foredoomed to failure. Teachers' interests may be aroused through such means as: (a) An outside speaker reports on the success of such a program. (b) A teacher on the staff who has become enthusiastic about a literature program, through observation in another school, reading on the topic, or attending a workshop or summer school, can report on the topic to his peers. (c) An inventory can be made of the status of the reading done by boys and girls in the school.

2. *Ground rules for work on the planning of the program should be laid early.* Such rules might include: (a) Every teacher will have an opportunity to participate in the planning of the program. Special teachers, such as those in music, art, and physical education, should be helped to see that they can make a contribution in planning the program. (b) There should be a division of

labor. Such allocation of responsibilities can probably best be made through organization into committees that report their recommendations back to the group with the possibility of eliciting suggestions for improvement on the plans presented. (c) Provisions should be made to familiarize teachers with the philosophy and structure of good literature programs. An orientation program will be a "must" in many school situations.

3. *Provisions should be made for a trial period in which a proposed program is launched.* During this period only some of the teachers—those most interested in serving in that phase of the program—may try out the program with their pupils. The purpose of such a trial period would be primarily to see "how it works" and to form a basis for further planning or replanning of the proposed curriculum. An alternative to having only a few teachers engage in the trial phase is to have all teachers work on only one segment of the total proposed plan—such as materials suggested by Ladder 3, earlier quoted, as proposed in *Reading Ladders for Human Relations,* which deals with "Appreciating Different Cultures."

4. *Plans should be drawn up during the planning period for the evaluation of the proposed program and "machinery" set up for possible future alteration of the program.* One such opportunity for evaluation is provided for by the trial period recommended in item three above. Even later, after the entire program has been put into effect, systematic means of evaluating and, if necessary, changing the program should be made. One point that should enter specifically into all evaluation of literature programs is the extent to which boys and girls voluntarily read quality literature.

TECHNIQUES FOR INTERESTING CHILDREN IN BOOKS

One of the best ways in which boys and girls can be interested in reading is through the type of planned literature program described in the preceding section. It can furnish the background for much voluntary reading of worthwhile literature; in fact, if it fails to produce this result the planned program falls far short of accomplishing its purpose.

General procedures for interesting the child in reading are scattered throughout preceding pages. Additional suggestions are given below.

1. *Storytelling by the teacher or pupils.* Under the heading "Development in Ability to Tell Stories" (see page 61 of chapter 4, "Guiding Growth in Oral Communication") points to note in storytelling are given.

4. Charlotte S. Huck and Doris Young Kuhn, *Children's Literature in the Elementary School,* 2nd ed. (New York: Holt, Rinehart and Winston, Inc., 1968), pp. 688-91. Used by permission of Holt, Rinehart and Winston.

The power of storytelling to arouse the children's interest in further reading of stories similar to those told them is considerable. Obviously, for storytelling to be effective as a medium for increasing the listener's desire to do worthwhile reading, the storytelling must be done according to certain criteria, such as those suggested in the reference given above.

2. *Oral reading by the teacher.* To introduce boys and girls to some worthwhile and highly interesting books the teacher may decide to read an entire book to the class, reading maybe for fifteen or twenty minutes daily. This type of reading used to be popular in schools of long ago as the first "period" in the school day, frequently, at the time, referred to as "opening exercises." Such reading could give a good start to the school day. However, the procedure can be followed just as effectively as a "closing exercise," in order to end the day with a pleasing activity that can be relaxing and at the same time, in many cases, inspiring.

Sometimes instead of reading the entire book to the class, the teacher may wish to read only the first chapter or two. If the book is highly interesting, he may find that many of the boys and girls would like to finish reading the book by themselves. In fact, a schedule may need to be worked as to who should get the book first, who next, and so on.

3. *Reports on books by members of the class.* If suggestions such as those given under "Book Reports" in chapter 4 (see page 60) and under the topic with the same name in chapter 5 (see page 104) are followed, both oral and written reports by boys and girls can be a means of interesting others in books.

4. *Commercially available visual aids.* Many visual aids on the market, such as motion pictures, filmstrips, tapes, and cassettes, can serve as incentive for reading. Their effectiveness depends to a considerable extent on how they are used. The reader is referred to the topic "Audiovisual Aids" in chapter 13, "Resources for the Language Arts." (See page 347.)

5. *Encouragement of use of the facilities of the public library.* To broaden the possible choice of reading material available to boys and girls and to stimulate them to use library resources during vacation periods the teacher may sponsor a trip to the public library. If the school library is not open during the summer months, to introduce the boys and girls to the resources of the public library may be an especially desirable practice. In cooperation with the librarian a program for summer reading could also be worked out.

6. *Dramatization of stories or parts of stories.* One of the most effective ways of enlivening a book report is to make use of dramatization. With the aid of one or more classmates, the reviewer may incorporate scenes from the book in his report as examples of what the book is about. The famous whitewashing-of-the-fence scene from *The*

Adventures of Tom Sawyer is an illustration of one that could well be presented.

7. *Other means of interesting boys and girls in books.* For suggestions of additional means of interesting boys and girls in books the reader is referred to the many other ideas discussed in this chapter, especially in the preceding section and in the two that follow, namely, "Games to Interest Children in Reading," and "Book Week." Many ideas are also presented under the topic "Independent Reading in Content Areas."

GAMES TO INTEREST CHILDREN IN READING

Sometimes it is difficult to distinguish between games and exercises that are not games. Some exercises suggested in this book may be classified by some as games. Others can be changed into games with only slight alteration. For a brief discussion on using educational games the reader is referred to "Games in the Language Arts." (See page 35.)

Additional suggestions for interesting boys and girls in independent reading are given below.

1. As a pupil describes a character from a story, the rest of the class guesses who is being described.

2. The pupils guess the title of stories suggested by headlines for newspapers such as: (a) Tom Boy Marooned on Rafters in Old Time Kitchen (Kate in Kate Seredy's *The Good Master*) and (b) Pig Rescued by a Spider (Wilbur in E.B. White's *Charlotte's Web*).

3. The boys and girls guess titles of stories represented by articles on a display table such as a paper doll representing a girl next to a thimble (for *Thimble Summer* by Elizabeth Enright) or a troll and a billy-goat, both made of clay (for "The Three Billy-Goats Gruff").

4. The pupils guess the titles of books that are presented in rebus form, such as these three illustrated in figure 10.4: *Crow Boy, The Door in the Wall,* and *The Witch of Blackbird Pond.*

5. The pupils make up and use in a contest rebuses representing titles of books. An example, in addition to those illustrated in figure 10.4 is: (a) a picture of a jungle and outline of a book (for *Jungle Book* by Rudyard Kipling).

6. The children name the designated characters of a story of which the title is given in answer to questions such as: (a) Who in *Little Women* married Laurie? (b) Who in *Charlotte's Web* saved Wilbur?

7. One or more pupils pantomime a scene from a story and the other pupils guess the title. For example, a pupil may stand "on all fours" and blow with all his might as he represents the wolf in "The Three Little Pigs."

8. The pupils match illustrations of book characters with phrases or sentences referring to the illustrations.

Figure 10.4. A Rebus (*Crow Boy, The Door in the Wall, The Witch of Blackbird Pond*).

For example, a picture of a toy rabbit made of cloth could be matched with these sentences: "The nursery magic had happened to him, and he was a toy no longer. He was real" from page 18 of *The Velveteen Rabbit* by Margery Bianco, published by Doubleday and Company.

9. A contest is held in solving crossword puzzles on books, which some of the pupils have constructed.

BOOK WEEK

Book Week, which comes during the first part of November, is an especially good time for concerted effort to help boys and girls become more interested in independent reading of worthwhile materials. It is sponsored by the Children's Book Council, which is composed of the children's book editors from a large number of the leading companies publishing children's books.

Guidelines

The teacher who wishes to help his pupils obtain the maximum benefits from Book Week should observe guidelines such as the following.

1. *Book Week should be used primarily for teaching purposes.* In schools where the administrative office personnel commands that each room do something to observe Book Week there is danger that some teachers may be tempted to put on a "show" as their means of following the injunction. The real purpose of Book Week can be defeated by emphasis on "putting on a program."

2. *Book Week should emphasize the beginning of a "Book Year."* The objective should be to interest the boys and girls in good reading the year round.

3. *Through educational Book Week activities parents can be made partners in the challenge of guiding the child in growth in independent reading.* Parents can be invited to programs that are planned in harmony with the true objective of Book Week. During Book Week special provisions, possibly through the Parent Teacher Association (PTA), can be made for discussion with parents of the problems involved in meeting the challenge of a "Book Year." In one school during a PTA meeting a librarian talked to the parents about book selection, had books on display, and distributed a list of titles of children's books as guide to parents for buying books for their children. Another procedure during Book Week that might bring good results is to set up a series of conferences for parents about the topic of the independent reading of children.

Procedures during Book Week

Many of the points listed on preceding pages of this chapter as suggestions for interesting boys and girls in books can be used effectively during Book Week. The teacher can also obtain many valuable ideas from: (a) The Children's Book Council, 175 Fifth Avenue, New York 10010 and (b) the October issue of the *Wilson Library Bulletin*, published at 950 University Avenue, Bronx, New York 10452. Another excellent source is the book review section of the Sunday edition of the *New York Times* issued during Book Week, which is exclusively devoted to a consideration of reading by boys and girls. Some professional periodicals also give attention to Book Week.

The Book Fair

Special mention is given here to one means of observing Book Week, namely, the book fair. It can, however, also be used at other times in the year.

A book fair can be a very simple or a rather complex undertaking. Only a relatively few books can be placed on exhibit, possibly only those that can be obtained from the public or school library. This collection may be supplemented by some books of their own that boys and girls may wish to include in the exhibit. Or a great many books may be displayed, many of which are borrowed from book stores that may be happy to cooperate.

The book fair may be strictly a book fair, in that only books are displayed. Or magazines, records or tapes on children's books, and other audiovisual aids, commercially available, may also be exhibited. Pupil-made charts or posters highlighting individual books or certain types of books (such as books on biography or animal stories, for example) can form part of the exhibit. Or boys and girls may make posters to encourage reading of any worthwhile type, with captions such as "Read Good Books" or "Good Books, Good Friends." In fact, any of the types of materials for interesting boys and girls in good reading that are described elsewhere in this chapter are also appropriate for use with a book fair. Programs can be given, consisting of puppet plays on books, other dramatizations, book reports, or other types of programs suggested in this chapter for Book Week or for otherwise interesting boys and girls in books.

The book fair may be put on by the boys and girls in one room or by an entire school. Sometimes, however, it is primarily the undertaking of an adult group. Parent organizations can decide upon a book fair as a major project.

Regardless of who puts on a book fair for school children—adults, boys and girls, or both groups together—requirements such as these should be met:

1. The chief objective should be to interest boys and girls in worthwhile reading.
2. There should be a variety of books on display, on different topics and of varying levels of difficulty.
3. Only worthwhile books should be exhibited.
4. The materials should be attractively arranged.
5. Care should be taken to avoid loss of books and other materials.
6. Provisions should be made to encourage a large number of persons to attend the fair—boys and girls and parents, and, in some instances, other adults.

If boys and girls put on or help put on a book fair, there should be wide participation on their part, so that every child has an opportunity to make a contribution to it, in terms of activities such as: arranging the exhibit, making illustrative material, participating in a program, or explaining the exhibit to visitors.

INDEPENDENT READING IN CONTENT AREAS

One of the problems in the teaching of reading in the elementary school is to help boys and girls read effectively in the area of the content subjects. Books devoted exclusively to methods of teaching reading usually discuss in some detail how skills especially needed in the content areas can be developed. In this chapter consideration is given to interesting the child in independent reading in the content subjects. Obviously no strict line of demarcation between the two types can or should be drawn.

What are some of the basic guidelines in stimulating growth in independent reading in the content areas? Three are briefly described following.

1. *The teacher should try to make available to the boys and girls a large amount of reading material in the various subject areas on different reading levels.* Purchase of materials for the room library should be supplemented by reference to books in the different areas in the school and public libraries if possible. Many

librarians welcome suggestions from teachers as to types of books that would fit with the subject matter in the content subjects taught in a given grade.

2. *The teacher should help boys and girls recognize the importance of reading in various areas.* While the teacher should emphasize the importance of much reading along the line of an individual's specialty, he should also discuss the narrowness that can result if a person confines himself too much to only one or two areas. Discussion should be supplemented by challenging reports on books of various types. In some instances it may also be desirable, in drawing up specifications for outside reading, to indicate that each child should assume responsibility for reading one or two books of each of a number of types of books for children such as books about history, geography, or science.

3. *The reading that the teacher recommends in the various areas should not be confined to those topics about which boys and girls are studying while in a given grade.* Although it is desirable that a rich collection of books on the topics the children are studying during a given school year be available and that the teacher encourage them to read along these lines, it is also important that the pupils read materials in the content areas other than those about which they are studying.

Books on History

Undoubtedly one reason why many boys and girls do not read many books dealing with history or having a historical background is that they have not been introduced to the good books in the field that would make interesting and significant outside reading for them.

Criteria for Selection. What criteria should the teacher keep in mind when recommending books dealing with history? Here are a few important questions that should be answered positively if a book is to be recommended.

1. *Is the book historically accurate?* A book is by no means to be excluded from consideration if it is historical fiction. However, even in historical fiction the background must be true to the facts of history. Marguerite de Angeli's *The Door in the Wall,* for example, while a story, has a background congruous with the history of the times.

2. *Are the theme and plot of a story constituting historical fiction adequate?* The fact that a story is based on history and can give the pupil an understanding of one or more periods of history does not constitute reason for accepting a poor theme or plot. The story should merit attention on its own—because it is a good story. The historical background should not overshadow the plot.

3. *Does the book give perspective resulting from a better understanding of the past?* A book for independent

Figure 10.5. A "Movie" or "Peep Show" to Illustrate a Book on Pioneer Life.

reading related to history should help the pupils appreciate the fact that we owe a debt to the past.

4. *Through reading this book will the reader be in a better position to live effectively in contemporary society?* To accomplish this implied objective the author does not need to resort to a clear explanation of the application of the problems of people of the past to those we face today. The content should frequently be presented so that the child himself, without being forced to a generalization involving the application of the problems discussed to present times, comes to an important understanding of how the knowledge of the past as given him in a book can throw light on present-day problems and their solution.

Suggested Procedures. How can the teacher interest boys and girls in reading material related to history as independent reading? How can he help them profit from such reading?

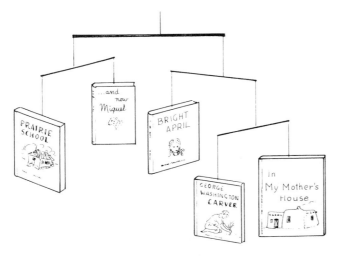

Figure 10.6. A Mobile to Illustrate Books Dealing with the Social Studies.

The first of these two questions is answered in part by discussions on preceding pages in which suggestions have been given for interesting boys and girls in books of any

types. General procedures for interesting boys and girls in reading books with historical background are: having available to boys and girls interesting and worthwhile books on history on various reading levels; putting up attractive exhibits of books in the classroom; having charts to interest them in books; reading to the class a part of a book (often the introductory part) in order to stimulate them to want to read the book; and having pupils give exciting and significant reports on books with a historical background.

A few specific suggestions for interesting pupils in books on history and for helping them profit from reading them are listed following.

1. After a pupil has read a book dealing with the history of a period, he may make a poster or an accordionlike picture folder or a notebook illustrating some of the learnings that he has acquired. For example, a book by Laura Ingalls Wilder may be illustrated by pictures authentically portraying the history of the times—by pictures of the interior of the home, of cooking utensils, of basic foods eaten, and of schoolhouse furnishings. If the display is made by means of a picture folder, on the space immediately preceding each picture, there may be written a quotation from the book explaining the point

Figure 10.7. An Illustration of an Indian Travois, to Interest Readers in Indian Life.

Figure 10.8. An Accordionlike Folder with Pictures Illustrating a Book.

that coincides with the history of the time that is illustrated. A picture of an Indian travois may interest children in books about Indians.

2. A date line can be made showing important historical happenings of the period on which a book is based. For example, for *Johnny Tremain* by Esther Forbes the events preceding and during the Revolutionary War can be shown on a time line. One suggestion for an interesting time line is actual use of a line (maybe a clothesline) strung across the room, to which are attached illustrations of important happenings of the story and placards with the names of the events and dates.

Figure 10.9. Part of a Time Line.

3. A frieze may be drawn showing significant events of the story with care taken that the details of the picture are in harmony with customs and habits of the people of the time.

4. After reading a book based at least in part on history, a pupil can study in reference books some of the topics suggested by the background of the story. For instance, after having read *Thanksgiving Story* by Alice Dalgliesh, the pupil can read authentic accounts of the voyage of the Mayflower and of the First Thanksgiving in Plymouth. The pupil can then make a booklet in which he reports on background events.

5. The pupil who plans to give a report on historical fiction can study about the lives of important men and women in history who lived at the time when the story took place. With the help of some of his classmates the reader may impersonate some of these people as he gives a report on the book and thereby makes history real to his audience.

6. One way in which readers can be helped to grasp historical sequence is by means of a series. of shadow boxes that can be made out of shoe boxes. For example, Lois Lenski's *Boom Town Boy* can be illustrated by a group of shadow scenes in which one of the shoe boxes can depict the farm before the discovery of oil, another during the construction of the first oil well, and the third after it was covered with wells.

Books on Geography

As in the case of books with a historical setting, so with those of a geographical setting, even the details of background must be true, regardless of whether the material is fiction or nonfiction. Also, as in the case of historical fiction, the story element must not be sacrificed in order to teach facts. In a fascinating story, such as the great classic of childhood *Heidi* by Johanna Spyri, the background can make a lasting impression upon boys and girls, for the heroine moves in a real world, one made significant to the child because Heidi lived there.

Books that deal with other countries should not place much emphasis on outmoded customs, such as the wearing of wooden shoes in Holland. However, the pronouncement often made by writers in the field of the teaching of social studies in the elementary school—that the likenesses rather than the differences among people around the world should be stressed—needs to be interpreted with caution. To be sure, the common humanity of all should be emphasized. Nevertheless, what makes one individual lovable and interesting is based to a considerable extent on his unique characteristics. So, too, with peoples of other countries.

Here are a few suggestions for stimulating interest in reading books with emphasis on the geography of a region. These ideas may be considered by the teacher in addition to the many others given in this and the preceding chapter on how to interest children in books of all types.

1. In the case of a book with a regional setting, the reporter can beforehand exhibit on a bulletin board a map showing the places at which the chief events of the story occurred.

Poster was made by Judith Cox.

Figure 10.11. Poster Suggesting Background by Means of Lines.

Poster was prepared by Cynthia Fish Cormany.

Figure 10.10. A Three-Dimensional Poster.

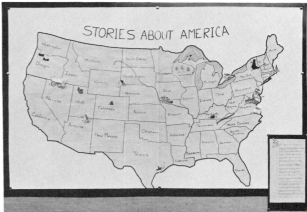

Poster was made by Gwen Stephens Meissner.

Figure 10.12. Map of the United States Illustrating Books about Our Country.

2. Dioramas showing the setting in which a major part of a book takes place can be especially effective as a motivating device in connection with books with a geographical setting. A scene showing the uncle's hut with the majestic Alps as background can be a stirring means of interesting the child in reading the book *Heidi*.

3. A display of travel folders, or even a make-believe travel bureau in the room, can interest children in reading about peoples in distant regions.

The teacher may wish to consult *Children's Books to Enrich the Social Studies* by Helen Huus (published by the National Council for the Social Studies). Since the titles are classfied according to theme, it will be relatively easy for the teacher to note books in areas needed in his room. He may suggest some of these as additions to the room or school or public library. Nancy Larrick's *A Teacher's Guide to Children's Books* published by Charles E. Merrill Publishing Company should also prove helpful.

Books on Science

During the last few decades many books on science for boys and girls have appeared on the market. Some of them have been outstanding in their contribution; others have been mediocre.

Criteria for Evaluation. For listings of excellent science books the reader is referred to the book by Nancy Larrick to which reference has already been made.

Another excellent source for the adult interested in locating good books on science is the professional book *Elementary School Science and How to Teach It* by Glenn O. Blough and Julius Schwartz, published by Holt, Rinehart and Winston, Inc. Books on the teaching of literature for children also give good listings or descriptions of books on science for boys and girls. Books excellent in this respect are the latest editions of *Children and Books* by May Hill Arbuthnot and Zena Sutherland and *Children's Literature in the Elementary School* by Charlotte S. Huck and Doris Young Kuhn.

A few criteria to apply when judging books on science for boys and girls are the following:

1. Is the book up-to-date in the facts presented?
2. Is the book accurate?
3. Is the book on the child's level of comprehension?
4. Is the book interesting?
5. Will reading the book interest the child in reading other books in the field of science?

Suggestions for Stimulating Interest. There are many ways in which to interest boys and girls in books on science, whether they deal with animal life, plant life, or facts in the realm of physics, chemistry, astronomy, or geology. A few are mentioned here.

1. An exhibit can be set up to intrigue boys and girls in trying a simple experiment with the directions for conducting it explained in written form. On the same table with the materials for experimentation one or more books dealing at least in part with the subject of the experiment can be exhibited with a caption such as this: "If you like to do experiments, here are some books you may enjoy."

2. An illustrated bulletin board entitled "Can You Answer These Questions?" may have challenging questions posted on it such as: "What makes an airplane move?" Several books on science may be placed on a table in front of the bulletin board. Each question on the bulletin board may be connected by a narrow ribbon to the book that gives the answer.

3. To interest boys and girls in books dealing with animals, the homes or habits of one or more of the animals can be represented. For example, a model showing a cross section of the home of a beaver can be displayed on the board. The exhibit, made from either clay or papier-mâché, could be about eighteen by twenty-four inches in size.

4. A chart entitled "Is It True?" can be used for listing various superstitions mingled with true facts. An illustrative chart may be used only for superstitions and facts about one topic such as the moon or travel in space. Near the chart can be placed a book with the sign "This book will tell."

5. A "migration" map can be made to interest boys and girls in books about birds. A map of the western hemisphere can be glued to a piece of white poster board. Migration routes of various birds such as the Arctic tern, the golden plover, and the robin can be indicated by ribbon or colored construction paper and then attached to the map with map tacks. A picture of each bird whose route is indicated can be fastened to the map or poster board.

6. Children can be interested in wildlife conservation by a mobile, to which are attached representations of animals in whose conservation there should be interest. For example, a fish can be illustrated by using a paper plate with the rippled edges cut so that they serve as fins and tail.

7. Below a sign "All about Aviation" books on aviators and aviation may be displayed.

8. To interest boys and girls in reading about magnetism, on a large piece of tagboard or mounting board headed "What does a magnet attract?" may be objects such as the following: (a) a piece of wood, (b) a thumbtack, (c) a nail, (d) a sponge, (e) a screwdriver, and (f) a piece of wire. Below each of these articles can be written the substance from which it is made. For example, under the piece of wire the word *steel* may be written. A magnet, attached by a cord to the background, can be used by the boys and girls to test which objects are attracted to it.

9. One exciting way in which to interest boys and girls in magnets is the construction of a "magnetic theater." The theater can be made from a cardboard box by cutting out one-half of the bottom and securing this piece of cardboard inside the box in the middle to serve as stage, as shown by the center lines in the accompanying figure. The backdrop can be illustrated with a scene to suit the story being dramatized. The piece of paper serving as backdrop can be slipped into a slit made across the top of the theater. The characters for the play can be made of cardboard and construction paper and then taped to a low stand containing a small piece of iron or steel. By moving a large magnet under the stage floor, the

Figure 10.13. A Magnetic Theater and "Actors."

characters can be made to move across the stage. The large magnet will attract the small magnets which are placed inside the stand supporting each character.

10. To interest boys and girls in reading books on electricity, illustrations of the following may be placed on a large piece of tagboard headed "Static or Current?": (a) a boy combing his hair and therby making it stand "on end," (b) a person being shocked when walking on a rug, (c) lightning, (d) a radio, (e) a flashlight, (f) a battery, (g) a doorbell.

11. A mobile may be used to interest the pupils in reading books dealing at least in part with electricity. The mobile may include pictures of the following mounted on tagboard: (a) an automobile, (b) a radio tower, (c) a telephone, (d) a flat iron, (e) an electric fan, (f) a stove.

Figure 10.14. A Mobile Showing Electricity at Work.

12. To interest boys and girls in learning about famous botanists some of the children may make a "hall of fame" from a large box cut in the manner indicated in the accompanying illustration. The "stage" can be covered with white shelf paper. The curtain shown in the illustration can be made of blue taffeta and suspended from a thin wire serving as curtain rod. The pedestals, also shown in the illustration, can be small tempera paint jars covered with white shelf paper. The pictures of botanists can be pasted onto a background of black construction paper and their names written on "name cards" pasted to the pedestals.

13. A bulletin board that can be constructed to interest boys and girls in reading about space travel can show how the different stages of a rocket work. The bulletin

Figure 10.15. A Hall of Fame of Botanists.

board can be made on blue poster board and can be entitled "Three-stage Rocket." The illustration of the rocket can be divided into four sections by using strips of gray construction paper to represent the rocket. The first section can show the rocket as a whole, the second section can show the first stage falling off, the third section can show the second part dropping, and the fourth section can show the third stage falling off with the capsule departing alone into space.

Books on Minority Groups

In general when we refer to the term *minority groups* we think not only of the opposite of *majority* but also of a group of people the majority have wrongly considered inferior.

In the past relatively few books for boys and girls have dealt with minority groups. Frequently those that have

Poster was made by Pamela Blazer.

Figure 10.16. Illustration of a Book about a Girl in a Minority Group.

been on the market for some time have not qualified in terms of the criteria discussed in the next paragraph.

Criteria for Evaluating Books. Some of the criteria by which we should evaluate books dealing with minority groups, in addition to those applying to all good books, are as follows:

1. The books should treat of the differences between the minority group and others as variations rather than abnormalties. Merely to follow the dictum of omitting reference to differences does little, if anything, toward approaching the ideal of brotherhood.

2. The books should show that many problems of life are identical in minority and majority groups.

3. The books should emphasize the fact that pain in one person is as hard to bear as pain in another and that joy is joy regardless of who is experiencing it.

4. The books should refer to any problems existing between majority and minority groups as being common problems. Emphasis should be put on the point of view that hurting someone brings harm to the person who inflicts the pain because of what it does to him as a person.

5. The books should be such that they are of assistance to boys and girls of both minority and nonminority groups. It would, as a rule, be unwise to have different literature for the groups and thus possibly widen rather than decrease the chasm existing between them.

6. Some of the books should show the contribution of a minority group to our heritage—literary, social, and spiritual.

Teaching Procedures. How can the teacher interest the pupils in the variety of good books available that deal with minority groups, whether the differences are in race, social standing, religion, or nationality? How can he help boys and girls profit from the reading of such books? The ingenious teacher will know many ways in which to apply to reading of this type of book the suggestions for interesting children in books given on preceding pages. Here are only a few procedures with specific application for use with books on minority groups.

1. The teacher can ask questions about a book that will help the readers imagine themselves in the place of characters of the story who are members of a minority group.

2. Skits can be put on in which the pupils take the role of a minority group.

3. The boys and girls can be given background for understanding peoples represented in books on minority groups.

4. The background for reading books on minority groups as well as their reading can be correlated with work in art, music, drama, and dance.

5. The teacher, preferably with the help of one or more pupils, can prepare a bulletin board on famous people of minority races. Marian Anderson and George Washington Carver serve as two examples of persons to whom references may be made on such a bulletin board.

6. As the boys and girls read biography of some of the great people of minority groups, they can be encouraged to make charts listing their contributions or to make displays representing important contributions these people have made.

7. The boys and girls can make a collection of suitable poetry or worthwhile stories about members of a minority race.

Books of Biography

Boys and girls enjoy reading good books of biography. It is well that this is the case for through biographies of people with sterling qualities the child can be inspired to emulation of them. Furthermore, since many biographies written for children put considerable emphasis on the background of the times in which the persons lived, much historical information is acquired in this pleasant manner.

There is considerable range in the difficulty of the reading material in biographies planned for boys and girls of the elementary school. Some are available in the easy-to-read style of books, such as those in the *Beginning-to-Read* series published by Follett Publishing Company. Others, as for example *The Landmark Series,* are primarily for the intermediate-grade child. Some of the excellent biographical material is in picture books such as those by Clara Ingram Judson and James Daugherty.

Biographies for boys and girls can be classified as either biographical fiction or true biography. Examples of the former are the *Childhood of Famous Americans Series,* published by Bobbs-Merrill; examples of books approximating the latter type are *Invincible Louisa* by Cornelia Meiggs and *Columbus* by Ingri and Edgar Parin d'Aulaire. Boys and girls may need guidance in distinguishing between points presented in these two types of biography.

Characteristics of Good Biographies. Some of the criteria by which books on biography for boys and girls should be judged are the same that should be applied to books of biography for adults. Other criteria are somewhat unique to books for younger readers. The list that follows contains both types.

1. A biography should be an authentic, truthful presentation of the life of an individual. In books for adults heavy documentation, which is not found in books for children, is often an index of authenticity of the facts related. In biographies for children the preface may give some indication of the source of the information.

2. A book on biography for children should not deal with problems beyond the realm of comprehension by the reader.

3. A biography for children should be written in a style that presents a suitable mood or background for recording the life of the person whose biography is being written.

4. A book of biography for children should not include the sordid or immoral. If an accurate biography cannot be written without such details, then the person's life is not a good choice.

5. A book of biography for children should be written about a person who is worthy of emulation. A person does not need to be flawless (for then there would be no biographies for boys and girls) but he should be a person who can serve as an example in many respects.

Teaching Procedures. The following points illustrate how boys and girls can be guided in reading biography.

1. Arranging a bulletin board. A bulletin board with the caption "Who's Who among American Women?" may have on it slips of paper with questions such as: (a) Who was the "Little Mother" of the prisoners? (b) What woman made the first solo transatlantic flight? On a nearby table can be placed attractive books of biography in which the answers to the questions can be found.

2. Dramatizing scenes from the lives of a few famous people such as (a) Jane Addams's ride with her father through slums, (b) Benjamin Franklin's arrival as a boy in Philadelphia, (c) Sacajawea's aid to Lewis and Clark.

3. Using a large map of the United States for indicating at appropriate places illustrations of something important in the lives of famous people. For example, a paper airplane can be placed at Little Falls, Minnesota, in recognition of Charles Lindbergh or a picture of Hull House, perhaps given a three-dimensional effect by a mounting on an accordionlike piece of paper, can be attached to the site of Chicago for Jane Addams.

4. Making objects or collecting them to represent something of importance about the person whose biography had been read in order to interest others in it, such as: (a) a collection of products, in connection with George Washington Carver that can be made from peanuts (cereal, flour, peanut butter) or (b) mottoes giving wise sayings of Benjamin Franklin.

Books on Religion

No listing of books for boys and girls in the elementary school would be complete without reference to books on religion. This fact remains true even though it has been ruled that religion as such is not to be taught in the public schools. The teacher may want to know books on the topic in order to furnish parents information on such books if they desire it. Furthermore, he may want to recommend to a child, within the boundaries of the religious beliefs of his home and church, suitable books on the subject.

Criteria for Books on Religion. First of all, books on religion should fulfill the general requirements of all good books as to illustration, format, and content. Additional criteria pertinent to all books dealing with religion are here listed. Still others are mentioned later on in this chapter in relation to the types of books on religion that are discussed.

1. In books for boys and girls only those concepts of religion should be presented that are somewhat within the power of the child to comprehend. To be sure, many of the concepts of religion are beyond man's total comprehension. Nevertheless, many can be stated so simply that they have meaning for the child.

2. Religious concepts should not be oversimplified. If they are made to seem simpler than they are, the child later may find himself in the unhappy situation of unlearning what he once learned.

Types of Books on Religion. The books on religion or related to religion which may be of value to boys and girls can be classified in the following manner.

1. *Bible Stories.* Many editions of the Bible, because of language problems, are difficult for boys and girls to read. Even modern versions have vocabulary beyond the comprehension of many boys and girls in the elementary school. Further difficulty in reading the Bible, or parts of it, for elementary school children lies in the fact that concepts difficult to comprehend are scattered among those that are simpler to grasp. For these reasons, books on stories of the Bible written for boys and girls can serve a real need. The use of the latter should not, however, keep the child from having some of the passages of the Bible read to him or from reading parts himself. The beauty of much of the language of some versions of the Bible has not been equalled in any edition of Bible stories.

2. *Books about Jesus.* Attempts to give a consecutive account of important events in the life of Jesus that boys and girls can read with comprehension, pleasure, and inspiration have resulted in various books on His life. They include a wide range of difficulty, from the very simple picture-story books to those read with profit by only the more advanced reader in the elementary school and by older people.

3. *Books about Bible characters other than Jesus.* The value of good books about Bible characters lies partly in the fact that strong characters, even though handicapped by human frailties, have been selected. As in other types of biography those points in the lives of persons selected as subjects for biography that are helpful and courageous should be emphasized, but only to the point of truthfulness. In a book about persons of the Bible the God-

Poster was made by Gretchen Schmidt Grier.

Figure 10.17.

loving character of the individuals should be highlighted so that they are presented as persons who, in spite of evil in their lives, nevertheless show that God did matter a great deal to them.

4. *Books about God.* Controversy also exists as to what books about God should be put into the hands of boys and girls. Some Christian people object to a child being given a book on religion that does not emphasize Jesus as the central figure. Similarly, objections to boys and girls reading books that tell about Jesus are raised by parents who are not Christians.

5. *Books of prayers.* One of the chief tests of any book of prayers for the adult or the child is whether it instills in the reader a worshipful attitude. In some books of prayers not only the words but also the accompanying illustrations help bring this about.

6. *Books of information about Bible lands.* Authenticity and clarity of presentation are two of the criteria that should be considered in books of this type. Importance of the facts selected constitutes another criterion.

7. *Other books of religious significance.* Books on persons other than Bible characters who were leaders in religious movements, such as Martin Luther and St. Francis of Assisi, are also written on a level of comprehension of older boys and girls in the elementary school. Books on religious holidays, although frequently emphasizing the secular rather than the religious elements (probably too much), also need to be mentioned in a well-rounded classification of books dealing with religion.

BOOKS OF POETRY

The teacher should make available poetry that will help the boys and girls achieve ever higher levels of appreciation. Some suggestions for interesting boys and girls in poetry and for elevating their taste are given on pages 121 to 123 under "Writing Poetry." Following are

listed a few suggestions about the selection of poetry for children.

1. Start with poetry approximately on the pupil's level of appreciation.

2. Provide the boys and girls with some poems about experiences, fanciful or actual, that they have had.

3. Do not make the mistake of thinking that a poem is suitable for a child because a child figures prominently in the poem. (For example, Eugene Field's "Little Boy Blue," though the main character is a boy, is an expression of an adult's grief at the death of a child.)

Figure 10.18.

Poster was made by Jean Shepherd.

Figure 10.19.

4. Include in the selection some books with poems that are humorous and also some that tell a story.

5. While a good anthology of poems is a desirable type of book to have in a classroom, also provide for the pupils some less ponderous-looking books than the typical anthology.

6. Make available to the boys and girls some books of poetry with wide margins, especially interesting looking print, and illustrations that are reprints from masters of the art.

VISUAL AIDS TO ENCOURAGE READING

Many visual aids that boys and girls can make to interest others in good books and provide for themselves values in connection with the reading they have done are described in preceding pages of this book. Additional suggestions are given here.

Bulletin Boards

Bulletin boards can be a valuable means of interesting boys and girls in books. While usually the pupils, rather than the teacher, should make the posters or other exhibits for the bulletin board, occasionally it may be advisable for the teacher to do so. Among the purposes that can be served if the teacher constructs one are these: (1) He can demonstrate media of which the boys and girls might not have thought for making a bulletin board, such as thin rope, cloth, papier-mâché. (2) He can set up a standard of excellence that can be approximated or achieved by the children. (3) He can help boys and girls see the value of bulletin boards in interesting others in books.

We can think of bulletin boards on books as falling under one of three classifications: (1) those illustrating one book only, such as the one entitled "The Bears of Hemlock Mountain," illustrated on page 273; (2) those dealing with a given type of book, such as one that could be made on the theme "Meet Famous Animal Characters," on which might be illustrated animals such as Bambi of the book by that title or "the Pooh" of *Winnie the Pooh;* (3) those designed to interest the children in good books of all or many types, with captions such as "Read Good Books" or "Reading Can Be Exciting."

Following are a few additional suggestions for bulletin boards.

1. The boys and girls should have a significant purpose in mind when constructing a bulletin board. "Let's all make a poster on a book" is not a challenging enough objective. A pupil might make a bulletin board for meaningful purposes such as these: (a) to make more interesting a book report he is giving or (b) to interest others in reading a book he has enjoyed.

2. A variety of materials can be used in constructing bulletin boards. Greater interest can be aroused through bulletin boards if they lack sameness in construction. Mention has already been made of rope, cloth, and papier-mâché. Others include: steel wool; sand glued to the background of a poster; cutout illustrations attached to the poster; three-dimensional objects constructed by the pupils and attached to the bulletin board or poster, (such as a simple steam shovel for *Mike Mulligan and His Steam Shovel* by Virginia Burton).

3. Standards in the construction of bulletin boards should be maintained. This statement is not to be interpreted as meaning that only near-perfect bulletin boards should be exhibited. However, slovenly work should be discouraged. Pupils should, for example, make application of what they know of balance and proportion; of their ability to do lettering; of their skill in pasting, drawing, and painting.

Displays

Displays such as those described here, which were made by college students, are illustrative of some that boys and girls could make in order to interest others in reading. It is, of course, not recommended that boys and girls reproduce these; these displays are to be suggestive only of others the children might make.

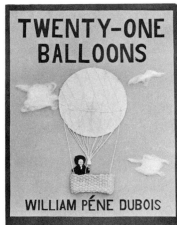

Poster was made by
Kathy Kappel Rose.

Figure 10.20.

Poster was made by Janice Sue Woods McPherson.

Figure 10.21.

Poster was made by Barbara Tener.

Figure 10.22.

Poster was made by Mary Stewart Rutchow.

Figure 10.23.

Poster was made by Nancy Howard Hickok.

Figure 10.24.

Poster was made by Kathryn Newman Feld.

Figure 10.25.

Bulletin Boards Dealing with One Book

Figure 10.26.

Display was made by Linda Deuble Lippincott.

Figure 10.27.

Display was made by Sue Kenworthy and Sandy Bardwell Lee.

Figure 10.28.

Display was made by Joan Kehl Royer.

Figure 10.29.

Display was made by Dorothy Wolfe.

Figure 10.30.

Display was made by Patti Tieken Johnson.

Figure 10.31.

Displays to Interest Children in Books

1. In one display a house was made out of a cardboard box and covered with white paper. (See page 274.) The roof was painted green and the words "COME VISIT WITH US," made of white paper, were glued to one side of the roof. The windows and a door were cut out and a piece of gray paper was used as backing for each. In front of the gray paper of some of the windows there is a book character, identified by name. An index card was placed near the house listing the various characters and the stories in which they are found. Some characters that were represented were Alice from *Alice in Wonderland*, Huck Finn from *The Adventures of Huckleberry Finn*, and Peter from *Peter Pan*. (See figure l0.30.)

2. A folder "Do You Know These Animal Characters?" was made out of poster paper folded in an accordionlike manner. The title was written on the first section of the folder. Pictures of animals from various animal stories had been cut out of white construction paper and colored the appropriate colors with crayon. These figures were pasted on the sections of the folder. The title of the story was written above each picture and the name of the author below it. On one side of the folder books for primary grades were illustrated and on the other side were books for intermediate grades. (See figure 10.28.)

3. A large world map was mounted on poster paper and placed on a table so that it leaned against a wall. Ribbons led from various points on the map to book jackets and to the characters that are displayed. The book jackets were made of colored pieces of construction paper. The title and the name of the author were written on each book jacket. The characters were made of cardboard. Each one also had a piece of cardboard behind it so that the figure stands up. The features were painted on the figures with poster paint. Cotton and wool material were used for the clothing and straw and yarn for the hair. (See figure l0.26.)

4. A three-dimensional castle was made out of cardboard. The castle was painted with poster paint and a drawbridge was cut in front so that it could be dropped as if it were real. Pieces of leather string were used for the chains of the bridge. The windows in the castle were cut out and a figure of Rapunzel was placed in a window, with her hair hanging out of the window almost to the ground. Various characters from fairy tales were placed around the castle. They were made of cardboard with another piece of cardboard attached to the back of each character to enable it to stand. (See figure l0.31.)

5. A large open "book" was made out of poster paper. On one side of the "book" were printed the title *Heidi* and the author's name *Johanna Spyri*, both in ink. A scene from the story was painted on the other side of the "book." The picture shows a mountain scene with a boy and girl in the foreground dressed in mountain attire playing with a goat. The "book" was propped up by a piece of cardboard and figures of goats made of cardboard were placed in front of it. These figures were painted with water colors. (See figure 10.29.)

6. A display entitled "Our Animal Friends" was made by placing the branch of a tree in a plastic container into which plaster of Paris was poured. The characters, such as a fish for Golden MacDonald's *The Little Island* (illustrated by Leonard Weisgard), a bear for Lynd Ward's *The Biggest Bear*, and a swallow for Leo Politi's *Song of the Swallow* were made from paper. These figures were suspended with black thread. (See figure 10.27.)

7. To interest children in reading history books dolls can be made out of cardboard and dressed in the costumes of different periods of history such as the Colonial, the Revolutionary, or the Medieval period. The clothing can be made of scraps of material. To each character a card can be attached giving the titles of several books about the period represented.

8. A map of the United States can be placed on a table. Characters made of cardboard can stand on the surface to represent a character from a book about a minority group in a given area of the United States. A card can be placed at each character's feet, with the title of the book and the name of the author.

9. The pupils can make dioramas or peep shows to illustrate scenes from a story. The characters can be three-dimensional little figures of clay, plastic, or wood or they can be paper doll representations. The furnishings for a scene can be made of paper, wood, or a variety of other materials. The scenery for the setting can be painted onto the interior sides of the box of the diorama.

Figure 10.32.

10. The pupils can make murals to illustrate scenes from books they like. In the primary grades, the boys and girls can draw the characters as well as parts of the

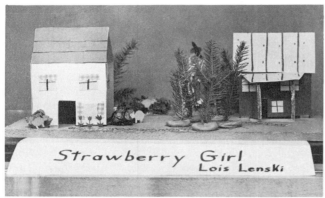

Display was made by Karen Whipkey Derusha.

Figure 10.33. Another Scene from a Book.

Figure 10.34. Making One's Own Bookmark.

scenery on paper and then cut them out and attach them to the appropriate spaces on the mural. Older pupils can draw or paint the parts of the mural directly onto the large paper roll. In some instances the paper may be divided into as many parts vertically as there are scenes to be represented. In other murals one scene may "run" into another without a distinct division of the mural into separate pictures.

11. Book mobiles of various types can "advertise" a single book, or they can illustrate books of a given kind (such as books of biography or animal stories) or they can be representative of a variety of types—possibly favorites of the child who made the mural or a book of each kind that would be good reading for the class.

Other Visual Aids

Reference is made following to a few additional types of visual aids the pupils can make for use in developing interest in good reading.

1. Book jackets. Original jackets for the books, drawn by the boys and girls, can portray for others in the class a reason why the person who drew the picture liked a given book.

2. Paper masks. Boys and girls enjoy transforming paper bags into masks to represent characters from a book they wish to portray.

3. Scrapbooks. The boys and girls may make notebooks or scrapbooks. In them can be included brief reports of books read by a pupil; pictures—either drawn by the pupil or cut from printed material—representing books that the owner has enjoyed; quotations from books; reports on how to take care of books; lists of books that the owner of the notebook or scrapbook would like to read; poems about books.

4. Bookmarks. Pupils can make a variety of bookmarks illustrating favorite books. Sometimes the picture can be drawn by the pupils; at other times pictures portraying scenes or characters from a book can be cut from

printed material advertising a book and then pasted onto the rest of the bookmark.

5. Puzzles. Puzzles on scenes from books or book characters can be made from the pictures on book jackets. Or boys and girls can draw the scenes or characters for the puzzles.

6. Puppets. Boys and girls are enthusiastic about making puppets and giving plays to interest others in books. (For a somewhat detailed description of puppets, the reader is referred to chapter 11.)

7. Collages. Collages of scenes from books can be made effectively by groups of boys and girls. Often for collages a variety of materials are used.

8. Transparencies. Transparencies can be made to accompany the giving of oral reports on books.

9. Dolls as book characters. Some girls will enjoy dressing dolls to represent characters of books they have enjoyed. An exhibit of the dolls can be used in a contest to see how many characters can be guessed by the other children in the room.

OTHER CONSIDERATIONS

For extensive treatment of topics so far discussed in this chapter and others related to the independent reading of boys and girls, the reader is referred to books on the teaching of literature such as *Children and Books* by May Hill Arbuthnot and Zena Sutherland and *Children's Literature for the Elementary School* by Charlotte S. Huck and Doris Young Kuhn. The additional topics discussed in these closing pages of this chapter indicate further points that need to be considered by the elementary school teacher and suggest a few ideas for dealing with them. Discussion follows on: (1) comic books, (2) keeping records of books read, (3) the learning resource center, (4) book selection, and (5) evaluation.

Comic Books

Comic books cannot be thought of as unimportant when it has been said that 90 percent of Americans ages eight through thirteen regularly read comic books. The importance is even clearer when we consider this 90 percent figure to be a "modest estimate." It was estimated some years ago that nearly one billion copies are distributed yearly in the United States alone. It is likely that more money is spent on the purchase of comics than on textbooks for the elementary and secondary schools. Though these figures may not be accurate, it is an established fact that a very large number of such books are read by boys and girls of elementary school age and beyond. It has been suggested that with the increase of some of the mass media of communication a decrease in interest in the comics has occurred. Let us hope that such is really the trend and that it will continue, with sharply dropping figures.

Arguments Given against Comic Books. Any unprejudiced evaluation of comic books, it seems to the writer, will need to take cognizance of the fact that, as in the case of other books, there is considerable variation between the best and worst. Among the worst types are those that deal with crime and deeds of horror and those in which sex plays a predominant role. In a different class are the watered-down classics or Bible stories and stories such as those of Donald Duck with funny antics of animals. Some arguments against the comics apply equally to both extremes of comics; others are acceptable only when characterizing the poorer types. However, when the large percent of comic books on the market that deal with deeds of crime and horror is kept in mind, the magnitude of the problem is self-evident.

Among the chief arguments given against the comics are the following.

1. The vocabulary of the comics usually is not such that the reader is likely to grow in a desirable command of the English language. In many instances it has a weakening effect.

2. The grammar used often is poor and the sentence structure frequently is not acceptable.

3. The spelling is at times not that accepted as standard.

4. The illustrations are frequently cheap and in some cases obscene and terrifying.

5. The illustrations do not follow accepted rules of techniques for illustrations for children.

6. The paper is poor and the print is hard on the eyes.

7. The reading lines, brief and irregular in length, counteract the establishment of effective eye movements in reading at a stage in reading progress (the intermediate grades, where the most avid readers of comics are found) when eye movements are being stabilized in many cases.

8. Many comic books deal with stories of horror and crime. In these typically the brawny man wins, methods used in committing crimes are demonstrated, techniques of torment are described and illustrated, and violent deaths are shown. These books can well give the child ideas for committing crimes. Furthermore, they can make boys and girls living in an overstimulated age tense with excitement of the undesirable kind. They are inimical to the development of sound and lasting standards of morality. They can lead to sadism and other types of delinquency. Books dealing with sex give children wrong ideas on that subject. The handsomeness of the men and the beauty of the women may give the reader a distorted idea of what is essential in love. The comics can be overstimulating in their effect on the sex life, especially for the age for which comics have the greatest appeal.

9. The illustrated classics are mediocre editions of the original. The same criticism can be made of those dealing with versions of Bible stories. The beauty of expression is lacking and the reader may obtain a false interpretation of some stories. There is reason to fear that reading the classics in comic books may decrease rather than increase the chances that the reader will later turn to the work of the masters.

10. The reading of comics is a waste of time and money.

11. The characters are often stereotyped, frequently either all good or all bad.

12. The comics are often used as a means of escape.

Arguments Given in Favor of the Comics. It is almost incomprehensible that some intelligent men and women, even some educators, have stated some of the arguments that they have given in favor of the comics. Their points are nullified in many instances through even a casual examination of a dozen comic books selected at random. The following are a few of the frequently cited arguments favoring comics. The sentences given in parentheses indicate the writer's reaction to the arguments as stated.

1. The books fill some of the child's needs, such as his desire for security, his need of using his imagination, and his longing for achievement. The very stereotyped nature of the characters has been advocated as an argument because they give a child security in that he knows what to expect. (In other literature we often condemn the use of stereotypes. Furthermore, the imagination of the child who reads many comics runs wild in areas where he might better not sojourn for the sake of his mental and spiritual health.)

2. The comics are the fairy tales of today. (The comic books can easily fill the child with horror that many of the fairy tales of long ago do not do. One reason for the difference is probably the fact that the "long-agoness" of fairy tales prevents the child from suffering from feelings of gruesomeness that are experienced when reading horror tales of stories with the immediacy of a modern setting.)

3. The children will outgrow their liking for comic books. (But surely it is important in the formative period of childhood that everything within reason be done to keep the child's mental and spiritual life healthy.)

4. The children learn to read by means of the comics. (Argument against this statement is that reading does not need to be learned through resorting to undesirable material. It is no more appropriate to use low-grade reading material to learn to read than it is to use vulgar speech as means of self-expression.)

5. Reading of books on crime will not cause the well-adjusted child to commit wrong deeds or add to delinquency as commonly defined. It is admitted by some people who use this argument that it may have that effect on a child who already has some emotional problems or a tendency to delinquency. (Surely this is poor argument for those of us who have seen the good and the bad intermingled in all children and in all adults whom we know. Since when, too, are we going to cease feeling responsibility for the weaker brother whom we have not yet even learned, in many instances, to identify?)

What to Do about the Comics. Under the leadership of Charles F. Murphy, the Association of Comic Books produced the Comics Code Authority for the alleged purpose of having reform come from within the comic industry. How ineffective the resulting reform has been can be judged by the reader who examines a random sampling of comic books bearing the seal of approval by the organization. If the Comics Code Authority formulated in 1954 has not brought the needed results, what can be done about the polluting types of comics?

1. The good books on the reading and interest levels of the boys and girls should be made readily accessible to them in large numbers.

2. Various procedures, many of which are described elsewhere in this book, should be used to interest the boys and girls in good books.

3. More books should be written emulating features of the comics which are not undesirable and which attract the children to them such as ease of material, adventure, and quick action in the stories.

4. Teachers should forbid boys and girls to read comics at school. Many educators would object to this point of view on the grounds that prohibiting the reading of a comic book makes it more sought after. The writer of this book argues that we do not hesitate to forbid children to use vile language at school for fear that they may consequently use it more out of school than otherwise.

5. Parents should forbid boys and girls to buy or read harmful literature at home. (The writer recognizes the difficulty of enforcement of this rule.)

6. The school and the home should try to give the child a background of values that will help him like that which is fine.

7. The school and the home should provide the child with many experiences that will help satisfy the needs some persons think the comics satisfy.

8. Teachers should try to help boys and girls become discriminating readers. This suggestion should not, however, be observed by having the children waddle in trash for a period of time.

9. Parents and teachers should examine the comic books on the newsstand and then take a firm position on the abolition of all undesirable comics from the newsstands of the community.

10. Parents and teachers should try to get laws passed that will forbid the sale of debasing literature. Why many persons with keen intelligence are specifically opposed to this suggestion is hard to comprehend. The argument seems to be that people do not become better through legal action. But we do favor laws against robbery, for example, even though we know that through the passing of the law, per se, the individuals who may be deterred from robbing may not be reformed. We know that forbidding the sale of tobacco to minors does not erase the desire in the younster who wants to buy tobacco, but we pass the law believing it wise not to ask children in their formative years to decide what is good for them in a matter of such moment.

Keeping Records of Books Read

Keeping records of books read, whether by the teacher or by the reader, can be valuable for two reasons, namely (1) to know or remember what books have been read and (2) to stimulate further reading. The first reason mentioned is of significance because an individual often finds it helpful to remember the exact title and author of a book he has read. To the teacher a record is of value in that he will know better how to guide further growth in reading. Records in reading can stimulate the pupil to further reading especially if he has set for himself (alone or through the influence of the teacher) a goal of wanting to read many good books. The incentive that keeping records furnishes even for adults can readily be noted as one observes how commonly the device is used in an attempt to inspire greater effort in United Appeals drives and in other campaigns.

Cautions for Record Keeping. In keeping records that

show books read by an individual, the following cautions should be noted.

1. Records that cause competition of the reader with others should be used sparingly, if at all. The child who has read only a few books (and sometimes for good reason) may feel discouraged if he is the one who lags behind as revealed in a posted chart showing the number or types of books read. Competition should be primarily with the reader's own past record.

2. When a pupil keeps record of the books or the number of books read, care must be taken, as a rule, that the number of pages read is in some way considered. If this caution is not observed, a child may avoid reading some of the longer books.

3. Provisions should be made that the child does not feel obligated to read every word in a book and, on the other hand, that he does not merely skim a book or parts of a book that he records as one he has read. One way in which pupils can be helped in this respect is through frank discussion of the degree of comprehension with which a book should be read in order to be recorded on a list.

4. Care should be taken that the child is not reading merely to have a good record of independent reading. If that is his objective, it is hardly one that will provide a lasting goal for adult reading.

5. A system of record keeping instigated by the teacher should not show only the number of books read. It should also give the titles or types of books read. It is often desirable to have a pupil indicate how many books in each of a number of categories he has read during the time while the record is being kept.

6. Records of children's reading should not be available only to the children. The teacher, too, should have access to them so that he can check (without the child feeling he is being investigated) on the accuracy of the report and so that he can ascertain whether the child's reading is on the level of what seems to be his ability.

Means of Keeping Records. Following are described types of records that can be kept of the reading done by the class or by an individual child.

1. A class record of books read can be kept in a file box. After a child has read a book, he can make a card for it if someone else in the room has not already made one for the book.

2. Small construction paper boats can be made for each child and attached to the bulletin board. The author and title of each book the child reads can be recorded on the sail of his boat. These can be arranged into a "classroom fleet."

3. A paper rocket for each pupil can be attached to a chart showing the planets of our solar system. The pupil's rocket ship can be moved from planet to planet as he reads an additional book.

4. The class can have a large class progress chart in the form of a bookworm. Made of paper, only the head of the worm should be displayed at first. When a child has completed a book not already listed, a new segment can be added onto the worm. The goal would be to see the worm grow as long as possible.

5. Each pupil can record on a card the title and author of every book he has greatly enjoyed. These cards can be placed in a pocket chart so other pupils can note the recommendations of their peers.

6. Each child in a room can construct a tagboard "book wheel." The wheel can be divided by lines into as many sectors as there are types of books to be designated (such as biography, animal stories) and each sector can be identified by the name of the type of book. On the back of the wheel each book a child reads can be listed, numbered in the order in which the book was read. On the proper sector of the wheel this code number can then be recorded. For example, if the first book a child has read during the school year is *The Biggest Bear* by Lynd Ward, he would number it *1* and record the figure *1* in the sector of the wheel reserved for animal stories. By means of such a "wheel" it can be noted at a glance whether the child is doing a variety of types of reading. Instead of keeping the list of books read with identifying numbers on the back of the wheel, each child can make a folder of tagboard, drawing the wheel on the right-hand side of the inside of the folder and keeping the list of books read on the opposite side.

The Learning Resource Center (The School Library)

With the recognition that visual materials, such as videotape recordings, films, filmstrips, and motion pictures, constitute an important resource for learning, many libraries, especially the larger ones, have been made a depository not only of books but also of a variety of other auditory and visual aids. Consequently the name *library* has frequently been changed to *learning resource center.* While recognition unquestionably needs to be given to the many material resources for learning in addition to books, some cautions need to be observed when school libraries are changed into learning resource centers. Care needs to be taken that the cost of the visual and auditory aids is not deducted from the budget otherwise justifiably used for books. Furthermore, the expense involved in adequately administering a program utilizing such aids should not reduce the amount of money that should be spent on books. Unless additional staff can be secured for assuring the wise purchase and use of the auditory and visual aids, it may decrease the effectiveness of the librarian if he needs to devote to that work part of the time he formerly used for his responsibility with books. Nor should the already limited space for housing books that is found in many schools be unduly sacrificed for storage of auditory and other visual aids. When precautions such as those suggested here are observed, it may not matter much whether books are housed with the other materials and whether the designation *library* or *learning resource center* is used.

A question that often arises in connection with a small school is whether there should be a room library or a school library. The answer probably is that preferably there should be both, though, to be sure, the accessibility of the latter—both in terms of physical placement of the school library and of ease with which it is possible for pupils to use it—needs to be considered when attempting to answer the question. A school library makes it possible for boys and girls in different grades of the elementary school to have access to the same books. The importance of this point is readily recognized as one is aware of the vast overlapping in reading ability and in interests among boys and girls in various grades. Furthermore, a well-equipped school library, with books well arranged and interestingly displayed, can serve as an important link between the resources of the school and the public libraries. However, the need of a room library must not be overlooked. Even if there is a school library, arrangements should be made for a sizeable number of suitable books to be kept in each classroom. These books can be ordered through budgetary provisions for room libraries, they may be secured "on loan" from the school or public library, or they may be obtained from all of these and other sources. Ready accessibility of the books in a room library and appropriateness of the books to the work being taken up in a given schoolroom are among arguments for room libraries.

Points, in addition to those heretofore discussed, that should be considered in relation to school and/or room libraries are listed below.

1. If possible there should be a librarian in each school. However, it needs to be borne in mind that the employment of a full-time librarian for a small school can probably not be justified. In such cases, alternatives to a full-time librarian that may be considered are: (a) having a librarian serve several schools if there is more than one school in a district, (b) engaging one teacher in a school for part-time work as librarian, along with other teaching responsibilities, (c) asking each teacher, if no librarian is available, to assume responsibilities in his own room library that might otherwise be allocated to a librarian. Elementary school teachers who have had a course in Literature for Children, as a large number have, should not find themselves at a loss as to how to proceed in guiding the independent reading of boys and girls without the assistance of a school librarian. Ob-

viously not as much can be expected in terms of results as if a librarian were available.

2. There should be close cooperation between the librarian and the teacher. A librarian should welcome suggestions from teachers as to books that would be particularly helpful to the boys and girls in the various rooms of the school, and the teacher should be receptive to information given by the librarian to help him become familiar with books on various topics. The librarian and teacher should work together on such matters as: (a) management of a room library, (b) provisions for story hour or book report activities, (c) development and operation of a library-skills program.

3. The library-skills development program should be carefully planned. It should be a schoolwide program so that there is no indiscriminate overlapping and so that gaps in the program can, to a considerable extent, be avoided. Part of the responsibility for the instigation and operation of such a program should lie with the librarian. But he alone cannot carry it out effectively. The room teacher needs to assume an important role in this respect. Suggestions for developing some of the types of "library skills" are given in chapter 9, under the topic "Skills in Locating Information and Using It." (See page 248.)

Book Selection

As indicated earlier in this chapter the selection of books for a school library should be a cooperative undertaking for school librarians and teachers. Boys and girls, too, can be given a voice in choosing books for the room or school library, but the final decision on recommendations made by boys and girls should rest with the adults—the teacher and the librarian.

Since such a vast number of books for boys and girls are available and since the number is rapidly increasing, no librarian and assuredly no teacher can have a personal acquaintance with anywhere near all books. Consequently it is fortunate that there are various published aids for book selection, among them: *Best Books for Children,* latest edition (R.R. Bowker); *Children's Books: Awards and Prizes,* latest edition (Children's Book Council); *Notable Children's Books,* latest edition (American Library Association); and *Sources of Good Books and Magazines for Children,* compiled by Winifred C. Ladley (International Reading Association, 1970). Books listed under "Books on Literature for Children" also give help on book selection. (See page 334.)

Quite a number of periodicals evaluate current books for children. Included in this group are: *The Booklist* (American Library Association); *Childhood Education*

Figure 10.35. A Reading Center.

(Association for Childhood Education, International); *Elementary English* (National Council of Teachers of English); *Reading Teacher* (International Reading Association); and *Wilson Library Bulletin* (H.W. Wison Company). Some of the leading newspapers of the country also at times publish reviews of books for children.

Evaluation

The success of the literature program, as in the case of all other school programs, should be judged in terms of the objectives that have been set. However, only insofar as the objectives are sound, can the results, if they are in harmony with the objectives, be considered desirable. In various parts of this chapter indications have been given as to what should be attained through guidance of boys and girls in their development of interests and tastes in reading. In the light of these, the teacher can get some help in judging the effectiveness of the program through means such as the following:

1. Observing the extent to which the pupils read worthwhile materials when left "on their own"

2. Noting whether the boys and girls read a variety of materials (such as biography, science, history) as part of their independent reading activity

3. Being cognizant of the extent to which boys and girls make comments that reveal an increase in interests and an elevation in tastes in what they read

4. Noting whether reading has an effect on the behavior of boys and girls, as, for example, whether a book giving a sympathetic treatment of a minority group seems to result in a greater appreciation of members of that group with whom they come into contact

5. Observing whether the pupils have increased sensitivity to good style of writing.

FOR STUDY AND DISCUSSION

1. Devise a questionnaire for help in determining what books to recommend to an individual who is asked, either orally or in writing, the questions you have formulated. Indicate the grade level for which you have planned the instrument.

2. How might you proceed in guiding a child so that he will develop more refined tastes in his reading?

3. Suggest ways in which the teacher can assist a child, through books, to grow in understanding of himself and of others.

4. It has been claimed that the teacher who in an appropriate manner starts reading to his pupils books of the universal appeal of *Doctor Dolittle* by High Lofting or *The Wind in the Willows* by Kenneth Grahame need not fear that many children able to read such books will

not be eager to read them. What are other books in this category that you would recommend for oral reading of the introductory chapter by the teacher?

5. Devise a game that can be used to interest boys and girls in reading worthwhile books.

6. In this chapter are given suggestions for planning a literature program for the elementary school. Enlarge upon any of the suggestions given, showing how they could be implemented in the planning stage of the program.

7. Construct one or more visual aids to be used to interest boys and girls in books.

8. Plan a Book Week program for any grade of the elementary school.

9. Examine a professional book such as *Children and Books* by May Arbuthnot and Zena Sutherland or *A Teacher's Guide to Children's Books* by Nancy Larrick, for suggested readings for boys and girls in any one area of the content subjects. Then read in that area and write brief reviews, possibly on cards, of each book read. Include among other points in your reviews your evaluation of each book. (Some of the other books listed under "References" will suggest additional sources for help in choosing worthwhile books. The reader is also referred to chapter 13 for further listings in the area of literature for children.)

10. Toward the end of the chapter suggestions for evaluating the success of efforts to guide boys and girls in reading worthwhile books are given. Can you think of additional ones?

REFERENCES

Arbuthnot, May Hill, and Sutherland, Zena. *Children and Books*, 4th ed. Chicago: Scott, Foresman and Company, 1972.

Burrows, Alvina Treut; Monson, Diane L.; and Stauffer, Russell G. *New Horizons in the Language Arts*. New York: Harper & Row, 1972.

Chambers, Dewey W. *Literature for Children: Storytelling and Creative Drama*. Dubuque, Iowa: Wm. C. Brown Company Publishers, 1970.

Gans, Roma. *Common Sense in Teaching Reading*. Indianapolis, Ind.: The Bobbs-Merrill Company, 1963.

Huck, Charlotte, and Kuhn, Doris. *Children's Literature in the Elementary School*. New York: Holt, Rinehart and Winston, Inc., 1968.

Huus, Helen. *Children's Books to Enrich the Social Studies*. Washington, D.C.: National Council for the Social Studies, 1961.

Jacobs, Leland B. *Literature with Young Children*. New York: Teachers College Press, Columbia University, 1965.

Reid, Virginia M., ed. *Reading Ladders for Human Relations.* 5th ed. Washington, D.C.: American Council on Education, 1972.

Ruggs, Corinne. *Bibliotherapy.* Newark, Del.: International Reading Association, 1968.

Smith, James A. *Creative Teaching of Reading and Literature in the Elementary School.* Boston: Allyn and Bacon, Inc., 1967.

Spache, George. *Sources of Good Books for Poor Readers.* Newark, Del.: International Reading Association, 1966.

Whitehead, Robert. *Children's Literature: Strategies of Teaching.* Englewood Cliffs, N.J.: Prentice-Hall, Inc., 1968.

3

SPECIALIZED PROCEDURES
AND RESOURCES

11

Creativity Through Dramatic Expression and Choral Speaking

Creative expression constitutes an essential component of a successful language arts program. We have emphasized its role in various parts of this book, and in chapter 5, "Guiding Growth in Oral Communication," we have paid special attention to creative writing. In this chapter we are discussing two other means of expressing creativity through language arts activities, namely, dramatic expression and choral speaking.

DRAMATIC EXPRESSION

During the past few decades elementary school teachers have become increasingly cognizant of the role of dramatic expression—which provides communication through speech and movement—as a vital part of the language arts curriculum. Trends that seem to be characteristic are:

1. A greater number of elementary school teachers take college courses or attend workshops pertaining at least in part to creative dramatics, it would seem.
2. Books and articles in periodicals, dealing exclusively or in part with creative dramatics in the elementary school classroom, have been appearing on the market in greater numbers.

Values of Dramatic Expression

Although the values of dramatic expression vary somewhat from one type of dramatics to another, the variance is probably more one of degree than of kind. Listed here are those which more or less pertain to several types of creative dramatics, while on subsequent pages of this chapter attention is drawn, as the types of dramatic expression are discussed, to the contributions each can make.

Provision for Emotional Expression. One of the chief values of creative dramatics lies in the opportunity it affords for emotional expression. Children, hemmed in by myriads of regulations—many necessary, some not—need the freedom of self-expression that dramatic expression can so well supply. Without some independence the child's world, far from being a happy, carefree one, might be well-nigh intolerable.

It is indeed fortunate that the simplest, freest, most spontaneous means of dramatic expression, namely, dramatic play, is almost second nature to the child who, when one minute he plays he is a horse, for all practical effects (that is, for effects on the child's emotional nature) *is* a horse whinnying as he gallops through the dining room, even though the next moment ascending the steps to the second floor, he may be an airplane zooming upward into space. What matter physical restrictions when the spirit is free to abide wheresoever it chooses!

In dramatic play or in more structured dramatization, an observing adult can at times gain insight into the child's emotional life. Care must be taken that neither teacher nor parent assumes diagnostic responsibilities that would baffle an expert psychiatrist, for it is easy to make serious errors in associating dramatic expression with specific underlying and deep-seated psychic deviations. However, persistence in choice of certain roles may well indicate a need. The girl who almost invariably wants to be a princess may have a feeling of deep inferiority. The child who shows cruelty in his dramatic play may be in need of help in freeing himself of asocial impulses.

Development of Personality Traits. Through various types of creative dramatics opportunity for increased self-control, greater poise, and more self-confidence is given. The freedom of movement encouraged by liberating dramatic expression fosters gracefulness which in turn affects physical characteristics. One of the greatest boons of creative dramatics lies in its effects upon the imagination. In the young child ample opportunity to engage in creative dramatics gives the imagination of the child free reign. Continued participation in dramatics helps prevent the undesirable inhibitions that typically thwart the imagination of the child as he passes toward adolescence and later into adulthood. Boys and girls receiving the full benefits of creative dramatics at its best may be helped to know even when they are grownups how:

Of the magic things of life, never to tire,

And how, to renew, when it is low, the lamp of my desire.[1]

Expansion of the Environment. Through dramatics, whether it is the dramatic play of the three-year-old who is playing that he is an Arabian steed or the twelve-year-old who participates in a Mexican fiesta, there is need for effective dramatization, of knowledge of the situations dramatized, obtained either firsthand through observation or indirectly through pictures, conversation, reading, and the like. The near can become fascinating and the faraway clear and intriguing.

Growth in Sympathetic Understanding. As the child's environment expands through creative dramatics and through related activities, he is provided with the chance to develop in ability to put himself in the place of another, especially when under the guidance of a wise adult. When the bully who is given the role of the bullied, when the boy or girl who once thought of Indians as savages takes the part of an Indian lad or lass as a day on a reservation is dramatized, or when the girl who had been prejudiced against Orientals takes part in a dramatization of "Matsayama's Mirror," the children can hardly avoid developing a feeling of warmth toward the people they portray, for true dramatics is not to *seem* to be but to *be*.

Development of Language Skills. What better reason can there be for boys and girls to develop some of the language arts skills than that afforded by dramatics? The child who has talked almost inaudibly begins to recognize the value of speech that can readily be heard. Even exercises, if necessary, to get a suitable intonation, to achieve proper pitch, or to speak with convincing tempo make sense to the participant eager to do his best. Exercises in the use of exact words to express feeling can become surprisingly important. The script for a dramatization and letters of invitation to a play constitute but a few of the opportunities for written communication provided by creative dramatics.

Means of Motivation. In the preceding paragraph reference is made to the power of motivation of dramatics in the area of the language arts. Similarly the social studies, science, art, music, physical education, and health can be vitalized through dramatic expression as the pupils dramatize a folk tale of a foreign country, put on skits showing scenes from the lives of great men and women of science, plan a backdrop for a puppet show, learn songs for use in a pageant, play games of boys and girls in faraway times or places, or make up a good-health play showing the constituents of a balanced diet.

Development of Work Habits. Important work habits can be formed or reinforced through dramatics. Cooperation, perseverance, critical thinking with need to come to decisions, and participation in evaluation, for example, can be practiced in meaningful situations.

Influence on Class Atmosphere. Repeatedly it has been observed that the whole atmosphere in a classroom can be affected favorably through introduction of dramatics. Boys and girls who previously had lacked interest in school may frequently engage happily in other activities of the school day that formerly had been only boring to them. Pride in the room, joy in teacher and peers, and enthusiasm for school are often the result.

Variation of Procedure. Dramatics can help avoid the sameness in teaching procedure that seems to be one of the reasons why some boys and girls do not like school.

1. Author unknown.

Dramatic activities provide not only variety but pleasant variety. To the boys and girls "the play's the thing."

Provision for Enjoyment. Very important among the values of creative dramatics is the fun provided. As "beauty is its own excuse for being," so is the pure, wholesome, unadulterated fun that can result from creative expression in dramatics.

Dramatic Play

Dramatic play, as the term is used here, refers to the spontaneous play that is characteristic of the young child, in which he lives—not merely acts—the part he is portraying. The girl engages in dramatic play when she *is* the mother dressing the baby. The boy takes part in dramatic play when he *is* the engine that pulls the long heavy cars up an almost impossibly steep ascent. For dramatic play no talent is needed beyond that common to childhood. There is no audience to please. The joy of the actor is its reason for being. While props can be used, they are far from essential, and simple props are much to be preferred to the elaborate. The role of a child may change swiftly as after a few minutes of being an air-plane—without even a need for transformation, without a fairy wand to make the change—he becomes the milk-man, a spider, or even a rock. Or the same role, as mother, for example, may be continued for week after week.

Values. All of the results indicated under "Values of Dramatic Expression" probably can be achieved, at least to some extent, in dramatic play. Among those to which dramatic play can contribute especially are: (1) provi-sion for emotional expression, (2) development of per-sonality traits, (3) expansion of the environment, and (4) growth in sympathetic understanding. It is through dramatic play that the child can try out the life he observes around him and that which his vivid imagina-tion creates for him. It is through this medium of expres-sion that he can be what he wants to be, ruled by his own spirit not by the physical laws of existence. With utter, joyous abandon he can surmount problems and short-comings of all types.

Role of the Teacher. Maybe the most important func-tion the teacher can fulfill in connection with the dramatic play of the young is not to interfere with it. He should avoid interference by arranging the school pro-gram so that ample time is provided, by refraining from "directing" the child's play, and by making no untoward remarks about his activities, such as referring to them as "dear," "darling," or "amusing." He can help by setting aside places in the schoolroom where dramatic play can "germinate" and develop. He can provide facilities such as a playhouse unit with its simple household furnishings or a make-believe store. He can help make available to **the child large blocks, found in both the kindergarten** and first-grade room, from which the children can con-struct houses, stores, post offices, airplanes, boats, trains, trucks, tractors, or whatever fancy dictates. The teacher can make accessible one or more boxes of simple props such as an apron for grandmother, a piece of cloth for baby's blanket, high-heeled shoes for mother, long skirts for the ladies, and veiling, hats, pocketbooks for a variety of purposes.

The teacher can also perform an important role by:

1. Conducting discussion that stimulates dramatic play

2. Providing pupils with experiences that lead to dramatic play (such as taking children to a zoo, a farm, or a bakery)

3. Participating, usually only on invitation, in dramatic play (such as tending to the baby when mother needs to cook, being a guest at supper in the playhouse, or playing the role of a customer in a store)

4. Giving some (but only a few) suggestions as to how dramatic play can be carried on effectively within the limitations of time and space

5. Helping maintain a classroom attitude conducive to freedom without license and with respect for personality

6. Observing the child at his play in order to try to note his needs and his satisfactions.

Sequence. The teacher who wisely endeavors to guide the child in dramatic play will do well to keep in mind points stressed in the following sequence listed by Mildred Donoghue:[2]

Solitary play—The child plays alone with little or no atten-tion to other children. Although he may show interest in others, he will not play with them.

Parallel play—The child still plays independently but alongside of other children, and he enters into the same types of activities that they do. There is very little conversation.

Associate play—Children playing in the playhouse may share some ideas and materials, and their activities may be similar. One child sets the table while another feeds the baby. Each plays according to his interests.

Cooperative play—Late in the first year of school (first grade or kindergarten, depending on the school organization) a more organized type of play may appear. The play period may be lengthened and the same interest may carry over for several days. Two to five children may play together.

In interpreting the suggestions given in the above listing, the teacher will need to bear in mind that: (1) some of the boys and girls have passed through one or more of the stages before they enter school; (2) some pupils may omit one of the stages; (3) there may be variation in the characteristics of one or more of the stages outlined, as far as any one pupil is concerned.

2. Mildred R. Donoghue, *The Child and the English Language Arts,* (Dubuque, Iowa: Wm. C. Brown Company Publishers, 1971), p. 83.

Role-Playing. Role-playing can be thought of as one type of dramatic play, often of more complexity, however, than other forms of dramatic play. Typically in role-playing two or more participants enact, without previous rehearsal, a social situation that presents a problem. It may be centered on a problem that one or more of the boys and girls have encountered. For example, the theme of such an activity may be the arguments of two pupils each of whom is demanding the right to be the first to use a desired cassette. Or the dramatization may be centered around the treatment of an adult who has been asked to give a talk to the class. Although as a rule, the type of problem situation in which some members of the class actually find themselves probably furnishes the most desirable theme, there are times when the teacher may wish to introduce situations that have not actually occurred in the lives of any of the pupils. He may relate an event or read part of a story to the class, stopping at a crucial point to have different children dramatize what would constitute a desirable continuation of the activity described and, possibly, what would be an undesirable ending for it. If the subject of the dramatic play is one that none of the members of the class has actually experienced, it should, nevertheless, be one that is on the children's level of comprehension—similar at least in some respects to one that the boys and girls might encounter.

The goal of the teacher in encouraging role-playing is often a more didactic one than when guiding other types of dramatic play. Besides trying to accomplish the objective of providing boys and girls opportunity for self-expression and the other aims listed earlier for dramatic play, he also desires to help the boys and girls gain more insight into the problems of human relationships and a greater incentive to act in socially and morally acceptable ways. Furthermore, by observing the actions and noting the remarks of the boys and girls taking part in the role-playing, as in other dramatization, the teacher can at times gain insight into the problems of some of the boys and girls. Care must, however, be taken that the teacher, in his interpretations, does not try to serve as a psychiatrist. The sociodrama of role-playing should not be used as psychodrama. There is danger when the teacher makes generalizations beyond his power to make correct ones.

Guidance in role-playing can, as in the case of most activities, be given in a variety of ways. The steps listed below are some worthy of consideration, with possible alteration, by the teacher.

1. The teacher brings to the attention of the class —unless a pupil has done so—a situation suitable for role-playing.

2. The class, under the guidance of the teacher, discusses the situation.

3. Selection of participants in the role-playing is made. Sometimes if the dramatization is based on one in which some of the pupils have been involved, it is desirable to encourage those individuals to act out in front of the class the roles they have taken. At other times the teacher might ask for volunteers to engage in the presentation. If no volunteers are available, the teacher may need to encourage participation on the part of pupils who are likely to act the required roles with success.

4. In some instances the teacher may confront the audience with a challenge as to what they should try to determine while the role-playing is taking place. They might be asked to try to think of various ways in which the situation could be resolved in a desirable manner.

5. If the participants in the role-playing are the pupils who had actually been involved in the problem situation being dramatized, they may be asked either to portray it as they have dealt with it in the "life situation" and/or they may be requested to show how it could be dealt with advantageously.

6. The class discusses the role-playing.

7. At times one or more groups of pupils—in addition to those who have participated in the original role-playing—might be asked to demonstrate other ways in which the problem involved in the situation could be dealt with. After such presentations discussion should follow.

Other Examples of Dramatic Play. Interspersed among the preceding pages of this chapter are examples of dramatic play in addition to those to which reference is made in the preceding paragraphs on role-playing. Still others are mentioned following.

1. Being an inanimate object, such as a river, the wind, a seashell, father's rocker, or an automobile

2. Being an animal, such as a dog, cat, elephant, duck, goose, robin, eagle, one of the Three Bears, or one (or all!) of the Three Little Pigs

3. Playing school, church, or Sunday school

4. Baking cookies, fixing baby's bottle, feeding the chickens, sewing a dress, or piloting a plane

5. Re-enacting parts of a trip to a farm, a fire station, a bakery, or a post office.

Dramatization

There is no strict line of demarcation that can be drawn between dramatic play and dramatization. However, some distinction can be made. While in dramatic play the accent is on *being*, in dramatization, even in the less formal types, there is recognition of the fact that something is being dramatized. The dramatic play of the four-year-old , for example, as he plays house is almost total identification with the role played, frequently with no concern about an audience. In dramatization there is a planned, though often extemporaneously planned, enactment of roles. There is a plot, often very simple, with a beginning and a definite ending.

Dramatization can be classified in a variety of ways, these among them: (1) impromptu dramatization, (2) dramatization of a pupil-planned play, and (3) dramatization of plays written by others. Suggestions for guiding boys and girls in dramatization of each of these three types follow.

Impromptu Dramatization. In the impromptu dramatization, which is sometimes almost entirely extemporaneous, there is relatively little, if any, preplanning. After a story has been read during reading class or after the teacher has told or read a story to the class, one child, in a room where pupil expression is encouraged, may ask, "May we play the story?" Even though only a few minutes may be available for following the suggestion, the teacher may assent and help the group to decide quickly what scenes to include, what characters are needed for each scene, and where the setting is to be. After two or three minutes' time, the play may be well on its way. At other times one or more scenes may be enacted even without any preliminary planning other than that of assignment of roles.

With similar lack of emphasis on preplanning the boys and girls can engage in dramatization, with or without words, of activities or scenes about which they have read or which they have seen in life situations. For example, a group of second-grade boys and girls, after having watched workmen build a house, may return to the classroom to decide to put on a pantomime showing the work of builders they have observed. One may be a carpenter, another a plumber, and still another an electrician or a painter. The class can be divided into groups of four (if four workmen are to be presented) with each group assigning one of its members to each of the roles and helping one another re-enact the part of a given workman. Then the groups may pantomime their parts as the audience (the members of the other groups) tell what each person is doing.

Another variation is to have pupils put on impromptu dramatizations of scenes about which they have studied in the content subjects, such as the social studies or the sciences. After having read and heard about life in a Pueblo village, for example, the class may decide on a dramatization of the life of a boy and girl in such a village. After only brief discussion of points that can be brought out in a dramatization, characters can be chosen, the scene dramatized, and a brief discussion held on points of excellence or needs for improvement. Thereupon, again one or more groups of characters may be chosen who in turn will enact scenes. After reading,

for example, about Thomas Edison's boyhood and early manhood, the class may determine which scenes would be good for dramatization and then divide into as many groups as there are scenes to be presented. Thereupon each group can plan its dramatization in a different part of the room. Then, for the entire class, the scenes can be presented in appropriate order.

In order to help boys and girls receive maximum benefit from impromptu dramatizations, the teacher should keep points such as the following in mind.

1. Presentation to the pupils of many types of subject matter that provide suitable background for dramatic presentation and encouragement in taking part in interesting activities can stimulate the desire to dramatize what they have seen or heard.

2. Because boys and girls become less and less interested in dramatic play (often because of the inhibitions adults have placed upon them) after the early school years, it is important that the teacher help them preserve the imaginativeness of childhood and develop it as they grow toward adolescence. At first a suggestion to dramatize often may need to come from the teacher if the boys and girls have been unaccustomed with teachers of previous years to take part in dramatizations.

3. Although there are many values that can be achieved through frequent participation in dramatizations, like most good things, they can be overdone. Boys and girls should not be allowed to participate in them so frequently that the excitement, novelty, and joy of participation wear off. To dramatize most of the stories in a reader would probably be more detrimental to the child's best growth and development than not to dramatize any.

4. The slapstick should be avoided in dramatizations. A desire to create a valuable contribution can be encouraged through a discussion beforehand of the mood to be portrayed or the attitude of the character or the style of expression most suitable. Wise use of praise following dramatization can also help set standards for subsequent ones.

5. Criticisms of a child's best effort should be given sparingly lest frustrations and inhibitions result. Emphasis should be placed primarily on points well done.

6. At times more than one dramatization of a scene or story could be given, with different pupils taking part.

7. Care should be taken that all boys and girls have opportunities for participation in dramatizations. The temptation to give a part to the child who seems best suited for it can prevent the child who may most need the help afforded by this type of language arts activity from being able to participate.

8. In impromptu dramatizations there usually is no **audience other than that consisting of the pupils who** are not in the dramatization. If a dramatization of this

type is given more than once by the same participants, it probably should no longer be classified as impromptu.

9. While it is not important and not possible that every child have the opportunity to take part in every dramatization (often there are not enough parts even if many pupils are intentionally included as characters with minor parts), as a rule no person should be given a part a second time before each child has been assigned one once.

Dramatization of Pupil-Planned Plays. As boys and girls progress to the upper-primary and intermediate grades, they can be increasingly interested in dramatization that involves more than extemporizing or impromptu presentation with relatively little preplanning. Careful preparation can take place both with stories that the children heard or read or with plays for which they themselves chose a theme and developed the plot.

1. *Dramatization of stories.* In addition to the values of dramatization already listed, dramatization of stories has this important value: boys and girls can gain greater appreciation of literature. If this objective is to be fulfilled, obviously it is important that the teacher guide the boys and girls accordingly. Suggestions for guidance follow.

Dramatization as a means of increasing pupils' appreciation of literature. One criterion to be observed in order that boys and girls can attain maximum appreciation of good literature through the dramatization of stories is that the stories chosen should be suitable and valuable. First of all, they should be worthwhile stories, as high on the pupils' level of appreciation as the class can dramatize with success. Dramatization of stories beyond the pupils' power of performance with reasonable success is likely not to instill in them a love of the story. Nor, on the contrary, will stories below the pupils' level of appreciation be likely to foster greater interest in good literature. Some of the requirements for stories for dramatization can be summarized thus:

The story should be ethically sound.

The story should be good literature.

The story should have vivid characters and swift moving action intermingled with suspense.

The story should consist of relatively few incidents.

The pattern of the story should be distinct, with a forceful beginning, an easily recognizable climax toward which all preceding events lead, and a satisfying ending.

The story should contain much action on which the theme should rest rather than chiefly on beauty of words or philosophy of background.

The characters should be interesting.

The story should have emotional appeal for the children.

Repetition of type of incident or of cause for incidents occurring with almost rhythmic quality in the development of the plot should be one of the points for which to watch in selecting a story for dramatization for the young child.

One way in which pupils can gain greatly in acquaintance with good literature and, it is hoped, with subsequent increased appreciation of it, is to have them read quite a number of good stories in order to decide which one or ones they consider most suitable for dramatization. Sometimes the entire class can be encouraged to read as many as they can, within a given period of time, of the stories listed by the teacher. At other times various committees or even individuals could assume responsibility for reading different stories and then later report to the class as to which they consider suitable for the purpose. However, it should be kept in mind that a teacher cannot truly delegate her responsibility for the selection of suitable stories. Nevertheless, by assisting the boys and girls in applying criteria such as those previously listed, he can use his final power to determine which selections to use, in a permissive rather than arbitrary manner. The reader may have noted that many of the well-known folktales fulfill the requirements listed. "Rumpelstiltskin," "The Three Golden Apples," and "Hänsel and Gretel" all qualify. Modern stories however, also can be used successfully, as, for example, parts of *Mary Poppins* or *Mr. Popper's Penguins*.

Steps in planning a dramatization of a story. After the story has been selected, what needs to be done next? There is no one series of steps that can be acclaimed as the one and only sequence to follow. The order of procedure here suggested, however, is one that can bring good results.

Drawing attention to the sequence of events in the story. The order of the happenings can be emphasized through questioning by the teacher or by listing of chief events on the chalkboard at the dictation of the boys and girls.

Drawing attention to the characters by asking for their names (to record on the chalkboard) and asking pertinent questions as to motive and actions of each.

Deciding upon scenes to dramatize and upon the order of these scenes, with emphasis on the action in each.

Determining characters needed for each scene and the role each plays within a given scene.

Discussing general content of what the various characters will need to say in order to portray the plot adequately.

Discussing what would make an effective beginning and a strong ending for the play.

Discussing ways in which the various characters can carry on the story through their words and their nonverbal responses.

Assigning roles, with care being taken that no pupil need play a part he does not want. (It may be impossible, however, for each pupil to get the part he likes best.)

Practicing scenes. (At times boys and girls not in a given scene may be engaged in other activities while others are practicing their parts. At other times the practicing may be done in front of classmates not in the play to obtain helpful suggestions from them.)

It is often advisable to have more than one pupil work on each of the parts of a play. Opportunity should, as a rule, be provided for each pupil assigned to a given role to be in one dramatization when it is presented to an audience.

Even in carefully preplanned dramatization, the lines frequently are not recorded. The general content of the dialogue should be discussed. There may well be variations each time the story is dramatized. On the other hand, there are times when it may seem advisable that the lines be recorded. A variety of procedures can be followed in the writing. For example, a committee under the direction of the teacher may work out dialogue for the first scene. That scene can then be presented to the class for suggestions, some of which may be incorporated in a rewriting of the parts. Thereupon another committee may proceed with work on the lines for the second scene, to be followed by still another committee or committees whose responsibility it is to write the script for the remainder of the play. Even when the script is written, it is not necessary that the lines be memorized. The script can be used merely as guide by the boys and girls.

The production. With dramatizations for which there has been careful preplanning, it seems only logical to have an audience for a final performance. Who should be invited should be determined in part by the complexity of the play. The audience may consist of another grade in the same building, the play may be given in an assembly program, or parents may be invited.

Elaborate costuming or stage settings should be avoided. In fact, in some of the best productions from the point of view of the growth and development of the performers, both costuming and stage properties may be lacking. If there is costuming, it is best to keep it so simple that the pupils themselves, not the parents and the teacher, have the experience involved in making the costumes. The same can be said about the stage setting. An apron to suggest that a girl is a grandmother, a hat to show that a boy is a man, long ears made of paper to show that the person is the bad wolf, often are enough. On the other hand if, for example, a play is worked out on the book *The Door in the Wall* by Marguerite De Angeli as a culmination for a unit on the Middle Ages, it may be that making costumes by the pupils after adequate research on the dress of that period of history can be a valuable means of integrating the work in the social studies with art. Similarly a study of the ways of living in the days of King Arthur might be reason for work on stage properties for a play adapted from the story of King Arthur and his knights. The background can, if desired, be satisfactorily presented through portrayal of scenes drawn on paper, possibly covering portable screens.

Evaluation. After the boys and girls have spent considerable time dramatizing a story, they are entitled to the benefit of evaluation. In using evaluative procedures it must be recognized that the emphasis should be placed not only on the product but also on the process of getting ready to give the play. The appraisal should be based to a large extent on self-evaluation, preferably in part at least, using criteria that the pupils have helped work out. Points that may be considered in such an evaluation include:

Did we work cooperatively with one another as we prepared the play?

Did we make good use of our time in our work on the play?

Did we tell the story well, arranging important points in a correct sequence?

Could we be heard easily in every part of the room?

Did we show by our actions how we felt about what we were saying?

Did the characters seem true to life?

Did the play have a strong beginning?

Did the play have a strong ending?

Probably more permanent values are gained if, after the final production, criticisms by others, including both the teacher and the children, are confined chiefly to favorable points. As a rule, suggestions for improvement may better be offered before the boys and girls give the play in front of an audience.

2. *Dramatization of original plays.* Though many boys and girls in the elementary school, especially in the lower grades, are greatly interested in dramatizing stories they have heard or read, they also like to plan the plot for plays they present. Sometimes the dramatization may be a series of episodes to illustrate points with a background in the content areas. For example, they may give a dramatization of (1) a Mexican market day, (2) life in Colonial times, (3) life on the Oregon trail, or (4) life during castle days.

Sometimes the dramatization may evolve around a story with a plot which the boys and girls themselves work out. The teacher will frequently need to help them decide on a worthy theme and develop a strong plot around the theme. A decision will need to be made as to what characters are necessary and what scenes to depict. The boys and girls may want to write the lines for their play or they may prefer putting on the play without use of any recorded lines. Occasionally a boy or girl may want to write a play as an individual creative writing project.

Dramatization of Plays Written by Others. Because of the many values that can be obtained through the very act of working out a play themselves, there has been a tendency among educators to look with disfavor on any dramatization that is not original with the boys and girls. This attitude hardly seems justifiable. There may well be times when boys and girls can achieve some of the objectives of dramatization through dramatizing a play written by others.

Many an adult who has been in a worthwhile high school or college play or has taken part in community theater will testify that values can accrue from taking part in a play that is published. From and through such activities can result increased cooperation, vicarious experiences with resulting lack of concentration on self, joy in active participation in a joint project, and insight into character development (in case the play is a worthy one).

Especially when plays are based in part on events or conditions in a background of social studies or science or health there is, at times, an advantage in dramatizing a play that has been written by a person who is well acquainted with the background. Unless boys and girls have studied rather extensively—more extensively than time often permits—for example, life in Colonial times, they may perpetuate through a pupil-created play ideas about that period of history that can be misleading or outright erroneous. On the other hand, they can receive and give a correct impression if they dramatize a play written by a person well acquainted with customs of Colonial times.

Puppetry

Puppetry is becoming more and more popular with boys and girls. It is well that this popularity exists for puppetry can serve as a decided aid to the elementary school child.

Values of Puppetry. Puppetry is an art form and, as such, one of its primary values lies in the achievement of objectives that active and passive participation in any art form should provide. Happily, however, it can also serve as the means of helping the elementary school child attain additional goals. Because many of these goals are in the field of the language arts a discussion of puppetry is included in this book.

1. *Value of puppetry as an art form.* First let us consider some of the values of puppetry as an art form, some of which are listed here and briefly commented upon.

Acquisition of a broader perspective. As with other art forms, there is a universality in the art of puppetry. Through teacher guidance the boys and girls can find out that the art has flourished in various times through past ages and that people in remotely distant parts of the world have had the little figures, known as puppets, representing humans and animals, as part of their cultural pattern. To give the boys and girls a better perspective of the role of the past as background for the present and to provide them with additional pleasure as they give puppet plays, the teacher may wish to acquaint them with facts such as these: (a) Relics of the long-distant past include dolllike figures with holes under the arms that were presumably used for attaching strings. (b) The Hindus, according to some sources, believed that the puppets had previously been gods and consequently they treated them with respect and reverence. (c) Beautiful puppets were created in China even during the legendary era. (d) Japan has produced puppets that are exquisite. (e) Among the relics of ancient Greece figures presumed to have been puppets have been found near what have been discovered to be little theaters. (f) Puppets seem to have been introduced into Italy from Greece following the Roman conquest. It is from the Latin word *pupa* that the word *puppet* seems to have been derived. (g) During the Middle Ages and, later puppets were used as actors in religious and morality plays. Many of them had the Nativity as their theme. It is claimed by some that the word *marionette* is a derivative of *mariolette*, the word meaning "little image of the Virgin Mary." (h) Puppeteers in medieval and postmedieval periods served as wandering messengers, as they traveled from town to town and city to city announcing the "news of the day" and providing entertainment. (i) During the feudal age puppet shows were a major source of entertainment in the courts of the nobility and in the living quarters of

Figure 11.1. Through Puppetry Many Worthwhile Objectives Can Be Achieved.

the common people. (j) The American Indian made extensive use of puppets in religious ceremonies. They also used them for entertainment. (k) Famous people of the past have been greatly interested in puppetry, among them the German poet Goethe, the great composer Franz Hayden, and Shakespeare.

Release from tension. Like other forms of art, participation in puppetry, whether either active or passive, can help an individual attain at least temporarily some freedom from tension. In an age so characterized by tensions as ours is, puppetry can be of real service in alleviating some tension.

Use of the imagination. Like other art forms, puppetry has the power to help an individual develop his imagination. As the pupil watches a puppet play or as he is involved in various steps in giving a puppet play, opportunity for considerable free play of the imagination can be given. Puppets—even when representing people or animals, to say nothing of inanimate objects or creatures of the imagination—do not portray the real, but an image of the real, removed from the actual by at least one step. This imaginative quality is achieved not only through the making of the puppets and the stage on which they perform but also in the words and the actions of the puppeteers. In fact, if a puppet looks too real, he loses one of the qualities that should characterize a puppet—the ability to serve as interpretation of the real, rather than a reproduction of it. Similarly, a puppet stage that presents a background that is photographic in detail fails to provide the proper setting for a puppet play, and the puppeteers who talk or act just like human beings lose their best role as actors. Imagination is therefore essential to the production and interpretation of a good puppet play. Undoubtedly it is this departure from the usual order of things that helps achieve the freedom from tension to which reference is made in the preceding paragraph.

Attainment of emotional satisfaction. Closely related to both freedom from tension and use of the imagination is the emotional reaction that can be achieved through puppetry. Through introduction to the fantasy that puppetry can so well provide, the spirit can be lifted beyond the mundane into the realms where the real is more than the practical.

Adaptation to individual differences. Engaging in puppetry can be beneficial to individuals with varying needs. A salutary effect on the shy child is that through it he may gain in self-confidence. As he manipulates a puppet or as he speaks the parts of one beyond the view of his audience, the child may be saved the embarrassment he might feel when taking part in a different type of dramatization. Hopefully such practice can prove to be a step toward greater self-assurance in other situations where he is not eclipsed by a puppet stage.

The retarded child can profit through puppetry. While working behind the scenes, slowness of reaction is not as likely to be as noticeable as if he were in full view of his audience. Furthermore he is saved the uneasiness of seeing any looks of impatience on faces of those waiting for the next step in the performance of the play. Consequently the retarded child may get an assurance that will carry over as he reacts in other situations. There are, moreover, so many ways in which the difficulty of the demands on a child can be adapted to his ability. Simple plays can be chosen and duties in the plays corresponding to the ability of the child can be assigned.

For the show-off, puppetry can be very beneficial. He, like the shy and the retarded child, can profit from not being in sight of his audience. What satisfaction is there to him if he has no one to perceive his antics?

To the physically handicapped, puppetry can be a great benefit. It can, in many instances, help him perform in an activity in which he can learn to excel. At times, too, it can serve as a means of inducing the child to make use of muscles that might atrophy were they not given the exercise provided by some of the activities required in puppetry.

2. *Value of puppetry as a group activity.* Although puppetry can be a solo performance, and as such have many values, typically it is a group activity, in which, in addition to those already mentioned, values such as the ones indicated below can be derived.

The child is given an illustration of the fact that "all are needed by each one." The importance of each person to the group project is clearly in evidence.

Practice in group planning is provided in a meaningful situation as the pupils select the play or determine on what to base their play, as they make the puppets, the stage, the scenery, and the props, as they determine details of the performance, and as they evaluate their work.

The satisfaction that comes from participating in a group, when the work on puppetry is well conducted, can be experienced by the child.

If through participation in puppetry at school the child becomes interested in working with puppets at home, his family may become a more close-knit group through viewing his plays or through familywide participation in puppetry.

Improved rapport among the members of the group and between the pupils and the teacher can be established as they work together on a common project in which there is great interest.

3. *Contribution as an aid to learning.* Participation in puppetry can serve as an asset in various curricular fields in addition to those to which reference has been made. It can be a means of helping boys and girls in speech training, reading (including research activities), writing, and listening. It can serve as motivation for development in some of the content areas as it gives purpose for some needed activities that might otherwise seem purposeless. It can add interest and understanding to literature as worthwhile stories are being played; it can serve as incentive for living according to laws of good health, when, for example, a puppet play shows the importance of the Basic Seven; it can throw light on periods remote in history as children study customs and costumes of the time, for example, when Robin Hood lived, in order to put on a puppet play on *Robin Hood and His Merry Men*; it can give meaning to science as scenes such as the invention of the telephone are dramatized; it can give reason for studying music so that suitable music to accompany the play will be selected; it can give purpose for studying various techniques of artistic production in order to be able to provide a stage setting that is attractive.

Kinds of Puppets. The difference between a puppet and a marionette should be made clear. The marionette is operated by strings; the puppet, as the term *puppet* is here used, is not. Because of the complexity of operating most marionettes, they are used relatively little in the

Figure 11.2. A Marionette.

elementary school. Consequently discussion in this book is confined almost exclusively to the puppet.

Puppets vary greatly, from the simple ones that even beginners in the elementary school can operate to the elaborate puppets used by professionals. In this chapter puppets are classified as to three types: (1) stationary puppets, (2) rod puppets, and (3) hand puppets.

Figure 11.3. Puppets to Fit Various Needs.

1. *Stationary puppets.* Stationary puppets, also called table puppets, are the simplest of all to operate. In a sense, they need no operator. The puppet is placed on the stage or representation of a stage, often on a table, and it usually remains there without movement while the

and it frequently remains there without movement while the puppeteer can concentrate on the thoughts he wishes to express. To be sure, the puppeteer can move the puppet by lifting him onto another part of the stage or pushing him to a different spot. Not only does the puppet often remain in one place but typically no parts of his body can be moved. He is, indeed, in those instances, stationary.

Stationary puppets, because of their simplicity of manipulation and, usually, of form, are used more frequently by the young child or the beginner in puppetry than by older or more advanced puppeteers. They may be effective in a one-character show, in which the puppet does all the speaking. However, more than one stationary puppet can be used in a puppet play. If actions are to be portrayed, in addition to lifting the puppet or pushing him by the puppeteer, they can be suggested by the words of the puppet or through background statements of the puppeteer. For example, if a one-puppet show is given on the story "Little Red Riding Hood," in which the wolf is the puppet, the introduction might be in words by the wolf, such as: "One lovely sunshiny morning when I was very hungry, I heard Little Red Riding Hood's mother say to her, 'Little Red Riding Hood, take this bread to your grandmother who is sick in bed. But do not stop to talk to anyone. Go directly to her home.'" Or the puppeteer might introduce the play by saying, "One lovely sunshiny morning Little Red Riding Hood's mother gave her a basket of "goodies" to take to her grandmother."

Many of the puppets described later under "Rod puppets" (see page 299) and "Hand puppets" (see page 299) can, with but slight alteration or without any modification other than unconnecting the stick, be used as stationary puppets.

A bottle can be transformed with water colors or construction paper in a variety of ways, one of which is illustrated here. In a similar manner an interesting looking stationary puppet can be made from a tin can. A variation from the tin can puppet illustrated here is made

Figure 11.4. A Puppet Head Made from a Bottle.

Figure 11.5. A Puppet Head Made from a Can.

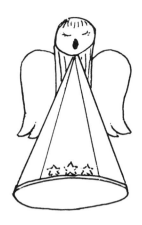

Figure 11.7. A Cone Puppet.

Figure 11.6. A Paper-Cup Puppet.

Figure 11.8. A Carved Puppet.

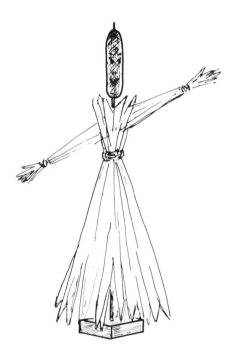

Figure 11.10. A Cattail Puppet.

Figure 11.9. A Box Puppet.

Stationary Puppets

Figure 11.11. Another Box Puppet.

by using the can as body of the puppet. It can be covered with cloth or paper to represent the puppet's clothing and a sock can be pushed through an opening in the top of the can. The sock can be stuffed, and facial features—either of felt, other cloth, or paper—can be sewed onto the sock. Yarn can be sewed on for hair.

Many other media that suit the child's fancy can be used for decoration. Instead of bottles or cans, articles such as blocks of wood, balloons, cones made of paper, paper dolls on a stand, cups, water glasses, or an interestingly formed branch made to stand up, can form the base of the puppet. (It should be noted that when painting on a surface that is likely to repel paint, such as glass, adding a little detergent to the paint often takes care of the difficulty.)

Figure 11.12. A Paper Bag Rod Puppet and a Paper Cone Rod Puppet.

Figure 11.13. Rod Puppets Made of Paper.

2. *Rod puppets.* The simplest of all nonstationary puppets is the rod or stick puppet. Basically, it is made of any one of many types of materials or a combination of several that are attached to a rod or stick, which controls the puppet. While there are several variations of the basic type of rod puppet, in its usual form it can make only a greatly limited number of motions. It can be moved upwards or downwards, forwards, backwards, or

sideways, either on one plane or on any number of planes. This limitation in movement provides for the ease in the operation of the rod puppet, but, at the same time, places restrictions on the expressiveness of the actions of the puppet. It is usually controlled from below the stage. However, it can be moved from above when, for example, an angel floats at the top of the stage area. Or the puppet can make its appearance from the side of the stage as when, for instance, an inquisitive character peeps from behind the side of a curtain.

The puppet can be made by attaching ready-made objects to the rod that controls the puppet. For example, pictures of men, women, children, animals, or inanimate objects can be cut out of catalogs, magazines, or other printed materials, pasted on cardboard to give desired firmness, and fastened to the control. Or materials can be purchased, such as paper dolls or paper reproductions of animals, for use as the puppet form. The ready-made materials need not necessarily be paper. Small rubber or plastic dolls or three-dimensional toy animals, of the type frequently available in a variety store, can be used.

The possibility of more creativity, however, can be provided if the pupils make their own puppets. They can draw a picture of the puppet on paper, paste it to cardboard, trim the cardboard to the size of the drawing, and then attach it to the controlling rod. They can decorate three-dimensional figures and attach them to a rod to form a puppet that is, to a considerable extent, one of their own making. In fact, they can form any flat or three-dimensional object to which a rod can be attached into a puppet. There is the wood-block rod puppet whose head is a small piece of wood with features painted on or attached. There is the rod puppet that can be made by attaching a head whose basic form consists of a ball of string. A rubber ball, with facial features attached, also can serve as head of a rod puppet. The head of a puppet made of soap can be attached to a rod. (It is recommended that the cake of soap be freshly unwrapped for then it is more malleable.) A puppet can be made by attaching a rod to a stuffed paper bag with features painted or pasted onto it.

The rod itself can be one of different materials. It should be chosen, in part, for the part the puppet is to play, for the motions through which it will go, and, partly, in terms of the material to be attached to it. It can be a tongue depressor, a doweling rod, or any other piece of wood of appropriate size and shape.

A variation of the usual rod puppet is the wooden spoon puppet in which the handle of the spoon serves as the rod. Another variation is the clothespin puppet. Wire pipe cleaners can serve as arms while features are drawn on and "hair" added.

3. *Hand puppets.* Hand puppets are moved directly by the hand, without use of a rod. A typical position of

Figure 11.14. A Styrofoam Puppet Head.

Figure 11.15. A Cloth Puppet.

Figure 11.16. A Paper Puppet with Movable Parts.

Figure 11.17. A Clothespin Puppet. (An adaptation of a rod puppet.)

Figure 11.18. A Corncob and Husk Puppet.

Figure 11.19. A Paper Bag Head.

Rod Puppets

the hand when operating a hand puppet is one in which the forefinger is inserted in the neck of the puppet, the thumb in one arm, and the second finger in the other arm, while· the two small fingers are closed. Another position of the hand places the forefinger and the second finger close together into the neck of the puppet, with the thumb controlling one arm and the two smaller fingers, also held close together, forming the control for the other arm. In still another position, with the forefinger in the neck, the thumb can control one arm and the smallest finger operate the other arm while the middle and ring fingers are folded down. (See Figure 11.20.)

There is possible an almost endless variety of types of hand puppets, a few of which will be briefly discussed. In most cases only the heads are described. For directions about dressing puppets the reader is referred to page 304.

Vegetable puppets are made from vegetables such as the potato, carrot, turnip, or onion. A hole big enough so that the puppeteer can control his puppet by sticking his forefinger into it can be cut with an apple corer. The features of the puppet can be made with ribbon, yarn, tacks, cloves, part of toothpicks, beads, nuts, or a miscellany of other materials.

Figure 11.21. A Potato Puppet.

Paper bag puppets can be made in many ways. The whole hand of the puppeteer can be put into a bag that has been decorated to show features. It can be tied around the puppeteer's hand at his wrist. Use of the hand within the bag and motion of the arm give movement to the puppet. A bag can

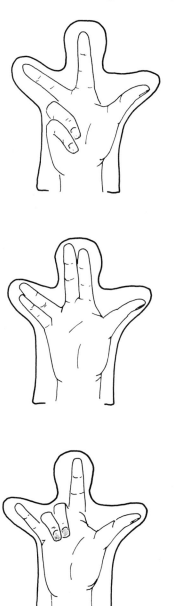

Figure 11.20. Hand Positions in Puppetry.

Figure 11.22. A Paper Bag Puppet.

also be used to portray the entire puppet, not just its head. In that case, after the features have been added to the upper part of the bag and a cord tied loosely around that part to form the neckline, holes can be made below the neckline. Through one of these the thumb projects as one arm and through the other another finger, other than the forefinger (which is used for head control), is used as the other arm.

Sock puppets are especially useful in portraying animals. Of these the stuffed sockhead puppet is perhaps the simplest. For control a four-inch paper tube can be inserted into the neck of the animal puppet. In addition the toe of a nylon stocking can be stuffed to form the head of a puppet, representing a human being. An alligator puppet can be made from an old sock by cutting around the toe end and lining the cut-open part with bright material to represent the jaws, to which are attached two pieces of cardboard for stiffening the mouth. Buttons can be used for eyes.

Figure 11.24. A Tin Can Puppet.

Figure 11.23. A Sock Puppet.

Figure 11.25. A Fist Puppet.

Tin-can puppets can also be made for use as a hand puppet, with features added in the form of paper hair, yarn, rope, pieces of paper, and the like. Care must be taken that the edges of tin cans are not sharp, lest puppeteers cut themselves.

Fist puppets can be made by painting or by pasting paper cutouts to the hand in fist formation.

Ring puppets can be made by attaching heads or entire puppets made of paper to a ring made *of* paper, slipped onto a finger.

Handkerchief puppets can be made by tying a man's white handkerchief around the hand at the wrist, to represent a ghost. (A ghost can also be made by tying a small piece of white cloth around one finger.)

Gourd puppets can be made by painting faces on

Figure 11.26. A Ring Puppet.

Figure 11.27. A Handkerchief Puppet.

Figure 11.28. A Gourd Puppet.

Figure 11.29. A Rag-Doll Puppet.

Figure 11.30. A Blockhead Puppet.

Figure 11.31. A Papier-Mâché Puppet Head.

gourds. Clothes can be fastened by a rubber band around the neck of the gourds.

The head of a *rag-doll puppet* can be cut from two oval pieces of cloth. The pieces can be sewed together, leaving a hole at one end through which the puppeteer's finger can control the puppet. After the sewing, the cloth should be turned inside out and the head stuffed with cloth, cotton, or crumpled paper, and then (or before) features should be added.

Blockhead puppets, for which a block is used for the head and nailed to a stick, are another interesting variation of the hand puppet.

Box puppets, similar to block puppets, can be made with a small box for the head of the character.

Papier-mâché puppets can be made simply or elaborately. One of the easiest ways of making it is to crumple paper and then with a string tie it into the general shape desired for the head. Over this basic form thinly cut strips of paper, dipped in paste, can then be applied. Through an opening left when putting on the strips, at the part that will form the neck of the puppet, the crumpled paper can be removed when the head has dried.

Pipe-cleaner puppets have as their base a piece of pipe cleaner onto which supplementary pieces are twisted for arms and for one leg. These can be bent as shown in the illustration. A wooden bead can serve as head. Or a loop of the main piece of the pipe cleaner can be the basic form for the head, to which a face of paper can be attached.

A peanut puppet is an interesting puppet that can be operated as a simple string puppet, as shown in the accompanying figure. The peanuts can be strung together with heavy thread. For a girl's dress a simple sleeveless blouse and a skirt made of cloth will suffice. The hair can be made of cloth or yarn and the features drawn on with a magic marker.

Dressing the Puppet. In some cases the dress of the puppet is made of the same material as the head. For example, in the case of the paper bag puppet the entire body can be made from a paper bag. In some of the vegetable puppets, too, such as the carrot puppet, the vegetable serves as the whole puppet. In a ghost puppet the handkerchief used for the head also represents the flowing robe.

In many cases, however, provisions need to be made for dressing the puppet. Perhaps the simplest dress is made of a piece of material with a hole cut in the center for the head. A circular piece of cloth for a skirt suffices. A rectangular piece can be sewed together at two ends, gathered at the top, and tied around the neck of the puppet. Out of the flowing dress an illusion of the arms can be made by using one or more fingers, as indicated in **finger positions illustrated on page 301**, or sleeves can be sewed onto the body of the puppet and holes cut at appropriate places in the robe as armholes. Another basic **dress pattern is illustrated in figure 11.35, in which the hands of the puppet are attached to the end of the sleeves as shown in the figure.**

Figure 11.32. A Pipe-Cleaner Puppet.

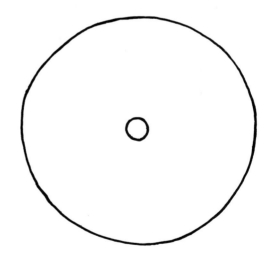

Figure 11.34. Circular Dress Pattern for Puppet.

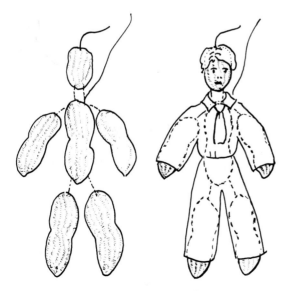

Figure 11.33. A Peanut Puppet.

Here are a few pointers to observe when fashioning the dress for puppets.

1. It is good to encourage beginners to test dress patterns by first cutting them out of paper.

2. There is danger of making the dress too skimpy. In the case of dresses for puppets representing girls or

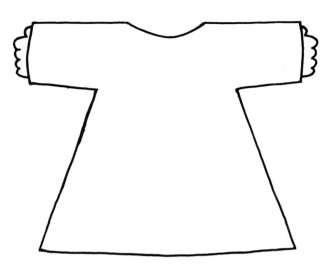

Figure 11.35. A Basic Dress Pattern for a Puppet.

women, the measurements should be related, in part, to the size of the hand of the puppeteer.

3. A woman's dress may consist of a full skirt that is attached to the waist of the basic dress pattern of the puppet.

4. To sew a dress to the puppet it can be turned inside out over the head of the puppet while being sewed to the head.

5. For the apparel of a woman puppet a straight-lined undergarment can be sewed to the neck of the puppet.

6. It is helpful to stuff the trousers of men puppets with crumpled cloth, paper, or cotton.

Puppet Stages. Puppet stages can be classified as temporary and permanent stages.

1. *Temporary stages.* Stages do not need to be elaborate. In fact, elaborateness of stage can interfere with the effectiveness of the play.

Here are suggestions for a few stages that can be used without bothering to make a permanent stage.

The surface of a table, with a cloth draped over it, may be used as the puppeteers stand in plain

view. This type of stage is particularly suited for stationary puppets.

A board can be placed across the top of two chairs with backs facing and a blanket draped over the board.

A box can be set on a table. The puppeteers present the show using the top of the box as the scene of action. This type is well suited for use with stationary puppets (see figure 11.38) but, with adaptation, it can also serve as stage for both rod and hand puppets if the top of the box is considered the stage.

A table can be placed on its side, with the top part facing the audience. A large piece of cloth can

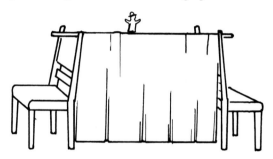

Figure 11.37. Two Straight Chairs Used in a Temporary Puppet Stage.

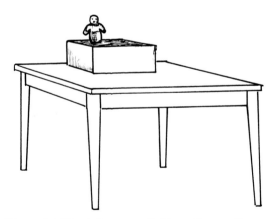

Figure 11.38. A Box on a Table as Puppet Stage.

Figure 11.36. A Top of a Table as Temporary Puppet Stage.

Figure 11.39. A Table on Its Side as Puppet Stage.

be strung as curtain around the sides or part of the sides and front of the stage so that the puppeteers can crouch behind the curtain.

A curtain can be drawn across the bottom half or so of a doorway by fastening it over a wire stretched across a doorway at whatever height is desired.

Figure 11.40. A Doorway as Puppet Stage.

The window stage, shown in the accompanying ilustrations, is another simple type of stage.

Figure 11.41. A Window as Puppet Stage.

A puppeteer can kneel on the seat of a high overstuffed chair. Kneeling on the seat of the chair he can manipulate his puppets so that they are visible to an audience facing the back of the chair. An empty picture frame can be fastened to the top of the back of such a chair to "frame" the action of the puppets.

A low three-part screen behind which the puppeteers are sitting can hide them from view as their puppets are visible over the top of the screen.

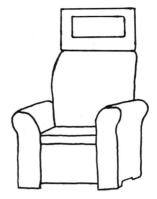

Figure 11.42. An Overstuffed Chair as Base for a Puppet Stage.

Figure 11.43. A Screen as Puppet Stage.

2. Permanent stages. As the term *permanent* is employed here it refers to any types of stage that cannot be quickly improvised without committing materials needed to future use as a stage. The degrees of "permanency" vary.

An opening to serve as proscenium can be cut into the upper part of the middle section of a three-fold screen. The two side parts of the screen can be arranged so that they are perpendicular to the middle section to hide the puppeteers from view. The puppeteers operate their puppets from a sitting position below the level of the bottom of the opening of the middle of the screen. A curtain can be drawn across the open part of the theater. Across the back of the lower part of the proscenium can be attached a shelf to serve as base of the stage.

A commonly used puppet stage is one made of a cardboard carton which has been painted on all sides after the top has been removed. The opening is the front of the stage. Part of the side on which the carton rests on a small table is cut out so that through the opening the puppeteers can operate their puppets. Often the back of the stage is removed for easier manipulation of puppets. In that case a backdrop is attached. A gathered strip of cloth fastened to the upper part of the front of the

Figure 11.44. Another Screen as Puppet Stage.

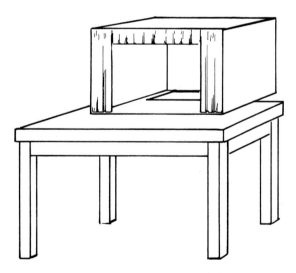

Figure 11.45. A Cardboard Carton as Puppet Stage.

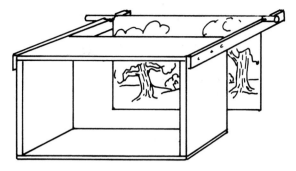

Figure 11.46. A Crate as Puppet Stage.

Figure 11.47. A Puppet Stage Made of Wood.

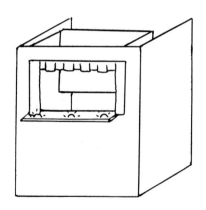

Figure 11.48. Another Puppet Stage Made of Wood.

stage can form part of the curtain. At each side of the front, draw curtains or pull-back curtains made of cloth can be fastened.

A stage can be constructed from an orange crate by knocking out the bottom and nailing two sticks to the crate so that they extend as shown in figure 11.46. To the end of these sticks the backdrop can be fastened.

Any wooden box of suitable size can be changed into a theater. Figure 11.47 shows the lower side taken out of the box and sawed into about half lengthwise, with one of the two pieces nailed under the box to form a shelf extending a few inches. The effect of a curtain can be achieved by attaching a piece of tagboard to the front of the theater.

A variation from the cardboard stage and the wooden box stage, is a stage built of wood. It can be made simply or rather elaborately with curtains, footlights, changes of backdrops fastened to the theater by a rod. Some teachers like to have one wooden theater in the room for use throughout the year whenever it seems to fit the needs of a production.

The puppet tray is one of the most interesting stages. It can be made from a flat cardboard box, into which two holes are cut. It is through these holes that the puppeteer operates his puppets. The box can be painted. Ribbons can be fastened to the corners so that the tray can be hung around the neck of the puppeteer.

Figure 11.49. A Puppet Tray Stage.

Scenery. The scenery, including the backdrop and the side "walls" of the interior as well as the stage setting, should help create the illusion that the little puppets are taking their audience into a fanciful world.

Care must be taken that the background is simple enough so that it truly serves as background and does not "steal the show" from the puppets. The scenery should be suggestive rather than realistic, as a rule. A few paper flowers are enough to indicate that it is spring. The scenery can be painted on a backdrop made of paper. The painted sides also can provide scenery. Usually it is not desirable to paint figures on the background.

In designing the scenery, the pupils need to give attention to proportionate size. A table in the front of the stage three inches high can hardly adequately serve as a dining table for puppets twelve inches tall.

If curtains are used, they should help create the atmosphere of fancy. Soft velvet or rich silk, possibly brocaded, helps give the impression of a world that is not commonplace. The draw-type curtain, one on each side of the stage, can be suspended by curtain rings from a rod above the proscenium. With a cord through these rings attached to hooks, the curtains can be pulled open and shut, or simple pull-back curtains can be used.

Figure 11.50. Indoor Setting for a Puppet Play.

Figure 11.51. Outdoor Setting for a Puppet Play.

Steps in Preparing and Presenting a Puppet Play. The steps in presenting a puppet play are basically similar to those that can be followed in connection with other types of dramatization; however, there is some variation.

If a puppet play is based on a story, one that is well adapted to puppetry should be chosen. The story should be worthwhile, a story that really does something or is likely to do something to the inner nature of the child. It should be dramatic and require but few characters. Those characters should be such that they can be shown in settings easily suggested in puppetry. Most stories need to be simplified before use in a puppet play. Some stories, however, such as "Little Red Riding Hood," "The Three Little Pigs," and "Snow White and the Seven Dwarfs" require comparatively little simplification. The conversation should be to the point and full of life.

When the story has been divided into scenes and the characters needed for each scene have been determined, assignment of parts may be made before or after the action of the scenes has been decided upon. In making the assignment one person sometimes is responsible for the manipulation of a puppet and another for the speaking of the parts. The stage setting can be discussed next. The lines of the story can be changed into play form by the boys and girls as they "ad lib" or individuals or committees may have the assignment of writing the parts. The pupils can read the parts, memorize them, or say them without memorization. Every performance of the play should be thought of as an opportunity for dramatic experiences, not merely as a time of rehearsal.

Somewhere between the steps indicated, the puppets should be made, the theater selected or constructed, the scenery—including both "interior walls" and stage furnishings—planned, and the plans executed. Regardless of when puppets and stage settings are made, the entire play, including scenes, stage settings, puppets, and lines, should be designed in relationship to each other before the details are perfected. The play should be characterized by unity.

Boys and girls enjoy putting on puppet plays of their very own, with a plot of their own making. In such plays, of course, the first step is to determine the theme. It may be based on personal experiences of one or more members of the group. After a primary grade class has been on a trip to a farm, they may, for example, decide to enact through puppetry some of their experiences. One puppet could represent all the boys and girls in the room as they meet, in the play, the various animals on the farm. The animals can be drawings on paper attached to dowel rods. The child puppet can be similarly constructed or it can be made more elaborately. Each of the animal puppets can tell him what it does to help the farmer and other people. A similar theme can be developed after a visit to a zoo. In the play various animals can tell interesting facts about themselves in answer to questions asked by the child puppet. A health puppet play can be planned, possibly showing what an emaciated looking, tired, unhappy child learned from various good foods, also in the form of puppets, in order to become a healthy, happy, strong child.

In making up an original plot, many boys and girls may need considerable guidance from the teacher. The amount should be determined by the skill of the class. With boys and girls who have had little experience in puppetry, the teacher may need to suggest the general theme while the pupils decide on the details. For example, in the health play to which reference is made in the preceding paragraph, after a study of a unit on the food we eat, the boys and girls may decide which foods the tired child should meet in the play and what each food should teach him.

Following are some other suggestions for topics for puppet plays:

1. A Christmas puppet show in which the pupils work out a series of simple skits showing what boys and girls can do to make others happy at Christmas

2. A Mother's Day play in which a boy and girl find out what different things they can do to make Mother happy not only on Mother's Day but the year around

3. A Thanksgiving play in which emphasis is put on reasons for gratitude

4. A puppet show telling important events in the life of an inventor

5. A play emphasizing good manners.

Puppet plays can also be worked out in connection with school subjects such as music, spelling, handwriting, social studies, speech, and foreign languages. For example, one or more puppets can explain the important points of posture to remember when writing.

Availability of Materials. If boys and girls are to be able to make puppetry a creative experience of maximum value, it is advisable to have a large variety of materials available so that they can use their imagination to the utmost. These materials are likely to be of greater value as

well as of greater diversity if the boys and girls have a part in collecting them. The smaller materials should be sorted as to type or function and stored in properly labeled drawers or boxes. Pupil responsibility in classification and keeping the collections in usable form is recommended.

The following list suggests a variety of materials, in addition to cartons and boxes of various types, that may be collected: pieces of cloth, including silk, cotton, velvet; pins, needles, and thread; scissors; hammers; coat hangers; glue and paste; paints, including tempera paints; paint brushes; paper, including crepe paper, construction paper of various colors, butcher paper, tagboard, beaver board, cardboard, corrugated paper, contact paper; mailing tubes and tubes from bathroom tissue or from paper toweling; paper doilies; buttons; paper clips and brass fasteners; beads; tinfoil; egg crates of a variety of types; pot cleaners; wood for carving; pipe cleaners; raffia and reed; leather; artificial flowers; pieces of fur; ribbons; braid; small pieces of doll's furniture; plasticine; styrofoam; lace; dowel rods; rulers; nails; plywood; balsa wood; ribbon; twine; crayons; sponges; netting; pictures of people, animals, and inanimate objects; gourds; twigs; wire; rope; old gloves; and used socks.

Other Suggestions. Here are a few additional suggestions for use in connection with puppetry.

1. Rod puppets of any kind that make good silhouettes can be used as shadow puppets. A light behind the scene of action throws the shadow on a translucent screen. The puppets can be made of a variety of materials—wood, plastic, cardboard, and lace doilies among them.

2. If the eyes of a puppet are close together, the puppet has an older or a shrewder expression than if they are farther apart.

3. For eyebrows of puppets representing children, only a small marking is needed, while strong and/or villainous characters need dark and shaggy eyebrows. Stitches of thread or yarn can produce the desired effects.

4. Pupils often need to be cautioned to hold their puppets erect and at stage level.

5. Puppeteers should speak their lines slowly and distinctly.

6. A puppet who is speaking should face his listeners, at least partially.

7. It is often effective to have a puppet as announcer of a puppet play.

8. Puppets can be used as mascots, to give assignments and to participate in panel discussions.

9. To obtain the illusion of thunder a sheet of tin can be placed on end, backstage, and then rattled.

CHORAL SPEAKING

Choral speaking, also referred to as choral reading and verse choirs, has become so common in the elementary school of this country that no longer is a definition of the term needed in a discussion of this type. Although preparation in directing verse choirs by means of college course or workshop on the topic is desirable, it is not essential. The wide-awake teacher can help her pupils gain some of the values of choral speaking without such specialized training. Books and magazine articles and references to the topic in various college courses in the preparation of teachers, especially in courses in literature for children and in methods of teaching the language arts, can furnish valuable background for the teacher or prospective teacher for his work with boys and girls.

Values of Choral Speaking

As the objectives that choral speaking can help fulfill which are named here indicate, a discussion of the topic could appropriately be taken up in various parts of this book—in connection with oral communication or reading, as well as in this chapter on dramatic expression.

1. Through choral speaking the interest of boys and girls in good poetry can be increased. Pupils who have never before felt the joy of reading poetry can be enthusiastic as they look through books on poetry for poems that they can suggest for reading by their verse choir. As they search for suitable poems and discover the treasures of poetry through choral reading some may develop a lasting interest in poetry.

2. Through choral speaking boys and girls can have the satisfaction of giving pleasure to an appreciative audience. When hearing verse spoken with sincerity, the members of the audience frequently show their happiness to the members of the choir by their response to the mood created by the verse choir. The resulting satisfaction to the participants in the choir is one not unlike that which the creative artist feels when he has awakened a responding emotion.

3. Choral speaking can help the participants and the audience to better interpretation of poetry. As the pupil works with an able teacher, the child is likely to add to his understanding of poetry both because of what the teacher says and does and because of deeper understandings that he acquires through interpretations made by his peers. Furthermore, members of an audience may get a better understanding of a familiar poem as they listen to the sincere speaking of it by a verse choir. Such interpretation of one poem may help them, like the participants, to increased appreciation of other poetry. If inspirational poetry is used, choral speaking can be a source of inspiration.

4. Participation in choral speaking can be a decided asset in the development of speaking abilities. While improvement in speech is an important by-product of verse speaking, it should not be considered the main purpose, even though there are many ways in which through choral speaking the pupil's ability in this facet of the language arts can be improved upon. Pupils can be helped to see purpose for speaking distinctly, pronouncing words correctly, using suitable tone quality, talking with correct pitch, and having good breath control and correct posture. Through choral speaking boys and girls can acquire the self-assurance needed to speak in front of an audience.

5. Taking part in choral speaking can serve as a valuable means of learning to work cooperatively with others. In choral speaking "all are needed by each one." The child recognizes the importance of having his voice blend with others. He can appreciate that successful performance is impossible unless each does his part.

6. Through choral speaking the shy, timid child and the overly aggressive one can be helped. The former, who may be afraid of taking part in a performance in which the spotlight may be on him for a while, can easily lose himself in a group activity such as choral speaking. Furthermore, confidence instilled in him through success in the activity can cause him to be less concerned about himself in the future, regardless of what the acitivity may be in which he engages. On the other hand, the aggressiveness of the too confident child may be tempered when participating in choral speaking, which could be ruined if he were not willing to submerge himself for the good of the group. The satisfaction he gets from joyous participation in choral speaking even though he is not in the limelight may help him at other times to prefer taking his part with a group rather than showing off.

7. Choral speaking can give release. It seems important that every individual express himself creatively. Some do so through music, others through art, others through writing, others through manual activities. Choral speaking can serve as an outlet for self-expression for every normal child, gifted or not.

8. Choral speaking can be a source of motivation for other worthwhile activities. It is easily conceivable that as a child who has lacked interest in school activities finds pleasure in choral speaking, he may develop a better attitude toward school work. Use of suitable poems, such as "Who Has Seen the Wind?" might make the work in primary grade science more interesting, while some of the poems by Carl Sandburg might well be used, along with music, to make a unit in the intermediate grades on Westward expansion more meaningful.

9. Through participation in choral speaking the child's vocabulary can be enlarged. This improvement can result especially if the teacher makes a point of explaining or has explained some of the words that may be unfamiliar. But choral reading should not become a

vocabulary drill. Not every so-called "unknown word" needs to be explained to boys and girls in order that they can understand and interpret a poem.

10. Through choral reading a participant can develop in poise. Through attention to the rhythm of a poem, through the opportunity afforded to participate in an activity that puts him in front of an audience without undue attention placed of him, he can develop in grace and ease of manner.

11. Not least but very important among the values that can be derived from choral speaking are the fun and the joy in the activity itself.

Guidelines

In spite of the many values that can be attained through choral speaking, some educators have not made use of it. A reason for this unpopularity with some may be that at times there is failure by teachers to live up to the underlying principles that should govern the use of choral speaking in the schoolroom. Suggestions such as the following should be observed.

1. Care should be taken to avoid overemphasis on words and rhythm. Important words should be emphasized but overemphasis can lead to loss of meaning or can make the speaking dramatic when simplicity of presentation should be an objective. While the participants should feel the rhythm of the poem and convey it in their interpretation, too much emphasis on rhythm can also cause loss of meaning.

2. Children's voices should be light and expressive. Loud strained voices not only can make the effect displeasing but also can cause permanent injury to vocal cords. A galloping pace, into which some choirs work themselves as they proceed giving a poem, should also be avoided. Rushing through a poem can be fatal to its meaning and beauty.

3. Overdramatization should be avoided. While with the very young child gesturing is evidence of uninhibited bodily response, frequently with the child in the upper-primary or intermediate grades it is put on for effect. When gesturing is not spontaneous, it spells insincerity and thus makes choral speaking lose its charm and much of its value.

4. Costuming and scenery should be kept very simple or not used at all. Costumes of any kind and scenery provided for the stage can easily detract from the boys and girls, the beauty of whose speech and manner should be allowed its full effect upon the audience. While some conductors like to have all the girls dress in white blouses and dark skirts and the boys in white shirts and dark trousers, clean and simple cotton dresses and shirts and trousers of any color can make the reading just as effective as similarity of apparel—maybe more effective. A

vase or two of flowers is all the decoration if any, that a verse choir needs.

5. The teacher who serves as leader of the group must exemplify certain characteristics not only at programs that may be given but throughout the work on choral speaking. He should have a love for poetry and must be able to convey his enthusiasm without trying to exhibit it in any way. True love of poetry must be lived, not forcibly demonstrated. Furthermore, he needs to exemplify in his posture, voice, and breath control those characteristics that make for success in verse speaking.

6. It is important that suitable poetry be chosen. For suggestions as to which literature is suitable the reader is referred to page 314.

7. The boys and girls should be encouraged to take part in selecting poems to be read and in planning and organizing choral speaking. They should not, as a rule, be asked to fit poems into a pattern devised by the teacher or found in a magazine article. Sometimes a pupil well suited to the work may even be chosen as conductor at the time of a performance. However, during practices the pupils should usually have the benefit of the teacher's conducting.

8. In choral speaking a final performance should not be the main objective, but the benefits that boys and girls can derive from work on it should constitute the chief aim. In fact, it is questionable whether choral speaking in the primary grades should culminate in a program. When it does seem desirable in the intermediate grades, care should be taken that the chief emphasis is on values gained from practices rather than on production of a polished program.

9. All boys and girls should have an opportunity to take part in choral speaking. If a child's voice comes out in a manner that interferes with the effectiveness of the choir, he may be cautioned, preferably in private, to keep his voice soft. It is questionable whether he should ever be given only a nonspeaking role, such as seating visitors or passing out programs. If the true objective of a verse choir is to help the boys and girls gain the values that should be reaped from choral speaking, the teacher will see his responsibility even to the pupils with characteristics that need developing in order for them to be effective participants in verse choirs.

10. Choral speaking should not be made the excuse for forcibly bringing in many voice or speech exercises during a time set aside for choral reading. The help given in this respect should, as a rule, fit right into the ongoing practice. The emphasis should be on clearly enunciating the words in the poem or prose selection to be read, rather than on drilling on the enunciation of many other words.

11. Care should be taken that the overconfident members of a verse choir do not dominate the scene. In

spite of the fact that choir work lends itself well to bringing out the shy child and discouraging showing-off by the aggressive member of the group, unless the teacher is consciously aware of his responsibility to help the one who wants to be seen and heard more than he should be, the possible desirable effects on his growth and development may be lost.

12. It is important that the participants in a choir can hear each other. Consequently a wedge-shaped formation is often to be preferred to the straight line.

Procedures in Choral Speaking

With these basic principles in mind, let us next turn our attention to the grouping for verse choirs.

Grouping. Even among children in the primary grades there are voices recognizable as higher or lighter than others. In the elementary school the division of a choir is often made into two groups, high and low (or light and heavy). Not infrequently, a third group—a medium group—is also established. Among elementary school children some boys and some girls are likely to be found in each of the three groups, for with young children not all boys' voices are low or medium nor are all girls' voices high or medium.

The teacher may be consciously taking note of the quality of the pupils' voices weeks before he starts choral speaking. Some teachers may want to pick out one of the highest and one of the lowest voices beforehand. When they begin the work on choral speaking, they may explain to the boys and girls that speaking voices can be grouped much as singing voices in a choir. The teacher may then point out the importance of having some high voices blend with others that are lower. It is important that he helps the children realize all voices are valuable in a good speaking choir. Next he may tell the class that he has already noticed that [name of pupil] has a rich low voice. while [name of a pupil] has a lovely high voice. Thereupon, he may have those two pupils count to ten or give the beginning of the ABC's or say a nursery rhyme such as "Mary had a little lamb." Next each of the other children in the room may be asked to do likewise as the teacher, often with the assistance of the boys and girls, divides the class into two or three groups. The boys and girls should understand that this grouping may not be perfect and that at times there may be changes made as their voices change or as the teacher, sometimes with the help of the class, for other reasons notes that a voice fits better with a different group.

Casting. The term *casting* is used in choral speaking to refer to the division of a given selection (usually a poem, but psalms and some other prose selections can also be used very effectively in the elementary school) into parts and assigning these to different groups or individuals. Commonly used methods of organization are given here.

1. *Unison speech.* This method of casting is not to be confused with the nonchoral reading done in concert when all pupils, without being grouped as to voices, speak all lines. When speaking in unison is a method of choral speaking, it means all groups say the same lines but that each group says them according to the voice specification of his division. Although having all choirs saying the lines in unison is the simplest form as far as structure is concerned, it is a very difficult method of choral speaking. In fact, speaking in choruses yet in unison probably constitutes the most difficult type of casting. There are problems in blending and in timing that are not as great in any other type of casting. As a rule unison speech should not be used in the elementary school for entire poems; if used it should usually be reserved for only short parts of selections.

2. *Refrain or chorus.* In poems in which there are refrains or choruses, the casting is often done by having one group read the refrains or choruses. The other parts can be read by one or two other groups. Sometimes the arrangement is solo-group or group-solo. At times the teacher might want to carry the solo part.

3. *Dialogue.* Poems in which considerable dialogue is used lend themselves well to two-part casting. Question-and-answer poems are particularly well suited for this type. One suitable arrangement is to give the question to the high voices and the response to the low.

4. *Line-a-child.* In line-a-child casting three or more children speak separate parts. Each child says at least one line as solo. Some lines may be spoken in unison.

5. *Line-a-choir.* In line-a-choir casting more than two choirs are used for separate parts.

6. *Solo-choir.* A variation from the two-part antiphonal casting is that in which one or more choirs as well as solo parts are used.

7. Other types. Various combinations and deviations from the types of casting described can be made for best interpretation of a poem according to the abilities and needs of a given group of boys and girls.

Suggested Methods. Here are some pointers as to methods of procedure in choral speaking.

1. Before the teacher starts work in choral speaking, with many boys and girls it may be advantageous to interest them in saying poetry by having the group, without any division into choirs, say enjoyable poems in concert.

2. After children's voices have been divided into groups and after a suitable poem has been selected, the teacher needs to present the poem to the class in such a way that the pupils will want to say it. Such an introduction can be made in a variety of ways. On a windy day the teacher may quietly start by saying, with good interpretation but not dramatically, the poem "Who Has

Seen the Wind?" There may be a very brief discussion in which some pupils name other signs by which they know that "the wind is passing by." A picture or a series of pictures showing children having fun on a windy day may be used as a point of reference. Then the teacher may say, as he repeats the poem, that some may like to join him in some of the lines. A suggestion from the teacher that the class say the poem by using the choirs into which the group has been divided may bring an enthusiastic response.

3. The problem of memorization can be avoided at the outset of choral speaking if at first the group uses only poems previously committed to memory.

4. Sometimes it is advantageous to have pupils note from a copy on the chalkboard or from one in their hands, the punctuation of a poem. It can then be determined which punctuation needs to be reflected in the voice.

5. Although it is not necessary that every word in a poem not in the pupils' vocabulary should be explained, since the pupils can get the meaning of some words without explanation, nevertheless it is probably safe to say that, as a rule, the boys and girls should be helped with words they cannot understand within the context of the poem. The words should not be presented as a formal drill in word study. A somewhat incidental approach is desirable. Sometimes when the teacher knows a few days or longer ahead of time that he will use a given poem in choral reading, he may in his conversation use one or more of the words of the poem that might otherwise cause a problem. He could use such a word, for example, in a sentence in which it has a built-in definition similar to the meaning of the word as it appears in the context of the poem. For instance, if the teacher plans to use the poem "Skating"[3] by Aileen L. Fisher, he may wish to prepare the pupils for the meaning of the word *wary* in the line "My feet are so wary," by using it in a sentence such as "After I saw how he had deceived one of his friends, I was wary of what he might do to me," before the poem is presented to the class. At that time the teacher might also wish to write the word on the chalkboard and possibly discuss it with the class after he has drawn attention to the fact that he has used a word that the pupils might want to add to their vocabulary.

Another technique the teacher may use is setting the mood for a poem and then saying before reading the poem that he would like to introduce the pupils to a few words whose meaning they will want to know in order to understand the poem. He may have these words written on the chalkboard, each in the context of a sentence that helps in their understanding. At times he may refer to a word he has written on the chalkboard as he tells the pupils he thinks he will not need to explain that word since he believes some or all of them may be able to

figure out the meaning when they hear it in the poem. If this approach to word study is used, it should be followed by attention to the word after the reading of the poem by the teacher. A bulletin board may be arranged with words that the boys and girls are learning, either in connection only with poems or also with other means of oral or written communication. Besides the verbal meaning of words such a chart could show illustrations of words that can be illustrated. Or a chart could be constructed with a caption such as "Can You Match Me?" with words to be emphasized in one column and the meaning or an illustration in the other.

6. The mood for a poem may be created by the teacher's reading it carefully, by discussion preceding the reading, by reading a series of poems before the one to be used for choral speaking is read—all of which are on the same topic such as snow, for example. A series of poems by the same author can be read before the one to be used in choral speaking is presented. Music and art can also serve as means of introduction to some poems.

7. One of the best ways to impress boys and girls with the need of good posture when speaking in a choir is for the teacher to set an example. A discussion of the importance of it may also be beneficial. Drawing attention at times to one or more participants with particularly good posture is another means that can be used effectively. The importance of good posture can also be shown in its relation to another important element of good choral speaking—breath control.

8. The need for good speech can be emphasized in somewhat the same manner as suggested in the preceding paragraph. Again the teacher should serve as a model in his own enunciation of words, clarity of speech, tone quality and pitch, pleasing variation, and lack of overemphasis on words. Help may need to be given with the pronunciation of words for even one mispronunciation can almost ruin a poem. The pupils should be helped to realize that unless the words can at all times be readily comprehended by the audience, unlike singing, the speaking is ineffective. The need for color in the voice and suitable pitch and tone in choral speaking can well give incentive for practice sessions that may be held at other times of the school day rather than during the period devoted to choral speaking.

9. To help pupils feel the rhythm of poetry, the teacher may read a number of poems in which the rhythm is marked. At times through suitable motions the boys and girls may express the rhythm of a poem that the teacher is reading. They may do whatever the rhythm suggests to them—tapping with pencils or feet, clapping, or skipping.

10. With shorter poems as a rule it is not necessary to give pupils a copy, for children usually can memorize

3. From *That's Why*, published by Thomas Nelson and Sons.

such poems with a rather small number of repetitions, especially if they have the intent to learn the poem. When poems are longer it is desirable that each pupil, if he can read, have a copy until he no longer needs one.

11. Just as in singing choirs, in speaking choirs it is important to have a good leader who will mark the time, indicate when different individuals or choirs are to begin, and the like. Like the leader of a singing choir, the conductor of a verse choir may indicate when tones are to be louder and when softer. It is recommended, however, that the leader not use a baton but directly communicate with the participants with his hands or fingers. As boys and girls work on the finer details of reading a poem, the teacher may find it desirable to use fewer and less conspicuous gestures as leader. Furthermore, if a performance is given before an audience, it may be unnecessary to have any guidance from the leader other than for the beginning and at the end of a poem.

12. It is at times necessary that the teacher help the boys and girls comprehend the general meaning of a poem and the relationship of the supporting parts to the general theme. Such help should, as a rule, be given before the pupils are asked to interpret the poem through choral speaking.

13. It is desirable to have the pupils stand when they take part in choral speaking, even during so-called practice periods.

Verse for Choral Speaking

There are various books on the market that contain poems designated as particularly appropriate for choral verse. Some suggest arrangements for casting of poems. A teacher should not be misled by such a listing. Frequently many poems in such a list would be good to use with some boys and girls; however, since different groups respond effectively to different poems, no one list can answer the question for the teacher or for the class, "What poems should we use for choral speaking?" (For a list of books designed for choral speaking the reader is referred to page 335 under "Books on Creative Expression.")

Whether a given poem is listed among those likely to be effective for choral reading or whether it is one that the teacher or a pupil finds in another source, the poem should meet the following criteria. It should:

1. Be a worthwhile poem, one that makes a desirable impression on boys and girls

2. Be on the level of understanding and appreciation of the pupils

3. Fit in well, either through conformity or by contrast, with other poems that the pupils have been or will be using for choral speaking

4. Be a poem which the teacher can present with enthusiasm

5. Have enough rhythm so that the boys and girls can feel and interpret it

6. Have melody

7. Be relatively short

8. Not end in tragedy.

FOR STUDY AND DISCUSSION

1. Name examples of dramatic play, other than those listed in this chapter, that children can engage in.

2. Write a script of a play for elementary school children on a story or part of a story that fulfills criteria for selection named in this chapter.

3. With two or more of your classmates present a short dramatization of a folktale.

4. A rather extensive listing of puppets is given in this chapter. After reading in other books dealing with puppetry, name, describe, and draw sketches of additional types, if possible.

5. Make one or more puppets.

6. What suggestions for stages for puppetry can you give in addition to those described or illustrated in this chapter? You may wish to construct a miniature puppet stage, possibly out of paper, unlike, in at least some respects, any of those illustrated in this chapter.

7. Find a poem suitable for speaking choirs in the primary grades and one appropriate for the intermediate grades. Indicate one desirable way in which each can be cast and be able to give reasons for your choice in casting.

8. Consult with your instructor about the possibility of serving as conductor of your class or of part of the group, as you demonstrate how boys and girls can be guided in choral speaking.

REFERENCES

Arbuthnot, May, and Sutherland, Zena. *Children and Books.* 4th ed. Glenview, Ill.: Scott, Foresman and Company, 1972.

Baird, Bill. *The Art of the Puppet.* New York: The Macmillan Company, 1965.

Batchelder, Marjorie. *The Puppet Theatre Handbook.* New York: Harper & Row Publishers, 1947.

Blackman, Olive. *Puppets into Actors.* New York: The Macmillan Company, 1949.

Carlson, Bernice W. *Act It Out.* Nashville, Tenn.: Abingdon Press, 1965.

Carlson, Ruth. *Literature for Children: Enrichment Ideas.* Dubuque, Iowa: Wm. C. Brown Company Publishers, 1970.

Chambers, Dewey W. *Literature for Children: Storytelling and Creative Drama.* Dubuque, Iowa: Wm. C. Brown Company Publishers, 1970.

Crosscut, Richard. *Children and Dramatics.* New York: Charles Scribner's Sons, 1966.

Henderson, Harold G. *An Introduction to Haiku.* New York: Doubleday & Company, Inc., 1958.

Menagh, H. Beresford. *Creative Dramatics in Guiding Children's Language Learning.* Dubuque, Iowa: Wm. C. Brown Company Publishers, 1967.

Rasmussen, Carrie. *Let's Say Poetry Together.* Minneapolis, Minn.: Burgess Publishing Company, 1962.

Ross, Laura. *Hand Puppets: How to Make and Use Them.* New York: Lothrop, Lee & Shepard Company, 1969.

Tichenor, Tom. *Tom Tichenor's Puppets.* Nashville, Tenn.: Abingdon Press, 1971.

Tiedt, Iris M., ed. *Drama in Your Classroom.* Urbana, Ill.: National Council of Teachers of English, 1974.

Torrance, E. Paul. *Creativity in the Classroom.* Dubuque, Iowa: Wm. C. Brown Company Publishers, 1970.

12

Adapting Instruction to Individual Differences

For effective teaching-learning situations, it is essential in the language arts, as in other areas, that the procedures used be adapted to individual differences. In Part One of this book, in the chapters on "Child Development and the Language Arts" and "Developmental Patterns," statements are made as to the existence of individual differences among boys and girls in their development, and some of the causes of these differences are discussed. In this chapter we will consider additional points related to individual differences of importance to the teacher when planning the program in the language arts. In the first part of the discussion attention is given to basic considerations in adapting instruction to the needs of individuals. Thereupon, suggestions are given for working with the gifted, the retarded, and the underachiever. The last parts of the chapter are devoted to a presentation of problems in the area of the language arts that confront the children from a culturally and economically disadvantaged background, as well as the ones who are bilingual with below-average skill in using the English language.

GUIDELINES FOR ADAPTING INSTRUCTION TO INDIVIDUAL DIFFERENCES

The following points, important in planning instruction adapted to individual differences in all areas, should serve as guidelines to the teacher.

1. One of the assets of the human race lies in the lack of uniformity of all its members.

2. Individual differences are likely to increase among individuals as they develop.

3. Good teaching is likely to result in greater increase in individual differences than poor teaching.

4. Each child has a right to be helped, if necessary, to feel that he can make a significant contribution and to be aided in making one.

5. Because of the great variations among boys and

girls, it is probably unwise to construct a list of minimum essentials for all boys and girls in any heterogeneously grouped class of pupils. It seems sounder to plan a continuum of steps in development along the various phases of skills, attitudes, and knowledge to be acquired.

6. Careful diagnosis should be made of individual differences.

DETERMINING INDIVIDUAL DIFFERENCES

Effective adaptation of instruction to individual differences makes mandatory knowledge of the variations that exist among the boys and girls whose development is to be guided. Without such information—incomplete though it will necessarily be—variation in the instructional program for different individuals in a group may, at times, be even worse than provision of a uniform curriculum for all.

Points to Consider in Diagnosis

Let us consider, then, some points according to which diagnosis should be made. (See also "Evaluation and Diagnosis" in chapter 3.)

1. *A variety of factors should be noted in diagnosis.* Important among these are the intelligence of the individual, his achievements in the area being studied, and his interests. On the basis of factors such as these, ascertainment of his needs can be approached.

2. *Diagnosis should be made of the needs of all the boys and girls.* It should not be reserved for the pupils who seem to be decidedly above or decidely below average. Each member of a class is entitled to an educational program adapted to his requirements.

3. *The optimum amount of time for diagnosis or the depth of it cannot be stated in definite terms.* However, it is certain that careful diagnosis of individual needs of the boys and girls within a classroom, although the process may seem quite time-consuming, can save much time in subsequent teaching-learning situations and can result in greater learning. For the puzzling cases among boys and girls within a classroom perhaps a detailed study should be made while less intensive study of others may suffice. In fact, for some the needed diagnosis may be of so complicated a nature that the classroom teacher who has recourse to a specialist in the area should make use of his services. For example, there are instances of reading problems that cannot adequately be handled by many classroom teachers without the assistance of a clinician.

4. *Diagnosis should be in terms of the objectives for instruction.* The goals thus set will assist the teacher in giving comprehensiveness to his attempts to diagnose the needs of his pupils.

5. *Participation by boys and girls in the evaluative process can be of decided value.* Self-evaluation can provide purpose for learning. To be most effective, the

boys and girls need to be cognizant of the goals to be accomplished. If those objectives are genuinely accepted by them as important, the educational outcome can be expected to be greater than if the pupils lack faith in the worthwhileness of the goals.

6. *Diagnosis should be a continuous process.* An initial diagnosis at the beginning of the school year should not end the process of appraisal. In fact, probably every teaching-learning situation provides some opportunity for evaluation.

Methods

Reference has been made to the fact that one of the points important in trying to fit a program of language arts instruction to the needs of individuals is knowledge of the intelligence of the learner. The standardized tests that are on the market and that give data on intelligence can be divided into group and individual tests. Among the recommended group tests are "The California Short-form Test of Mental Maturity" (California Test Bureau), "The Kuhlman-Anderson Intelligence Tests" (Educational Test Bureau), "The Lorge-Thorndike Intelligence Tests" (Houghton Mifflin Company), "The Pintner Non-language Primary Mental Abilities Test" (Science Research Associates). To get a clearer indication of the intelligence level, individual mental tests are frequently given. Since it is time-consuming to administer them and since some of them should be given only by especially qualified personnel in the field of testing, in many cases the use of individualized tests is restricted to a relatively few members of a class, those on whom it seems to be important to obtain a more accurate index of intelligence than can be provided by the group intelligence test. In fact, in many schools no individual intelligence tests are given. The tests on the market to be administered on an individual basis include among others, the "Stanford-Binet Intelligence Scale" (Houghton Mifflin Company) and the "Wechsler Intelligence Scale for Children" (Psychological Corporation).

Regardless of what type of test for appraising intellectual ability a child may be given, the teacher should be aware of the fact that none is anywhere near perfect as an instrument for measuring intelligence. It is for this reason and others that observation by the teacher of a child's manifestations of degree of intelligence should supplement information gained from one or more mental tests. The teacher can obtain insights into a pupil's mental ability in various ways, for example, by noting how his reactions indicating mental acuity compare with those of others in his age group, by obtaining data from parents, and by studying school records.

In addition to intelligence, knowledge of the achievement of the boys and girls in the area of language arts, can be of vital significance to the teacher in planning the language arts program. Suggestions for obtaining such data are given in chapter 3. For a discussion of that topic the reader is also referred to various other parts in chapters preceding this one, in which suggestions for evaluation are given in connection with a consideration of the various facets of the language arts program. Furthermore, the reader's attention is also directed to later discussion in this chapter.

BASIC PLANS FOR INDIVIDUALIZING INSTRUCTION

In order to adapt instruction to individual differences, two basic plans, often with overlapping between them, are in vogue. One is that of grouping; the other is that of adapting instruction to individual needs without grouping.

Organization for Homogeneous Grouping

Under the category of grouping, various plans have been followed, also with overlapping. Here is one classification of types of grouping.

Homogeneous Grouping Within a School. In some cases the grouping is made by dividing the total population of a school for a given grade into homogeneous groups, with the number depending in part, upon how many room teachers will be available to teach the pupils of a given grade. In other instances, the gifted pupils have been put into a room by themselves, often with some who are not in the same grade. Similarly, provisions are at times made for pupils who are slow learners or who are retarded for other reasons.

Homogeneous Grouping Within a Classroom. In many cases this type of grouping is done in only some of the subject areas. An example of homogeneous grouping within a classroom is the division into reading groups. At times the organization into groups is only temporary, as for instance with special-interest groups. An interest group might, while work is in progress on a unit on Modern Americans, be primarily responsible for making a "movie" to show the outstanding work of the persons studied. The homogeneity in interest groups consists of similarity of interest. Boys and girls of varying abilities often are included in the same group. In fact, one argument for interest groups is that they give the pupils the opportunity to work in some groups with others of different ability. Often while a child is a member of an interest group he also belongs to another group classified according to achievement, such as a reading group.

The Nongraded Plan. A plan that has greatly increased in popularity in recent times is the so-called nongraded plan. Although it seems to be in vogue more in the primary grades than in the intermediate, in a sizable number of schools it is the plan of organization for the entire elementary school. There are many other variations in this type of organization. One characteristic of this plan is that of not designating a child's grade while he is in the first three years of the elementary school. The child progresses as rapidly as he can during the three years ordinarily spent in the primary grades. In some schools pupils may be advanced into the intermediate grades after fewer than three years in the primary division or they may be detained more than the customary three. Where the nongraded plan is followed throughout the elementary school, frequently there is a division into nongraded primary and nongraded intermediate. When the plan is in operation in the intermediate grades, as in the primary grades, the number of years a pupil spends on that level may vary from child to child. Some may complete the intermediate-grade program in less, others in more, than the usual three-year time span.

Points to Consider When Grouping. Any teacher who expects grouping to be a panacea for all problems in adapting instruction to individual differences is, indeed, unduly optimistic. No matter what system of grouping is employed, even where there are only two persons in a group, there are bound to be individual differences that need to be considered for best teaching.

Here are some of the points to note when grouping, in addition to the one stressed in the preceding paragraph.

1. Even if the members of a group show relatively little variation in the criterion used for grouping (and often there is considerable range even in that respect), there are usually other ways, significant to learning, in which there are marked differences. For example, if pupils are classified according to intelligence, the differences in achievement, social maturity, and interest in work will make the group far from homogeneous. Or if the pupils are grouped according to achievement in one subject, there may be wide range in acheivement in other subjects, as well as in intelligence, age, social maturity, and interest.

2. Pupils need opportunity to associate with people who are unlike them in achievement or intelligence in order to be well equipped to take their places in a democracy.

3. Snobbery or feelings of inferiority may result from homogeneous grouping—snobbery on the part of those in the best group and feelings of inferiority on the part of those not in it.

4. The attitude toward the school of parents of children not in the highest groups is at times such that the parent-school relationship is impaired.

5. Parents of children not in the highest groups frequently put undue pressure on their children for greater achievement, and parents of children in the highest groups sometimes similarly put too much

pressure on their children to maintain their membership in such groups.

6. Flexibility in grouping is desirable. This point should be noted for various reasons, among them these: (a) Sometimes pupils are misplaced at the time the groups are organized, even according to the criterion used for classification. (b) Some pupils who seemed to belong in a given group at the beginning of the school year would, because of differences in learning rate and other factors, be placed to better advantage in a different group later in the year.

7. As a rule it is probably better not to try to hide the basis of grouping from boys and girls. Even first-grade children are likely to discover it before long. It is wiser for the teacher to explain the classification on a rational basis than for pupils to come to an irrational conclusion by themselves.

8. Each child has a right to be in a group in which he feels accepted.

9. Sociometric testing and the construction and use of sociograms may help the teacher discover how pupils in a group react toward one another.

Committee Work as a Means of Grouping. One method of temporary grouping that is used extensively even in classrooms where there is primarily heterogeneous division of pupils is the much used organization into committees. When it is wisely organized and executed, committee work can greatly add to the effectiveness of the program of language arts instruction.

1. *Values of committee work.* Some of the ways in which committee work can make contributions to the language arts curriculum are suggested here.

Through committee work instruction can be adapted to individual differences even though frequently this objective may not be the major reason for organizing a committee.

Opportunity for interest grouping can be provided through committees. However, uniformity of interest should not at all times be considered a requirement for membership in a committee. Sometimes membership can profitably be determined primarily by a divergence of interests and abilities that are needed in order to accomplish best the purpose for which the committee is organized and in order to help most in the all-around development of the participants.

Committee work gives boys and girls the opportunity to engage in small-group activities. The give-and-take in well-planned committee work is a significant experience for boys and girls, especially for the older children in an elementary school. Small-group participation provides opportunities

for socialization often not attainable through membership in large groups, such as an entire class.

Organization into committees makes possible a more flexible method of grouping than some other types of grouping. If a person is not well suited for work on the committee of his choice or of his assignment, the error in placement is likely not to be as serious as it might be in a group selection or assignment of longer duration.

2. *Guidelines for committee work.* Following are guidelines for organizing committees and for providing for effective functioning.

Committees should be organized to serve significant purposes—purposes accepted by the boys and girls as important.

Considerable planning for committee work by the teacher is important.

With pupils who are unaccustomed to working in committees the organization of the work should be very simple. As the boys and girls gain more familiarity with committee work, more complicated types of organization should be used. The first times pupils meet in committees the purpose may be as simple as to read orally to each other materials agreed upon beforehand. The chairman of each group may be appointed by the teacher in order to assure adequate leadership. The plan of procedure may be outlined and recorded on the chalkboard beforehand and directions given for (a) position of reader, (b) order of performance, (c) length of selection to be read by each individual, and (d) methods of helping pupils who need assistance.

Pupils should plan with the teacher for an orderliness conducive to work while engaged in committee activities.

While rotating chairmanships is desirable in many instances, care should be taken that those who serve as chairmen are competent. To assure good leadership, the teacher can plan with a chairman before a committee meeting some of the points in procedure and if necessary "coach" him in the performance of his responsibilities.

Frequently even when pupils are organized for committee work, much of the work can best be done individually. For example, in a committee responsible for making a notebook on writing friendly letters, the assignment for actual writing of a given letter can probably best be given to one individual even though that person may have received help from others in the group while planning the letter and later will receive aid from them in the evaluation of his efforts.

Adaptation of Instruction to Individual Differences Without Homogeneous Groupings

Because even in a so-called homogeneous group there are many variations among the individuals and because there are other disadvantages—in addition to the advantages—to such a grouping, some school systems do not subscribe to a plan in which pupils are grouped homogeneously throughout much or all of the school day. Many are of the opinion that more may be lost than gained by such a method of grouping. Such schools frequently attempt to adapt instruction to individual needs by making provision for some or much work on an individual basis. On the other hand, frequently in those schools much of the instruction consists primarily of group instruction. In still other instances it is a combination of whole-class instruction and individual instruction.

Earlier Attempts. Some of the earlier plans of adapting instruction without homogeneous grouping include the Winnetka plan by Carleton Washburne, the platoon school plan originated by William Wirt of Gary, Indiana, and the Dalton plan (or contract plan) developed by Helen Parkhurst in Dalton, Massachusetts. Although none of these plans was popular for a long period of time, some of them did emphasize some features of individualized instruction that have been adapted for other types of teaching situations, among them: extensive use of tests for survey and diagnostic purposes; development of many materials of instruction suited to individualization of work; emphasis on keeping careful records of each pupil's achievement; and encouragement of pupil participation in planning and executing the program.

More Recent Attempts. For the reading phase of the language arts a plan for Individualized Reading has been worked out by Jeanette Veatch. It will not be described here, because this book is not one on the teaching of reading for this book deals primarily with other facets of the language arts and only with those phases of reading instruction that have an especially marked bearing on teaching of the other facets of the language arts. Those interested in Jeannette Veatch's plan, characterized by "seeking, self-selection, and pacing" by the learner, may wish to consult one or more of these books by her: *How to Teach Reading with Children's Books* (Teachers College Press, Columbia University, 1964); *Individualizing Your Reading* (G.P. Putnam's Sons, 1959); and *Reading in the Elementary School* (The Ronald Press, 1959). Some additional organized attempts to adapt instruction to individual needs without homogeneous grouping of a class include "learning laboratories," programmed instruction, and "Individually Prescribed Instruction," each of which is briefly described in the following paragraphs.

1. *"Learning Laboratories."* Although so-called "learning laboratories" in the elementary school have been used primarily for the teaching of reading (as, for example, the Science Research Reading Laboratories, published by Science Research Associates), work with such "laboratories" need not be confined only to reading in the language arts area. Teachers can make up their own "laboratories" in various phases of the language arts curriculum. Typically a learning laboratory consists of practice materials arranged for the various levels of the elementary school, containing instructional materials, practice materials, answer keys, record sheets, as well as a teacher's manual. Pupils progress through these materials at their own speed. The similarity of such "laboratories" to phases of the Winnetka plan is marked. A teacher may wish to construct a laboratory for only one topic, such as, for example, writing a friendly letter, making the transition from manuscript to cursive writing, or studying the fable. (See also "Language Arts Laboratories," page 345.)

2. *Programmed instruction.* While used more with reading than with other phases of the language arts, programmed instruction in the language arts need not be confined to the teaching of reading. Though with some programs on the market teaching machines do form an integral part, programmed instruction does not necessarily involve the use of such machines. Many materials for programmed instruction are produced in booklet form, resembling somewhat in appearance the workbooks that have long been popular. Teachers can write their own programs on sheets of paper, not bound together in booklet form. The teacher can also produce programs by recording them on cassettes. The following are some of the points that characterize programmed materials or that are indicative of their use.

Through the use of programmed materials the learner can proceed at his own rate of learning.

Programmed materials are devised in such a manner that a pupil can do much of the work with them "on his own."

In writing programs the person constructing them divides the learnings to be acquired into small steps, often referred to as "frames."

A "frame" may consist of a brief explanatory presentation, followed by another "frame," in which the learner makes application of what has been explained to him. He does so, when no machine is used, by filling a blank in a sentence or in other ways supplying an answer—usually in an objectively constructed item. If the program is used with a teaching machine, instead of writing his response, the child punches a button or moves a lever to indicate his answer.

Through step-by-step development, the learner

is, in many programs, helped to arrive inductively at a generalization and then to make application of the generalization he has thus learned.

Since, in the program, the correct answer is given following each response by the child, he has the opportunity to check his work immediately.

Many programs provide opportunity for relearning through what is known as "branching," a strategy by means of which, if the child's answer is not the correct one, he is referred to "frames" that reteach the point he has missed.

There is a difference of opinion as to the value of much programmed instruction. Undoubtedly its desirability depends on factors such as the nature of the program, the extensiveness to which programmed instruction is used (too much can be detrimental to the achievement of some of the goals of a curriculum), and the manner in which it is done.

3. *"Individually Prescribed Instruction."* "Individually Prescribed Instruction" was systematically developed by Robert Glaser and associates with the Learning Research and Development Center of the Baldwin-Whitehall school district in the Oak Leaf School in Pittsburgh as experimental laboratory. Special features of the program include:

Upon entrance to the school—as early as kindergarten—the child is given general aptitude, intelligence, and reading readiness tests.

The test results are factors in determining the instructional materials with which the child will start.

A carefully worked out supply of materials, consisting of some commercially produced and others designed by the school system, are arranged in gradation of steps. Transparencies, filmstrips, recordings, and work sheets are among the materials used in the program.

Each child moves on at his own rate in the performance of the assignments individually prescribed for him on the basis of recognized needs and abilities.

SUGGESTIONS FOR INDIVIDUALIZING INSTRUCTION IN VARIOUS FACETS OF THE LANGUAGE ARTS

Regardless of whether the basic grouping in a school or classroom is homogeneously or heterogeneously planned, suggestions that are given below can, in many instances, be followed. We will note a few pertinent to the teaching of handwriting, spelling, reading, other phases of written communication, and oral communication. It is hoped that those to which reference is made will suggest many others to the reader.

Handwriting

The following are points pertinent to adapting instruction in handwriting to individual differences.

1. Boys and girls should be helped to understand when individuality in handwriting can be a decided detriment to ease in communication and that courtesy to the reader demands a clearly readable style of writing.

2. Careful diagnosis should be made of each pupil's needs and then individual or group attention should be the given to the problems.

3. Pupils may at times be grouped into sections such as the following: (a) those who are slow writers, (b) those who have particular problems with writing posture, (c) those who are left-handed, (d) those who have special problems with size, slant, beginning and /or ending strokes, spacing, or alignment, (e) those who have particular trouble with letter formations, and (f) those who have difficulty in achieving good format.

4. The program in handwriting should be so flexible that variation is possible in the time when individuals within a classroom make the transition from manuscript to cursive writing.

5. Each child should be competing with his own best record. Use of handwriting scales and diagnostic charts can be of considerable value in this respect.

Spelling

We will consider the topic of individualizing instruction in spelling according to: (1) factors in diagnosis, (2) spelling tests and scales, and (3) instructional procedures.

Factors in Diagnosis. If spelling is to be adapted to individuals, diagnosis is vital not only for pupils with pronounced difficulties but also for the average or above-average speller. How much time the teacher should spend on diagnosis cannot be stated with certitude. However, it is certain that careful diagnosis of the individual needs of the boys and girls within a classroom, although the process of making it may seem quite time-consuming, can often save much time in subsequent teaching-learning situations. For the puzzling cases perhaps a detailed study should be made while for the others less intensive study may suffice. Under all circumstances the initial diagnosis should not end the appraisal because evaluation should be continuous throughout the year. Factors such as the following should be considered in diagnosis of spelling status and needs.

1. *Intellectual ability.* Even though the correlation between intelligence and spelling ability is lower than it is between intelligence and some of the other school subjects, there is a positive relationship. It is seldom that the child with low intelligence is an excellent speller. It is

uncommon to find a very intelligent child who is unusually poor in spelling.

2. *Spelling ability.* Spelling ability can be checked by giving the pupils a presemester test in which a sampling of the words of the semester are included, or, in some instances, standardized tests or scales can be used effectively.

3. *Nature of spelling difficulties.* Study can be made through careful attention to the words a given individual misspells during spelling class and at other times. The pupil's errors in spelling can be recorded and the teacher, with the pupil, can look for any recurrent types of mistakes such as omitting so-called "silent letters" or not following the letter *q* in a given word by a *u*.

4. *Pupil's method of study.* The following and similar points about a pupil's method of study may be investigated.

> Does he pay good attention during periods when the teacher is helping the class?
>
> Does he begin to study spelling promptly when time is provided for such study?
>
> Does he make good use of his study period?
>
> Does he observe recommended steps for learning to spell a word?

5. *Attitude toward spelling.* Insight into the child's attitude can sometimes be gained through noting his verbal response when time for spelling is announced or by observing his bodily response during spelling class. Whether or not the pupil has pride in being a good speller can sometimes be gathered by the meticulousness (or lack of it) with which he does his work in spelling.

6. *Skill in reading.* Data gained through checking a pupil's reading are of significance in diagnosing some factors regarding spelling. It should be noted that at times skill in phonic analysis may cause problems in spelling. His ability in phonics can be tested by means such as these:

> The teacher asks the pupil to name words beginning with a sound that starts a word he gives.
>
> The teacher asks the pupil to write the letter with which each word in a series he names begins or ends.
>
> The pupils name various spellings of the same phonogram.

7. *Physical well-being.* Vision, hearing, and general health are factors important to spelling.

8. *Pronunciation.* The child who mispronounces a word is more likely to misspell it than the one who pronounces it correctly. To check the ability to pronounce words correctly the teacher can ask the child to read a list of words or a selection orally or he can ask the child to repeat words after him.

9. *Handwriting.* Errors in spelling are at times traceable to illegible handwriting. Slowness in writing may also cause a pupil to receive a poor mark on a spelling test. Consequently, analysis of a pupil's handwriting in terms of legibility and observation of the time it takes him to write are important points to check.

10. *Errors in correcting.* A child's deficiency in spelling may be due to the fact that he makes errors in checking his work. Rechecking of papers by the teacher is needed for diagnosis as well as for other purposes.

11. *Materials.* Careful study of materials of instruction is important in terms of validity of the word lists, provisions for individual differences, suggestions for method of study, and provisions for review and testing.

12. *Methods of teaching.* The teacher should, first of all, critically examine his own methods of teaching spelling. Furthermore, if a pupil has special difficulties in spelling that do not seem to be accounted for by other factors showing up in the diagnosis, it might be desirable for the teacher to inquire (tactfully, of course) into methods of teaching spelling used with a pupil during the preceding school years. The inaccuracy of pupil reports on what actually took place should be borne in mind by the teacher if this suggestion is followed.

Spelling tests and scales. Some teachers use standardized tests or scales to ascertain a pupil's level in spelling. Others prefer those provided in manuals accompanying spelling books and some that they themselves made from words in the spelling lists. If spelling scales or standardized tests are used, it is advisable to check the words for frequency of use as established by research unless evidence on the validity of a test or scale for a desired purpose is given, making further checking by the teacher unnecessary. (Some commerical tests and scales are listed in chapter 13; see page 346.)

Instructional Procedures. The following are a few ways of adapting instruction in spelling to individual differences.

1. Some spelling books have a differentiated list of words, with a small number of words of high frequency of use and relatively low difficulty, for all the pupils to study. They have additional words for the pupils of average ability, and still more for those of above-average ability. In some spellers the extended activities show similar differentiation.

2. When individual lists of words are used, the pupils can be encouraged by the teacher to study as many words as they should be expected to learn without undue stress or strain.

3. In the use of standardized and nonstandardized lists, the teacher can help each pupil diagnose his types of errors or difficulties. Some common types are: substitution of certain letters, repetitions, reversals, lack of knowledge of phonics, application of limited knowledge of phonics to nonphonetic elements of words,

illegible handwriting, lack of speed in writing (if words are dictated).

4. The teacher can encourage the pupils to keep a record of their spelling achievement and discuss it from time to time with them.

5. The teacher can help the pupils individually in studying spelling according to recommended steps. He may ask each child, while in individual conference, to explain how he proceeds as he studies several words.

6. The teacher can ask the individual how much time he spends studying spelling and then make needed recommendations.

7. The teacher can try to help a child determine whether his spelling difficulty lies primarily in lack of immediate or delayed recall of the spelling of words.

8. Some pupils may be allowed during part or all of a spelling period to help their classmates.

9. The pupils can be grouped for help when common problems exist.

10. The teacher can teach some pupils by the study-test plan and others by the test-study-test plan if such differentiation seems advantageous.

11. The teacher can have available, either obtained from commercial materials or made by the teacher, work sheets of various types, with emphasis on different skills important in spelling, such as making applications of generalizations, finding the spelling of words in a dictionary, or matching graphemes with phonemes.

12. Some of the boys and girls may at times during spelling class be allowed to engage in other activities if they have mastered the spelling learnings to be acquired during a given spelling period.

Reading

Only a few suggestions are given below for adapting instruction in reading to individual differences, since this book deals primarily with teaching facets of the language arts other than reading.

1. Accepted beyond question by specialists in the field of elementary school reading is the fact that some of the work in reading should be individualized. Argument is only in relation to the extent of individualization and to the methods to be followed.

2. Programmed learning (see page 321) in the area of reading has thus far consisted chiefly if not exclusively, of developmental or pratice-type material. Objective-type questions based on the material are asked. True-false statements and multiple-choice responses have been used extensively. Furthermore, the programs have dealt primarily with the more mechanical skills of reading. Phonic exercises, work on structural analysis, skill in locating materials, and work on factual comprehension seem to lend themselves better to program-

ming than does work of the more interpretative types. Little has been done, it seems, with "reading between the lines" and with "reading beyond the lines"—aspects of comprehension that are highly significant but much more difficult than factual data to be tested by a device such as programmed learning. To be sure, more can be done in programmed learning than has been to develop skills such as the ability to predict outcomes or the ability to arrive at generalizations, for objective tests can be devised to test some aspects of these abilities. However, since to many matters of interpretation there is no one single acceptable answer and since discussion is often very desirable when determining the answers to thought questions, something beyond programmed learning needs to be provided in the development of such competencies.

In consideration of the question "Can the elementary school make effective use of programmed learning when guiding boys and girls toward growth in reading?" the following responses can be made.

> The elementary school teacher will do well to look into the matter of programmed learning, preferably, if feasible, participating in the preparation of materials in addition to studying some commercial programs.

> Since the type of skills used rather extensively in programmed learning in reading is limited chiefly to the more mechanical aspects of the concept of programmed learning, it would seem that there is need for radical revision of the concept of programmed learning, as held by some teachers, if it is to supplant to a considerable extent some of the other methods used in teaching reading.

3. Through the independent reading of boys and girls excellent opportunity is afforded for adapting part of the reading program—some would claim much or all of it—to individual differences. Chapter 10, "Guiding Growth in Independent Reading," offers many suggestions in this regard.

Other Phases of Written Communication

Scattered throughout chapters 5 and 6 are presented ideas that the teacher can apply as he tries to adapt instruction in other areas of written communication to individual differences. Only a few examples of how this objective can be attained are mentioned here.

1. In creative writing (see page 115) much opportunity for adapting learning to individual needs and interests can be provided.

2. As the teacher tries to foster development in the skills of written work—such as capitalization and punctuation—he can make careful diagnosis of the child's

level of achievement and of his particular problems. For instance, he can check papers written by the boys and girls to determine whether he evidenced any shortcomings in the matter of punctuation or capitalization. Following diagnosis, reteaching—frequently on an individual basis—may be indicated.

3. In the case of boys and girls not writing up to capacity, the teacher can try to determine whether an undesirable attitude on the part of the learner is the cause or part of the cause for the problem. If it is, the teacher may be able to help the pupil by showing him the significance of the activities in which he engages. Of course, if this procedure is to be followed successfully, it will be highly important that the activities really be worthwhile.

Oral Communication

As in the case of "Other Phases of Written Composition," discussed earlier only a few examples are given below as to how the work in oral communication can be adapted to individual differences. Many ideas dealing with oral communication that can be utilized in an attempt to meet the needs of individual boys and girls in this important area of the language arts are presented in other parts of this book.

1. The teacher can observe errors in usage made by various pupils as they talk, either informally or in more formal situations. Thereupon, he can attempt to provide reteaching or additional practice to suit the needs of the individuals.

2. Choice in topics for talks by the boys and girls can meet the interests of the pupils.

3. In dramatizations boys and girls can be given roles that suit their needs and level of ability.

GUIDING THE GIFTED CHILD

On any grade level the child who has above-average intelligence or is singularly endowed in some other respects should be helped to improve beyond the norm of his class. He can be provided with reading material of difficulty commensurate with his ability to read. He can be guided in developing the reading skills required for his expanding field of interest. In handwriting provisions can be made for improving the quality and increasing the rate beyond that of the average. Greater efficiency and increased artistry in both so-called functional and creative writing can also be encouraged. The pupil can be assisted in developing beyond the class norms in various forms of oral communication. Furthermore, provisions can be made without unduly interfering with the work that the child is likely to do in succeeding

grades in a well-planned and intelligently executed program of the language arts.

The following are additional points that should be observed when guiding the gifted child.

1. Care should be taken that the gifted child does not consider himself more important than his peers who are not blessed with as much ability as he possesses.

2. Care should be taken that the classmates of the gifted child do not become alienated from him. While, to be sure, there are instances when the bright child is admired by his peers, there are also many in which he has the disapproval of others in his group. Also for this reason, the teacher must guard against highlighting the accomplishments of the gifted.

3. In making provisions for work for the gifted, the assignment of additional work along the same level of difficulty on which his peers are working often is not the best procedure. For example, the gifted third-grade child who is considerably above his classmates in reading should not be encouraged to do a great amount of his independent reading of books on the level of comprehension of the average third-grade pupil. Rather, he should be stimulated to read more difficult materials.

4. In planning the work for the gifted, the curriculum to which he will be exposed in later years should be taken into consideration. If a teacher works in a school with a somewhat lockstep system of curriculum organization (i.e., one in which the gifted child would do, let us say, regular fourth-grade work regardless of whether or not he has already mastered it), the teacher, in order to avoid boredom for the child in the following school year, is advised to try very hard not to have the pupil do work that he is likely to have to repeat the following year.

5. Double promotions should not be given to the gifted child unless careful attention has been paid not only to his intellectual level but also to his social, emotional, and physical maturity. Enrichment, rather than acceleration, is often desirable.

6. The gifted child should be aided in accepting the responsibility incumbent upon the person possessing "many talents." The challenge of the responsibility, however, not its burden, should be emphasized with many children of superior ability.

7. The gifted child should not be exploited. Sometimes the pupil who is particularly capable in a certain activity, such as dramatics, art, or music, is given a part in a disproportionate number of dramatic productions, is chosen to make most of the posters in the room, or is asked to sing solo parts again and again. Participation in such activities should be distributed in the best interests of both the gifted pupil and the other boys and girls, who should not be deprived of their share in such activities.

While every gifted child should be helped in the development of a specialty, he should also be given a broad education that provides him with opportunity to participate in many types of activities.

WORKING WITH THE RETARDED PUPIL

The problem of the retarded learner in the area of the language arts cannot be neglected in any effective curriculum.

Points to Keep in Mind when Searching for Reasons for Retardation

The teacher should be cognizant of the following points.

1. Attention should be paid not merely to the immediate but also to the long-time factors that contribute to retardation.

2. Symptoms must not be confused with causes. While the former are often of great value in diagnosis, unless the underlying causes are discovered, any resulting remedial work is likely to lack in effectiveness.

3. Usually no one single factor constitutes the total reason for a deficiency. As a rule a constellation of factors, sometimes closely interwoven, is at the root of the trouble. No diagnostician should stop his search as soon as he has located one underlying factor.

4. Frequently a primary cause of retardation in a language art, especially if the difficulty is of long duration, results in one or more secondary causes which may in turn greatly influence the productivity of the individual. Illness, for example, with resulting irregularity in school attendance, may be the original cause. It may result in lack of interest in learning, which even by itself is significant enough to bring about grave learning problems.

Common Causes of Retardation

Common among the causes of retardation are:
1. Low intelligence
2. An undesirable environment at school and/or at home
3. Poor physical or mental health
4. An inadequate experience background
5. Lack of interest in developing skill in the language arts
6. Poor methods of teaching.
The possibility of a brain lesion should not be excluded before examination when there is a serious difficulty unexplainable by other possible causes.

Guidelines for Working with the Retarded

Methods used with the retarded learner should be in harmony with the following recommendations to the teacher.

1. Be encouraging, but not beyond the point of truthfulness.

2. Stimulate the pupil so that he will want to improve.

3. Find an appropriate time of the day for remedial work. Do not use physical education, art, or music periods for remedial work. When these periods are used for that type of work the child is robbed of participation in activities he particularly enjoys. Furthermore, do not schedule remedial work for a time of day when the child is likely to be tired.

4. Use suitable materials of instruction. They should, if possible, be on both the interest and ability level of the learner.

WORKING WITH THE CULTURALLY AND ECONOMICALLY DISADVANTAGED CHILD

One group of boys and girls in our elementary schools, as well as on other rungs of the educational ladder, who are increasingly receiving special attention are the culturally and economically disadvantaged. They are found in vast numbers in localized areas, such as the inner city or remote agricultural or mining regions. However, they are not confined to such districts. Unless a teacher is employed in suburbia, and frequently even there, he is likely to have at least one child in his room who could be classified as culturally or economically disadvantaged. Consequently the problems of the disadvantaged child should be a matter of universal concern for all elementary school teachers.

How to help the culturally and economically deprived child is a problem of special magnitude when guiding the language experiences of boys and girls. Probably in no other area of the elementary school curriculum is the effect of deprivation as pronounced as in the language arts. It is a problem of magnitude in both the receptive (listening and reading) and the expressive (speaking and writing) phases of communication.

Problems in Communication

While there are those who claim that each child comes to school with adequate language skills to meet his needs, this point can be challenged. The argument can easily center around the term *adequate to his needs*. Surely it must be acceded that not all boys and girls come to school with a language background equally adequate for social and economic advancement in our society. Whether such advancement should be the goal is a question for philosophical consideration; that it is sought by many is a matter of fact.

When speaking of the socially and economically underprivileged child there is, to be sure, the danger of creating a stereotype that is not based on reality. Among all groups of people there are many significant differences in all aspects of living. Individuals who comprise any group show marked variation. In a sense there is no such person as *the* underprivileged child; instead there are underprivileged children, who often, but not invariably, have certain characteristics in common, among them those of special significance in the development of communication skills.

Boys and girls from homes that are economically and culturally deprived, in comparison with other boys and girls, frequently have:

1. A more limited vocabulary
2. A different vocabulary
3. A more restricted experience background of significance to school learnings
4. Less desire to express themselves verbally
5. The tendency to speak in less developed sentences.

Explanation of some of the points listed above may be of value. While it is true that the child from a deprived home is likely to have a more limited vocabulary than the one from a home on a higher level, it must be remembered that the former often has many expressive terms at his command that his peers from other types of homes may not know. At times this difference is so great that for the underprivileged boy or girl the language used at school—the one to which he listens, in which he is expected to express himself orally and in writing, and the one he encounters in his reading—is so different from his own that he is confronted with a problem somewhat similar to that of the child from a non-English-speaking home, namely that of learning a second language.

In some respects, undoubtedly, the child from a disadvantaged home may have a wider background of experience than the one brought up in a more favorable home. Often he has come to grips more intensely with the hard facts—frequently with the sordid facts—of life, from which effort is made to protect the boy and girl in more advantaged homes. Often in the hard school of experience he has acquired an experience background unknown to a large extent to his peers who have grown up in a different kind of environment. Nevertheless, many of his experiences are not the type that schools seemingly designed for the perpetuation of middle-class ideals will build upon. In general, too, the child of the disadvantaged home has traveled less than the one from a middle-class home. Furthermore, even if the culturally disadvantaged child has traveled considerably—like the migrant child, for example—he has often not absorbed as much from his travels as other more economically and culturally favored children would, since his attention frequently has not been drawn to points that would be of relevance to the formal education that he will receive or receives at school.

Causes of Shortcomings

Research has confirmed what common sense often told us, that among the causes of the deficits related to the language development of the underprivileged child are the following:

1. Less communication between the mother and child in the crucial preschool years
2. Inadequate models of oral expression at home and in the neighborhood environment
3. Comparative lack of objects—books included—that stimulate the child to intellectual and language development
4. Lack of incentive for improvement of speech due to the attitude of adults with whom the child comes into contact at home and in his neighborhood
5. Lack of understanding on the part of the teacher of the problems encountered by the child.

Guidelines for the Teacher

One understanding that the teacher should have is that not all economically disadvantaged children are culturally disadvantaged. Although frequently the culturally disadvantaged child comes from a home in which money is a great problem, there are many homes that are economically disadvantaged in which culture is much more in evidence than in some homes in which economical deprivation does not exist. We are using the term *culture,* in the preceding sentence, as somewhat synonymous with the word *refinement.* With that connotation for the word *culture* we can all think of homes that are lacking it though money is no special problem.

What then can the school do to help the disadvantaged child in his language development? Here are some pointers for teachers.

1. Build upon the language equipment with which the child comes to school.
2. Recognize the fact that helping boys and girls from deprived backgrounds to develop communication skills more in keeping with those that have been accepted as standard speech is a delicate task. As the teacher attempts to do so, he must proceed with caution. An individual's language is such a personal attribute that criticism of it can cause great injury to the child.
3. Try to understand the child who is culturally different.
4. Help the child to realize that to be different does not mean to be inferior.
5. Help all the boys and girls in the class to recognize the fact that all people are of equal importance and worth.
6. Provide many opportunities for the child to enrich his background of experience and to verbalize about that which he experiences.
7. Guard against making unnecessary remarks that could reasonably be interpreted by a child as a criticism of his background.
8. Bear in mind that all English—including so-called "standard English"—is really dialect.

9. As teacher, learn the chief characteristics of the dialect one or more of your pupils use.

10. Accept, in the early stages of instruction in the language arts and in other phases of the school program, the child's dialect, thereby making the transition to "standard English" a gradual process.

11. Try to motivate the boys and girls to want to develop skill in communicating in accordance with generally accepted standards of speech.

12. Explain to the pupils that different standards of speech are appropriate for different occasions, but that the vulgar and irreligious are to be barred at all times.

References

The teacher who is perplexed by problems of assisting the child from a disadvantaged home could advisedly read some of the many writings currently being produced on the topic. A large number particularly suited to the needs of the elementary school teacher has been appearing during late years in *Elementary English,* one of the official organs of the National Council of Teachers of English. The reader is also referred to books on the subject listed in chapter 13, "Resources for the Language Arts." (See page 336.)

WORKING WITH THE CHILD FROM THE NON-ENGLISH-SPEAKING HOME AND WITH THE BILINGUAL CHILD

It has been estimated that "four million children and adolescents in this country are native speakers of languages other than English."[1] While many of these are clustered in various cultural centers, such as in Spanish-speaking areas of the Southwest, some are interspersed in the school population throughout the country. In the homes of some of these children, to be sure, some English is spoken; in other homes a non-English language is used exclusively. Obviously the problems in the program of the language arts should differ for these two groups.

Not infrequently teachers seemingly have taken for granted that the child from a non-English-speaking home or from one in which English is a second language is also a culturally disadvantaged individual. While, to be sure, many of the homes in which English is not the major language are to be found among the culturally and/or economically disadvantaged, some of the children from non-English-speaking homes have a background that is culturally equal to or superior to the average child from homes in which English is the chief mode of communication. Obviously the child from a non-English-speaking home who is also culturally disadvantaged has a serious problem in schools in which the instruction is given in English.

The situation of the child who comes to school with a bilingual background needs the special attention of the teacher, as does the one from a non-English-speaking home. In many instances the child is not adept in the use of the English language during the early stages of school instruction. It is not a question as to whether there are advantages in learning two languages—a point generally accepted as fact. The number of schools in which a language other than English is being taught as a second language—chiefly French or Spanish—is indicative of the rather widespread assumption that it is desirable for a young child to learn a second language. (It should be noted that such instruction is generally not given to the child upon entrance to school.) The point about which we are concerned here is that, regardless of later advantages, when the bilingual child starts classes conducted in English, he is often handicapped in language expression until his use of the English language has become on par with that of other boys and girls of his ability.

With recognition of the problems of the bilingual child or the one who comes from a non-English-speaking home, several theories have been advanced as to desired procedure for helping him upon entrance to school. Furthermore, some or all of these theories have been put into practice in some schools. However, currently, no one broad plan for dealing with the situation has been scientifically established as the best way of proceeding. For insight into methods that have been used, the reader is referred to many of the books on the teaching of the language arts in the elementary school that now deal in part with this problem and to the books that treat in more detail with problems of the culturally disadvantaged and the bilingual child and the one from non-English-speaking homes. (See page 336.) Suffice it here to present a few guidelines for working with such children.

1. If the child is also from a culturally disadvantaged home, the teacher should recognize the immensity of the problem the pupil faces when he becomes a member of a school in which the sole or primary means of communication is English. In such a case the teacher needs to observe with care suggestions, such as those presented earlier under "Working with the Culturally and Economically Disadvantaged Child."

2. The teacher should seek to understand the culture of the child and to appreciate the contribution it can make.

3. The teacher should make certain that he correctly pronounces the name of a child from a different language group, since to the child, acceptance may be closely linked with such ability on the part of the teacher.

4. The teacher should learn at least a few words from

---

1. Mildred R. Donoghue, *The Child and the English Language Arts* (Dubuque, Iowa: Wm. C. Brown Company Publishers, 1971), p. 387.

the basic language of the child, not only to communicate better with him but also to show him that he recognizes the value of the child's language.

5. The school should provide special instruction to the child and it should give that instruction not as an extracurricular activity but as a schooltime project.

6. The approach to instruction of the child in English should be through oral communication. However, reading and writing should not be postponed until considerable excellency is achieved in speaking and listening, for skill in the various facets of the language arts can reinforce each other.

7. Considerable use of visual aids in educational media, such as realia, pictures, tapes, discs, and filmstrips should be made.

8. The teacher should acquaint himself with the audiolingual method (sometimes referred to as the aural-oral method of teaching) for assisting the child in learning English, for that method is considered by many as the most advantageous one. Donoghue[2] lists and describes the following as "instructional strategies" pertinent to the audiolingual method, reference to some of which has been made above.

The four skills are developed in turn. Language is sound so the ear and the tongue are trained first and the skills of listening and speaking are developed before the skills of reading and writing.

The spoken language has primacy. Language is initially speech and any structural or lexical item to be learned is first presented orally. Since the beginning stages of listening and speaking are basic to the later stages of literacy, teachers cannot afford to give only superficial attention to the oral nature of language and rush the pupils into reading and writing prematurely.

Words are presented in meaningful context. Since effective communication demands responses in situations simulating true life, the sounds of a second language are best given meaning by relating them to actions and objects contained in such situations. For instructional purposes structural patterns, not word lists, are deemed significant, for communication relies on patterns instead of on separate or isolated words.

Reading and writing are secondary derivatives. Language is not writing. Many language communities in the world have never developed an orthography with its subsequent demand for reading. Elementary TESOL [an organization for *Teaching* (or *Teachers*) of *English* to *Speakers* of *Other Languages*] pupils read and write only what they have already heard and said. Written language is never used to explain the spoken language since reading and writing serve to reinforce and not to replace the acquired audiolingual skills.

Grammar is taught inductively. Language is pattern and the children develop speaking skills through oral imitation of whole language patterns modeled by the teacher. Grammatical generalizations or descriptions are presented only after oral mastery of patterns has been acquired by the class and only when such generalizations will help learning and ensure retention.

Repetitive drill is used to instill language habits. Language in reality is a complex combination of varied sensory and motor habits which can and must become automated as much as

possible through response and repetition. The use of electromechanical aids for the large amount of needed drill can save the teacher's time and voice while it simultaneously promotes automatization.

Basic language patterns are overlearned. Language learning signifies overlearning of the structural patterns through repeated practice. Such "internalizing" or overlearning precedes manipulations whereby structures can be adapted and varied to demonstrate independent speech.

Speech is rendered at the conversational tempo of the native. In order that the children can become accustomed to the intonation and rhythm of the second language, normal tempo is maintained in the classroom from the beginning whenever the second language is used in dialogues or pattern practice.

Culture study is an essential part of language learning. The anthropological concept of culture which stresses daily social patterns of the native speakers is a vital aspect of second language study. Children must learn to respond in realistic situations which are culturally accurate and which closely approximate contemporary life.

Contrastive linguistics is a tool for the teacher. Comparative analysis of contrastive linguistics compares the native tongue of the learner with the language introduced in the classroom. Such information about the differences between languages should not be presented in organized form to children. However, it is useful to the teacher in her planning and preparation because it points up areas of interference and unusual difficulty; one such area, for example, for Spanish-speaking children is the English use of the *expressed* pronoun as the subject of a statement or question, since the Spanish language uses verbal inflection to indicate person and number.

FOR STUDY AND DISCUSSION

1. Read in one or more professional magazines or books, articles or sections that deal with the topic of sociometric measurement. What procedures might you follow in making a sociogram? What cautions would you observe, in applying to grouping, data about pupils whose ratings are indicated on a sociogram? What benefits would you expect to derive from construction of a sociogram?

2. Write a hypothetical description of a gifted child in the upper-primary grades whom you might consider for possible double promotion. Indicate which points in the description give reason for double promotion and which may constitute arguments against it. State what your verdict about double promotion would be in the case you described.

3. Suggest ways in which boys and girls can be stimulated to engage in self-evaluation.

4. Since the Winnetka plan and the Dalton plan have greatly influenced some phases of current procedures for adapting instruction to individual differences, read in one or more professional books on teaching in the elementary school descriptions and evaluations of those plans for adapting instruction to individuals. What application of them do you recognize in some of the more recently developed plans?

2. Ibid., pp. 391-93.

5. Indicate how you might make use of committee work when teaching any phase of the language arts program other than reading.

6. It is suggested earlier in this chapter that "care should be taken that the classmates of the gifted child do not become alienated from him." (See page 321.) Name ways in which such care can be taken.

7. What means might you as teacher employ to determine whether a given child falls into any one or two of these categories: culturally disadvantaged, economically deprived, or bilingual?

8. Suggest teaching procedures beyond those enumerated in this chapter that might be of value in helping motivate the economically and culturally disadvantaged child to improve his language.

REFERENCES

The reader is referred to the list of books dealing with teaching the disadvantaged child that is given in chapter 13. (See page 336.) Many books on the general topic of teaching the language arts in the elementary school also contain valuable information on how to meet needs of individual pupils, the following among them:

Burns, Paul C.; Broman, Betty; and Wantling, Alberta L. *The Language Arts in Childhood Education,* 2nd ed. Chicago: Rand McNally & Company, 1971.

Ruddell, Robert B. *Reading-Language Instruction: Innovative Practices.* Englewood Cliffs, N.J. Prentice-Hall, Inc., 1974.

Smith, James A. *Adventures in Communication: Language Arts Methods.* Boston: Allyn and Bacon, 1972.

Strickland, Ruth G. *The Language Arts in the Elementary School,* 3rd ed. Lexington, Mass.: D.C. Heath and Company, 1969.

13

Resources for the Language Arts

A large number of resources, both human and material, are at the disposal of the teacher of the language arts. The ideas the teacher has gleaned through his years of living; materials he has collected; the background of the boys and girls he is teaching; the individuals in any community who can add to the enrichment of the language arts program; the places, natural and man-made, that can give increased meaning or provide background for the development of greater skill and artistry in the use of the skills of communication; the physical appearance of the classroom and the atmosphere permeating the room—these and many other factors, together with what are commonly referred to as materials of instruction—need to be considered in any comprehensive report on the resources at the command of the teacher of the language arts.

It is not, however, the purpose of this chapter to present an all-inclusive listing of resources. In earlier chapters of this book reference is made to the significance of some of the types of resources listed in the preceding paragraph. In this chapter attention is focused on materials that can be procured commercially.

BOOKS

The first part of this section deals with professional books for teachers and the last three with books for boys and girls, including trade books, textbooks, and reference books.

Books for Teachers

Some of the references for teachers included here have also been listed at the end of the preceding chapters. The reader may wish to supplement the listing of professional books given in this and earlier chapters by perusal of the catalogs of publishers on the teaching of the language arts.

Books on the Language Arts: A General Bibliography. In this general bibliography are not included the books listed on subsequent pages in this chapter under the more specific headings such as "Books on Teaching Reading" or "Books on Creative Expression."

Andersen, Dan A. "Teaching Handwriting." *What Research Says to the Teacher: Number 4.* Washington, D.C.: National Education Association, 1968.

Anderson, Paul S. *Resource Materials for Teachers of Spelling.* Minneapolis, Minn.: Burgess Publishing Company, 1963.

Anderson, Verna; Anderson, Paul S.; Ballantine, Francis; and Howes, Virgil M., eds. *Readings in the Language Arts.* New York: The Macmillan Company, 1968.

Applegate, Mauree. *Easy in English.* New York: Harper & Row, 1960.

Burns, Paul C. *Improving Handwriting Instruction in Elementary Schools.* Minneapolis, Minn.: Burgess Publishing Company, 1968.

Burns, Paul C.; Broman, Betty, L.; Wantling, Alberta Lowe. *The Language Arts in Childhood Education,* 2nd ed. Chicago: Rand McNally & Company, 1971.

Burns, Paul C., and Schell, Leo M., eds. *Elementary School Language Arts: Selected Readings.* Chicago: Rand McNally & Company, 1969.

Burrows, Alvina Treut; Monson, Diane L.; and Stauffer, Russell G. *New Horizons in the Language Arts.* New York: Harper & Row, 1972.

Carlson, Ruth Kearney. *Writing Aids Through the Grades.* New York: Teachers College Press, Columbia College, 1970.

DeStefano, Johanna S., and Fox, Sharon E., eds. *Language and the Language Arts.* Boston: Little, Brown and Company, 1974.

Donoghue, Mildred R. *The Child and the English Language Arts,* 2nd ed. Dubuque, Iowa: Wm. C. Brown Company Publishers, 1975.

Eisenson, Jan, and Ogilvie, Mardel. *Speech Correction in the Schools.* New York: The Macmillan Company, 1963.

Fitzgerald, James A. *The Teaching of Spelling.* Milwaukee, Wis.: Bruce Books, 1951.

Freeman, Frank N. *Guiding Growth in Handwriting.* Columbus, Ohio: The Zaner-Bloser Company, 1965.

Gates, Arthur I. *A List of Spelling Difficulties in 3876 Words.* New York: Teachers College Press, Columbia University, 1937.

Greene, Harry, and Petty, Walter. *Developing Language Skills in Elementary Schools,* 4th ed. Boston: Allyn and Bacon, Inc., 1971.

Hanna, Paul, et al. *Spelling: Structure and Strategies.* Boston: Houghton Mifflin Company, 1970.

Herrick, Virgil E. *New Horizons for Research in Handwriting.* Madison, Wis.: University of Wisconsin Press, 1963.

Hildreth, Gertrude. *Teaching Spelling.* New York: Holt, Rinehart and Winston, Inc., 1955.

Hodges, Richard E. *What's New in Language Arts?: Spelling.* Washington, D.C.: National Education Association, 1970.

Horn, Thomas D., ed. *Research on Handwriting and Spelling.* Urbana, Ill.: National Council of Teachers of English, 1966.

Jones, Anthony, and Mulford, Jeremy, eds. *Children Using Language: An Approach to English in the Elementary School.* Urbana, Ill.: National Council of Teachers of English. 1971.

King, Martha L.; Emans, Robert; and Cianciolo, Patricia J., eds. *The Language Arts in the Elementary School.* Urbana, Ill.: National Council of Teachers of English, 1973.

Knight, Lester N. *Language Arts for the Exceptional: The Gifted and the Linguistically Different.* Itasca, Ill.: F.E. Peacock Publishers, Inc., 1974.

Lamb, Pose, ed. *Guiding Children's Language Learnings.* Dubuque, Iowa: Wm. C. Brown Company Publishers, 1967.

Lewis, Thomas R., and Nichols, Ralph G. *Speaking and Listening.* Dubuque, Iowa: Wm. C. Brown Company Publishers, 1965.

McCullough, Constance. *Handbook for Teaching the Language Arts.* rev. ed. Scranton, Pa.: International Textbook Company, 1969.

Moffett, James A. *Student-Centered Language Arts Curriculum, Grades K-6: A Handbook for Teachers.* Boston: Houghton-Mifflin Company, 1968.

Myers, Emma Harrison. *The Whys and Hows of Teaching Handwriting.* Columbus, Ohio: The Zaner-Bloser Company, 1963.

Petty, Walter T., ed. *Issues and Problems in Elementary Language Arts: A Book of Readings.* Boston: Allyn and Bacon, Inc., 1968.

Pflaum, Susanna. *The Development of Language and Reading in the Young Child.* Columbus, Ohio: Charles E. Merrill Publishing Company, 1974.

Phillips, Gerald M., et al. *The Development of Oral Communication in the Classroom.* Indianapolis, Ind.: The Bobbs-Merrill Company, Inc., 1970.

Possien, Wilma M. *They All Need to Talk.* New York: Appleton-Century-Crofts, 1969.

Robinson, H. Alan, and Burrows, Alvina Treut. *Teacher Effectiveness in Elementary Language Arts: A Progress Report.* Urbana, Ill.: National Council of Teachers of English, 1974.

Ruddell, Robert B. *Reading-Language Instruction: Innovative Practices.* Englewood, N.J.: Prentice-Hall, Inc., 1974.

Smith, Genevieve. *A Programed Text: Spelling by Principles.* New York: Appleton-Century-Crofts, 1966.

Smith, James A. *Adventures in Communication: Language Arts Methods.* Boston: Allyn and Bacon, Inc., 1972.

———. *Creative Teaching of the Language Arts in the Elementary School.* Boston: Allyn and Bacon, Inc., 1967.

Strickland, Ruth G. *The Language Arts in the Elementary School.* Lexington, Mass.: D.C. Heath and Company, 1969.

Taylor, Elvin. *A New Approach to Language Arts in the Elementary School.* West Nyack, N.Y.: Parker Publishing Company, 1970.

Tidyman, Willard F.; Smith, Charleen; and Butterfield, Marguerite. *Teaching the Language Arts.* New York: McGraw-Hill Book Company, 1969.

Trauger, Wilmer K. *Language Arts in the Elementary Schools.* New York: McGraw-Hill Book Company, 1963.

Wagner, Guy; Hosier, Max; and Blackman, Mildred. *Listening Games.* Darien, Conn.: Teachers Publishing Corporation, 1962.

Zaner-Bloser Company, The, *Writing on the Board.* Columbus, Ohio: The Zaner-Bloser Company, 1958.

Books on Teaching Reading. Because of the close relationship of reading to the other language arts, a listing of some of the books dealing with the teaching of reading is included here.

Aukerman, Robert C. *Approaches to Beginning Reading.* New York: John Wiley & Sons, Inc., 1971.

Beery, Althea; Barrett, Thomas C.; and Powell, William R., eds. *Elementary Reading Instruction.* Boston: Allyn and Bacon, Inc., 1969.

Bond, Guy L., and Bond Wagner, Eva. *Teaching the Child to Read.* 4th ed. New York: The Macmillan Company, 1966.

Bush, Clifford L., and Huebner, Mildred H. *Strategies for Reading in the Elementary School.* New York: The Macmillan Company, 1970.

Chall, Jeanne S. *Learning to Read: The Great Debate.* New York: McGraw-Hill Book Company, 1967.

Cohen, S. Alan. *Teach Them All to Read.* New York: Random House, Inc., 1969.

Dallmann, Martha; Rouch, Roger L.; Chang, Lynette Y.C.; and DeBoer, John J. *The Teaching of Reading,* 4th ed. New York: Holt, Rinehart and Winston, Inc., 1974.

Darrow, Helen F., and Howes, Virgil M. *Approaches to Individualized Reading.* New York: Appleton-Century-Crofts, 1969.

Davis, Bonnie M., comp. *A Guide to Information Sources for Reading.* Newark, Del.: International Reading Association, 1972.

Dawson, Mildred A., ed. *Developing Comprehension.* Newark, Del.: International Reading Association, 1968.

———. *Teaching Word Recognition Skills.* Newark, Del.: International Reading Association, 1970.

Doman, Glenn. *How to Teach Your Child to Read.* New York: Random House, 1964.

Douglass, Malcolm P., ed. *Reading in Education: A Broader View.* Columbus, Ohio: Charles E. Merrill Publishing Company, 1973.

Downing, John. *The Initial Teaching Alphabet.* New York: The Macmillan Company, 1964.

Durkin, Dolores. *Children Who Read Early.* New York: Teachers College Press, Columbia University, 1966.

———. *Teaching Them to Read.* Boston: Allyn and Bacon, Inc., 1970.

Durr, William P., ed. *Reading Instruction: Dimensions and Issues.* Boston: Houghton Mifflin Company, 1967.

Ekwall, Eldon E. *Locating and Correcting Reading Difficulties.* Columbus, Ohio: Charles E. Merrill Company, Inc., 1970.

———. *Psychological Factors in the Teaching of Reading.* Columbus, Ohio: Charles E. Merrill Publishing Company, 1973.

Frost, Joe L. *Issues and Innovations in the Teaching of Reading.* Glenview, Ill.: Scott, Foresman and Company, 1967.

Fry, Edward. *Reading Instruction for Classroom and Clinic.* New York: McGraw-Hill Book Company, 1972.

Gans, Roma. *Common Sense in Teaching Reading.* Indianapolis, Ind.: The Bobbs-Merrill Company, Inc., 1963.

Gray, William S. *On Their Own in Reading.* Glenview, Ill.: Scott, Foresman and Company, 1960.

Hall, Mary Anne. *Teaching Reading as a Language Experience.* Columbus, Ohio: Charles E. Merrill Publishing Company, 1970.

Harris, Albert J. *How to Increase Reading Ability.* New York: David McKay Company, 1970.

Harris, Albert J., and Sipay, Edward R. *Effective Teaching of Reading.* 2nd ed. New York: David McKay Company, 1971.

Heilman, Arthur W. *Principles and Practices of*

Teaching Reading. 2nd ed. Columbus, Ohio: Charles E. Merrill Publishing Company, 1972.

Henderson, Richard L., and Green, Donald Ross. *Reading for Meaning in the Elementary School.* Englewood Cliffs, N.J.: Prentice-Hall, Inc., 1969.

Herbert, Harold L. *Teaching Reading in Content Areas.* Englewood Cliffs, N.J.: Prentice-Hall, Inc., 1970.

Herr, Selma E. *Learning Activities for Reading,* 2nd ed. Dubuque, Iowa: Wm. C. Brown Company Publishers, 1970.

Herrick, Virgil E., and Nervovig, Marcella. *Using Experience Charts with Children.* Columbus, Ohio: Charles E. Merrill Publishing Company, 1964.

Karlin, Robert. *Teaching Elementary Reading: Principles and Strategies.* New York: Harcourt Brace Jovanovich, 1971.

Lee, Dorris M., and Allen, R.V. *Learning to Read through Experience.* New York: Appleton-Century-Crofts, 1963.

Lillard, Paula Polk. *Montesorri: A Modern Approach.* New York: Schocken Books, 1972.

Moburg, Larry. *Inservice Teacher Training in Reading.* Reading Information Series. Newark, Del.: International Reading Association, 1972.

Morrison, Ida E. *Teaching Reading in the Elementary School.* New York: The Ronald Press, 1968.

Moyle, Donald, and Moyle, Louise. *Modern Innovations in the Teaching of Reading.* Newark, Del.: International Reading Association, 1971.

National Society for the Study of Education. *Innovation and Change in Reading Instruction.* Sixty-Seventh Yearbook, part II. Edited by Helen Robinson. Chicago: University of Chicago Press, 1968.

Sartain, Harry, comp. *Individualized Reading,* rev. ed. Newark, Del.: International Reading Association, 1970.

Schubert, Delwyn G., and Torgerson, Theodore L., eds. *Readings in Reading.* New York: Thomas Y. Crowell Company, 1968.

Sebesta, Sam Leaton, and Wallen, Carl J., eds. *The First R: Readings on Teaching Reading.* Chicago: Science Research Associates, 1972.

Smith, Nila Banton. *Reading Instruction for Today's Children.* Englewood Cliffs, N.J.: Prentice-Hall, Inc., 1970.

Spache, Evelyn B. *Reading Activities for Child Involvement.* Boston: Allyn and Bacon, Inc., 1972.

Spache, George D., and Spache, Evelyn B. *Reading in the Elementary School,* 3rd ed. Boston: Allyn and Bacon, Inc., 1972.

Staiger, Ralph, and Sohn, David A., eds. *New Directions in Reading.* New York: Bantam Books, 1967.

Stauffer, Russell G. *Directing Reading Maturity as a Cognitive Process.* New York: Harper and Row, 1969.

Veatch, Jeannette. *Reading in the Elementary School.* New York: The Ronald Press, 1966.

Vilscek, Elaine, ed. *A Decade of Innovation: Approaches to Beginning Reading.* Proceedings of the Twelfth Annual Convention, vol. 12, part 3. Newark, Del.: International Reading Association, 1971.

Witty, Paul A., ed. *Reading for the Gifted and the Creative Student.* Newark, Del: International Reading Association, 1970.

Books on Literature for Children. The following are a few of the many books on literature for children. Some are anthologies while others are books devoted primarily to the teaching of literature for children. For additional professional material the reader is referred to books in the preceding listing. Many of those contain chapters on means of interesting children in reading. Additional books of help in guiding boys and girls in the development of lasting, worthwhile interests in reading are listed under "Sources for Book Selection," page 337.

Arbuthnot, May Hill, and Sutherland, Zena. *Children and Books,* 4th ed. Chicago: Scott, Foresman and Company, 1972.

Behn, Harry. *Chrysalis: Concerning Children and Poetry.* New York: Harcourt Brace Jovanovich, 1968.

Carlson, Ruth Kearney. *Literature for Children: Enrichment Ideas.* Dubuque, Iowa: Wm. C. Brown Company Publishers, 1970.

Catterons, Jane, ed. *Children and Literature.* Newark, Del.: International Reading Association, 1970.

Chambers, Dewey W. *Literature for Children: Storytelling and Creative Drama.* Dubuque, Iowa: Wm. C. Brown Company Publishers, 1970.

Cianciolo, Patricia. *Literature for Children: Illustrations in Children's Books.* Dubuque, Iowa: Wm. C. Brown Company Publishers, 1970.

Cullinan, Bernice E. *Literature for Children: Its Discipline and Content.* Dubuque, Iowa: Wm. C. Brown Company Publishers, 1971.

Dietrich, D.M., and Mathews, V.H., eds. *Development of Lifetime Reading Habits.* Newark, Del.: International Reading Association, 1968.

Fenwick, Sara Innis, ed. *A Critical Approach to Children's Literature.* Chicago: University of Chicago Press, 1967.

Hazard, Paul. *Books, Children and Men.* Boston: Horn Book, Inc., 1960.

Huck, Charlotte, and Kuhn, Doris. *Children's Literature in the Elementary School.* 2nd ed. New York: Holt, Rinehart and Winston, Inc., 1968.

Jacobs, Leland B. *Literature with Young Children.* New York: Teachers College Press, Columbia University, 1965.

Kingman, Lee, ed. *Newbery and Caldecott Medal Books, 1956-65.* Boston: Horn Book, Inc., 1964.

Painter, Helen W. *Poetry and Children.* Newark, Del.: International Reading Association, 1970.

Reid, Virginia M., ed. *Reading Ladders for Human Relations,* 5th ed. Washington, D.C.: American Council on Education, 1972.

Ruggs, Corinne. *Bibliotherapy.* Newark, Del.: International Reading Association, 1968.

Sawyer, Ruth. *The Way of the Storyteller.* New York: The Viking Press, 1962.

Spache, George D. *Sources of Good Books for Poor Readers.* Newark, Del.: International Reading Association, 1966.

Whitehead, Robert. *Children's Literature: Strategies of Teaching.* Englewood Cliffs, N.J.: Prentice-Hall, Inc., 1968.

Books on Creative Expression. Many suggestions for creative expression are interspersed among the chapters of the books listed elsewhere in this bibliography. To those the reader is referred as well as to the following which deal primarily with creativity of various types—creativity in writing, creativity in dramatic expression (including puppetry), creativity through choral speaking.

Applegate, Mauree. *Freeing Children to Write.* New York: Harper & Row, Publishers, 1963.

———. *When the Teacher Says, "Write a Poem."* New York: Harper & Row, Publishers, 1965.

———. *When the Teacher Says, "Write a Story."* New York: Harper & Row, Publishers, 1965.

Association for Childhood Education International. *Creative Dramatics.* Washington, D.C.: Association for Childhood Education International, 1961.

Baird, Bil. *The Art of the Puppet.* New York: The Macmillan Company, 1965.

Bamman, Henry A.; Dawson, Mildred A.; and Whitehead, Robert J. *Oral Interpretation of Children's Literature,* 2nd ed. Dubuque, Iowa: Wm. C. Brown Company Publishers, 1971.

Batchelder, Marjorie. *The Puppet Theatre Handbook.* New York: Harper & Row, Publishers, 1947.

Brown, Helen A., and Heltman, Harry J. *Choral Reading for Fun and Recreation.* Philadelphia: Westminster Press, 1956.

Burrows, Alvina; Jackson, Doris; and Saunders, Dorothy. *They All Want to Write.* New York: Holt, Rinehart and Winston, Inc., 1964.

Carlson, Bernice. *Act It Out.* Nashville, Tenn.: Abingdon Press, 1965.

Chambers, Dewey W. *Literature for Children: Storytelling and Creative Drama.* Dubuque, Iowa: Wm. C. Brown Company Publishers, 1970.

Crosscut, Richard. *Children and Dramatics.* New York: Charles Scribner's Sons, 1966.

Henderson, Harold G. *An Introduction to Haiku.* New York: Doubleday & Company, Inc., 1958.

Howard, Vernon. *Puppet and Pantomime Plays.* New York: Sterling Publishing Company, Inc., 1962.

Kamerman, Sylvia, ed. *Dramatized Folk Tales of the World.* Boston: Plays, Inc., 1971.

Kerman, Gertrude. *Plays and Creative Ways with Children.* New York: Harvey House, Inc., 1961.

Kosinski, Leonard V., ed. *Readings on Creativity and Imagination in Literature and Language.* Urbana, Ill.: National Council of Teachers of English, 1968.

Menagh, H. Beresford. *Creative Dramatics in Guiding Children's Language Learning.* Dubuque, Iowa: Wm. C. Brown Company Publishers, 1967.

Pratt, Lois H. *The Puppet Do-It-Yourself Book.* New York: Exposition Press, 1957.

Rasmussen, Carrie. *Let's Say Poetry Together.* Minneapolis, Minn.: Burgess Publishing Company, 1962.

Raubicheck, Letitia. *Choral Speaking Is Fun.* New York: Noble & Noble Publishers, Inc., 1955.

Ross, Laura. *Hand Puppets: How to Make and Use Them.* New York: Lothrop, Lee & Shepard Company, 1969.

Severn, Bill. *Shadow Magic.* New York: David McKay Company, Inc., 1959.

Siks, Geraldine B. *Children's Literature for Dramatization.* New York: Harper & Row, Publishers, 1964.

Taylor, Loren E. *Puppetry, Marionettes, and Shadow Plays.* Minneapolis, Minn.: Burgess Publishing Company, 1965.

Tichenor, Tom. *Tom Tichenor's Puppets.* Nashville, Tenn.: Abingdon Press, 1971.

Tiedt, Iris M., ed. *Drama in Your Classroom.* Urbana, Ill.: National Council of Teachers of English, 1974.

Torrance, E. Paul. *Creativity in the Classroom.* Dubuque, Iowa: Wm. C. Brown Company Publishers, 1970.

Walter, Nina. *Let Them Write Poetry.* New York: Holt, Rinehart and Winston, Inc., 1962.

Worrell, Estelle. *Be a Puppeteer: The Lively Puppet Book.* New York: McGraw-Hill Book Company, 1969.

Books Dealing with Diagnosis and Remediation. In addition to many of the books listed under "Books on the

Language Arts" (see page 331) and "Books on Teaching Reading" (see page 333), which deal with the topic of diagnosis and remediation, the following additional references may be helpful to the reader.

Barrett, Thomas, ed. *The Evaluation of Children's Reading Achievement*. Newark, Del.: International Reading Association, 1967.

Bond, Buy L., and Tinker, Miles A. *Reading Difficulties: Their Diagnosis and Correction*, 2nd ed. New York: Appleton-Century-Crofts, 1968.

Brown, Frederick G. *Principles of Educational and Psychological Testing*. Hinsdale, Ill.: The Dryden Press, Inc., 1970.

Burns, Paul C. *Diagnostic Teaching of the Language Arts*. Itasca, Ill.: F.E. Peacock Publishers, Inc., 1974.

Buros, Oscar K., ed. *Mental Measurements Yearbook*, latest edition. Highland Park, N.J.: Gryphon Press.

Dechant, Emerald V. ed. *Detection and Correction of Reading Difficulties: Readings and Commentary*. New York: Appleton-Century-Crofts, 1970.

Delacato, Carl H. *New Starts for the Child Who Can't Read*. New York: David McKay Company, 1970.

Ebel, Robert L. *Measuring Educational Advancement*. Englewood Cliffs, N.J.: Prentice-Hall, Inc., 1970.

Fierson, Edward C., and Barbe, Walter B., comp. *Educating Children with Learning Disabilities*. New York: Appleton-Century-Crofts, 1967.

Gronlund, Norman E. *Measurement and Evaluation in Teaching*. New York: The Macmillan Company, 1965.

Johnson, Marjorie S., and Kress, Roy A. *Informal Reading Inventories*. Newark, Del.: International Reading Association, 1965.

Kaphart, Newell G. *The Slow Learner in the Classroom*. 2nd ed. New York: Schocken Books, 1971.

Otto, Wayne, and Koenke, Karl. *Remedial Teaching: Research and Comment*. Boston: Houghton Mifflin Company, 1969.

Potter, Thomas, and Rae, Kenneth. *Informal Reading Diagnosis: A Practical Guide for the Classroom Teacher*. Englewood Cliffs, N.J.: Prentice-Hall, Inc., 1972.

Wilson, Robert M. *Diagnostic and Remedial Reading for Classroom and Clinic*, 2nd ed. Columbus, Ohio: Charles E. Merrill Publishing Company, 1972.

Books Dealing with Linguistics. The subject of linguistics in relation to its application to the elementary school program is discussed in many of the recent books on the teaching of the language arts. The books listed here deal with linguistics.

Anderson, Paul S. *Linguistics in the Elementary School Classroom*. New York: The Macmillan Company, 1971.

Corcoran, Gertrude. *Language Arts in the Elementary School: A Modern Linguistic Approach*. New York: The Ronald Press, 1970.

Dechant, Emerald V. *Linguistics, Phonics and the Teaching of Reading*. Springfield, Ill.: Charles C. Thomas, Publishers, 1969.

Durkin, Dolores. *Phonics, Linguistics and Reading*. New York: Teachers College Press, Columbia University, 1972.

Fedor, Jerry A., and Katz, Jerrold J. *The Structure of Language*. Englewood Cliffs, N.J.: Prentice-Hall, Inc., 1964.

Hanna, Paul R.; Hanna, Jean S.; Hodges, Richard E.; and Rudort, Edwin H., Jr. *Phoneme-Grapheme Correspondence as Cues to Spelling Improvement*. Washington, D.C.: U.S. Department of Health, Education and Welfare, 1968.

Lamb, Pose. *Linguistics in Proper Perspective*. Columbus, Ohio: Charles E. Merrill Publishing Company, 1967.

LeFevre, Carl A. *Linguistics, English, and the Language Arts*. Boston: Allyn and Bacon, Inc., 1970.

Savage, John F., ed. *Linguistics for Teachers: Selected Readings*. Chicago: Science Research Associates, 1973.

Books Dealing with the Teaching of the Disadvantaged and the Culturally Different. The deep concern with the teaching of the disadvantaged and the culturally different in our population has resulted in many articles on the subject that have appeared in professional periodicals. Books on it are also appearing in large numbers, these among them:

Allen, Vernon L. *Psychological Factors in Poverty*. Chicago: Markham Publishing Company, 1970.

Baratz, Joan C., and Shuy, Robert W., eds. *Teaching Black Children to Read*. Washington, D.C.: Center for Applied Linguistics, 1969.

Bentley, Robert H., and Crawford, Samuel D., eds. *Black Language Readers*. Glenview, Ill.: Scott, Foresman and Company, 1973.

Broderick, Dorothy. *The Image of the Black in Children's Fiction*. Ann Arbor, Mich.: R.R. Bowker Order Department, 1973.

Cullinan, Bernice, ed. *Black Dialects and Reading*. National Council of Teachers of English, 1974.

Dennison, George. *The Lives of Children: The Story of the First Street School*. New York: Random House, Inc., 1969.

Fantini, Mario, and Weinstein, Gerald. *Making Urban*

Schools Work: Social Realities and the Urban School. New York: Holt, Rinehart and Winston, Inc., 1968.

Figurel, J. Allen, ed. *Better Reading in Urban Schools.* Newark, Del.: International Reading Association, 1972.

Frost, Joe L., and Hawkes, Glenn R., eds. *The Disadvantaged Child.* Boston: Houghton Mifflin Company, 1966.

Hardy, William G. *Communication and the Disadvantaged Child.* Baltimore: Williams and Wilkins Company, 1970.

Horn, Thomas D., ed. *Reading for the Disadvantaged: Problems of the Linguistically Different Learners.* New York: Harcourt Brace Jovanovich, Inc., 1970.

Janowitz, Gayle. *Helping Hands: Volunteer Work in Education.* Chicago: University of Chicago Press, 1965.

Labov, William. *The Study of Nonstandard English.* Urbana, Ill.: National Council of Teachers of English, 1970.

Noar, Gertrude. *Teaching the Disadvantaged: What Research Says to the Teacher.* Washington, D.C.: National Education Association, 1967.

O'Brien, Carmen. *Teaching the Language-Different Child to Read.* Columbus, Ohio: Charles E. Merrill Publishing Company, 1973.

Passow, A. Harry. *Education in Depressed Areas.* New York: Teachers College Press, Columbia University, 1968.

———. *Reaching the Disadvantaged Learner.* New York: Teachers College Press, Columbia University, 1970.

Shuy, Roger W. *Discovering American Dialects.* Urbana, Ill.: National Council of Teachers of English, 1967.

Spache, George D. *Good Reading for the Disadvantaged: Multi-Ethnic Resources.* Morristown, N.Y.: The Garrard Publishing Company, 1970.

Thonis, Eleanor W. *Teaching Reading to Non-English Speakers.* New York: The Macmillan Company, 1970.

Watt, Lois B., comp. *Literature for Disadvantaged Children: A Bibliography.* OE-37019. Washington, D.C.: U.S. Department of Health, Education and Welfare, 1968.

Williams, Frederick. *Language and Poverty.* Chicago: Markham Publishing Company, 1970.

Trade Books for Boys and Girls

With the large number of books for boys and girls on the market—some excellent, others ordinary, and still others banal—it is important that both teacher and parent know where to turn for guidance in selection.

Sources for Book Selection. Fortunately there are many excellent sources of information to which to turn for help. Two good sources for book lists are: (1) Children's Services Division of the American Library Association, 50 East Huron Street, Chicago, Illinois 60611 and (2) The Children's Book Council, 175 Fifth Avenue, New York, New York 10010. The United States Office of Education also issues bibliographies of books for boys and girls. Among books on the teaching of literature for children that contain many suggestions for excellent books for boys and girls are *Children and Books* by May Arbuthnot and Zena Sutherland (Scott, Foresman and Company, 1972) and *Children's Literature in the Elementary School* by Charlotte Huck and Doris Kuhn (Holt, Rinehart and Winston, Inc., 1968.)

The following are some of the publications printed periodically that evaluate currently written books for children:

> *The Booklist* (American Library Association)
> *Book Review Digest* (H.W. Wilson Company)
> *Bulletin of the Center for Children's Books* (University of Chicago Press)
> *Chicago Sunday Tribune*
> *Childhood Education* (Association for Childhood Education)
> *Elementary English* (National Council of Teachers of English)
> *Horn Book Magazine* (Horn Book, Inc.)
> *New York Herald-Tribune Book Review*
> *New York Times Book Review*
> *Parents Magazine* (Parents Magazine Press)
> *Publisher's Weekly* (Children's Book Number, R.R. Bowker Company)
> *Reading Teacher* (International Reading Association)
> *School Library Journal* (R.R. Bowker Company)
> *Young Readers Review* (Box 137, Wall Street Station, New York, N.Y. 10005).

The following sources are also recommended. It will, however, be noted that, as the copyright dates indicate, some of them do not include recent books.

Adventuring with Books: A Booklist for Elementary Schools. Edited by Elizabeth Guilfoile. Champaign, Ill.: National Council of Teachers of English, 1960.

Aids in Choosing Books for Your Children. New York; Children's Book Council, latest edition.

Annotated Bibliography of Selected Books with High Interest and Low Vocabulary Level. Indianapolis Public Schools.

Annual List of Children's Literature. American Library Association, latest edition.

Books for Children. American Library Association, latest edition.

Books for Slow Readers. Holiday House.

Children's Books: Awards and Prizes. Children's Book Council, latest edition.

Children's Books for Schools and Libraries. R.R. Bowker Company, latest edition.

Children's Books in Print. R.R. Bowker Company, latest edition.

Children's Books Suggested as Holiday Gifts. New York Public Library, latest edition.

Distinguished Children's Books. American Library Association, latest edition.

A Graded List of Books for School Libraries. Harcourt Brace Jovanovich.

Guide to Information Sources for Reading. International Reading Association, 1972.

Index to Children's Poetry. H.W. Wilson Company, latest supplement.

An Index to Young Readers' Collective Biographies. R.R. Bowker Company, 1970.

The Negro in Schoolroom Literature. Center for Urban Education, 1967.

Notable Children's Books of . . . . American Library Association, latest edition.

Paperbound Book Guide for Elementary Schools. R.R. Bowker Company, latest edition.

A Parent's Guide to Children's Reading. Nancy Larrick. Doubleday and Company, 1969.

Reading Ladders for Human Relations, 5th ed. American Council on Education, 1972.

Sources of Good Books and Magazines for Children. International Reading Association.

Subject Index to Poetry for Children and Young People. American Library Association.

A Teacher's Guide to Children's Books. Charles E. Merrill Publishing Company, 1960.

Book Awards. The two best-known awards in the field of literature for boys and girls are the Newbery Medal and the Caldecott Medal. The Newbery Medal books date back to 1922 when Frederic C. Melcher made possible the award, given annually for the most distinguished book of the year in the field of literature for children. Himself a publisher, he named the award after the famous publisher of books for children, John Newbery. In 1939, also through the generosity of Mr. Melcher, the first Caldecott Medal was awarded. It is named after Randolph Caldecott, well-known illustrator of books for children during an earlier era. This award is given annually to the book judged to be the most distinguished picture book for children published during the year. Additional awards include:

The Jane Addams Children's Book Award. (Given by the Jane Addams Peace Association, 345 East 46th Street, New York, New York 10017.)

Book-World Chidren's Spring Book Festival Award. (Presented by the newspaper of that name, for two meritorious books selected, one for the younger age group and the other for the older age group, as well as one for a picture book.)

Boston Globe-Horn Book Awards. (Awarded by *The Boston Globe,* Boston, Massachusetts 02107, and *The Horn Book Magazine,* 585 Boylston Street, Boston, Massachusetts 02116.)

Child Study Association of American Children's Book Award. (Given by the Children's Book Committee of the Child Study Association of America, 50 Madison Avenue, New York, New York 10010.)

Charles W. Follett Award. (Awarded by the sons of Charles W. Follett; the Follett Publishing Company, 1010 West Washington Boulevard, Chicago, Illinois 60607.)

William Allen White Children's Books Award. (Presented by the William Allen Memorial Library, Kansas State Teachers College, Emporia, Kansas 66801.)

Laura Ingalls Wilder Award. (Administered by the Children's Services Division of the American Library Association, 50 East Huron Street, Chicago, Illinois 60611.)

For further information on book awards, the reader is referred to the latest edition of *Literary and Library Prizes,* published by the R.R. Bowker Company and to *Children's Books: Awards and Prizes,* published periodically, available through The Children's Book Council, 175 Fifth Avenue, New York, New York 10017.

1. The Newbery Medal books. For the following books the Newbery Medal has been awarded.

1922 Van Loon, Hendrik. *The Story of Mankind.* New York: Liveright Publishing Corporation.

1923 Lofting, Hugh. *The Voyages of Doctor Dolittle.* Philadelphia: J.B. Lippincott Company.

1924 Hawes, Charles Boardman. *The Dark Frigate.* Boston: Little, Brown and Company.

1925 Finger, Charles J. *Tales from Silver Lands.* New York: Doubleday and Company, Inc.

1926 Chrisman, Arthur. *Shen of the Sea.* New York: E.P. Dutton and Company, Inc.

1927 James, Will. *Smoky.* New York:Charles Scribner's Sons.

1928 Mukerji, Dhan Gopal. *Gay-Neck.* New York: E.P. Dutton and Company, Inc.

1929 Kelly, Eric P. *The Trumpeter of Krakow.* New York: The Macmillan Company.

1930 Field, Rachel. *Hitty, Her First Hundred Years.* New York: The Macmillan Company.

1931 Coatsworth, Elizabeth. *The Cat Who Went to Heaven.* New York: The Macmillan Company.

1932 Armer, Laura Adams. *Waterless Mountain.* New York: David McKay Company, Inc.

1933 Lewis, Elizabeth Foreman. *Young Fu of the Upper Yangtze.* New York: Holt, Rinehart and Winston, Inc.

1934 Meigs, Cornelia. *Invincible Louisa.* Boston: Little, Brown and Company.

1935 Shannon, Monica. *Dobry.* New York: The Viking Press, Inc.

1936 Brink, Carol Ryrie. *Caddie Woodlawn.* New York: The Macmillan Company.

1937 Sawyer, Ruth. *Roller Skates.* New York: The Viking Press, Inc.

1938 Seredy, Kate. *The White Stag.* New York: The Viking Press, Inc.

1939 Enright, Elizabeth. *Thimble Summer.* New York: Holt, Rinehart and Winston, Inc.

1940 Daugherty, James. *Daniel Boone.* New York: The Viking Press, Inc.

1941 Sperry, Armstrong. *Call It Courage.* New York: The Macmillan Company.

1942 Edmonds, Walter. *The Matchlock Gun.* New York: Dodd, Mead & Company.

1943 Gray, Elizabeth Janet. *Adam of the Road.* New York: The Viking Press, Inc.

1944 Forbes, Esther, *Johnny Tremain.* Boston: Houghton Mifflin Company.

1945 Lawson, Robert. *Rabbit Hill.* New York: The Viking Press, Inc.

1946 Lenski, Lois. *Strawberry Girl.* Philadelphia: J.B. Lippincott Company.

1947 Bailey, Carolyn Sherwin. *Miss Hickory.* New York: The Viking Press, Inc.

1948 DuBois, William Pene. *The Twenty-One Balloons.* New York: The Viking Press, Inc.

1949 Henry, Marguerite. *King of the Wind.* Chicago: Rand McNally & Company.

1950 De Angeli, Marguerite. *The Door in the Wall.* New York: Doubleday & Company, Inc.

1951 Yates, Elizabeth. *Amos Fortune, Free Man.* Alladin Books.

1952 Estes, Eleanor, *Ginger Pye.* New York: Harcourt Brace Jovanovich, Inc.

1953 Clark, Ann Nolan. *Secret of the Andes.* New York: The Viking Press, Inc.

1954 Krumbold, Joseph. *And Now Miguel.* New York: Thomas Y. Crowell Company.

1955 DeJong, Meindert. *The Wheel on the School.* New York: Harper & Row, Publishers.

1956 Latham, Jean Lee. *Carry On, Mr. Bowditch.* Boston: Houghton Mifflin Company.

1957 Sorenson, Virginia. *Miracles on Maple Hill.* New York: Harcourt, Brace, Jovanovich, Inc.

1958 Keith, Harold. *Rifles for Watie.* New York: Thomas Y. Crowell Company.

1959 Speare, Elizabeth George. *The Witch of Blackbird Pond.* Boston: Houghton Mifflin Company.

1960 Krumgold, Joseph. *Onion John.* New York: Thomas Y. Crowell Company.

1961 O'Dell, Scott. *Island of the Blue Dolphins.* Boston: Houghton Mifflin Company.

1962 Speare, Elizabeth George. *The Bronze Bow.* Boston: Houghton Mifflin Company.

1963 L'Engle, Madeline. *Wrinkle in Time.* New York: Farrar, Straus & Giroux, Inc.

1964 Neville, Emily Cheney. *It's Like This, Cat.* New York: Harper & Row, Publishers.

1965 Wojciechowska, Maia. *Shadow of a Bull.* New York: Atheneum Publishers.

1966 de Trevino, Elizabeth Borten. *I, Juan de Pareja.* New York: Farrar, Straus & Giroux, Inc.

1967 Hunt, Irene. *Up a Road Slowly.* Chicago: Follett Publishing Company.

1968 Konigsburg, E.L. *From the Mixed-Up Files of Mrs. Basil E. Frankweiler.* New York: Atheneum Publishers.

1969 Alexander, Lloyd. *The High King.* New York: Holt, Rinehart and Winston, Inc.

1970 Armstrong, William H. *Sounder.* New York: Harper & Row, Publishers.

1971 Byars, Betsey. *Summer of the Swans.* New York: The Viking Press, Inc.

1972 O'Brien, Robert C. *Mrs. Frisby and the Rats of NIMH.* New York: Atheneum Publishers.

1973 George, Jean C. *Julie of the Wolves.* New York: Harper & Row, Publishers.

1974 Fox, Paula. *The Slave Dancer.* Scarsdale, N.Y.: Bradbury Press.

1975 Hamilton, Virginia. *M.C. Higgins the Great.* New York: Macmillan.

2. The Caldecott Medal books. The Caldecott Medal has been awarded to the following books on page 340.

1938 Lathrop, Dorothy. *Animals of the Bible.* Philadelphia: J.B. Lippincott Company.

1939 Handforth, Thomas. *Mei Li.* New York: Doubleday & Company, Inc.

1940 D'Aulaire, Ingri and Edgar. *Abraham Lincoln.* New York: Doubleday and Company, Inc.

1941 Lawson, Robert. *They Were Strong and Good.* New York: The Viking Press, Inc.

1942 McCloskey, Robert. *Make Way for Ducklings.* New York: The Viking Press, Inc.

1943 Gray, Elizabeth Janet. *Adam of the Road.* New York: The Viking Press, Inc.

1944 Thurber, James (with Louis Slobodkin, illustrator). *Many Moons.* New York: Harcourt Brace Jovanovich, Inc.

1945 Field, Rachel (with Elizabeth Orton Jones, illustrator). *Prayer for a Child.* New York: The Macmillan Company.

1946 Petersham, Maud and Miska. *The Rooster Crows.* New York: The Macmillan Company.

1947 MacDonald, Golden (with Leonard Weisgard, illustrator). *The Little Island.* New York: Doubleday and Company, Inc.

1948 Tresselt, Alvin (with Roger Duvoisin, illustrator). *White Snow, Bright Snow.* New York: Lothrop, Lee & Shepard Co., Inc.

1949 Hader, Berta and Hader, Elmer. *The Big Snow.* New York: The Macmillan Company.

1950 Politi, Leo. *Song of the Swallows.* New York: Charles Scribner's Sons.

1951 Milhous, Katherine. *The Egg Tree.* New York. Charles Scribner's Sons.

1952 Lipkind, William (with Nicolas Mordvinoff, illustrator). *Finders Keepers.* New York: Harcourt Brace Jovanovich, Inc.

1953 Ward, Lynd. *The Biggest Bear.* Boston: Houghton Mifflin Company.

1954 Bemelmans, Ludwig. *Madeline's Rescue.* New York: The Viking Press, Inc.

1955 Perrault, Charles (with Marcia Brown, illustrator). *Cinderella: or the Little Glass Slipper.* New York: Charles Scribner's Sons.

1956 Langstaff, John (with Feodor Rojankovsky, illustrator). *Frog Went a-Courtin.* New York: Harcourt Brace Jovanovich, Inc.

1957 Udry, May (with Marc Simont, illustrator). *A Tree Is Nice.* New York: Harper & Row, Publishers.

1958 McCloskey, Robert. *Time of Wonder.* New York: The Viking Press, Inc.

1959 Cooney, Barbara. *Chanticleer and the Fox.* New York: Thomas Y. Crowell Company.

1960 Ets, Marie Hall. *Nine Days to Christmas.* New York: The Viking Press, Inc.

1961 Robbins, Ruth (with Nicolas Sidjakov, illustrator). *Baboushka and the Three Kings.* Berkeley, Calif.: Parnassus Press.

1962 Brown, Marcia. *Once a Mouse.* New York: Charles Scribner's Sons.

1963 Keats, Ezra Jack. *The Snowy Day.* New York: The Viking Press, Inc.

1964 Sandak, Maurice. *Where the Wild Things Are.* New York: Harper & Row, Publishers.

1965 deRegniers, Beatrice Schenk (with Beni Montresor, illustrator). *May I Bring a Friend?* New York: Atheneum Publishers.

1966 Leodhas, Sorche Nic (with Nonny Hogrogian, illustrator). *Always Room for One More.* New York: Holt, Rinehart and Winston, Inc.

1967 Ness, Evaline. *Sam, Bangs, and Moonshine.* New York: Holt, Rinehart and Winston, Inc.

1968 Emberley, Barbara (with Ed Emberley). *Drummer Hoff.* Englewood Cliffs, N.J.: Prentice-Hall, Inc.

1969 Ransome, Arthur (retold by, with Uri Shulvitz, illustrator). *The Fool of the World and the Flying Ship.* New York: Farrar, Straus & Giroux, Inc.

1970 Steig, William. *Sylvester and the Magic Pebble.* New York: Simon & Schuster, Inc.

1971 Haley, Gail E. *A Story—a Story: An African Tale.* New York: Atheneum Publishers.

1972 Hogrogrian, Nonny. *One Fine Day.* New York: The Macmillan Company.

1973 Mosel, Arlene (retold by, with Blair Lent, illustrator). *The Funny Little Woman.* New York: E.P. Dutton and Company, Inc.

1974 Zemach, Havre (retold by, with Margot Zemach, illustrator). *Duffy and the Devil.* New York: Farrar, Straus & Giroux, Inc.

1975 McDermott, Gerald. *Arrow to the Sun.* New York: The Viking Press.

Book Club Selections. Book clubs for children have gained in popularity. They have the advantages and the disadvantages rightly associated with book clubs for adults. A few are named following. For a longer list and for information on each club included, the reader is referred to *Literary Market Place,* published by the R.R. Bowker Company, a copy of which is available in many libraries. Interested persons may wish to write to the sponsors of the clubs for details of membership.

Arrow Book Club. (Scholastic Book Services, 50 West 44th Street, New York, New York 10036).

The Bookplan. (46 Jane Street, New York, New York 10014)

Grow-With-Me Book Club. (Doubleday and Company, 501 Franklin Avenue, Garden City, New York 11530)

Junior Literary Guild. (277 Park Avenue, New York, New York 10017)

Parents' Magazine's Read Aloud and Easy Reading Program. (Division of Parents' Magazine Enterprises, Inc., 52 Vanderbilt Avenue, New York, New York 10017)

The Weekly Reader Children's Book Club. (One for each of these age levels: 5-7; 7-10; 10-13; (Xerox Family Educational Services, 245 Long Hill Road, Middletown, Connecticut 06457)

"Easy-To-Read" Books. Relatively many so-called "easy-to-read" books have been appearing on the market. These are designed for the beginning reader and not for the retarded person. Probably the best known of these books are those by Dr. Seuss, such as *Green Eggs and Ham* (published as one of the Beginner Book series by Random House in 1960) and *The Cat in the Hat Comes Back.* (published by Houghton Mifflin Company in 1958). Controlled vocabulary and simplicity of sentence structure characterize these "easy-to-read books," which range in difficulty so that some are suitable for the better reader in the second half of the first grade while others have been rated on a third-grade reading level.

Severe criticism has been hurled by some authorities in the field of literature for children against the "easy-to-read books" on the claim that they lack literary value. While recognizing the fact that these books have not contributed to the classic literature of the day, other educators point out that they nevertheless can make a significant contribution to reading if used wisely. An argument advanced by those defending the books is that when young children have a severely limited reading vocabulary, they cannot read the books of enduring values for the stories in those books are not couched in a vocabulary that the child recognizes in print. These people can argue that since the "easy-to-read books" help the boys and girls learn to read, unless they are undesirable in content, they can be of value in the achievement of a worthy goal. So that the primary grade children will not be deprived of enjoyment and learning from the great stories of childhood—written in the more difficult reading vocabulary—defenders of the "easy-to-read books" could favor the teacher's making much use of the classics at this early stage of development by reading and telling the boys and girls those stories that have enduring value, thereby supplementing the reading by the child of books of not-so-good quality.

The following publishers, in addition to Houghton Mifflin Company and Random House, mentioned in connection with Dr. Seuss books, are among those that publish books of the "easy-to- read" type: Benefic Press (Beckley-Cardy Company); Follett Publishing Company; Grosset & Dunlap; Harper & Row; Holt, Rinehart and Winston; Steck Company; and the Southwest Regional Laboratory for Educational Research and Development.

Books for the Retarded Reader. The "easy-to-read books" for the beginning reader are not to be confused with books for the retarded reader. Some of the latter type have been in print a long time although there still is a great lack in this area. To be sure, the retarded reader may enjoy some of the books designed as "easy-to-read" for the normal reader.

The big problem with books for the retarded reader is to be able to provide him with books written in his narrowly limited vocabulary but nevertheless on his interest level, and, in many cases, on his intelligence level. (It must not be forgotten, however, that many intelligent boys and girls are retarded in reading.)

The following series are among the many written with the retarded reader in mind:

Air-Space-Age series. (Benefic Press, Beckley-Cardy Company)

American Adventure series. (Harper & Row)

Basic Vocabulary series. (Garrard Publishing Company)

Beginning-to-Read Biographies. (G.P. Putman's Sons)

The Cowboy Sam series. (Benefic Press, Beckley-Cardy Company)

Landmark Books. (Random House, Inc.)

Reader's Digest Skill Builders. (Reader's Digest Services)

Space Age Books. (Bowmar Publishing Company).

Some of the publishers, in addition to those to which reference is made in the preceding paragraphs, that publish books with high interest-low vocabulary are: The Bobbs-Merrill Publishing Company; The Children's Press; Doubleday and Company; Field Educational Publications; D.C. Heath and Company; Melmont Publishers (Children's Press); William Morrow and Company; Science Research Associates; Scott, Foresman and Company; Webster Publishing Company; and Wheeler Publishing Company.

Textbooks for Boys and Girls

It is with pride that publishers of the outstanding language arts series can point to their productions. As both authors and publishers keenly realize, the last word is far from having been said in textbook production in the field. They are striving for improved instructional materials of all types for boys and girls. Yet these books, with supplementary materials, have improved so much that many criticisms that used to be voiced against them can no longer justifiably be applied; in many cases the criticism should lie not in the books themselves as much as in the misuse of them.

Reading Textbooks. Reading series differ in various respects—in burden of vocabulary, in nature and quality of the stories and other articles, in format, and in underlying educational theory. Each publishing company will point out some of the unique features of its basal readers. Free literature highlighting the points of excellence of each series is available from the publishers.

The publishers of some of the outstanding textbooks in reading are listed following.

Allyn and Bacon, Inc.
American Book Company
The Bobbs-Merrill Company, Inc.
Ginn and Company
Harper & Row, Publishers
D.C. Heath and Company
Holt, Rinehart and Winston, Inc.
Houghton Mifflin Company
Laidlaw Brothers
J.B. Lippincott Company
Lyons and Carnahan
The Macmillan Publishing Company
Pitman Publishing Corporation
Science Research Associates
Scott, Foresman and Company
The L.W. Singer Company, Inc.

Many of the publishers of reading textbooks have more reading books than those that are included in their basal reading series. Upon request the publishers will supply the teacher or prospective teacher with a list of their publications in the field of elementary school reading, including, in many instances, supplementary reading series, workbooks, teachers' manuals, and other teaching aids.

Other Language Arts Textbooks. Although there has been a tendency to integrate the work in "language," spelling, and handwriting, many of the textbooks in these areas continue to deal with a specific phase of the language arts. There are many textbooks or workbooks in spelling, consumable books in handwriting, and both hardback and consumable English books.

As in the case of reading textbooks, various companies stress different points in their programs in spelling, handwriting, and English. Some series of spellers, for example, make it relatively easy to adapt instruction within a grade to levels of spelling ability. Another differentiating feature lies in the role that linguistics plays in the spelling program advocated and incorporated in a spelling series. Handwriting books and English books similarly differ in emphases. For information on the unique features of the various textbooks, the reader may wish to write to some of the publishing companies in-

dicated in the following listings of well-known series of spellers, handwriting materials, and other language arts books.

1. Publishers of spelling series

   Allyn and Bacon, Inc.
   Follett Publishing Company
   Ginn and Company
   Harcourt Brace Jovanovich, Inc.
   Harper & Row, Publishers
   Houghton Mifflin Company
   Lyons and Carnahan
   McGraw-Hill Book Company
   Charles E. Merrill Publishing Company
   Silver Burdett Company
   The L.W. Singer Company, Inc.

2. Publishers of handwriting series

   Allyn and Bacon, Inc.
   Benefic Press
   The Bobbs-Merrill Company
   The Macmillan Publishing Company
   McCormick-Mathers Publishing Company, Inc.
   Noble & Noble, Publishers, Inc.
   The A.N. Palmer Company
   Charles Scribner's Sons
   E.C. Seale and Company
   Zaner-Bloser, Inc.

3. Publishers of language series

   Allyn and Bacon, Inc.
   American Book Company
   The Economy Company
   Follett Publishing Company
   Ginn and Company
   Harcourt Brace Jovanovich, Inc.
   Harper & Row, Publishers
   D.C. Heath and Company
   Holt, Rinehart and Winston, Inc.
   Houghton Mifflin Company
   Laidlaw Brothers
   The Macmillan Publishing Company
   McCormick-Mathers Publishing Company
   The L.W. Singer Company, Inc.

Reference Books for Boys and Girls

Much emphasis is placed in the modern elementary school on the use of reference books. Publishers are meeting the growing demand for dictionaries and encyclopedias for boys and girls. Selected reference books are named here.

Picture Dictionaries. Many picture dictionaries can be found on the counters of book stores and of book departments of other stores. Some are here listed.

McIntire, Alta. *The Follett Beginning-to-Read Picture Dictionary.* Chicago: Follett Publishing Company.

Monroe, Marion, and Greet, W.C. *My Little Pictionary.* Chicago: Scott, Foresman and Company.

Moore, Lillian. *Child's First Picture Dictionary.* New York: Grosset & Dunlap.

———. *The Golden Picture Dictionary.* New York: Simon and Schuster.

Scott, Alice. *Picture Dictionary for Boys and Girls.* Garden City, N.Y.: Garden City Publishing Company.

Scott, Alice, and Center, Stella. *The Giant Picture Dictionary for Boys and Girls.* Garden City, N.Y.: Doubleday & Company.

Walpole, Ellen. *Golden Dictionary.* Racine, Wis.: Golden Press.

Other Dictionaries. Some of the dictionaries used by boys and girls, other than picture dictionaries, are listed below.

The Holt Basic Dictionary of American English. New York: Holt, Rinehart and Winston, Inc.

The Holt Intermediate Dictionary of American English. New York: Holt, Rinehart and Winston, Inc.

Thorndike-Barnhart Beginning Dictionary. Chicago: Scott, Foresman and Company.

Thorndike-Barnhart Junior Dictionary. Chicago: Scott, Foresman and Company.

Webster's A Dictionary for Boys and Girls. New York: American Book Company.

Webster's Elementary Dictionary. New York: American Book Company.

Webster's New World Dictionary. New York: American Book Company.

The Winston Dictionary for Schools. New York: Holt, Rinehart and Winston, Inc.

The World Book Dictionary. Chicago: Field Enterprises Educational Corporation, two volumes.

Encyclopedias. Encyclopedias for boys and girls include the following:

Book of Knowledge. New York: Grolier Society, Incorporated.

Britannica Junior Encyclopedia. Chicago: Encyclopedia Britannica.

Childcraft. Chicago: Field Enterprises Educational Corporation.

Compton's Pictured Encyclopedia. F.E. Compton Company.

The Golden Book Encyclopedia. New York: Golden Press.

The Golden Book Encyclopedia. New York: Golden Press.

My First Picture Encyclopedia. New York: Grosset & Dunlap, Inc.

Pictorial Encyclopedia of American History. Chicago: Children's Press.

World Book Encyclopedia. Chicago: Field Enterprises Educational Corporation.

Young People's Science Encyclopedia. Chicago: Children's Press.

PERIODICALS FOR BOYS AND GIRLS

In the 1970 edition of *The Dobler World Directory of Youth Periodicals,* compiled by Lavinia Dobler and Muriel Fuller (distributed by Muriel Fuller, P.O. Box 193, New York, New York 10017), nearly a thousand periodicals for boys and girls, with a combined circulation of more than 100,000,000 are listed. The following publications also contain listings of periodicals for boys and girls.

Association for Childhood Education International. *Guide to Children's Magazines, Newspapers, Reference Books.* Association for Childhood Education International.

Dobler, Lavinia G. *The Dobler International List of Periodicals for Boys and Girls.* Distributed by Muriel Fuller, P.O. Box 193, New York, New York 10017.

Graves, Eileen P., ed. *Ulrich's Periodicals Directory.* R.R. Bowker Company.

Martin, Laura K., *Magazines for School Libraries.* New York: R.R. Bowker, Inc.

H.W. Wilson Company. *Reader's Guide to Periodical Literature.* Bronx, N.Y.: H.W. Wilson Company.

Periodicals for Class Use

Two publishers put out a series of periodicals that are ordered in large quantities by individual classrooms, with a subscription often for each child. One of these companies is Xerox Education Publications (formerly American Education Publications), 245 Long Hill Road, Middletown, Connecticut 06457; the other is Scholastic Magazines, Inc., 50 West 44th Street, New York, New York 10036.

Periodicals by the Xerox Education Publications include *My Weekly Reader,* with seven editions, kindergarten through grade six. The same company also publishes *Current Events,* which is designed for grades six to eight. *Read Magazine,* also published by this company, is suitable for use in grades six to nine.

Scholastic Magazines publishes among others, the following that are used extensively in class situations:

News Pilot (for grade one)
News Ranger (for grade two)

News Trails (for grade three)

News Explorer (for grade four)

Newstime (for grades five and six)

Other Periodicals

The following are among the periodicals of wide circulation, single copies of which are frequently ordered for classrooms or libraries or subscribed to in homes.

American Girl, The. Girl Scouts of the United States, 830 Third Avenue, New York, N.Y. 10022

Boys' Life. Boy Scouts of America, U.S. Highway #1, North Brunswick, N.J. 08902.

Child Life. Saturday Evening Post Company, Inc., 1100 Waterway Boulevard, Indianapolis, Ind. 46206.

Children's Digest. Parents' Magazine Enterprises, Inc., 52 Vanderbilt Avenue, New York, N.Y. 10017.

Highlights for Children. Highlights for Children, Inc., 2300 West Fifth Avenue, Columbus, Ohio 43216; also 803 Church Street, Honesdale, Pa. 18431.

Jack and Jill. Saturday Evening Post Company, Inc., 1100 Waterway Boulevard, Indianapolis, Ind. 46206.

National Geographic Magazine. National Geographic Society, 17 and M Street, N.W., Washington, D.C. 20036.

Popular Mechanics Magazine. Hearst Corporation, 224 West 57th Street, New York, N.Y. 10019.

Summertime. Scholastic Magazines, Inc., 50 West 44th Street, New York, N.Y. 10036.

Young Miss (formerly *Calling All Girls*). Parents' Magazine Enterprises, Inc., 52 Vanderbilt Avenue, New York, N.Y. 10017

OTHER READING MATERIALS

Even a quick glance at the advertising pages of professional magazines for elementary school teachers indicates the large number of materials in print, other than textbooks and periodicals, that are claimed to be valuable in teaching reading or the other language arts. An examination of the publicity materials of many publishing companies and distributors of elementary school supplies also reveals the abundance of such literature. Some of these aids have stood up favorably after scrutiny of research techniques and/or after evaluation in terms of sound educational practice. At the other extreme on the scale of desirability are some that sound dangerously close to quack procedures.

Evaluation

A listing of such reading materials that can be given in limited space cannot be comprehensive. An evaluation of them in this chapter would necessarily show many inaccuracies, for the worth of the material is to a considerable extent a function of the purpose for which it

is intended by the user and the methods employed in using it. It is suggested that the reader make his own evaluation as he studies the literature on a given aid, asking himself questions such as these:

1. Is it designed, according to the publicity material on it, to serve a purpose that is important to me? (Care should be exercised so that unsupported claims of publishers or distributors do not mislead the examiner in his appraisal.)

2. Is there evidence to indicate that the claimed purpose of the material is being accomplished through use of it.

3. Is use of the material in harmony with what we know from the field of child growth and development?

4. Is use of the material in harmony with accepted principles of teaching?

5. Is the time that needs to be spent in the use of the materials reasonable?

6. Can the materials be used without constant supervision by the teacher? (It is not necessarily a score against an aid if constant supervision is needed; however, it is important to note if a teacher is looking for an aid that can be used primarily as a "seatwork activity.")

7. Is the cost of the material in favorable proportion to its usefulness?

When considering possible use of materials dealing with the development of skills in word recognition, the teacher should pay particular attention to the role that phonics plays. He will want to make certain that according to his best insights phonics is neither overemphasized or underemphasized and that methods used in teaching it are in harmony with the teaching principles he accepts.

One further word of caution needs to be expressed. While it is important that a teacher try to justify the use of materials he selects in terms of his best understanding of educational principles and procedures, such consideration should not keep him from refusing to experiment with the new. If all teachers were reluctant to try out materials until their value has been established beyond a doubt, educational progress would be retarded.

Sources of Materials

The teacher in search of materials of instruction of the types to which reference is here made—including reading-readiness materials and those for the development of work-study-skills—is advised to write, first of all, for publication lists to the publishing company whose program in reading and in other language arts he is following. An inquiry as to what materials beyond the basal series the company has will likely bring a quick response. If the request is for descriptive literature that will most likely be complied with rapidly also, especially if the teacher indicates that he already is using some of the company's material. Furthermore, the teacher or college student intent upon making a study of available materials may write to any of the publishers of language arts materials listed on preceding pages of this chapter. Some of the publishers and/or distributors of such teaching material in the language arts are given in the following listing.

Beckley-Cardy Company
Benefic Press (A division of Beckley-Cardy Company)
The Economy Company
Expression Company
Garrard Publishing Company
E.M. Hale and Company
Harlow Publishing Company
Judy Publishing Company
Kenworthy Educational Service
McCormick-Mathers Publishing Company
Charles E. Merrill Publishing Company
Noble & Noble Publishers
F.A. Owen Publishing Company
Platt and Munk
Teachers College Press, Columbia University
Reader's Digest Services
Science Research Associates
Society for Visual Education
George Wahr Publishing Company
Webster Publishing Company.

Language Arts Laboratories

Programs in the form of materials for the development of skills have made a considerable impact during recent years on the teaching of the language arts. One such is the *EDL Study Skills Library,* published by the Educational Developmental Laboratories. Science Research Associates has several programs, among them the *SRA Reading for Understanding Laboratory;* the *SRA Reading Laboratory;* the *Basic Composition Series,* of which one part "Writing Skills" is for grades five and six and the other for grades seven and eight, published by Science Research Associates; and the *Spelling Word Power Laboratory.* Charles E. Merrill Publishing Co. has a programmed course entitled *Building Reading Power.*

The *EDL Study Skills Library* consists of materials for grades four to nine. The *SRA Reading for Understanding Laboratory,* designed for grades three through twelve, is comprised of 4,000 selections that deal primarily with the development of comprehension skills. The materials are arranged in order of difficulty. The *SRA Reading Laboratory,* for grades one through thirteen, stresses various skills of reading, including rate. On the lower levels considerable emphasis is placed on phonics as a means of achieving growth in word recognition.

Publicity material, available to teachers and prospective teachers for the asking, gives detailed information on the programs incorporated in the language arts laboratories.

TESTS

To secure a comprehensive listing and evaluation of standardized tests on the markets, the reader is advised to consult the most recent edition of the *Mental Measurements Yearbook,* edited by Oscar K. Buros and published by the Gryphon Press and *Tests in Print* (latest edition) by the same editor and publisher.

Mental Tests

Mental tests, or intelligence tests, can be classified according to those designed to test one individual at a time and those that are usable in group-testing situations. Much of the individual testing in the elementary school is done by means of one or more of the following tests. (It should be noted that for satisfactory administration of individual tests it is important that a person especially trained in that area should give them.)

Arthur Point Scale of Performance Tests by Grace Arthur, for use with children with language handicaps (Psychological Corporation).

Stanford-Binet Intelligence Scale revised by Lewis M. Terman and Maud A. Merrill (Houghton Mifflin Company).

Wechsler Intelligence Scale for Children by David Wechsler (Psychological Corporation).

A few of the well-known group intelligence tests for elementary school pupils are:

The California Test of Mental Maturity by Elizabeth T. Sullivan, Willis W. Clark, and Ernest W. Tiegs (California Test Bureau).

Cattell Culture Fair Intelligence Tests (Bobbs-Merrill Company).

The Kuhlman-Anderson Intelligence Tests by F. Kuhlman and Rose G. Anderson (Personnel Press).

The Lorge-Thorndike Intelligence Tests by Irving Lorge and Robert L. Thorndike (Houghton Mifflin Company).

Otis Quick-Scoring Mental Ability Tests by Arthur S. Otis (Harcourt Brace Jovanovich, Inc.

The Pintner-Cunningham Primary Test by Rudolph Pintner and Bess Cunningham (Harcourt Brace Jovanovich, Inc.).

The Pintner Non-Language Primary Mental Test (Teachers College Press, Columbia University).

SRA Primary Mental Abilities by L.L.Thurstone and Thelma G. Thurstone (Science Research Associates).

Reading Readiness Tests

Among much-used tests that test readiness for beginning reading are the following:

Gates Reading Readiness Tests. Teachers College Press, Columbia University.

The Harrison-Stroud Reading Readiness Profiles. Houghton Mifflin Company.

Lee-Clark Readiness Test. California Test Bureau.

Metropolitan Readiness Test. Harcourt Brace Jovanovich.

Monroe Reading Aptitude Tests. Houghton Mifflin Company.

Murphy-Durrell Diagnostic Reading Readiness Test. Harcourt Brace Jovanovich.

Scholastic Reading Readiness Test. Scholastic Testing Service.

Webster Reading Readiness Test. Webster Publishing Company.

Reading Tests

Some of the following tests of reading ability of boys and girls in the elementary school are primarily survey tests; others are chiefly diagnostic. Some check a variety of reading skills; a few are limited to one phase of reading.

American School Reading Tests by Willis E. Pratt and Stanley W. Lore (Bobbs-Merrill Company).

Botel Reading Inventory by Morton Botel (Follett Publishing Company).

California Reading Tests by Ernest W. Tiegs and Willis W. Clark (California Test Bureau).

Diagnostic Reading Scales by George D. Spache (California Test Bureau).

Diagnostic Reading Tests by Guy L. Bond, Theodore Clymer, and Cyrile Hoyt (Lyons and Carnahan).

Durrell Analysis of Reading Difficulty by Donald D. Durrell (Harcourt Brace Jovanovich).

Durrell-Sullivan Reading Capacity and Achievement Tests by Donald D. Durrell and Helen Sullivan (Harcourt Brace Jovanovich).

Flash-X Sight Vocabulary Test by George D. Spache and Stanford E. Taylor (Educational Developmental Laboratories).

Gates Advanced Primary Reading Tests (Type AWR, word recognition; Type APR, paragraph reading) by Arthur I. Gates (Teachers College Press, Columbia University).

Gates Basic Reading Tests (Type GS, reading to appreciate general significance; Type UD, reading to understand precise directions; Type ND, reading to note details; Type RV, reading vocabulary; Type LC, level of comprehension) by Arthur I. Gates (Teachers College Press, Columbia University).

Gates-McKillop Reading Diagnostic Tests by Arthur I. Gates and Anne S. McKillop (Teachers College Press, Columbia University).

Gates Primary Reading Tests (Type PWR, word recognition; Type PSR, sentence reading: Type PPR, paragraph reading) by Arthur I Gates (Teachers College Press, Columbia University).

Gates Reading Survey by Arthur I. Gates (Teachers College Press, Columbia University).

Gilmore Oral Reading Test by John V. Gilmore (Harcourt Brace Jovanovich).

Gray Standardized Oral Reading Check Tests by William S. Gray (Public School Publishing Company).

Gray Standardized Oral Reading Paragraph Tests by William S. Gray (Public School Publishing Company).

Iowa Every-Pupil Tests of Basic Skills: Silent Reading Comprehension by H.F. Spitzer et al. (Houghton Mifflin Company).

Iowa Silent Reading Tests by Harry A. Greene, A.N. Jorgensen, and Victor H. Kelley (Harcourt Brace Jovanovich).

Kelley-Greene Reading Comprehension Test by Victor H. Kelley and Harry A. Greene (Harcourt Brace Jovanovich).

Lee-Clark Reading Test by J. Murray Lee and Willis W. Clark (California Test Bureau).

Metropolitan Achievement Tests: Reading by Gertrude Hildreth and others (Harcourt Brace Jovanovich)..

Peabody Library Information Test by Louis Shores and Joseph E. Moore (Educational Test Bureau).

Primary Reading Profiles by James B. Stroud and Albert N. Hieronymus (Houghton Mifflin Company).

Roswell-Chall Diagnostic Reading Test of Word Analysis Skills by Florence G. Roswell and Jeanne S. Chall (Essay Press).

SRA Achievement Series: Reading by Louis P. Thorpe et al. (Science Research Associates, Inc.).

SRA Reading Record by Guy T. Buswell (Science Research Associates, Inc.).

Stanford Achievement Test: Reading by Truman L. Kelley et al. (Harcourt Brace Jovanovich).

Spelling Tests and Scales

Some standardized tests dealing with various elementary school fields of learning include a part on testing of spelling, as, for example, the *Metropolitan Achievement Test* and the *Stanford Achievement Test*, both published by Harcourt Brace Jovanovich, and the *California Achievement Tests* by the California Test Bureau.

Data on some spelling scales are given below.

Ashbaugh, Ernest J., *Iowa Spelling Scales* (Bureau of Educational Research and Service).

Ayers, Fred C., *Ayers Standardized Spelling Scale* (The Steck Company).

Dolch, Edward W., *Dolch List of the Two Thousand Commonest Words for Spelling* (Garrard Publishing Company).

Gates, Arthur I., *A List of Spelling Difficulties in 3876 Words* (Teachers College Press, Columbia University).

Greene, Harry A., *The New Iowa Spelling Scale* (Bureau of Educational Research and Service, University of Iowa).

Morrison, J. Cayce, and McCall, William A., *Morrison-McCall Spelling Scale* (Harcourt Brace Jovanovich).

Handwriting Scales

Titles of some of the handwriting scales are given in the following list:

Freeman, Frank N., *Correlated Scales* (The Zaner-Bloser Company).

———, *New Scientific Evaluation Scales* (The Zaner-Bloser Company).

———, *Print to Script (Manuscript) Measuring Scales* (The Zaner-Bloser Company).

Hildreth, Gertrude, *Metropolitan Primary Cursive Handwriting Scale* (Harcourt Brace Jovanovich).

———, *Metropolitan Primary Manuscript Handwriting Scale* (Harcourt Brace Jovanovich).

Leamer, E.W., *Leamer Handwriting Scale* (Public School Publishing Company).

West, Paul, *American Handwriting Scale* (A.N. Palmer Company).

Other Language Arts Tests

One source of published tests for the evaluation of language arts abilities such as capitalization, punctuation, and correct usage is that provided by some publishers of language arts books produced in consumable form. Some workbooks contain end tests to precede and follow work on the units in the workbooks. Some also include tests to be given at the beginning or end of the year. Other publishers supply separate booklets with their books, which can be used to appraise the success with which the users of the series have mastered the learnings to be acquired through the use of the books. When using any language arts series the teacher is advised to write to the publisher for information as to the availability of tests to accompany the series.

The following is a listing of some standardized tests that are not planned specifically for the users of a given series of books in the language arts.

The Clapp-Young English Test: The Clapp-Young Self-Marking Tests (Houghton Mifflin Company).

Iowa Every-Pupil Test of Basic Skills: Basic Language Skills (Houghton Mifflin Company).

Iowa Language Abilities Test (Harcourt Brace Jovanovich, Inc.).

Metropolitan Achievement Tests: English Test (Harcourt Brace Jovanovich, Inc.).

SRA Achievement Series: Language Arts (Science Research Associates).

AUDIOVISUAL AIDS

Although this section deals only with films, filmstrips, and recordings, there are many other audiovisual aids to learning in the area of the language arts which the teacher should use. Provisions should be made, for example, for opportunities for viewing still pictures (including slides), examining realia, watching television, listening to radio broadcasts, and going on field trips.

For a comprehensive presentation of audiovisual aids to learning, the reader is referred to chapters on the subject in many professional books on teaching methods and to books dealing exclusively with the subject of audiovisual education.

Films

The films in the language arts may be classified as to (1) films for the teacher and (2) films for boys and girls.

Films for the Teacher. Films for the teacher include (1) those that provide guidance in using films, such as *Choosing a Classroom Film* by McGraw-Hill Book Company and *Film and You* available through Bailey Films and (2) those that give professional information on one or more phases of the language arts such as:

Good Speech for Gary (McGraw-Hill Book Company).

Gregory Learns to Read (produced in the Detroit Public Schools; available through Syracuse University.)

How Your Child Learns to Read (produced in the Salt Lake City Schools; available from the Board of Education, Salt Lake City).

Individualizing Reading in the Classroom (Columbia University).

The Lively Art of Picture Books (Distributed by Children's Services Division, American Library Association or Weston Woods Studios).

New ETV Handwriting Programs (six films, on the transition from manuscript to cursive writing, to accompany the Guiding Growth in Handwriting series. The Zaner-Bloser Company).

They All Learn to Read (available through Syracuse University).

Films for Boys and Girls. Motion pictures in the area of the language arts that are designed for use by boys and girls may be classified as to (1) films that tell stories, (2) films that provide background for language arts experiences, and (3) films that give help in development of skills in the language arts.

1. *Films that tell stories.* Films on stories have been produced in series and singly. An example of a series are the films entitled *Picture Book Parade,* available through Weston Woods Studios, Weston, Connecticut. Some of the titles of books in the series are: *In the Forest* by Marie Hall Ets; *Magic Michael* by Louis Slobodkin; and *Pancho* by Berta and Elmer Hader.

Examples of films on single stories or books are: *Little Red Riding Hood,* modern puppet version (Encyclopedia Britannica Films); *Night before Christmas* (Encyclopedia Britannica Films); *Heidi* (Teaching Films Custodians); *Perfect Tribute* (Teaching Films Custodians); *Little Red Hen* (Coronet Films); *Three Little Pigs* (Coronet Films); *Andy and Lion* (Weston Woods Studios); and *Rumpelstiltskin* (Coronet Films).

2. *Films that provide background.* Since the subject matter of language arts experiences is all of life, the many films suitable for pupils in areas such as the social studies, health, and science—to name only a few—in a sense provide background for development in the area of the language arts. For example, *Animals and Their Homes* (Coronet Films) can be used to enhance the reading of stories about animals or to furnish information for a report the pupils may wish to write. Of similar value are titles as diverse as *Milk* (Encyclopedia Britannica Films), *Minerals and Rocks* (Encyclopedia Britannica Films), *Children of Germany* (Encyclopedia Britannica Films), *How Weather is Forecast* (Coronet Films), and *Visit with Cowboys* (Encyclopedia Britannica Films). Information to serve as interesting background for Robert McCloskey's books for children is furnished by the film *Robert McCloskey* (Weston Woods Studio). The films *Writing through the Ages* (Encyclopedia Britannica Films) and *Between the Lines* (Modern Talking Pictures Services, Inc.), both on the intermediate-grade level, give background on the development of written communication.

3. *Films for the development of skills.* The majority of the films for the development of language arts skills for elementary school boys and girls are on the intermediate-grade rather than the primary-grade level. They include a great diversity of topics, as illustrated by the small sampling of Coronet films that follows.

How to Prepare a Class Report
Improve Your Handwriting
Improve Your Pronunciation
Improve Your Reading
Improve Your Spelling

Know Your Library
Verbs: Recognizing and Using Them.

Filmstrips

Filmstrips for use in connection with language arts activities include, among many others;

The Comma Series (Society for Visual Education)

Basic Primary Phonics (Society for Visual Education)

Filmstrips for Practice in Phonetic Skills (Scott, Foresman and Company)

Goals in Spelling Series (Popular Science Publishing Company, Audio-Visual Division)

How to Use an Encyclopedia (McGraw-Hill Book Company)

Learning to Use the Dictionary (eight filmstrips; Pacific Production, 414 Mason Street, San Francisco)

Picture Book Parade Filmstrip Series (Frederick Warne)

Use Your Library (Society for Visual Education)

Using a Dictionary (Webster Publishing Company

Your Library: A Treasure Chest (Society for Visual Education).

Recordings

One of the excellent series of recordings for boys and girls is that known as Enrichment Records, to accompany Landmark Books by Random House. (Filmstrips are also available for use with these books.)

Another worthwhile series of records is that produced by the National Council of Teachers of English. Titles in this series include among others: *Children's Arabian Nights,* with selections from "Aladdin and the Wonderful Lamp," "Ali Baba and the Forty Thieves," and others; and *Grimm's Fairy Tales,* featuring "Rumpelstiltskin," "Briar Rose," "The Elves and the Shoemaker," and others. The records by the National Council of Teachers of English also include such titles as *The House at Pooh Corner, Now We Are Six, Rip Van Winkle,* and *Just So Stories.* Two other series are the *Folkways Records,* available from Folkways Records and Service Corporation, and *My First Golden Record Library,* distributed by Golden Records.

Newbery Award Record, Inc. are the distributors of records to interest boys and girls in reading some of the Newbery award winners. Among those available are recordings on: *The Wheel on the School* (Meindert DeJong), *Call It Courage* (Armstrong Sperry), *The Matchlock Gun* (Walter D. Edmonds), *Amos Fortune, Free Man* (Elizabeth Yates), *Caddie Woodlawn* (Carol Brink), *Ginger Pye* (Eleanor Estes), *The Trumpeter of Krakow* (Eric Kelly), *Invincible Louisa* (Cornelia Meigs), and *Thimble Summer* (Elizabeth Enright).

Examples of a few other recordings for children are:

Alice in Wonderland (with *Many Moons* and *The Eager Piano* on the reverse side; Columbia Records).

Andersen's Fairy Tales (in three volumes, with "The Nightingale," "The Emperor's New Clothes," "The Steadfast Tin Soldier" in Volume I; Educational Record Sales).

Choral Speaking for Intermediate Grades (Educational Record Sales).

Communities and Community Helpers (Educational Record Sales).

Fun with Speech Sounds (Coronet Films).

Handwriting Demons (National Council of Teachers of English)

Hansel and Gretel (Educational Record Sales).

Importance of Making Notes (Coronet Films).

It's Your Library (Vocational Guidance Films).

Let's Be Firemen (Educational Record Sales).

Let's Pronounce Well (Coronet Films).

Let's Read Poetry (Bailey Films).

Let's Try Choral Reading (Young America Films).

Make Way for Ducklings (by Robert McCloskey; Weston Woods Studios).

Making Sense with Outlines (Coronet Films).

Sound-filmstrip sets are on the market in increasing numbers. In these sets records are synchronized with filmstrips. *Crow Boy* by Taro Yashima, *Petunia* by Roger Duvoisin, *Little Tim* and *the Brave Sea Captain* by Edward Ardizonne, and *The Three Billy Goats Gruff* by Marcia Brown comprise one such set, available from Weston Woods Studios.

Guides to Selection

Many state universities and state departments of education have catalogs of their audiovisual materials. Additional guides to selection of such materials are:

Aids in Selection of Materials for Children and Young People (American Library Association).

An Annotated List of Recordings for the Language Arts (National Council of Teachers of English).

Choosing a Classroom Film (McGraw-Hill Book Company).

Directory of 3660 16mm Film Libraries (by Seerley Reid, Anita Carpenter, and Annie Dougherty; United States Printing Office).

Educational Film (now on cards; American library Assoication).

Educational Film Guide (out of print, however, still used by Frederic A. Krahm; H.W. Wilson Company).

Educational Filmstrip Guide (out of print, however, still used by Frederic A. Krahm; H.W. Wilson Company).

Educational Television Guidebook (by Phillip Lewis; McGraw-Hill Book Company).

Educational Television Motion Pictures, Descriptive Catalog (National Education Television Film Service, Audiovisual Center, University of Indiana, Bloomington, Indiana).

Educator's Guide to Free Films (Educators Progress Service).

Educator's Guide to Free Filmstrips (Educators Progress Service).

Educator's Guide to Free Slidefilms (Educators Progress Service).

Educator's Guide to Free Tapes and Recordings (Educators Progress Service).

Guides to Newer Media (by Margaret L. Rufswold and Carolyn Gauss; American Library Association).

National Tape Recording Catalog (National Tape Library or some state universities, among them the National Tape Depository, Audiovisual Center, University of Colorado, Boulder, Colorado 20004).

New Media Index (McGraw-Hill Book Company).

Sources of Information on Educational Media (by John A. Moldstad; United States Printing Office).

UCLA Children's Film Series (Children's Theater Committee, Theater Arts Department, University of California, Los Angeles).

The following helpful indices, published periodically, are available through the National Information Center for Education Media, University of Southern California, University Park, Los Angeles 90007:

NICEM Index to Educational Audio Tapes
NICEM Index to Educational Records
NICEM Index to Educational Video Tapes
NICEM Index to 8mm Cartridges
NICEM Index to Filmstrips
NICEM Index to Overhead Transparencies
NICEM Index to Producers and Distributors
NICEM Index to 16mm Educational Films.

Producers and Distributors

In the preceding paragraph reference is made to an excellent listing of producers and distributors of many visual aids, namely the *NICEM Index to Producers and Distributors*. Another source of information on addresses is the *Index to Instructional Media Catalogs*.

In addition to the many state universities and the state departments of education that distribute audiovisual aids, some are available through book companies, consuls, and other agencies. A few of the book companies that have one or more types of audiovisual aids for sale are:

Benefic Press
Garrard Publishing Company
Harcourt Brace Jovanovich, Inc.

Harper & Row, Publishers
Charles E. Merrill Publishing Company
Houghton Mifflin Company
McGraw-Hill Book Company
Macmillan Publishing Company
Scott, Foresman and Company.

Following are the names and addresses of a few of the many additional distributors of audiovisual aids.

American Library Association, 50 East Huron Street, Chicago, Ill. 60611.

American Museum of Natural History, Central Park West at 79th Street, New York, N.Y. 10024.

Bailey Film Association (BFA Educational Media), 11559 Santa Monica Boulevard, Los Angeles, Calif. 90025.

Bowmar Records, 622 Rodier Drive, Glendale, Calif. 91207.

Budget Films, 4590 Santa Monica Boulevard, Los Angeles, Calif. 90029.

Caedmon Records, Inc. (Division of Houghton Mifflin), 110 Tremont Street, Boston, Mass. 02107.

Child Study Association of America, 50 Madison Avenue, New York, N.Y. 10010.

Churchill Films, 622 North Robertson Boulevard, Los Angeles, Calif. 90069.

Coronet Instructional Media, 65 East South Water, Chicago, Ill. 60601.

Educational Development Corporation, Learning Resource Division, 202 Lake Miriam Drive, Lakeland, Florida 33803.

Educational Film Library Association, 17 West 60th Street, New York, N.Y. 10023.

Educational Reading Services, 64 East Midland Avenue, Paramus, N.J. 07652.

Educational Record Sales, 157 Chambers Street, New York, N.Y. 10017.

Educators Progress Service, Randolph, Wis. 53956.

Encyclopedia Britannica Educational Corporation, 425 North Michigan Avenue, Chicago, Ill. 60611.

Enrichment Teaching Materials, 246 Fifth Avenue, New York, N.Y. 10001.

Eye Gate House, Inc., 146-01 Archer Avenue, Jamaica, N.Y. 11435.

Field Enterprises Educational Corporation, 510 Merchandise Mart Plaza, Chicago 60654.

Miller-Brody Productions, Inc., 342 Madison Avenue, New York, N.Y. 10017.

National Council of Teachers of English, 1111 Kenyon Road, Urbana, Ill. 61801.

Oxford Films, Inc., 1136 North Las Palmas Avenue, Hollywood, Calif. 90038.

Parents' Magazine Films, Inc., 52 Vanderbilt Avenue, New York, N.Y. 10017.

Pyramid Film Productions, P.O. Box 1048, Santa Monica, Calif. 90406.

Spoken Arts, 310 North Avenue, New Rochelle, N.Y. 10801.

Sterling Educational Films, 241 East 34th Street, New York, N.Y. 10016.

Teaching Film Custodians, 25 West 43rd Street, New York, N.Y. 10036.

Texture Films, Inc., 1600 Broadway, New York, N.Y. 10019.

U.S. Government Printing Office (Division of Public Documents), Washington, D.C. 20402.

Weston Woods Studios, Inc., Weston, Conn. 06880.

H.W. Wilson Company, 950 University Avenue, Bronx, N.Y. 10452.

ADDRESSES OF PUBLISHERS AND DISTRIBUTORS

In this last part of the chapter addresses of publishers and distributors of materials for teaching or learning the language arts are given. Because of the changes constantly being made in addresses of publishers and distributors, the reader may find it advisable to refer to the listing of publishers and distributors given in the most recent edition of *Books in Print*, published by R.R. Bowker Company, which is available in many libraries.

Abelard-Schuman, Ltd., 257 Park Avenue, New York, New York 10010.

Abingdon Press, 201 Eighth Avenue, South, Nashville, Tennessee 37202.

Allyn and Bacon, Inc., 470 Atlantic Avenue, Boston, Massachusetts 02210.

American Book Company (A division of Litton Educational Publishing Company, Inc.) 450 West 33rd Street, New York, New York 10001.

American Council on Education, One Dupont Circle, N.W., Washington, D.C. 20036.

American Education Publications (See Xerox Education Publications.)

American Heritage Publishing Company, 1221 Avenue of the Americas, New York, New York 10036.

American Library Association, 50 East Huron Street, Chicago, Illinois 60611.

Appleton-Century-Crofts, Inc. (See Prentice-Hall International, Inc.)

Association for Childhood Education International, 3615 Wisconsin Avenue, N.W., Washington, D.C. 20016.

Atheneum Publishers, 122 East 42nd Street, New York, New York 10017.

Bantam Books, Inc., 666 Fifth Avenue, New York, New York 10019.

Beckley-Cardy Company, 10300 West Roosevelt Road, Westchester, Illinois 60153.

Benefic Press (A division of Beckley-Cardy Company) 10300 West Roosevelt Road, Westchester, Illinois 60153.

Bobbs-Merrill Company, Inc. (Subsidiary of Howard W. Sams and Company) 4 West 58th Street, New York, New York 10019; *also* 4300 West 62nd Street, Indianapolis, Indiana 46268.

R.R. Bowker, Inc. (A Xerox Education Company) 1180 Avenue of the Americas, New York, New York 10036.

Bowmar Publishing Company, 622 Rodier Drive, Glendale, California 91201

Bradbury Press, Inc., 2 Overhill Road, Scarsdale, New York, 10583.

Wm. C. Brown Company Publishers, 2460 Kerper Boulevard, Dubuque, Iowa 52001.

Bruce Books (*formerly* Bruce Publishing Company) 866 Third Avenue, New York 10022.

Bureau of Educational Research (See University of Iowa Press.)

Burgess Publishing Company, 7108 Ohms Lane, Minneapolis, Minnesota 55435.

Cambridge University Press, 32 East 57th Street, New York, New York 10022.

Center for Applied Linguistics, 1611 North Kent Street, Arlington, Virginia 22209.

Center for Urban Education, 105 Madison Avenue, New York, New York 10016.

Chandler Publishing Company (College division of Intext, Inc.) 257 Park Avenue, South, New York, New York 10010.

Child Study Press (c/o Child Study Association of America, Inc.) 50 Madison Avenue, New York, New York 10010.

Children's Book Council, 175 Fifth Avenue, New York, New York 10010.

Citation Press (Imprint of Scholastic Book Services) 50 West 44th Street, New York, New York 10036.

Coward, McCann and Geoghegan, Inc., 200 Madison Avenue, New York, New York 10016.

Criterion Books, Inc., 257 Park Avenue South, New York, New York 10010.

Crowell, Collier and Macmillan, 866 Third Avenue, New York, New York 10022.

T.S. Denison and Company, Inc., 5100 West 82nd Street, Bloomington, Minnesota 55437.

Denoyer-Geppert Company (A subsidiary of Times Mirror Company) 5235 Ravenswood Avenue, Chicago, Illinois 60640.

Doubleday and Company, Inc., 501 Franklin Avenue, Garden City, New York 11530.

Dryden Press, The (A division of Holt, Rinehart and Winston, Inc.) 901 North Elm, Hinsdale, Illinois 60521

Duell, Sloan and Pearce, 1716 Locust Street, Des Moines, Iowa 50336.

Economy Company, The, 1901 North Walnut, Oklahoma City, Oklahoma 73125.

Education Center for Children's Books, Regenstein Library, University of Chicago, Chicago, Illinois 60637.

Educational Publishers, Inc., 1525 North State Parkway, Chicago, Illinois 60610.

Educational Testing Service, 20 Nassau Street, Princeton, New Jersey 08540.

Educators Progress Service, Inc., Randolph, Wisconsin 53956.

Encyclopedia Britannica Education Corporation, 425 North Michigan Avenue, Chicago, Illinois 60611.

Expression Company, 155 Columbus Avenue, Boston, Massachusetts 02116.

Farrar, Straus and Giroux, Inc., 19 Union Square West, New York, New York 10003.

Fearon Publishers, 6 Davis Drive, Belmont, California 94002.

Field Enterprises Educational Corporation, 510 Merchandise Mart Plaza, Chicago, Illinois 60654.

Follett Publishing Company, 1010 West Washington Boulevard, Chicago, Illinois 60607.

Garrard Publishing Company, 1607 North Market Street, Champaign, Illinois 61820.

Ginn and Company, 191 Spring Street, Lexington, Massachusetts 02173.

Golden Press (Imprint of Western Publishing Company) 850 Third Avenue, New York, New York 10022.

Grolier, Inc., 575 Lexington Avenue, New York, New York 10022.

Grosset & Dunlap, Inc., 51 Madison Avenue, New York, New York 10010.

E.M. Hale and Company, 1201 South Hastings Way, Eau Claire, Wisconsin 54701.

C.S. Hammond, Inc., 515 Valley Street, Maplewood, New Jersey 07040.

Harcourt Brace Jovanovich, Inc., 757 Third Avenue, New York, New York 10017.

Harlow Publishing Corporation, 212 East Gray, Norman, Oklahoma 73069.

Harper & Row, Publishers, Inc., 10 East 53rd Street, New York, New York 10022.

Harvard University Press, 79 Garden Street, Cambridge, Massachusetts 02138.

Harvey House, Inc., Publishers (See E.M. Hale and Company.)

Hastings House Publishers, Inc., 10 East 40th Street, New York New York 10016.

Hayes School Publishing Company 321 Penwood Avenue, Wilkinsburg, Pennsylvania 15221.

D.C. Heath and Company, College Department, 125 Spring Street, Lexington, Massachusetts 02173.

Heritage Press, Avon, Connecticut 06001.

Highlights for Children, Inc., 2300 West Fifth Street, Columbus, Ohio 43216; *also* 803 Church Street, Honesdale, Pennsylvania 18431.

Holiday House, Inc., 18 East 56th Street, New York, New York 10022.

Holt, Rinehart and Winston, Inc., 383 Madison Avenue, New York, New York 10017.

Horn Book, Inc., 585 Boylston Street, Boston, Massachusetts 02116.

Houghton Mifflin Company, 2 Park Street, Boston, Massachusetts 02107.

Indiana University Press, Bloomington, Indiana 47401.

Initial Teaching Alphabet Publications, Inc. (A division of Pitman Publishing Corporation) 6 East 43rd Street, New York, New York 10017.

Instructor Publishing Company, Inc. (*formerly* the F.A. Owen Publishing Company) Dansville, New York 14437.

International Reading Association, 800 Barksdale Road, Newark, Delaware 19711.

Intext Educational Publishers, 257 Park Avenue South, New York, New York 10016.

Charles A. Jones Publishing Company, Village Green, Worthington, Ohio 43085.

Judy Publishing Company, The, Box 5270, Main Post Office, Chicago, Illinois 60680.

Kansas State College, Bureau of Educational Measurements, Emporia, Kansas 68802.

Kenworthy Educational Service, Inc., Box 3031, Buffalo, New York 14205.

Keystone View Company (See Mast Development Company.)

Alfred A. Knopf, Inc. (A subsidiary of Random House) 201 East 50th Street, New York, New York 10022.

Laidlaw Brothers (A division of Doubleday and Company, Inc.) Thatcher and Madison, River Forest, Illinois 60305.

J.B. Lippincott Company, East Washington Square, Philadelphia Square, Philadelphia, Pennsylvania 19105.

Little, Brown and Company, 34 Beacon Street, Boston, Massachusetts 02106.

Liveright Publishing Corporation, 386 Park Avenue, South, New York, New York 10016.

Longmans, Green and Company, Inc. (A division of the David McKay Company) 750 Third Avenue, New York, New York 10017.

Lothrop, Lee & Shepard Company (A division of William Morrow and Company, Inc.) 105 Madison Avenue, New York, New York 10016.

Lyons and Carnahan, 407 East 25th Street, Chicago, Illinois 60616.

McCormich-Mathers Publishing Company, Inc. (A division of Litton Educational Publishing, Inc.) 450 West 33rd Street, New York 10001.

McGraw-Hill Book Company, 1221 Avenue of the Americas, New York, New York 10036.

David McKay Company, Inc., 750 Third Avenue, New York, New York 10017.

Macmillan Publishing Company, Inc., 866 Third Avenue, New York, New York 10022.

Markham Publishing Company (Rand McNally College Publishing Company) P.O. Box 7600, Chicago, Illinois 60680.

Mast Development Company, 2212 West 12th Street, Davenport, Iowa 52803.

Melmont Publishers, Inc. (A division of Children's Press) 1224 West Van Buren Street, Chicago, Illinois 60607.

Charles E. Merrill Publishing Company, 1300 Alum Creek Drive, Columbus, Ohio 43216.

Julian Messner, Inc., (A division of Simon & Schuster, Inc.) 1 West 39th Street, New York, New York 10018.

William Morrow and Company (A division of Scott, Foresman and Company), 105 Madison Avenue, New York, New York 10016.

National Council of Teachers of English, 1111 Kenyon Road, Urbana, Illinois 61801.

National Education Association, 1201 Sixteenth Street, N.W., Washington, D.C. 20036.

Thomas Nelson, Inc., 30 East 42nd Street, New York, New York 10017.

Noble & Noble, Publishers, Inc., 1 Dag Hammarskjold Plaza, New York, New York 10017.

Odyssey Press (Distributors: Bobbs-Merrill Company, Inc.) 4300 West 62nd Street, Indianapolis, Indiana 46268.

Ohio Scholarship Tests (See The Ohio State University Press.)

Ohio State University Press, The, 2070 Neil Avenue, Columbus, Ohio 43210.

F.A. Owen Publishing Company (See Instructor Publishing Company.)

Oxford University Press, Inc., 200 Madison Avenue, New York, New York 10016.

A.N. Palmer Company, 1720 West Irving Park Road, Schaumburg, Illinois 60172.

Parents' Magazine Press, Bergenfield, N.J. 07621.

Parker Publishing Company (A division of Prentice-Hall, International, Inc.) West Nyack, New York 10994.

Parnassus Press, 4080 Halleck Street, Emeryville, California 94608.

George Peabody College for Teachers, Division of Surveys, 21 Avenue "S," Nashville, Tennessee 37203.

F.T. Peacock Publishers, Inc., 401 West Irving Park, Itasca, Illinois 60143.

Personnel Press, Inc. (A division of Ginn and Company) 191 Spring Street, Lexington, Massachusetts 02173.

Pitman Publishing Corporation, 6 East 43rd Street, New York, New York 10017.

Platt and Munk Publishers, 1055 Bronx River Avenue, Bronx, New York 10472.

Plays, Inc., 8 Arlington Street, Boston, Massachusetts 02116.

Prentice-Hall International, Inc., Englewood Cliffs, New Jersey 07632.

Public School Publishing Company (Test division of Bobbs-Merrill Publishing Company) 4300 West 62nd Street, Indianapolis, Indiana 46268; *also* 4 West 57th Street, New York, New York 10019.

G.P. Putnam's Sons, 200 Madison Avenue, New York, New York 10016.

Rand McNally & Company, P.O. Box 7600, Chicago, Illinois 60680.

Random House, 201 East 50th Street, New York, New York 10022.

Reader's Digest Association, Pleasantville, New York 10570.

Ronald Press Company, The, 79 Madison Avenue, New York, New York 10016.

Scholastic Book Services, 50 West 44th Street, New York, New York 10036.

Science Research Associates (A subsidiary of IBM, College Division) 1540 Page Mill Road, Palo Alto, California 94304.

Scott, Foresman and Company, 1900 East Lake Avenue, Glenview, Illinois 60025.

Charles Scribner's Sons, 597 Fifth Avenue, New York, New York 10017.

Silver Burdett Company (A division of General Learning Corporation) 250 James Street, Morristown, New Jersey 07960.

Simon & Schuster, Inc., 630 Fifth Avenue, New York, New York 10020. The address for the order department is 1 West 39th Street, New York, New York 10018.

Society for Visual Education, Inc. (A subsidiary of Graflex, Inc.) 3750 Monroe Avenue, Rochester, New York 14603.

Spencer International Press, Inc. (A division of Grolier, Inc.) 575 Lexington Avenue, New York, New York 10022.

Stanford University Press, Stanford, California 94305.

Steck-Vaughn Company, The, Box 2028, Austin, Texas 78767.

Sterling Publishing Company, Inc., 419 Fourth Avenue, New York, New York 10016.

Frederick A. Stokes Company (*see* J.B. Lippincott Company.)

Teachers College Press, Columbia University, 1234 Amsterdam Avenue, New York, New York 10027.

Charles C. Thomas, Publishers, 301-327 East Lawrence Avenue, Springfield, Illinois 62703.

United States Government Printing Office (Division of Public Documents) Washington, D.C. 20402.

University of California Press, 2223 Fulton Street, Berkeley, California 94720.

University of Chicago Press, 5801 Ellis Avenue, Chicago, Illinois 60637.

University of Florida Press, 15 Northwest 15th Street, Gainesville, Florida 32601.

University of Iowa Press, Graphic Services Building, Iowa City, Iowa 52242.

University of Minnesota Press, 2037 University Avenue, S.E., Minneapolis, Minnesota 55455.

Vanguard Press, Inc., 424 Madison Avenue, New York, New York 10017.

Viking Press, Inc., The, 625 Madison Avenue, New York, New York 10022.

George Wahr Publishing Company, 304 1/2 South State Street, Ann Arbor, Michigan 48108.

Henry Z. Walck, Inc., 19 Union Square, West, New York, New York 10003.

Franklin Watts, Inc., (A division of Grolier, Inc.) 845 Third Avenue, New York, New York 10022.

Van Nostrand Reinhold Company (A division of Litton Educational Publishing, Inc.) 450 West 33rd Street, New York 10001.

Western Reserve Press, 3530 Warrensville Ctr. Road, Cleveland, Ohio 44122.

Westminster Press, The, Witherspoon Building, Philadelphia, Pennsylvania 19107.

Wilcox and Follett Publishing Company (See Follett Publishing Company.)

John Wiley & Sons, Inc., 605 Third Avenue, New York, New York 10016.

Williams and Wilkins Company, 428 East Preston Street, Baltimore, Maryland 21202.

H.W. Wilson Company, The, 950 University Avenue, Bronx, New York 10452.

World Publishing Company, The, 110 East 59th Street, New York, New York 10022.

Xerox Education Publications, 245 Long Hill Road, Middletown, Connecticut 06547.

Zaner-Bloser, Inc., 803 Church Street, Honesdale, Pennsylvania 18431

FOR STUDY AND DISCUSSION

1. Consult the reference librarian in your college as to various volumes, such as *Books in Print*, that give information on books published in the United States and note methods of indexing, type of information given, and other matters of interest to you.

2. Examine some of the standardized tests listed in this chapter. Make a record of types of questions asked in reading readiness tests, in reading tests, and in other language arts tests.

3. Become familiar with the classification of tests in *Tests in Print* by Oscar K. Buros, published by the Gryphon Press.

4. Send to a company for a few free or inexpensive materials that should prove helpful in teaching the language arts.

5. If you have access to an audiovisual department, make arrangements to view one or more aids in the field of the language arts. Be able to give your evaluation of the aid(s) that you selected. If you think an aid is worthwhile, be able to explain in detail how it may be used effectively.

6. Start a picture collection that should be of value to you in teaching the language arts in the elementary school.

7. Read parts or all of one or more of the professional books listed in the first part of this chapter. Be able to tell your classmates of important learnings that you acquired through your reading.

Index

The names of authors and editors occurring on pages 332 to 340 are not included in this index unless reference is also made to them elsewhere in the book. Nor are the tests and authors of tests given on pages 345 to 347 included unless reference to them is also made in other pages of the book.